AF777445

EXCHANGE RATE ECONOMICS

Exchange Rate Economics

Selected Essays

Ronald MacDonald

Adam Smith Professor of Political Economy, University of Glasgow, UK

Edward Elgar

Cheltenham, UK • Northampton, MA, USA

© Ronald MacDonald 2009

All rights reserved. No part of this publication may be reproduced, stored in a retrieval system or transmitted in any form or by any means, electronic, mechanical or photocopying, recording, or otherwise without the prior permission of the publisher.

Published by
Edward Elgar Publishing Limited
The Lypiatts
15 Lansdown Road
Cheltenham
Glos GL50 2JA
UK

Edward Elgar Publishing, Inc.
William Pratt House
9 Dewey Court
Northampton
Massachusetts 01060
USA

A catalogue record for this book
is available from the British Library

Library of Congress Control Number: 2009936734

FSC
Mixed Sources
Product group from well-managed
forests and other controlled sources
www.fsc.org Cert no. SA-COC-1565
© 1996 Forest Stewardship Council

ISBN 978 1 84376 198 3

Printed and bound by MPG Books Group, UK

Contents

Acknowledgments

The author wishes to thank the following who have kindly given permission for the use of copyright material.

Blackwell Publishing, for permission to reproduce: MacDonald, R., 'Exchange Rate Behaviour: are Fundamentals Important?', *Economic Journal*, **109** (459), 1999, F673–F691; MacDonald, R. and Ricci, L.A., 'The Real Exchange Rate and the Balassa–Samuelson Effect: the Role of the Distributional Sector', *Pacific Economic Review*, **10** (1), 2005, 29–48; MacDonald, R. and Torrance, T.S., '£M3 Surprises and Asset Prices', *Economica*, **54** (216), 1987, 505–15; MacDonald, R. and Marsh, I.W., 'Combining Exchange Rate Forecasts: What is the Optimal Consensus Measure?', *Journal of Forecasting*, **13**, 1994, 313–32

Elsevier, for permission to reproduce: Taylor, M.P. and MacDonald, R., 'The Monetary Model of the Exchange Rate: Long-run Relationships, Short-run Dynamics and How to Beat a Random Walk', *Journal of International Money and Finance*, **13** (3), 1994, 276–90; Husted, S. and MacDonald, R., 'Monetary-based Models of the Exchange Rate: a Panel Perspective', *Journal of International Financial Markets, Institutions and Money*, **8** (1), 1998, 1–19; MacDonald, R. and Marsh, I.W., 'Currency Spillovers and Tri-polarity: a Simultaneous Model of the US Dollar, German Mark and Japanese Yen', *Journal of International Money and Finance*, **23** (1), 2004, 99–111; Frömmel, M., MacDonald, R. and Menkhoff, L., 'Markov Switching Regimes in a Monetary Exchange Rate Model', *Economic Modelling*, **22** (3), 2005, 485–502; MacDonald, R., 'Panel Unit Root Tests and Real Exchange Rates', *Economics Letters*, **50** (1), 1996, 7–11; Juselius, K. and MacDonald, R., 'International Parity Relationships Between the USA and Japan', *Japan and the World Economy*, **16** (1), 2004, 17–34; Clark, P.B. and MacDonald, R., 'Filtering the BEER: a Permanent and Transitory Decomposition', *Global Finance Journal*, **15** (1), 2004, 29–56; MacDonald, R. and Ricci, L.A., 'Real Exchange Rates, Imperfect Substitutability, and Imperfect Competition', *Journal of Macroeconomics*, **29** (4) 2007, 639–64; MacDonald, R. and Marsh, I.W., 'Currency Forecasters are Heterogeneous: Confirmation and Consequences', *Journal of International Money and Finance*, **15** (5), 1996, 665–85; Bénassy-Quéré, A., Larribeau, S. and MacDonald, R., 'Models of Exchange Rate Expectations: How Much Heterogeneity?', *Journal of International Financial Markets, Institutions and Money*, **13** (2) 2003, 113–36; Anthony, M. and MacDonald, R., 'On the Mean-reverting Properties of Target Zone Exchange Rates: Some Evidence from the ERM', *European Economic Review*, **42** (8), 1998, 1493–523; Hallwood, C.P., MacDonald, R. and Marsh, I.W., 'Crash! Expectational Aspects of the Departures of the United Kingdom and the United States from the Inter-war Gold Standard', *Explorations in Economic History*, **34** (2), 1997, 174–94; Hallwood, C.P., MacDonald, R. and Marsh, I.W., 'Realignment Expectations and the US Dollar, 1890–1897: Was There a "Peso

Problem"?', *Journal of Monetary Economics*, **46** (3), 2000, 605–20; Bordo, M.D. and MacDonald, R., 'Interest Rate Interactions in the Classical Gold Standard, 1880–1914: Was There Any Monetary Independence?', *Journal of Monetary Economics*, **52** (2), 2005, 307–27

MIT Press Journals, for permission to reproduce: MacDonald, R. and Marsh, I.W., 'On Fundamentals and Exchange Rates: a Casselian Perspective', *Review of Economics and Statistics*, **79** (4), 1997, 655–64; MacDonald, R., 'Long-run Purchasing Power Parity: is it for Real?', *Review of Economics and Statistics*, **75** (4), 1993, 690–95

The American Statistical Association, for permission to reproduce: La Cour, L. and MacDonald, R., 'Modeling the ECU Against the U.S. Dollar: a Structural Monetary Interpretation'. Reprinted with permission from the *Journal of Business and Economic Statistics*, **18** (4), 2000, 436–50. All rights reserved.

Oxford University Press, for permission to reproduce: MacDonald, R. and Torrance, T.S., 'Expectations Formation and Risk in Four Foreign Exchange Markets', *Oxford Economic Papers*, **42** (3), 1990, 544–61

Every effort has been made to trace all the copyright holders but if any have been inadvertently overlooked the publishers will be pleased to make the necessary arrangements at the first opportunity.

Introduction

This book brings together some of the papers I have written on exchange rate issues over the last twenty years or so. Although I have written many more than the 22 papers reproduced here, these are, I believe, representative of the kind of issues my research has pursued in this area. I have organised the chapters under four section headings: monetary fundamentals and exchange rate forecasting; equilibrium exchange rates: purchasing power parity and the real exchange rate; expectations formation, news and risk; the economics of fixed exchange rates and credibility issues.

The chapters contained in Part I, on monetary fundamentals, are all essentially geared towards answering the puzzle raised in the seminal paper by Meese and Rogoff (1983). In sum, using a number of variants of the monetary model, the latter found that none of these variants could outperform a random walk in an out of sample forecasting context, and this so-called 'exchange disconnect' is discussed in some detail in Chapter 1. This result has always seemed rather disturbing to me as an educator since I, and I'm sure every other lecturer of International Finance, will at some stage teach the classic open economy macro models which all have at their heart monetary fundamentals. My own work in this area has demonstrated that careful attention to long run relationships and, particularly, parsimonious dynamics can convincingly overturn this result and this is illustrated in the chapters with Lisbeth la Cour, Ian Marsh and Mark Taylor. The most convincing of these for me is that with Ian Marsh, in Chapter 3, where we demonstrate that a suitably parsimonious dynamic ECM model can out-perform a random walk in an out of sample forecasting exercise relative to a random walk. These results seem all the more powerful because, in contrast to the original work of Meese and Rogoff and others, we actually forecast all of the variables used to explain the exchange rate, rather than simply employing actual data outcomes. We also demonstrate that the kind of empirical models estimated have good directional forecasting ability and are far superior to the vast majority of professional forecasters.

The other key theme considered in Part I concerns the existence of long-run cointegrating relationships amongst monetary fundamentals and the exchange rate. This topic is interesting in itself since a number of papers (see MacDonald (2007) for a survey) use the Engle–Granger cointegration method and do not find any evidence of such long-run relationships. The chapters contained in Part I find clear evidence of cointegrating relationships using either a FIML estimator, applied to single country data (Chapters 2, 3, 5 and 6) or a variety of panel estimators (Chapter 4). Chapter 5 with Lisbeth la Cour, tries to address the thorny issue of multiple cointegrating vectors in the context of the monetary model, using a specific-to-general approach, while the chapter with Michael Froemmel and Lukas Menkhoff demonstrates the benefits of using a Markov-switching approach when estimating the monetary model.

Long-run exchange rate relationships are also the main theme of Part II, and although cointegrating methods again feature here in terms of the estimation, the focus is more on what the economics literature has to say about long-run theoretical relationships between exchange rates and fundamentals. Purchasing power parity is often the relationship that economists first turn to in order to get a fix on a country's equilibrium exchange rate and the extent of any implied misalignment. In Chapter 8 I show that using the standard interpretation of PPP, in terms of the nominal exchange rate–relative price relationship, that a version of PPP is in the data, in a long-run cointegration sense, for US dollar and DM bilateral exchange rates but that the nature of PPP does not conform to the standard textbook definition, in the sense that the coefficient on relative prices is often far from unity. I believe I was the first to stress the importance of distinguishing between this 'weak form' of PPP and the fact that 'strong form' PPP is more prevalent for DM-based bilaterals than USD bilaterals. In Chapter 9 I provide a test of PPP by examining the unit root properties of the real exchange rate, using non-stationary panel methods and annual data for the post Bretton Woods period. I was one of the first to suggest such a test (see MacDonald (2007) for a comprehensive overview of this literature) and indeed in an earlier paper (see MacDonald (1988)) had argued the advantages of using low frequency annual data in testing the PPP hypothesis. My own panel unit root tests and that of others, of the time series properties of the real exchange rate, are part confirmation of the so- called PPP puzzle of Rogoff. This puzzle arises because the high volatility of nominal exchange rates observed for currencies when they are flexible, combined with sticky prices, seems consistent with a monetary interpretation of the exchange rate (such as that provided in the classic Dornbusch (1976) model), whereas statistically significant mean reversion of the real exchange rate reported in Chapter 9, and in other chapters, turns out to be too slow to be consistent with a monetary interpretation of PPP (this is because it takes about four years for half of the effect of a nominal shock on the real exchange rate to be extinguished, whilst monetary neutrality should work through to prices in around two years, implying a half life of one year – see MacDonald (2007) for a further discussion).

In Chapter 10, I demonstrate with Katarina Juselius that using the information contained in the slow mean reversion of the real exchange rate is crucial in understanding failures of various parity conditions, such as the Fisher condition and real interest rate parity. In Chapter 12 Luca Ricci and I try to understand the PPP puzzle by conditioning the real exchange rate on productivity effects and also a measure of productivity in the distribution sector, using panel cointegration methods. We show that although total factor productivity shocks from the traded goods sector do have a statistically significant effect on the real exchange rate, they do not work in the way predicted by the classic Balassa–Samuelson hypothesis. We also demonstrate that relative productivity in a country's distribution sector has a statistically significant effect on the real exchange rate and, indeed, is an important variable in explaining the PPP puzzle. The failure of productivity to work in the way predicted by the Balassa–Samuleson hypothesis, led Luca and I to argue that, in order to understand the linkages between real exchange rates and productivity, we need to move away from the neoclassical trade paradigm, where goods entering international trade are regarded as perfect substitutes, to a paradigm in which goods are imperfectly substitutable across countries. That is the topic of Chapter 13 in which we show that, allowing for product differentiation and using a variant of the New Trade Theory model of Helpman and Krugman (1985), produces a new variable, which we label 'efficiency', and which we show has a statistically significant effect on the real exchange rate.

The fact that there are systematic movements of real exchange rates suggests that Purchasing Power Parity is never going to provide a good measure of a country's equilibrium exchange rate and that an approach which explicitly allows for deviations from PPP is going to be crucial to providing sensible measures of equilibrium for policy makers. One such approach is the behavioural equilibrium exchange rate (BEER) model that I developed with Peter Clark (see Clark and MacDonald (1999)). In this approach a theoretical model of the real exchange rate is estimated using cointegration methods and the equilibrium value of the exchange rate constructed using the significant, or stationary, cointegrating relationships and the implied misalignment (which can either be 'current' or 'total') can then be backed out. The chapter by Peter Clark and myself reprinted in Chapter 11 takes the BEER approach one step further and uses it to construct a permanent equilibrium exchange rate which has also proved useful to policy makers for measuring disequilibrium.

The first paper I published in a refereed journal (MacDonald, 1983) examined the impact of new information on the excess return between spot and forward exchange rates. This work was motivated by the more general foreign exchange market literature which examines the role of expectations formation and risk on the exchange rate determination process. Part III contains a selection of my papers in this area. The first, in Chapter 14, co-authored with Tom Torrance, examines the impact of unanticipated and anticipated economic news, generated using survey-based expectations rather than estimated news, at the time of a monetary announcement. We find that monetary surprises have a significantly positive effect on the change in asset prices. In Chapter 15 I have reproduced a paper that again Tom and I wrote which focuses on using survey-based data on expectations to get a fix on whether it is risk or expectational errors, whatever their source, which explain the so-called forward premium puzzle. We find, and in contrast to much of this literature emanating from US authors, that *both* risk and expectational factors are the source of the biasedness of the forward premium in explaining exchange rate changes.

Much of the macroeconomics literature in Chapters 14 and 15 assume that agents' expectations are homogeneous and therefore attention is focused on the mean or perhaps the median as the central measure of expectations. In Chapter 16 I have reprinted an article with Ian Marsh in which we had access to the expectations of individual forecasters in the foreign exchange market. Using some standard tests, and a new test, we demonstrate that forecasters' expectations are not homogeneous as many theoretical and empirical studies assume. In Chapter 17 Ian and I follow this empirical finding of heterogeneity up by trying to improve the accuracy of the individual forecasts by pooling them. Chapter 18 with Agnes Bénassy-Quéré and Sophie Larribeau, uses disaggregate survey expectations to examine the degree of heterogeneity in exchange rate expectations formation.

Although it may at first blush seem odd to apply methods widely used in determining flexible asset prices to the treatment of fixed exchange rates, Krugman (1991) has argued that there are few, if any, fixed exchange rate regimes in which the exchange rate is in fact rigidly fixed, and so the application of such methods is sensible enough. The target zone literature, which applies a variant of the monetary approach to the exchange rate/ balance of payments to understand the determination of fixed exchange rates, has become the workhorse in this literature. A key aspect of the target zone literature concerns the credibility of a fixed exchange rate and in Chapter 19 in Part IV the paper by Myrvin Anthony and myself provides a very simple test of credibility in a target zone regime, namely we test for the mean reverting properties of exchange rates in the (narrow band) experience of the ERM period and show that lack of mean reversion is associated with a lack of credibility. This result seems intuitive enough given the assumptions underlying the target zone model. Chapter 20 I co-authored with Paul Hallwood and Ian Marsh, and in which we examine the credibility of the pound sterling and US dollar in the run up to their departure from the inter-war gold standard. In Chapter 21, another with Paul Hallwood and Ian Marsh, we provide a way of unravelling the sources of an apparent lack of credibility of a fixed exchange rate system into expectational failures, a peso effect (the probability that an exchange rate parity change will happen in sample but it does not) or a risk premium. For the well-known example of the lack of credibility for the US dollar in the 1880s we show that the largest part of the lack of credibility was due to a peso effect (with the risk premium and explaining a much smaller proportion of the lack of credibility).

The final chapter in the book provides another twist to the credibility concept, namely it follows up on an idea of Lars Svensson (1994) that if an exchange rate is regarded as credible then it should be possible for the central bank of that currency to have some, albeit limited and transitory, independence in the operation of monetary policy. Mike Bordo and I demonstrate that the central banks of the UK, US and France all had such independence conferred on them during the classical gold standard period; in a further paper, Mike and I demonstrate that a similar story held for the inter-war gold standard experience (see Bordo and MacDonald (2003)). Hali Edison and I (Edison and MacDonald (2003)) used the same methodology to estimate the degree of monetary independence for the ERM experience and, interestingly, found that currencies which were known to be credible had a similar degree of monetary independence conferred on them as in the classical gold standard period (see Bordo and MacDonald (2009) for a complete selection of papers on the topic of credibility in different exchange rate regimes of the international monetary system).

References

Bordo, M.D. and R. MacDonald (2003), 'The Inter-war Gold Exchange Standard: Credibility and Monetary Independence', *Journal of International Money and Finance*, **22** (1), 1–32.

Bordo, M.D. and R. MacDonald (2005), 'Violations of the "Rules of the Game" and the Credibility of the Classical Gold Standard, 1880–1914', *Journal of Monetary Economics*, **52**, 307–27.

Bordo, M.D. and R. MacDonald (2009), *Credibility in Three Regimes of the International Monetary System*, Cambridge: Cambridge University Press.

Clark, P.B. and R. MacDonald (1999), 'Exchange Rates and Economic Fundamentals: a Methodological Comparison of BEERs and FEERs', in R. MacDonald and J.L. Stein (eds), *Equilibrium Exchange Rates*, Boston: Kluwer.

Dornbusch, R. (1976), 'Expectations and Exchange Rate Dynamics', *Journal of Political Economy*, **84**, 1161–76.

Edison, H.J. and R. MacDonald (2003), 'Credibility and Interest Rate Discretion in the ERM', *Open Economies Review*, **14**, 351–68.

Helpman, E. and P. Krugman (1985), *Market Structure and Foreign Trade*, Cambridge, MA: MIT Press.

Krugman, P. (1991), 'Target Zones and Exchange Rate Dynamics', *Quarterly Journal of Economics*, **56**, 669–82.

MacDonald, R. (1983), 'Some Tests of Rational Expectations Hypothesis in the Foreign Exchange Market', *Scottish Journal of Political Economy*, **30**, 235–50.

MacDonald, R. (1988), 'Purchasing Power Parity: Some Long-run Evidence from the Recent Float', *The Economist*, **136**, 239–52.

MacDonald, R. (2007), *Exchange Rate Economics: Theories and Evidence*, London: Taylor and Francis.
Meese, R. and K. Rogoff (1983), 'Empirical Exchange Rate Models of the Seventies: Do They Fit Out of Sample?', *Journal of International Economics*, **14**, 3–24.
Svensson, L. (1994), 'Why Exchange Rate Bands? Monetary Independence in Spite of Fixed Exchange Rates', *Journal of Monetary Economics*, **33** (1), 157–99.

PART I

MONETARY FUNDAMENTALS AND EXCHANGE RATE FORECASTING

[1]

The Economic Journal, 109 (*November*), F673–F691. © Royal Economic Society 1999. Published by Blackwell Publishers, 108 Cowley Road, Oxford OX4 1JF, UK and 350 Main Street, Malden, MA 02148, USA.

EXCHANGE RATE BEHAVIOUR: ARE FUNDAMENTALS IMPORTANT?

Ronald MacDonald

One of the most controversial issues in the international economics literature concerns the role of economic fundamentals in explaining exchange rate behaviour. We interpret this controversy as having three different aspects. The first concerns the relationship between exchange rates and fundamentals in the 'long-run'. The second, the usefulness of fundamentals in producing out-of-sample forecasts which dominate a random walk, and the third controversy concerns the relative importance of shocks to real and nominal fundamentals in explaining real exchange rate variability (this, as we shall see, is related to the first). Controversies one and two, therefore, may be thought of as relating to the first moment of exchange rate behaviour, while the third is associated with the second moment.

The first controversy may be motivated by referring to Fig. 1, which portrays the logarithm of the real and nominal exchange rates of the mark-dollar

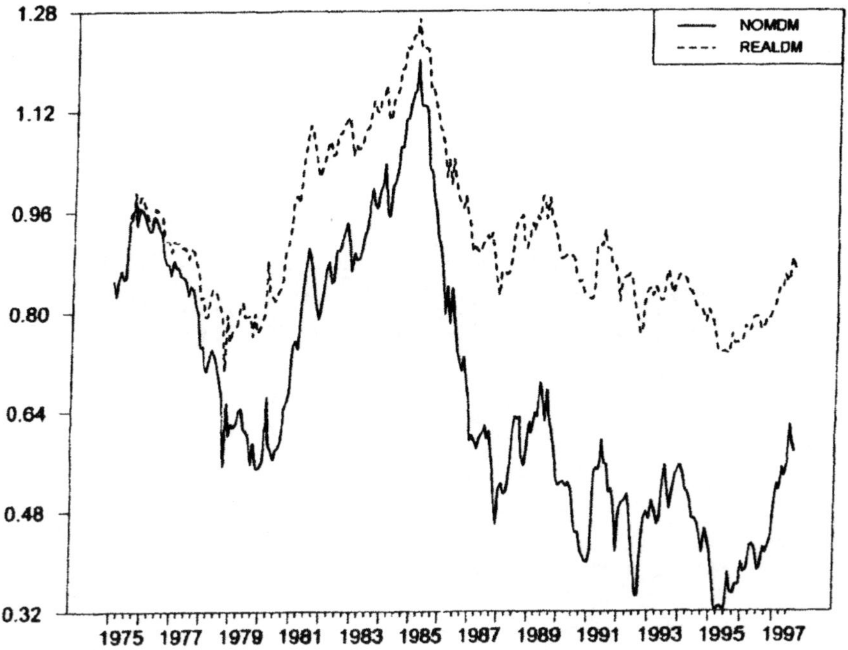

Fig. 1. *German Mark-US dollar, Real and Nominal*

exchange rate. Purchasing power parity (PPP) – the proposition that the equilibrium level of an exchange rate is determined by some measure of relative prices – is the relationship economists often reach for first when thinking about the determination of equilibrium exchange rates. However, Fig. 1 indicates that PPP does not hold on a short-run basis, since real and nominal exchange rates are clearly not independent (they have a correlation coefficient which exceeds 0.9). But does PPP have any validity as a long-run concept, or does it have to be modified in some way to explicitly recognise the real determinants of exchange rates?

The concept of PPP has had something of a roller coaster ride in the academic literature. For example, for the 1920's and 1930's experiences with floating exchange rates PPP is thought to have considerable validity (Frenkel, 1978), while for the recent floating period the initial verdict was that PPP had 'collapsed' (Frenkel, 1981). Recently, however, there has been a considerable resurgence of interest in PPP and there is a controversy in the profession over the usefulness of the concept. In particular, although it can be demonstrated that exchange rates gravitate towards a version of PPP, the adjustment speed is regarded as too slow to be consistent with a traditional form of PPP (see Rogoff (1995)). That is the first controversy addressed in this paper.

Perhaps the most controversial issue in the economics of exchange rates concerns the shorter term behaviour of exchange rates. From Fig. 2 we note

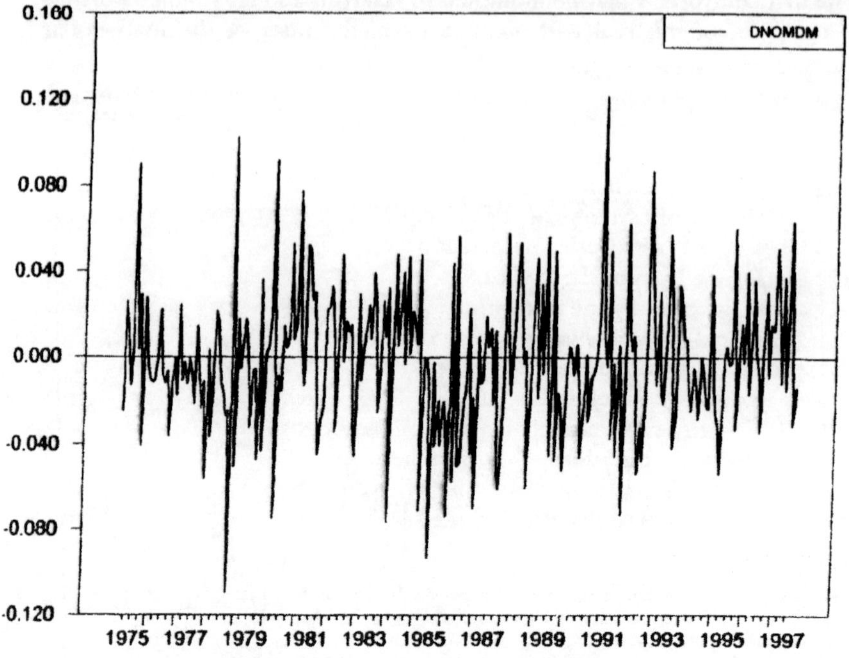

Fig. 2. *First Difference of German Mark-US Dollar*

© Royal Economic Society 1999

that the logarithmic change of the DM-dollar exchange rate displays considerable randomness. Indeed, the proposition that exchange rates follow *approximate* random walks has become something of a stylised fact in the international economics literature. However, the emphasis on approximate is important, since even simple eyeball econometrics of Fig. 2 suggest that there is some predictability in exchange rate behaviour (in both the level and variance of the series). Although randomness of asset prices, such as the exchange rate, is often taken to be an indication of market efficiency[1], in the sense that all available information is discounted into the price, predictability of exchange rate movements is also consistent with efficiency if the equilibrium return is time-varying. However, in one of the most widely cited papers in the international economics literature, Meese and Rogoff (1983) demonstrated that a whole range of fundamentals-based exchange rate models were unable to outperform a simple random walk in an out-of-sample forecasting exercise.

The Meese and Rogoff result has had an enduring effect on the profession. For example, Frankel and Rose (1995) in their recent authoritative overview of the state of play in the exchange rate literature concluded that: '..the Meese and Rogoff analysis at short horizons has never been convincingly overturned or explained. It continues to exert a pessimistic effect on the field of empirical exchange rate modelling in particular and international finance in general'. Such pessimism led Frankel and Rose to advocate a move away from fundamentals-based models towards models which focus on market microstructure variables. However, I believe such pessimism is unfounded and demonstrate in this paper that there is ample evidence to support the proposition that standard exchange rate models have clear forecastability at horizons as short as two months ahead. That is the second controversy I address in this paper.

The third controversy is not unrelated to the previous two and concerns the cause(s) of the real exchange volatility captured in Fig. 1. Is this volatility simply a reflection of asymetrical adjustment speeds in goods and asset markets?[2] The so-called 'sticky-price' explanation for real exchange rate volatility, first attributable to Dornbusch (1976), has been very influential in the profession. However, it has not gone uncontested. An alternative view argues that the real (and nominal) volatility we observe in Fig. 1 is generated by real shocks, such as productivity and preference shocks. So, for example, a productivity shock can change the nominal exchange rate which, for an unchanged internal relative price ratio, also changes the real exchange rate.

A further twist to the third controversy concerns the issue of regime volatility. In particular, it is not just that real and nominal exchange rates exhibit similar volatility under floating rates, it is also that real and nominal

[1] Of course it is widely accepted that randomness of price movement is neither a necessary nor sufficient condition for market efficiency. However, for pedagogic purposes it is useful to refer to the randomness criterion at this point.

[2] That is, prices of commodities are sticky in comparison to the relative prices of currencies and so a nominal shock, by imparting volatility into the nominal exchange rate, imparts a similar degree of volatility into the real exchange rate.

© Royal Economic Society 1999

rates are much more volatile in the recent floating regime than in the Bretton Woods regime, despite there being no notable change in the volatility of the underlying fundamentals. Since Flood and Rose (1999) address this controversy in some detail I do not pursue it in great depth here, although I do try to reconcile it with my conclusion that exchange rates are forecastable at short horizons.

In sum, my paper focuses on the usefulness of fundamentals in explaining exchange rates at long and short horizons, and the sources of real exchange rate variability. I do not examine the very short-run behaviour of exchange rates – that is daily or intra-day – since at this frequency it is now generally accepted that exchange rates are driven by market microstructure considerations rather than traditional economic fundamentals.

1. Fundamentals and Long-run Exchange Rates

A natural starting point for any discussion of the relationship between exchange rates and fundamentals is the concept of purchasing power parity (PPP). The familiar log-form expression for absolute PPP is:

$$s_t = p_t - p_t^*, \tag{1}$$

where s_t denotes the home currency price of a unit of foreign exchange, p_t, denotes a price level and an asterisk denotes a foreign magnitude (lower case letters denote logarithmic values). The restrictions necessary for this condition to hold continuously are well known (see, for example, Dornbusch (1988) and MacDonald (1995)). However, most researchers would go with a less restrictive version of PPP, which simply relies on a real exchange rate being mean-reverting. This may be interpreted as in the spirit of Cassel (1928), the formulator of modern PPP, who recognised that there are a number of factors – interest differentials and foreign exchange market intervention[3] – which prevent an exchange rate from always being at its PPP-defined value; nevertheless, PPP would act as a focal point towards which exchange rates would gravitate. Since the speed of gravitation has become such a crucial issue in this literature, it is perhaps worth noting that Cassel believed that disturbances to PPP would be extinguished after one year.

By defining the real exchange rate as $q_t = s_t - p_t + p_t^*$, Casselian PPP may be described using the following expression:

$$q_t = \rho q_{t-1} + \alpha + \varepsilon_t, \qquad 0 < \rho < 1. \tag{2}$$

As long as ρ is less than one, a current disturbance to the nominal exchange rate/relative price configuration, due to, say, a liquidity effect (à la Dornbusch (1976)) will eventually be offset – the real exchange rate is mean-reverting. In this traditional view of PPP, it is arbitrage in tradable goods which forces the PPP equality. A view diametrically opposite to this is efficient markets PPP

[3] See Officer (1976) for a detailed discussion of the Casselian view of PPP.

© Royal Economic Society 1999

(EMPPP), which relies on arbitrage in bond markets for its prediction that real exchange rates should follow a random walk (with drift) process:

$$q_t = q_{t-1} + \alpha + \varphi_{t+k}. \tag{3}$$

These alternative interpretations of PPP have been tested in one of two ways: by focussing on the nominal exchange rate – relative price relationship or by examining the time series properties of real exchange rates. In terms of the former set of tests, recent work has concentrated on the application of cointegration methods to an equation such as (4):

$$s_t = \beta + \alpha_0 p_t + \alpha_1 p_t^* + \varphi_t. \tag{4}$$

If s_t, p_t, and p_t^* are integrated of order one – I(1) – then weak-form PPP (MacDonald, 1993) exists if the residual term from an estimated version of (4) is stationary – I(0). Strong-form PPP exists if, in addition to weak-form holding, homogeneity is also satisfied: $\alpha_0 = 1$ and $\alpha_1 = -1$.[4] Using robust estimators, such as those of Johansen and Phillips and Hansen, there is now growing support for weak-form PPP when US dollar bilaterals are examined and strong-form PPP seems to hold for DM-based bilaterals. The average half-life to emerge from these kinds of studies is around 3 years (MacDonald, 1995). The superior performance of PPP when DM-based exchange rates are used is a recurring theme in the literature and was first noted by Frenkel (1981) in the context of a traditional regression based test of PPP. The effect may be attributed to a number of factors: the existence of the ERM has attenuated the volatility of DM bilaterals relative to US dollar bilaterals, thereby producing a higher signal-to-noise ratio; the geographical proximity of European countries facilitates greater goods arbitrage and therefore makes it more likely that PPP will occur; the relative openness of European countries, in terms of their trade making up a greater proportion of their collective national output than in the United States.

Univariate unit root tests, such as the Dickey Fuller statistic, have been employed to test (3) against (2), and for the recent float these produce even slower adjustment speeds (half-lives of around 20 years – see MacDonald (1995)) than those estimated for the nominal exchange rate relationship. However, it is now widely accepted that univariate unit root tests have relatively low power to reject the null when it is in fact false. One way the power, and also the size, of such tests may be improved is by increasing the span of the data. A number of papers have therefore taken approximately 100 years of annual data and find significant evidence of mean reversion with the half-life adjustment speed being approximately four years. However, such studies bring with them their own specific problems. For example, the basket used to construct the price indices is likely very different at the beginning and end of the sample;[5] they also

[4] The distinction between weak- and strong-form PPP is seen to be important because the existence of transportation costs and different price weights across countries means that 'there are no hypotheses regarding the specific values of α_0 and α_1 except that they are positive and negative.' (Patel, 1990).

[5] This may be viewed as the temporal analogue to the spatial problem that arises in comparing price indices at a particular point in time.

© Royal Economic Society 1999

suffer from amalgamating data from very different exchange rate regimes, a factor which may affect the statistical properties of the real exchange rates.

This has led researchers to increase the data span by introducing a cross sectional dimension into the tests and, in particular, moving to panel data sets. Such tests involve testing the null hypothesis that each individual series is I(1), against the alternative that all of the series taken as a panel are stationary. Studies which have adopted this approach find evidence of mean reversion which is very similar to that reported in long time spans of annual data, namely half-lives of four years.

So both single country nominal cointegration regressions and real rate regressions with extended data spans demonstrate that real exchange rates are mean-reverting. It is worth noting that the degree of mean reversion in the nominal cointegration studies is recovered from a bilateral pairing for the recent float, whereas the comparable half-lives for real exchange rates can only be achieved when panel methods are used. However, even adjustment speeds of 3 to four years are not viewed as fast enough to be consistent with traditional PPP (Rogoff, 1995). But before abandoning PPP completely, are there explanations for the relatively slow mean reversion which are not necessarily inconsistent with the basic PPP hypothesis?

First, it is well known, and indeed widely accepted by proponents of PPP, that transactions costs in the form of transportation costs can create a neutral band within which it is unprofitable to arbitrage away potentially profitable trading opportunities. Indeed, a number of studies have indicated that transportation costs represent a statistically significant explanation for PPP deviations.[6] This idea has been pushed further by, for example, Dumas (1992) who demonstrates that in the presence of proportional transaction costs deviations from PPP should follow a non-linear mean-reverting process, with the speed of mean reversion depending on the magnitude of the deviation from PPP. A number of researchers have demonstrated that allowing for non-linear adjustment processes produces mean reversion numbers which are much closer to speeds consistent with traditional PPP: for example, Obstfeld and Taylor (1997) show adjustment speeds as low as 12 months for aggregate CPI based real exchange rates and only two months for deviations from the law of one price. This would seem to be an important finding, as 12 months is of course the time frame which Cassel cited as the horizon within which currencies should revert to PPP.

A similar explanation for the relatively slow mean reversion in real exchange rates may be gleaned from studies which emphasise a more microeconomic or industrial organisation perspective. For example, the existence of menu costs (Delgado, 1991), the entry and exit decisions of firms (Baldwin and Krugman, 1989) and the pricing to market models of Dornbusch (1987) and Marston (1990) are relevant here. Although these models have not been the focus of such intense empirical scrutiny as the non-linear models, readers who are

[6] The existence of other factors such as the uncertainty of the permanence of the shock and the so-called sunk costs of the activity of arbitrage may widen the bands over-and-above the width associated with simple trade restrictions (see Dixit (1989) and Krugman (1989)).

© Royal Economic Society 1999

members of frequent flyer programmes will recognise that they contain more than a grain of truth! Therefore, recognition of the current framework within which international trade is conducted – the pricing structure of firms and the costs of arbitrage – seems to make PPP consistent with the Casselian interpretation.

However, knowing that it is, say, non-linear adjustment which is responsible for the relatively slow mean reversion in PPP equations is perhaps not particularly helpful to a policy-maker interested in having a long-run exchange rate relationship for assessment purposes; that is, in trying to gauge how near or how far away a currency is from its equilibrium value. So can fundamentals be used to define a long-run equilibrium relationship which policy makers could sensibly use?

An alternative approach to achieving higher adjustment speeds than those obtained from simple PPP relationships, involves explicitly modelling deviations from PPP in terms of the real determinants of exchange rates. Indeed, it may well be the case that the large real exchange rate movements which non-linear threshold models pick up is in fact the effect of (linear) real shocks on the real exchange rate. Since this approach to modelling long-run exchange rates is also quite controversial we give a brief description of it here.

One approach which explicitly recognises that there may be deviations from PPP which are not consistent with a traditional interpretation is Williamson's (1985) Fundamental Equilibrium Exchange Rate, or FEER. The latter is defined as the real exchange rate consistent with internal-external balance in the medium run,[7] and is usually calculated using a full scale macro-model or, in a partial equilibrium setting, using an estimated trade equation. However, the approach is rather intractable, the implied exchange rate is never revealed (and therefore one has no way of knowing if it is statistically well-founded), and it also suffers from having a normative structure imposed on it from the outset. An alternative approach involves taking a standard theoretical model for the real exchange rate and estimating the implied reduced form. This approach has been labelled a Behavioural Equilibrium Exchange Rate (BEER), since it does not involve any normative elements (See Clark and MacDonald (1998)). Since the BEER approach fits more readily into the mainstream literature, we focus on a simple version of it here.[8] Consider the condition of real uncovered interest parity:

$$\Delta q^e_{t+1} = r_t - r^*_t, \tag{5}$$

where r_t denotes a real interest rate.[9] It is relatively easy to rearrange this into an equilibrium condition for the real exchange rate as:

[7] Internal balance is defined as an economy being at full employment with low inflation, while external balance is taken to be a 'sustainable' current account. The medium run is defined as a period of five years hence.

[8] These alternative approaches to modelling the equilibrium exchange rate are discussed in some detail in MacDonald and Stein (1999).

[9] It is straightforward to include a risk premium in (5) but it turns out this typically has an insignificant effect on the results.

© Royal Economic Society 1999

$$q_t = \overline{q}_t - (r_t - r_t^*), \tag{6}$$

where $\overline{q}_t$ is the systematic (or 'long-run') component of the real exchange rate and is driven by factors such as productivity differences across countries, net foreign asset accumulation and terms of trade effects.[10] Although it is not an uncontroversial finding, a number of papers report the existence of significant long-run relationships using this expression, especially when a relatively rich set of variables is used to model $\overline{q}_t$. Perhaps, most interestingly, the half-lives calculated from these single country expressions are as short as one year, thereby suggesting that it may be real factors which explain the relatively slow mean reversion in studies of real exchange rates which simply condition on the past history of the real exchange rate (as in unit root-based studies). The estimated value of the equilibrium exchange rate backed out from this kind of model, is reported in Fig. 3 for the US dollar. This relationship may shown to be statistically well-founded[11] and therefore could potentially be used to assess 'how close' or 'how far' the dollar is from equilibrium (additionally, such

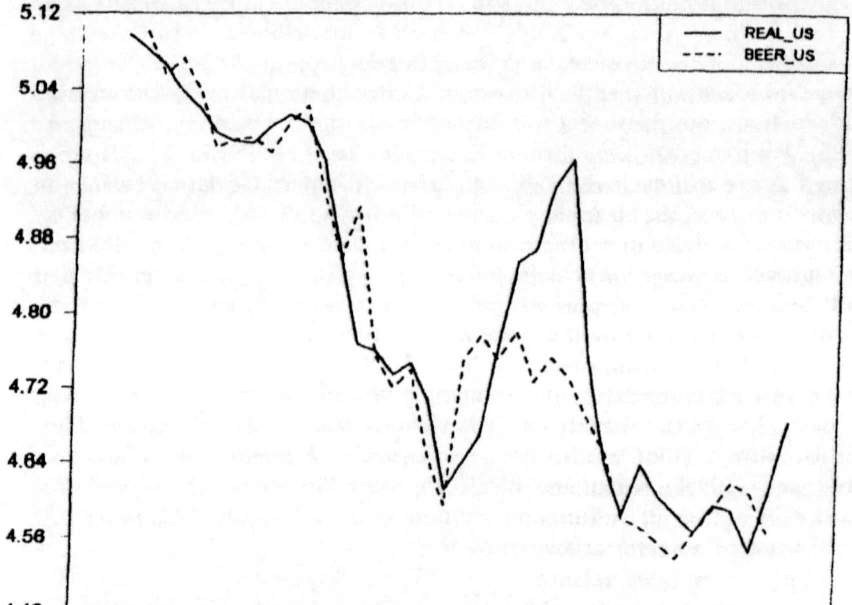

Fig. 3. *US Actual Real Exchange Rate and BEER*

[10] We view (6) as a simple and convenient apparatus for thinking about the determination of equilibrium real exchange rates. There may be other, more theoretically rigorous apparatus which we could have used (see, for example, MacDonald (1998)), although these would produce a very similar reduced form relationship to that presented here.

[11] In the sense of passing an array of statistical tests for stability and in-sample goodness of fit. Additionally, these kinds of models can be used to outperform a random walk at horizons as short as one quarter ahead (see MacDonald (1998)).

© Royal Economic Society 1999

models can be used to construct simple counterfactuals, along the lines of the normative FEER-based approach).

In sum, then, it is our contention that we do know a great deal about the long- run behaviour of exchange rates, using either the benchmark PPP model or a model which explicitly incorporates real factors. It would seem that the finding in favour of PPP-based models is of more interest to academics than to policy makers. For the latter group of consumers the BEER class of models is perhaps of more interest for assessment purposes. Either way, fundamentals can be used to say something positive about long-run exchange rate movements.

2. Fundamentals and Short-run Exchange Rate Movements

In moving from long- to short-run exchange rate relationships, the emphasis shifts from concerns about the existence of equilibrium, and reversion to such equilibrium, to the ability of an exchange rate model to outperform a random walk in an out-of-sample forecasting contest. Here the benchmark is:

$$s_t = s_{t-1} + \kappa + \varepsilon_t, \tag{7}$$

where κ is a constant (drift) term and ε_t is a random disturbance. Although it has become something of a stylised fact to think of the log of the spot exchange rate as following a random walk, there is nevertheless evidence to suggest that monthly exchange rate changes do have some predictability. However, despite this, Meese and Rogoff (1983) (M+R), in their path-breaking study, demonstrated that a comprehensive range of exchange rate models were unable to outperform the benchmark given by (7). More specifically, M+R took the simple flex-price monetary model, which relates an exchange rate to relative money supplies, relative income levels and relative short term interest rates, the Dornbusch-Frankel model (which essentially adds a long term interest differential to the flex-price model) and the Hooper-Morton model (which adds a wealth term and a risk premium to the Dornbusch-Frankel model). These models were all estimated in static form: that is, the variables entered the equations in levels terms and only very limited dynamics were included, if at all. Additionally, M+R considered a wide array of univariate models and a vector autoregression comprising exchange rates, relative short-term interest rates, relative inflation rates, and the current account. The currencies studied were the dollar-mark, dollar-pound, dollar-yen and the trade weighted dollar, and the sample period was March 1973 to November 1980, with the out-of-sample forecasts conducted over the sub-period December 1976 to November 1980. Out-of-sample forecasting accuracy was determined using the mean bias, mean absolute bias and the root mean square error criteria.

In summary, M+R were unable to outperform a random walk at horizons of between one and 12 months ahead, although in four instances (out of a possible 224) the VAR model produced a ranking which was above the random walk at the longer horizons (one out-performance at 6 months and three out-

© Royal Economic Society 1999

performances at 12 months), although this is still a number which is less than that expected by chance. The M+R finding has been interpreted as a particularly telling indictment against fundamentals-based models since in their forecasting exercises M+R deliberately gave such models an unfair advantage by using actual data outcomes of the fundamentals, rather than forecasting them simultaneously with the exchange rate. As we noted in the introduction, the M+R finding has had an enduring effect on the profession, with researchers asserting it still has not been overturned or explained. Indeed, the finding has assumed something akin to the persistence of an I(1) series. But, just as the availability of new and powerful methods of testing unit roots means that real exchange rates no longer appear to be I(1) processes, we would argue that the M+R finding is no longer valid in the light of new econometric methods for addressing issues of simultaneity and dynamic interactions.

One clue to the poor performance of the reduced forms used in the M+R study is the possibility of structural instability and, indeed, much of the predictability contained in Fig. 2 appears to be episodic. Hence a more appropriate way of addressing the performance of structural models would be to allow the coefficients to evolve over time and this has been done in a number of studies (see Wolff (1987) and Schinasi and Swamy (1987)). These studies report a consistent outperformance of a random walk at horizons as short as one or two months. Another clue to the poor out-of-sample forecasting performance reported by M+R relates to the dynamic properties of the data. As we noted in Section 1, although deviations from PPP are mean-reverting there is nevertheless considerable persistence in the behaviour of real exchange rates and this would need to be incorporated into any exchange rate modelling exercise. The same may be said for other 'structural' relationships, such as money demand functions, which underpin many exchange rate models, such as the monetary model. Although in one of their models, M+R did allow for rich dynamic interactions using a VAR, it is now well known that such systems tend to be overparameterised in terms of their use of information (indeed, M+R in a footnote cited this as a potential reason for the poor performance of the VAR model). Researchers have demonstrated that parsimonious exchange rate models are capable of beating a random walk (see, for example, MacDonald and Taylor (1994))

Perhaps one reason why studies like those noted above, and the other studies which outperform a random walk at short horizons,[12] are not taken completely seriously is that, as in the original M+R study, most continue to use actual data outcomes for the forecasted variables.[13] However, research exists which suggests that even forecasting all of the fundamental variables simultaneously with the exchange rate produces forecasts which are superior to a random walk. Since the idea that it is impossible to beat a random walk at short horizons is so deeply entrenched in the psyche of international economists it is

[12] It seems to be widely accepted that a random walk can be beaten at long horizons – that is horizons greater than 3 years. See Mark (1995) and Chinn and Meese (1996).

[13] Which does not seem unreasonable given that this was the metric devised by Meese and Rogoff.

© Royal Economic Society 1999

perhaps worth spending a little time illustrating how the martingale model may be beaten.

Perhaps the most convincing demonstration of being able to outperform a random walk has been provided by MacDonald and Marsh (1997) (M+M). M+M take a very simple extension of PPP, which they christen Casselian PPP, and construct fully dynamic and simultaneous out-of-sample forecasts. In particular, they show that by conditioning nominal exchange rates on relative interest rates, in addition to relative prices, that the homogeneity of exchange rates in relative prices cannot be rejected. That is, using the following vector:

$$\mathbf{x} = [s_t, p_t, p_t^*, i_t, i_t^*]'$$

M+M identify two long-run relationships – one relating to the exchange rate and relative prices and the other an interrelationship amongst interest rates, prices, and the exchange rate. Using these long-run relationships they then build simultaneous econometric models which facilitate the simultaneous forecasting of exchange rates, relative inflation and relative interest rates. In contrast to Meese and Rogoff, all of the forcing variables are forecast *ex-ante* using the model. This, combined with the fact that the short- and long-run coefficients are not updated during the out-of-sample exercise, means that the fundamentals-based model is subjected to a very stringent out-of-sample forecasting test. The dynamic error correction models are estimated for the bilateral US dollar rates of the mark, pound and yen, for the period January 1974 to December 1992, with the last 24 observations being saved for the out-of-sample exercise.[14] In addition to assessing the performance of their models against a random walk, using the root mean square error criterion, M+M also use a directional ability test and compare their forecasts to the 3 and 12 month forecasts of over 150 professional forecasters. The reason for introducing a measure of directional ability is because it is possible for a forecaster to produce a very low (high) RMSE statistic, but consistently get the direction of the exchange rate change wrong (correct). Since financial market users of forecasts are primarily interested in directional ability a successful model should also be deemed to have passed this criterion. The comparison of academic forecasts with a wide array of professional forecasters is, to our knowledge, a unique aspect of the study and has not been attempted before.

The main findings of MacDonald and Marsh are as follows. First, in terms of the RMSE ratio of the fundamentals-based model relative to a random walk, the model for the pound sterling is less than one from a horizon as short as two months ahead, while the yen out-performs at three months ahead and the DM at four months; many of these out-performances are statistically significant (most other studies do not address the issue of statistical significance). Directional ability rises rapidly above 0.5 for all currencies after 2 months and rises as high as 0.8 for all currencies, with the yen yielding 0.9 at the longer horizons.

[14] There is nothing special about this sample period in the sense of the chosen currencies exhibiting obvious trends.

© Royal Economic Society 1999

The M+M models also do exceptionally well against the professional forecasters, since for the yen their model forecasts dominated all of the professional forecasters in terms of the RMSE, the pound sterling was second and the DM forecast was fifth.[15] In fact across currencies and horizons no forecaster is able to beat the model based approach. This would seem to be an especially strong finding given that M+M did not update their models during the out-of-sample period, a luxury afforded to the professionals. A sceptic may be tempted to dismiss the M+M study by arguing it merely reflects the sample period chosen. However, in a follow up study MacDonald and Marsh (1999) use the same vector of variables as above, but a longer sample and are still able to produce results which dominate a random walk.

The sample period in M+M (1999) runs from January 1983 to December 1997, with the last 24 observations reserved for out-of-sample forecasting, and the currencies examined are the German mark and Japanese yen against the US dollar. The econometric methods used are the multivariate cointegration methods discussed above, the novelty being that the model is treated as tri-polar; that is to say disequilibrium in either the yen-dollar or mark-dollar markets not only affects 'own' inflation and interest rate but also the inflation rate and interest rates in the other system. The out-of-sample forecasting results obtained from these models are summarised in Table 1.

At each horizon in Table 1 we report the ratio of the model root mean square error to that of a random walk, and the proportion of correct directional forecasts. A good performance would be indicated by an error ratio less than unity and directional ability in excess of 50%. We believe these results to be impressive, and they underscore what we said above about the ability of relatively simple fundamentals- based models to outperform a random walk. The mark forecasts are seen to outperform a random walk at all horizons, while the yen forecasts start to beat a random walk at a horizon of 3 months. The RMSE ratios are statistically below one from horizon four onwards in the case of the mark and horizon 6 onwards for the yen. Directional ability is satisfactory throughout and indeed for the yen it reaches 100% by horizon 9,

Table 1

Forecasting Performance of Tri-polar Model.

	Deutschemark		Japanese Yen	
Horizon	RMSE Ratio	Direction	RMSE Ratio	Direction
1	0.969	56	1.120	52
3	0.973	60	0.912	80
6	0.885**	69.6	0.721*	78
9	0.917**	65	0.545**	100
12	0.906***	88	0.440***	100

where: *, ** and *** denote, respectively, significance at the 10, 5 and 1% levels. Source: MacDonald and Marsh (1999).

[15] Since the professional forecasters only supply 3 and 12 month forecasts, only these forecasts featured in the comparison.

© Royal Economic Society 1999

(see Johansen and Juselius (1992) for an alternative application of this model).

3. Real Exchange Rate Variability: Sticky Prices, Real Shocks or What?

The evidence in Fig. 1, and our discussion in section 1, clearly indicate that PPP does not hold on a continuous basis. An important controversy in the exchange rate literature is what causes deviations from PPP. Is it simply a reflection of liquidity disturbances interacting with sticky goods prices to produce nominal exchange rate overshooting (as articulated by Dornbusch (1976))? Or is it, in fact, real disturbances – such as supply side and preference shocks – which are driving real exchange rates (as proposed by Stockman (1988))? In the former interpretation, volatility in the nominal exchange rate drives volatility in the real exchange rate, while in the latter it is volatility in the real rate which drives volatility in the nominal rate.

Two groups of papers shed some light on the potential sources of real exchange rate movements. First, there are papers which examine the relative importance of geographic considerations, and, in particular, their implications for transportation costs, compared to nominal exchange rate volatility. In sum, this work demonstrates that although transaction costs are statistically important, the existence of national borders, and therefore the nominal exchange rate link, is the key driving force of real exchange rate volatility. For example, in a comparison of US and Canadian prices Engel and Rogers (1996) show that for distance to generate as much volatility as the border, the cities would have to be 75,000 miles apart! Although this line of work is interesting it does not, however, explicitly focus on the contribution of real shocks. An important strand in the real exchange rate literature attempts to decompose real exchange rate volatility into volatility associated with the business cycle and volatility due to supply side and/or preference shocks using structural vector autoregressions (SVAR). Since this approach has generated considerable controversy, we discuss it briefly here.

The base-line SVAR approach involves specifying a vector autoregressive model for the vector $\Delta \mathbf{x}_t$, where $\Delta \mathbf{x}_t \equiv [\Delta y_t, \Delta q_t, \pi_t]'$ and Δy denotes the change in relative output (home versus foreign), Δq is the change in the real exchange rate and π represents relative inflation. The VAR is then inverted to give the following moving average representation:

$$\Delta \mathbf{x}_t = \mathbf{C}_0 \boldsymbol{\varepsilon}_t + \mathbf{C}_1 \boldsymbol{\varepsilon}_{t-1} + \mathbf{C}_2 \boldsymbol{\varepsilon}_{t-2} + \ldots, \tag{8}$$

where $\mathbf{C}_0$ is the 3 by 3 matrix that defines the contemporaneous structural relationship among the systems 3 variables. By imposing the identification methods of Blanchard and Quah (1989) on the long-run matrix $\mathbf{C}(1)$, the system's disturbances may be interpreted as structural shocks. In particular, $\boldsymbol{\varepsilon}_t \equiv [z_t, \delta_t, \nu_t]'$ denotes the 3×1 vector of the above system's three structural disturbances, where z_t represents the supply shock, δ_t is the demand shock and v_t is the nominal shock. Clarida and Gali (1995), who first proposed this approach as a way of decomposing real exchange rates into real and nominal

© Royal Economic Society 1999

components, used a modified version of the Mundell-Fleming-Dornbusch (MFD) model[16] to motivate the imposed long-run restrictions. They are: money shocks do not influence the real exchange rate or relative output in the long run; only supply shocks are expected to influence relative output levels in the long run; both supply and demand shocks are expected to influence the real exchange rate in the long-run.

The punch-line from the SVAR approach is that it is business cycle related components which explain the vast majority of the residual variance of real exchange rates, with supply side/preference shocks only contributing a minsicule amount. Table 2, from MacDonald and Swagel (1998), makes the point. It shows variance decompositions from SVARs for the German mark, Japanese yen and the pound sterling over the period January 1975 to December 1997. If the business cycle related component is interpreted as the sum of the demand and nominal shocks then these variance decompositions demonstrate strikingly that the business cycle component constitutes approximately 90% of the variance of the exchange rates at all forecast horizons for Japan and the United Kingdom, while for Germany the corresponding percentage is 75.[17] So the SVAR result indicates that the key to understanding real exchange rate variability lies in asymmetric adjustment in goods markets relative to asset markets and has little to do with supply side shocks.

However, this kind of finding has proved to be controversial and has not gone unchallenged. There are at least three well documented sources of controversy relating to the kind of results portrayed in Table 2 (see, for example, Stockman (1995)). First, the basic identification procedure used forces all of the temporary shocks, including temporary fiscal and oil price shocks, to have a monetary origin. Of course in practice, or in the data, this is unlikely to be the case. Second, in setting up the identifying assumptions, it is

Table 2

Variance Decompositions from the Structural VAR – Bilateral Results.

Germany			Japan			UK			
Supply	Demand	Nominal	Supply	Demand	Nominal	Supply	Demand	Nominal	Horizon (quarters)
18.23	68.95	12.82	2.53	57.73	39.73	9.64	90.08	0.27	1
(7.51)	(7.21)	(2.77)	(3.78)	(7.20)	(7.29)	(9.05)	(9.04)	(0.06)	
18.52	60.83	20.65	5.49	55.84	38.61	9.84	82.18	7.97	4
(6.32)	(6.40)	(3.97)	(3.97)	(7.02)	(7.12)	(8.18)	(8.02)	(1.75)	
24.28	54.96	20.76	8.42	49.66	41.91	12.36	75.55	12.08	12
(5.13)	(5.83)	(3.75)	(3.70)	(6.46)	(6.98)	(7.81)	(7.58)	(3.68)	
25.96	53.89	20.14	11.44	47.95	40.61	12.15	73.89	13.98	20
(5.17)	(5.83)	(3.65)	(3.81)	(6.23)	(6.80)	(7.76)	(7.52)	(3.69)	
26.18	53.74	20.07	11.58	47.82	40.59	12.20	73.39	14.40	40
(5.18)	(5.83)	(3.64)	(3.83)	(6.22)	(6.79)	(7.52)	(7.41)	(2.74)	

Note: standard errors in ( )

[16] Modified to be stock-flow consistent and exhibit long-run neutrality of money. The particular version is a stochastic version of Obstfeld's representation of the Mundell-Fleming-Dornbusch model.

[17] In the original Clarida-Gali study, none of the supply-side effects were statistically significant although most are in the MacDonald-Swagel study.

© Royal Economic Society 1999

assumed that the innovations to demand and supply are uncorrelated, which, for a variety of reasons, seems implausible (i.e. an increase in aggregate demand raises investment, which raises the future capital stock and supply, as well as demand). Third, in the original CG study, supply shocks only have a miniscule effect on relative output and this raises the question of whether it is the way supply shocks are specified, rather than the absence of important nominal effects that is to blame.

A number of studies have taken on board the first and last of the above criticisms and find that supply side real shocks put in a much more respectable showing – to around one third of the total residual variance (see MacDonald (1998) for an extended discussion). However, even in these studies, it is unclear if they are sufficiently encompassing to exhaust the data of the richness of shocks they actually contain. This leads into the final controversy relating to volatility, namely that of regime volatility which is often taken as evidence against the view that real forces drive the real exchange rate. Since this is taken as a separate controversy by Flood and Rose, I do not address this topic in great detail here. Rather, my motivation is to discuss the topic in relation to how it impinges on some of the other work discussed above, particularly that relating to forecasting.

In a nutshell, the regime volatility point is that in moving from a system of fixed to flexible exchange rates the volatility of the underlying economic fundamentals remains about the same, while the volatility of the nominal exchange rate increases dramatically. The issue of regime volatility has been formalised by Flood and Rose (1995) and in their paper for this Controversy they propose an explanation in terms of a portfolio balance effect which can provide a link to the changing structure of the foreign exchange market as it moves from fixed to flexible rates. How, though, does their result tie up with the forecastability of exchange rates, I noted in the previous section, which I argued kicks in at horizons as short as one month?

In trying to understand the apparent paradox between the work of Flood and Rose and our discussion in the previous section, it is useful to refer to Table 3.

In Table 3 we note the coefficients of variation of three series for a number of representative countries. The series are: the log of the bilateral US dollar exchange rate; the log of the ratio of the country's consumer price index

Table 3

Coefficients of Variation of Exchange Rates and Fundamentals.

Country	Exchange Rate	Relative Prices	Interest Differential
France	18.16	8.32	199.38
Germany	16.23	2.51	54.52
Japan	14.58	2.79	146.49
Switzerland	16.73	3.78	40.40
UK	22.36	5.17	56.91

© Royal Economic Society 1999

(CPI) to the US CPI; the difference between the country's three month euro-interest rate and that of the United States (interest rates are expressed as a proportion). The data set runs from January 1980 through to December 1997 and all of the variables have been first differenced. We note that exchange rates are between two and eight times more volatile than relative prices. This kind of result is often cited to make the point that exchange rates are much more volatile than economic fundamentals, and, of course, the finding is entirely consistent with what we said in Section 1 (this kind of result would also occur if we took other standard fundamentals such as money supplies and current accounts). However, the key thing to note from Table 3 is that interest differentials are much more volatile than exchange rates. Indeed, the excess volatility of interest rates with respect to exchange rates is similar in magnitude to the excess volatility of exchange rates to prices, the range for the former being between two and ten. So Table 3 makes the point that in trying to understand the behaviour of exchange rates it is more appropriate to take an asset price perspective than a commodity price perspective. Indeed, the insight that exchange rates should be thought of as asset prices is a fundamental contribution of the asset approach to the exchange rate.

One key contribution of the asset approach literature is that exchange rates are inherently forward looking – today's price is inextricably linked with the price in the next period, and so on. Although Flood and Rose (1995) use an asset market framework for their volatility comparisons, it is unclear if their approach fully captures the forward looking nature of these prices as expressed in, say, a forward looking monetary equation. Indeed, one way of reconciling the forecastability of exchange rates at short horizons, noted in the previous section, with the regime volatility result is to say that the kind of models producing good out-of-sample forecasts involve very rich data dynamic interactions. It is well known that these kinds of backward looking models can be equivalently interpreted as forward looking equations (feedback and feed-forward mechanisms). So it may be that it is the failure, at least in part, to capture this forward looking aspect which gives the regime volatility result.

A second way of tying up the out-of-sample forecasting results with the regime volatility issue is to note that the interest differential is equal to the sum of the expected exchange rate change and the portfolio balance effect. Therefore, so long as one incorporates this in an exchange rate modelling exercise it should capture the evolution of the effects Flood and Rose refer to in their paper.

A third way of reconciling the out-of-sample forecasting results with the regime volatility result is to focus on the time dimension. If one takes a typical bank with a foreign exchange dealing room, then the Frankel and Froot (1990) description of how foreign exchange rate trades take place is probably very realistic. On a daily basis, and indeed on any frequency up to a month, exchange rate movements are dominated by non-fundamentals such as chartist techniques and market microstructure factors. However, as we move beyond a month, traditional fundamentals become important in the dealings of banks, particularly if they have treasury exposure, and the usefulness of fundamentals

© Royal Economic Society 1999

becomes more and more pronounced the longer the horizon the bank is interested in forecasting. Using essentially static methods and monthly data it is perhaps not surprising that there is not a role for traditional fundamentals. Models which incorporate long-run cointegrating relationships are more likely to capture the low frequency trends in exchange rates and therefore are perhaps more likely to be successful at allowing traditional fundamentals to breathe. This seems to be borne out by the fact that forecastabilty in these kinds of models (on average) kicks in at about one quarter ahead. At the end of the day, then, it seems that what this controversy amounts to is a disagreement over the appropriate horizon at which traditional fundamentals come into play. The difference between my work and that of Flood and Rose may be thought of as lying in the timing – their interpretation of when fundamentals become more important would be much longer than mine.

4. Concluding Comments

In this paper I have focused on a controversy which is central to the international economics literature, namely the role and usefulness of traditional economic fundamentals in explaining exchange rate behaviour. Three aspects of this controversy were addressed: the ability of fundamentals to explain or capture the longer run trends in the behaviour of exchange rates; the ability of fundamentals to produce exchange rate forecasts which are an improvement over the simple martingale model; the sources of real exchange rate variability and, in particular, reconciling such with regime volatility.

In terms of the simplest fundamentals-based model, namely PPP, there is now considerable evidence to suggest that this construct is a useful device for capturing long-run exchange rate behaviour. In particular, for bilateral exchange rates during the recent float we know that weak-form PPP holds for US-based bilateral exchange rates, while strong-form PPP holds for most DM-based bilaterals. The adjustment speeds in these nominal relationships indicate half-lives of about 3 years. In contrast, studies which focus on bilateral real exchange rate behaviour find adjustment speeds which are painfully slow (around 20 years). However, when these bilaterals are stacked into a panel the adjustment speed drops to a half-life of about 4 years, very similar to that recovered from single country nominal studies. Nevertheless, such adjustment speeds are still regarded as too slow to be consistent with a traditional form of PPP. We have argued that there are ample ways of reconciling such half-lives with traditional PPP. For example, non-linearities, which can arise because of the existence of transaction costs, is one story which gives clean adjustment speeds consistent with traditional PPP. The persistence may also be explained by appealing to menu costs and the pricing to market policies of companies, factors which are well known in the theoretical literature but to date have not been fully explored in empirical studies.

Although PPP still seems to have considerable merit as a long-run construct, it is probably not very helpful from an assessment perspective. In particular, this is because knowing that PPP 'works' when, say, a non-linear adjustment

© Royal Economic Society 1999

has been made is not very helpful to a policy maker who needs a long-run exchange rate relationship for assessment purposes. However, although PPP has been resurrected of late and may be made consistent with a traditional interpretation, it is nevertheless probably not very useful for assessment purposes. Using models which explicitly recognise deviations from PPP appear to give appealing exchange rate relationships which may be exploited for assessment purposes.

I have also contended that fundamentals have a clear and significant role to play in determining the in-sample and out-of-sample performance of exchange rate models, such as the monetary model. This issue, as I have stressed, is at the core of the debate over the usefulness of fundamentals in explaining exchange rate behaviour. I contend that the Meese and Rogoff paradigm no longer rules the roost, and argue that there is now sufficient evidence to support the view that exchange rates are predictable at horizons as short as one month ahead. I believe there are various ways of reconciling this finding with the view that exchange rates seem to be excessively volatile during the recent float.

In sum, both short and long-run exchange rate modelling is alive and well. This is clearly a relief, at the very least, for those of us who have to teach fundamentals-based models in the classroom.

University of Strathclyde

References

Baldwin, R. and Krugman, P. (1989), 'Persistent trade effects of large exchange rate shocks', *Quarterly Journal of Economics*, vol. 104, pp. 635–54.

Blanchard, O. and Quah, D. (1989), 'The dynamic effects of aggregate demand and supply disturbances', *American Economic Review*, vol. 79, pp. 655–73.

Cassel, G. (1928), *Foreign Investments*, Lectures of the Harris Foundation, University of Chicago Press.

Chinn, M. and Meese, R. (1996), 'Banking on currency forecasts: how predictable is the change in money?', *Journal of International Economics*, vol. 38, pp. 161–78.

Clarida, R. and Gali, J. (1995), 'Sources of real exchange rate fluctuations: how important are nominal shocks?', *Carnegie-Rochester Series on Public Policy*, vol. 41, pp. 1–56.

Clark, P. B. and MacDonald, R. (1998), 'Exchange rates and economic fundamentals: a methodological comparison of BEERs and FEERs' IMF Working Paper 98/67 (May).

Delgado, F. A. (1991), 'Hysteresis, menu costs and pricing with random exchange rates', *Journal of Monetary Economics*, vol. 28, pp. 461–84.

Dixit, A. K. (1989), 'Hysteresis, import penetration, and exchange rate pass through', *Quarterly Journal of Economics*, vol. 104, pp. 205–28.

Dornbusch, R. (1976), 'Expectations and exchange rate dynamics', *Journal of Political Economy*, vol. 84, (December) pp. 1161–76.

Dornbusch, R. (1987) 'Exchange rates and prices', *American Economic Review*, vol. 77, pp. 93–106.

Dornbusch, R. (1988), 'Purchasing power parity', in *The New Palgrave: A Dictionary of Economics*, New York: Stockton Press.

Dumas, B. (1992), 'Dynamic equilibrium and the real exchange rate in a spatially separated world', *Review of Financial Studies*, vol. 5, pp. 153–80.

Engel, C. and Rogers, J. H. (1996), 'How wide is the border?', *American Economic Review*, vol. 86, pp. 1112–25.

Flood, R. and Rose, A. K. (1995), 'Fixing exchange rates: a virtual quest for fundamentals', *Journal of Monetary Economics*, vol. 36, pp. 3–37.

Flood, R. and Rose, A. K. (1999), 'Understanding exchange rate volatility without the contrivance of macroeconomics', ECONOMIC JOURNAL, vol. 109, (November), pp. F660–72.

© Royal Economic Society 1999

Frankel, J. and Froot, K. (1990), 'The US dollar in the eighties: the expectations of chartists and fundamentalists' *Economic Record*, Special Issue, pp. 24–38.

Frankel, J. and Rose, A. (1995), 'A survey of empirical research on nominal exchange rates' in (E. Grossman and K. Rogoff, eds), *The Handbook of International Economics*, vol. 3, Amsterdam: North Holland.

Frenkel, J. (1978), 'Purchasing power parity: doctrinal perspectives and evidence from the 1920's', *Journal of International Economics*, vol. 8, pp. 169–91.

Frenkel, J. (1981) 'Flexible exchange rates, prices and the role of "news": lessons from the 1970s', *Journal of Political Economy*, vol. 89, (August), pp. 665–705.

Johansen, S. and Juselius, K. (1992), 'Testing structural hypothesis in a multivariate cointegration analysis of the PPP and the UIP', *Journal of Econometrics*, vol. 53, pp. 211–24.

Krugman, P. (1989), *Exchange Rate Instability*, Cambridge MA: MIT Press.

MacDonald, R. (1993) 'Long-run purchasing power parity: is it for real?' *Review of Economics and Statistics*, vol. 75 (November), pp. 690–5.

MacDonald, R. (1995) 'Long-run exchange rate modeling: a survey of the recent evidence', *Staff Papers*, International Monetary Fund, vol. 42(3), pp. 437–89.

MacDonald, R. (1998), 'What do we really know about real exchange rates?', Oestereichische Nationalbank, Working paper 28, forthcoming as Chapter 2 of MacDonald and Stein (1999).

MacDonald, R. and Marsh, I. W. (1997), 'On Casselian PPP, cointegration and exchange rate forecasting' *Review of Economics and Statistics*, vol. 79 (November), pp. 655–64.

MacDonald, R. and Marsh. I. W. (1999), *Exchange Rate Modelling*, Amsterdam: Kluwer Academic Press.

MacDonald, R. and Stein, J. (1999), *Equilibrium Exchange Rates*, Amsterdam: Kluwer.

MacDonald, R. and Swagel, P. (1998), 'Real exchange rates and the business cycle' forthcoming as IMF working paper.

MacDonald, R. and Taylor, M. P. (1994), 'The monetary model of the exchange rate: long-run relationships, short-run dynamics and how to beat a random walk', *Journal of International Money and Finance*, vol. 13, pp. 276–90.

Mark, N (1995), 'Exchange rates and fundamentals: evidence on long-horizon predicatability', *American Economic Review*, vol. 85, pp. 201–18.

Marston, R. (1990), 'Pricing to market in Japanese manufacturing', *Journal of International Economics*, vol. 29, pp. 217–36.

Meese, R. and Rogoff, K. (1983), 'Empirical exchange rate models of the seventies: do they fit out of sample?', *Journal of International Economics*, vol. 14, pp. 3–24.

Obstfeld, M. and Taylor, A. M. (1997), 'Nonlinear aspects of goods-market arbitrage and adjustment: Hecksher's commodity points revisited', *Journal of Japanese and International Economies*, vol. 11, pp. 441–79.

Officer, L. H. (1976), 'The purchasing power parity theory of exchange rates: a review article', *Staff Papers*, International Monetary Fund, vol. 23, March, pp. 1–60.

Patel, J. (1990), 'Purchasing power parity as a long-run relation', *Journal of Applied Econometrics*, vol. 5, October-December, pp. 367–79.

Rogoff, K. (1995), 'The purchasing power parity puzzle', *Journal of Economic Literature*, vo. 34, pp. 647–68.

Schinasi, G. and Swami, P. (1987), 'The out-of-sample forecasting performance of exchange rate models when coefficients are allowed to change', Discussion Papers of the Federal Reserve System, No 301, Washington DC.

Stockman, A. (1988), 'Real exchange rate variability under pegged and floating nominal exchange rate systems: an equilibrium theory', *Carnegie Rochester Conference Series on Public Policy*, vol. 29, pp. 259–94.

Stockman, A. (1995), 'Sources of real exchange-rate fluctuations: a comment', *Carnegie Rochester Conference Series on Public Policy*, vol. 41, pp. 57–65.

Williamson, J. (1985), *The Exchange Rate System*, Washington, DC: Institute for International Economics.

Wolff, C. (1987), 'Time-varying parameters and the out-of sample forecasting performance of structural exchange rate models', *Journal of Business and Economics Statistics*, vol. 5, pp. 87–97.

© Royal Economic Society 1999

[2]

The monetary model of the exchange rate: long-run relationships, short-run dynamics and how to beat a random walk

RONALD MACDONALD

University of Strathclyde, Glasgow GL4 0LN, UK

AND

MARK P. TAYLOR

University of Liverpool, Liverpool L69 3BX, UK
and Centre for Economic Policy Research, London, UK

The monetary model is re-examined for the sterling–dollar exchange rate. First, it is demonstrated, using a multivariate cointegration technique, that an unrestricted monetary model is a valid framework for analyzing the long-run exchange rate. Second, we find, once proper account has been taken of the short-run data dynamics, that an unrestricted monetary model outperforms the random walk and other models in an out-of-sample forecasting contest. (JEL F31).

Modeling and forecasting the exchange rate is a hazardous occupation. Not only have the empirical exchange rate models developed over the last two decades proved notoriously fickle in their in-sample behavior when presented with different data sets and sample periods, they have also been shown to have inferior out-of-sample forecasting ability compared to naive models such as a random walk (Meese and Rogoff, 1983). The object of the present paper is to demonstrate that at least one of the main exchange rate models—the monetary model—does not behave as badly as is widely thought if it is given better treatment. In particular, we show that by treating the monetary model as a long-run equilibrium condition, and allowing for short-run dynamics, a monetary-type exchange rate equation can be found which has robust in-sample properties and forecasts well out-of-sample.

Since the inception of floating exchange rates in 1973, the asset approach to the exchange rate has become the dominant theoretical model of exchange rate determination.[1] Within the asset approach, there are essentially two alternative views of the appropriate assets to model. In the monetary models, non-money

* The authors are grateful to the UK ESRC for research funding under grant number R00002937. The authors wish to thank two anonymous referees and James Lothian for constructive comments on an earlier draft of the paper, although the usual disclaimer applies.

0261-5606/94/03 0276–015 © 1994 Butterworth-Heinemann Ltd

assets are assumed to be perfect substitutes and the exchange rate is determined by relative excess money supplies. In the portfolio balance class of models, non-money assets are assumed to be imperfect substitutes and have an important role to play, through the risk premium channel, in the determination of the exchange rate. The empirical evidence on asset approach exchange rate models has, to say the least, afforded them very little support; both their in-sample performance, judged by standard goodness-of-fit criteria and estimated coefficient signs, and their out-of-sample forecasting ability are usually seen as very poor (MacDonald and Taylor, 1992).

In this paper we re-examine the monetary class of models for the sterling–dollar exchange rate during the recent float. In particular, we examine the long- and short-run properties of the monetary model. Our approach is novel in a number of ways. First, we use a multivariate cointegration technique to test for the existence of a long-run relationship underpinning the monetary equation. In contrast to previous work, which uses a less appropriate methodology, we find evidence of cointegration. Our finding of cointegration facilitates an examination of the short-run monetary model using a dynamic error correction model. Our chosen error correction model satisfies a battery of in-sample diagnostics and also easily outperforms a random walk model, over a two-year post-estimation sample period, using dynamic forecasts. We believe that this latter finding is of some significance and suggests that previous exchange rate forecasting attempts may have been unsuccessful due to their failure to model the data dynamics adequately and in imposing inappropriate coefficient restrictions.[2]

The outline of the remainder of this paper is as follows. In Section I we discuss the monetary model and, in particular, the model's empirical validity. The data set used and some multivariate cointegration tests are presented in Section II. The monetary model's short-run dynamics are reported in Section III where some out-of-sample forecasting results are also presented. The paper closes with a concluding section.

I. The monetary model of exchange rate determination: a brief review of the evidence

A typical flexible-price monetary approach (FLMA) reduced form equation may be written as (for further discussion, see Bilson, 1978; Frenkel, 1976; and Hodrick, 1978):

$$\langle 1 \rangle \qquad s_t = \beta_1 m_t + \beta_2 m_t^* + \beta_3 y_t + \beta_4 y_t^* + \beta_5 i_t^l + \beta_6 i_t^{l*} + \gamma_t,$$

where s_t is the spot exchange rate (home currency price of foreign currency), m_t denotes the domestic money supply, y_t denotes domestic income, i_t^l denotes the long-term domestic interest rate, corresponding foreign magnitudes are denoted by an asterisk, γ_t is a disturbance term, and all variables, apart from the interest rate terms, are expressed in natural logarithms.

If the FLMA is correct, then it is expected that β_1 and β_2 should equal, respectively, +1 and −1, β_3 and β_4 should, respectively, be negative and positive with numerical values equal to income elasticities from domestic and foreign money demand functions, and β_5 and β_6 should, respectively, be positive and negative with numerical values similar to those from interest rate semi-elasticities in money demand functions. The domestic (foreign) interest rate has a positive (negative) influence on the exchange rate essentially because interest rates reflect inflation premia in this model; an increase in expected inflation results in agents switching from domestic currency into domestic and foreign bonds, generating a domestic currency depreciation.

Frankel (1979) has suggested that the view of the relationship between interest rates and the exchange rate portrayed in the simple FLMA is unrealistic, especially in the short term. He incorporates a real interest rate differential to capture the liquidity effects of monetary policy. The real interest rate is normally captured by an interest rate with a short-term maturity, since such rates are seen as rapidly reflecting the liquidity effects of monetary policy. Frankel's reduced form, usually referred to as the real interest rate differential (RID) model, is noted here as equation ⟨2⟩:

$$\langle 2\rangle \qquad s_t = \beta_1 m_t + \beta_2 m_t^* + \beta_3 y_t + \beta_4 y_t^* + \beta_5 i_t^l + \beta_6 i_t^{l*} + \beta_7 i_t^s + \beta_8 i_t^{s*} + v_t,$$

where i_t^s denotes a short-term interest rate. In the RID model, the coefficients on the variables entering the FLMA have the same interpretation; however, the key distinguishing feature separating the two models is the presence of home and foreign short-term interest rates, which are expected to have coefficients which are, respectively, negative and positive.

Equations ⟨1⟩ and ⟨2⟩ have been estimated by numerous researchers for the recent floating exchange rate experience. Early tests of equations ⟨1⟩ and ⟨2⟩ by, *inter alia*, Hodrick (1978), Bilson (1978) and Frankel (1979) tended to be supportive of the FLMA and RID models in that estimated coefficients largely confirmed priors and the equations had reasonable in-sample forecasting performance (in terms of basic diagnostics such as R^2 and Durbin–Watson statistics). Such tests were conducted with data up to around the end of 1978 and tended to be static or have very limited dynamics (such as partial adjustment terms).

Numerous other researchers have estimated versions of ⟨1⟩ and ⟨2⟩ for the period after 1978, again using static models or limited dynamics. The models have not performed well in the period beyond 1978, with estimated coefficients often wrongly signed or insignificant, and having poor in-sample performance (MacDonald and Taylor, 1992). Perhaps the most serious indictment against the monetary class of models is the finding by Meese and Rogoff (1983) that they fail to outperform a simple random walk in an out-of-sample forecasting contest. However, one major problem with previous empirical implementations of the monetary model is that they practically all fail properly to capture the dynamic data generating processes for the time series in question. One of the novel features of this paper is that we attempt to improve the forecasting performance of the monetary class of models by properly modeling such dynamics.

As a preliminary exercise to modeling the dynamics of the monetary model, we also test for the long-run relationship between the exchange rate and the monetary variables. Strictly speaking, the RID model incorporates short-run influences (through short-run real interest rates), only the FLMA may be tested in a long-run setting. A number of researchers (see, *e.g.*, Meese, 1986; Boothe and Glassman, 1987; McNown and Wallace, 1989) have tested for the validity of the monetary model in a long-run context using the two-step cointegration methodology proposed by Engle and Granger (1987). Thus, aside from differences in specification, a test for cointegration involves testing whether the residuals in

⟨1⟩ are stationary. The broad conclusion to emerge from this body of work is that exchange rates are not cointegrated with the standard vector of monetary variables. Since, if anything, the FLMA is a long-run model (given the manifest short-term deviations from PPP) this would tend to be a particularly injurious piece of evidence against its validity. However, we argue below that a cointegrating set may not previously have been unearthed for the monetary model because of the reliance by previous researchers on the Engle–Granger two-step methodology. A further novel aspect of our work is the estimation of a monetary cointegration vector using an appropriate multivariate estimation technique.

II. Multivariate cointegration: is there a long-run monetary model?

II.A. A multivariate cointegration procedure

In order to model short-run exchange rate dynamics in terms of monetary variables, we first seek to determine if there exists a long-run monetary relationship. As we have indicated, previous estimates of a long-run monetary model have been unsuccessful. However, previous tests, which rely on the Engle–Granger (1987) two-step methodology, suffer from a number of deficiencies. In order to test for cointegration we use the multivariate cointegration technique proposed by Johansen (1988).[3] This technique is superior to the simpler regression-based technique because it fully captures the underlying time series properties of the data, provides estimates of all of the cointegrating vectors that may exist among a vector of variables, and offers a test statistic for the number of cointegrating vectors which has an exact limiting distribution. This test may therefore be viewed as more discerning in its ability to reject a false null hypothesis.

The Johansen estimation test procedure is by now well known. The tests used are the TRACE Statistic, which tests for at most r cointegrating vectors among a system of $N > r$ time series, and the λMAX statistic, which tests for exactly r cointegrating vectors against the alternative hypothesis of $r+1$ cointegrating vectors (Johansen, 1988). The TRACE and λMAX statistics have non-standard distributions under the null hypothesis, although approximate critical values have been tabulated by Johansen (1988), Johansen and Juselius (1990) and Osterwald-Lenum (1990).[4]

A further advantage of using the Johansen methodology is that it allows direct hypothesis tests on the coefficients entering the cointegrating vectors. We may therefore test certain priors which have been widely discussed in the monetary approach literature. The novel feature of the present tests is that they are robust to the non-stationarity of the data; previous tests, which use the levels of the variables and standard t-tests or F-ratios, are not. The most common, and perhaps most important, restriction to test on ⟨1⟩ is whether there is proportionality between relative monies and the exchange rate. Additionally, a number of researchers have imposed equal and opposite coefficients on relative income and interest rate terms, although this has been criticized by Haynes and Stone (1981) and Rasulo and Wilford (1980). The latter restriction, on relative interest rates, is especially important since, if it does not hold, the forward substitutions which are now fairly commonplace in the literature should not be imposed (see MacDonald and Taylor, 1992). The hypotheses which we test on the monetary model are summarized in Table 1. In addition, we also tested exclusion restrictions on the various arguments—*i.e.* the exchange rate, money supplies, output and interest rates.

II.B. The data and some long-run results

The data for this study, relating to the dollar–sterling exchange rate and UK and US macroeconomic variables, are all taken from the IFS data tape, are monthly and run from January 1976 through December 1990.[5] Specifically, the exchange rate used is line ag (expressed as pounds per dollar), the chosen monetary aggregate is M1, line 34, the income measure is industrial production, line 66c, the long-term interest rates is line 61, and the short-term interest rate is line 60c. The money supply and industrial production series are seasonally adjusted. Because of collinearity between short- and long-term interest rates, we included only long-term rates in the cointegration analysis, although the effect of short-term rates on the short-run dynamics is considered in the next section. The last 24 data points—January 1989 through December 1990—were reserved for post-sample forecasting tests, and all estimations were initially carried out with data ending in December 1988.

In order to implement the Johansen procedure, a lag length must be chosen for the VAR and the orders of integration of the series entering the VAR must be determined. Our procedure for choosing the optimal lag length was to test down from a general 13-lag system until reducing the order of the VAR by one lag could be rejected at the 5 per cent level, using a likelihood ratio statistic. The residuals from the chosen VAR were then checked for whiteness. If, at this stage, the residuals in any equation proved to be non-white, we sequentially chose a higher lag structure until they were whitened; a twelfth-order lag satisfied these criteria. The orders of integration of the series were determined using standard Dickey–Fuller and Phillips–Perron statistics. We report the former in addition to the latter because there is now a growing consensus that the Dickey–Fuller class of statistics have better small-sample properties (see Campbell and Perron, 1992).

In Table 2, our tests for a unit root indicate that all series are I(1) processes.[6] As a preliminary to our multivariate tests we tested the FLMA model using the Engle–Granger two-step method and our results are reported here as equation ⟨3⟩:

$$\langle 3\rangle \quad s_t = -0.471m_t + 1.036m_t^* - 0.733y_t - 0.284y_t^* - 0.052i_t^l + 0.0041i_t^{l*}$$

$$\text{CRDW} = 0.11 \qquad \text{CRDF} = -2.03 \qquad \text{CRADF}(6) = -2.17$$

TABLE 1. Some commonly imposed monetary restrictions.

$$s_t = \beta_1 m_t + \beta_2 m_t^* + \beta_3 y_t + \beta_4 y_t^* + \beta_5 i_t^l + \beta_6 i_t^{l*} + \gamma_t$$

$H_1: \beta_1 = -\beta_2 = 1$	$H_4 = H_1 \cap H_2$	
$H_2: \beta_3 + \beta_4 = 0$	$H_5 = H_1 \cap H_3$	$H_7 = H_1 \cap H_2 \cap H_3$
$H_3: \beta_5 + \beta_6 = 0$	$H_6 = H_2 \cap H_3$	

TABLE 2. Tests for a unit root in the data.

	Dickey–Fuller				Phillips–Perron			
	Level τ_μ	First Difference τ_μ	Level τ_τ	First Difference τ_τ	Level $Z(\tau_\mu)$	First Difference $Z(\tau_\mu)$	Level $Z(\tau_\tau)$	First Difference $Z(\tau_\tau)$
m^*	−0.56(1)	−8.34	−2.62(1)	−8.32	−0.70	−11.53	1.75	−11.51
y^*	−0.77(12)	−2.71(12)	−3.03(12)	−2.74(12)	−0.66	−8.77	−2.57	−8.74
i^{s*}	0.63(12)	−3.31(12)	−2.36(12)	−3.55(12)	−2.23	−10.83	−2.10	−10.81
i^{l*}	−1.58(6)	−7.64(6)	−1.56(6)	−7.63(6)	−2.08	−9.79	−3.48	−10.81
m	0.66(1)	−18.58	−2.36(1)	−18.59	0.48	−18.08	−2.82	−18.09
y	−1.15(1)	−17.09	−2.58(1)	−17.06	−1.18	−17.35	−2.93	−17.33
s	−1.63	−9.35	−1.09	−13.83	−1.82	−13.94	−1.51	−13.97
i^s	−2.40	−11.64	−2.42	−11.61	−2.85	−11.45	−2.89	−11.43
i^l	−1.64(4)	−5.36(4)	−1.45(4)	−5.43(4)	−1.89	−10.95	−1.66	−10.94

Notes: The symbols m, y, s, i^s, i^l, denote, respectively, the narrow money supply, industrial production, the spot exchange rate, the short-term interest rate, and the long-term interest rate (see the text for data source and exact definition). The reported numbers in the columns headed Dickey–Fuller are standard Dickey–Fuller statistics for the null hypothesis that the sum of the coefficients in the autoregressive representation of the variable sum to unity. τ_μ is a test statistic allowing for constant mean; τ_τ is a test statistic allowing for trend in mean. Numbers in parenthesis after these statistics indicate the lag length used in the autoregression to ensure residual whiteness. The reported numbers in the columns headed Phillips–Perron are Dickey–Fuller statistics, with the modification suggested by Phillips (1987). In constructing these statistics we have allowed for up to twelfth-order autocorrelation and used a Bartlett lag window to ensure positive definiteness (Newey and West, 1987). For both sets of statistics, the null hypothesis is that the series in question is I(1). Approximate critical value at the 5 per cent level for τ_μ and $Z(\tau_\mu)$ is −2.89, with rejection region $(\phi|\phi < -2.89)$; the 5 per cent rejection region for τ_τ and $Z(\tau_\tau)$ is $(\phi|\phi < -3.43)$. (See Fuller, 1976.)

Where CRDW, CRDF and CRADF denote, respectively, the Durbin–Watson, Dickey–Fuller and Augmented Dickey–Fuller statistics based on the residuals from the cointegrating regression, the number in parentheses after the CRADF denotes the lag length used to construct the statistic. These results confirm the findings of other researchers who test asset approach reduced forms (MacDonald and Taylor, 1992)—the coefficients are all, apart from that on domestic income, wrongly signed and the CRDW, CRDF and CRADF statistics are all insignificant at standard significance levels. MacKinnon (1991) has estimated response surfaces for the critical values of the CRDF statistic for cointegrating equations with up to six variables. The 5 per cent critical value implied for our sample size and a six-variable equation by MacKinnon's estimates is −4.815. For a seven-variable system this would be larger in absolute size, so that the null hypothesis of non-cointegration clearly cannot be rejected using the CRDF or CRADF statistics. Similarly, a 5 per cent critical value of 0.386 for CRDW, suggested by the Monte Carlo evidence of Engle and Granger (1987), also suggests non-cointegration on our evidence.

In Table 3 we report the TRACE and maximum eigenvalue statistics obtained using Johansen's multivariate maximum likelihood technique for estimating cointegrating relationships. On the basis of these statistics, we may reject the hypothesis that there are no cointegrating vectors: there would appear to be up to three such relationships. Our finding of at least one cointegrating vector indicates that the monetary model would seem to have some long-run validity. This result contrasts sharply with the findings of other researchers (see *inter alia* Meese, 1986; McNown and Wallace, 1989), who have been unable to discover even a long-run relationship for the monetary variables, and our two-step result reported as equation ⟨3⟩. The fact that we are also unable to obtain a cointegration relationship for our sample period using the two-step methodology suggests that the multivariate results are due to the use of a more powerful technique rather than being sample-specific.

This finding of cointegration allows us to proceed to some tests of popularly imposed monetary restrictions summarized in Table 1. Interestingly, we find that

TABLE 3. Results of Johansen maximum likelihood estimation.

Number of cointegrating vectors	λMAX	Trace	5 per cent critical values λMAX	5 per cent critical values Trace
$r \leqslant 6$	0.00	0.00	9.24	9.24
$r \leqslant 5$	8.37	8.38	15.67	19.96
$r \leqslant 4$	16.97	25.35	22.00	34.91
$r \leqslant 3$	23.83	49.18	28.14	53.11
$r \leqslant 2$	48.13*	97.31*	34.40	76.07
$r \leqslant 1$	50.12*	147.44*	40.30	102.14
$r = 0$	74.43**	221.87*	46.45	131.70

Notes: r denotes the number of cointegrating vectors. The 5 per cent critical values of the maximum eigenvalue (λMAX) and the Trace statistics are taken from Osterwald-Lenum (1990). The vector autoregressions included a constant. An asterisk denotes significance at the 5 per cent level.

all of the restrictions are rejected at standard significance levels (Table 4). Thus, although we have found some support for the monetary model, in that the variables which that approach suggests are important in determining the exchange rate are, indeed, cointegrated with the exchange rate, our analysis also suggests that the relationship may not be quite as simple as the basic FLMA suggests. However, taking the cointegrating vector which corresponds to the second largest eigenvalue, we have:

$$\langle 4\rangle \qquad s_t = 0.209m_t - 0.498m_t^* - 0.098y_t + 0.646y_t^* + 0.035i_t^l + 0.086i_t^{l*}$$

where an asterisk denotes a US variable.

Equation ⟨4⟩ does not, in fact, do great violence to the monetary model in the sense that all of the coefficients, apart from that on the US interest rate, are of the expected sign and are at least numerically close to satisfying the monetary restrictions. A drawback with the Johansen analysis is that it requires coefficient restrictions to be tested on the *full* set of significant cointegrating vectors. Thus, it is possible—and, in the light of ⟨4⟩, plausible—that a cointegrating vector may yet exist which satisfies some or all of the restrictions in Table 1.

A number of authors have recently applied the cointegration methodology to estimate long-run money demand functions in the UK and the USA (Hendry and Ericsson, 1991; Miller, 1991; Hafer and Jansen, 1991; MacDonald and Taylor, 1991), and have found some evidence of long-run stability. Thus, our finding of evidence in favor of a long-run monetary model implies indirect evidence in favor of long-run purchasing power parity (PPP), since PPP forms the link between stable domestic money demand and the monetary exchange rate equation. Direct evidence on long-run PPP is notoriously mixed, although recent evidence tends to support the existence of long-run reversion to PPP (Abuaf and Jorion, 1990; Lothian and Taylor, 1992; MacDonald, 1993 and Pippenger, 1993).[7]

In Table 5, we report test statistics for exclusion restrictions on the exchange rate, money supplies, output and interest rates in the cointegrating relationship. In each case, the restrictions are easily rejected.

TABLE 4. Tests of some popular monetary restrictions.

H_1	46.31 (0.00)
H_2	13.55 (0.00)
H_3	35.34 (0.00)
H_4	67.64 (0.00)
H_5	85.48 (0.00)
H_6	49.66 (0.00)
H_7	114.91 (0.00)

Note: H_1 to H_7 denote the hypotheses summarized in Table 1. The numbers not in parenthesis are χ^2 statistics with degrees of freedom equal to rxk, where r denotes the number of cointegrating vectors and k is the number of restrictions. The numbers in parenthesis are marginal significance levels, accurate to two decimal places.

TABLE 5. Tests of exclusion restrictions.

Exchange rate	27.90 (0.00)
Money supplies	48.47 (0.00)
Output	36.17 (0.00)
Interest rates	67.20 (0.00)

Notes: Figures not in parenthesis are χ^2 statistics with two degrees of freedom (one for the exchange rate restriction). Figures in parenthesis are marginal significance levels, accurate to two decimal places.

III. Short-run dynamics and out-of-sample forecasting performance: can we outwit a random walk?

In this section we use the long-run multivariate relationships derived in the previous section to model the short-run exchange rate dynamics for the sterling–dollar exchange rate. The short-run dynamic equation is then used to construct out-of-sample forecasts, which are compared to a number of alternative forecasting models.

Following the now familiar general-to-specific modeling strategy, we initially estimated a twelfth-order autoregressive distributed lag of the nominal exchange rate on home and foreign money, industrial production and short- and long-term interest rates, for the period 1974:1 to 1988:12. To this was added one lag of an 'error correction' term (ecm), formed from the cointegrating relationship reported in ⟨4⟩:

$$\langle 5\rangle \quad \text{ecm}_{t-1} = s_{t-1} - 0.209m_{t-1} + 0.498m^*_{t-1} + 0.098y_{t-1} - 0.646y^*_{t-1} - 0.035i^l_{t-1} - 0.086i^{l*}_{t-1}$$

We then sequentially imposed statistically insignificant restrictions in order to reduce the dimensions of the parameter space. The final parsimonious specification we arrived at was as follows:

$$\langle 6\rangle \quad \underset{}{\Delta s_t} = \underset{(0.005)}{-0.017\Delta i^{l*}_{t-3}} + \underset{(0.003)}{0.008\Delta i^s_t} + \underset{(0.003)}{0.006\Delta^2 i^{s*}_t} \underset{(0.008)}{-0.026\text{ecm}_{t-1}} \underset{(0.017)}{-\ 0.052}$$

$$R^2 = 0.14; \quad \sigma = 3\%; \quad \eta_1[24,148] = 1.03(0.43);$$

$$\eta_{2,1-3}[3,145] = 0.77(0.51); \quad \eta_{2,3-6}[4,144] = 0.87(0.48);$$

$$\eta_{3,1}[1,146] = 1.27(0.26); \quad \eta_{3,1-3}[3,142] = 2.02(0.11);$$

$$\eta_4[1,147] = 1.16(0.28); \quad \eta_5[12,124] = 0.66(0.78); \quad \eta_6[14,133] = 0.91(0.55).$$

Where R^2 is the coefficient of determination; σ is the standard error of the regression; figures in parentheses below coefficient estimates are estimated heteroscedastic-consistent standard errors (White, 1980); η_1 is the predictive failure test statistic (Chow, 1960); $\eta_{2,1-3}$ and $\eta_{2,3-6}$ are, respectively, Lagrange multiplier serial correlation test statistics which test for serial correlation from lags one to three and three to six; $\eta_{3,1}$ and $\eta_{3,1-3}$ are Lagrange multiplier test statistics for first and third-order ARCH effects in the residuals; η_4 is a RESET misspecification test statistic; η_5 is a heteroscedasticity test statistic based on the quadratic form of the regressors; and η_6 is a general (White, 1980) test for functional form misspecification and heteroscedasticity. The η statistics are distributed as central F under the relevant null hypothesis, with degrees of freedom in square brackets and marginal significance levels in parenthesis.[8] Our chosen equation easily passes this battery of equation diagnostics. Perhaps most impressively, the equation also passes the out-of-sample forecasting test for the 24 month period up to 1990:12 (η_1). This seems a powerful result, given the fact that the equation was estimated only for the period up to 1988:12.

In Figure 1, the actual and fitted values of the change in the exchange rates over the period 1976:1 to 1988:12 and out-of-sample forecasting periods are reported; the actual and fitted values for the out-of-sample period are reported in Figure 2. Further evidence of the goodness of fit of our estimated equation is revealed by these figures. Thus, in Figure 1 the predicted exchange rate change from the model tracks the actual exchange change well and manages to get a considerable number of turning points correct. More significantly, the model is also able to get most of the out-of-sample turning points correct. The model's directional performance would, we believe, be attractive to an investor considering taking a speculative position in the dollar or pound. In Figure 2 notice that only one out of the twenty-four observations of the actual exchange rate change falls outside the two standard error bars, an outcome which could occur by chance even if the model is correctly specified.

We also tested for sequentially including the first and third cointegrating vectors in the preferred equation. This yielded Lagrange multiplier statistics of 0.814 (for the first cointegrating vector), and 3.525 (for the second cointegrating vector). Both of these statistics have a central F distribution under the null hypothesis with marginal significance levels of 37 and 7 per cent, respectively.

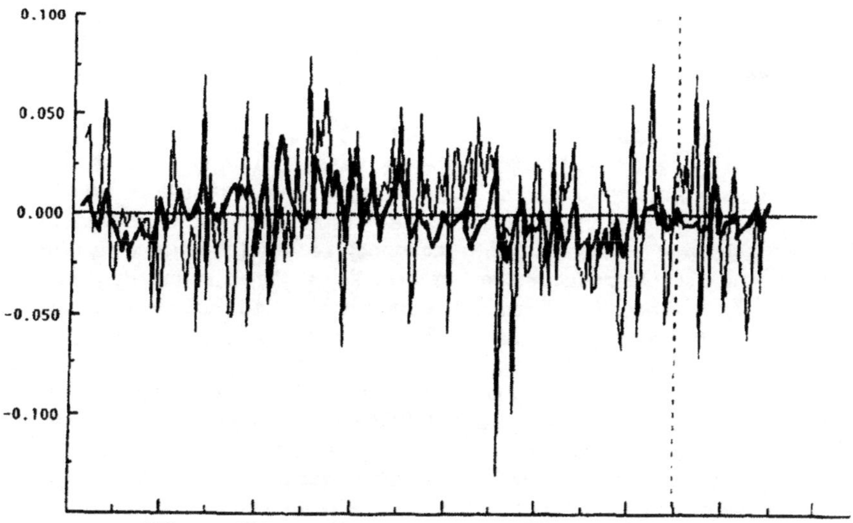

FIGURE 1. Actual and fitted values.
Δs_t = —— Fitted = ▬▬

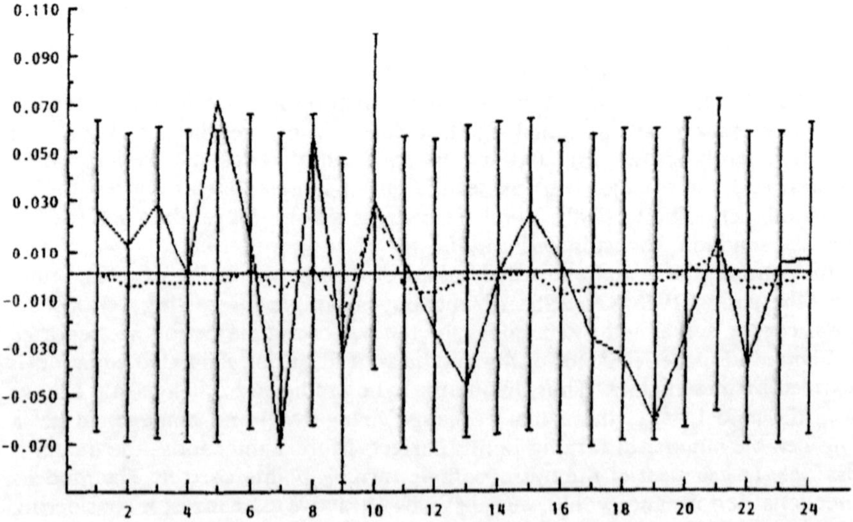

FIGURE 2. Forecasts and two standard error bars.
Δs_t = —— Forecast = - - -

The next set of tests of our preferred model's adequacy involved testing whether it encompassed an alternative model often adopted in empirical work, namely a version of equation ⟨2⟩ estimated in first differences. We refer to our preferred equation as model 1 and the alternative model as model 2. We calculated four encompassing test statistics: the Cox, Ericsson IV, Sargan and Joint Model test statistics. These four statistics are reported in Table 6. Interestingly, all four statistics indicate that model 1 encompasses model 2 but that model 2 does not encompass model 1. This gives further support for our approach.

The last stage of testing for the adequacy of our estimated model entailed considering its out-of-sample forecasting performance. We conducted this in the following way. The model reported as equation ⟨6⟩ above was estimated up to the end of 1988. This estimated equation was then used to forecast the exchange rate for five forecasting horizons, namely one, three, six, nine and twelve months ahead over the period 1989:1 to 1990:12. The estimated values of the level of the exchange rate were then fed back into the model (*i.e.* into the error correction term) and a further set of forecasts made; our forecasts are therefore fully dynamic. This process was continued for all remaining observations and root-mean-square error (RMSE) statistics were calculated over the five forecasting horizons. As a comparison, we computed RMSE statistics for a number of alternative models: a simple random walk, a simple random walk with drift, the simple FLMA equation in differences (equation ⟨2⟩ in first differences), our preferred equation with the error correction term omitted, and our preferred equation augmented to include all three cointegrating vectors as error correction terms lagged once. The parameters for these models were also sequentially re-estimated as described above.

The results from the forecasting exercise are reported in Table 6, and are of considerable interest: in all instances the estimated model clearly outperforms

TABLE 6. Encompassing tests.

Null hypothesis: Model 1 Encompasses Model 2	Test	Null hypothesis: Model 2 Encompasses Model 1
$1.857 \sim N(0, 1)$ (0.06)	Cox	$-7.431 \sim N(0, 1)$ (0.00)
$1.792 \sim N(0, 1)$ (0.07)	Ericsson IV	$6.808 \sim N(0, 1)$ (0.00)
$6.383 \sim \chi^2$ (6) (0.38)	Sargan	$17.680 \sim \chi^2$ (4) (0.00)
$1.067 \sim F(6, 141)$ (0.39)	Joint model	$4.895 \sim F(4, 141)$ (0.00)

Note: Figures in parenthesis below test statistics are marginal significance levels.

TABLE 7. Out of sample forecasts: random walk versus the monetary model.

Forecast horizon (months):	1	3	6	9	12
RMSE for random walk	0.035	0.061	0.093	0.114	0.132
RMSE for random walk with drift	0.035	0.062	0.096	0.119	0.142
RMSE for ECM monetary model	0.032	0.057	0.082	0.094	0.105
RMSE for first-differenced monetary model	0.035	0.063	0.104	0.137	0.167
RMSE for augmented ECM monetary model	0.033	0.059	0.082	0.092	0.096
RMSE for dynamic non-ECM model	0.033	0.058	0.091	0.112	0.138

the random walk model (with or without a drift term) across the range of forecasting horizons. Our model also clearly dominates the other versions of the monetary model, described above, except for two horizons (9 and 12 months) with the augmented ECM monetary model. We attribute the slightly superior long-horizon performance of this model, which is after all essentially a less parsimonious version of our preferred model, to the extra information it contains due to the inclusion of the two extra cointegrating vectors. It is also interesting to note that the type of equation that has often been estimated in the literature—the first difference version of ⟨2⟩—fails to outperform a random walk at any of the forecasting horizons.

Finally, we note that the degree of improvement in the root-mean-square forecast error of the monetary error correction model over the random walk model rises as the forecasting horizon is extended, from about 8.5 per cent at the one-month horizon to over twenty per cent at the twelve-month horizon. Statistically, this may be attributed to the effect of the error correction term. Economically, it suggests the increasing importance of economic fundamentals at longer horizons.

IV. Conclusions

In this paper we have re-examined the monetary model using data for the sterling–dollar exchange rate. A number of novel findings were reported. In particular, we demonstrated that there were up to three statistically significant cointegrating vectors between the exchange rate and domestic and foreign money supplies, industrial outputs and long-term interest rates. This finding contrasts sharply with the cointegration results of a number of other researchers, and we attribute it to our use of a more appropriate estimation methodology. This technique facilitated tests of some popular restrictions imposed on monetary reduced forms. Such restrictions were shown to be rejected by the data when imposed on the full set of cointegrating vectors, although at least one of the significant cointegrating relationships was not greatly different from what the monetary approach would predict. Using this unrestricted estimated cointegrating vector, a dynamic error correction model was fitted to the data which was shown to perform well in terms of both in-sample and out-of-sample criteria. Indeed, the monetary error correction model was demonstrated to outperform random walk forecasting mechanisms (the usual metric for exercises of this kind) at all five forecasting horizons examined, with the degree of improvement over the random walk rising steadily as the forecasting horizon was extended. The monetary error correction model also outperformed a range of alternative models including a standard monetary model equation.

We believe that our results are significant, contrasting with much, if not all, of the extant empirical evidence on this issue. Overall, our approach suggests that the monetary class of exchange rate models, interpreted carefully and with allowance made for complex short-run dynamics, may still be usefully applied, and warrants further research.[9]

Notes

1. The first papers on this approach appeared in the June 1976 edition of the *Scandinavian Journal of Economics*. Useful surveys of the approach are given by Boughton (1988), Isard (1988), and MacDonald and Taylor (1992).
2. Interestingly, previous attempts to incorporate dynamics into the monetary model, by introducing partial adjustment terms, have met with some, albeit limited, success (Woo, 1985; Somanath, 1986).
3. See Cuthbertson *et al.* (1992) for an accessible introduction to cointegration analysis and the Johansen technique.
4. The critical values recorded in Johansen's 1988 paper are for a VAR without an intercept term. Johansen (1990) reports critical values for VAR systems with a constant for systems of up to 5 variables. These critical values have been extended by Osterwald-Lenum (1990) for systems of up to 11 variables. We utilize these latter critical values in the present study.
5. Shiller and Perron (1985) and Lothian and Taylor (1992) demonstrate that the total length of the sample period, rather than the frequency of observation, is the important factor when examining the long-run properties of time series. Moving to higher-frequency observations would, therefore, be unlikely to affect the results qualitatively.
6. For two of the series (US industrial production and US long-term interest rate) there is some evidence of stationarity around a trend. However, given the power of such tests, we would argue that this evidence is slight and consider these series to be I(1) processes.
7. Using the dollar–sterling data used in this paper for the period January 1976 to December 1988, together with data on UK and US consumer price indices (from IFS), we were also able to find evidence of long-run PPP using the Johansen technique.
8. Under the appropriate null hypothesis. See Cuthbertson *et al.* (1992) for a discussion of modern regression diagnostics.
9. An anonymous referee has suggested that our success in forecasting the exchange rate may be due to the relative stability of the dollar–sterling real exchange rate over the 1988–90 period. Further empirical work might, therefore, check our findings for other exchange

rates and time periods. The present authors have found similar results for the dollar–mark exchange rate over the same period (MacDonald and Taylor, 1993).

References

ABUAF, NISO, AND PHILIPPE JORION, 'Purchasing Power Parity in the Long Run,' *Journal of Finance*, March 1990, **45**: 157–174.

BILSON, JOHN F. O., 'Rational Expectations and the Exchange Rate,' in Jacob A. Frankel and Harry G. Johnson, eds, *The Economics of Exchange Rates*, Reading, MS.: Addison-Wesley, 1978.

BOOTHE, PAUL AND DEBRA GLASSMAN, 'Off the Mark: Lessons for Exchange Rate Modeling,' *Oxford Economic Papers*, September 1987, **39**: 443–457.

BOUGHTON, JAMES M., 'The Monetary Approach to Exchange Rates: What Now Remains?' *Princeton Studies in International Finance*, No. 171, Princeton, New Jersey: Princeton University, 1988.

CAMPBELL, JOHN Y. AND PIERRE PERRON, 'Pitfalls and Opportunities: What Macroeconomists Should Know About Unit Roots,' NBER Technical Working Paper No. 100, 1992.

CHOW, GREGORY C., 'Tests of Equality Between Sets of Coefficients in Two Linear Regressions,' *Econometrica*, May 1960, **28**: 591–605.

CUTHBERTSON, KEITH, STEPHEN G. HALL, AND MARK P. TAYLOR, *Applied Econometric Techniques*, Ann Arbor: University of Michigan Press, and London: Phillip Allan, 1992.

ENGLE, ROBERT F., AND CLIVE W. J. GRANGER, 'Cointegration and Error Correction: Representation, Estimation and Testing,' *Econometrica*, March 1987, **55**: 251–276.

FINN, MARY G., 'Forecasting the Exchange Rate: A Monetary or Random Walk Phenomenon?' *Journal of International Money and Finance*, June 1986, **5**: 181–220.

FRANKEL, JEFFREY A., 'On the Mark: A Theory of Floating Exchange Rates Based on Real Interest Differentials,' *American Economic Review*, May 1979, **64**: 610–622.

FRENKEL, JACOB A., 'A Monetary Approach to the Exchange Rate: Doctrinal Aspects and Empirical Evidence,' *Scandinavian Journal of Economics*, May 1976, **78**: 200–224.

FULLER, WAYNE A., *Introduction to Statistical Time Series*, New York: Wiley, 1976.

HAFER, ROBERT W., AND DENNIS W. JANSEN, 'The Demand for Money in the United States: Evidence from Cointegration Tests,' *Journal of Money, Credit and Banking*, May 1991, **23**: 155–168.

HAYNES, STEPHEN E., AND JOE A. STONE, 'On the Mark: Comment,' *American Economic Review*, December 1981, **71**: 1060–1067.

HENDRY, DAVID F., AND NEIL R. ERICSSON, 'An Econometric Analysis of UK Money Demand,' *American Economic Review*, February 1991, **81**: 8–38.

HODRICK, ROBERT J., 'An Empirical Analysis of the Monetary Approach to the Determination of the Exchange Rate,' in Jacob A. Frenkel and Harry G. Johnson, eds, *The Economics of Exchange Rates*, Reading, MS: Addison-Wesley, 1978.

ISARD, PETER, 'Exchange Rate Modeling: An Assessment of Alternative Approaches,' in Ralph C. Bryant, Dale W. Henderson, Gerald Holtham, Peter Hooper, and Stephen A. Symansky, eds, *Empirical Macroeconomics for Interdependent Economics*, Washington: Brookings Institution, 1988.

JOHANSEN, SOREN, 'Statistical Analysis of Cointegration Vectors,' *Journal of Economic Dynamics and Control*, June/September 1988, **12**: 231–254.

JOHANSEN, SOREN, 'Estimation and Hypothesis Testing of Cointegration Vectors in Gaussian Vector Autoregressive Models,' *Econometrica*, July 1989, **59**: 1551–1580.

JOHANSEN, SOREN, AND KATARINA JUSELIUS, 'Maximum Likelihood Estimation and Inference on Cointegration—With Applications to the Demand for Money,' *Oxford Bulletin of Economics and Statistics*, May 1990, **52**: 169–210.

LOTHIAN, JAMES R., AND MARK P. TAYLOR, 'The Behavior of the Real Exchange Rate: The Recent Exchange Rate Float from the Perspective of the Past Two Centuries,' manuscript, International Monetary Fund, Washington, 1992.

MACDONALD, RONALD, 'Long-run Purchasing Power Parity: Is it for Real?,' *Review of Economics and Statistics*, November 1993 (forthcoming).

MACDONALD, RONALD, AND MARK P. TAYLOR, 'A Stable U.S. Money Demand Function, 1874–1975,' *Economics Letters*, October 1991, **39**: 191–198.

MacDonald, Ronald, and Mark P. Taylor, 'Exchange Rate Economics: A Survey,' International Monetary Fund *Staff Papers*, March 1992, **39**: 1–57.

MacDonald, Ronald, and Mark P. Taylor, 'The Monetary Approach to the Exchange Rate: Rational Expectations, Long-Run Equilibrium and Forecasting,' International Monetary Fund *Staff Papers*, March 1993, **40**: 89–107.

MacKinnon, James, 'Critical Values for Cointegration Tests,' in Robert F. Engle and Clive W. J. Granger, eds, *Long-Run Economic Relationships*, Oxford: Oxford University Press, 1991.

McNown, Robert, and Myles Wallace, 'Co-Integration Tests for Long Run Equilibrium in the Monetary Exchange Rate Model,' *Economics Letters*, December 1989, **31**: 263–267.

Meese, Richard A., 'Testing for Bubbles in Exchange Markets: A Case of Sparkling Rates?,' *Journal of Political Economy*, April 1986, **94**: 345–373.

Meese, Richard A., and Kenneth Rogoff, 'Empirical Exchange Rate Models of the Seventies: Do They Fit Out of Sample?,' *Journal of International Economics*, February 1983, **14**: 3–74.

Miller, Stephen M., 'Monetary Dynamics: An Application of Cointegration and Error-Correction Modeling,' *Journal of Money, Credit and Banking*, May 1991, **23**: 139–154.

Newey, Whitney K., and Kenneth D. West, 'A Simple, Positive Definite Heteroskedasticity- and Autocorrelation-Consistent Covariance Matrix,' *Econometrica*, May 1987, **55**: 703–708.

Osterwald-Lenum, M., 'Recalculated and Extended Tables of the Asymptotic Distribution of Some Important Maximum Likelihood Cointegrating Test Statistics,' mimeo (University of Copenhagen, 1990).

Phillips, Peter C. B., 'Time Series Regression With a Unit Root,' *Econometrica*, March 1987, **55**: 277–301.

Pippenger, Michael K., 'Cointegration Tests of Purchasing Power Parity: the Case of Swiss Exchange Rates,' *Journal of International Money and Finance*, February 1993, **12**: 46–61.

Putnam, Bluford H., and John R. Woodbury, 'Exchange Rate Stability and Monetary Policy,' *Review of Business and Economic Research*, 1979, **15**: 1–10.

Rasulo, James A., and D. Sykes Wilford, 'Estimating Monetary Models of the Balance of Payments and Exchange Rates: A Bias,' *Southern Economic Journal*, July 1980, **47**: 136–146.

Schwert, G. William, 'Effects of Model Specification on Tests for Unit Roots in Macroeconomic Data,' *Journal of Monetary Economics*, July 1987, **20**: 73–103.

Shiller, Robert J., and Pierre Perron, 'Testing the Random Walk Hypothesis: Power versus Frequency of Observation,' *Economics Letters*, 1985, **18**: 381–386.

Somanath, V. S., 'Efficient Exchange Rate Forecasts: Lagged Models Better than the Random Walk,' *Journal of International Money and Finance*, June 1986, **5**: 195–220.

White, Halbert, 'A Heteroskedasticity-Consistent Covariance Matrix Estimator and a Direct Test for Heteroskedasticity,' *Econometrica*, February 1980, **48**: 55–68.

Woo, Wing T., 'The Monetary Approach to Exchange Rate Determination Under Rational Expectations,' *Journal of International Economics*, February 1985, **18**: 1–16.

[3]

ON FUNDAMENTALS AND EXCHANGE RATES: A CASSELIAN PERSPECTIVE

Ronald MacDonald and Ian W. Marsh*

Abstract—Using an expanded version of the purchasing-power-parity condition we construct simultaneous equation models for three key exchange rates which incorporate meaningful long-run equilibrium relationships and complex short-run dynamics. We show that fully dynamic out-of-sample forecasts from these models are capable of significantly outperforming those of a random walk model over horizons as short as 3 months, and that they are also more accurate than the vast majority of professional forecasts.

I. Introduction

THE MEESE and Rogoff (1983) finding that fundamentals-based models of the exchange rate fail to beat a random walk in an out-of-sample forecasting exercise has generated considerable pessimism about the usefulness of macroeconomic variables in explaining exchange rates. It has led, for example, to renewed interest in speculative bubbles and fads and, more recently, the development of market microstructure hypotheses as nonfundamental explanations (see, for example, the references in Frankel and Rose (1994)).

Although the Meese and Rogoff conclusion has been confirmed by a number of authors (see, for example, Diebold et al. (1994) and Engel (1994)), a recent strand of the literature suggests that fundamentals-based models of the exchange rate can outperform a random walk, particularly over relatively long horizons (see Chinn and Meese (1995), MacDonald and Taylor (1994), and Mark (1995)). Despite this positive evidence, however, there is still a widespread perception that the random walk paradigm rules the roost over shorter horizons. This view is amply summarized by Frankel and Rose (1994) who, in their overview of the fundamentals-based exchange rate literature, conclude: ". . . the Meese and Rogoff analysis of *short horizons* has never been convincingly overturned or explained. It continues to exert a pessimistic effect on the field of empirical exchange rate modeling in particular and international finance in general" (p. 23, emphasis added).

The main message of our paper is that the pessimism widely expressed regarding fundamentals-based exchange rate modeling is misplaced. We demonstrate that a purchasing-power-parity (PPP)-based exchange rate model can be used to deliver a sensible in-sample performance and, most tellingly, significantly outperform a random walk and the vast majority of professional exchange rate forecasts over horizons as short as 3 months. More specifically, we seek to build on recent contributions to exchange rate modeling in the following ways. First, taking as our point of departure the recent literature on long-run exchange rate modeling, we use a simple version of PPP to produce sensible long-run exchange rate relationships for the bilateral U.S. dollar rates of the German mark, the U.K. pound, and the Japanese yen (see Edison (1991)). Second, the derived long-run relationships are used to produce (short-run) dynamic models which have sensible economic properties and satisfy a range of stringent econometric tests. Third, these dynamic exchange rate models are used to produce out-of-sample exchange rate forecasts. Unlike most previous work using such structures, our dynamic models are fully simultaneous and are not given any unfair informational advantage over a simple random walk. Fourth, we present tests of statistical significance of our out-of-sample forecasts. Again, almost all such previous work in this area neglects to provide significance tests of forecasting ability. Fifth, in addition to comparing our forecasts with those of a random walk model (which has become the academic benchmark), we provide an alternative metric based on the performance of a large international panel of professional exchange rate forecasts.

The outline of the remainder of this paper is as follows. We first advocate a method for obtaining sensible long-run exchange rate relationships for bilateral exchange rates, using only data from the recent float. We describe the data in section IV and the results of our long- and short-run exchange rate modeling in section V. In section VI our out-of-sample forecasts are evaluated, and the paper ends with some concluding comments.

II. Casselian Purchasing Power Parity and the Long-Run Exchange Rate

In this section we present a brief overview of recent research on long-run exchange rate modeling and how it relates to the long-run relationship used in this paper.

Recently there has been renewed interest in modeling long-run exchange rates using versions of PPP. One of the best-known proponents of PPP was Cassel. (For a summary of Cassel's work see Officer (1976).) He viewed PPP as a long-run condition to which the actual exchange rate tended once disturbances, real or nominal, had evaporated. In the Casselian view, the real exchange rate should be a mean-reverting process. This proposition has been tested using two related methods. Define s as the nominal exchange rate defined as domestic currency per unit of foreign currency and p as the domestic price level. Let an asterisk denote a foreign variable and lowercase letters indicate that the level of a variable has been transformed using the natural

Received for publication October 10, 1995. Revision accepted for publication September 23, 1996.

* University of Strathclyde.

The authors would like to thank Peter Clark, Rebecca Driver, David Hendry, Soren Johansen, Peter Spencer, two anonymous referees, and the Editor, Richard Caves, for many useful comments, and Mike Sykes of Consensus Economics for providing some of the data. The usual disclaimer applies. Financial support from the Nuffield Foundation and the ESRC (Grant R000232945) is gratefully acknowledged.

© 1997 by the President and Fellows of Harvard College and the Massachusetts Institute of Technology

logarithm operator. With reference to the regression equation (1),

$$s_t = \alpha + \beta p_t - \beta^* p_t^* + \xi_t \qquad (1)$$

a number of researchers have used cointegration methods to test the validity of the hypothesis that ξ_t is stationary or $I(0)$, and that symmetry ($\beta = \beta^*$) and homogeneity ($\beta = \beta^* = 1$) conditions are satisfied.[1] An alternative strand of research involves imposing symmetry and homogeneity on the exchange rate–relative price relationship and testing whether the real exchange rate is a mean-reverting process.[2] That is, in estimating

$$q_t = \alpha + \rho q_{t-1} + \epsilon_t \qquad (2)$$

where $q_t = s_t - p_t + p_t$ it would be expected that ρ lies between zero and unity.

A useful way of categorizing the estimates of equations (1) and (2) is to consider first the results using long-time-series spans of annual data (around 100 years) and, second, those for the recent floating period. When one takes long time spans of data, there is considerable evidence to support PPP in the sense that homogeneity and symmetry restrictions cannot be rejected and the residuals from an estimated version of equation (1) are stationary (see MacDonald (1995a)). Also, estimates of equation (2) using such data spans indicate relatively rapid mean reversion of real exchange rates. A typical half-life for a deviation from PPP to be corrected is 4 years (see Frankel (1986)). When using data from the recent floating period the results are rather different. Thus in terms of equation (1) there is considerable evidence to suggest that the residual series is mean reverting, but the homogeneity and symmetry restrictions are usually strongly rejected (see, for example, Cheung and Lai (1993a), Kugler and Lenz (1993), and MacDonald (1995a)). Also, although there is some evidence of mean reversion in real rates for the recent float, the process is painfully slow (and only starts to occur after 8 years).

One way to improve on these results, estimated using only data from the recent float, is to take a group of exchange rates and treat them as a panel. Defining $w_t' = \{p_t, p_t^*\}$, the idea here is that for an individual country the condition $E(w_t, \xi_t) = 0$ is likely to be violated (because deviations from PPP are correlated with the price differential). By taking a panel sample, the researcher increases the variability of the price differential relative to the PPP deviation (as represented by the disturbance), and hence any bias in the coefficient estimates should disappear as the panel dimensions increase (see Davutyan and Pippenger (1985)). This line of research has in fact been successful in the sense that symmetry and homogeneity restrictions cannot be rejected (see MacDonald (1988), Flood and Taylor (1996), and Frankel and Rose (1995)) and panel real exchange rates exhibit relatively rapid mean reversion (see Frankel and Rose (1995) and MacDonald (1996)). Although these results are interesting, they do not address the issue of how a sensible long-run relationship may be obtained for an individual currency using just data from the recent floating period. One way of approaching this is to ask what are the factors that produce a violation of $E(w_t, \xi_t) = 0$ for the recent float, and does conditioning on such factors, in addition to relative prices, allow one to satisfy the homogeneity condition?

An alternative way of considering this last point is to distinguish between what may be referred to as a "true" equilibrium position and an "empirical" equilibrium. The former concept may be defined in the following way. In some time frame, which may be referred to as the "long long run" (Breuer (1994)), it would be expected that long-term international money markets are in equilibrium (perhaps because net savings are at their desired level) and any real shocks that occur in a succession of short runs cancel out and PPP holds. This is the kind of equilibrium captured in the empirical studies discussed above, which use long runs of annual data. However, if the data span provided by the recent float is insufficient for true equilibrium to be reached, the empirical equilibrium should attempt to capture these other factors. We believe that this distinction is one that is in the spirit of Cassel's (1928) view of PPP. Cassel argued that since factors such as capital flows and "exogenous" elements would keep the exchange rate away from this value in the short to medium term, the attainment of absolute PPP pertains only in the (long) long run.

We propose capturing the concept of Casselian PPP using the following equilibrium relationship:

$$s_t = p_t - p_t^* - \gamma(i_t - i_t^* - \Delta s_{t+k}^e) + \xi_t \qquad (3)$$

where in addition to the terms already defined, i is the yield on bonds with maturity k, Δ is the difference operator, and superscript e denotes expectations such that Δs_{t+k}^e represents the expected change in the exchange rate over the subsequent k periods.[3,4] Although this kind of representation of the equilibrium exchange rate may be unfashionable from the perspective of open economy macromodels, from an empirical perspective, and especially for a period such as the recent float, it seems unreasonable to force stock-flow equilibrium, particularly with respect to long-term capital movements. It may be that such nonzero capital account effects reflect productivity differentials, expected inflation differentials, or the influence of relative monetary policies. Although these

[1] See, for example, Kugler and Lenz (1993) and MacDonald (1993).

[2] See, for example, Adler and Lehman (1983) and Roll (1979).

[3] It is straightforward to demonstrate that this kind of relationship may be derived from a simple balance of payments equilibrium condition, consisting of the sum of the current balance (a function of competitiveness) and the capital account (a function of expected interest yields). See MacDonald and Marsh (1996) for a fuller discussion.

[4] Defining $z_t' = \{p_t, p_t^*, i_t, i_t^*\}$, then the orthogonality condition that $E_t(z_t, \xi_t) = 0$ is now more likely to hold than in the relative price case discussed above.

underlying factors are not explicitly modeled in this paper, we believe that they may have persistent effects on exchange rates.

The empirical model we estimate is clearly not intended to be complete. However, the simplifications made do allow us to address the common and important empirical finding of nonhomogeneity of prices and to provide a firm foundation from which we can produce exchange rate forecasts that are, we believe, impressive.

III. The Econometrics of Small, Nonstationary Systems

Our modeling strategy follows recent developments in the econometric literature, in particular, the work of Clements and Mizon (1991), Hendry and Mizon (1993), and Johansen (1988). Essentially, this process involves starting with a general VAR model specified in levels from which the cointegrating relationships are recovered, and then simplifying the full VAR structure until a parsimonious simultaneous system is obtained. The final set of linear simultaneous equations then incorporate both long-run relatinships and short-run dynamics. The process of moving from the general VAR (a prerequisite of the Johansen method) to the parsimonious system is discussed in more detail below.

The familiar error correction form of a VAR is

$$\Delta x_t = \sum_{i=1}^{p-1} \Gamma_i \Delta x_{t-i} + \Pi x_{t-1} + \psi D_t + v_t \tag{4}$$

where $x = [s, p, p^*, i, i^*]$, D_t contains deterministic components (constant-trend, centered seasonal dummies and event dummies) and v_t is assumed to have mean zero, be homoskedastic, and serially uncorrelated.[5] The order of the VAR, p, is assumed finite to exclude moving-average components, and the parameters Γ_i, ψ, and Σ (the covariance matrix of v) are assumed constant. Π is interpreted as the matrix of long-run responses. If the data cointegrate, Π must be of reduced rank, $r < N$, where N is the number of variables in x. It can be factored such that

$$\Pi = \alpha\beta' \tag{5}$$

where β and α are $p \times r$ matrices, which give the cointegrating vectors (empirical long-run relationships) and the associated adjustment matrix, respectively (see Johansen (1988) and Johansen and Juselius (1990, 1992)). Due to the reduced-form nature of the cointegrating vectors there is an increasing trend toward performing transformations and imposing restrictions on the estimated cointegrating space to reveal "meaningful economic relationships." In this paper we can bring the economic model outlined in section II to bear on the problem.

[5] The expected long-run change in the exchange rate is not included in the vector of variables since this will be $I(0)$ under the weakest assumptions of rationality.

The imposition of restrictions on the cointegrating vector of the adjustment matrix will change the estimated short-run dynamics of equation (4) and the coefficients of the deterministic variables. These new coefficients are denoted by a tilde. If we also denote the restricted cointegration space by $\tilde{\Pi} = \tilde{\alpha}\tilde{\beta}'$, the constrained VAR (CVAR) can be written as

$$\Delta x_t = \sum_{i=1}^{p-1} \tilde{\Gamma}_i \Delta x_{t-i} + \tilde{\Pi} x_{t-1} + \tilde{\psi} D_t + w_t. \tag{6}$$

The CVAR is an intermediate stage in the modeling of the system. The next step is to make the system more parsimonious by exclusion restrictions on $\tilde{\Gamma}_i$. If we denote the coefficient on the lth lag ($l \leq p$) of the kth variable in the jth equation ($k, j \leq N$) of the CVAR by $\tilde{\Gamma}_{j,k,l}$, we test for valid reductions in the dimensions of the system, which take the form of the restriction that $\tilde{\Gamma}_{j,k,l}$ equals zero for all $j = 1, \ldots, N$. These restrictions are imposed on the basis of the t-ratio of an individual coefficient. More specifically, if a t-ratio is less than 2, the relevant variable is dropped from the equation. After the imposition of all such unrejected restrictions, the parsimonious VAR (PVAR) can be written as

$$\Delta x_t = \sum_{i=1}^{p-1} \breve{\Gamma}_i \Delta x_{t-i} + \tilde{\alpha}\tilde{\beta}' x_{t-1} + \breve{\psi} D_t + u_t \tag{7}$$

where a breve denotes a new matrix of coefficients following these restrictions.

The final stage in the procedure is to move from this reduced-form PVAR to simultaneous econometric models (SEMs) of the individual equations in the system. The simultaneous models are not unique and are normally governed by economic considerations rather than statistical distributions, but can be given, for instance, by

$$A_0 \Delta x_t = \sum_{i=1}^{p-1} A_i \Delta x_{t-i} + \alpha\tilde{\beta}' x_{t-1} + \varphi D_t + \mu_t. \tag{8}$$

In the final SEM, each equation is fully specified in that it may have contemporaneous as well as lagged dynamic terms, and may contain long-run equilibria ($\tilde{\beta}' x_{t-1}$) where the speed of adjustment is given by the coefficients in a. A key advantage of this modeling strategy is that it results in a full system of equations, rather than a single reduced form. This allows us to use what we believe is a stringent test of forecast ability since predicted values of all terms (exchange rates, prices, and interest rates) are used rather than actual data values.

IV. Data and Preliminary Results

Our exchange rate models contain five variables each—the spot exchange rate s, defined as the end-of-period home currency price of a unit of foreign (U.S.) currency (International Financial Statistics line 61), home and foreign consumer prices indices p and p^*, respectively (IFS line 64), and home and foreign long-term interest rates i and i^*. The definition of the latter is country-specific. Thus, for the United States we measure i^* by the yield on constant maturity 10-year U.S. Treasury bonds (IFS line 61), while we measure i by the yield on 10-year government bonds for Japan (Nikkei data service), 10-year government bonds for the United Kingdom Financial Statistics, CSO), and 9–10-year government bonds for Germany (Bundesbank). We have tried to match the maturity structures of the long bonds as closely as possible, although there will clearly be different risk characteristics reflected in the yields.

The survey data used in our out-of-sample forecast comparison are taken from Consensus Economics Inc. of London and consist of disaggregated forecasts for the spot value of the German mark, the Japanese yen, and the U.K. pound 3 and 12 months ahead. The Consensus survey, conducted by fax on the first Monday of every month, covers more than 150 commercial and investment banks, forecasting agencies, and industrial companies from the G7 countries. The first survey took place in September 1989, and our data end in November 1992. Further details of the survey can be found in MacDonald and Marsh (1993).

The nonsurvey time-series data run from January 1974 through to December 1992. In order to maintain comparability with the Consensus panel members, the initial determination of the model will only use data up to September 1989, that is, those observations available to forecasters when they made their first predictions in October 1989. This leaves 189 observations for model estimation.

All of the exchange rates and price series have been transformed using the natural logarithmic operator. The interest rate series are expressed in decimal form and we have included seasonal dummies as additional deterministic series. Visual inspection of the series and augmented Dickey–Fuller statistics (not reported) indicate that each series is nonstationary in levels but stationary after first differencing. We now proceed to model systems for the United Kingdom, Japan, and Germany, following the strategy outlined in section III.

V. From the Unrestricted VAR to the Restricted SEM

A. Long-Run Relationships

For the United Kingdom the Akaike and Schwarz information criteria indicate that a four-lag system adequately captures the dynamics of the system. However, there remains evidence of three substantial but explanable outliers: October 1976 for U.K. interest rates (relating to the sterling exchange rate crisis); July 1979 for U.K. prices (VAT increase); and May 1980 for U.S. interest rate (relating to the Federal Reserve Board's switch to monetary targeting). Each of these outliers is eliminated using dummy variables. The Japanese model needs just three lags in the VAR to capture the dynamics and three dummies in the U.S. interest rate equation (April 1980, December 1984, and January 1985) to reduce nonnormality. The first dummy is clearly due to the Fed's switch in policy, and the latter two may be related to the end of the dramatic appreciation of the dollar. More severe problems are encountered with the (three-lag) German model, and six dummies have to be included (February and April 1980 (Fed switch), February and November 1981, June 1982, and January 1985 (dollar downturn)).[6]

TABLE 1.—JOHANSEN COINTEGRATION ANALYSIS

	Germany		United Kingdom		Japan	
	λ_{max}[a]	Trace[a]	λ_{max}	Trace	λ_{max}	Trace
$r \leq 4$	2.43	2.43	2.22	2.22	1.76	1.76
$r \leq 3$	7.97	10.39	13.25	15.47	13.67	15.34
$r \leq 2$	16.31	26.70	15.88	31.34	17.14	32.57[b]
$r \leq 1$	25.36	52.06[b]	28.73[b]	60.07[b]	22.59	55.16[b]
$r = 0$	44.84[b]	96.89[b]	44.60[b]	104.67[b]	66.84[b]	122.01[b]
	Vector 1	Vector 2	Vector 1	Vector 2	Vector 1	Vector 2
	Standardized Eigenvectors β[c]					
s	1.000	1.000	1.000	1.000	1.000	1.000
p	−36.905	0.078	−2.332	−0.021	−10.655	−1.518
p^*	17.131	0.935	4.425	0.254	6.124	1.329
i	2.936	31.011	46.158	0.073	23.648	−14.622
i^*	12.319	−14.614	−27.368	−4.177	−15.883	−0.777
	Standardized Loadings α					
s	0.004	−0.009	−0.021	−0.064	0.003	−0.035
p	0.002	0.001	0.004	−0.002	0.004	−0.000
p^*	0.001	−0.003	0.000	−0.003	−0.000	−0.004
i	−0.000	−0.002	−0.003	0.000	−0.000	0.004
i^*	0.000	−0.000	−0.001	−0.004	0.000	−0.003

Notes: [a] Maximum eigenvalues λ_{MAX} and trace texts for number of cointegrating vectors
[b] Significant at the 5% level based on critical values taken from Osterwald-Lennum (1992).
[c] Two most significant vectors are arranged by decreasing size of eigenvalue for each country, normalized on exchange rate term.

The diagnostics indicate an absence of serial correlation in the VAR for all three currencies.[7] There is, however, evidence of nonnormality in some of the equations, reflecting a degree of excess kurtosis in the data (particularly the interest-rate series). Since Cheung and Lai (1993b) and Gonzalo (1994) demonstrate the robustness of the Johansen procedure to nonnormality, we make no further modeling provisions, but note that our results should be qualified in this respect.[8]

The estimated trace and maximum eigenvalue statistics are reported in table 1 for the three systems. On the basis of the trace tests, all three currencies produce evidence of at least two significant cointegrating relationships, while using the maximum eigenvalue test only one vector is significant

[6] Clements and Mizon (1991) advocate the use of dummy variables as an alternative to enlarging the system dramatically. However, we note that there is inevitably a tradeoff between adding extra variables to the model and excluding periods in which the model does not capture the dynamics by including dummies.

[7] To conserve space, these are not given here but are detailed in a working paper available from the authors on request.

[8] The use of further dummy variables might have eradicated this nonnormality, but the properties of the Johansen procedure in the presence of several deterministic dummy variables is unknown.

TABLE 2.—THEORETICAL RESTRICTIONS ON COINTEGRATING VECTORS

Hypothesis	Economic Interpretation	Implied Restriction on β
A	PPP forms a cointegrating vector	$\beta_1 = (1, -1, 1, 0, 0)'$
B	PPP augmented by interest differentials forms a cointegrating vector	$\beta_1 = (1, -1, 1, m, -m)'$
C	PPP augmented by unconstrained interest rates forms a cointegrating vector	$\beta_1 = (1, -1, 1, m, n)'$

for Germany and Japan.[9] As Cheung and Lai (1993b) find the trace test to be more robust to nonnormality, we favor a finding of multiple cointegration vectors. We do not use the Cheung and Lai (1993b) finite-sample critical values, which reduce the evidence of two cointegrating vectors, since their use is less than universally accepted. We prefer to combine the standard test statistics with commonsense interpretation of the size of the eigenvalues and plots of the cointegrating relationships. On this basis we will proceed on the assumption of two cointegrating vectors for each country.

We also report in table 1 the standardized eigenvectors and the loadings α. In terms of the normalized eigenvectors we note that the coefficients on prices are correctly signed in 11 out of 12 cases (negative on the home price level and positive on the foreign price level), although many deviate markedly from a value of unity in absolute terms. As noted above, however, it is not clear how to interpret these vectors, but researchers have found that the imposition of testable restrictions on the space spanned by the vectors can reveal more meaningful relationships. Based on our model in section II, three nested hypotheses about the nature of the long-run relationships suggest themselves—PPP by itself may be a cointegrating relationship, PPP augmented by long-term interest differentials may cointegrate (accounting for the distinction between true and empirical concepts of equilibrium), and PPP augmented by unconstrained interest rates may form a stationary relationship. These restrictions are summarized in table 2, and the test results are given in table 3.[10] For the United Kingdom and Japan, only the hypothesis that PPP augmented by unconstrained interest rates is stationary cannot be rejected at the 5% level. For Germany, the more restrictive hypothesis B (interest rates enter as a differential) cannot be rejected.[11] These results underscore the point made in section II: in a period in which net long-term capital movements are likely to be nonzero,

[9] In estimating the German model over the full in-sample period, January 1974 to September 1989, only one significant but uninterpretable cointegrating vector could be found. A plot of the vector revealed that turbulence at the very start of the period seemed to be the cause. We therefore estimate the German model over the slightly smaller sample period of January 1975 to September 1989.

[10] Since the economic theory outlined in section II explains only one long-term relationship, we test restrictions on only cointegrating vector. The second vector remains as a reduced form.

[11] See Edison et al. (1994) for a discussion of the characteristics of these likelihood ratio test restrictions.

TABLE 3.—RESTRICTIONS ON COINTEGRATION VECTORS

	Germany		United Kingdom		Japan	
Hypothesis	Test Statistic	Marginal Significance	Test Statistic	Marginal Significance	Test Statistic	Marginal Significance
A	11.88	0.01	14.69	0.00	20.19	0.00
B	4.06	0.35	13.93	0.00	6.64	0.04
C	0.88	0.13	2.74	0.10	0.17	0.68
	β_1	β_2	β_1	β_2	β_1	β_2
	Standardized Restricted Cointegrating Vectors[a]					
s	1.000	1.000	1.000	1.000	1.000	1.000
p	−1.000	−51.429	−1.000	−1.039	−1.000	−5.225
p^*	1.000	23.841	1.000	1.597	1.000	3.248
i	7.329	7.354	−25.218	−1.083	−18.186	0.203
i^*	−7.329	17.772	8.202	−3.747	0.840	−6.521
	α_1	α_2	α_1	α_2	α_1	α_2
	Standardized Adjustment Vectors					
s	−0.049	0.001	0.043	−0.118	−0.031	0.003
p	0.002	0.001	−0.007	0.011	−0.005	0.009
p^*	−0.004	0.001	−0.001	−0.003	−0.003	−0.001
i	−0.003	−0.000	0.006	−0.007	0.004	0.000
i^*	−0.002	0.000	0.002	−0.007	−0.003	0.000

Notes: Hypotheses are distributed χ^2 with 3, 2, and 1 degrees of freedom, respectively. The results of imposing the most stringent, acceptable restriction for each country are detailed in the lower part
[a] Normalised on the exchange rate.

the exchange rate versus relative price configuration will be established only when long-term bond yields are incorporated into the cointegrating set.[12]

B. *A Parsimonious Representation*

Having determined the long-run economic relationships, the next step is to establish a parsimonious representation of the system. Each constrained VAR contains seven endogenous variables (changes in the exchange rate, domestic and foreign prices, domestic and foreign interest rates, and two error correction terms), together with dummy variables and constants. The endogenous variables are determined by five stochastic equations and two identities. The CVARs are simplified by sequentially removing insignificant variables based on F-tests. The regressors which remain in the PVARs are all significant at the 5% level. Encouragingly, all error correction terms and dummy varibles prove highly significant.

The residual diagnostics for the three PVARs show no significant deterioration from the original VARs, but despite removing a large number of insignificant lagged terms, they are still rather large, containing 75, 65, and 50 parameters, respectively, for the German, U.K., and Japanese models (excluding seasonal dummies). The final step in our modeling strategy, therefore, involves determining the individual

[12] Given that short- and long-term interest rates are cointegrated, it is not surprising that Johansen and Juselius (1992) found similar evidence in their study of the effective sterling exchange rate using bill/euro rates to augment PPP. Our results are not substantially changed if short rates are used, but the economic arguments outlined above lead us to prefer bond yields.

TABLE 4.—SEM EQUATIONS: GERMANY

	A_0					A_i							a	
	Δs_t	Δp_t	Δp_t^*	Δi_t	Δi_t^*	Δs_{t-1}	Δp_{t-1}	Δp_{t-1}^*	Δi_{t-1}	Δi_{t-2}	Δi_{t-1}^*	Δi_{t-2}^*	$ECM1_{t-1}$	$ECM2_{t-1}$
Δs_t	−1				2.566		5.087	−4.092				1.307	−0.040	
					(2.430)		(4.178)	(3.956)				(2.280)	(2.207)	
Δp_t		-1					0.202							0.001
							(2.973)							(7.301)
Δp_t^*			−1					0.451		0.138			−0.006	0.001
								(6.697)		(1.952)			(4.467)	(2.441)
Δi_t				−1		0.012			0.204		0.152		−0.004	−0.001
						(2.947)			(3.090)		(4.392)		(3.788)	(3.394)
Δi_t^*	−0.063				−1					−0.386	0.316		−0.006	
	(2.207)									(2.955)	(3.914)		(2.521)	

Notes: A constant and seasonal dummies are included in all equations in the system. To conserve space equation-specific dummies are not reported. Hendry and Mizon encompassing text [$\chi^2(48)$] equals 53.82.

simultaneous equations of the system in an effort to reduce the dimensionality and sample dependence of the system while increasing its robustness to change.

C. Simultaneous Models

Ideally, the equations in the simultaneous econometric models should be economically meaningful and interpretable. Unfortunately, theoretical exchange rate models are not particularly explicit about the short-run dynamics, with the exception of the overshooting model. Furthermore, the variables have been chosen to explain exchange rates and not with the whole system in mind. However, while we may not have prior hypotheses about parameter values or even signs, we do have some expectations regarding the relationships between variables. For example, we would expect a high degree of simultaneity in the system, primarily because it contains three highly related asset prices. We might also expect that the U.S. variables would react primarily to U.S. events, particularly in the sterling model in which the United Kingdom can probably be considered "small." Besides the dynamics in A_i, we also have an interest in the adjustment coefficients on the cointegrating relationships, since these tie the short-run dynamics to the long-run equilibria. These are particularly important as there is no explicit causality in a PPP model which instead merely describes an equilibrium condition. In a floating regime it is usually assumed that the exchange rate adjusts to equate prices, but if prices react to competitiveness changes imposed by shifts in the exchange rate, PPP becomes a theory of price setting (see Frankel (1981)). Whether prices or exchange rates (or both, or even interest rates) are adjusting to restore equilibrium will be revealed by the coefficients in the a matrix. Some guide as to the likely significance of terms in a is given by the adjustment matrices in the lower panel of table 3 (i.e., the $\tilde{\alpha}$ matrix in equation (6)).

Since there is relatively little economic knowledge that can be applied to determining the short-run dynamic structures, we follow the explorative identification process outlined in Johansen and Juselius (1994). Essentially a series of alternative structures is imposed on A_0, which give insight into the true nature of the system. These include the unrestricted reduced form (where A_0 is the identity matrix), the unrestricted simultaneous equations form (where A_0 is unrestricted and the system is estimated equation by equation in ordinary least squares (OLS)), plausible unrestricted triangular forms (where A_0 is upper triangular and imposes certain causality chains), and restricted simultaneous equations forms (where A_0 contains sufficient exclusion restrictions to identify the equations when estimated by full-information maximum likelihood (FIML)). In the final SEM equations exclusion restrictions are imposed on A_0, A_i, a, and, in light of these experiments, the whole system is estimated by FIML. The final equations are reported in tables 4–6.

The models are much more parsimonious than the CVARs, with just 27, 27, and 18 estimated parameters for the

TABLE 5.—SEM EQUATIONS: UNITED KINGDOM

	A_0					A_i								a	
	Δs_t	Δp_t	Δp_t^*	Δi_t	Δi_t^*	Δp_{t-1}	Δp_{t-3}	Δp_t^{*-1}	Δi_{t-1}	Δi_{t-1}^*	Δi_{t-2}^*	Δi_{t-3}^*	Δi_{t-4}^*	$ECM1_{t-1}$	$ECM2_{t-1}$
Δs_t	−1		−5.541	2.959											−0.076
			(3.826)	(3.354)											(4.410)
Δp_t	−0.119	−1		0.433	−0.551	0.266	0.157							−0.006	
	(3.014)			(2.508)	(2.304)	(4.734)	(3.006)							(6.104)	
Δp_t^*	0.053	0.097	−1					0.646				0.125			
	(2.930)	(2.193)						(9.426)				(2.928)			
Δi_t				−1	0.441	0.122			0.362					0.007	−0.010
					(2.687)	(2.254)			(6.036)					(5.744)	(4.178)
Δi_t^*			0.476		−1					0.195	−0.297		−0.124		
			(4.047)							(2.929)	(4.324)		(1.949)		

Notes: See notes to table 4. Hendry and Mizon encompassing text [$\chi^2(38)$] equals 38.62.

TABLE 6.—SEM EQUATIONS: JAPAN

	A_0					A_1					a	
	Δs_t	Δp_t	Δp_t^*	Δi_t	Δi_t^*	Δs_{t-1}	Δp_{t-1}^*	Δp_{t-2}^*	Δi_{t-1}^*	Δi_{t-2}^*	$ECM1_{t-1}$	$ECM2_{t-1}$
Δs_t	−1				2.739							
					(2.739)							
Δp_t		−1						0.547				0.007
								(7.085)				(8.775)
Δp_t^*			−1		0.353		0.507			0.065	−0.005	
					(2.138)		(6.818)			(1.923)	(3.804)	
Δi_t			0.348	−1	0.190	0.019					0.006	
			(2.843)		(2.221)	(3.374)					(3.884)	
Δi_t^*		−0.188	0.496		−1				0.293	−0.222		
		(1.914)	(3.709)						(4.557)	(3.360)		

Notes: See notes to table 4. Hendry and Mizon encompassing text [$\chi^2(32)$] equals 29.24.

German, U.K., and Japanese models, respectively. As expected, a high degree of simultaneity is found in each model, with contemporaneous terms significant in 11 out of 15 equations. Without discussing each model in detail, we note the following points about the short-run dynamics of the exchange rate equations, all of which are consistent with theory and expectations: short-run price elasticities are much greater than unity, consistent with overshooting; rising domestic (U.S.) prices cause the exchange rate to depreciate (appreciate); and interest rate effects are also typically large and contemporaneous, with rising U.S. rates causing a depreciation of the currency. Finally, we note that the Japanese yen does not adjust toward equilibrium and error correction is instead performed by prices and the domestic interest rate. In the other two countries the exchange rate equations contain correctly signed *ECM* (Error Correction Mechanism) terms, but since these also appear in several other equations of the system, single-equation reduced-form modeling would not be appropriate. It is clear, however, that the adjustment coefficients are much larger (in absolute terms) in the exchange rate equations. This indicates that the German and British exchange rates are adjusting to remove disequilibria rather than prices or interest rates.

Given the data-driven identification procedure followed, an important test statistic is the ability of the SEM to parsimoniously encompass the PVAR (see Clements and Mizon (1991)). Essentially, the final system of equations must contain roughly the same amount of information as the PVAR from which they are derived given the restrictions imposed. Each of our SEMs encompasses its relevant PVAR easily (see tables 4–6), and they are therefore deemed to be acceptable parameterizations of the original VARs.

VI. Beating a Random Walk and the Crème de la Crème of Forecasters: Some Out-of-Sample Forecasting Results

As we noted in the introduction, the bottom line on any exchange rate modeling is how well forecasts from an estimated model perform relative to a random walk, based on the metric of root mean squared errors (RMSEs). Since Meese and Rogoff's seminal paper this has become the measure by which an exchange rate model is judged.

Though no academic journal has published a forecasting model with such impressive performance, it is entirely conceivable that such a model has been developed but is instead being used by market participants. A potentially useful comparison can therefore be made with the 3- and 12-month predictions of the Consensus panel of forecasters. Since the response rate of each panelist is seldom perfect, only those forecasters who produced at least 20 predictions were included, resulting in between 93 and 107 forecasters over the 3-month horizon (81 to 91 over 12 months).

Previous forecasting exercises have typically given the modeled exchange rate the benefit of the doubt in the sense that the actual outcomes of the regressors, rather than forecast outcomes, have been used. In this paper we do not give our exchange rate models an unfair advantage over the random walk. In particular, we compute fully dynamic multi-step-ahead predictions from the SEMs, in which the forecast values of each variable are fed back into the system to calculate projections for the subsequent period. (This is done for both levels and changes of variables, so the *ECM* terms are based on the forecast values of the variables.) Furthermore, we only estimate each model once. The estimated coefficients remain fixed throughout the forecasting period, rather than being updated, as is common in other papers. This, we believe, offers an especially stringent test of our models' out-of-sample forecasting performance.

Table 7 gives the ratio of the RMSE of exchange rate forecasts from the estimated model to that of four alternative benchmark forecasts for each currency over a range of horizons. The first column, as is standard in the literature, uses the driftless random walk. The second and third columns use, respectively, the median forecast from our panel of forecasters, and the median of the 10 forecasters who prove most accurate when evaluated over the full sample for each currency–horizon combination (and whose identities, therefore, remain constant each period). Note that this latter benchmark is based on an expost selection of the best panelists and so is an especially severe test of our models' abilities. In an attempt to see whether the long-run equilibria are important, we compare the model's forecasts to the forecast performance of a parsimonious differenced

TABLE 7.—DYNAMIC FORECAST PERFORMANCE

	Deutsche Mark					Pound Sterling					Japanese Yen				
Horizon	R.W. (1)	Median Panel (2)	Median Best (3)	DPVAR (4)	Direct. (5)	R.W. (1)	Median Panel (2)	Median Best (3)	DPVAR (4)	Direct. (5)	R.W. (1)	Median Panel (2)	Median Best (3)	DPVAR (4)	Direct. (5)
1	1.081			0.946*	0.500	1.007			0.910*	0.553	1.059			0.991	0.500
2	1.059			0.968	0.541	0.990			0.873*	0.649	1.034			0.976	0.541
3	1.003	0.923	1.055	0.938	0.583	0.929*	0.894*	0.960	0.830*	0.694*	0.974	0.893*	1.025	0.961	0.528
4	0.929			0.897*	0.657	0.871*			0.791*	0.829*	0.952			0.946	0.514
5	0.894*			0.877**	0.735**	0.854*			0.782*	0.882*	0.957			0.932	0.618
6	0.877*			0.879	0.818*	0.854*			0.787*	0.788*	0.949			0.912	0.656
7	0.879**			0.891**	0.781	0.853*			0.790*	0.750*	0.912			0.885	0.750*
8	0.881**			0.906	0.710	0.837*			0.772*	0.774*	0.843*			0.824	0.742**
9	0.901			0.910	0.700^{NA}	0.812*			0.750*	0.767*	0.818*			0.758**	0.833**
10	0.914			0.904	0.655^{NA}	0.806*			0.749*	0.793*	0.771*			0.697*	0.897*
11	0.903			0.886	0.571^{NA}	0.802*			0.755*	0.786*	0.682*			0.608*	0.929^{NA}
12	0.889	0.845	1.070	0.882	0.556^{NA}	0.805*	0.760*	0.945	0.754*	0.741‡	0.618*	0.889	1.450*	0.539*	0.963^{NA}

Notes: Column (1) ratio of model RMSE to random walk RMSE; column (2) ratio of model RMSE to RMSE of median forecast from full panel; column (3) ratio of model RMSE to RMSE of median forecast from best 10 panel members; column (4) ratio of model RMSE to RMSE of PVAR specified only in differences; column (5) proportion of model forecasts of which direction of change was correct. Significance of the Diebold-Mariano test statistic (columns (1)–(4)) and of the Cumby–Modest test statistic (column (5)) is indicated by * (5% level) or ** (10% level). For NA see text.

VAR (i.e., versions of equation (7) with no *ECM* terms) for each currency. The results are given in table 7 under the columns headed DPVAR. The significance of each of these measures of relative forecast accuracy is tested using the Diebold–Mariano (1995) procedure, in which the squared error differential (model forecast minus benchmark) is regressed on a constant.

As an additional test of forecasting ability, the fifth column also gives the proportion of forecasts that predict the direction of change correctly. Due to the overlapping nature of the forecasts at horizons in excess of 1 month, significance tests of directional ability are not straightforward. As an alternative we compute Cumby–Modest (1987) statistics, whereby the actual appreciation in the exchange rate is regressed on a constant and an indicator variable, which takes a value of +1 if the currency is expected to appreciate and −1 if a depreciation is predicted. Forecasts that predict the direction of change in the spot rate relative to its sample mean will be revealed by a significantly positive coefficient on the indicator variable. Intuitively, the Cumby–Modest approach says the model provides value if it predicts the sign of subsequent large changes correctly, even if it gets the direction wrong on average.[13]

Consider first the comparisons with the random walk. For the 1-month horizon the random walk dominates across all three currencies. For horizons greater than 1 month, however, the relative accuracy of the models improves such that for each currency the ratio falls below unity. The outperformance typically improves as the forecast horizon lengthens, suggesting that the long-run equilibria are important. The pound sterling model is significantly more accurate than a random walk at the 5% level for all horizons greater than 2 months. For the yen, superiority is evident from the 8-month horizon, and for the mark for the 5- to 8-month horizons.

Comparing the model with the forecast panel we note that over 3 months, the RMSE ratios of the sterling and yen models are less than unity. The U.K. pound predictions rank second when added to the group of forecasters (the best performing forecaster's RMSE ratio was 0.89), and the yen predictions come out in first place. The Deutsche mark model RMSE ratio is marginally greater than unity, placing it tenth. Recall that German reunification took place in the middle of our forecast period and that while the panelists ought to have made allowance for this in their predictions, no such concessions were made in producing the model forecasts. That the model still ranks so highly is testament to its resilience to change and lack of sample dependence, two of the goals of the simultaneous econometric modeling technique used. In fact the model interprets the prereunification rise in German bond yields as a monetary tightening and consequently predicts a relative fall in German inflation.[14] Since the dynamics of the German exchange rate equation contain an approximate inflation differential term, this is translated into a mark appreciation. A similar effect is felt through the error correction term. Thus the model correctly predicts a rise in the mark in the run-up to unification, without any knowledge of what was actually driving the system.

Over the longer horizon the comparison with our panelists becomes more stringent than with a random walk since several professional forecasters return subunity RMSE ratios. It is therefore especially pleasing to find that the model forecasts still rank highly. The yen model records the lowest RMSE ratio of the three currencies at this horizon and is ranked tenth in terms of our panel. The sterling model comes second while the mark model ranks eighth. No forecaster ranks as consistently highly as the econometric models, across currencies and horizons.

[13] The regression nature of this test allows us to correct for overlapping forecasts by the use of generalized method of moments (GMM) standard errors, using a lag length of $k - 1$, where k is the forecast horizon.

[14] This is not apparent from the SEM, but in reduced form the rise in interest rates feeds through with a two-period lag into *ECM2*, which then affects the German inflation equation.

In terms of the median forecaster benchmark measures, the sterling model is significantly better than the full panel median at both the 3- and the 12-month horizons. It is also more accurate than the median of the ex post selected top 10 forecasters, although not significantly so. The yen model is significantly more accurate than the panel median over 3 months, though not over the longer horizon. Indeed, despite the model's low RMSE ratio over 12 months, the median top 10 forecast is significantly more accurate. This would seem to indicate that the model does not contain at least one factor that determines the path of the yen, but which is incorporated by a substantial subgroup of the panel. The mark model outperforms the panel median but is marginally less accurate than the median of the best forecasters. None of the out performance is significant, even though, as noted above, the professionals might be expected to have incorporated information about reunification, which was denied to the model.

So where does this forecasting accuracy come from? Table 7 shows that the differenced VARs (columns labeled DPVAR) typically perform marginally worse than the random walk, and are uniformly less accurate than the models, which include long-run equilibria over each forecast horizon. These results confirm that the error correction terms are important both in sample (since they are significant in the SEMs) and out of sample (where they improve forecast performance). At this point some comments on the yen model are warranted. Since the SEM shows that the change in the exchange rate is solely a function of the contemporaneous change in U.S. bond yields, it would be correct to say that simply knowing the path of U.S. interest rates is sufficient for us to forecast the yen–dollar rate more accurately than the random walk. However, this is of course meaningless from a practical forecaster's point of view. The forecasts from our system are made from the reduced-form versions of the SEMs, and because of the complex nature of the A_0 matrix, the reduced-form exchange rate equation does contain several significant dynamic terms as well as both *ECM* terms. The forecasting ability of the system then comes from rather more than the simple representation of table 6.

Turning now to the tests of the ability to predict the sign of exchange rate changes, note that the proportions of correct directional forecasts are never below 0.5, the expected number under pure chance. Indeed, from performance over short horizons not inconsistent with no directional forecast ability, the proportions rise to between two-thirds and approximate perfection over those horizons where the earlier RMSE tests indicate forecast ability. Over some longer horizons the Cumby–Modest test is not possible since the model always forecasts a movement in the currency in one direction (e.g., the model always predicts an appreciation of the yen over 12-month horizons, which in fact turns out to have been correct in all but one instance). These instances are denoted by the superscript NA in table 7.

Our results contrast with the extant literature on forecasting the exchange rate. They suggest that the "longer" horizon, over which the exchange rate is related to fundamental variables, starts at around 3 months. This contrasts markedly with the recent results of Chinn and Meese (1995) and Mark (1995), where reasonable forecasting performance only begins at around 3 years.

VII. Conclusions

In this paper we have sought to build on recent exchange rate modeling in a number of ways. In particular, we have taken the recent empirical finding that there exists some form of long-run PPP for the recent float, and we have attempted to explain why empirically estimated relationships for bilateral exchange rates do not conform to a traditional interpretation of PPP. Our explanation lay in what we have referred to as Casselian PPP: the idea being that when considering data from the recent float, long-term capital flows may explain deviations from PPP. Indeed, we demonstrated, using three currencies, that when an exchange rate is conditioned on long bond yields, in addition to relative prices, the hypothesis of homogeneity cannot be rejected. The main focus of our work, however, concerned exchange rate forecasting. Based on the Casselian PPP relationships, we adopted a simultaneous-equation modeling strategy to produce dynamic exchange rate models. These models were shown to produce significantly better forecasts than the benchmark random walk and also the vast majority of professional forecasters polled by a commercial survey-gathering agency. As we noted, our methods are especially stringent since we constructed fully simultaneous forecasts of each variable in our model and held the model coefficients constant in our out-of-sample forecasting exercise. We believe that our combined findings of a sensible long-run empirical exchange rate relationship and the ability to produce statistically superior forecasts with a very simple exchange rate model represent a substantial contribution to the literature on the economics of exchange rates.

One way in which our work could be extended is in terms of explaining the factors which the long-term interest rates are actually reflecting: are they picking up productivity and demographic effects or something else? One potentially fruitful avenue of research in this respect would be to estimate the stock-flow exchange rate models of Mussa (1984) and Krugman (1985). These models also use the balance of payments equilibrium condition and detail the factors that prevent an exchange rate from returning to its equilibrium value in the time frame referred to in this paper. The implementation of these models for the recent float should be the next stage in the rehabilitation of fundamentals-based models of the exchange rate.[15]

[15] Initial estimates of the stock-flow consistent models have been made by Faruqee (1994) and MacDonald (1995b).

REFERENCES

Adler, M., and B. Lehman, "Deviations from Purchasing Power Parity in the Long Run," *Journal of Finance* (1983), 1471–1487.

Breuer, J. B., "An Assessment of the Evidence on Purchasing Power Parity," in J. Williams (ed.), *Estimating Equilibrium Exchange Rates* (Washington, DC: Institute for International Economics, 1994).

Cassel, G., *Foreign Investments* (Chicago, IL: University of Chicago Press, 1928).

Cheung, Y. W., and K. S. Lai, "Long-Run Purchasing Power Parity during the Recent Float," *Journal of International Economics* 34 (1993a), 181–192.

——— "Finite-Sample Sizes of Johansen's Likelihood Ratio Tests for Cointegration," *Oxford Bulletin of Economics and Statistics* 55 (1993b), 313–328.

Chinn, M. D., and R. A. Meese, "Banking on Currency Forecasts: How Predictable Is Change in Money?," *Journal of International Economics* 38 (1995), 161–178.

Clements, M. P., and G. E. Mizon, "Empirical Analysis of Macroeconomic Time Series: VAR and Structural Models," *European Economic Review* 35 (1991), 887–917.

Cumby, R. E., and D. M. Modest, "Testing for Market Timing Ability," *Journal of Financial Economics* 19 (1987), 169–189.

Davutyan, N., and J. Pippenger, "Purchasing Power Parity Did Not Collapse during the 1970s," *American Economic Review* 75 (1985), 1151–1158.

Diebold, F. X., J. Gardeazabal, and K. Yilmaz, "On Cointegration and Exchange Rate Dynamics," *Journal of Finance* 49 (1994), 727–735.

Diebold, F. X., and R. S. Mariano, "Comparing Predictive Ability," *Journal of Business and Economic Statistics* 13 (1995), 253–263.

Edison, H., "Forecast Performance of the Exchange Rate Models Revisited," *Applied Economics* 23 (1991), 187–196.

Edison, H., J. Gagnon, and W. Melick, "Understanding the Empirical Literature on Purchasing Power Parity: The Post-Bretton Woods Era," mimeo, Board of Governors of the Federal Reserve System, Washington, DC (1994).

Engel, C., "Can the Markov Switching Model Forecast Exchange Rates?," *Journal of International Economics* 36 (1994), 151–165.

Faruqee, H., "Long-Run Determinants of the Real Exchange Rate: A Stock-Flow Equilibrium Approach," IMF working paper 94/90 (1994).

Flood, R. P., and M. P. Taylor, "Exchange Rate Economics: What's Wrong with the Conventional Approach?," in J. A. Frankel, G. Galli, and A. Giovannini (eds.), *The Micro-Structure of Foreign Exchange Markets* (Chicago, IL: University of Chicago Press, 1996).

Frankel, J. A., "International Capital Mobility and Crowding out in the U.S. Economy: Imperfect Integration of Financial Markets or of Goods Markets," R. Hafer (ed.), *How Open Is the U.S. Economy?* (Washington, DC: AEI, 1986).

——— "Flexible Exchange Rates, Prices and the Role of 'News'," *Journal of Political Economy* 89 (1981), 665–705.

Frankel, J. A., and A. K. Rose, "A Survey of Empirical Research on Nominal Exchange Rates," NBER working paper 4865 (1994).

——— "A Panel Project on Purchasing Power Parity: Mean Reversion within and between Countries," NBER working paper 5006 (1995).

Gonzalo, J., "Five Alternative Methods of Estimating Long-Run Equilibrium Relationships," *Journal of Econometrics* 60 (1994), 203–233.

Hendry, D. F., and G. E. Mizon, "Evaluating Dynamic Econometric Models by Encompassing the VAR," in P. C. B. Phillips (ed.), *Models, Methods, and Applications of Econometrics: Essays in Honor of A. R. Bergstrom* (Oxford, UK: Blackwell, 1993).

Johansen, S., "Statistical Analysis of Cointegration Vectors," *Journal of Economic Dynamics and Control* 12 (1988), 231–254.

Johansen, S., and K. Juselius, "Maximum Likelihood Estimation and Inference on Cointegration—With Applications to the Demand for Money," *Oxford Bulletin of Economics and Statistics* 55 (1990), 169–210.

——— "Testing Structural Hypotheses in a Multivariate Cointegration Analysis of the PPP and UIP for UK," *Journal of Econometrics* 53 (1992), 211–244.

——— "Identification of the Long-Run and the Short-Run Structure. An Application to the ISLM Model," *Journal of Econometrics* 63 (1994), 7–36.

Krugman, P. R., "Is the Strong Dollar Sustainable?" in *The U.S. Dollar—Recent Developments, Outlook and Policy Options* (Kansas City, KS: Federal Reserve Bank of Kansas City, 1985).

Kugler, P., and C. Lenz, "Multivariate Cointegration Analysis and the Long-Run Validity of PPP," this REVIEW 75 (1993), 180–187.

MacDonald, R., "Purchasing Power Parity: Some 'Long-Run' Evidence from the Recent Float," *De Economist* 136 (1988), 239–252.

——— "Long-Run Purchasing Power Parity: Is It for Real?," this REVIEW 75 (1993), 690–695.

——— "Long-Run Exchange Rate Modeling: A Survey of the Recent Evidence," *International Monetary Fund Staff Papers* 42 (1995a).

——— "Asset Market and Balance of Payments Characteristics: An Eclectic Exchange Rate Model for the Dollar, Mark and Yen," IMF working paper 95/55 (1995b).

——— "Panel Unit Roots and Real Exchange Rates," *Economics Letters* 50 (1996), 7–11.

MacDonald, R., and I. W. Marsh, "Combining Exchange Rate Forecasts: What Is the Optimal Measure?," *Journal of Forecasting* 13 (1993), 313–332.

——— "On Casselian PPP, Cointegration and Exchange Rate Forecasting," discussion paper, University of Strathclyde (1996).

MacDonald, R., and M. P. Taylor, "The Monetary Model of the Exchange Rate: Long-Run Relationships, Short-Run Dynamics and How to Beat a Random Walk," *Journal of International Money and Finance* 13 (1994), 276–290.

Mark, N. C., "Exchange Rates and Fundamentals: Evidence on Long-Horizon Predictability," *American Economic Review* 85 (1995), 201–218.

Meese, R. A., and K. Rogoff, "Empirical Exchange Rate Models of the Seventies: Do They Fit out of Sample?," *Journal of International Economics* 14 (1983), 3–24.

Mussa, M., "The Theory of Exchange Rate Determination," in J. F. O. Bilson and R. Marston (eds.), *Exchange Rate Theory and Practice* (Chicago, IL: University of Chicago Press, 1984).

Officer, L., "The Purchasing Power Parity Theory of Exchange Rates: A Review Article," *International Monetary Fund Staff Papers* 23 (1976), 1–60.

Osterwald-Lennum, M., "A Note with Fractiles of the Asymptotic Distribution of the Maximum Likelihood Cointegration Rank Test Statistics: Four Cases," *Oxford Bulletin of Economics and Statistics* 54 (1992), 461–472.

Roll, R., "Violations of Purchasing Power Parity and Their Implications for Efficient International Commodity Markets," in M. Sarnat and G. Szego (eds.), *International Finance and Trade*, vol. 1 (Cambridge, MA: Ballinger, 1979).

ELSEVIER

Journal of International Financial Markets, Institutions and Money 8 (1998) 1–19

Journal of
INTERNATIONAL
FINANCIAL
MARKETS,
INSTITUTIONS
& MONEY

Monetary-based models of the exchange rate: a panel perspective[1]

Steven Husted [a,*], Ronald MacDonald [b]

[a] *Department of Economics, University of Pittsburgh, Pittsburgh, PA 15260, USA*
[b] *Department of Economics, University of Strathclyde, Glasgow, G4 0LN, UK*

Received 1 September 1997; accepted 1 February 1998

Abstract

In this paper we re-examine the monetary model of the exchange rate in a panel context. In particular, we examine three panel data sets constructed for the US dollar, German mark and Japanese yen exchange rates using annual data for the recent floating experience. Amongst our findings are: compelling evidence of cointegrating relationships in all three panels; an ERM effect, in the sense that the mark denominated panel produces point estimates of monetary approach coefficients which are close to their priors; relatively rapid speeds of adjustment to the monetary approach equilibrium (half-lives of between 3 and 6 years).
© 1998 Elsevier Science B.V. All rights reserved.

Keywords: Panel cointegration; Monetary models of exchange rates; Long-run exchange rate behaviour

JEL classification: C33; F31; F41

1. Introduction

Modeling the determinants of long-run, or equilibrium, exchange rates is currently extremely fashionable (see Froot and Rogoff, 1995; MacDonald, 1995). In many ways this work has been inspired by recent developments in the time series literature, rather than any new theoretical interest in the determinants of long-run exchange

* Corresponding author. Tel: 001 412 648 1757; Fax: 001 412 648 3011 e-mail: husted1@pitt.edu
[1] We are grateful to an anonymous referee and the editor, Ike Mathur, for helpful comments. A preliminary version of this paper was presented at the conference on 'Equilibrium Exchange Rates' held at the Univerity of Strathclyde, December 1996. We would like to thank conference participants Menzie Chinn, Peter Clark, Andrew Hughes Hallet, Peter Isard, Nelson Mark and Simon Wren-Lewis for their helpful comments. We also received helpful comments from participants during a presentation at the IMF Research Department semianr series.

1042-4431/98/$19.00 © 1998 Elsevier Science B.V. All rights reserved.
PII S1042-4431(98)00021-3

rates. Nevertheless, this work is interesting since, in summary form, it suggests that sensible long-run relationships can be derived, particularly when the span of the data is increased from the recent floating period to a period encompassing around one hundred years of annual data [see Froot and Rogoff (1995) and MacDonald (1995) for surveys of this literature]. By sensible long-run relationships we mean, for example, when a researcher conditions an exchange rate on relative prices she finds that the exchange rate is homogeneous with respect to relative prices and that the adjustment to equilibrium, following a disturbance, takes around eight years to complete. One key problem, though, in extending the data span on an historical basis is that it may expose the investigated relationship to destabilising regime changes. Also, for relationships which involve price indices (and indeed non-indexed variables) it is not clear how homogeneous these are over long historical periods in which the underlying basket must have changed dramatically.

An alternative way of increasing the span of the data in testing equilibrium exchange relationships involves utilising panel data sets for the recent float (MacDonald, 1988, 1996; Chinn and Johnston, 1996; Frankel and Rose, 1996). Such tests have focussed exclusively on purchasing power parity (MacDonald, 1988; Frankel and Rose, 1996) and the time series properties of real exchange rates (Chinn and Johnston, 1996; Jorion and Sweeney, 1996; MacDonald, 1996; Wu, 1996), In terms of panel PPP tests, researchers find that homogeneity restrictions hold and that the implied real exchange rate is strongly mean-reverting with around one-half of a disturbance to PPP being extinguished after 4 years.[2] Given these results, in this paper we propose contributing to the panel exchange rate literature by re-examining the monetary model of the exchange rate in a panel context using data from the recent floating period. In particular, we estimate the monetary exchange rate model using four different panel data sets: an international dollar-based data set, consisting of 21 countries; a European sample against both the US dollar and the German mark; and an international data set based on the Japanese yen. Previous panel tests involving the PPP relationship have concentrated on US dollar bilaterals, but we believe it is of interest to examine the two other key bilateral rates since they may give very different results (i.e. the yen is usually viewed as a currency susceptible to productivity biases).[3]

The outline of the remainder of this paper is as follows. In Section 2, we present a brief overview of the monetary model and also discuss previous 'long-run' empirical work on this relationship. In Section 3 we present an overview of the econometrics of panel data sets, particularly as it relates to testing long-run relationships. Our data set is discussed in Section 4. Section 5 is our results section which is in two

[2] These results are identical to those obtained with long runs of historical data

[3] It has been demonstrated (see O'Connell (1996)) that if each exchange rate in the panel is assumed to have common serial correlation properties, and country and time effects are included in the regression, then panel regression results should be invariant to the choice of numeraire currency. However, since the assumption of a common serial correlation pattern is relaxed inthis paper the choice of numeraire currency may well be imprtant.

parts: Section 5.1 containing the various single country results; and Section 5.2 containing the various panel results. Section 6, the conclusion, completes the paper.

2. Exchange rate models

The simplest variant of the monetary model takes as its starting point absolute purchasing power parity (PPP), in which the exchange rate is determined by relative prices:

$$s_t = p_t - p_t^*, \tag{1}$$

where s_t denotes the spot exchange rate (home currency price of a unit of foreign exchange), p_t denotes a consumer price level and an asterisk denotes a foreign magnitude. Lower case letters in this and future expressions indicate that a variable is written in logs (the exception being interest rates). On using standard money market equilibrium conditions, Eq. (1) may be transformed into a monetary approach equation. The money market equilibrium conditions for the home and foreign country are given by Eqs. (2) and (3), respectively:

$$m_t - p_t = \alpha y_t - \beta i_t, \tag{2}$$

$$m_t^* - p_t^* = \alpha^* y_t^* - \beta^* i_t^*, \tag{3}$$

where m denotes the money supply, y is real income, i is the interest rate, α is the income elasticity of demand for money and β is the interest rate semi-elasticity. On rearranging Eqs. (2) and (3) for the home and foreign price levels and substituting into Eq. (1), a monetary approach equation may be derived which is the long-run solution for the flex-price monetary model of Bilson (1978), Frenkel (1978) and Hodrick (1978) and the sticky price monetary model of Dornbusch (1976) and Frankel (1979). This equation is reported here as Eq. (4)[4]

$$s_t = m_t - m_t^* - \alpha y_t + \alpha^* y_t^* + \beta i_t - \beta^* i_t^* \tag{4}$$

Eq. (4) asserts that an exchange rate in equilibrium is driven by relative excess money supplies. This equation may be re-expressed as a reduced form, as:

$$s_t = \omega_1 m_t + \omega_2 m_t^* + \omega_3 y_t + \omega_4 y_t^* + \omega_5 i_t + \omega_6 i_t^* + u_t, \tag{5}$$

where the ωs are the parameters to be estimated and u_t is a disturbance term. The strict form of the monetary model implies $\omega_1 = -\omega_2 = 1$, ω_3 and ω_4 should take on values which are close to estimated income elasticities from money demand functions and ω_5 and ω_6 should take on values close to interest rate semi-elasticities from the demand for money. The hypothesised values of ω_1 and ω_2 would be those expected, in equilibrium at least, by proponents of both the flex-price and fix-price monetary models. However, it is important to note that even within the tradition there is a

[4] This kind of reduced form may also be derived from the generalised asset pricing model of Lucas (1982).

view which indicates that these coefficients may be less than one in absolute value; this view is attributable to Mussa (1976).

Meese (1986), Baillie and Selover (1987), Boothe and Glassman (1987); Kearney and MacDonald (1990) all estimate Eq. (5), or simplified versions thereof using the Engle–Granger two step methods (Engle and Granger, 1987), and find no evidence of a long-run relationship in the sense that the residual series is an I(1) process. Further, the estimated coefficients are often very different from their prior values in terms of magnitude and sign. However, subsequent to these studies, MacDonald and Taylor (1993), MacDonald and Taylor (1994) have demonstrated using the multivariate methods of Johansen (1988), that a long-run version of the pure monetary model Eq. (4) can be defined for the recent float, in the sense that the residuals are I(0) and point estimates are close to their a priori values. However, the speed of adjustment in such relationships proves to be painfully slow.

3. Econometric methods

The approach adopted in this paper to estimate Eq. (5) involves exploiting panel data sets defined with respect to the US dollar, the German mark and the Japanese yen. The use of panel data in the current context has a key advantage over single equation estimates and this may be illustrated using the simple PPP Eq. (1), expressed here in regression format as:

$$s_t = \tau_0 p_t + \tau_1 p_t^* + \mu_t, \tag{6}$$

for PPP to be a valid long-run, or equilibrium, relationship μ should be an I(O) process (weak-form PPP) and $\tau 0 = -\tau 1 = 1$ (strong-form PPP). An alternative way of expressing this is as:

$$q_t = \alpha + \delta q_{t-1} + \mu_t \tag{7}$$

where $q_t \equiv s_t - p_t - p_t^*$ and for PPP to hold as a long-run relationship δ should be significantly less than one. In testing either Eq. (6) or Eq. (7) it is now widely accepted that low frequency data, such as annuual data, have a much higher signal-to-noise ratio than monthly data in the context of estimating an equilibrium relationship (Shiller and Perron, 1985). However, in trying to estimate, say, a PPP relationship for the recent floating period with annual data, a researcher will have only approximately 23 useable observations. Although this may be sufficient to obtain homogeneity, it is unlikely that it will produce evidence of a cointegrating relationship (i.e. a stationary residual series) or, in the context of the real exchange rate autoregression Eq. (7), statistically significant mean-reversion. The way to increase the power of such tests involves increasing the span of the data (see MacDonald, 1995). One way the span may be increased simply involves lengthening the historical time series of the data (see Diebold et al., 1991). However, such an approach is fraught with difficulty — there may be several exchange rate regime changes throughout the period and the definition of the explanatory variables may have changed beyond all recognition from the beginning to the end of the sample. An alternative way to increase the span of the data involves expanding the panel dimensions. In a univariate context,(Levin and Lin, 1992, 1993) have demonstrated that a substantial increase in power may be obtained by testing an equation like Eq. (7) in a panel context. Pedroni (1995) has made a similar case for estimating cointegrating relationships in a panel context. Therefore, we propose using panel methods to estimate the monetary model, Eq. (5), since the same kind of arguments discussed above should apply to this relationship.

Our testing methods may be illustrated by starting with the following standard panel context. Pedroni (1995) has made a similar case for estimating cointegrating relationships in a panel context. We therefore propose using panel methods to estimate the monetary model Eq. (5), since the same kind of arguments discussed above should apply to this relationship.

Our testing methods may be illustrated by starting with the following standard panel framework.

$$s_{it} = \alpha + \beta' x_{it} + \left\{ \sum_{i} \gamma_i D_i \right\} + \left\{ \sum_{t} \delta_t D_t \right\} + u_{it}, \tag{8}$$

where the i subscript indicates that the data have a cross-sectional dimension (running from 1 to N), x_{it} is a matrix, consisting of any of the sets of explanatory variables from the models noted above, D_i and D_t denote, respectively, country-specific and time-specific fixed effect dummy variables (although not noted here, it is straightforward to incorporate random effects into Eq. (8)). In a standard panel setting a number of modeling strategies are available for the disturbance term: it may be assumed random, heteroscedastic, autoregressive (with either a common autoregressive terms across individual panel members or different autoregressive terms across members), it may be spatially correlated or some combination of these assumptions may be used.

However, the key feature of recent work with panel data sets relates to the potential non-stationarity of the data. If the dependent and explanatory variables in Eq. (8) are stationary, then Eq. (8) would represent an appropriate way to estimate the desired relationship. If, however, the variables in Eq. (8) are non-stationary, then it has to be determined if they form a cointegrating set or not. If they are I(1) and not cointegrated, an appropriate way to proceed simply involves recasting Eq. (8) with the dependent and independent variables in first differences. If, however, s_{it} and x_{it} are cointegrated, then simply specifying Eq. (8) in difference form would be inappropriate since information pertaining to the long-run relationship would be lost.

In the single equation setting, determining the existence of cointegration amongst a vector of non-stationary variables is relatively straightforward, since there are a number of alternative estimators available (see Campbell and Perron, 1991 for a discussion of the merits of a range of different estimators). Unfortunately, cointegration in the panel context is not well developed. Pedroni (1995) has proposed the panel equivalent of the Engle-Granger two step method and tabulated critical values for the two variable case. Since our models contain at least six variables Pedroni's critical values cannot be used (indeed it is unclear if his methods can be extended beyond the bivariate case). We propose the following method which involves an application of the Levin and Lin unit root test.

The Levin and Lin method involves assuming that the x_{it} matrix in Eq. (8) is simply equal to a scaler, defined as the lagged dependent variable. The stationarity of the exchange rate may be gauged by the estimated t-ratio on the lagged dependent variable. In circumstances where all of the deterministic elements in Eq. (8) are excluded apart from the single constant term, α, Levin and Lin demonstrate that the t-statistic converges to a standard normal distribution. Including individual-specific effects (either or both) but excluding time-specific intercepts, Levin and Lin (1992) demonstrate that the t-ratio converges to a non-central normal distribution, with substantial impact on the size ofthe unit root test. However, Levin and Lin (1993) argue that unless there are very strong grounds for exclusion, time specific intercepts should always be included in these kind of panel tests. The reason for this is that the inclusion of such dummies is equivalent to subtracting the cross section average in each period. This subtraction may be dispensed with in cases where the units in the panel are independent of each other; however, in cases where this is not the case such a subtraction is vital to ensure independence across units.[5]

Since the Levin and Lin (1993) method is not well known we briefly summarise it here. The first step involves subtracting the cross-section mean, $\bar{s}_{it}=(1/N)\cdot\Sigma_{i=1}^{N} s_{it}$, from the observed series. In the following steps the term s_{it} is interpreted as having been adjusted by $\bar{s}_{it}$. Under the null hypothesis of a unit root Levin and Lin, allow for three different deterministic settings: model 1, in which the mean of s is zero for all individuals; model 2, in which s is assumed to have a non-zero mean; and model 3, in which in addition to a non-zero mean a time trend is included in the deterministic set. Step two involves performing Eqs. (9a) and (9b) on the demeaned data

$$\Delta s_{it}=\sum_{L=1}^{pi}\hat{\pi}_{iL}\Delta s_{it-L}+\hat{\alpha}_{mi}d_{mt}+\hat{e}_{it}, \tag{9a}$$

$$s_{it-1}=\sum_{L=1}^{pi}\hat{\phi}_{iL}\Delta s_{it-L}+\hat{\alpha}_{mi}d_{mt}+\hat{e}_{it-1}, \tag{9b}$$

where the d represents the deterministic elements. The following regression is then constructed based on the generated residuals from Eqs. (9a) and (9b)

$$\hat{e}_{it}=\delta_i\hat{v}_{it-1}+\epsilon_{it}. \tag{10}$$

The t-ratio calculated on the basis of Eq. (10) is the panel equivalent to an augmented Dickey Fuller statistic (Dickey and Fuller, 1979). In order to control for heterogeneity across individuals both $\hat{e}_{it}$ and $\hat{v}_{it-1}$ are deflated by the regression

[5] Subtracting the cross sectional mean reduces the potentially problematic effect that contemporaneous correlations can have in a panel unit root context; see O'Connell (1996). We further address the issue of contemporaneous correlation by using a seemingly unrelated regression correction in one of our panel cointegration tests.

standard error from Eq. (10); these adjusted errors are labeled $\hat{e}_{it}$ and $\hat{v}_{it-1}$. Under the null hypothesis these normalised innovations should be independent of each other and this may be tested by running the following regression:

$$\tilde{e}_{it} = \delta \tilde{v}_{it-1} + \tilde{\varepsilon}_{it}, \tag{11}$$

Under the null hypothesis that $\delta_i = 0$, for all $i = 1,\ldots,N$, the asymptotic theory in Section 4 of Levin and Lin indicates that the regression t-statistic, $t\delta$ has a standard normal distribution for model 1, but diverges to negative infinity for models 2 and 3. However, Levin and Lin demonstrate that the following adjusted t-ratio has a $N(0,1)$ distribution and the critical values of the standard normal distribution can be used to test the null hypothesis that δi for all $i = 1,\ldots,N$:

$$t_\delta^* = \frac{t_\delta - N\tilde{T}\hat{S}_{NT}\sigma\tilde{\epsilon}^{\,2} RS\hat{E}(\hat{\delta})\mu_{mT}^*}{\sigma_{mT}^*}, \tag{12}$$

where $\hat{S} = (1/N)\sum_{i=1}^{n} \hat{q}$, and $\hat{q}_i = \hat{\sigma}_{yi}/\hat{\sigma}_{ei}, \hat{\sigma}_{ei}$, is the residual standard error from Eq. (11) and $\hat{\sigma}_{yi}$ is an estimate of the long-run standard deviation, RSE(δ) is an estimate of the standard error of $\hat{\delta}$ (the latter being a least squares estimate), $\hat{\delta}\epsilon$ is

Table 1
Two-step MAER cointegration results: all countries, US dollar

	M	M*	Y	Y*	i	i*	α	R^2	ADF	PP	k
Australia	−0.54	1.19	0.50	−0.64	0.013	−0.014	−3.26	0.94	−3.85	−3.31	1
Austria	0.83	0.99	−3.01	−2.97	−0.004	0.030	39.02	0.68	−4.2	−3.09	1
Belgium	0.13	1.80	−4.30	−2.37	0.017	0.024	48.10	0.44	−4.65	−2.82	1
Canada	−0.18	0.34	2.02	−2.09	−0.038	0.039	3.71	0.70	−2.67	−2.67	0
Denmark	0.42	0.61	3.27	−5.87	−0.008	0.041	23.9	0.5	−4.43	−2.92	1
Finland	−0.18	1.98	−2.10	−2.24	0.003	0.029	20.43	0.58	−3.67	−2.86	1
France	0.99	0.24	−5.25	1.24	0.067	−0.045	27.8	0.70	−3.38	−3.49	1
Germany	0.16	1.03	−3.28	−1.72	0.0015	0.004	32.70	0.68	−4.37	−3.03	1
Greece	0.47	2.10	−1.28	−2.87	−0.039	0.028	24.39	0.96	−1.49	−2.31	2
Iceland	1.48	−1.93	−0.15	−3.17	−0.008	0.001	41.12	0.99	−2.93	−2.93	0
Ireland	0.89	1.5	−2.68	−3.17	−0.008	0.007	24.15	0.72	−3.53	−3.20	1
Italy	0.90	0.58	−9.44	5.41	0.070	0.010	76.84	0.97	−5.28	−4.22	1
Japan	−0.15	0.17	0.60	−3.14	−0.004	0.016	24.67	0.92	−3.40	−3.40	0
Netherlands	0.18	0.99	−2.82	−1.85	−0.015	0.019	26.47	0.70	−4.60	−3.06	1
New Zealand	−0.01	0.97	1.45	−2.30	0.025	0.002	7.23	0.88	−4.43	−2.09	1
Norway	−0.21	1.26	−0.76	−1.28	0.026	−0.003	10.26	0.57	−3.74	−2.93	1
Portugal	−0.72	3.20	−1.79	0.69	0.038	0.016	−1.77	0.97	−4.09	−3.01	1
Spain	1.03	1.13	−6.99	−0.66	0.002	−0.020	68.37	0.83	−2.95	−2.87	2
Sweden	0.71	0.64	−2.44	−1.72	0.014	−0.008	25.17	0.69	−2.95	−2.57	1
Switzerland	−0.57	0.51	0.27	−2.37	−0.002	0.001	18.24	0.70	−3.72	−3.26	1
UK	0.40	0.46	−2.16	−0.09	−0.015	−0.008	9.72	0.54	−2.75	−2.75	0

Notes: the numbers in columns headed M, M*, Y, Y*, i, i* and α are, respectively, the coefficients on domestic money, foreign money, domestic income, foreign income, the domestic interest rate, the foreign interest rate and the estimated constant. R^2 denotes the coefficient of determination. ADF, augmented Dickey Fuller statistic; PP, the Phillips–Perron t-ratio and k the lag length used to construct ADF. The approximate 5% critical value for ADF and PP is −5.53 (source MacKinnon, 1991).

the estimated standard error of regression Eq. (11), $\bar{T} \equiv (T - \bar{p} - 1)$ is the average number of observations per individual in the panel and $\bar{p} \equiv (1/N)\sum_{i=1}^{N} p_i$ is the average lag order for the individual ADF statistics. σ^*_{mT} and μ^*_{mT} represent the mean and standard deviation adjustments, respectively, and are tabulated in Table 1 of Levin and Lin for different deterministic specifications ($m = 1,2,3$).

We propose applying the tests of Levin and Lin to the residuals from Eq. (5). In particular, we report adjusted (ALL) and unadjusted (LL) Levin and Lin statistics and construct these on the basis of no deterministic elements and a country-specific constant. We believe it is important to report t-ratios for both deterministic specifications since, as we shall see, all of our cointegrating relationships already have some assumptions about the deterministic elements built in. The use of Levin and Lin t-ratios, of course, leaves us open to criticism that we intend applying these tests to a generated residual rather than an actual series (although it should be noted that Frankel and Rose (1996) in their panel tests of PPP use a more primitive version of the Levin and Lin t-ratio, which does not adjust the data for cross-sectional means).

We propose addressing the generated residual issue using a method proposed by Hansen (1990). He highlights what he refers to as 'the curse of dimensionality', which is that in a residual-based cointegration test, the cointegrating vector is random, imparting randomness into the generated residual series, and that this randomness is a function of the number of variables in the system. The particular implication that this has is to give 'dramatic reductions in power' as the number of variables in the system increases, rendering cointegration tests ineffective in moderate sample sizes with moderately large systems. The reason that the test distributions depend on the dimensionality of the system is because they involve estimation of all n unit roots in the system. The central element of Hansen's estimation method is now illustrated.

The Hansen procedure may be illustrated in the following way. Consider a variable y_t and an $n-1$ dimensional vector x_t, all variables are assumed to be I(1) processes and the null hypothesis is that there is no cointegration amongst the variables. Consider the following two-equation system

$$y_t = x_t'\alpha + u, \tag{13}$$

$$u_t = \rho u_{t-1} + \epsilon_t, \tag{14}$$

which may be estimated sequentially by least squares, and the least squares estimators are: $\hat{\alpha}$ and $\hat{\rho}$. By quasi-differencing the data.

$$y_t^* = y_t - y_{t-1}\hat{\rho}, \tag{15}$$

$$x_t^* = x_t - x_{t-1}\hat{\rho}, \tag{16}$$

the so-called Cochrane-Orcutt estimator may be derived by applying OLS to the following transformed equation.

$$y_t^* = x_t^*\bar{\alpha} + \bar{\epsilon}_t. \tag{17}$$

These estimates will be consistent and asymptotically normal if both variables are covariance stationary and the conditional expectation of the residual series is zero. Park and Phillips (1988) demonstrate that if the untransformed values of x and y are I(1) and the series are cointegrated then $\tilde{\alpha}$ converges stochastically to the cointegrating vector and $\bar{\rho} \rightarrow_p \rho < 1$.

Hansen's innovation is to analyze this estimator in the context of integrated variables which are not cointegrated. As demonstrated by Phillips and Ouliaris (1990), under the null of no cointegration $T(\hat{\rho}-1)$ has a limiting distribution (implying that $\hat{\rho} \rightarrow_p 1$ at rate T). This means that y_t^* and x_t^* are asymptotically first differences of y_t and x_t and $\tilde{\alpha}$ estimates the regression coefficient of Δy_t upon Δx_t. The first theorem of Hansen (1990) is: Theorem 1. Under the null hypothesis of no cointegration

$$\tilde{\alpha} \rightarrow_p \alpha \equiv [E(\Delta x_t \Delta x_t')]^{-1} E(\Delta x_t \Delta y_t). \quad (18)$$

This theorem demonstrates that under the null hypothesis of no cointegration, the Cochrane-Orcutt estimate of α converges to a constant and not to a random variable as in the case of the least squares (i.e. Engle–Granger) estimator. Hence a test of cointegration based on Cochrane-Orcutt residuals will not display the 'curse of dimensionality'. Hansen goes on to demonstrate that the distributions of the Dickey Fuller and augmented Dickey Fuller statistics are identical to the univariate unit root case. Three of the estimators used in this paper exploit a Cochrane-Orcutt type correction. Additionally, one of these estimators involves a GLS correction for contemporaneous correlation and, therefore, we also address the point made by O'Connell (1996) that a failure to control for cross-sectional dependence in a panel unit root test can have a dramatic effect on statistical size (we also control for cross-sectional dependence by subtracting cross-sectional means — see footnote 4). In general, then, our approach involves using a wide variety of panel estimators to ensure that the result generated using a specific estimator is simply a function of that estimator.

4. Data

The data for this study are collected from the International Monetary Fund's *International Financial Statistics* CD-ROM disc, and are for the sample period 1973–1994. The exchange rate is defined as the home currency price per unit of foreign currency (line ae), money supplies are M1 (line 34)[6], income terms are real GDP (line 99b.p), interest rates are short rates (line 60 or 61) and all variables, apart from the interest rate terms, have been converted into natural logarithms. Exchange rates and interest rates are end of period; other variables are period averages.

Eq. (5) is estimated for four groups of countries. The first group consists of 21 OECD countries relative to the United States. The countries in this group are:

[6] MO, Line 34, was used for the UK, and broad money, line 38a, for Sweden.

Australia, Austria, Canada, Denmark, Finland, France, Germany, Greece, Iceland, Ireland, Italy, Japan, Netherlands, New Zealand, Norway, Portugal, Spain, Sweden, Switzerland and the United Kingdom. The second group comprises the (17) European countries in the group listed above. These countries are: Austria, Belgium, Denmark, Finland, France, Greece, Iceland, Ireland, Italy, Netherlands, Norway, Portugal, Spain, Sweden, Switzerland and the United Kingdom. A third grouping comprises the European countries relative to Germany while the fourth grouping consists of the countries in group 1 relative to Japan.

5. Results

5.1. Single country two-step cointegration results

As motivation for our panel results, we report in Tables 1–3 individual country estimates of the cointegrating vectors, using the two-step estimator of Engle and Granger. In addition to the standard augmented Dickey Fuller (ADF) residual-based *t*-ratio test statistic we also constructed a Phillips–Perron *t*-ratio (PP) which has a non-parametric correction for serial correlation and heteroscedasticity. Since the latter is often a feature of foreign exchange market data, the latter test may be regarded as a more discriminating test for cointegration. The tag length, *k*, of the ADF statistic was chosen using the following procedure. An ADF was estimated for each country using alternatively 0 to 3 lags (since the data are annual, 3 lags

Table 2
Two-step MAER cointegration results: European sample, German mark

	M	M*	Y	Y*	i	i*	α	R^2	ADF	PP	*k*
Austria	−0.07	0.04	−0.37	0.38	−0.002	−0.001	1.89	0.60	−3.97	−4.97	2
Belgium	0.51	−0.14	2.31	−1.78	−0.011	0.01	−6.09	0.83	−2.02	−2.02	0
Denmark	0.30	0.03	1.11	−1.21	0.015	0.007	1.35	0.97	−2.77	−4.95	1
Finland	−0.01	0.53	−0.25	0.05	−0.004	−0.004	−1.02	0.91	−2.57	−2.44	2
France	0.32	−0.38	0.60	1.25	0.015	−0.022	−13.72	0.98	−4.38	−3.63	1
Greece	1.06	−1.08	−1.22	2.86	0.003	−0.003	−7.33	0.99	−3.43	−3.43	0
Iceland	0.78	0.57	1.22	−3.45	−0.001	−0.01	17.38	1.00	−4.67	−4.67	0
Ireland	0.40	−0.43	0.47	1.01	0.013	−0.03	−8.02	0.98	−3.68	−4.39	3
Italy	0.38	0.13	−0.35	0.84	0.019	−0.024	−0.64	0.98	−3.35	−2.77	2
Netherlands	−0.23	−0.15	−0.57	0.56	0.003	−0.001	−0.90	0.90	−3.98	−4.34	3
Norway	0.09	−0.1.	0.27	1.07	0.008	−0.009	−8.68	0.96	−5.24	−3.96	1
Portugal	0.95	−2.08	1.44	3.49	0.03	−0.06	−30.25	0.99	−4.50	−3.73	1
Spain	0.95	0.30	−4.10	0.68	0.003	−0.023	32.42	0.97	−2.11	−4.78	2
Sweden	0.72	0.18	−0.93	−0.12	−0.012	−0.007	3.45	0.97	−5.55	−4.95	1
Switzerland	−0.81	−0.55	0.59	2.27	−0.007	−0.013	−14.04	0.79	−5.29	−5.29	0
UK	0.26	−0.35	−0.42	2.67	−0.002	−0.04	17.55	0.94	−3.93	−7.99	3

Notes: see Table 1.

Table 3
Two-step MAER cointegration results: all countries, Japanese yen

	M	M*	Y	Y*	i	i*	α	R^2	ADF	PP	*k*
Australia	−1.21	0.69	4.69	0.97	−0.026	−0.018	−47.98	0.96	−4.75	−4.75	0
Austria	1.41	−0.52	−3.22	1.23	0.020	−0.021	4.12	0.87	−3.21	−2.55	3
Belgium	0.96	−0.85	−3.95	3.37	0.010	−0.020	−7.15	0.89	−3.11	−3.11	0
Canada	−0.12	0.31	2.50	0.96	−0.025	−0.01	−17.13	0.94	−3.81	−3.48	3
Denmark	1.08	−0.78	0.15	−0.54	0.002	−0.027	0.07	0.93	−2.40	−2.40	0
Finland	0.19	0.15	0.20	0.32	0.003	−0.042	−11.04	1.00	−6.50	−3.89	0
France	0.37	0.20	−5.37	3.55	0.011	−0.034	−7.08	0.95	−3.95	−3.95	0
Germany	1.22	−0.90	−4.1.1	1.79	0.01.5−	−0.035	7.30	0.83	−4.57	−4.57	0
Greece	1.46	−2.14	−0.89	0.36	0.04	−0.069	17.60	0.99	−4.14	−4.14	0
Iceland	1.34	0.27	0.31	4.34	−0.002	−0.009	46.34	1.00	−6.50	−6.50	0
Ireland	0.60	0.08	−1.02	1.06	−0.012	−0.024	−17.07	0.96	−3.10	−3.50	0
Italy	0.70	0.51	−1.96	0.46	0.009	−0.003	8.89	0.97	−3.81	−3.81	1
Netherlands	−0.42	0.37	−1.25	1.68	−0.033	−0.004	−20.16	0.87	−3.46	−3.46	0
New Zealand	−0.07	0.40	1.29	1.53	0.008	−0.014	−34.12	0.99	−3.55	−3.55	0
Norway	0.40	−0.80	1.67	−0.11	0.011	−0.031	−5.36	0.97	−5.31	−5.31	0
Portugal	1.27	−1.53	−0.52	0.57	0.044	−0.075	5.15	0.99	−4.39	−4.39	0
Spain	−0.02	1.10	−3.53	2.74	−0.006	−0.035	−9.80	0.95	−4.54	−4.54	0
Sweden	1.09	−0.79	−1.56	1.48	−0.017	−0.043	−8.24	0.95	−3.60	−3.60	0
Switzerland	−0.82	−0.53	2.61	0.86	−0.039	−0.028	−20.39	0.75	−4.37	−4.37	0
UK	0.52	−0.30	0.22	1.06	−0.037	−0.019	−18.07	0.98	−4.14	−4.14	0
US	−0.17	0.15	3.14	−0.60	−0.016	0.004	−24.67	0.92	−3.40	−3.40	0

Notes: see Table 1.

was regarded as sufficiently long to ensure residual randomness). The value of k was then picked on the basis of the t-values on the lag coefficients.

For the US-based bilaterals there is no evidence of cointegration in any of the equations using either the ADF or PP tests. The 5% per cent critical value used here is −5.53, which was calculated on the basis of six variables (MacKinnon (1991) critical values do not extend beyond six variables). A total of 13 of the coefficients on the home money supplies are correctly signed, but remarkably only one of the coefficients on the US money supply term is correctly signed. This 'sign failure' is repeated across the other variables: only 3 and 6, respectively, of the coefficients on the foreign income and interest rate terms are correctly signed, although a much higher proportion of the coefficients on the domestic variables are correctly signed (16 in the case of income and 11 in the case of the interest rate). For the DM bilaterals there is one rejection of the null of no cointegration using the PP statistic (UK pound sterling), and there is a much higher proportion of correctly signed coefficients compared with the US bilaterals, with a large number ofthe coefficients on the foreign (i.e. Gerinan) variables correctly signed (for the foreign interest rate 14, for foreign income 12, and for foreign money 9). Interestingly, there are two relationships — for Greece and the Netherlands — in which all of the variables enter with the correct sign and for Greece the magnitude of the coefficient values is close to the prior values. A further seven relationships have all but one of the coefficients correctly signed.[7] The Japanese results are closer to those for the DM-based bilaterals in the sense that there is a good strike record of correctly signed coefficients, and there is a single instance in which the null of no cointegration is rejected using the PP (for Iceland).

To sum up the single equation estimates: there is little evidence of significant long-run relationships, in the cointegration sense, irrespective of the specification of the exchange rate relationship. There is, however, some evidence that, particularly for DM- and yen-based equations, the majority of variables enter the long-run relationships with correctly signed coefficients. Does the picture alter when we move to our panel data sets?

5.2. Panel results

5.2.1. Panel estimators

Before turning to a detailed discussion of our results we first define the range of different panel estimators used to estimate each of the models. For the 'traditional' panel tests we have opted to report the results from four estimators (we have used other estimators, including random effects, but their output is qualitatively similar to those reported here): OLS with fixed effects, that is individual intercepts for each unit (denoted in the Tables by $\alpha_i \neq \alpha_j$); Maximum Likelihood estimates with fixed effects and a common AR1 process specified for the error term [this is denoted in the tables as MAX 1 ($\rho_i = \rho_j$)]; Maximum Likelihood with fixed effects and an AR1 process which differs across individual units [represented in the Tables by MAX 2 ($\rho_i \neq \rho_j$)]; finally, we use a maximum likelihood estimator which allows fixed effects, differing AR1 processes across individual units, contemporaneous residual correlation and a correction for heteroscedasticity (this is labeled 'POOL' ($\rho_i \neq \rho_j$) in the tables). Given that the dependent variable is different for each individual in the panel, estimators with a common intercept are not considered.

The above-noted 'traditional' panel models facilitate testing for cointegration between exchange rates and various fundamentals. As an alternative check on the existence of cointegration, we propose estimating error correction models (ECMS) in a panel context. Four sets of ECM results are reported in the Tables. The ECMs are calculated with the current lagged change and two lagged changes of all the variables in the model, as well as the lagged equilibrium error. The latter is constructed with fixed effects [ECM ($\alpha_i \neq \alpha_j$)] and using the pooled estimator referred to above [ECM(Pool)]. The number not in brackets in the γ column of each of the tables refers to the adjustment speed of the coefficient on the ECM. We also estimate the ECM model using non-linear least squares [reported as ECM (NL) in the tables], the non-linearity arising from the joint estimation of both the α (adjustment) and β (cointegration) coefficients (which enter the expression multiplicatively). In addition to providing a check on the existence of cointegration the estimates derived from the ECMs provide direct estimates ofthe adjustment speed back to equilibrium following a disturbance to the equilibrium relationship.

[7] They are France, Iceland, Italy, Norway, Portugal, Spain and the United Kingdom.

However, as is now well known in the context of standard cointegration analysis, the above-noted estimators do not necessarily generate coefficient or standard error estimates which are uncontaminated by serial correlation and endogeneity. As a means of producing coefficient estimates and standard errors which are uncontaminated by such potential nuisance parameters, we propose implementing the Phillips and Loretan (1991) estimator in a panel context. In particular, we present a set of Phillips–Loretan estimates each having one lead and one lag of the variables, plus fixed effects, and these are labeled [Phil–Lor ($\alpha_i \neq \alpha_j$)]. The t-ratios we refer to are based on the Phillips–Loretan estimates and are reported in round brackets.

5.2.2. *Panel monetary approach equations*

The panel monetary approach results are presented in Tables 4–7. In all, 90 out of a total of 144 coefficients are correctly signed. The contrast between the US dollar and yen based systems and the DM system is quite marked. In particular, it is the US and yen-based results which bring the coefficient strike record down: the average across Tables 4, 5 and 7 is 20 out of 36, whereas 28 out of 36 coefficients are correctly signed in the DM-based system (Table 6). An inspection of the source of this is that the signs on the US and yen variables are wrongly signed (most notably, the US income term, but also the money and interest rate terms). Excluding the US variables from the score sheet, we note that of the home variables only 4 out of 36 coefficients in the two US-based systems are wrongly signed. In terms of the domestic money supply, it is especially noteworthy that this is positive in all but one instance, and

Table 4
Unrestricted monetary approach equations: all countries, US dollar

Method	M	M*	Y	Y*	i	i*	γ	R^2	DW	ρ
OLS	0.80	0.39	−0.59	−3.07	0.021	0.003	-	0.73	0.58	-
($\alpha_i \neq \alpha_j$)										
MAX 1	0.48	−0.03	−0.71	−0.41	0.003	−0.002	-	0.91	1.46	0.9
($\rho_i = \rho_j$)										
MAX 2	0.60	0.03	−1.01	−0.65	0.004	0.003	-	0.90	1.19	-
($\rho_i \neq \rho_j$)										
POOL	0.73	−0.21	−0.94	−0.61	0.006	−0.003	-	0.96	1.21	-
($\rho_i \neq \rho_j$)										
Phil-Lor	0.41	2.87	0.34	−9.61	0.064	0.006	-	0.97	0.71	
ECM							−0.032	0.53		
($\alpha_i \neq \alpha_j$)							(2.39)			
ECM							−0.037	0.58		
(Pool)							(2.80)			
ECM	−0.21	6.48	1.10	−19.92	0.053	0.237	−0.08			
(NL)	(1.23)	(4.74)	(5.29)	(4.97)	(2.64)	(4.70)	(5.86)			

Notes: the panel estimator is noted in the first column (see text for an explanation). The columns labeled M, M*, Y, Y*, i, i* and R^2 have the same interpretation as in Table 1; DW denotes the Durbin Watson statistic. The column labeled γ contains the estimated adjustment speed on the error correction term. t-ratios are reported in round brackets. The numbers in the column labeled ρ are the estimates of the autocorrelation coefficient.

14 *S. Husted, R. MacDonald / Int. Fin. Markets, Inst. and Money 8 (1998) 1–19*

Table 5
Unrestricted monetary approach equations: European countries, US dollar

Method	M	M*	Y	Y*	i	i*	γ	R^2	DW	ρ
OLS	0.86	0.40	−0@80	−3.03	0,016	0.005	—	0.99	0.58	—
$(\alpha_i \neq \alpha_j)$										
MAX 1	0.61	−0.16	−0.90	−0.27	0,003	−0.003	—	0.92	1.51	0.89
$(\rho_i = \rho_j)$										
MAX 2	0.76	−0.05	−1.17	−0.74	0,003	0.003	—	0.91	1.26	—
$(\rho_i \neq \rho_j)$										
POOL	0.85	−0.26	−1.15	−0.69	0.007	-0.004	—	0.97	1.31	—
$(\rho_i \neq \rho_j)$										
Phil-Lor	0.74	1.56	−0−37	−6.49	0.04	0.026	—	1.00	0.81	
$(\alpha_i \neq \alpha_j)$	(24.5)	(1.62)	(1.47)	(2.13)	(10.2)	(4.21)				
ECM							−0.158	0.63		
$(\alpha_i \neq \alpha_j)$							(4.97)			
ECM							−0.179	0.71		
(Pool)							(6.09)			
ECM	0.59	2.31	0.65	−9.29	0.024	0.077	−0.298			
(NL)	(7.88)	(6.64)	(1.18)	(8.93)	(3.61)	(7.05)	(12.85)			

Notes: see Table 4.

Table 6
Unrestricted monetary approach equations: European countries, German mark

Method	M	M*	Y	Y*	i	i*	γ	R^2	DW	ρ
OLS	0.82	−0.53	−0.34	0.64	0.016	0.015	—	0.89	0.46	–
$(\alpha_i \neq \alpha_j)$										
MAX 1	0.45	−0.12	0.34	0.26	0.004	−0.008	—	0.97	1.89	0.96
$(\rho_i = \rho_j)$										
MAX 2	0.69	−0.26	0.21	0.10	0.005	0.007	—	0.97	1.70	–
$(\rho_i \neq \rho_j)$										
POOL	0.76	−0.44	−0.07	0.29	0.009	−0.007	—	0.97	1.62	-
$(\rho_i \neq \rho_j)$										
Phil – Lor	0.75	−0.38	−0.37	−0.12	0.041	−0.043		0.99	1.55	
$(\alpha_i \neq \alpha_j)$	(17.5)	(0.2)	(1.06)	(.02)	(7.3)	(2.1)				
ECM							−0.094	0.34		
$(\alpha_i \neq \alpha_j)$							(2.85)			
ECM							−0.055	0.17		
(Pool)							(2.52)			
ECM	0.26	0.85	0.35	−4.07	0.03	−0.118	−0.135			
(NL)	(1.8)	(0.38)	(0.41)	(0.53)	(2.12)	(1.28)	(4.47)			

Notes: see Table 4.

in a number of cases it is numerically close to plus one (and therefore the perverse sign so prevalent in many monetary approach studies — see Frankel (1982) — does not appear in this study). The DM-based system does particularly well with a number of the systems having either all, or all but one, of the coefficients correctly signed (the Pool estimator has all of the coefficients correctly signed). We attribute

Table 7
Unrestricted monetary approach equations: all countries, Japanese yen

Method	M	M*	Y	Y*	i	i*	γ	R^2	DW	ρ
OLS ($\alpha_i \neq \alpha_j$)	0.78	−0.54	0.25	0.24	0.017	−0.041	—	0.90	0.66	—
MAX 1 ($\rho_i = \rho_j$)	0.68	−0.09	0.22	−0.08	0.002	−0.017	—	0.96	2.03	0.82
MAX 2 ($\rho_i \neq \rho_j$)	0.72	0.02	0.14	−0.16	0.003	0.017	—	0.95	1.80	
POOL ($\rho_i \neq \rho_j$)	0.82	−0.35	0.23	−0.04	0.00	−0.022	—	0.80	1.77	
Phil–Lor	0.46	−1.35	0.34	1.39	0.081	−0.19	—	0.95	0.70	
($\alpha_i \neq \alpha_j$)	(7.77)	(0.58)	(4.9)	(.48)	(7.35)	(3.1)				
ECM							−0.032	0.53		
($\alpha_i \neq \alpha_j$)							(2.39)			
ECM							−0.023	0.58		
(Pool)							(1.67)			
ECM	−1.02	30.83	2.40	−34.86	0.028	1.23	−0.03			
(NL)	(1.23)	(2.03)	(2.83)	(1.91)	(.48)	(2.37)	(2.84)			

Notes: see Table 4.

the different success rate in the two systems to the fact that German Bundesbank placed greater emphasis on money market developments throughout the period and, furthermore, that the German simple sum aggregate was less prone to instabilities introduced by financial deregulation than the US simple sum measures (see Chrystal and MacDonald, 1995 for a discussion).

The γ (i.e. adjustment) coefficients derived from the ECM models reveal relatively slow adjustment for the full sample of countries against the US dollar and Japanese yen, but a much faster speed for both the European samples: around −0.1 (half-life of 6 years) from the OLS-ECM and approx −0.2 (half-life of 3 years) from the two non-linear systems. Notice also that the non-linear ECM estimator produces an adjustment speed for the full sample against the US dollar which is approximately double that for the linear variant. Apart from one instance, the ECM terms are all statistically significant at the 5% level or better. There would seem to be two conclusions to draw from these speed of adjustment results. First, the particular exchange rate regime makes a difference to the estimated adjustment speed. Currencies which were on quasi-fixed regimes produced faster adjustment speeds, both against the currency to which they were anchored (the DM) and also relative to the currency with which they were floating (the US$). Second, the estimator used, in particular the non-linear estimator, clearly makes a difference to both the magnitude ofthe adjustment speed and also its significance.

The Levin–Lin t-ratios for the monetary model are presented in Table 8. The numbers not in brackets are constructed on the basis of a constant entering the deterministic set, while those in square brackets have no deterministic elements. All of the reported estimators, including the one with an explicit correction for contemporaneous correlation (POOL), tum in very small unadjusted t-ratios, the smallest

Table 8
Levin–Lin t-ratios for monetary approach equations

	Full-$		Euro-$		Euro-DM		Yen	
Method	LL	ALL	LL	ALL	LL	ALL	LL	ALL
OLS	−5.13	1.61	−4.37	1.48	−4.74	0.93	−5.19	1.48
$(\alpha_i \neq \alpha_j)$	[−5.61]	[−5.39]	[−4.64]	[−4.46]	[−4.92]	[−4.73]	[−5.46]	[−5.25]
MAX 1	−25.02	−18.76	−22.82	−17.24	−21.25	−16.14	−20.09	−14.12
$(\rho_i = \rho_j)$	[−20.84]	[−19.92]	[−19.27]	[−18.41]	[−17.24]	[−16.47]	[−18.78]	[−17.9]
MAX 2	−15.89	−10.47	−15.16	−10.65	−16.08	−11.64	−15.28	−9.54
$(\rho_i \neq \rho_j)$	[−14.18]	[−13.56]	[−13.26]	[−12.68]	[−14.69]	[−14.04]	[−14.36]	[−13.7]
POOL	−20.5	−14.7	−19.49	−14.42	−17.68	−12.65	−21.65	−15.81
$(\rho_i \neq \rho_j)$	[−20.12]	[−19.22]	[−18.18]	[−17.5]	[−17.5]	[−16.72]	[−20.97]	[−20.0]

Notes: the columns haeded Full-$, Euro-$, Euro-DM and Yen repesent the three different samples discussed in the text: all countries against the dollar, European countries against the dollar, European countries against the mark and all countries against the yen, respectively. LL and ALL denote, respectively, the unadjusted and adjusted Levin and Lin statistics. The numbers not in brackets are constructed on the basis of a constant entering the deterministic set, while those in square brackets have no deterministic elements. See Table 4 for other definitions.

being for the estimators which exploit GLS corrections for residual correlation. The t-ratios rise after implementing the recommended Levin–Lin correction, but all apart from one are smaller than the required critical value of −2.0. Even recognising that the Levin and Lin statistics are designed for univariate tests on nongenerated data, we believe these statistics are large enough, in absolute value, to convincingly reject the null of no cointegration. The similarity of the results across different estimators indicates that our finding of cointegration is not dependent on a particular technique,

6. Summary and conclusions

In this paper we have been concerned to test the monetary model of the exchange rate, as an equilibrium relationship, for US dollar, German mark and Japanese yen bilateral exchange rates, using panel econometric methods. In sum, we believe that the monetary approach acquits itself well in the panel context. More specifically, we report evidence of significant long-run relationships for all of the panel combinations, with many of the monetary coefficients being correctly signed and of a plausible magnitude, this being especially so for DM-based relationships. The results derived from estimators which control for the most complex error structures uniformly do best in terms of having many correctly signed and sized coefficients; the estimated output coefficients are perhaps the exception having values which often differ from their interpretation as income elasticities of the demand for money (this perhaps being indicative of the fact that measured output is a poor proxy for the transactions demand for money). Interestingly, the half-lifes of our best monetary models are still faster than the half-lifes other researchers have noted using panel PPP tests (see Frankel and Rose, 1996).

The full sample of countries against the yen and the dollar produced very similar results, in terms of sign patterns and adjustment speeds, and this contrasted with the pattern for the European currencies against the dollar and mark. One reason the European countries may do better relates to the fact that most of these countries were on some sort of managed DM-based system (either explicitly or implicitly) for much of this period. Also, to the extent that the monetary approach is seen as a PPP-based approach, the estimates of monetary exchange rate equations based on the mark are likely to fare better than their dollar or yen counterparts simply because the geographic distances[8] for the European countries is in general much less than the pairings based on the dollar and yen, although, of course, as Mussa (1976) notes, monetary reduced forms may be derived without resorting to PPP. We conclude by noting that our panel monetary approach results would seem to give some credence to international reform proposals which rely on the coordination of monetary policies across countries (see, for example, McKinnon, 1984).

References

Baillie, R., Selover, D., 1987. Cointegration and models of exchange rate determination. International Journal of Forecasting 3, 43–51.

Bilson, J.F.O., 1978. Rational expectations and the exchange rate. In: Frenkel, J.A., Johnson, H.G. (Eds.), The Economics of Exchange Rates: Selected Studies, Addison-Wesley, Reading, MA.

Boothe, P., Glassman, D., 1987. Off the mark: lessons for exchange rate modeling. Oxford Economic Papers 39, 443–457.

Campbell, J.Y., Perron, P., 1991. Pitfalls and opportunities: what macroeconomists should know about unit roots. In: Blanchard, O.J., Fischer, S. (Eds.), NBER Economics Annual 1991, MIT Press, Cambridge, pp. 141–201.

Chinn, M., Johnston, L., 1996. Real exchange rate levels, productivity and demand shocks. Evidence from a panel of 14 countries, Working Paper #5709, NBER.

Chrystal, K.A., MacDonald, R., 1995. Exchange rates, financial innovation and divisia money: The sterling/dollar rate, 1972–1990. Journal of International Money and Finance 14, 493–513.

Dickey, D., Fuller, W.A., 1979. Distribution of the estimators for autoregressive time series with a unit root. Journal of the American Statistical Association 74, 427–431.

Diebold, F.X., Husted, S., Rush, M., 1991. Real exchange rates under the gold standard. Journal of Political Economy 99, 1252–1271.

Dornbusch, R., 1976. Expectations and exchange rate dynamics. Journal of Political Economy 84, 1161–1176.

Engel, C., Rogers, J.H., 1996. How wide is the border? American Economic Review 86, 1112–1125.

Engle, R., Granger, C., 1987. Cointegration and error correction. Representation, estimation and testing. Econometrica 55, 251–276.

Frankel, J., 1979. On the mark: a theory of floating exchange rates based on real interest differentials. American Economic Review 69, 610–622.

Frankel, J., 1982. The mystery of the multiplying marks: a modification of the monetary model. Review of Economics and Statistics 64, 515–519.

Frankel, J., Rose, A., 1996. A panel project on purchasing power parity: mean reversion within and between countries. Journal of International Economics 40, 209–224.

Frenkel, J., 1978. A monetary approach to the exchange rate. Doctrinal aspects and empirical evidence.

[8] Geographic distance has been shown to be an important reason for PPP violations by a number of researchers; see for example, Engel and Rogers (1996) and Wei and Parsley (1995).

In: Frenkel, J.A., Johnson, H.G. (Eds.), The Economics of Exchange Rates: Selected Studies, Addison-Wesley, Reading, MA.

Froot, K.A., Rogoff, K., 1995. Perspectives on ppp and long-run real exchange rates. In: Obstfeld, M., Rogoff, K. (Eds.), Handbook of International Economics, vol. 3, North Holland, Amsterdam, pp. 1647–1688.

Hansen, B., 1990. A powerful simple test for cointegration using Cochrane-Orcutt, Working Paper, University of Rochester.

Hodrick, R., 1978. An empirical analysis of the monetary approach to the determination of the exchange rate. In: Frenkel, J.A., Johnson, H.G. (Eds.), The Economics of Exchange Rates: Selected Studies, Addison-Wesley, Reading, MA.

Johansen, S., 1988. Statistical analysis of cointegrating vectors. Journal of Economic Dynamics and Control 12, 231–254.

Jorion, P., Sweeney, R., 1996. Mean reversion in real exchange rates: evidence and implications for forecasting. Journal of International Money and Finance 15, 535–550.

Kearney, C., MacDonald, R., 1990. Rational expectations, bubbles and monetary models of the exchange rate: the Australian/US dollar rate during the recent float. Australian Economic Papers 29, 1–20.

Levin, A., Lin, C.F., 1992. Unit roots in panel data: asymptotic and finite sample properties, Working Paper, University of California.

Levin, A., Lin, C.F., 1993. Unit roots in panel data: asymptotic and finite sample properties, [revised] Working Paper, University of California.

Lucas, R., 1982. Interest rates and currency prices in a two-country world. Journal of Monetary Economics 16, 335–360.

MacDonald, R., 1988. Purchasing power parity: some long run evidence from the recent float. De Economist 136, 239–252.

MacDonald, R., 1995. Long-run exchange rate modeling: a survey of the recent evidence. Staff Papers, International Monetary Fund 42, 437–489.

MacDonald, R., 1996. Panel unit root tests and real exchange rates. Economics Letters 50, 711

MacDonald, R., Taylor, M.P., 1993. The monetary approach to the exchange rate: rational expectations, long-run equilibrium and forecasting. Staff Papers, International Monetary Fund 40, 89–107.

MacDonald, R., Taylor, M.P., 1994. The monetary model of the exchange rate. Long-run relationships short-run dynamics and how to beat a random walk. Journal of International Money and Finance 13, 276–290.

MacKinnon, J., 1991. Critical values for cointegrating tests. In: Engle, R.F., Granger, C.W.J. (Eds.), Long-run Economic Relationships: Readings in Cointegration, Oxford University Press, Oxford, pp. 267–276.

McKinnon, R., 1984, An International Standard for Monetary Stabilization, Institute for International Economics, Washington, DC.

Meese, R., 1986. Testing for bubbles in exchange markets. A case of sparkling rates? Journal of Political Economy 94, 345–373.

Mussa, M., 1976. The exchange rate, the balance of payments and monetary and fiscal policy under a regime of controlled floating. Scandinavian Journal of Economics 2, 229–248.

O'Connell, P.G.J., 1996. The overvaluation of purchasing power parity, mimeo, Harvard University.

Park, J.Y., Philips, P.C.B., 1988. Statistical inference in regressions with integrated processes: Part I. Econometric Theory 4, 468–497.

Pedroni, P., 1995. Panel cointegration: asymptotic and finite sample properties of pooled time series tests with an application to the ppp hypothesis, mimeo, Indiana University.

Phillips, P., Loretan, M., 1991. Estimating long-run economic equilibria. Review of Economic Studies 58, 407–436.

Philips, P.C.B., Oularis, S., 1990. Asymptotic properties of residual based tests for cointegration. Econometrica 58, 165–193.

Shiller, R., Perron, P., 1985. Testing the random walk hypothesis: power versus frequency of observation. Economics Letters 18, 381–386.

Wei, S.J., Parsley, D., 1995. Purchasing power disparity during the floating rate period, Working Paper #5032, NBER.

Wu, Y., 1996. Are real exchange rates nonstationary? Evidence from a panel-data test. Journal of Money Credit and Banking 28, 54–63.

[5]

Modeling the ECU Against the U.S. Dollar: A Structural Monetary Interpretation

Lisbeth La Cour
Department of Economics, Copenhagen Business School, DK 1366 Copenhagen K, Denmark (*llc.eco@cbs.dk*)

Ronald MacDonald
Department of Economics, University of Strathclyde, Glasgow G4 OLN, United Kingdom (*r.r.macdonald@strath.ac.uk*)

The proposal that a reformed international monetary system be designed around currency blocs has gained some popularity of late. In Europe, the formation of the Euro formalizes the existence of a DM-based currency block. Little academic research has been conducted, however, on the properties of composite currencies such as the Euro. In this article, we examine the properties of the precursor to the Euro—namely, the ECU—against the U.S. dollar using a monetary framework. The article has several novel features: Our modeling strategy involves starting with underlying equilibrium conditions rather than a final reduced form; uses divisia money rather than the more conventional simple-sum money; interprets, in an economic sense, the long-run relationships; and produces an appealing forecasting performance.

KEY WORDS: Divisia money; Exchange-rate modeling; Forecasting.

Proposals for the reform of the international monetary system, such as those of McKinnon (1988) and Williamson (1985), stem from an inherent dissatisfaction with the recent experience of generalized floating exchange rates. Such proposals have at their heart the proposition that exchange-rate arrangements should be based on currency blocs or zones: For example, in the McKinnon plan there is a yen bloc, based on Pacific Rim currencies; a dollar bloc, based on the Americas; and a European zone, based on the deutsche mark (DM) (or the Euro). Given the renewed interest in European monetary integration in political fora and, in particular, the irrevocable locking of key European currencies in 1999, the latter zone has recently acquired special significance. It is therefore of interest from the relatively narrow European perspective, but also from the wider perspective of international monetary reform, to ascertain if a composite European currency has sensible properties vis-à-vis other key currencies, such as the U.S. dollar. That is the purpose of this article.

In particular, we econometrically examine the determinants of the (European Currency Unit) ECU–U.S. dollar exchange rate over the period January 1982 to December 1994. We focus on the ECU because it is available on a historical basis for a sufficiently long time span to allow us to implement the kind of testing methods advocated in this article. We are not predicting that the Euro will behave in the same way as the ECU. Rather our main objective is to offer an alternative approach to exchange-rate modeling other than that currently adopted in the literature. Given that the Euro will compose around 85% of the ECU, however, it does not seem unreasonable to suppose that they will behave in a similar fashion. The framework used is a variant of the monetary model of exchange-rate determination that has been widely exploited in the exchange-rate literature. Such a model is seen as having special relevance in the context of European monetary integration because the monetary policy of the European central bank is likely to be similar to that of the Bundesbank, and therefore this will ultimately have implications for the exchange rate. Indeed, given that the external value of the ECU may exhibit excess volatility, or at the very least behave in an unpredictable way, European monetary policy may have to use the ECU as an intermediate target of policy rather than let it be determined by the vagaries of international capital movements with all that this might imply for European competitiveness [of course, in reform proposals such as that of McKinnon (1988), targeting the exchange rate is a central element of the proposal].

In implementing the monetary model for the ECU, we have chosen divisia money as the appropriate monetary aggregate. In both European union (EU) (see Spencer 1997) and U.S. (see Belongia and Chalfont 1989) money-demand studies, divisia money has been demonstrated to have superior properties over simple-sum monetary aggregates. Furthermore, Chrystal and MacDonald (1995) demonstrated the superior performance of divisia money in the context of a reduced-form monetary-approach equation. In an earlier version of this article, however, we used both divisia and simple-sum money and found that there was little difference between the two aggregates (the simple-sum results are available from the authors on request).

Our modeling strategy involves using a "bottom-up" approach to defining an exchange-rate relationship rather than the "top-down" approach so often employed when estimating exchange-rate relationships. By this we mean that we first of all consider the statistical properties of the underlying equilibrium relationships, such as money-market equilibrium and purchasing power parity (PPP), and then build our exchange-rate relationship on the basis of these. Although other studies (e.g., MacDonald and Taylor 1992,

© 2000 American Statistical Association
Journal of Business & Economic Statistics
July 2000, Vol. 18, No. 4

1993) have built monetary-approach exchange-rate relationships using the equilibrium relationships used here, they did not pretest these relationships before establishing the final reduced form. We refer to research that starts, in a statistical sense, with the final reduced form as the "top-down" approach. We believe it is advantageous to first analyze the underlying relationships because this should give a better insight into the properties of the final exchange-rate relationship. Relatedly, and in contrast to much extant exchange-rate modeling, we attempt to interpret, in an economic sense, the cointegrating vectors produced in our econometric modeling. One particular advantage of our approach is that it should reveal the source of any potential instabilities in the final exchange-rate relationship.

The outline of the remainder of this article is as follows. In Section 1, we briefly outline our framework and the econometric testing methods employed. Section 2 contains a discussion of the dataset used and our estimates of the stochastic properties of the data. In Section 3 we present our analysis of the long-run relationships for three sectors (two money-market and an exchange-rate relationship) and the long-run relationships for our complete model. In Section 4 an estimate of the "equilibrium" ECU is presented, while in Section 5 the dynamic interactions contained in our complete model are examined in the context of an impulse-response analysis. The forecasting performance of our model is presented in Section 6, and the article closes with a concluding section.

1. ECONOMIC FRAMEWORK AND ECONOMETRIC MODELING METHODS

The model we propose takes as its starting point the monetary model of exchange-rate determination. Although this model is well known, it is worth presenting here briefly to give a backdrop against which our modeling strategy may be compared. The backbone of the monetary model, as the label implies, relates to conditions of money-market equilibrium in the home and foreign countries. We take a standard Cagan (1956) money-demand relationship of the form, $M^D = Y^\alpha \exp^{-\beta i}$, and, on setting the demand for money equal to the supply and transforming it logarithmically, we obtain

$$m_t - p_t = \alpha y_t - \beta i_t \tag{1a}$$

and

$$m_t^* - p_t^* = \alpha y_t^* - \beta i_t^*, \tag{1b}$$

where m denotes the money supply, p the price level, y real income, and i an interest rate, and where α is the income elasticity of demand for money, β is the interest-rate semielasticity, and an asterisk denotes a foreign magnitude; lowercase letters in this, and future, expressions indicate that a variable is written in logs (the exception being interest rates, which are expressed as fractions) and, for simplicity, the income elasticities and interest-rate semielasticities are assumed to be the same across countries [see Bilson (1978) for a discussion of this relationship in the context of the monetary model of the exchange rate). The so-called flex-price monetary approach (e.g., see Frenkel 1976; Bilson 1978; Hodrick 1978) assumes that absolute PPP holds continuously:

$$s_t = p_t - p_t^*, \tag{2}$$

where s_t denotes the spot exchange rate (home currency price of a unit of foreign exchange).

On rearranging (1a) and (1b) for the home and foreign price levels and substituting into (2), a flex-price monetary-approach equation may be derived:

$$s_t = m_t - m_t^* - \alpha(y_t - y_t^*) + \beta(i_t - i_t^*). \tag{3}$$

Equation (3) asserts that in equilibrium an exchange rate is driven by relative excess money supplies [this kind of reduced form may also be derived from the generalized asset-pricing model of Lucas (1982)]. Holding other variables fixed, an increase in the domestic money supply produces an equiproportionate increase in the exchange rate, whereas an increase in domestic income produces a currency appreciation (because its influence occurs through the demand for money). In the flex-price monetary model, an increase in the domestic interest rate, ceteris paribus, generates a currency depreciation because interest rates track expected inflation. This may be seen by writing the standard Fisher decomposition for domestic and foreign interest rates:

$$i_t = E_t r_t + E_t \Delta p_{t+k} \tag{4a}$$

and

$$i_t^* = E_t r_t^* + E_t \Delta p_{t+1}^*, \tag{4b}$$

where E_t denotes a conditional expectation $E_t = E(\cdot|I_t)$, I_t is the information set, r_t is the real interest rate, Δ represents the first-difference operator, and, therefore, Δp_{t+k} represents the $t+k$ inflation rate. In the flex-price monetary model, the expected real interest rates are assumed to be constant and hence the nominal interest rates are measures of expected inflation. Given that the uncovered interest-rate parity condition is also assumed to hold in this class of model,

$$E_t \Delta s_{t+k} = i_t - i_t^*, \tag{5}$$

the interest differential in (3) also represents the expected inflation differential. Because of its reliance on PPP, however, the flex-price monetary model must be regarded as having limited applicability for the recent floating-exchange-rate period in which violations of PPP have been manifest and persistent (e.g., see MacDonald 1995). A more attractive variant of the monetary model is the sticky-price approach (Dornbusch 1976; Frankel 1979), which has as its long-run solution (3) but allows for short-run deviations from PPP. Because the approach used in this article is in the spirit of the sticky-price monetary model, we discuss it briefly here. The variant of the sticky-price model due to Frankel (1979) assumes that the actual exchange rate evolves according to the following equation:

$$E_t \Delta s_{t+k} = \phi(\bar{s} - s)_t + (E_t \Delta p_{t+k} - E_t \Delta p^*_{t+k}), \quad 0 < \phi < 1. \quad (6)$$

On using (5) in (6) and rearranging, we may obtain

$$s_t = \bar{s}_t - \frac{1}{\phi}\left[(i_t - E_t \Delta p_{t+k}) - (i^*_t - E_t \Delta p^*_{t+k})\right] \quad (7a)$$

or

$$s_t - p_t + p^*_t = -\frac{1}{\phi}\left[(i_t - E_t \Delta p_{t+k}) - (i^*_t - E_t \Delta p^*_{t+k})\right], \quad (7b)$$

where $\bar{s}_t$ is the long-run, PPP-determined, equilibrium exchange rate. Equation (7a) demonstrates that the current spot rate will deviate from the long-run rate as a proportion of the real interest differential. The long-run spot rate is assumed to be given by (3) or, one step removed, (2). On using (2) we see that another interpretation of the sticky-price monetary approach is to say that it explains movements in the real exchange rate in terms of a real interest differential. This latter interpretation is essentially the one used to define the exchange-rate sector in our model. Using (3) and (4), instead of (2), in (7a), we obtain

$$s_t = m_t - m^*_t - \alpha(y_t - y^*_t) + \beta(E_t \Delta p_{t+k} - E_t \Delta p^*_{t+k}) - \frac{1}{\phi}\left[(i_t - E_t \Delta p_{t+k}) - (i^*_t - E_t \Delta p^*_{t+k})\right]. \quad (8)$$

This equation is often reexpressed as the following reduced form:

$$s_t = \varphi_1 m_t + \varphi_2 m^*_t + \varphi_3 y_t + \varphi_4 y^*_t + \varphi_5 i^s_t + \varphi_6 i^{s,*}_t + \varphi_5 i^l_t + \varphi_6 i^{l,*}_t + u_t, \quad (9)$$

where the s and l superscripts indicate that the interest rates are of short and long maturity, respectively. In this kind of reduced form, the long interest rates are assumed to capture expected inflation and the short rates the liquidity, or real, effects of monetary policy. In early empirical applications of (3) and (8), the relationships were, in general, estimated in a static form, although some limited dynamics were sometimes allowed (in terms of a partial adjustment mechanism). Additionally, it was assumed that all of the right-side variables were exogenous, although some researchers allowed for simultaneous interactions between the exchange rate and relative money supplies or interest rates using simultaneous equation estimators [for a comprehensive overview of this early literature, see MacDonald (1988)]. The model was generally assessed in terms of how close the income elasticities and interest-rate semielasticities were to hypothesized priors (as estimated from money-demand equations) and in terms of its goodness of fit. Although there is some evidence that these models performed quite well for the 1970s, their performance in the 1980s and 1990s has generally been regarded as dismal. Perhaps the most telling indictment against such models is their failure to beat a random walk in an out-of-sample forecasting context (Meese and Rogoff 1983).

More recent research on (9) has involved an explicit recognition of the stationarity issues relating to an appropriate empirical implementation. For example, several researchers have tested for cointegration in (9) and reported results supportive of the monetary approach (e.g., see MacDonald and Taylor 1993, 1994). (Support for the approach is usually adduced if there is evidence of at least one statistically significant cointegrating relationship and the implied coefficients are close to their prior values.) There are, however, problems in the way previous tests have interpreted the cointegrating relationships, and this will be discussed in greater detail.

Our modeling strategy takes the preceding framework, and particularly the sticky-price monetary model, as its point of departure. In essence we use the monetary model as scaffolding that may be manipulated in such a way as to produce an appealing structure for the ECU–dollar exchange rate. As in recent tests of the monetary model, we use cointegration methods to analyze the long- and short-run behavior of the ECU. Our approach contains several novel features, however, compared to other work using this class of model.

First, in implementing monetary models researchers have, generally speaking, taken the final reduced form as their starting point. In this article, we propose starting with the basic building blocks of the monetary model, such as the underlying money-market relationships, and testing these separately before building our final exchange-rate model. This has the advantage that potential problems can be detected at source rather than trying to unravel the causes of a poorly specified exchange-rate equation. Furthermore, this approach, by pretesting the underlying relationships, should give insight into the kind of restrictions that can be placed on the gross system. The approach, though, does have the potential disadvantage that the estimates in the subsystems may be biased because they omit variables that appear in the more general model. We do ensure, however, that our subsystems are free from serial correlation, so our implicit assumption, that the first differences of the variables appearing in the subsystems are orthogonal to the variables not included (but which appear in the more general system), does have some support. Furthermore, in a qualitative sense the coefficients in the more general system are similar to the coefficients identified in the subsystems. At the very least, therefore, we believe that this approach is instructive of what the final system should look like and in this sense is a useful tool for data analysis.

Second, as is now well known, PPP does not perform at all well on a single currency basis using data from the recent floating period (e.g., see Froot and Rogoff 1995; MacDonald 1995). Indeed, as we shall demonstrate, the (logarithm of the) real exchange rate for the ECU, $s_t - p_t + p^*_t$, is an I(1) process, and this in itself represents a violation of PPP. This means that deviations from PPP have to be explicitly recognized in our modeling, and we offer a method of doing this here that is in the spirit of the sticky-price monetary model. In recognition of this violation of PPP, we focus on the real exchange rate in terms of real money balances rather than the nominal exchange rate in terms of nominal money balances.

Third, one aspect of Equation (1) that is often overlooked is that a model of the money-demand relationship based on just three variables—real money, income, and an interest rate—imposes both long-run price homogeneity and short-run price homogeneity in dynamic equations (e.g., see, La Cour 1996). The latter feature of the model is, we believe, unattractive, and we propose relaxing it here. A straightforward way of doing this is to introduce inflation into the datasets for the home and foreign money markets. This also opens the possibility of interpreting the inflation rate as an opportunity cost of holding money as in

$$m_t - p_t = \alpha y_t - \beta i_t - \gamma \Delta p_t \qquad (1a')$$

and

$$m_t^* - p_t^* = \alpha y_t^* - \beta i_t^* - \gamma \Delta p_t^*, \qquad (1b')$$

where Δ is the first-difference operator and Δp has the interpretation of the inflation rate.

Fourth, given that there are several potentially nonstationary variables entering an equation such as (9), there may be multiple cointegrating vectors, and it is therefore crucial to place some economic interpretation on these because the cointegrating vectors will not be uniquely determined (although the cointegrating space will be uniquely determined). The existence of multiple cointegrating vectors has been a particular problem in the exchange-rate studies mentioned previously. For example, MacDonald and Taylor (1993) found evidence of three statistically significant cointegrating vectors in their application of the German mark–U.S. dollar exchange rate but based their dynamic short-run analysis on only the most significant vector, although it is not clear if this indeed represents an exchange-rate relationship. In this article we explicitly test for the number of cointegrating vectors and attempt to place some structure on each of the significant vectors by conducting various hypothesis tests [following the approach of Johansen and Juselius (1992a,b)].

The nine-dimensional vector of variables that composes our most general, or "gross," system is

$$x_t^{g'} = [(s_t - p_t + p_t^*), (m_t - p_t), (m_t^* - p_t^*), y_t, y_t^*, i_t^l, i_t^{l,*}, \Delta p_t, \Delta p_t^*)], \qquad (10)$$

where the g superscript denotes gross. This equation may be seen to be in the spirit of the sticky-price monetary approach discussed previously, and we will give further justification for this specification in Section 3.

The cointegration methods we propose are based on the work of Johansen (1995). Specifically, consider the $(n \times 1)$ vector of variables $\mathbf{x}_t$ [where $\mathbf{x}_t$ contains the variables entering (10) and also different subsets of these variables] and assume that it has a vector autoregressive (VAR) representation of the form

$$\mathbf{x}_t = \eta D_t + \sum_{i=1}^{p} \Pi_i \mathbf{x}_{t-i} + \varepsilon_t, \qquad (11)$$

where ε is an $(n \times 1)$ vector of white-noise disturbances with mean 0 and covariance matrix Ξ, η is the matrix of coefficients of the deterministic variables [dimension $(n \times k)$], and D_t is the vector of deterministic variables [dimension $(k \times 1)$]. In our analysis, these include a constant and 11 centered seasonal dummies (i.e., $k = 1 + s$ and s is the number of centered seasonal dummies, which is 11 in our case). Expression (11) may be reparameterized into the vector error-correction mechanism (VECM) as

$$\Delta \mathbf{x}_t = \eta D_t + \sum_{i=1}^{p-1} \mathbf{\Phi}_i \Delta \mathbf{x}_{t-i} - \mathbf{\Pi} \mathbf{x}_{t-1} + \varepsilon_t, \qquad (12)$$

where Δ denotes the first-difference operator, $\mathbf{\Phi}_i$ is an $(n \times n)$ coefficient matrix (equal to $-\sum_{j=i+1}^{p} \mathbf{\Pi}_j$), and $\mathbf{\Pi}$ is an $(n \times n)$ matrix (equal to $\sum_{i=1}^{p} \mathbf{\Pi}_i - I$) whose rank determines the number of cointegrating vectors. If $\mathbf{\Pi}$ is of either full rank, n, or zero rank, $\mathbf{\Pi} = 0$, then either all of the series are stationary or there is no cointegration among the elements in the long-run relationship (in these instances it will be appropriate to estimate the model in, respectively, levels or first differences). If, however, $\mathbf{\Pi}$ is of reduced rank, r (where $r < n$), then there will exist $(n \times r)$ matrices α and β such that $\mathbf{\Pi} = \alpha\beta'$, where β is the matrix whose columns are the linearly independent cointegrating vectors and the α matrix is interpreted as the adjustment matrix, indicating the speed with which the system responds to last period's deviation from the r equilibrium relationships defined by the β's. Hence the existence of the VECM model, relative to say a VAR in first differences, depends on the existence of cointegration. Furthermore, the so-called Granger representation theorem (see Engle and Granger 1987) implies that, if cointegration exists among a group of variables, an error-correction representation must also exist.

2. DATA SOURCES

In this section, we provide some detail on the construction and definitions of variables used in this study. The full sample period runs from January 1982 to December 1994 (monthly observations), with the last 24 observations being retained for an out-of-sample forecasting analysis. The data for the European area were supplied by Peter Spencer and were discussed in some detail by Spencer (1997). The methods used to weight the data were outlined by Artis, Bladen-Hovell, and Zheng (1993). In short, the countries included in the EU aggregates are Austria, Belgium, Denmark, France, Germany, Ireland, Italy, the Netherlands, and Spain. The average (U.S. dollar) nominal exchange rates from 1980 are used to convert these into a common currency (see appendix A of Artis et al. 1993). A similar procedure is used to convert individual income series into an EU aggregate. In this regard it is worth noting that individual-country data on gross domestic product (GDP) are only available on a quarterly basis. To obtain a monthly income series, the individual GDP series were interpolated using monthly industrial production and the methods of Chow and Lin (1971).

Interest rates—both "dual" for divisia and a "long" rate—were weighted using the weights contained in the ECU, and consumer prices were aggregated using GDP weights [again both of these weighting procedures follow Artis et al. (1993)]. Although such prices are usually seen as most appropriate for defining real money balances, there remains a controversy in the exchange-rate literature over the appropriate price series to use for a PPP calculation [e.g., see Frenkel (1980) or Dornbusch (1988) for an overview of these issues], with some authors preferring a measure that most closely reflects traded-goods prices. The recent empirical literature on PPP (see MacDonald 1995), however, suggests that violations of PPP are equally likely regardless of the price series used.

For the nine countries, 18 monetary components were used to construct divisia monetary measures. For most of the countries these consisted of both M1 and quasimoney as extracted from the International Monetary Fund's International Financial Statistics (IFS). The main exceptions to this were Germany, where the standard Bundesbank series was used, and Belgium, where only a single monetary aggregate was available. National banking statistics for M2 were used for the Netherlands, France, Denmark, and Italy to construct a measure of retail interbank balances as an alternative to quasimoney (as M2–M1). Spencer (1997) demonstrated that the ECU divisia series satisfies the generalized axiom of revealed preference. The U.S. divisia and user cost series are taken from the Federal Reserve Bank of St. Louis's database [accessible on the Internet; for further details on the construction of this series see Anderson, Jones and Nesmith (1997)].

User costs were constructed for each of the monetary components by taking the relevant government bond yield and subtracting the deposit rates (although, as we shall see, we do not use these rates in the systems reported in this article). The U.S. income, price, and interest-rate series are from the IFS CD-ROM disk (lines 99b.r, 64, and 61, respectively). Most of the data series used in our analysis are seasonally adjusted. Because the EU money and income series are seasonally unadjusted, we included 11 centered seasonal dummies in our VAR systems (these were also included in systems that did not contain EU money or income to model any uncorrected seasonality).

Before conducting a detailed analysis of the long-run relationships in each of the sectors, we present some evidence on the stochastic properties of the variables studied. The model used for testing the univariate unit-root properties of our data is the following augmented Dickey–Fuller (ADF) equation:

$$\Delta z_t = \alpha_0 + \gamma z_{t-1} + \sum_{i}^{p} a_i \Delta z_{t-i} + e_t, \tag{13}$$

where z is one of the series we want to investigate, α_0 is a constant, and the residual term, e, is assumed to be iid $\sim N(0, 1)$. For $z = (m - p)$ and $\Delta(m - p)$ (i.e., the levels and differences of EU real money balances) a set of centered seasonal dummies was also included in the regression equation (the seasonal dummies were not significant in the EU income series—the other seasonally unadjusted series—and were therefore dropped from the final estimated relationship). These latter series are seasonally unadjusted, and without the dummies too many lags would be required to ensure that the residual terms appear as white noise. In each equation, the number of included lagged differences was decided as the smallest number necessary to make the residuals appear white noise on the basis of the Ljung–Box test statistic for 33 autocorrelations (which is one quarter of the sample size). The null hypothesis of a unit root is $\gamma = 0$. The results from estimating (13) for each of the series are presented in Table 1.

The results in the top half of Table 1 give the clear impression that the majority of variables (i.e., the variables that appear in the final model) are I(1) processes. The exception is the European price level, which appears to be I(2); the U.S. price level appears to be close to I(2). In what follows we decided to analyze this series as if it were in fact I(2). This is attractive from a statistical point of view because it gives a consistency to the treatment of the two monetary sectors, which is important when we come to model the complete, or gross, system. For example, if the EU price series is the only I(2) process in the real exchange-rate relationship, then this would require that the real exchange rate be I(2). The latter does not seem a plausible interpretation. It is also attractive from a theoretical perspective because real money balances are the appropriate monetary variable. None of the unit-root results reported in Table 1 are affected by the inclusion of a deterministic time trend into the estimated version of (13).

3. RESULTS FOR THE LONG-RUN STRUCTURE

3.1 Money-Market Building Blocks

In this section, we examine the long-run relationships stemming from our money-market conditions. In particular, we examine the properties of the following vector, which represents a subset of the gross vector, (10):

$$x_t^{m'} = [(m_t - p_t), y_t, i_t, \Delta p_t]', \tag{14}$$

Table 1. Unit-Root Tests

Series	No. of lagged differences	Test statistic	Unit root?
$s - p + p^*$	0	−1.04	Yes
$m - p$	3	−1.32	Yes
$m^* - p^*$	1	−.57	Yes
y	2	−.89	Yes
y^*	1	−1.25	Yes
i	7	−2.37	Yes
i^*	0	−1.64	Yes
Δp	11	−2.69	Yes
Δp^*	6	−4.13	No
$\Delta(s - p + p^*)$	0	−10.91	No
$\Delta(m - p)$	2	−4.73	No
$\Delta(m^* - p^*)$	0	−6.51	No
Δy	1	−12.67	No
Δy^*	0	−8.40	No
Δi	6	−3.40	No
Δi^*	0	−8.80	No
$\Delta^2 p$	10	−6.49	No
$\Delta^2 p^*$	5	−8.77	No

NOTE: The critical value of the ADF test are approximately −3.51 (1% level), −2.89 (5% level), and −2.56 (10% level) (see Fuller 1978).

where variables have the same interpretation as before. Note that, as before, this relationship has the constraint that money enters in real terms imposed, a constraint that is not rejected (using at least a 1% significance level) by the data for any of our money-market systems. The appropriate interest rate in a divisia study is the so-called divisia dual, or user cost. Because this is not the relevant interest rate for capital account transactions and hence the determination of the exchange rate, however, we also experimented with long rates in our divisia systems. Because long rates produced very similar results in the two divisia-based systems and because we are ultimately interested in an exchange-rate relationship, we only report the long-rate results in this article (although it would have been relatively straightforward to link the long rate to the dual rate from the money-demand equation, using a term structure relationship, but this would unnecessarily complicate the definition of the full system without adding anything to the analysis). All of our systems are constructed with four lags for each of the variables because this lag structure was sufficient to produce random residuals.

In Table 2, we present a variety of multivariate misspecification test statistics for the EU- and U.S.-based models. In particular, we present a multivariate Godfrey (1988) Lagrange multiplier (LM)-type of statistic for first- and fourth-order autocorrelation [LM(1) and LM(4)] and a Doornik and Hansen (1994) multivariate normality test [NM(8)], where the numbers in parentheses are p values. In general these statistics indicate an absence of serial correlation, although there is some evidence of nonnormality in each of the systems. To establish the source of this nonnormality, we experimented with dummy variables to capture large outliers. In general, the addition of two dummy variables to each model system proved sufficient to produce insignificant normality statistics. Because in other respects these results are qualitatively similar to those reported here, we do not discuss them further.

Our tests of the rank of each of the systems are presented in Table 3. The null hypothesis of rank order r is noted in column 1. On the basis of a 95% significance level, there is evidence of two cointegrating vectors for the EU model, whereas for the U.S. system there is clear evidence of one cointegrating vector, the second vector being marginal at the 90% level (the second vector is significant at the 80% level). Given the small-sample problems associated with the Johansen trace test and the fact that choosing one cointegrating vector will be too little to identify our desired money-market relationships, however, we decided to proceed with the analysis based on two cointegrating vectors for both the United States and Europe. Indeed, graphing the chosen cointegrating vectors seems to support the impression of two stationary relationships for each system. Furthermore, it turns out that in each case we are able to identify in an economically meaningful way both of these relations—a property that even more strongly supports our choice of cointegration rank (see Johansen 1995). In each of these models an unrestricted constant is included, thereby allowing for both linear trends in the data and intercepts in the cointegrating relationships (we explicitly tested for a deterministic trend in the cointegrating relations, and in each case we could not reject the null hypothesis that the trend was 0).

Table 2. Misspecification Tests

Test	Europe	U.S.
LM(1)	16.64 (.41)	10.74 (.83)
LM(4)	12.65 (.70)	8.61 (.93)
NM(8)	20.36 (.01)	18.08 (.02)

Table 3. Trace Tests for Cointegration Rank in Money Market Systems

H_0: r	Europe	U.S.	Trace90	Trace95
0	53.98	72.40	43.84	47.21
1	30.47	23.73	26.70	29.38
2	13.92	11.16	13.31	15.34
3	4.43	1.81	2.71	3.84

Having established the existence of two cointegrating vectors in each system, our next task involved interpreting the vectors. That is, because it is now accepted that multiple cointegrating vectors, and even single cointegrating vectors, are hard to interpret, we attempt to place some structure on each of the significant vectors. To this end, we implement joint hypothesis tests of the following form on the full cointegrating space (see Johansen and Juselius 1992a,b):

$$\text{Hypothesis: } \beta = \{H_1\phi_1, H_2\phi_2\};$$

this can be seen as the joint selection of two stationary relationships that are fully specified and identified. The results from this testing strategy are reported in Table 4. The standard errors reported in Table 4, and in other tables, are the square roots of the relevant diagonal elements in the observed Fisher information matrix [they are therefore the standard errors advocated by Johansen (1995) rather than normal standard errors reported in a linear regression equation]. Furthermore, in this table and all future tables containing cointegration results, a "1" denotes a normalizing restriction and a "0" denotes a "real" restriction.

In the case of the EU divisia system, we note that the first vector may be restricted to a very simple stationary relationship consisting of real money balances and the opportunity cost dual term. That is, it has the form given by the following equation:

$$m_t - p_t = -10.55 * \text{long}_t. \tag{15}$$

Therefore, real divisia balances are negatively related to the opportunity cost variable, as standard monetary theory

Table 4. Divisia-based Cointegration Relationships

	$m-p$	y	long	Δp	Interpretation
Europe	1	0	10.55 (1.89)	0	Money relation
	0	0	−.406 (.04)	1	Fisher relation
U.S.	1	0	6.63 (.67)	0	Money relation
	0	0	−.058 (.03)	1	Fisher relation

NOTE: Numbers in parentheses are standard errors, calculated as the square root of the relevant diagonal elements in the observed Fisher information matrix.

would predict. The fact that income is insignificant in this money-demand relation is quite unexpected but probably has to do with the lack of variation in this variable for the relatively short time span of our sample period. The insignificance of income may alternatively (or additionally) reflect measurement errors imparted from our use of industrial production as our measure of income. From a policy perspective, the existence of such a simple long-run money-market equilibrium condition must be appealing. For the second vector, we find a stationary relationship between inflation and the interest rate, as suggested by the Fisher relationship [in the Fisher relationships reported here we do not restrict the vector to be $(1, -1)$; however, we do impose and test this restriction in the full system]. The test of the joint hypothesis that these two vectors define the cointegration space has a chi-squared distribution with 2 df—$\chi^2(2)$. This may be seen in the following way. The total number of restrictions, including normalizations, is 6—3 from the first vector (the 1 on money and the 2 zero restrictions) and 3 from the second vector (the 1 on inflation and the 2 zero restrictions). With two cointegrating vectors we can obtain four (i.e., 2^2) restrictions for free (by normalization), so we subtract this number from the total to get two "real" restrictions. The estimated $\chi^2(2)$ statistic has a value of .93 and a p value of .63. Other restrictions tests reported later are computed in a similar manner.

It is noteworthy that the U.S.-based divisia system has very similar properties to the EU system: The first vector consists of a stationary relationship between real money balances and the interest rate, and the second stationary vector picks out a positive relationship between inflation and the nominal interest rate (the magnitude of this coefficient being smaller than in the EU case). The test of the joint hypothesis that these two vectors define the cointegration space is a chi-squared statistic, with 2 df (for the reasons noted in the context of the EU money-demand system) and has an estimated value of .30, with a p value of .86. On the basis of the standard errors reported in parentheses, all of the variables are significantly different from 0.

The fact that income does not appear in either EU or U.S. long-run relationships seems to conflict with traditional money-demand theory in which real income enters as a scale variable (e.g., see Laidler 1992). In addition to the previously noted restrictions being statistically acceptable, however, it is also the case that for both divisia systems real income is weakly exogenous on the basis of the appropriate chi-squared test statistics, which are 3.82 (p value .43) for the EU system and 3.90 (p value .42) for the U.S. system. (The restricted cointegrating vectors for simple-sum money are very similar to those for divisia money and are not reported in the text; they are available from the authors on request.) Furthermore, the likelihood ratio test statistics (which have an approximate chi-squared distribution, with 2 df) for the exclusion of income from the cointegrating space are .10 for the EU system and .03 for the U.S. system. Because the 5% critical value for these statistics is 5.99, income may be legitimately excluded from both sets of long-run relationships (in fact, this proved to be the case irrespective of the chosen rank; income could also be excluded if the rank was chosen as 1 or 3).

The restricted alpha matrix corresponding to the divisia system indicated that, for both the EU and U.S. systems, real money balances adjust significantly to disequilibrium in the first vector and inflation adjusts significantly to disequilibrium in vector 2 (this and other adjustment matrices are available from the authors on request).

3.2 Exchange-Rate Building Block

As we noted in Section 1, trying to empirically implement an exchange-rate model based on the flex-price monetary model for the recent float is going to be a nonstarter, given the well-known failure of PPP to hold for this period. Hence we adopt a variant of the sticky-price monetary model discussed in Section 1.

To make sense of the PPP relationship for individual currencies, both Johansen and Juselius (1992a,b) and MacDonald and Marsh (1997) advocated conditioning the nominal exchange-rate/relative-price configuration onto an appropriate interest differential. The intuition being that, because interest differentials have been nonzero throughout the recent floating period, failure to incorporate them into the conditioning information set will produce a misspecified exchange-rate relationship (Johansen and Juselius justified this in terms of the open interest parity condition, while MacDonald and Marsh argued on the basis of a balance-of-payments equilibrium relationship). Hence, for our exchange-rate sector, we propose examining the following subsystem:

$$x_t^{ppp'} = [(s_t - p_t + p_t^*), i_t, i_t^* \Delta p_t, \Delta p_t^*]',$$

which captures the interest rate–PPP relationship noted previously and also potentially the "closed" Fisher relationship between nominal interest rates and inflation. Our interpretation of the monetary approach is therefore more in the spirit of Mussa (1979) than Frenkel (1976) and Bilson (1978). In Table 5, the portmanteau tests for residual whiteness are presented, and these indicate an absence of serial correlation, although again, as in the monetary sector, there is some evidence of residual nonnormality.

The results for the rank properties of the exchange-rate subsector are presented in Table 6, and these indicate the existence of up to three cointegrating vectors.

As in the money-market systems, we try to interpret the three cointegrating relationships by imposing and testing identifying restrictions on the complete cointegrating space. These are of the following form:

$$\text{Hypothesis: } \beta = \{H_1\phi_1, H_2\phi_2, H_3\phi_3\},$$

Table 5. Exchange-Rate Misspecification Tests

LM(1)	*LM(4)*	*N(10)*
31.78 (.16)	21.23 (.68)	39.19 (.00)

Table 6. Rank of Exchange-Rate Subsector

$H_0: r$	Trace	Trace90	Trace95
$r = 0$	104.51	64.74	68.68
$r \leq 1$	51.99	43.84	47.21
$r \leq 2$	27.17	26.70	29.38
$r \leq 3$	9.44	13.31	15.34
$r \leq 4$	1.47	2.71	3.84

and our estimates of the restricted forms are reported in Table 7. In particular, we restrict the first vector to be the exchange-rate relationship, which is driven by an interest differential. We note that, as in the traditional flow model of the capital account (as exemplified in the seminal Mundell–Fleming model), the real exchange rate is negatively related to the domestic interest rate and positively related to the foreign rate (when the vector is written as an equation). The absolute magnitude of the semielasticity on the U.S. interest rate is much larger than that on the European rate (although, as we shall see, the relative size is reduced in the full model). This may in part reflect the fact that, of the two currencies composing our exchange-rate measure, it was only the U.S. dollar that was actually traded during the sample period and, furthermore, the U.S. bond market was much deeper than that of our synthetic ECU bond. The second and third vectors are restricted to be Fisher relationships in which the home and foreign interest rates are positively related to the respective inflation rates [at this point we do not restrict these vectors to be $(1, -1)$, although they are restricted in the gross system discussed later]. We note that all of the coefficients, apart from that on the domestic interest rate in the first relationship and the coefficient in the foreign interest-rate relationship, are statistically different from 0. The chi-squared test of the joint hypothesis that the three vectors define the cointegration space has a test statistic of .76, with 2 df, producing a p value of .68. In this system we impose a total of 11 $(3 + 4 + 4)$ restrictions. We then subtract from this the 9 $(= 3^2)$ restrictions, which are fulfilled simply due to normalization to obtain the 2 df.

3.3 Analysis of the "Gross" Dataset: Putting the Building Blocks Together

Having established the existence of what we believe are attractive money-market relationships and an exchange-rate relationship, we now turn our attention to the gross structure containing the data from both the money and exchange-rate sectors. Our expectation in this large system is that it

Table 7. Exchange-Rate Sector Cointegration Relationships

$s - p + p$	i	i^*	Δp	Δp^*	Interpretation
1	1.939	−11.115	0	0	Exchange-rate relation
	(1.69)	(1.71)			
0	−.31	0	1	0	Home Fisher relation
	(.04)				
0	0	−.036	0	1	Foreign Fisher relation
		(.04)			

NOTE: Numbers in parentheses are standard errors, calculated as the square root of the relevant diagonal elements in the observed Fisher information matrix.

Table 8. Gross System Misspecification Tests

LM(1)	LM(4)	LM(12)	LM(13)	N(14)
55.33	38.66	42.28	47.23	38.09
(.25)	(.86)	(.73)	(.55)	(.00)

will have a rank equal to 5—that is, an exchange-rate relationship, two real money-market relationships, and two Fisher equations. Furthermore, from a theoretical perspective (Johansen 1995) we would expect to be able to place the same set of restrictions on the gross systems as we had in our subsystems. Our testing framework is fully simultaneous and features the long-run relationships constructed in the last section, plus an exchange-rate relationship. Our attention, therefore, focuses on the following vector, introduced and defined earlier:

$$x_t^{g'} = [(s_t - p_t + p_t^*), (m_t - p_t), (m_t^* - p_t^*), \quad i_t^l, i_t^{l,*}, \Delta p_t, \Delta p_t^*], \quad (16)$$

where variables have the same interpretation as before. In Section 3.1, we found that income was insignificant in the long-run EU and U.S. money-demand relationships. Furthermore, for both systems income proved to be weakly exogenous. To keep the dimensions of the gross system tractable, we have used these findings to justify the exclusion of income from (16).

In Table 8 a set of portmanteau statistics, for a range of lag lengths, indicates an absence of serial correlation, although there is again some evidence of residual nonnormality.

In Table 9 we present the cointegration rank results for the system (16), and these indicate the existence of up to five cointegrating vectors (the fifth vector being marginally significant). A plot of the fifth vector supports the impression that it is stationary. Note that in choosing the rank of our seven-dimensional system to be 5, we are entirely consistent with the analysis of the subsystems in Sections 3.1 and 3.2.

Having established the existence of up to five cointegrating vectors for our exchange-rate relationship, we next attempt to impose and test identifying restrictions on the full cointegration space. In particular, we attempt to test if the restricted cointegrating vectors defined for our subsectors also hold in the gross system. These are of the following form:

$$\text{Hypothesis: } \beta = \{H_1\phi_1, H_2\phi_2, H_3\phi_3, H_4\phi_4, H_5\phi_5\}.$$

Table 9. Rank of Gross System

$H_0: r$	Trace	Trace90
$r = 0$	166.1	117.23
$r \leq 1$	113.1	89.37
$r \leq 2$	74.91	64.74
$r \leq 3$	45.12	43.84
$r \leq 4$	19.48	26.70
$r \leq 5$	7.27	13.31
$r \leq 6$	.79	2.71

Table 10. Cointegration Relationships in Gross System

$s-p+p^*$	i^l	i^{l*}	$(m-p)$	(m^*-p^*)	Δp	Δp^*
1	$19.51_{(1.63)}$	$-46.58_{(2.77)}$	0	0	0	0
0	$3.50_{(.66)}$	0	1	0	0	0
0	0	$15.78_{(1.15)}$	0	1	0	0
0	−1.00	0	0	0	1	0
0	0	−1.00	0	0	0	1

NOTE: Numbers in parentheses are standard errors, calculated as the square root of the relevant diagonal elements in the observed Fisher information matrix.

Table 10 contains our estimates of the restricted forms of the five cointegrating vectors.

The first vector represents our exchange-rate relationship. We find that the nominal exchange-rate/relative-price configuration is only stationary when the long bond yields enter the cointegrating set. This is consistent, in a somewhat different context, with the findings of Johansen and Juselius (1992a) and MacDonald and Marsh (1997), who used nominal interest rates to generate a stationary measure of the real exchange rate. It is also consistent with the wider literature on PPP in which real rates defined for the recent float appear nonstationary and only a weak-form version of PPP holds. That is, in a regression context in which the nominal exchange rate is conditioned on relative prices, the residual term is mean reverting, but the coefficients on relative prices are far from their a priori values—see MacDonald (1993). As in the traditional flow model of the capital account (as exemplified in the seminal Mundell–Fleming model), the real exchange rate is negatively related to the domestic interest rate, but the foreign rate is positively related. As in the exchange-rate subsystem, the magnitude of the U.S. interest rate semielasticity is greater than the corresponding EU elasticity, although the relative difference is greatly reduced. Vectors 2 and 3 are interpretable as EU and U.S. money-demand relationships, which have the same specifications as those reported in Table 4, although there are some differences in the magnitude of the coefficients. The fourth and fifth vectors are, respectively, the Fisher conditions for the EU and the United States. Here these have been restricted as $(1,-1)$ vectors, which is what a strict interpretation of the Fisher condition implies (rather than the coefficients simply being correctly signed, as we had in the subsystems). On the basis of the reported standard errors, all of the coefficients are statistically different from 0. A test of the joint hypothesis that the five vectors define the cointegration space has a chi-squared test statistic of 9.41, with 6 df, producing a p value of .15. In this system we impose a total of 31 $(5+6+6+7+7)$ restrictions. We then subtract the $25(=5^2)$ restrictions that are fulfilled due to normalization to obtain 6 df.

4. AN ESTIMATE OF THE EQUILIBRIUM ECU

Recently a huge literature has developed around testing equilibrium exchange-rate relationships [see MacDonald (1995) for overviews]. This literature is primarily concerned with issues of mean reversion in real exchange rates and estimating cointegrating relationships between exchange rates (both real and nominal) and sets of fundamentals. Increasingly, both policy makers and practitioners have been using such estimated relationships to address issues of exchange-rate misalignment and also for assessment purposes. A measure of the real equilibrium ECU exchange rate may be obtained from our model by summing the five divisia-based cointegrating relationships, using the appropriate alpha coefficients. Because our estimated constant terms lie in the dynamic component of the VECM, we had to construct constants for each of the cointegrating relationships. This was achieved by decomposing the unrestricted constant into its alpha and alpha orthogonal directions, using the result of Johansen (1995, p. 81).

Our measure of the real equilibrium ECU is reported in Figure 1, along with the actual value of the real ECU for our sample period. The figure indicates periods when the real ECU was undervalued—the early 1980s and again in the early 1990s (and also during the dramatic appreciation of the ECU from 1985 to 1987)—and periods when it was overvalued, particularly 1987 to 1990. Knowing where the ECU, or its successor the Euro, is in relation to the underlying equilibrium could be potentially useful for several policy exercises, most notably perhaps for those who advocate a new international monetary system based on greater fixity of key currencies. Of course, the equilibrium derived in Figure 1 sidesteps the issue of the appropriateness of the underlying fundamentals, but nevertheless we believe that this kind of exercise is illustrative of the kind of equilibrium relationship our modeling strategy could be used to generate. It would be straightforward, for example, to generate a different measure of equilibrium based on some "desired" measures of the underlying fundamentals.

5. AN IMPULSE–RESPONSE ANALYSIS AND DYNAMIC INTERACTIONS

To gauge the dynamic interactions in our model and, in particular, to examine the effects of monetary impulses on the real exchange rate, we calculated impulse-response functions for our divisia-based systems. The construction of such systems is "nonstandard" in the current application because we are exploiting a VECM model rather than a standard VAR in first differences. There are two recommendations in the literature for the construction of impulse responses in the presence of cointegrating vectors. The first follows Lutkepohl (1993) and involves reparameterizing the VAR in levels and constructing the analysis on this basis. The problem with this approach is that any restrictions imposed on the cointegrating vectors will be lost in the process. A second method, originally advocated by Hendry and Mizon (1993), is more in tune with the analysis here because it involves reparameterizing the restricted error-correction terms (into a term in first differences and a lagged-levels term). Having reparameterized the systems, a standard Choleski decomposition may be used to generate orthogonal errors. The particular Choleski decomposition used involves the following ordering of the variables: $\Delta p^*, i^{l*}, m^*, \Delta p, m, i^l, (s-p+p^*)$. This ordering is intended to capture the relative exogeneity of the variables. It is, of course, well known that impulse-response functions

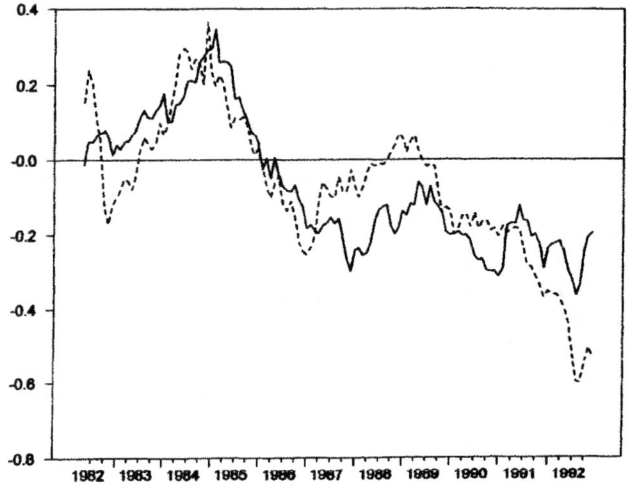

Figure 1. Equilibrium ECU Real Exchange Rate: ———, Real ECU/USD; – – –, Equilibrium.

are sensitive to the particular ordering used; however, our experimentation with different orderings gave qualitatively similar pictures. We consider two shocks to these systems. The first is a standardized 1% shock to European money (Fig. 2) and the second is a standardized 1% shock to U.S. money (Fig. 3).

We note that initially the real exchange rate appreciates by about .8% in response to the home monetary shock, this being rapidly offset between quarters 2 and 3 with a further offset between periods 3 and 4 when the currency appreciates again. The main impression from this figure is one of exchange-rate volatility imparted by the monetary shock. Note that the real exchange-rate change returns to 0 after four years, which is a relatively rapid adjustment compared to the relatively long persistence observed when researchers examine, on an individual basis, the time series properties of real exchange rates. The home long rate initially falls by about four basis points in response to the monetary increase, and this liquidity effect produces a fall in the U.S. interest rate, by a larger amount (10 basis points); the domestic inflation rate also initially falls. We note that European inflation exhibits considerable volatility before returning to 0.

Interestingly, the U.S. monetary impulse (Fig. 3) produces an initial real exchange-rate overshoot of the opposite sign to the long-run effect of money in this model. The overshoot is, however, rapidly offset, although we again note indications of volatility as the exchange-rate changes dampen out. The U.S. long rate again exhibits a liquidity effect in response to the monetary impulse, and this is also reflected in a fall in the EU rate. The EU and U.S. inflation rates also appear highly volatile here.

6. FORECASTING AND THE RANDOM WALK

Ever since the seminal paper by Meese and Rogoff (1983), it has become something of a benchmark for an exchange-rate model that it should be able to outperform a simple random walk in an out-of-sample forecasting exercise. Although Meese and Rogoff were unable to outperform a random walk using a variety of fundamentals-based models and bilateral exchange rates, several more recent works have demonstrated that the random-walk paradigm can be beaten for bilateral exchange rates at long horizons [i.e., horizons from about 36 months out—e.g., see Chinn and Meese (1995) and Mark (1995)] and also at short horizons [from about three months out—e.g., Wolff (1987); MacDonald and Taylor (1993, 1994); MacDonald and Marsh (1997)]. How then do our monetary models of the ECU perform in an out-of-sample context?

In constructing our out-of-sample forecasts, we used the 24 data points saved from our complete dataset—namely, for the period January 1993 to December 1994. The criterion used to gauge the relative performance of our model with that of a random walk is the industry standard—namely, the root mean squared error (RMSE). Before examining these results, however, we present in Figure 4 the dynamic one-step-ahead out-of-sample forecasts for each of the equations, along with the 5% confidence bands. These are quite impressive because only 5 (out of 168) of the forecasted values lie outside the bands (there are none outside the bands in the exchange-rate equation), and the directional ability of the forecasts is good. The formal one-step-ahead restrictions test for the restricted VECM model (which takes account of the variance of the estimated pa-

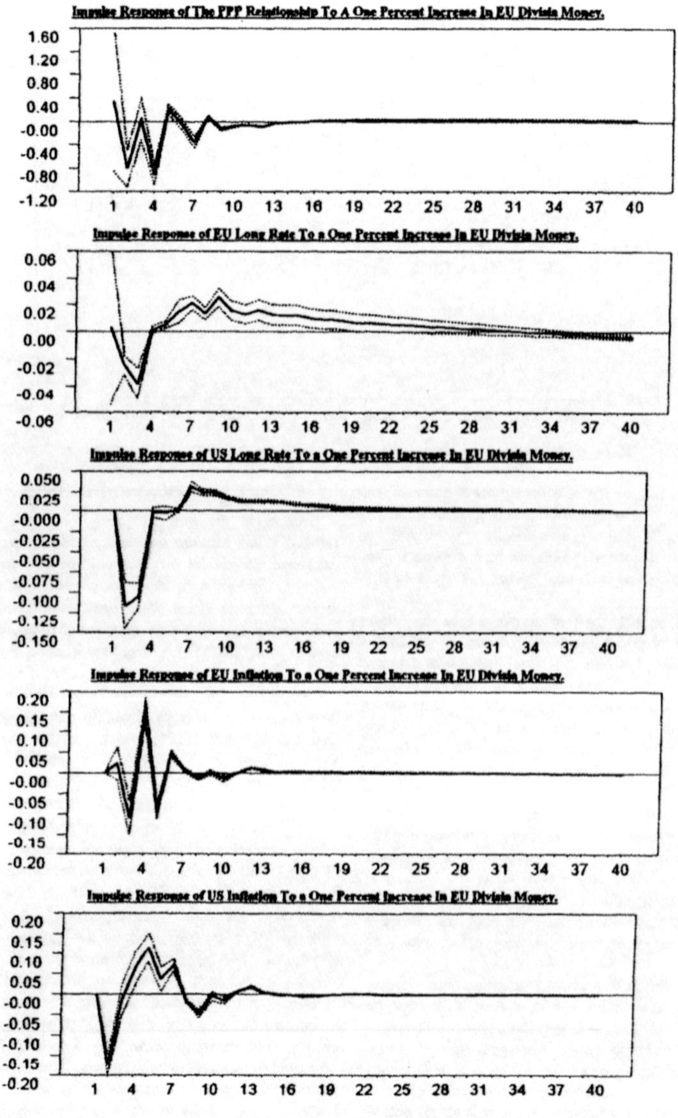

Figure 2. A 1% Increase in EU Divisia Money.

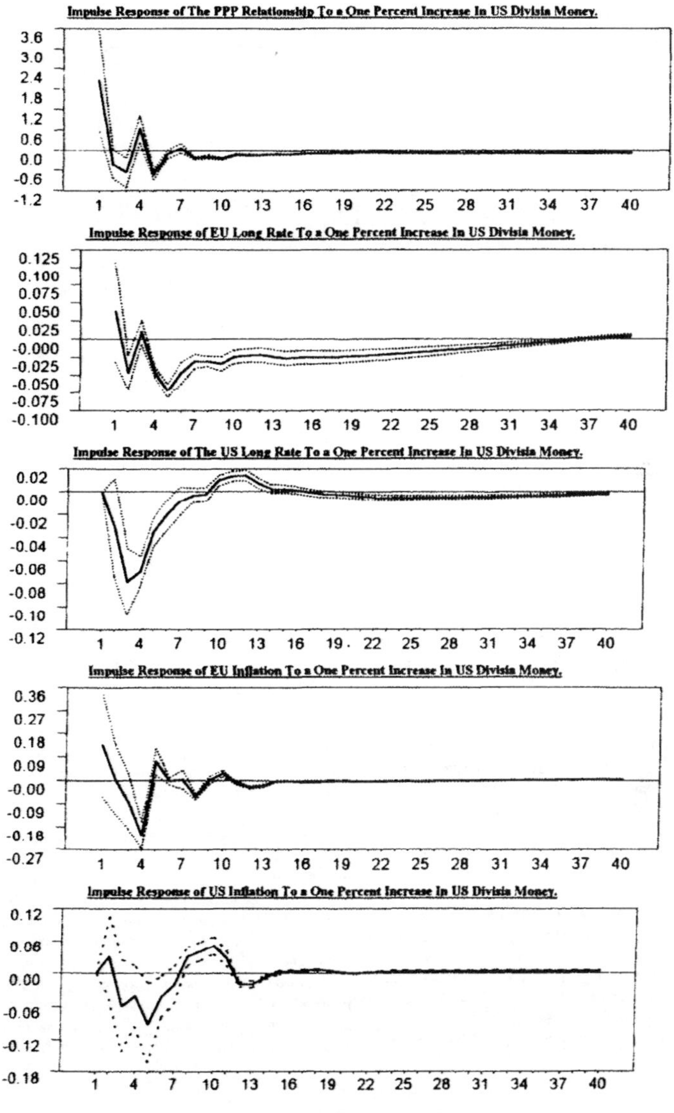

Figure 3. A 1% Increase in U.S. Divisia Money

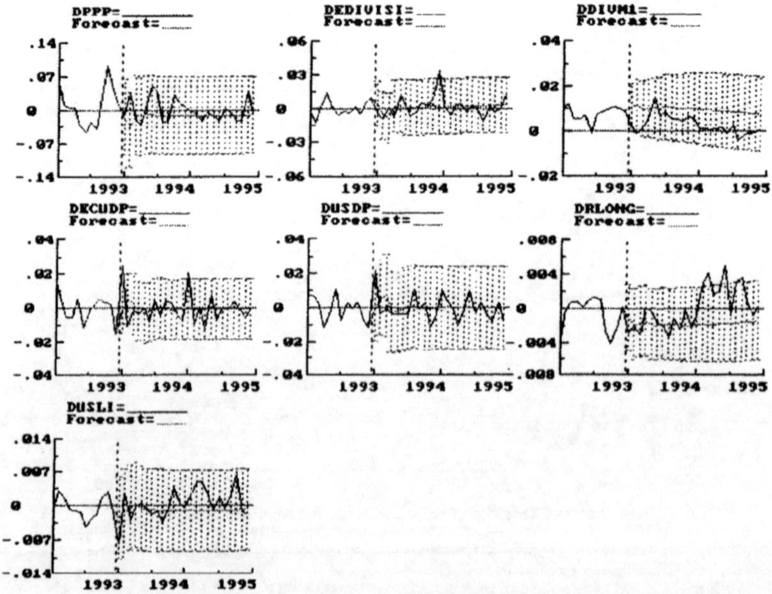

Figure 4. One-Step-Ahead Out-of-Sample Forecasting Performances.

rameters and their correlation) has a p value of approximately .5.

In Table 11, we present the ratio of the model RMSE to the RMSE obtained from a random walk, for horizons 1–12 months. It is worth stressing that the model RMSE's are obtained from a fully dynamic, simultaneous version of the model, with all of the restrictions imposed on the cointegrating space. The ratios indicate that at a horizon one month ahead the structural model is incapable of outperforming a random walk. By four months, however, the divisia-based system is (just) outperforming a random walk and from horizon 6 onward it convincingly beats a random walk. We believe that our ability to dominate a random walk at such relatively short forecast horizons stems in large measure from the modeling strategy adopted. In particular, our approach captures both the long-run equilibrium relationships, to which exchange rate and the other variables are reverting, and the short-run dynamics, which are a crucial element in trying to track exchange rates when they are away from equilibrium. We believe that this kind of modeling approach has applicability for other exchange rates as well. For example, using related methods,

Table 11. Root Mean Squared Error Ratios

Horizon	*1*	*4*	*6*	*8*	*12*
Ratio	1.74	.99	.75	.56	.51

MacDonald and Taylor (1994) and MacDonald and Marsh (1997) demonstrated that dynamic error-correction models and structural econometric models can be used to produce out-of-sample forecasts that dominate a random walk. The results reported in this section, therefore, add to the growing body of evidence that suggests that exchange rates do have some predictability when methods that capture the underlying data-generation process are used, and this should act as a useful counterpoint to the pessimism noted by Frankel and Rose (1995) in their survey of exchange-rate modeling (in particular, these authors argued that it is almost a stylized fact that structural exchange-rate models are incapable of beating a random walk at horizons of less than three years).

We also compared the forecasting performance of the restricted VECM model with that of the unrestricted VECM (i.e., the VECM with five unconstrained cointegrating vectors). This system performed as well as the restricted system, and this is perhaps not surprising given that the statistical satisfaction of our chosen restrictions means that they are close to the parameter values in the unrestricted case. This does not, however, imply that it is uninformative to impose our chosen restrictions in the first place. To compare our results with the underlying economic structure we started from, we need to be able to identify the estimated model structure to see how close it actually conforms to the underlying model. In this sense, we are more readily able to trust our predictions if they are based on some explicit model. Furthermore, of course, and as we stated earlier, our approach to restricting the vectors has other advantages, among which are its ability to track any weak links in the underlying model structure.

7. SUMMARY AND CONCLUSION

In this article we have attempted to model the ECU–U.S. dollar exchange rate over the period January 1982 to December 1994 using a variant of the monetary model of the exchange rate. Although the monetary model has been investigated fairly extensively for other currencies, it has not to our knowledge been applied to the external value of the ECU (or indeed to other composite currencies). In contrast, however, to the extant literature on exchange-rate modeling we have proposed building an exchange-rate model from the underlying equilibrium relationships rather than taking the final exchange-rate relationship as our starting point—what we referred to as the bottom-up approach. This approach is seen to have certain advantages, such as providing information about the properties of the complete model.

The econometric methods used to implement our model are those of Johansen (1995). Although this method has been fairly widely adopted to test exchange-rate models, previous research in the exchange-rate literature has sidestepped the issue of interpreting estimated cointegrating vectors. In this article, we have sought to interpret all of the estimated cointegrating vectors, and we note that none of our interpretations can be rejected in a statistical sense.

In assessing the monetary model, we chose two measures of money—namely, divisia and simple sum—a choice that reflects the increased interest in the usefulness of divisia money in a European context. Both measures of money produced very similar results, so we concentrated on the results for divisia money (with the simple-sum results available from the authors on request). Having defined sensible long-run equilibria from our EU system, we then analyzed the dynamic interactions among the variables using an impulse-response analysis. This analysis revealed that the external value of the ECU was more sensitive to U.S. monetary shocks than European monetary shocks (the former shock produced an exchange-rate overshoot, whereas the latter produced an undershoot) and that the shocks imparted fairly persistent volatility into the ECU. The equilibrium relationships were also used to construct an equilibrium measure of the ECU, and this approach may be of interest to those concerned with exchange-rate assessment. We also analyzed the out-of-sample forecasting performance of our models, and these demonstrated an ability to convincingly beat a random-walk model at horizons of four months and greater, a finding that contrasts sharply with the conclusions of Frankel and Rose (1995).

We therefore advocate our approach to exchange-rate modeling as a useful antidote to conventional reduced-form modeling and highlight the potential usefulness of divisia money in the exchange-rate process of the ECU.

ACKNOWLEDGMENTS

We are grateful to two anonymous referees and an associate editor for their helpful comments on an earlier draft of this article. Additionally, the first author is grateful to Carlsbergfondet for financial support, and the second author thanks both the ESRC and INQUIRE for financial assistance.

[Received February 1998. Revised October 1999.]

REFERENCES

Anderson, R. G., Jones, B. E., and Nesmith, T. D. (1997), "The Special Report on the Monetary Services Index Project of the Federal Reserve Bank of St Louis," *The Federal Reserve Bank of St. Louis Review*, 79.

Artis, M. J., Bladen-Hovell, R. C., and Zhang, W. (1993), "A European Money Demand Function," in *Policy Issues in the Operation of Currency Unions*, eds. P. Masson and M. P. Taylor, Cambridge, U.K.: Cambridge University Press, pp. 240–263.

Belongia, M., and Chalfont, J. (1989), "The Changing Empirical Definition of Money: Some Estimates From a Model of the Demand for Money Substitutes," *Journal of Political Economy*, 97, 387–397.

Bilson, J. F. O. (1978), "Rational Expectations and the Exchange Rate," in *The Economics of Exchange Rates*, eds. H. G. Johnson and J. A. Frenkel. Reading, MA: Addison-Wesley, pp. 75–96.

Cagan, P. (1956), "The Monetary Dynamics of Hyperinflation," in *Studies in the Quantity Theory of Money*, ed. M. Friedman, Chicago: University of Chicago Press.

Chinn, M., and Meese, R. (1995), "Banking on Currency Forecasts: How Predictable Is the Change in Money?" *Journal of International Economics*, 38, 161–178.

Chow, G., and Lin, A. (1971), "Best Linear Unbiased Interpolation, Distribution and Extrapolation of Time Series by Related Series," *Review of Economics and Statistics*, 53, 372–375.

Chrystal, K. A., and MacDonald, R. (1995), "Exchange Rates, Financial Innovation and Divisia Money: The Sterling-Dollar Rate 1972–1990," *Journal of International Money and Finance*, 14, 493–514.

Doornik, J., and Hansen, H. (1994), "A Practical Test of Multivariate Normality," unpublished paper, Oxford University, Nuffield College.

Dornbusch, R. (1976), "Expectations and Exchange Rate Dynamics," *Journal of Political Economy*, 84, 1161–1176.

——— (1988), "Purchasing Power Parity," in *The New Palgrave Dictionary of Economics*, Stockton Press: New York, pp. 56–74.

Engle, R., and Granger, C. (1987), "Cointegration and Error Correction: Representation, Estimation and Testing," *Econometrica*, 55, 251–276.

Fuller, W. A. (1976), *Introduction to Statistical Time Series Analysis*, New York: Wiley.

Frankel, J. (1979), "On the Mark: A Theory of Floating Exchange Rates Based on Real Interest Differentials," *American Economic Review*, 69, 610–622.

Frenkel, J. (1976), "A Monetary Approach to the Exchange Rate: Doctrinal Aspects and Empirical Evidence," *Scandinavian Journal of Economics*, 78, 200–224.

——— (1980), "Exchange Rates, Prices, and Money: Lessons From the 1920's," *American Economic Review, Papers and Proceedings*, 70, 235–242.

Godfrey, L. G. (1988), *Misspecification Tests in Econometrics*. Cambridge, U.K.: Cambridge University Press.

Hendry, D., and Mizon, G. E. (1993), "Evaluating Econometric Models by Encompassing the VAR," in *Models, Methods and Applications of Econometrics*, ed. P. C. Phillips, Oxford, U.K.: Blackwell.

Hodrick, R. (1978), "An Empirical Analysis of the Monetary Approach to the Exchange Rate," in *The Economics of Exchange Rates*, eds. H. G. Johnson and J. A. Frenkel, Reading, MA: Addison-Wesley, pp. 97–116.

Johansen, S. (1995), *Likelihood-based Inference in Cointegrated Vector Autoregressive Models*, Oxford, U.K.: Oxford University Press.

Johansen, S., and Juselius, K. (1992a), "Testing Structural Hypothesis in a Multivariate Cointegration Analysis of the PPP and the UIP for the UK," *Journal of Econometrics*, 53, 211–244.

——— (1992b), "Maximum Likelihood Estimation and Inference on Cointegration—With Applications to the Demand for Money," *Oxford Bulletin of Economics and Statistics*, 52, 169–210.

La Cour, L. F. (1996), "The Problems of Measuring 'Money': Results From an Analysis of Divisia Monetary Aggregates for Denmark," mimeo, University of Copenhagen, Institute of Statistics.

Laidler, D. (1992), *The Demand for Money*, New York: HarperCollins.

Lucas, R. E. (1982), "Interest Rates and Currency Prices in a Two-Country World," *Journal of Monetary Economics*, 10, 335–360.

Lutkepohl, H. (1993), *Introduction to Multiple Time Series Analysis*, Berlin: Springer-Verlag.

MacDonald, R. (1988), *Floating Exchange Rates: Theories and Evidence*, London: Unwin-Hyman.

——— (1993), "Long-Run Purchasing Power Parity: Is it For Real?" *Review of Economics and Statistics*, 75, 690–695.

——— (1995), "Long-Run Exchange Rate Modeling: A Survey of the Recent Evidence," *Staff Papers, International Monetary Fund*, 42, 3, 437–489.

MacDonald, R., and Marsh, I. W. (1997), "On Fundamentals and Exchange Rates: A Casselian Perspective," *Review of Economics and Statistics*, 79, 655–664.

MacDonald, R., and Taylor, M. P. (1993), "The Monetary Approach to the Exchange Rate: Rational Expectations, Long-Run Equilibrium and Forecasting," *International Monetary Fund Staff Papers*, 40, 89–107.

——— (1994), "The Monetary Approach to the Exchange Rate: Long-Run Relationships, Short-Run Dynamics, and How to Beat a Random Walk," *Journal of International Money and Finance*, 13, 276–290.

McKinnon, R. (1988), "Monetary and Exchange Rate Policies for International Financial Stability: A Proposal," *Journal of Economic Perspectives*, 2, 83–103.

Mark, N. (1995), "Exchange Rates and Fundamentals: Evidence on Long-Horizon Predictability," *American Economic Review*, 85, 201–218.

Meese, R., and Rogoff, K. (1983), "Empirical Exchange Rate Models of the Seventies: Do They Fit Out of Sample?" *Journal of International Economics*, 14, 3–24.

Mussa, M. (1979), "Empirical Regularities in the Behaviour of Exchange Rates and Theories of the Foreign Exchange Market," in *Policies for Employment, Prices and Exchange Rates* (Carnegie-Rochester Conference Series on Public Policy), eds. K. Brunner and A. H. Meltzer, Amsterdam: North-Holland, pp. 1–50.

Spencer, P. (1997), "Should the ECB Adopt a Divisia Monetary Aggregate?" *European Economic Review*, 41, 1403–1419.

Williamson, J. (1985), *The Exchange Rate System*, Washington, DC: Institute for International Economics.

Wolff, C. (1987), "Time-Varying Parameters and the Out-of Sample Forecasting Performance of Structural Exchange Rate Models," *Journal of Business & Economic Statistics*, 5, 87–97.

Available online at www.sciencedirect.com
SCIENCE @ DIRECT•
Journal of International Money and Finance
23 (2004) 99–111
ELSEVIER
Journal of International Money and Finance
www.elsevier.com/locate/econbase

Currency spillovers and tri-polarity: a simultaneous model of the US dollar, German mark and Japanese yen☆

Ronald MacDonald [a,*], Ian W. Marsh [b]

[a] *Department of Economics, University of Strathclyde and CESifo, 100 Cathedral Street, Glasgow G4 0LN, UK*

[b] *Cass Business School, 106 Bunhill Row, London EC1Y 8TZ, UK*

Abstract

This paper presents a simultaneous model of exchange rates between the US dollar, German mark and Japanese yen. In addition to incorporating long-run equilibria and short-run dynamics, the model is designed to capture complex interaction between currencies not normally considered in exchange rate models. The model is demonstrated to be an economically and statistically superior forecasting tool over relatively short horizons, thereby demonstrating that the random walk paradigm no longer rules the roost.
© 2003 Elsevier Ltd. All rights reserved.

JEL classification: F31; G15

Keywords: Tri-polarity; Exchange rate forecasting; Purchasing power parity

1. Introduction

The advent of the European monetary integration means that the international monetary system is now characterized by a tri-polar currency structure, consisting of the US dollar, Japanese yen and euro. Recently, there has been considerable interest in policy circles regarding the operation and design of this system. Should it continue to be effectively a freely floating system, a managed float (based perhaps

☆ The authors are grateful to two anonymous referees and the co-editor, Michael Melvin, for helpful comments on an earlier draft of this paper.

* Corresponding author. Tel.: +44-141-548-3861; fax: +44-141-552-5589.
E-mail address: r.r.macdonald@strath.ac.uk (R. MacDonald).

0261-5606/$ - see front matter © 2003 Elsevier Ltd. All rights reserved.
doi:10.1016/j.jimonfin.2003.08.003

on a target zone arrangement) or one of complete fixity? In this paper, we seek to shed some light on the operation of the new system by considering a tri-polar exchange rate model consisting of the US dollar, Japanese yen and German mark, which may be regarded as the antecedent to the new system. Because of the different operational objectives of the European Central Bank relative to the Bundesbank, the euro may, of course, have different properties to the mark. Nevertheless, we believe that the study of the dollar–mark–yen system is useful, both in terms of indicating how a tri-polar network may be modelled, and also in suggesting how such a system may behave in terms of its long- and short-run properties.

Our tri-polar exchange rate system represents an extension of the joint modelling of exchange rates, interest rates and prices by Johansen and Juselius (1992), Juselius (1995), Juselius and MacDonald (2000), and MacDonald and Marsh (1997, 1999). We extend this literature in two main ways. First, we seek to interpret all the significant cointegrating vectors in an economic and statistical sense (MacDonald and Marsh, 1997, for example, only focus on the first significant vector). Second, and as we have noted, we use a tri-polar structure, rather than a single currency analysis, which has been the norm in this literature, in order to capture currency spillovers. Although little research has been undertaken on modelling exchange rate spillovers (other than by accounting for contemporaneous correlation between exchange markets), it seems a natural component of an exchange rate model since it is widely accepted that currency markets are not independent.

One of the main contributions of this paper is the emphasis laid on the complex dynamic interactions among the variables in an exchange rate system. One of the deficiencies of many fundamental-based models is that they often neglect the dynamics inherent in the exchange rate process. Even if exchange rate models do incorporate dynamics, they are often very limited in scope. The econometric methods proposed here ensure a very rich dynamic specification for the exchange rate relationship and also for the equations of the other fundamental variables driving the exchange rate. Our exchange rate model is assessed using standard statistical criteria and also by what has become the benchmark by which an exchange rate model is judged, namely its ability to outperform a random walk model in an out-of-sample forecasting exercise.

The outline of the remainder of this paper is as follows. In the next section, we present a motivational discussion for the modelling approach adopted. In Section 3, the econometric methods are briefly outlined and our estimated long-run cointegration relationships discussed. The out-of-sample forecasting results are presented in Section 4. The paper ends with a concluding section.

2. Motivation and related research

Long-run purchasing power parity (PPP) forms the basis of our modelling exercise. Since, in one form or another, it is an assumed condition for many exchange rate models, PPP has received vast attention in the academic literature. While there is now general agreement that PPP does not hold in the short-run, except for case of (near) hyperinflation, as a long-run proposition, the evidence is much more favourable (see, for example, Froot and Rogoff, 1995; MacDonald, 1995). However, the fact that the majority of empirical papers on PPP reject the restrictions of proportionality and symmetry is rather worrying for a PPP-based study. While measurement errors may partly account for the difference between estimated and theoretical values, the divergence is sufficiently large for us to conclude that something more than measurement errors is at hand. In line with Cassel's synthesis of PPP and asset demand approaches to the exchange rate, we shall augment the traditional PPP relationship (see Holmes, 1967, for further discussion).

The particular approach used here to augment PPP is discussed in some detail by Johansen and Juselius (1992), Juselius (1995), MacDonald and Marsh (1997), and Juselius and MacDonald (2000) and essentially entails supplementing the PPP relationship with an interest differential. Johansen and Juselius (1992) and Juselius (1995) motivate such a model in terms of combining PPP with a UIP condition, while MacDonald and Marsh (1997) have labelled this approach to exchange rate modelling as Casselian PPP. The latter follows from Cassel's emphasis on the role of capital flows in preventing an exchange rate from always being at its PPP determined level. In the work of Johansen and Juselius (1992), Juselius (1995), MacDonald and Marsh (1997) and Juselius and MacDonald (2000), the Casselian approach is shown to produce stationary combinations of exchange rates, relative prices and interest differentials. However, in all these papers, currency markets are analysed separately. The main novelty in the present paper is to note that currency markets are closely linked and so any statistical analysis should explicitly recognize this in our econometric modelling. For the US dollar bilateral exchange rates of the Japanese yen and German mark, our tri-polar approach amounts to analysing the following data vector:

$$x_t = \left(s_t^{\mathrm{GER}}, s_t^{\mathrm{JAP}}, p_t^{\mathrm{GER}}, p_t^{\mathrm{JAP}}, p_t^{\mathrm{US}}, i_t^{\mathrm{GER}}, i_t^{\mathrm{JAP}}, i_t^{\mathrm{US}}\right)', \tag{1}$$

where s denotes the (log) bilateral spot exchange rate against the US dollar, p denotes the (log) price level and i the short-term interest rate and the superscripts have an obvious interpretation. We then propose testing hypotheses on this vector which allow us to partition the long-run cointegrating space into two long-run stationary relationships of the form:

$$\beta^{\mathrm{GER}} x_t = \omega_1^{\mathrm{GER}}\left(i_t^{\mathrm{GER}} - i_t^{\mathrm{US}}\right) - \omega_2^{\mathrm{GER}}\left(p_t^{\mathrm{GER}} - p_t^{\mathrm{US}}\right) + s_t^{\mathrm{GER}},$$

$$\beta^{\mathrm{GER}} x_t = \omega_1^{\mathrm{JAP}}\left(i_t^{\mathrm{JAP}} - i_t^{\mathrm{US}}\right) - \omega_2^{\mathrm{JAP}}\left(p_t^{\mathrm{JAP}} - p_t^{\mathrm{US}}\right) + s_t^{\mathrm{JAP}}.$$

Although there are no spillovers from one currency market to the other in these long-run relationships, there may nevertheless be information contained in the joint process from the two markets which is important in defining the long-run and would be ignored by simply conditioning on the information set from one market. However, direct spillovers do appear in the short-run dynamic equations. For example, the dynamic equation for the Japanese yen exchange rate would have the following form:

$$\begin{aligned}\Delta s_t^{\mathrm{GER/JAP}} &= \gamma_0 + \sum_{i=1}^{l}\gamma_{1i}\Delta s_{t-i}^{\mathrm{GER}} + \sum_{i=1}^{l}\gamma_{2i}\Delta s_{t-i}^{\mathrm{JAP}} + \sum_{i=1}^{l}\gamma_{3i}\Delta p_{t-i}^{\mathrm{GER}} \\ &+ \sum_{i=1}^{l}\gamma_{4i}\Delta p_{t-i}^{\mathrm{JAP}} + \sum_{i=1}^{l}\gamma_{5i}\Delta p_{t-i}^{\mathrm{US}} + \sum_{i=1}^{l}\gamma_{6i}\Delta i_{t-i}^{\mathrm{GER}} + \sum_{i=1}^{l}\gamma_{7i}\Delta i_{t-i}^{\mathrm{JAP}} \\ &+ \sum_{i=1}^{l}\gamma_{8i}\Delta i_{t-i}^{\mathrm{US}} + \alpha_1\beta^{GER}x_{t-1} + \alpha_2\beta^{JAP}x_{t-1} \qquad (2)\end{aligned}$$

where l represents the lag length of the differenced VAR. Hence, spillovers arise both through dynamic interactions and also through the significance of the cointegrating relationships (the alphas). As we shall see in our empirical section, both these effects turn out to be important in our analysis.

3. Econometric methods and results

3.1. *Econometric modelling*

In this section, we briefly outline the econometric methods used to estimate our exchange rate models. In short, we use a vector autoregressive (VAR) model to determine the number of cointegrating relationships and to define the cointegrating vectors. This part of our analysis is based on the methods of Johansen (1995). The familiar VAR representation is:

$$x_t = \sum_{i=1}^{l+1} A_i x_{t-i} + \psi D_t + v_t, \qquad (3)$$

which may be reparameterized into the VECM representation as:

$$\Delta x_t = \sum_{i=1}^{l} \Gamma_i \Delta x_{t-i} + \Pi x_{t-1} + \psi D_t + v_t, \qquad (4)$$

where x is a vector of variables entering the system, D_t contains deterministic components (constant, trend, centred seasonal dummies and event dummies) and v_t is assumed to have mean 0, be homoscedastic and serially uncorrelated. The order of the VAR is assumed finite to exclude moving average components, and the parameters A_i, Γ_i, ψ, and Σ (the covariance matrix of v) are assumed constant. Π is interpreted as the matrix of long-run responses. If the data cointegrate, Π must be of reduced rank, $r < n$, where n is the number of variables in x and it may be factored as (see Johansen, 1995):

$$\Pi = \alpha\beta',$$

where β and α are $n \times r$ matrices, which give the cointegrating vectors (empirical long-run relationships) and associated adjustment matrix, respectively. Due to the reduced form nature of the cointegrating vectors, there is an increasing trend towards performing transformations and imposing restrictions on the estimated cointegrating space to reveal 'meaningful economic relationships'.

The imposition of restrictions on the cointegrating vector or adjustment matrix will change the estimated short-run dynamics of Eq. (4) and the coefficients of the deterministic variables. These new coefficients are denoted by a tilde. If we also denote the restricted cointegration space by $\bar{\Pi} = \bar{\alpha}\bar{\beta}'$, the constrained VAR (CVAR) can be written as:

$$\Delta \mathrm{x}_t = \sum_{i=1}^{l} \tilde{\Gamma}_i \Delta \mathrm{x}_{t-i} + \bar{\Pi} x_{t-1} + \psi \mathrm{D}_t + \mathrm{w}_t, t \tag{5}$$

This is the full vector form of the dynamic equation (4) above.

3.1.1. Long-run equilibria in the tri-polar system

Our eight variable system comprises two bilateral exchange rates (dollar–mark and dollar–yen), three price indices and three short-term interest rates. The expected exchange rate changes are not included in the vector of variables as these will be I(0) under the weakest assumptions of rationality. The data run from January 1983 through September 1998 and are extracted from the IMF's International Financial Statistics CD-ROM. The start date for estimation is set to exclude turbulence in the interest rate markets in the early 1980s caused by changes in the Federal Reserves' operating procedures, and which necessitated the use of many intervention dummies in our previous work (MacDonald and Marsh, 1997). The final data point in our sample was chosen to be September 1998, rather than December 1998, in order to exclude some market turbulence in the run up to European Monetary Union in January 1999. Just two dummies are needed in this system (1985:11 and 1986:01), primarily to remove two outliers in the Japanese interest rate series. Four lagged levels in the VAR, chosen after performing a battery of tests, centred seasonal dummies and an unconstrained constant are included in the system. Some of the tests indicated a shorter lag length, but we chose to include the maximum amount of relevant information albeit at the possible cost of estimation accuracy.

The interest rates used in this study are short-term (3 months) eurocurrency interest rates rather than the long-term bond yields used in our previous work (MacDonald and Marsh, 1997). There are two justifications for this. First, short-term rates have been used successfully by other authors who exploit similar systems (Fisher et al., 1990; Johansen and Juselius, 1992; Lee et al., 1994). Second, factors such as taxation, duration and liquidity effects can cause bond yields to differ from the pure interest rate which we would like to observe. These factors are not only less prevalent in the short-term euromarkets, but are also more similar between currencies leading to, we hope, a better proxy for capital flows.

Consumer prices are our preferred price measure for Germany and the US, while for Japan, we use the wholesale price index. This change is motivated primarily by the marked differences in behaviour of the Japanese consumer and wholesale price

Table 1
Johansen cointegration analysis—tri-polar system

Null hypothesis	Trace	Trace critical (95%)
$r = 0$	186.92	165.58
$r \leq 1$	133.87	131.70
$r \leq 2$	91.66	102.14
$r \leq 3$	60.93	76.07
$r \leq 4$	37.62	53.12
$r \leq 5$	19.00	34.91
$r \leq 6$	7.90	19.96
$r \leq 7$	2.52	9.24

Note: Trace critical values from Osterwald-Lenum (1992).

indices. In many countries, these proxies for 'the' price level follow similar trends. For Japan over the period studied they do not, and our use of the wholesale index produces results which are more in conformity with the basic model. In particular, we are able to impose the correct coefficient restrictions on the Japanese systems when the Japanese WPI is used, but not with the CPI. We have no good explanation for this finding, but note that there is a controversy in the PPP literature as to the appropriate price series to use in a PPP calculation (see, for example, Frenkel, 1981), and our tests seem to indicate that for Japan, the appropriate series is the wholesale price index. It could be that distribution costs are much important for Japan than for the other countries in our sample and that this drives an important wedge between the CPI and WPI, rendering the CPI an inappropriate price measure for Japan (see MacDonald and Ricci, 2001 for a further discussion of the importance of distribution costs in PPP calculations).

Diagnostic tests (not reported here to save space but available from the authors on request) indicate that the residuals are random, but that there are normality problems in our system. Reassuringly, this is due to kurtosis, rather than to skewness, and therefore should not affect our results (see Paruolo, 1995). Incorporating further dummy variables into the VAR models proved unsuccessful in removing this kurtosis.

The Johansen cointegration Trace test results are detailed in Table 1. These indicate two significant relationships, a finding supported by the presence of two noticeably larger eigenvalues and an analysis of the roots of the companion matrix (not reported).[1]

Although a number of the coefficients are correctly signed in the unrestricted cointegrating relationships reported in Table 2, the relationship does not conform closely to the hypothesized relationships. However, it may be that coefficients which appear quite large in absolute terms in the two equations (say, the Japanese price coefficient in the first vector and the coefficient on the German price series in

[1] In particular, the number of roots close to unity in the companion matrix was the same as the number of common stochastic trends in the cointegrated VAR, namely 6.

Table 2
The normalized cointegration relationships and the adjustment matrices

	Standardized beta vector		Standardized alpha vector	
	Vector 1	Vector 2	Vector 1	Vector 2
s^{ger}	1	0.034	−0.019 (1.57)	0.006 (1.28)
s^{jap}	−0.235	1	−0.000 (0.05)	0.014 (2.77)
p^{ger}	5.691	16.073	−0.000 (0.34)	−0.001 (4.53)
p^{jap}	−1.285	−15.230	−0.000 (0.34)	0.002 (3.02)
p^{US}	−3.292	−9.885	−0.002 (4.36)	−0.000 (2.04)
i^{ger}	0.043	−0.204	−0.395 (4.86)	0.090 (2.70)
i^{jap}	−0.001	0.227	−0.050 (0.69)	−0.80 (0.28)
i^{US}	−0.083	0.130	0.135 (1.21)	0.044 (0.98)

Note: Numbers in parenthesis are numerical t-values.

the second) are in fact insignificantly different from 0. Exclusion and homogeneity restrictions are formally tested below. The normalized alpha terms indicate clear adjustment to the two disequilibrium errors. For example, both US prices and the German interest rate adjust significantly to the first disequilibrium error. The German exchange rate also adjusts (negatively) to this error, although the significance is quite weak. The pattern of adjustment is much richer with respect to the second disequilibrium error, with all the prices adjusting in addition to the German interest rate and Japanese yen. The evident spillovers we are picking up here would seem to reinforce the use of the tri-polar framework.

Tests of the restrictions implied by the theory are summarized in Table 3. Simple PPP (with symmetry and proportionality imposed) is rejected for both exchange rates (see hypothesis A1–A3). Casselian PPP cannot be rejected for either exchange rate (hypothesis B1 and B2), and the tests would seem to indicate that PPP augmented by the relevant interest differential is an acceptable description of both cointegrating relationships (hypothesis B3).

Table 3
Restrictions on cointegration space—tri-polar system

Hypothesis	Economic interpretation	Implied restrictions	Distributions	Test statistic
A1	PPP for Germany	$\beta_1 = (1,0,-1,0,1,0,0,0)'$	$\chi^2(6)$	32.44 (0.00)
A2	PPP for Japan	$\beta_2 = (0,1,0,-1,1,0,0,0)'$	$\chi^2(6)$	31.60 (0.00)
A3	PPP holds for both	$\beta_1 = (1,0,-1,0,1,0,0,0)'$, $\beta_2 = (0,1,0,-1,1,0,0,0)'$	$\chi^2(12)$	74.99 (0.00)
B1	PPP plus interest differential for Germany	$\beta_1 = (1,0,-1,0,1,m,0,-m)'$	$\chi^2(5)$	2.65 (0.75)
B2	PPP plus interest differential for Japan	$\beta_2 = (0,1,0,-1,1,0,n,-n)'$	$\chi^2(5)$	8.29 (0.14)
B3	PPP plus interest differential for both	$\beta_1 = (1,0,-1,0,1,m,0,-m)'$, $\beta_2 = (0,1,0,-1,1,0,n,-n)'$	$\chi^2(10)$	18.48 (0.05)

Note: Numbers in parenthesis in the final column are p-values.

Table 4
Loadings associated with restricted cointegrating vectors

Variable	CV_1	CV_2
s^{ger}	−0.016 (1.08)	−0.004 (0.67)
s^{jap}	0.013 (0.88)	−0.021 (3.18)
p^{ger}	0.002 (2.38)	0 (0.34)
p^{jap}	0 (0.11)	−0.001 (1.89)
p^{US}	−0.001 (1.74)	0.001 (2.01)
i^{ger}	−0.429 (4.31)	0.110 (2.57)
i^{jap}	0.104 (1.23)	−0.071 (1.88)
i^{US}	0.019 (0.14)	−0.023 (0.38)

Note: Numbers in parenthesis are *t*-values.

The final restricted cointegrating vectors are as follows:

$$CV_1 = s_t^{GER} - p_t^{GER} + p_t^{US} + 0.135(i_t^{GER} - i_t^{US}),$$

$$CV_2 = s_t^{JAP} - p_t^{JAP} + p_t^{US} + 0.375(i_t^{JAP} - i_t^{US}).$$

These vectors closely accord with the view discussed in Section 2 that interest differentials reflect capital mobility. It may seem surprising that the unconstrained estimates reported in Table 2, which seem to be quite far from the hypothesized priors, can be constrained to such tightly defined relationships. However, the constrained estimates take account of the variance of the coefficients, something that cannot be gleaned from an inspection of the point estimates themselves.[2] The loadings matrix associated with the two cointegrating vectors, reported in Table 4, shows the importance of the tri-polar nature of the system. In particular, the fact that German interest rates, and to a lesser extent US prices, significantly adjust to remove disequilibrium in both cointegrating vectors implies that disturbances will be transmitted around the whole system, even if a shock occurs to just one leg. For example, if there is a shock to Japanese prices which pushes CV_2 out of equilibrium, not only will Japanese variables act to restore equilibrium, but so will US prices and even German interest rates. Since both these latter terms help to form CV_1, disequilibrium spills from one exchange rate to another. This seems to confirm the conventional wisdom on how foreign exchange markets work, although it has not to our knowledge been demonstrated formally before in the context of this kind of model.

The fact that US interest rates appear to be weakly exogenous in the above systems is perhaps not surprising given that US interest rates are usually seen as leading (i.e. pushing) world financial markets. Indeed, a formal test that the two alpha terms in the US interest rate equation are insignificant (plus hypothesis B3) produces a chi-squared statistic (with 12 degrees of freedom) of 18.69 and an associa-

[2] Indeed, one good reason for explicitly testing the constraints is that the unconstrained estimates may simply reflect collinearity amongst the variables entering our VAR.

ted p-value of 0.10. That US prices appear to be adjusting in the above systems is probably intuitive enough given the large US current account imbalances necessitating relative price adjustments between the US and its trading partners. The formal test that the alpha terms on the two error correction terms in the US price equation produces a chi-squared statistic of 21.91 and a p-value of 0.04.

One issue which we have not addressed in the above modelling is the potential I(2) ness of our price series. For example, Juselius and MacDonald (2000) have demonstrated that in the kind of modelling framework used here that prices are likely to be I(2). However, they also note that, despite this, the real exchange rate is an I(1) process. Since in our constrained model we work with the real exchange rate, we do not pursue the I(1) vs. I(2) issue in this paper although we believe it is an interesting topic for future research, particularly in instances when the degree one homogeneity of the nominal exchange rate in relative prices is not satisfied.[3]

4. Forecast accuracy

While the equilibrium estimates for the tri-polar model look plausible, ever since Meese and Rogoff (1983), the real test of the validity of an exchange rate model lies in its forecasting power.

The above analysis has been performed on the system estimated up to September 1998. To allow the computation of out-of-sample forecasts, the entire model was reestimated over the period January 1983–December 1995. The long-run cointegrating relationships were reimposed, namely PPP augmented by interest differentials, but the coefficients on the interest differentials were reestimated. Out-of-sample forecasts for 1–12 months ahead were then made. One observation was then added to the end of the sample and the entire process repeated, including estimation of the model. The final estimation is for the period January 1983–September 1998. The free coefficients in the cointegrating relationships and the short-run dynamics were therefore allowed to change over time. The coefficient on the interest differential in the German relationship varies between 0.107 and 0.134, while the coefficient on the Japanese differential in the second vector lies in the range 0.172–0.361. The relative stability of the German vector strengthens our belief that we have captured a meaningful relationship. However, the movements in the Japanese coefficient may indicate that we have excluded an important variable from our simple model, and we question the appropriateness of (short-term) interest rates as a proxy for capital flows in the Japanese case. Further refinements of the model might usefully employ somemeasure of stock market performance which may be qualitatively more important for Japanese capital flows.

[3] An anonymous referee has pointed out that the existence of I(2) trends will affect the critical values of the Trace statistics. However, and as we have noted, the estimated eigenvalues and the roots of the characteristic polynomial from our system seem to support the existence of two stationary cointegrating vectors.

Table 5
Out-of-sample forecasting performance of tri-polar model

Horizon	Deutsche mark				Japanese yen			
	RMSE ratio (model)	Direction (model)	RMSE ratio (VAR)	Direction (VAR)	RMSE ratio (model)	Direction (model)	RMSE ratio (VAR)	Direction (VAR)
1	0.952	60.61	0.970	60.61	1.137	45.45	1.226	45.45
2	0.927	65.63	1.010	65.63	1.100	59.38	1.286	31.25
3	0.946	61.29	1.073	61.29	0.984	67.74	1.327	29.03
4	0.927^{1}	70.00	1.145	50.00	0.911	70.00	1.370	20.00
5	0.902^{1}	65.52	1.190	34.48	0.848^{2}	79.31	1.385	10.34
6	0.890^{3}	71.43	1.218	42.86	0.793^{3}	71.43	1.410	14.29
7	0.885^{3}	62.96	1.240	25.93	0.699^{3}	85.19	1.436	11.11
8	0.925^{2}	61.54	1.272	19.23	0.641^{3}	92.31	1.443	7.69
9	0.956	56.00	1.305	8.00	0.621^{3}	100.00	1.437	4.00
10	0.945	70.83	1.319	4.17	0.582^{3}	95.83	1.442	0.00
11	0.930^{3}	65.22	1.318	13.04	0.568^{3}	100.0	1.443	4.35
12	0.935^{2}	81.82	1.313	13.64	0.555^{3}	100.0	1.444	4.55

Notes: The superscripted numbers 1, 2 and 3 in the columns labelled RMSE ratio are 10%, 5% and 1% significance levels calculated using the Diebold–Mariano test statistic with a correction for serial correlation imparted by the overlapping forecasts.

As in the original Meese and Rogoff study, and in many articles since, we take the driftless random walk as the benchmark against which we judge our model. The forecast performance is detailed in Table 5. For each horizon, it gives the ratio of the RMSE of the exchange rate forecasts from our preferred model with the weak exogeneity of US interest rates imposed,[4] to those from a random walk model, the proportion of correct directional forecasts, and the RMSE ratio of a VAR set up in differences but with no cointegrating vectors. Good performance would be indicated by an RMSE ratio less than unity and directional ability in excess of 50%. The significance of the relative forecast accuracy of the model compared to that of the random walk alternative is tested using the Diebold–Mariano (1995) procedure.

The results are clearly impressive. For the deutsche mark, the forecasts from the tri-polar model are both more accurate than the random walk and more likely to correctly suggest the direction of change than chance would suggest at all forecast horizons. The relative accuracy becomes statistically significant at the 4-month forecast horizon. The yen forecasts become significantly more accurate than the random walk at the 5-month horizon. In terms of directional forecast ability, the yen forecasts again prove better than pure chance would suggest at all horizons over 1-month. Without seeking to denigrate the results, we would point out that over the longer forecast intervals, the yen consistently depreciated over the forecast period which explains the exceptional directional ability shown by the model from the 8-month forecast horizon. However, the model can only be asked to forecast reality, and we feel that the impressive predictions of the more volatile German unit validate its performance.

The RMSE ratios for the differenced VAR (i.e. no cointegrating relationships) are clearly inferior to both the VECM formulation and a random walk. The importance of including the cointegrating vectors is made apparent by this forecasting exercise. Furthermore, the importance of imposing restrictions to reveal meaningful economic relationships, as noted in Section 3.1 above, is made clear by considering the forecast performance of the model with unrestricted cointegrating vectors. Although not reported in Table 5 to save space, the RMSE ratio of the unconstrained system was greater than unity for both exchange rates at all horizons, and the directional ability noticeably inferior to that of the constrained model for the both rates at all horizons in excess of 1 month. These results confirm the finding in the literature that the use of restrictions on the cointegrating relationships improves the long-run forecast performance of error correction models and also extends it to encompass short horizons.

[4] The results are in fact very similar when the alpha terms on the US interest rates are left unrestricted.

5. Conclusions

In this paper, we have sought to model the mark, dollar and yen using a simultaneous tri-polar structure, which allows for spillovers between the currencies. The modelling strategy may be judged successful since we produced an interpretable exchange ratio model with desirable economic properties. Most significantly, perhaps, when confronted with what is taken to be the most severe test of an exchange rate model—its out-of-sample forecasting ability—the model is capable of producing predictions which compare extremely well to two industry standard benchmarks. This performance is statistically significant and, we believe, of practical relevance—forecasts from models closely related to those presented here are currently used by corporate entities as part of their financial decision-making processes.

Given the current interest in academic and policy circles in the behaviour of the tri-polar relationship between the euro, dollar and yen, we believe our results are suggestive of the functioning of such a system. Our approach suggests, for example, that such a system will exhibit both long- and short-run predictability (and the interaction amongst variables accords with economic intuition) and this may be useful from the perspective of setting target zone bands and monitoring their evolution over time. Furthermore, our analysis suggests that shocks to the system, originating in the system itself, do not create excess exchange rate volatility. This in turn may give comfort to those who favour a freely floating structure for the tri-polar grouping since it seems to imply that the system will be more stable than a system based on multiple bilateral relationships.

References

Diebold, F.X., Mariano, R.S., 1995. Comparing predictive ability. Journal of Business and Economic Statistics 13, 253–263.

Fisher, P.G., Tanna, S.K., Turner, D.S., Wallis, K.F., Whitley, J.D., 1990. Econometric evaluation of the exchange rate in models of the UK economy. Economic Journal 100, 1230–1244.

Frenkel, J.A., 1981. Flexible exchange rates, prices and the role of 'news'. Journal of Political Economy 89, 665–705.

Froot, K.A., Rogoff, K., 1995. Perspectives on PPP and long-run real exchange rates. In: Jones, R.W., Kenen, P.B. (Eds.), In: Handbook of International Economics, vol. 3. North Holland, Amsterdam.

Holmes, J.M., 1967. The purchasing power parity theory: in defence of Gustav Cassel. Journal of Political Economy 75, 686–696.

Johansen, S., 1995. Likelihood-based Inference in Cointegrated Vector Autoregressive Models. Oxford University Press, Oxford.

Johansen, S., Juselius, K., 1992. Testing structural hypothesis in a multivariate cointegration analysis of the PPP and the UIP for the UK. Journal of Econometrics 53, 211–244.

Juselius, K., 1995. Do purchasing power parity and uncovered interest rate parity hold in the long-run? An example of likelihood inference in a multivariate time series model. Journal of Econometrics 69, 211–240.

Juselius, K., MacDonald, R., 2000. International Parity Relationships Between Germany and the United States: A Joint Modelling Approach. Global Economic Institutions Working Paper No. 50.

Lee, K., Pesaran, M.H., Shin, Y., 1994. Exchange Rate, Price and Interest Rate Dynamics in the UK: An Application of the Generalised Impulse Response Analysis. Mimeo, University of Cambridge.

MacDonald, R., 1995. Long-run exchange rate modeling. International Monetary Fund Staff Papers 42, 437–489.

MacDonald, R., Marsh, I.W., 1997. On fundamentals and exchange rates: a Casselian perspective. Review of Economics and Statistics 79, 655–664.

MacDonald, R., Marsh, I.W., 1999. Exchange Rate Modelling. Kluwer, Dordrecht.

MacDonald, R., Ricci, L., 2001. PPP and the Balassa Samuelson Effect: The Role of the Distribution Sector. IMF Working Paper No. 01/38.

Meese, R., Rogoff, K., 1983. Empirical exchange rate models of the seventies: do they fit out of sample? Journal of International Economics 14, 3–24.

Osterwald-Lenum, M., 1992. A note with fractiles of the asymptotic distribution of the maximum likelihood cointegration test statistics: four cases. Oxford Bulletin of Economics and Statistics 54, 461–472.

Paruolo, P., 1995. On the determination of integration indices in I(2) systems. Journal of Econometrics 72, 313–356.

Available online at www.sciencedirect.com
SCIENCE DIRECT
Economic Modelling 22 (2005) 485–502
Economic Modelling
www.elsevier.com/locate/econbase

Markov switching regimes in a monetary exchange rate model

Michael Frömmel[a,*], Ronald MacDonald[b], Lukas Menkhoff[c]

[a]*Department of Economics, Universität Hannover, Königsworther Platz 1, Hannover 30167, Germany*
[b]*University of Strathclyde, United Kingdom*
[c]*Universität Hannover, Germany*

Accepted 7 July 2004

Abstract

This paper extends the real interest differential (RID) model of Frankel [Am. Econ. Rev. 69 (1979) 610] by introducing Markov regime switches for three exchange rates, over the years 1973–2000. Evidence of a non-linear relationship between exchange rates and underlying fundamentals is provided. It turns out that one of the estimated regimes represents exactly the RID case. The key fundamental which determines regimes turns out to be the interest rate. The established relationship is shown to be stable in several respects: regimes are highly persistent, provide a much better description of the data than alternatives and are robust towards several modifications.
© 2004 Elsevier B.V. All rights reserved.

JEL classification: F31

Keywords: Markov switching model; Monetary model of the exchange rate; Real interest differential model (Frankel, 1979)

1. Introduction

Exchange rate modelling has received a new lease of life as a result of simple monetary models having well-defined long-run properties (see, for example, MacDonald and Taylor.

* Corresponding author.
E-mail address: froemmel@gif.uni-hannover.de (M. Frömmel).

0264-9993/$ - see front matter © 2004 Elsevier B.V. All rights reserved.
doi:10.1016/j.econmod.2004.07.001

1994). Knowing that fundamentals matter in the long-run (see also Mark, 1995; MacDonald, 1999), attention has shifted to shorter-term horizons. Although the verdict on the importance of fundamentals is still ambivalent (see, for example, Frankel and Rose, 1995) new approaches, many of them building on non-linear relationships between fundamentals and exchange rates, seem to offer more hope at this horizon. In this paper, we contribute to these efforts by re-examining the monetary model in a time-varying coefficients context using a Markov switching approach. Amongst other things, we show that for a relevant sample of exchange rates regime switching properties provide substantial explanatory power beyond a constant coefficients approach.

The poor explanatory power of structural exchange rate models (see, for example, Frankel and Rose, 1995) provides a natural motivation to search for a more sophisticated modelling of the fundamental determinants of exchange rates. Many of these approaches incorporate non-linearities, which have been indicated for exchange rates for some time now (see, for example, Hsieh, 1989). There are at least four strands in the literature, each postulating a characteristic link: First, linear models can be modified by allowing for the non-linear formulation of coefficients (see, for example, Meese and Rose, 1991). Second, the relation between fundamentals and exchange rates can be expressed in an error correction framework, based on statistically derived cointegration vectors (MacDonald and Taylor, 1994; MacDonald and Marsh, 1997). Third, a similar idea of the long-term stable influences and short-term dynamics is captured in threshold approaches which assume mean-reverting properties of exchange rates (e.g. Kilian and Taylor, 2003). Fourth, there has been a presumption in the literature that coefficients may be time-varying (some general thoughts on unstable processes are given in Hendry and Clements, 2003). Whereas earlier studies assume these coefficients evolve smoothly (Wolff, 1987; Schinasi and Swamy, 1989), we draw on the idea of changing regimes. This approach seems to be more appealing for two reasons. First, it fits in with the observation that exchange rate models perform well for some sub-periods, whereas they do not for other periods (Meese, 1986, 1990; Faust et al., 2003), and, second, there is recent empirical support for the view that fairly sudden regime changes occur (Frydman and Goldberg, 2001).

The power of the Markov switching approach for exchange rate modelling was first demonstrated by Engel and Hamilton (1990) and Engel (1994). These studies used a time series approach, with two regimes, and applied their models to three currencies. Despite the success of these studies in capturing the dynamic evolution of exchange rates there are very few studies which have applied the Markov-switching approach to a fundamental exchange rate model. The exceptions are Marsh (2000), who uses a Markov switching model (MSM) for daily exchange rate data, with interest rate differentials as the only fundamental. He concludes that this approach does not provide superior forecasts for exchange rates in comparison with a pure time series Markov switching model. Bessec (2003) uses a Markov switching error correction model to describe adjustments to PPP in the European Monetary System. Clarida et al. (2003) apply a Markov switching multivariate model to weekly spot and forward rates of four major exchange rates. They come to the conclusion that allowing for regime switches in an error correction framework provides forecasts which significantly outperform linear models. De Grauwe and Vansteenkiste (2001) use monthly data for high and low inflation countries' exchange rates for the period 1973–1998. Regressing the exchange rate on a set of fundamentals, they show that the coefficients switch significantly between the two states examined for high inflation countries but not for industrialised countries.

In this paper, we demonstrate significant regime changes in a monetary exchange rate model for the three most important currency markets, namely the bilateral US Dollar (USD) values of the D-Mark, Yen and Pound (see Bank for International Settlements, 2002). Our paper differs from the study of De Grauwe and Vansteenkiste (2001)—which is similar in that it considers fundamentals—in several respects: First, the use of a regime switching approach in modelling exchange rate fundamentals is explicitly based on a market microstructure approach. This provides a substantial motivation for applying regime changes to the major markets. Second, the modelling follows Frankel (1979) real interest rate differential exchange rate approach, which has been a widely used variant of the monetary approach. Third, our findings are seen to be robust to several modifications. Fourth, the Markov switching monetary exchange rate model does not systematically provide forecasting power. In summary, our results can be seen as further evidence in favour of non-linear modelling of fundamentals.

The paper is structured as follows: Section 1 motivates the approach of time-varying fundamentals and in particular regime switching fundamentals by referring to the market microstructure literature. In Section 2, the Markov switching methodology is described. Section 3 presents the estimation results for three major exchange rates, which are further discussed in Section 4. Robustness checks are performed in Section 5, and Section 6 summarizes our main findings.

2. On the regime switching character of fundamentals

Traditional applications of the monetary exchange rate model rely on a single state relationship between fundamentals and exchange rates. As we have noted, our application of the monetary model relaxes the assumption of a single state. The monetary models can be derived on an ad hoc basis, using Cagan style money demand functions or from an optimising model. In this paper, we use the extended monetary model, first established by Frankel (1979), and referred to as the "real interest rate difference model (RID)". This model nests both the flexible price and the sticky price monetary model, within it, and may be represented by the following equation:

$$e_t = c + \alpha(m_t - m_t^*) + \beta(y_t - y_t^*) + \gamma(i_t^s - i_t^{s*}) + \delta(i_t^l - i_t^{l*}) + \varepsilon_t \qquad (1)$$

where e_t denotes the log of the spot rate at time t, defined as the home currency price of a unit of foreign currency (in our study, the US Dollar is the foreign currency), m_t the log of the money supply, y_t is the log of output, i_t^s is the short-term interest rate, which captures liquidity effects in this model and i_t^l is the long-term interest rate which captures expected inflation. The asterisk represents the foreign country which is the United States in our study. From a monetary perspective, one would expect the estimated coefficient on the relative money supply term to be close to one and the income elasticity, β, should be estimated negative. The coefficient on the short-term interest rate is also expected to be negative, while the expected inflation term should exhibit a positive influence on the exchange rate.

An abstract relation as simple as the monetary model is perhaps most useful as a long-run relationship, but is unlikely to capture the full dynamic interrelationships between fundamentals and exchange rates. One major criticism in this respect is the observation of foreign exchange market professionals that the importance of fundamental factors appears to change over time. What has been viewed as anecdotal evidence of the market in the past has recently become the subject of systematic market microstructure research (see, for example, Lyons, 2001). Three studies can be used to substantiate the claim of an unstable relationship between fundamentals and exchange rates. In similarly designed questionnaire surveys in the US (Cheung and Chinn, 2001) and in the UK (Cheung et al., 1999), foreign exchange dealers were asked which announcement of fundamentals they regarded as most important for their market. The fundamentals referred to were, unemployment, an interest rate, the inflation rate, the trade deficit, GDP and a category "other". The response from these surveys is summarised in Table 1, and it reveals some interesting insights. First, fundamentals are of different importance to professionals; second, the relative importance of fundamentals between the two countries is very similar, but the difference over time is enormous. Indeed—as the lower part of Table 1 indicates—the difference over time is clearly larger than the difference between the two countries. To put this last finding into numbers, the average absolute difference between countries for the ten cases (five fundamentals times two points in time) is 5.7 percentage points, but the average absolute difference over time for ten cases (five fundamentals times two countries) is 15.4 percentage points and thus three times larger.

These findings substantiate convincingly that market participants regard the importance of fundamentals as time-varying. What is not clear, however, are possible reasons for this instability. In this respect, another questionnaire survey conducted in 1992, and analysed by Menkhoff (1998), provides further illumination. In this survey, FX dealers and international fund managers in Germany were explicitly asked why fundamentals might attract different attention over time. Table 2 presents the exact question and response

Table 1
The impact of economics announcements on the FX market

		Unemployment rate	Interest rate	Inflation	Trade deficit	GDP	Other	
USA	1996/1997	33.0	30.9	18.3	9.9	2.1	4.2	
UK	1998	27.0	46.7	19.7	2.5	0.0	1.6	
USA	1991/1992	16.3	22.8	10.9	37.5	3.8	0.5	
UK	1993	9.2	29.2	9.2	45.8	3.3	0.8	
Differences between countries								
USA–UK	Now	6.0	−15.8	−1.4	7.4	+2.1	–	∅ 5.65
USA UK	5 years ago	7.1	6.4	1.7	−8.3	+0.5		
Differences over time								
Change USA		16.7	8.1	7.4	−27.6	−1.7	–	∅ 15.39
Change UK		17.8	17.5	10.5	−43.3	−3.3	–	

Data sources: **Cheung and Chinn (2001)** for USA; **Cheung et al. (1999)** for UK.

Table 2
Time-varying importance of fundamentals as seen by FX professionals

Question: Are economic variables regarded differently over time by market participants? Do you agree with the following statements?

( ) There are often variables in the foreground, which emphasise the actually most urgent problem.
( ) There are often variables in the foreground, which are just fashionable but not directly related to fundamental problems.
( ) The attention does not change over time.

	Most urgent problem	Fashions	No change over time
Agree fully	20.6	23.6	3.6
:	40.0	32.7	3.0
:	24.8	19.4	9.1
:	9.1	13.3	5.5
:	3.6	6.7	16.4
Disagree fully	1.8	4.2	62.4
Number n	165	165	165

Data source: Menkhoff (1998).

statements which the professionals were asked to evaluate with different degrees of (dis)agreement. Consistent with the evidence given above is the fact that the "no change over time" statement is denied by almost 85% of respondents.

Interestingly, moreover, is the evaluation of the other two statements which formulate alternative sources of instability. The first alternative stresses that changing attention reflects the "most urgent problem", whereas the second alternative regards changing attention as a sign of "fashions", that is of non-fundamental influences. Although both answers attract clear agreement, the "most urgent problem" alternative receives even more than 85% agreement, and the "fashions" alternative more than 75%. In addition, the latter responses show more extreme responses at both ends of the spectrum, thereby indicating less consensus. We interpret these additional findings as not only supporting time-varying importance of fundamentals, but also as linking changing importance to fundamental real world problems. Changing fundamental scenarios can in principle be detected by a regime switching approach.

The identification of regimes is simplified by the limited number of relevant fundamentals that is quite stable over time and that can be related to the monetary model. Regarding the number of fundamentals, the list in Table 1 includes a category "other" which would capture further factors but which hardly received any attention by respondents. This is confirmed by the German survey study which includes a list of ten fundamentals. Fundamentals being related to the monetary model receive the highest ranks.

These results, however, do not indicate where the regime switches come from. There would seem to be two main explanations: First, the traders could cause the regime switches themselves. That is, the exchange rate is driven by those fundamentals which are given most attention to by the traders and the exchange rate therefore reflects the traders' views. These are not necessarily related to changes in the fundamentals' importance. Second, another possible explanation could be that the time series processes governing the fundamentals evolve over time. In this case, the traders' assessments will change, too, but they would just reflect the actually differing importance of fundamentals.[1]

However, survey evidence on the behaviour of foreign exchange participants strongly suggests that instability over time in the relationship between fundamentals and exchange rates matters. The modelling of time-varying fundamentals is thus more than justified from this literature and the particular regime-switching approach seems to be reasonable.

3. The Markov switching methodology

The Markov switching model has been popularised by Hamilton (1989), although it was originally motivated by Goldfeld and Quandt (1973). For our aim it is convenient to consider it as a switching regression (for this particular form of the MSM, see Hamilton, 1994, Chap. 19):

$$r_t = \begin{cases} \beta_1 z_t + \varepsilon_t, & \text{if } s_t = 1 \\ \beta_2 z_t + \varepsilon_t, & \text{if } s_t = 2 \end{cases} \tag{2}$$

where r_t is the time series to be explained, in our case, the 12-month percentage change of an exchange rate, z_t is a vector of exogenous regressors, β_i is a vector of real numbers, whose values depend on the non-observable state variable s_t and ε_t is Gaussian white noise. The state variable s_t is assumed to follow an ergodic first-order Markov process and is characterised by the matrix Π consisting of the transition probabilities p_{ij} from state i to state j:

$$\Pi = \begin{bmatrix} p_{11}p_{21} \\ p_{12}p_{22} \end{bmatrix}, \ p_{ij} = Pr(s_t = j|s_{t-1} = i) \tag{3}$$

Once the coefficients of the model and the transition matrix have been estimated, the probability $Pr(s_t{=}j|r_1,\ldots,r_T)$ of being in state j, based on the knowledge of the complete series, can be calculated for each date (for details of the algorithm, see Kim and Nelson, 1999). This series of probabilities will be referred to as the *smoothed probabilities*, in contrast to the series of probabilities $Pr(s_t{=}j|r_1,\ldots,r_t)$ of being in state j based on the information up to date t—the *filter probabilities*—which is also calculated. It is straightforward to show that for the last date, that is $t{=}T$, the smoothed probability equals the filter probability.

In our investigation, the vector z_t of fundamentals in Eq. (2) is chosen according to the real interest differential monetary model (RID), as presented in the previous section. In this context, the set of fundamentals covers relative changes in money supply (Δm_t), industrial production (Δy_t), the money market interest rate (Δi_t^s), as the short-term interest rate, and

[1] As one referee has stated, the RID model is a semi-reduced form. Frydman and Goldberg (2001) argue that the regime switches may occur through structural changes in the economy, e.g., instabilities of the money demand function, or through changes in expectation functions, although this would not be consistent with rational expectations.

the government bond yield (Δi_t^l) as the long-term interest rate. Eq. (1) can therefore be rewritten as:

$$r_t = \begin{cases} c_1 + \alpha_1 \Delta m_t + \beta_1 \Delta y_t + \gamma_1 \Delta i_t^s + \delta_1 \Delta i_t^l + \varepsilon_t, & s_t = 1 \\ c_2 + \alpha_2 \Delta m_t + \beta_2 \Delta y_t + \gamma_2 \Delta i_t^s + \delta_2 \Delta i_t^l + \varepsilon_t, & s_t = 2 \end{cases}, \qquad (4)$$

with state-depending coefficients. For comparative purposes, the RID variant of the monetary model is also estimated with constant coefficients, which serves as a benchmark model and the null hypothesis for the tests.

Testing a MSM against a linear alternative is not straightforward because under the null hypothesis of a constant coefficient model without regime switches, only one regime governs the exchange rate and the transition probabilities are not identified. Garcia (1998) gives asymptotic critical values for Hansen's (1992, 1996) test for a couple of simple MSMs with two regimes. The set of models discussed by Garcia, however, does not include a model with exogenous regressors and a constant variance over the two regimes as used in our investigation. So his critical values are not valid for our model.

We therefore rely on Wald tests as used by, for instance, Engel and Hamilton (1990), Engel (1994) and Dewachter (1997). The Wald tests allow for testing two hypotheses. The first one tests against the null of $p_{11}+p_{22}=1$; that is, it tests for systematically alternating regimes (as opposed to arbitrarily switching between regimes). The second one tests against the null of identical parameters in the different states. The latter test also facilitates testing which coefficients differ for the regimes. Both tests in combination test for Markov switching against the null hypothesis of a linear model. However, due to the problems mentioned above, the results have to be interpreted with caution.

4. Data and estimation results

For the estimation we use monthly data from January 1974 to October 2000[2] for four industrialised countries (the United States, Germany, United Kingdom, Japan) from the IFS database by the International Monetary Fund.[3] The estimation was performed in GAUSS.

For the German money stock and industrial production, possible structural breaks due to German reunification in 1990 merit some additional consideration. For M2, a structural break is detected in June 1990, which means the money stock is shifted upwards. In contrast, the series of industrial production does not show any significant break around reunification. This may be due to the low level of industrial production in Eastern Germany during reunification, compared to Western Germany. Therefore, structural breaks

[2] For Germany, a shorter series up to December 1998 was used due to the introduction of the EURO in January 1999.

[3] The following series have been used (replace ccc by country code): ccc.RF.ZF (exchange rate); ccc.39MBC (money for Germany and the US), ccc.59MC.ZF (money for the UK), ccc.34.BZF (money for Japan), ccc.66...CZF (industrial production), ccc.60B...ZF (short term interest rate); ccc.61...ZF (government bond yield). The UK does not report an M2 money series, which we use for Germany, Japan and the US. Therefore for the UK we use M0 as the money stock variable.

have been considered only for the series for M2. The calculations have been performed using both, the corrected and the original series. As the results do not substantially differ, we subsequently rely on the results for the original series. This approach may be justified by the consideration that the increase in money supply, not being accompanied by an increase in output, would also have affected the exchange rate.

Each fundamental is calculated as the difference of the percentage change during the last 12 months in the home country versus the percentage change for the same horizon in the United States. This approach is applied for two reasons: First, it avoids seasonal effects in the data and reduces the noise from short-term movements in the exchange rates and the fundamentals and therefore promises more stable results.[4] Smoothing the time series by applying year-to-year changes is commonly used by statistical offices and central banks for growth rates of fundamentals to focus on their trend behaviour. To achieve comparable data, we apply yearly changes to the exchange rate, too.

Although this approach does not affect the frequency of the data, a major disadvantage is that it leads to some serial correlation in the residuals. This autocorrelation is considerable, but dies out after few months. We therefore rely on heteroskedasticity and autocorrelation consistent standard errors (Newey and West, 1987). These do not only correct for autocorrelation but also for heteroskedasticity and we do not need the form of autocorrelation to be more precisely specified. Second, Frankel's model is based on a version of purchasing power parity PPP (Frankel, 1979, p. 612). Absolute PPP, however, is not a particularly useful construct, due to well-known market imperfections. Therefore, it is straightforward to work with changes in exchange rates and fundamentals, as is done in empirical work on PPP.

For example, the relative change in the money supply is calculated as (the other fundamentals are calculated analogously):

$$\Delta m_t = \frac{m_t^{\text{home}} - m_{t-12}^{\text{home}}}{m_{t-12}^{\text{home}}} - \frac{m_t^{\text{USA}} - m_{t-12}^{\text{USA}}}{m_{t-12}^{\text{USA}}} \tag{5}$$

Table 3 shows the estimation results for the constant coefficients RID for the exchange rates of the Deutsche Mark (DEM), the Japanese Yen (JPY) and the Pound Sterling (GBP), all against the US Dollar.

The results are heterogeneous and hardly consistent with theory. The expected signs from the theoretical model are given in the last column for comparison. First, we note that the coefficient on the money supply term is significant, but wrongly signed, relative to the theoretically derived expectation, for the Deutsche Mark and the Pound Sterling, whereas it is correctly signed, although not significant, for the Yen. Second, the sign of the coefficient on the short-term interest rate differential is significantly positive for the Deutsche Mark, significantly negative for the Yen and insignificant for the Pound. The long-term interest rate differential has the correct sign and is significant only for the

[4] The use of quarterly changes in the respective variables, instead of overlapping annual changes severely lowers the significance of the results, due to noise and seasonal effects in the data and the lower number of observations (never more than 108) which are then available for estimation. The results are not given here, but available from the authors on request.

Table 3
Estimation results for the constant coefficient RID model

	DEM/USD	JPY/USD	GBP/USD	Expected signs
Intercept: c	−0.0166	0.0108**	0.0239	n.a.
Money: α	−0.1922*	0.0006**	−0.8296*	>0
Industrial production: β	−0.5023*	−0.0627**	−0.4233	<0
Short-term interest rate: γ	0.0435**	−0.0292	−0.0006	<0
Long-term interest rate: δ	−0.0890	0.0112	0.1086	>0

Asterisks refer to level of significance, *10%, **5%, ***1%, Newey–West HAC standard errors.

Pound, but not for the other exchange rates. Only for the coefficient on industrial production do we find the correct sign and significance in accordance with theory. These results are in line with early empirical findings. For example, Dornbusch (1980), Boothe and Glassmann (1987) find that the initial relationship reported by Frankel breaks down as soon as the sample is extended beyond 1978.

The results are substantially better when the restriction of constant coefficients is abandoned. Table 4 provides estimation results for the real interest differential model with Markov switching coefficients.

It is worth mentioning that the MSM distinguishes regimes which are highly persistent. The probability of remaining in the present state is always between 91% and 97%, most probabilities being close to 95%. The smoothed probabilities are given in Fig. 1 in

Table 4
Estimated coefficients for the MSM

	DEM/USD	JPY/USD	GBP/USD
State 1			
c_1	0.0893***	−0.0414***	−0.0688***
α_1	0.1600*	0.0082	0.2045
β_1	−0.5958***	−0.1845***	−0.7344***
γ_1	−0.0860***	−0.0272	−0.0006
δ_1	0.1654***	0.1172**	0.1762**
State 2			
c_2	−0.1179***	0.0282***	0.1290***
α_2	0.0390	0.0003*	−0.8722***
β_2	−0.3895	0.0204	−0.5401***
γ_2	0.0317	−0.0028	−0.0088***
δ_2	−0.1022	−0.0070	0.2810***
p_{11}	0.9494***	0.9137***	0.9697***
p_{22}	0.9556***	0.9726***	0.9590***
$P(s_t=1)$	0.4676	0.2410	0.5747
$P(s_t=2)$	0.5324	0.7590	0.4253
Expected duration of the regimes (in months)			
Regime 1	19.8	11.6	33.0
Regime 2	22.5	36.5	24.4

Asterisks refer to level of significance, *10%, **5%, ***1%, Newey–West HAC standard errors.

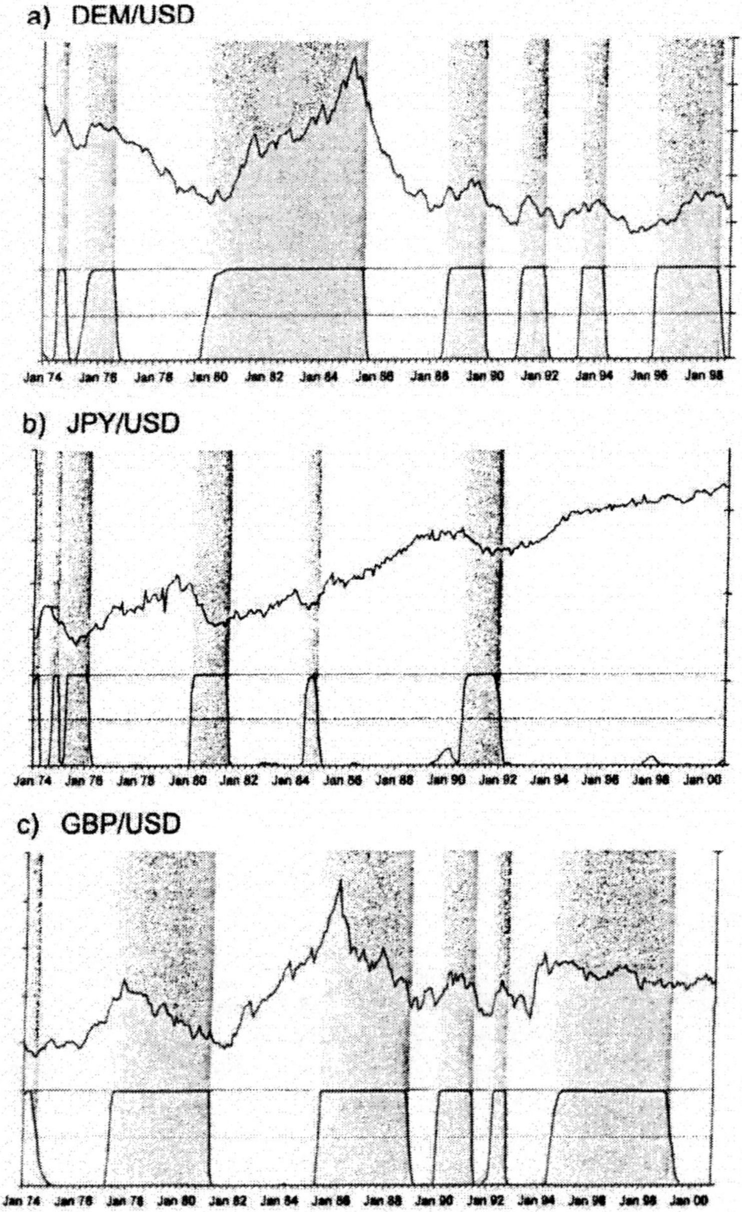

Fig. 1. Smoothed probabilities of being in state 1 (lower line) and exchange rate. (a) DEM/USD. (b) JPY/USD. (c) GBP/USD. The grey areas mark periods for which the process is more likely to be in state 1 (in favour of the RID) than in state 2, that is, $P(s_t=1|r_1...r_T)$ exceeds 0.5.

graphical form and show the comparatively low number of regime switches due to the high persistence: There are 7 periods where the process is in state 1 for the DEM/USD, 11 for the JPY/USD and 10 for the GBP/USD.

For all exchange rates, one regime is identified within which the estimates are fully consistent with Frankel's model: All coefficients are correctly signed and, in most cases, significant at least at the 10% level. The RID regime is given in Table 4 as 'State 1' and covers, respectively, 47% and 57% of the whole sample for the DEM/USD and the GBP/USD, but only 24% for the JPY/USD. This finding is consistent with the notion that the RID model is a useful explanation of exchange rates in certain periods. There are other periods, however, where exchange rate determinants either have a clearly different degree of influence—leading to different coefficients—or have a different sign. According to the approach chosen there is always a second regime, that is 'State 2', which we now discuss.

A first insight in this respect is that the signs in state 2 are different from state 1 and are heterogeneous for the three exchange rates. Turning to each exchange rate, the DEM/USD and the JPY/USD are different concerning the significance of the parameters in state 2. Except for the constant, which is significant at the 1% level for each single estimation, only the changes in output are significant at the 10% level. This means that both rates are characterised by a regime 1 which is consistent with theory (but occurs less frequently for the case of the DEM/USD), and a second one which is hardly connected to any changes in the fundamentals considered here.

The picture is different for the GBP/USD rate, which also shows highly significant estimations in the second regime. But while the signs for changes in output are in accordance with the RID model for both rates, the GBP/USD shows a negative coefficient on the changes in the money supply. This particular result is contrary to our expectations.

In summary, the MSM has been proven to be useful in several respects. First, there are two significant regimes which can be identified and this indicates the usefulness of a regime switching approach. Second, regimes have a length of roughly two years, which leaves open the possibility that they are caused by major real world economic issues whose impact lasts for some time. Third, one of these regimes has coefficients which conform to the RID model, confirming earlier findings of appropriate monetary exchange rate modelling in certain periods only. Fourth, the second regime reveals some complexity as coefficients have different signs from regime 1 and are heterogeneous for the three exchange rates. This complexity fits in with the failure of simple models to explain exchange rates. Despite these results, two more challenges have to be overcome: From a statistical viewpoint, does the MSM provide a superior modelling to alternatives, and from an economic viewpoint, can the regimes identified be linked to economic characteristics?

5. Discussion of results

Using a univariate exchange rate specification, Engel and Hamilton (1990) were the first to demonstrate the power of MSM in explaining exchange rate behaviour. One may thus expect that our fundamental-based version of the MSM provides a better fit to the data than competing models do.

Table 5 shows some conventional measures of fit for the MSM with fundamentals, a standard MSM without fundamentals, a constant coefficients model and a simple random walk with drift. For all models, the coefficients have been estimated based on the whole sample period and the expectations based on these models have been compared with realised exchange rate changes. The expected returns for the two Markov switching models are calculated as:

$$E[r_t] = \sum_{i=1}^{2} E[r_t|s_t = i]Pr(s_t = i|r_1, \ldots, r_t) \tag{6}$$

Calculating the expected returns for the linear model and the random walk with drift is straightforward.

Both MSM models, with and without fundamentals, generate lower errors than the classical models and the MSM with fundamentals performs best. Fig. 2 shows plots of the estimated exchange rate changes from the constant coefficient model and the MSM with fundamentals in comparison with the actual exchange rate changes. The MSM tracks the data much better than the constant coefficient model.

Statistical superiority is, however, a necessary but not a sufficient condition for satisfying model adequacy. It is therefore of interest to determine if the regimes can be linked to some characteristics of the economic environments. As a first step in examining this issue we refer to the Wald tests, reported in Table 6, which allow us to better assess the significance of differences in the coefficients. It can be seen that the intercepts differ significantly between the states for all of the exchange rates. The many significant results for the slope coefficients show that the regime changes are in fact caused by different fundamentals for the exchange rates. In addition to the insights from Table 4, we are now

Table 5
Fit of the MSM in comparison with competing models

	DEM/USD	JPY/USD	GBP/USD
Markov switching RID model			
RMSE	0.06075	0.02324	0.06042
MAE	0.04767	0.01822	0.04663
Pure Markov switching model			
RMSE	0.06527	0.02449	0.06486
MAE	0.04692	0.01995	0.05102
Constant coefficient RID model			
RMSE	0.11992	0.03821	0.11367
MAE	0.09872	0.02869	0.09059
Random walk with drift			
RMSE	0.12402	0.04123	0.12434
MAE	0.10230	0.03026	0.10167

RMSE: root mean squared error. MAE: mean average error.

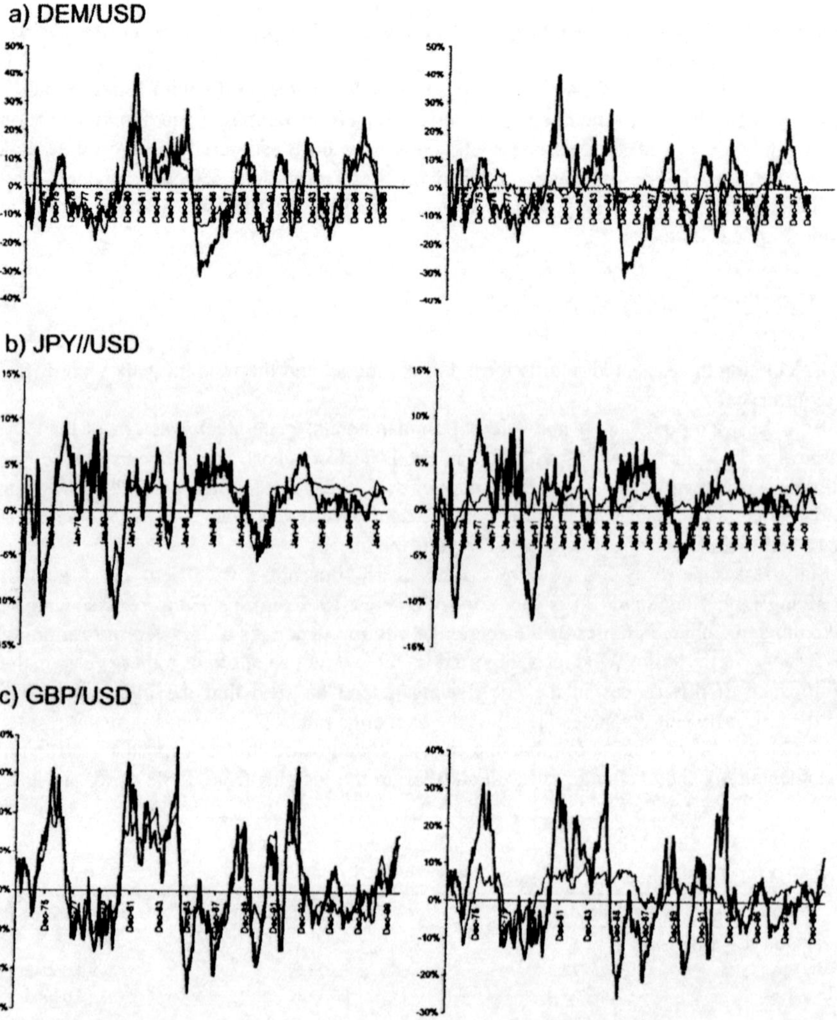

Fig. 2. Fit of estimated models to actual percentage 12-month changes. (a) DEM/USD. (b) JPY/USD. (c) GBP/USD. Bold line: Actual percentage change in exchange rate; thin line: fitted by RID with Markov switching coefficients (left-hand figure), fitted by constant coefficient RID (right-hand figure).

in a position to say something about characteristic differences between regimes, indicating which differences in fundamentals are decisive.

The DEM/USD and the JPY/USD differ in the coefficients for the short-and the long-term interest rates, whereas there is no significant difference in the coefficients for changes in money supply and production between the regimes. This means that the regime dependence is mainly driven by the assessment of interest rates, whereas the influence of

Table 6
Wald test results for transition probabilities and coefficients

H_0	DEM/USD	JPY/USD	GBP/USD
$p_{11}=1-p_{22}$	10.058***	7.300***	8.433***
$c_1=c_2$	8.745.685***	66.358***	1.829.783***
$\alpha_1=\alpha_2$	0.984	0.002	308.819.285***
$\beta_1=\beta_2$	0.980	1.023	23.680***
$\gamma_1=\gamma_2$	24.862***	8.276***	0.453
$\delta_1=\delta_2$	15.935***	4.809**	15.467***

The Wald statistics given in the table have been calculated using the asymptotic covariance matrix. Asterisks refer to level of significance: **5%, ***1%.

money and output does not differ substantially. The case of the GBP/USD is somewhat different, as only long-term interest rates are also significantly different between regimes but not short-term rates. Some of the dynamics for this currency are instead captured by money supply and output. As an interim summary, the most important although not all relevant differences between regimes appear to be linked to differences in interest rate changes.

6. Robustness checks

To ensure our results are stable, and in particular to confirm the existence of two significantly different regimes, we check the robustness of our results. In particular, we vary four elements of our baseline model: the exact definition of variables, the differencing frequency (originally 12-month changes), the fundamental variables set and the sample period. Finally, we test for out-of-sample forecasting power.

First, we check whether the results are related to the exact definition of fundamentals. For this reason, several fundamentals are substituted for similarly defined ones. There are no major differences in the results, when M2 is substituted by M3 for the money supply. This also applies when other proxies for inflation expectations are used, such as realised inflation data. For both indices of producer and consumer prices, the results do not differ.

Second, using 6- or 3-month changes, instead of 12-month changes, does not affect most of the signs of the estimated coefficients, but the coefficients mostly become insignificant. This may indicate that exchange rates fluctuate around the model-based estimations in the short run or that there are time lags of several months between changes in the fundamentals and those in the exchange rate.

Third, the set of fundamental variables is changed by omitting the second interest rate, thus converting the RID approach to the standard monetary model, and by adding a proxy for trade volume. Adding the relative percentage changes of imports and exports as a proxy for trade volume only slightly affects the values of the existing variables. However, imports as well as exports are significantly related to changes in the exchange rate for all rates and regimes other than regime 2 for the JPY/USD rate. Omitting the long-term interest rate does not substantially influence the coefficients of the remaining variables, but the fit of the model gets slightly worse.

Table 7
Performance of out-of-sample forecasts based on competing models

	DEM/USD	JPY/USD	GBP/USD
Markov switching RID model			
1 month	0.0291	0.0093	0.0298
6 months	0.0945	0.0188	0.0754
12 months	0.1724	0.0379	0.1159
Pure Markov switching model			
1 month	0.0239 (−4.5914***)	0.0079 (−0.2062)	0.0250 (−3.2604***)
6 months	0.0817 (−2.5786**)	0.0147 (−0.3306)	0.0718 (−1.2023)
12 months	0.1239 (−1.9937*)	0.0234 (−0.4982)	0.1001 (−2.2351**)
Constant coefficient RID model			
1 month	0.0264 (−1.9279*)	0.0083 (−2.7424***)	0.0419 (5.2685***)
6 months	0.0936 (−0.3396)	0.0655 (3.6607***)	0.0983 (3.8782***)
12 months	0.1917 (0.0578)	0.2006 (3.5413***)	0.1835 (3.9745***)
Random walk			
1 month	0.0228 (−5.2933***)	0.0076 (−3.5322***)	0.0237 (−4.4309***)
6 months	0.0736 (−4.1238***)	0.0142 (−2.4539***)	0.0623 (−13.3567***)
12 months	0.1141 (−3.0134***)	0.0203 (−3.2203***)	0.0843 (−5.8335***)

The alternatives are compared with the Markov switching RID model using the asymptotic test by Diebold and Mariano (1995) against the null hypothesis of no difference in forecast accuracy (using the absolute forecast error as loss function). The test statistic S_1 is given in parentheses. Positive values of S_1 indicate that the Markov switching RID model performs better than the alternative and vice versa. Asterisks refer to level of significance: **5%, ***1%.

Fourth, we re-estimate the results shortening the sample period successively for two years each.[5] For regime 1, this does not affect the signs of the estimated coefficients, but their size differs over time. While the influence of the money supply and the output variable becomes larger when the sample is shortened, there are only minor changes for the short-term interest rate. The long-term interest rate, which serves as our proxy for inflation expectations, finally becomes insignificant when the sample ends before 1990. For regime 2, the results are different: The coefficients for relative changes in the money supply and output become insignificant, whereas the interest rates do not change their sign, being highly significant. This behaviour suggests that the structure of our findings is somewhat sensitive with respect to the exact sample period. In particular, when sample periods differ markedly, some characteristics of the regimes may change and this is perhaps to be expected in light of the earlier literature claiming high instability in the exchange rate fundamentals relationship.

This finding raises doubts about the ability of the RID model with Markov switching coefficients to provide out-of-sample forecasts which significantly outperform those of a random walk. To explicitly assess the model's forecastability, we estimate the model over a rolling sample of 10 years and calculate the conditional expectations of the returns for the

[5] The results are given for the DEM/USD rate. Results for the other rates are similar and available from the authors on request.

next 1–12 months. The forecasts of the Markov switching RID model are then compared to those generated by the competing models using the asymptotic test by Diebold and Mariano (1995).[6] The monetary model with time-varying coefficients is outperformed by random walk forecasts in the short-run but improves the forecasts of the constant coefficient RID model in most cases (see the results in Table 7). Even the pure time series Markov switching model without fundamentals generates forecast errors exceeding those by the random walk. The fact that Markov switching models are able to describe the data well, but produce poor forecasts, is in line with many empirical works (Dacco and Satchell, 1999). This leads to the conclusion that, although the MSM captures most of the structural instability in the coefficients, there is still some additional source of time variation left. It has, however, to be stated that our results are strongly in favour of a non-linear relationship between exchange rates and macroeconomic fundamentals. These findings are in line with other recent studies as surveyed by Neely and Sarno (2002) or Cheung et al. (2002).

7. Conclusions

In this paper, we have re-examined the RID variant of the monetary model using a Markov-switching framework. The motivation for our work is based on three strands in the exchange rate literature: A number of studies indicate some influence of the monetary model's fundamentals on exchange rates, results from the market microstructure literature suggest a time-varying influence of a limited set of fundamentals on the exchange rate, and, finally, a MSM approach has been proven much better at describing exchange rates than linear approaches. The overall results are highly supportive of our chosen approach.

First, there appear to be two highly persistent regimes that can be identified for the three exchange rates under investigation. Second, one of the regimes shows exactly the coefficients as forecast by the RID model. Third, the MSM significantly improves the quality of the estimation over some alternatives and the best model is the model combination of a RID approach with Markov switching regimes. The fundamentals that differentiate the two regimes are in large part but not only interest rates. Finally, we demonstrate that this outcome is quite robust against several modifications to sample periods, definitions, measurement and even the exact set of variables.

However, our results also show that there is always a second regime that is difficult to explain theoretically. Moreover, the other regimes are heterogeneous which is consistent with earlier literature indicating that there are complex influences in exchange rate determination. Finally, structural stability is not good enough to systematically produce out-of-sample forecasting ability.

[6] The Diebold–Mariano test allows to compare just the forecast of a model with the forecast of exactly one other model. **Harvey and Newbold (2000)** propose a modified Diebold–Mariano-type test, allowing to compare a forecast with the combined forecast of a group of competitors, which could be appealing in our case. However, as our results indicate that the Markov Switching RID does not outperform the Random Walk out of sample, one will always find a combination including the Random Walk forecast, which is not outperformed by the Markov Switching RID.

Taking Rogoff (2001) verdict as a benchmark that "explaining the yen, dollar and euro exchange rates is still a very difficult task, even ex post", we claim some progress. Fundamentals matter and despite limitations mentioned, our contribution is in line with high frequency studies which indicate some non-linear fundamental influences on exchange rates. It is up to further research in improving exchange rate explanation beyond the present promising indications.

Acknowledgements

We would like to thank Menzie Chinn, Olaf Hübler, Stefan Niermann and two anonymous referees for helpful suggestions. Financial support by the Deutsche Forschungsgemeinschaft is gratefully acknowledged.

References

Bank for International Settlements (2002), Triennial Central Bank Survey, Foreign Exchange and Derivatives Market Activity in 2001, Basel.

Bessec, Marie, 2003. Mean-reversion vs. adjustment to PPP: the two regimes of exchange rate dynamics under the EMS, 1979–1998. Economic Modelling 20, 141 – 164.

Boothe, Paul, Glassmann, Debra, 1987. Off the mark: lessons for exchange rate modelling. Oxford Economic Papers 39, 443 – 457.

Cheung, Yin-Wong, Chinn, Menzie D., 2001. Currency traders and exchange rate dynamics: a survey of the US market. Journal of International Money and Finance 20, 439 – 471.

Cheung, Yin-Wong, Menzie D. Chinn and Ian W. Marsh (1999), How Do UK-Based Foreign Exchange Dealers Think Their Market Operates? CEPR Discussion Papers 2230, London.

Cheung, Yin-Wong, Menzie D. Chinn and Antonio G. Pascual (2002), Empirical Exchange Rate Models of the Nineties: Are Any Fit to Survive? NBER Working Paper Series 9393, Cambridge, Massachusetts.

Clarida, Richard H., Sarno, Lucio, Taylor, Mark P., Valente, Giorgio, 2003. The out-of-sample success of term structure models as exchange rate predictors: a step beyond. Journal of International Economics 60, 61 – 83.

Dacco, Roberto, Satchell, Steve, 1999. Why do regime-switching models forecast so badly? Journal of Forecasting 18, 1 – 16.

De Grauwe, Paul and Isabel Vansteenkiste (2001), Exchange Rates and Fundamentals, CESifo Discussion Papers No. 577, Munich.

Dewachter, Hans, 1997. Sign predictions of exchange rate changes: charts as proxies for bayesian Inferences. Weltwirtschaftliches Archiv 133 (1), 39 – 55.

Diebold, Francis X., Mariano, Roberto S., 1995. Comparing predictive accuracy. Journal of Business and Economic Statistics 13, 253 – 262.

Dornbusch, Rudiger, 1980. Exchange rate economics: where do we stand? Brookings Papers on Economic Activity 1, 143 – 194.

Engel, Charles, 1994. Can the Markov switching model forecast exchange rates? Journal of International Economics 36, 151 – 165.

Engel, Charles, Hamilton, James D., 1990. Long swings in the dollar. Are they in the data and do markets know it? American Economic Review 80, 689 – 713.

Faust, Jon, Rogers, John H., Wright, Jonathan H., 2003. Exchange rate forecasting: the errors we've really made. Journal of International Economics 60, 35 – 59.

Frankel, Jeffrey A., 1979. On the mark: a theory of floating exchange rate based on real interest differentials. American Economic Review 69 (4), 610 – 622.

Frankel, Jeffrey A., Rose, Andrew K., 1995. Empirical research on nominal exchange rates. In: Grossman, Gene, Rogoff, KennethHandbook of International Economics, vol. 3. Amsterdam, North-Holland, pp. 1689 – 1729.

Frydman, Roman, Goldberg, Michael D., 2001. Macroeconomic fundamentals and the DM/$ exchange rate: temporal instability and the monetary model. International Journal of Finance and Economics 6 (4), 421–435.

Garcia, Rene, 1998. Asymptotic null distribution of the likelihood ratio test in Markov switching models. International Economic Review 39 (3), 763–788.

Goldfeld, S.M., Quandt, R.E., 1973. A Markov model for switching regressions. Journal of Econometrics 1, 3–16.

Hamilton, James D., 1989. A new approach to the economic analysis of non-stationary time series and the business cycle. Econometrica 57 (2), 357–384.

Hamilton, James D., 1994. Time Series Analysis. Princeton University Press, Princeton.

Hansen, Bruce E., 1992. The likelihood ratio test under nonstandard conditions: testing the Markov switching model of GNP. Journal of Applied Econometrics 7, 62–81.

Hansen, Bruce E., 1996. Erratum: the likelihood ratio test under nonstandard conditions: testing the Markov switching model of GNP. Journal of Applied Econometrics 11, 195–198.

Harvey, David, Newbold, Paul, 2000. Tests for multiple forecast encompassing. Journal of Applied Econometrics 15, 471–482.

Hendry, David F., Clements, Michael P., 2003. Economic forecasting: some lessons from recent research. Economic Modelling 20, 301–329.

Hsieh, David A., 1989. Testing for non-linear dependence in daily foreign exchange rate changes. Journal of Business 62, 339–368.

Kilian, Lutz, Taylor, Mark P., 2003. Why is it so difficult to beat the random walk forecast of exchange rates? Journal of International Economics 60, 85–107.

Kim, C.J., Nelson, Charles R., 1999. State Space Models with Regime Switching: Classical and Gibbs Sampling Approaches with Applications. MIT Press, Massachusetts.

Lyons, Richard, 2001. The Microstructure Approach to Exchange Rates. MIT Press, Massachusetts.

MacDonald, Ronald, 1999. Exchange rate behaviour: are fundamentals important? Economic Journal 109 (459), 673–691.

MacDonald, Ronald, Marsh, Ian W., 1997. On fundamentals and exchange rates: a Casselian perspective. Review of Economics and Statistics 79 (4), 655–664.

MacDonald, Ronald, Taylor, Mark P., 1994. The monetary model of the exchange rate: long-run relationships, short-run dynamics and how to beat a random-walk. Journal of International Money and Finance 13 (3), 267–276.

Mark, Nelson, 1995. Exchange rates and fundamentals: evidence on long-horizon predictability. American Economic Review 85 (1), 201–218.

Marsh, Ian W., 2000. High-frequency Markov switching models in the foreign exchange market. Journal of Forecasting 19, 123–134.

Meese, Richard A., 1986. Testing for bubbles in exchange markets: a case of sparkling rates? Journal of Political Economy 94 (21), 345–373.

Meese, Richard A., 1990. Currency fluctuations in the post-Bretton Woods era. Journal of Economic Perspectives 4 (1), 117–134.

Meese, Richard A., Rose, Andrew K., 1991. An empirical assessment of nonlinearities in models of exchange rate determination. Review of Economic Studies 58 (3), 603–619.

Menkhoff, Lukas, 1998. The noise trading approach—questionnaire evidence from foreign exchange. Journal of International Money and Finance 17, 547–564.

Neely, Christopher J., Sarno, Lucio, 2002. How well do monetary fundamentals forecast exchange rates? Review-Federal Reserve Bank of St. Louis 84 (5), 51–74.

Newey, Whitney K., West, Kenneth D., 1987. A simple, semi-definite, heteroskedasticity and autocorrelation conistent covariance matrix. Econometrica 55, 703–708.

Rogoff, Kenneth, 2001. The failure of empirical exchange rate models: no longer new, but still true. Economic Policy Web Essay 1 (1).

Schinasi, G.J., Swamy, P.A.V.B., 1989. The out-of-sample forecasting performance of exchange rate models when coefficients are allowed to change. Journal of International Money and Finance 8, 375–390.

Wolff, Christian, 1987. Time-varying parameters and the out-of-sample forecasting performance of structural exchange rate models. Journal of Business and Economic Statistics 5, 87–97.

PART II

EQUILIBRIUM EXCHANGE RATES: PURCHASING POWER PARITY AND THE REAL EXCHANGE RATE

[8]

NOTES

LONG-RUN PURCHASING POWER PARITY: IS IT FOR REAL?

Ronald MacDonald*

Abstract—In this paper we re-examine the purchasing power parity concept using data from the recent experience with floating exchange rates. In particular, we utilise the recently developed multivariate cointegration methodology to test for a long-run relationship between exchange rates and relative prices and also to test for the proportionality of the exchange rate with respect to relative prices. In contrast to much other research, we demonstrate that there is a long-run relationship between a number of bilateral U.S. dollar exchange rates and their corresponding relative prices. The proportionality of the exchange rate to relative prices does not, however, receive support from the data. This finding may be attributable to the use of measured price series rather than the "true" series.

I. Introduction

The purchasing power parity (PPP) view of the determination of the exchange rate has been fundamentally called into question by the empirical evidence from the recent experience with flexible exchange rates.[1] For example, a number of researchers, such as Enders (1988), Patel (1990) and Taylor (1988), have used cointegration techniques to test for *long-run* PPP, and have demonstrated that long-run PPP does not hold. Other researchers, such as Adler and Lehman (1983) and Roll (1979), have demonstrated that real exchange rates contain unit roots and therefore a current change in the real exchange rate is permanent. This evidence is entirely complementary to the cointegration tests which effectively tests for a unit root in the real exchange rate without imposing equal and opposite coefficients on relative prices (this is discussed in more detail below).

In this paper we propose some evidence which indicates that PPP does seem to hold as a long-run phenomenon. In particular, we use recently developed multivariate cointegration techniques to test for the number of cointegrating vectors in five cases, each consisting of a U.S. bilateral exchange rate, and "home" and "foreign" prices. We argue that our cointegration tests are an improvement over previous such tests and, significantly, we find that our estimation strategy clearly reveals important cointegrating relationships. Such relationships are robust to changes in the sample period. A further novelty of our study entails tests of the proportionality restrictions implied by the model. Such restrictions tests are facilitated by our use of the multivariate technology.

II. Purchasing Power Parity: A Brief Overview of the Recent Evidence

Under a number of fairly restrictive assumptions it can be demonstrated that the condition of absolute PPP should hold for a country's bilateral exchange rate (see Hallwood and MacDonald, 1986, for a further discussion):

$$s_t = p_t - p_t^* \tag{1}$$

where p_t denotes the price level in the domestic country, s_t denotes the spot exchange rate (home currency price of a unit of foreign exchange), an asterisk denotes a foreign magnitude and lower case letters denote natural logarithms. Absolute PPP implies that an increase (decrease) in the home (foreign) price level should result in an equiproportionate rise (fall) in the exchange rate. An alternative way of expressing absolute PPP is to say that the real exchange rate, $q_t = (s_t - p_t + p_t^*)$, should continually equal zero.

In testing PPP a researcher is immediately faced with the issue of the appropriate price series to use. Most researchers in fact use either the consumer price or producer price indices. Such measured prices in all probability deviate from the "true" price measure by a, perhaps substantial, measurement error. In addition, such series also contain important non-tradeable elements and are constructed differently from country to country. In terms of the above discussion this means that relative measured prices need not have an equiproportionate effect on the exchange rate and this

Received for publication August 5, 1991. Revision accepted for publication February 24, 1992.

* The University of Strathclyde.

This paper was begun whilst I was a visiting scholar in the research department of the IMF, and I am grateful for the hospitality extended by the IMF. I should also like to thank Walter Enders, the editor and two anonymous referees for their helpful comments on an earlier draft of this paper.

[1] MacDonald (1988) contains a survey of the empirical evidence on PPP.

Copyright © 1993

will be compounded if transaction and trade restrictions are important[2]; in terms of equation (2) β and β^* need not equal unity

$$s_t = \beta p_t - \beta^* p_t^* + \varphi_t \qquad (2)$$

and, indeed, there can be no hypothesis about the coefficients on the relative prices (all that one can say is that β and β^* should be positive).[3] This makes it all the more important that in testing PPP one does not impose restrictions with respect to the β's. However, if PPP is to have any validity, the error term in (2), φ_t, should be stationary (we discuss this concept in more detail below). Thus although few proponents of PPP (see, for example, Officer, 1976, for a useful discussion of the views of the traditional proponents of PPP) would argue for a strict adherence to PPP, they would assert that shocks to the nominal exchange rate which cause non-zero values of the real exchange rate will be corrected in the long run; the real exchange is a mean-reverting process.

A number of researchers (see, *inter alia*, Roll, 1979, Adler and Lehmann, 1983, and MacDonald, 1985) have examined the null hypothesis that a variety of real exchange rates contain a unit root and are unable to reject the null (the nature of these studies means that they force β and β^* in 2 to be unity and therefore ignore the issue referred to above). However, Abuaf and Jorion (1990) have argued that such tests are likely to have low power against the alternative of a stable near random walk model. By carefully modelling the time series properties of a system of real exchange rate, Abuaf and Jorion show that there is some evidence of mean reversion in real exchange rates.

An alternative way of testing whether real exchange rates are stationary or not has involved exploiting the cointegration methodology proposed by Engle and Granger (1987). In terms of equation (2), if the exchange rate and relative prices *are* cointegrated the estimated residuals (i.e., the $\hat{\varphi}$'s) should form a stationary series. One of the main advantages in using the cointegration methodology as opposed to testing for unit roots in the real exchange rate is that it does not restrict β to equal one and β^* to equal minus one. As we have indicated, this may well be important when measured price series are utilised.

For the recent experience with flexible exchange rates the cointegration methodology has been applied to aggregate price data by Enders (1988), Taylor (1988) and Patel (1990). These authors test for cointegration between bilateral dollar exchange rates and prices using the Engle-Granger two-step methodology (the first two authors impose the restriction that $\beta = -\beta^*$, whilst the latter allows them to be unrestricted). Only Patel reports (slight) evidence that the null hypothesis of non-cointegration cannot be rejected: therefore these papers may be summarised by saying that there is no long-run tendency for exchange rates and relative prices to settle down on an equilibrium track.[4] A disadvantage of these studies is that the use of the two-step methodology precludes testing for proportionality of the β's with respect to the exchange rate.[5]

In this paper we present some further tests of the PPP hypothesis using cointegration techniques. Our approach has, however, a number of advantages over previous tests. First, other researchers generally impose the restriction $\beta = -\beta^*$; however, a number of factors discussed above, may drive a wedge between these two coefficients and they should therefore be estimated unconstrained. We estimate the β's in an unconstrained fashion and indeed test for the validity of the restriction. Such tests are facilitated, despite the fact that we are dealing with non-stationary variables, by our use of the multivariate cointegration methodology proposed by Johansen (1988). The Johansen technique is superior to the simpler regression based tests, noted above, because it fully captures the underlying time series properties of the data, provides estimates of *all* the cointegrating vectors that exist within a vector of variables and offers a test statistic for the number of cointegrating vectors. This test may therefore be viewed as more discerning in its ability to reject a false null hypothesis.

III. Econometric Methodology, Data and Results

Our econometric results are based on Johansen's multivariate cointegration methodology for extracting up to r cointegrating vectors from a vector of variables (in our case consisting of s_t, p_t and p_t^*). Since this methodology is now well known we do not present it here. Instead, we simply note two test statistics used to determine the number of cointegrating vectors. In our application the likelihood ratio, or Trace, test statistic (LR1) for the hypothesis that there are at most r

[2] See Taylor (1988) and Patel (1990) for a discussion of the importance of transportation costs and measurement error in violating degree one homogeneity of the exchange rate with respect to relative prices.

[3] See Patel (1990) for a useful discussion of the problems in using measured price series.

[4] Choudry, McNown and Wallace (1991) find some evidence of cointegration for the Canadian dollar in the 1950s.

[5] Huizinga (1987) applies the variance ratio methodology to ten US dollar bilateral exchange rates for the recent floating experience. He reports some qualitative evidence that real exchange rates exhibit mean reverting properties but cannot statistically reject the random walk model for these rates.

distinct cointegrating vectors is

$$LR1 = T \sum_{i=r+1}^{n} \ln(1 - \hat{\lambda}_i) \qquad (3)$$

where $\hat{\lambda}_{r+1}, \ldots, \hat{\lambda}_n$ are the $n - r$ smallest squared canonical correlations between the X_{t-k} and ΔX_t series (where $X_t = [s_t, p_t, p_t^*]'$), corrected for the effect of the lagged differences of the X_t process (for details of how to extract the $\hat{\lambda}_i$'s see Johansen 1988). Additionally, the likelihood ratio statistic for testing at most r cointegrating vectors against the alternative of $r + 1$ cointegrating vectors is given by (4):

$$LR2 = T \ln(1 - \lambda_{r+1}). \qquad (4)$$

Johansen (1988) shows that (3) and (4) have a non-standard distribution under the null hypothesis. He does, however, provide approximate critical values for the statistic, generated by Monte Carlo methods.[6]

An additional advantage of using the Johansen methodology is that it allows direct hypothesis tests on the coefficients entering the cointegrating vectors. We may therefore test the proportionality of the exchange rate to relative prices. The novel feature of the present tests is that they are robust to the non-stationarity of the data; previous tests, which use the levels of the variables and standard t-tests or F-ratios, are not. Using the notation of Johansen and Juseleius (1990), the hypothesis tests which we implement are of the general form:

$$H_3: \Pi = \alpha\varphi' H' \text{ (or } \beta = H\varphi) \qquad (5)$$

where H is an $n \times s$ matrix, with $s \geq r$ and φ is the corresponding $s \times r$ weighting matrix.

In this paper we use the above methodology to test what we refer to as strong-form and weak-form PPP. Strong-form PPP refers to the situation where there is at least one cointegrating vector between an exchange rate and the corresponding relative prices *and* the proportionality restrictions are satisfied. As we have indicated, such restrictions may not be satisfied because of factors such as measurement error and transportation costs. Given the high probability that the price series used in our empirical analysis are not the "true" price series, we would tend to emphasize the weak-form version of PPP. The latter places no restrictions on the cointegrating vector and simply requires that the exchange rate and relative prices be cointegrated. This latter definition of PPP is, we believe, of considerable importance since if it does not hold, as other researchers have found, then it may have important implications for the current account of the balance of payments and also theoretical models which rely on some form of long-run PPP.

The data for this study were obtained from Datastream who, in turn, use International Financial Statistics (IFS) as their original source. The exchange rates used are all bilateral U.S. dollar rates of the Canadian dollar, French Franc, German mark, Japanese yen and U.K. pound, all IFS line RF (except the U.K. which is line RH).[7] Two alternative price series were used, namely, a wholesale price index, line 63, and a consumer price index, line 64. The data period runs from January 1974 to June 1990 (all lags are generated within this sample period) and all the variables are converted into natural logarithms.

As a preliminary exercise to our multivariate cointegration tests, we investigated the orders of integration of the series using standard Augmented Dickey-Fuller statistics.[8] The estimated Dickey Fuller statistics are reported in table 1 for the levels and first and second differences of the variables. All of the exchange rate series appear to have a single unit root in that although

TABLE 1.—TESTS FOR A UNIT ROOT

	L		Δ		Δ^2	
	t_μ	t_τ	t_μ	t_τ	t_μ	t_τ
CNS	−1.89	−0.52	−3.06	−3.56	−9.22	−9.21
CNWP	−1.27	−0.54	−2.52	−2.83	−27.44	−27.56
CNCP	−1.21	−1.31	−1.90	−2.85	−7.79	−7.77
FRS	−1.37	−1.07	−10.61	−10.69	−20.49	−20.43
FRWP	0.31	−3.47	−3.72	−3.85	−23.84	−23.78
FRCP	−1.12	−1.04	−1.37	−2.03	−7.89	−7.86
GRS	−0.67	−1.25	−10.90	−10.93	−20.38	−20.32
GRWP	−0.95	−1.52	−2.79	−2.99	−9.54	−9.67
GRCP	−0.67	−1.89	−1.74	−1.94	−7.84	−7.83
JPS	−0.48	−2.08	−4.19	−4.17	−8.42	−8.41
JPWP	−1.86	−1.52	−3.46	−3.53	−5.87	−5.83
JPCP	−1.93	−2.01	−3.90	−4.38	−10.90	−11.31
UKS	−1.69	−1.19	−9.17	−9.21	−17.65	−17.60
UKWP	−2.36	−2.86	−1.91	−2.36	−6.87	−7.01
UKCP	−2.56	−2.38	−1.90	−2.76	−7.17	−7.17
USWP	1.65	−1.96	−2.68	−2.94	−7.92	−7.91
USCP	−0.71	−2.02	−1.77	−1.92	−8.32	−7.86

Note: The mnemonics in the first column have the following interpretation. The first two letters denote the country (CN = Canada, FR = France, GR = Germany, JP = Japan, UK = United Kingdom, US = United States of America) and the remaining letters indicate an exchange rate (S), a wholesale price index (WP) and a consumer price index (CP). L, Δ and Δ^2 denote, respectively, the level, first difference and second difference of the series. t_μ is the Augmented Dickey Fuller (ADF) t-ratio, and t_τ is the ADF t-ratio, with allowance for a time trend. The null hypothesis is that the series in question contains a unit root in its autoregressive representation. The 5% critical values for t_μ and t_τ are, respectively, −2.89 and −3.45.

[6] The critical values recorded in Johansen's 1988 paper are for a VAR without an intercept term or seasonal dummies. Since these were included in our empirical analysis, we used the critical values for (3) and (4) reported in Johansen and Juselius (1990).

[7] All currencies are originally expressed as the home currency per unit of foreign currency, except for the U.K. pound. The reciprocal of the published U.K. pound rate was utilised.

[8] The lag lengths for the ADF statistics were chosen to ensure that the residuals in the autoregressive representation of any one series were white noise.

we cannot reject the null of a unit root when these variables appear in levels, we can reject the null when the variables enter as first differences (deterministic time trends do not appear to be important for these variables). The picture is, however, less clear-cut for the price series. Thus, in first differences 3 of the price series (*FRWP*, *JPWP* and *JPCP*) appear stationary at the 5% level while a further 3 appear stationary at the 10% level; the remaining 6 price series require to be second differenced before the null hypothesis of non-stationarity may be rejected. On the face of it some of our price series would seem to be $I(2)$ series. Although, therefore, our price and exchange rate series may be integrated of different orders (i.e., $I(1)$ and $I(2)$), it is still possible for these variables to interact in such a way as to produce an $I(0)$ series (this would clearly not be the case if we had three variables integrated of orders $I(3)$, $I(2)$ and $I(1)$).[9] However, we present the unit root tests more for motivational purposes than as a definitive statement since it is not entirely clear that inferences from such tests are reliable in small samples; we believe that a better basis for examining the issue of unit roots in a vector of variables is given by the multivariate cointegration testing method, to which we now turn.

All of our multivariate cointegration tests were implemented using a twelfth-order lag in the underlying VAR; the VAR also contained a constant and eleven seasonal dummies. The choice of a twelfth-order system was sufficient to ensure residual whiteness and account for any seasonality not captured by the seasonal dummies. In table 2 we report our estimates of the trace and maximum eigenvalue statistics (equations (3) and (4), respectively) for our full sample period. Interestingly, all but two of the country/price combinations reveal evidence of at least one unique cointegrating vector; for the U.K. there would appear, on the basis of the trace statistic, to be two cointegrating vectors. There is an absence of cointegration for the Canadian dollar and the Japanese yen, when consumer prices are used but not when wholesale prices are utilised. Given the discussion in section II, our finding of cointegration for so many currency/price combinations would seem to be an important one. On the basis of these results, and a variety of sub-sample results,[10] we would appear to have strong support for weak-form PPP.

TABLE 2.—MULTIVARIATE COINTEGRATION RESULTS, FULL SAMPLE

		Consumer Prices TRACE	Consumer Prices λ MAX	Wholesale Prices TRACE	Wholesale Prices λ MAX
	$r \leq 2$	1.66	1.66	3.00	3.00
CN	$r \leq 1$	7.22	5.56	9.79	6.79
	$r = 0$	26.73	19.51	32.37^a	22.58^a
	$r \leq 2$	6.55	6.55	1.14	1.14
FR	$r \leq 1$	14.72	8.16	9.18	10.32
	$r = 0$	34.71^a	19.99	18.29	28.62^b
	$r \leq 2$	4.07	4.06	0.74	0.74
GR	$r \leq 1$	15.97	11.90	7.71	6.97
	$r = 0$	49.77^b	33.80^b	34.61^a	26.90^b
	$r \leq 2$	4.85	4.85	0.90	0.90
JP	$r \leq 1$	18.02	13.17	6.87	7.67
	$r = 0$	40.27^b	22.24^a	17.32	25.08^a
	$r \leq 2$	7.75	7.75	5.74	5.74
UK	$r \leq 1$	27.14^b	19.38	17.47	11.72
	$r = 0$	63.12^b	35.98^b	42.72^b	25.25^a

Note: The letters in column 1 have the same interpretation as in table 1. r denotes the number of cointegrating vectors. The 1% and 5% critical values of the maximum eigenvalue (λ *MAX*) and the *TRACE* statistics are taken from Johansen and Juselius (1990). The underlying vector autoregressions included a constant and 12 seasonal dummies.
^{a}Significant at the 5% level.
^{b}Significant at the 1% level.

In table 3a we present tests, for the full and two sub-samples, of the homogeneity hypothesis that a one per cent increase in relative prices results in an equiproportionate increase in the dollar bilateral exchange rate. The likelihood ratio statistics reported in table 3a have a chi-square distribution, with degrees of freedom equal to the number of restrictions times the number of cointegrating vectors. For the full sample, the homogeneity restrictions are rejected in all cases. For the sub-sample periods, the results are rather less clear cut. In a bid to determine if the rejection of strong-form PPP is attributable to transportation costs and trade restrictions, we estimated the homogeneity restrictions for three European cross rates implicit in our dollar bilateral (it is also expected that the construction of the price series for these cross rates are more similar).[11] The results, reported in table 3b, tend to support this hypothesis, since for three of the country/price combinations we cannot reject the strong-form version of PPP.[12]

Some supporting evidence for our finding that the homogeneity restrictions are rejected, is given in table 4, where we report the estimates of the different cointegrating vectors (all normalised on the spot exchange rate). These estimates support the restriction tests in table 3 in that although all, apart from Canadian consumer prices, have coefficients which are correctly signed, most are numerically quite far from their prior

[9] See Granger (1986), for support of this contention. See also Johansen (1992) for a discussion of how to implement multivariate cointegration tests when the set of variables under consideration consists of both $I(1)$ and $I(2)$ variables.

[10] The subsample results are not reported in the current paper, but are available from the author on request. For all of the country/subsample combinations investigated, we found evidence of at least one cointegrating vector in each case.

[11] I am grateful to an anonymous referee for suggesting this point.

[12] For all country/price combinations there was evidence of at least one cointegrating vector.

TABLE 3.—TESTS OF HOMOGENEITY RESTRICTIONS

	CPW	WPW	CP1	WP1	CP2	WP2
	a. Dollar Bilateral Rates					
CN	13.92 (0.00)	14.96 (0.00)	27.19 (0.00)	20.93 (0.00)	4.44 (0.11)	6.21 (0.04)
FR	9.28 (0.01)	14.04 (0.00)	4.52 (0.10)	NA	25.76 (0.00)	NA
GR	23.24 (0.00)	19.27 (0.00)	23.68 (0.00)	8.84 (0.01)	2.55 (0.28)	7.58 (0.02)
JP	16.11 (0.00)	11.52 (0.00)	1.82 (0.40)	14.86 (0.00)	12.92 (0.00)	22.31 (0.00)
UK	25.32 (0.00)	15.08 (0.00)	12.06 (0.02)	44.77 (0.00)	7.14 (0.02)	35.91 (0.00)
	b. European Cross Rates					
UKGR	1.97 (0.37)	6.17 (0.05)				
UKFR	2.52 (0.28)	24.69 (0.00)				
GFR	13.69 (0.00)	32.02 (0.00)				

Note: The column headings denote the price series used, as defined in table 1, a *W* after a price series name indicates that the whole sample has been used to calculate the statistics, a 1 denotes the subsample 1974, 1 to 1981, 12 and a 2 denotes the subsample 1982, 1 to 1990, 12. The row headings denote the countries as defined in table 1. The numbers not in parentheses are χ^2 statistics with degrees of freedom equal to $r \times k$, where r denotes the number of cointegrating vectors and k is the number of restrictions. The numbers in parentheses are marginal significance levels.

TABLE 4.—MAXIMUM LIKELIHOOD ESTIMATES OF NORMALISED COINTEGRATION VECTORS

	Consumer Prices		Wholesale Prices	
	β	β^*	β	β^*
CN	−6.115	6.857	1.016	−0.805
FR	4.454	−5.022	1.211	−0.799
GR	15.166	−7.825	65.984	−37.594
JP	4.268	−3.992	2.403	−1.753
UK	0.712	−1.180	0.403	−1.353

Note: β and β^* are the maximum likelihood estimates of the coefficients on, respectively, the domestic and U.S. price levels

TABLE 5.—MAXIMUM LIKELIHOOD ESTIMATES OF ADJUSTMENT SPEEDS

	Consumer Prices	Wholesale Prices
	α	α
CN	−0.021	−0.005
FR	−0.074	−0.141
GR	−0.030	0.002
JP	−0.010	−0.053
UK	−0.002	−0.011

Note: The α's denote the first element of the normalised adjustment vector.

values.[13] Strong-form ppp does not therefore appear to hold.[14]

As we have argued, our finding of cointegration for the majority of currencies indicates that some form of PPP holds; the discussion based on tables 3 and 4 indicates that it is the weak version. However, one interesting issue concerns how rapidly long-run PPP is attained. Our multivariate cointegration estimates give insight into this question since they provide estimates of the α matrix, defined in Johansen (1988). The coefficients of this matrix can be interpreted as the weights with which PPP disequilibrium is corrected in each of our three equations.[15] In table 5 the α's from the equation for the change in the exchange rate for the full sample period are reported, and all, apart from German wholesale prices, are negative. The adjustment speeds tend to vary across countries. For example, on the basis of the consumer price indices France has the most rapid adjustment speed (around 7% of any deviation from PPP is extinguished in the current month) whilst the UK has the lowest.

Summary and Conclusions

In this paper we have re-examined the purchasing power parity concept using data from the recent experience with floating exchange rates. In particular, we utilised the recently developed multivariate cointegration methodology to test what we have referred to as weak-form and strong-form PPP. We have demonstrated, *inter alia*, that weak form PPP receives very strong support from the data, whilst strong-form PPP receives practically no support. Our finding of weak-form PPP, that the long-run nominal exchange rate is tied down by relative prices, is one which contrasts with much previous research but confirms the recent

[13] An anonymous referee has suggested that the implausible point estimates are the result of explosive residuals. The idea is that although we can reject the null of unit roots in the residuals from our VARs (i.e., the null of no cointegration) in most cases, this does not rule out the possibility of a root greater than unity. In order to shed some light on this issue, we plotted the residuals from the cointegrating relationships and these suggested that the residuals were not explosive (due to space constraints these plots are not reported in the paper but are available from the author on request).

[14] Since a number of the β coefficients seem to be equal and opposite in sign, we also constructed likelihood ratios to formally test the hypothesis that the sum of β plus β^* was zero. Only in the case of France (for both measures of the price series) were we unable to reject this hypothesis at the 5% level.

[15] Because of space constraints we do not report the adjustment coefficients for the implied price equations.

work of Huizinga (1987) and Abuaf and Jorion (1990). The tide would seem to be turning in favour of some form of purchasing power parity!

REFERENCES

Abuaf, N., and P. Jorion, "Purchasing Power Parity in the Long-run," *The Journal of Finance* 45 (1990), 157–173.

Adler, M., and B. Lehmann, "Deviations from Purchasing Power Parity in the Long-run," *The Journal of Finance* 5 (381) (1983), 1471–1487.

Choudry, T., R. McNown and M. Wallace, "Purchasing Power Parity and the Canadian Float in the 1950's," this REVIEW 73 (3) (1991), 558–562.

Enders, W., "ARIMA and Cointegration Tests of PPP Under Fixed and Flexible Exchange Rates," this REVIEW 70 (Aug. 1988), 505–508.

Engle, Robert, and C. W. J. Granger, "Cointegration and Error Correction: Representation, Estimation and Testing," *Econometrica* 55 (1987), 251–276.

Fuller, Wayne, A., *Introduction to Statistical Time Series* (New York: Wiley, 1976).

Granger, C. W. J., "Developments in the Study of Cointegrated Economic Variables," *Oxford Bulletin of Economics and Statistics* 48 (3) (1986), 213–228.

Hallwood, P., and Ronald MacDonald, *International Money: Theory, Evidence and Institutions* (Oxford: Blackwell, 1986).

Huizinga, J., "An Empirical Investigation of the Long-run Behaviour of Real Exchange Rates," *Carnegie Rochester Conference Series on Public Policy* 27 (1987), 149–214.

Johansen, Søren, "Statistical Analysis of Cointegration Vectors," *Journal of Economic Dynamics and Control* 12 (1988), 231–254.

———, "Testing Weak Exogeneity and the Order of Cointegration in UK Money Demand Data," *Journal of Policy Modeling* 14 (1992), 313–334.

Johansen, Søren, and K. Juselius, "Maximum Likelihood Estimation and Inference on Cointegration—With Applications to the Demand for Money," *Oxford Bulletin of Economics and Statistics* 52 (1990), 169–210.

MacDonald, Ronald, "Do Deviations of the Real Effective Exchange Rate Follow a Random Walk?," *Economic Notes* 14 (1) (1985), 63–69.

———, *Floating Exchange Rates: Theories and Evidence* (London: Unwin Hyman, 1988).

Officer, C. H., "The Purchasing Power Parity Theory of Exchange Rates: A Review Article," *IMF Staff Papers* 23 (1976), 1–60.

Patel, J., "Purchasing Power Parity as a Long-Run Relation," *Journal of Applied Econometrics* (1990), 367–379.

Roll, R., "Violations of Purchasing Power Parity and Their Implications for Efficient International Commodity Markets," in M. Sarnat and G. Szego (eds), *International Finance and Trade* 1 (Cambridge, MA: Ballinger, 1979).

Taylor, Mark P., "An Empirical Examination of Long-run Purchasing Power Parity Using Cointegration Techniques," *Applied Economics* 20 (1988), 1369–1382.

[9]

ELSEVIER

Economics Letters 50 (1996) 7–11

economics letters

Panel unit root tests and real exchange rates

Ronald MacDonald

Department of Economics, University of Strathclyde, Glasgow G4 0LN, UK

Received 6 February 1995; accepted 16 April 1995

Abstract

Using two real exchange rate data sets, we implement a new form of unit root test. In particular, we use a panel unit root test to jointly test for a unit root in a group of OECD real exchange rates for the recent floating experience. In contrast to many other unit root tests using a similar data set, we are able to reject the null hypothesis of a unit root.

Keywords: Exchange rates; Panel unit roots

JEL classification: C12; C23; F31

1. Introduction

Testing for a unit root in real exchange rates has become a popular pastime.[1] The existence of such a root has important implications for the 'traditional' interpretation of purchasing power parity (PPP)[2] and also for many theoretical models of the balance of payments and exchange rate. Thus, for example, if a real exchange rate does indeed contain a unit root, as it should according to proponents of the efficient markets PPP (EMPPP) (see, for example, Adler and Lehman, 1983; Roll, 1979), it means that a current shock to the real rate is permanent, whereas a proponent of traditional PPP would posit that such shocks will only have a transitory effect and therefore the real rate should be mean-reverting. Further, the existence of a unit root in a real exchange rate has unpleasant consequences for the balance of payments: from a position of current account balance a real appreciation of the exchange rate will, ceteris paribus, generate a permanent deficit on the current account (necessitating a permanent capital account surplus).

[1] Surveys of this literature are to be found in Breur (1994), Froot and Rogoff (1995) and MacDonald (1995).

[2] By which we mean the view that asserts that PPP holds as a long-run equilibrium relationship, although there may be deviations in the short run.

0165-1765/96/$12.00 © 1996 Elsevier Science S.A. All rights reserved

SSDI 0165-1765(95)00730-X

Generally speaking, when considering data for the recent floating experience (i.e. post 1973), researchers have been unable to reject the null of a unit root (see, inter alia, Meese and Rogoff, 1988; Mark, 1990; Edison and Pauls, 1993). One response to such rejection has been to say that the tests do not encompass a sufficiently long time-span to capture the mean reversion necessary to reject the null hypothesis. Therefore, researchers have advocated using data sets with a much longer time-span than the recent float and, additionally, using low frequency data (i.e. annual data) (see, inter alia, Frankel, 1988; Kim, 1990). One advantage of using annual data is that these have a relatively high signal-to-noise ratio compared with monthly data (see Shiller and Perron, 1985). Tests that have used long time-spans of annual data have been able to reject the null of a random walk. However, we would argue it is still of interest to determine whether exchange rates are mean-reverting for the recent floating period.

In this paper, we offer a new test of the unit root hypothesis in real exchange rates, based on two annual data sets for the recent floating experience.[3] The novelty in our present work is that we increase the span of the data by jointly testing for a unit root across a large number of currencies; i.e. we increase the power of the test by pooling across currencies rather than extending the time-series dimensions of the data set. The structure of the paper is as follows. In the next section, we briefly outline the method used to construct our panel unit root tests. In Section 3, we note our data sources and present some standard unit root tests alongside our panel unit root results.

2. Panel unit root tests

The idea of increasing the data span of, say, an annual time-series data set using pooled/cross-section methods has been proposed in the context of unit root testing by Quah (1994) and Levin and Lin (1995). The latter authors, for example, demonstrate that implementing a unit root test on a pooled cross-section data set, rather than performing separate unit root tests for each individual series, can provide 'dramatic improvements in statistical power'. The Levin–Lin test is designed to evaluate the null hypothesis that each individual series is I(1), versus the alternative hypothesis that all the series considered as a panel are stationary. The Levin–Lin test may be viewed as especially attractive, since it facilitates the incorporation of a wide variety of individual-specific, or heterogeneous, effects under the null. Their testing method produces a single *t*-ratio for the panel and this statistic is shown to have standard normal distribution. We propose using the method of Levin and Lin to test for the existence of a unit root in two real exchange rate panel data sets.

The method of Levin and Lin (1995) may be briefly summarised as consisting of the following stages. Under the null hypothesis, it is assumed that each country's real exchange

[3] Using traditional panel methods, MacDonald (1988) demonstrates, with annual data from the recent float for the US dollar bilateral exchange rates of the pound sterling, French franc, German mark, Japanese yen and Swiss franc, that the hypothesis of relative PPP cannot be rejected (in the sense that the slope coefficient from an equation of the exchange rate change on the relative price change is insignificantly different from unity).

rate contains a unit root and the first difference of the real exchange rate follows a stationary ARMA process. Under the alternative hypothesis, all the real exchange rates, taken as a group, are assumed to be stationary. Within the class of stationary ARMA models, Levin and Lin consider three variants (Models 1–3), each distinguished by the deterministic variables included: in Model 1, no deterministic variables are included; in Model 2, a constant is included; in Model 3, the deterministic list includes both a constant and a time trend. The null hypothesis may be tested against the given alternatives, by performing the following regression:

$$\breve{e}_{it} = \delta \breve{v}_{it-1} + \breve{\varepsilon}_{it}, \tag{1}$$

where $\breve{e}_{it}$ and $\breve{v}_{it-1}$ are normalised residuals constructed from two auxiliary regressions.[4] Under the null hypothesis that $\delta_i = 0$, for all $i = 1, \ldots, N$, the asymptotic theory of Levin and Lin indicates that the regression t-statistic on δ (t_δ), has a standard normal distribution for Model 1, but diverges to negative infinity for Models 2 and 3. However, Levin and Lin provide a corrected value of t_δ, which we label At_δ, which is shown to have a standard normal distribution under the null.

3. Data sources, unit root tests and conclusions

The data used in this paper are annual, and consist of 17 OECD real rates based on a wholesale price index (WPI), and 23 OECD real rates based on a consumer price index (CPI), all over the period 1973–1992.[5] In our empirical tests, all the exchange rates are expressed as natural logarithms. As a preliminary exercise, we estimated standard augmented Dickey–Fuller (ADF) test statistics for each real exchange rate, using the two annual data sets. These results are presented in Table 1 and indicate very little evidence of rejection of the null of a unit root; using a 5% critical value there are three real exchange rates, based on

[4] In particular,

$$\hat{e}_{it} = \Delta q_{it} - \sum_{L=1}^{p} \hat{\pi}_{iL} \Delta q_{it-L} - \hat{\alpha}_{mi} d_{mt}$$

and

$$\hat{v}_{it-1} = q_{it-1} - \sum_{L=1}^{p_i} \hat{\phi}_{iL} \Delta q_{it-L} - \hat{\alpha}_{mi} d_{mt},$$

where q_{it} denotes a real exchange rate for country i, Δ is the first difference operator, d represents a vector of deterministic variables (defined by Models 1–3), $\breve{e}_{it}$ and $\breve{v}_{it-1}$ are the normalised equivalents of $\hat{e}_{it}$ and $\hat{v}_{it-1}$, where the normalisation consists of scaling $\hat{e}_{it}$ and $\hat{v}_{it-1}$ by the standard error from the regression, $\hat{e}_{it} = \delta \hat{v}_{it-1} + \hat{e}_{it}$ (such normalisation allows for the existence of heterogeneity across real rates). A total of $N\tilde{T}$ observations are used in regression (1), where $\tilde{T} = (T - \bar{p} - 1)$ is the average number of observations for each real exchange rate in the panel and $\bar{p} = 1/N \sum_{i=1}^{N} p_i$ is the average lag length from an individual augmented Dickey–Fuller regression and N denotes the number of real exchange rates.

[5] The number of currencies entering each data set are determined by the number of OECD countries with consistent price data for the recent floating experience. All data are sourced from the IMF's International Financial Statistics CD-Rom disc (December 1993).

Table 1
Augmented Dickey–Fuller statistics

	WPI		CPI			WPI		CPI	
	t_μ	t_τ	t_μ	t_τ		t_μ	t_τ	t_μ	t_τ
Australia	−7.81	−11.37	−2.63	−2.54	Israel	−1.54	−1.90	−1.32	−1.74
Austria	−0.01	−1.08	−2.10	−2.01	Italy	−0.32	−1.83	−1.51	−1.62
Belgium	−0.25	−0.99	−1.67	−1.99	Japan	−0.61	−3.33	−1.75	−2.34
Canada	−2.06	−3.25	−2.58	−2.49	Luxembourg	−1.86	−1.50	–	–
CIP	−0.16	1.22	−2.17	−2.09	Malta	−1.05	−0.67	–	–
Denmark	−0.45	−2.59	−2.88	−2.67	Netherlands	2.18	−0.70	−1.76	−1.69
Finland	−1.96	−1.98	−2.68	−1.71	Norway	−1.31	−3.38	−2.60	−2.50
France	−2.09	−2.00	–	–	Portugal	−1.54	−3.07	–	–
Germany	−0.71	−2.09	−1.66	−4.83	Spain	−3.54	−3.42	−1.89	−1.90
Greece	−4.62	−4.22	−4.83	−4.50	Sweden	−0.14	−2.62	−2.65	−2.58
Iceland	−1.41	−2.52	–	–	Switzerland	−1.71	−1.63	−1.95	−1.87
Ireland	−1.54	−1.90	−2.39	−2.45	UK	−2.07	−1.62	−2.11	−2.39

Notes: The numbers are estimated augmented Dickey–Fuller statistics calculated from an autoregression for the real exchange rate; t_μ and t_τ indicate, respectively, the inclusion of a constant and constant plus time trend in the autoregression. WPI and CPI indicate, respectively, that a wholesale and consumer price measure have been used in the construction of a real exchange rate. The 1% and 5% critical values of t_μ and t_τ are: −3.81 and −3.02 (t_μ); −4.50 and −3.69 (t_τ) (Source: MacKinnon, 1991).

WPIs, that are stationary around a constant (Australian dollar, Greek drachma and Spanish peseta) and two CPI-based real rates that are stationary (the Greek drachma is again stationary around a constant and the German mark appears stationary around a trend). Our tests for a unit root in individual real exchange rates for the recent float are consistent with other tests for this period using higher frequency data (i.e. monthly) (see, for example, Mark, 1990).

In Table 2, we present our estimates of At_δ, the corrected t-ratio from (1), calculated for Model 2 and Model 3.[6,7] The results are, we believe, of considerable interest, since they

Table 2
Panel unit root tests

	Model 2		Model 3	
	t_δ	At_δ	t_δ	At_δ
CPI	−9.91*	−3.30*	−12.29*	−2.23*
WPI	−9.86*	−4.35*	−12.25*	−3.65*

Notes: With regard to terms not previously defined, the numbers in the columns labelled t_δ and At_δ are, respectively, the unadjusted and adjusted (using formula (16) of Levin and Lin, 1995) t-ratios on δ in Eq. (1). The 'Model 2' and 'Model 3' labels denote the deterministic specification used to calculate t_δ and At_δ. The statistic At_δ is distributed asymptotically as a standard normal variable. An asterisk denotes significance at the 5% level.

[6] These estimates were computed using the panel unit root programme kindly provided by Alex Hoffmeister.
[7] We have not considered Model 1, because we do not believe that imposing a zero mean on the time-series properties of real exchange rates is an attractive proposition.

indicate that, regardless of the chosen deterministic specification, or the price measure used to construct real exchange rates, real exchange rates are stationary around a constant (and a constant plus time trend). Therefore, these results parallel recent work using long runs of annual data: when the span of the data set used to construct real exchange rate unit root tests is increased, the null hypothesis that real exchange rates contain a unit root is easily rejected. Here, though, we can reject the null across all the key currencies for the recent floating experience. Our result may be interpreted as a further blow against efficient markets PPP and a confirmation of a more traditional form of PPP.

Acknowledgements

I am indebted to David Coe for bringing this test to my attention, Alex Hoffmeister for the use of his panel unit root programme and Ian Marsh for assistance with data management.

References

Adler, M. and B. Lehmann, 1983, Deviations from purchasing power parity in the long run, The Journal of Finance 38, 1471–1483.

Breur, J., 1994, Purchasing power parity: A survey of and challenge to recent literature, in: J. Williamson, ed., Fundamental equilibrium exchange rates, in press.

Edison, H. and D. Pauls, 1993, A re-assessment of the relationship between real exchange rates and real interest rates: 1974–1990, Journal of Monetary Economics, 165–188.

Frankel, J. A., 1988, International capital flows and domestic economic policies, in: M. Feldstein, ed., The United States in the world economy (Chicago University Press, Chicago).

Froot, K. A. and K. Rogoff, 1995, Perspectives on PPP and long-run real exchange rates, in: G. Grossman and K. Rogoff, eds., Handbook of international economics, Vol. 3 (North-Holland, Amsterdam).

Kim, Y., 1990, Purchasing power parity in the long-run: A cointegration approach, Journal of Money Credit and Banking 22, no. 4, 491–503.

Levin, A. and C.-F. Lin, 1995, Unit root tests in panel data: Asymptotic and finite sample properties, Journal of Econometrics in press.

MacDonald, R., 1988, Purchasing power parity: Some 'long run' evidence from the recent float, De Economist 136, no. 2, 239–252.

MacDonald, R., 1995, Long-run exchange rate modelling: A survey of the recent evidence, Working Paper WP/95/14, International Monetary Fund.

MacKinnon, J., 1991, Critical values for co-integration tests, in: R.F. Engle and C.W.J. Granger, eds., Long-run economic relationships (Oxford University Press, Oxford).

Mark, N., 1990. Real and nominal exchange rates in the long-run: An empirical investigation, Journal of International Economics, 115–136.

Meese, R. and K. Rogoff, 1988, Was it real? The exchange rate–interest rate differential relation over the modern floating-rate period, The Journal of Finance, XLIII, no. 4.

Quah, D., 1994, Exploiting cross section variation for unit root inference in dynamic data, Economics Letters 44, 9–19.

Roll, R., 1979, Violations of purchasing power parity and their implications for efficient international commodity markets, in: M. Sarnat and G. Szego, eds., International Finance and Trade 1 (Ballinger, Cambridge, MA).

Shiller, R. and P. Perron, 1985, Testing the random walk hypothesis: Power versus frequency of observation, Economics Letters 18, 381–386.

Available online at www.sciencedirect.com

SCIENCE DIRECT

ELSEVIER

Japan and the World Economy
16 (2004) 17–34

Japan and the WORLD ECONOMY

www.elsevier.com/locate/econbase

International parity relationships between the USA and Japan

Katarina Juselius[a,*], Ronald MacDonald[b]

[a]*Institute of Economics, University of Copenhagen, Studiestraede 6, Copenhagen K 1455, Denmark*
[b]*Department of Economics, University of Strathclyde, Strathclyde, Denmark*

Received 7 July 2000; received in revised form 11 November 2002; accepted 3 December 2002

Abstract

Based on multivariate cointegration analysis we show that key parity conditions between the USA and Japan do not hold as stationary relations and that this is related to the nonstationarity of the real exchange rate. The latter seems almost exclusively to be related to similar nonstationary movements in interest rates. We obtain strong empirical results suggesting a reversal of the standard linkages, as predicted by the term structure of interest rates and the Fisher condition, between short and long interest rates and interest rates and inflation. Our findings may be important for the conduct of monetary policy, which is usually thought to be transmitted through short-term interest rates. Altogether, the empirical results suggest that it is agents' behavior in the foreign exchange market, rather than in the goods market, which is crucial for the determination of the exchange rate.
© 2003 Elsevier Science B.V. All rights reserved.

JEL classification: E31; E43; F31; F32

Keywords: PPP; UIP; Fisher parity; Term spread; Cointegration

1. Introduction

The introduction of a common European currency in 1999 is likely to have significantly changed the working of the international monetary system. In order to evaluate the future impact of the new currency area it is important to have a good empirical understanding of how the international transmission mechanisms worked in the preceding system, namely the post-Bretton Woods system. In this regard it is of particular interest to study how the external value of the yen and euro area worked relative to the dollar during the recent floating experience. This euro–dollar relationship was addressed in Juselius and

* Corresponding author. Tel.: +45-3532-3068.
E-mail address: katarina.juselius@econ.ku.dk (K. Juselius).

0922-1425/$ – see front matter © 2003 Elsevier Science B.V. All rights reserved.
doi:10.1016/S0922-1425(03)00003-3

MacDonald (2000), hereafter JMa, where international parity conditions—purchasing power parity (PPP), uncovered interest rate parity (UIP), the term structure (TS), and the Fisher parities—were studied for the USA and Germany, where the latter country represented the euro area. The purpose of this paper is to focus on the international parity conditions between the US and Japan, building on the findings in JMa.

The basic empirical design adopted in JMa will be repeated here for the US–Japanese case. This approach has the additional advantage of testing the empirical findings in JMa as prior hypotheses. Hence, we will frequently refer to the results of JMa when interpreting the empirical results. Nevertheless, we will also try to empirically isolate those relationships which seem unique for the US–Japanese case. As we shall see, there are some important differences between the results for the US–Japanese and US–German systems.

An important finding in JMa was that the very slow, though significant, price adjustment towards sustainable levels of real exchange rates, was compensated by corresponding changes in the spread of the long-term bond rates. Related to this was the strong empirical support for the weak exogeneity of the long-term bond rates, signifying the importance of the large US trade deficits (i.e. the low levels of US savings) and, hence, their linkage to international finance. The results pointed to a reversal of the standard linkages contained in the term structure of interest rates and in the Fisher relationship. In terms of the former, we found that the linkage ran from the long to short end of the market, while in terms of the Fisher condition the linkage was from nominal interest rates to the inflation rate.

These results should be of concern for the conduct of monetary policy as the transmission mechanism in normally thought to run from the short end of the yield curve to the long end. In the words of Blinder (1997, p. 242):

> Unfortunately the model miserably fails a variety of empirical tests (see Campbell, 1995). Economists are thus in desperate need of a better model of the term structure. More than academic completeness is at stake here, for the absence of a usable term structure severely handicaps the conduct of monetary policy, which works its will on the economy through short-term rates of interest rates.

Clearly if one of the important conditions of monetary policy has changed, prompting for a modified theoretical explanation, then it seems likely that we would find that other relationships do not work according to theory either. Since the theoretical basis of international macroeconomics builds strongly on these parity conditions, one would expect the international transmission mechanisms (nominal as well as real) to be significantly different from standard theoretical assumptions. This was also the conclusion in JMa where the empirical findings generated a number of new hypotheses which we will here confront against new data.

The outline of the remainder of this paper is as follows. In Section 2 we present a motivational overview of some international parity relationships which feature prominently in our empirical analysis. Section 3 defines the statistical model and the data and discusses the 'general-to-specific' approach in econometric modelling versus the 'specific-to-general' approach in the choice of information. Section 4 discusses a small model comprising inflation rates, real exchange rates, and bond yields and presents stationarity tests of the hypothetical parity relationships. Section 5 extends the small VAR model to include libor interes rates and discusses the choice of cointegration rank and its implications for the economic analysis. Section 6 discusses long-run weak exogeneity in both the small and large models and its implications for long-run feedback and its reversal. Section 7 presents a fully identified structure of long-run parity relations and the short-run adjustment structure. Section 8 contains the final impact of permanent shocks to the variables of the system and Section 9 discusses the role of the short-term interest rates in the large model. Section 10 summarizes the findings and concludes. To conserve space we refer from time to time to the discussion paper version of this paper (Juselius and MacDonald, 2002, hereafter JMb) which contains a comprehensive range of figures and a longer discussion of the empirical results and econometric methods used here.

2. Price adjustment, interest rates and exchange rates: a motivational discussion

The results in JMa strongly rejected the stationarity hypothesis of individual parity conditions for the US–Germany. However, when the conditions were modelled interdependently, stationarity was recovered. Our key finding was that the nonstationarity of the 'simple' parity relationships was primarily related to the nonstationarity of the real exchange rate and the long-term bond rate differential. A hypothetical explanation is that the lack of (or very slow) adjustment to a stationary purchasing power parity (PPP) steady-state has contributed to the large trade deficits between the US and Europe versus Japan. The financing of the latter has caused the long-term bond yield differential to move in a correspondingly nonstationary manner. Thus, the theoretical assumption of stationary parity conditions appears to be a special case of a more general formulation allowing for persistent deviations from steady-state and, hence, market failure in a simple model framework.

JMa demonstrated that the stationarity assumption underlying the theoretical parity conditions is consistent with two common stochastic trends: a general price trend reflecting permanent shocks to demand and supply, and a trend reflecting differences in policy between the two countries. This simple model did not obtain any empirical support and the theoretical assumption of two common driving trends had to be replaced by the empirically consistent finding of four common trends. Hypothetically the two additional trends were assumed to be: (1) a trend describing relative national savings behavior and (2) a 'financial/safe haven' trend capturing the role of the dollar as a world reserve currency.

The strong-form of the purchasing power parity (PPP) condition is captured by:

$$P = P^*S,$$

and the departure from the PPP parity by:

$$ppp_t = p_t - p_t^* - s_t, \tag{1}$$

where p_t is the log of the domestic price level, P_t, p_t^* the log of the foreign price level, P_t^*, and s_t denotes the log of the spot exchange rate, S_t, measured as yen/\$. Strong-form PPP requires that the ppp_t term (or, equivalently, the negative of the real exchange rate) is a stationary, steady-state relation implying that the spot exchange rate should mirror the development of relative prices. As is common for other currencies, a visual inspection of the spot rate/relative price relationship for Japan, reported in the upper panel of Fig. 1, indicates that this is not the case.

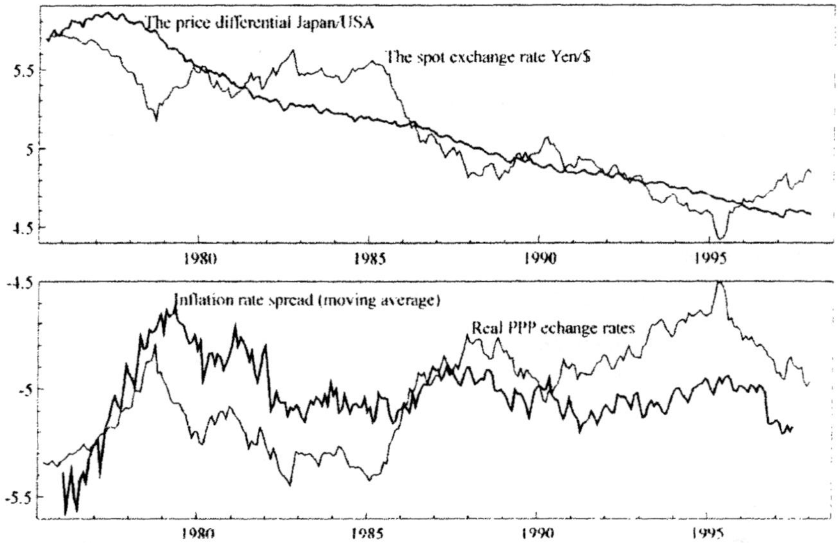

Fig. 1. The Japan-US price differential and the spot exchange rate (upper panel) and the *ppp* term and the inflation rate differential (lower panel).

If adjustment towards strong-form PPP takes place exclusively in the goods market we would have the following adjustment relations, for, respectively, home and foreign inflation:

$$\Delta p_t = \omega_1(\Delta p_t^* + \Delta s_t) - \omega_2 ppp_{t-1} + v_t, \tag{2}$$

$$\Delta p_t^* = \omega_3(\Delta p_t - \Delta s_t) + \omega_4 ppp_{t-1} + v_t, \tag{3}$$

and the adjustment for the spot exchange rate would be:

$$\Delta s_t = \omega_5(\Delta p_t - \Delta p_t^*) + \omega_6 ppp_{t-1} + v_t, \tag{4}$$

where v_t is a generic stochastic error component. We assume that (4) can be used to form expectations of the future change in the period-t exchange rate:

$$E_t^e \Delta_l s_{t+l} = \omega_5 E_t^e(\Delta_l p_t - \Delta_l p_t^*) + \omega_6 E_t^e(p_{t+l} - p_{t+l}^* - s_{t+l}), \tag{5}$$

where E_t^e stands for an economic expectation in a wide sense. For example we do not assume model based rational expectations, but allow agents to form incomplete knowledge expectations (Frydman and Goldberg, 2002). We also assume that $\{E_t^e(\Delta_l p_t - \Delta_l p_t^*) - (\Delta_l p_t - \Delta_l p_t^*)\} \sim I(0)$ and $E_t^e(p_{t+l} - p_{t+l}^* - s_{t+l}) - (p_{t+l} - p_{t+l}^* - s_{t+l}) \sim I(0)$, i.e. forecast errors do not drift off systematically. Furthermore, if $\{((\Delta_l p_t - \Delta_l p_t^*)/l) - (\Delta p_t - \Delta p_t^*)\} \sim I(0)$ and $\{(p_{t+l} - p_{t+l}^* - s_{t+l}) - (p_t - p_t^* - s_t)\} \sim I(0)$, then

$$E_t^e \Delta_l s_{t+l} = \omega_5(\Delta p_t - \Delta p_t^*) + \omega_6(p_t - p_t^* - s_t) + v_t, \tag{6}$$

and the expected change in the future spot exchange rate can be expressed as a function of the present deviation from PPP and the inflation rate differential at time t.

A connection between PPP, which arises from conditions in goods markets, and uncovered interest rate parity (UIP), which arises from conditions in capital markets, can be found by first expressing the expected change in the exchange rate in terms of the long-term interest rate spread:

$$E_t^e \Delta_l s_{t+l} = i_t^l - i_t^{l*} + v_t, \tag{7}$$

and then inserting (6) in (7) we obtain:

$$(i_t^l - i_t^{l*}) = \omega_5(\Delta p_t - \Delta p_t^*) + \omega_6(p_t - p_t^* - s_t) + v_t. \tag{8}$$

We now have a relationship combining the two parity conditions, where $\omega_5 = 1$ delivers a relationship between real interest rates and ppp_t.

The condition for v_t to be stationary in (8), when ppp_t is nonstationary, is that the stochastic trend movements in the *ppp* term are compensated by similar movements in either the bond rate differential, the inflation rate differential, or both. The lower panel of Fig. 1 gives the graphs of ppp_t together with the inflation rate differential.

From (4) we see that ppp_t and the US–Japan inflation rate differential should move in opposite directions to secure steady-state behavior. When this is not the case (8) predicts a compensating movement in the US–Japan bond rate differential. Fig. 1 shows that the inflation rate differential has more often moved in line with the *ppp* term rather than in the opposite direction. But, contrary to the US–German case, the *ppp* term and the bond rate differential have not moved as closely together as expected. This is particularly so at the beginning of the sample period. The extended empirical analysis reported in JMb interpreted this adjustment as a transition towards a more market determined steady-state.

Using a similar line of argument to that used to derive (8) we can obtain the following relationship between the short spread, the inflation rate spread and the *ppp* term:[1]

$$(i_t^s - i_t^{s*}) = \omega_7(\Delta p_t - \Delta p_t^*) + \omega_8(p_t - p_t^* - s_t) + v_t.$$

The term structure relationship between short- and long-term interest rates predicts that short rates 'drive' long rates. The standard expectations model of the term structure implies that the term spread (TS), or yield gap, should be stationary. The TS is defined as:

$$(i_t^l - i_t^s) = v_t. \tag{9}$$

However, in the context of an open economy the stationarity assumption of (9) is based on the *ceteris paribus* assumption of a stationary real exchange rate. Since ppp_t behaves in a nonstationary manner in our sample period we do not expect the TS to hold empirically as a stationary relationship.

Finally, the simple Fisher condition states that the real interest rate r_t is constant or at least stationary:

$$r_t = (i_t - E_t^e \Delta p_{t+1}) + v_t. \tag{10}$$

[1] As in the case of long rates, there is no clear evidence of comovements between libor rates and the *ppp* term.

Again, the stationarity of (10) is based on the *ceteris paribus* assumption of a stationary real exchange rate. When this is not the case it is an empirical question whether real interest rate parity holds between the home and foreign country or whether the parity condition is related to ppp_t:

$$(i_t - E_t^e \Delta p_{t+1}) - (i_t^* - E_t^e \Delta p_{t+1}^*) + \omega_9 \, ppp_t + v_t. \tag{11}$$

The purpose of the econometric analyses in Sections 4–6 is to shed further light on the linkages between these relationships in an open economy context using data for Japan and the United States.

3. The econometric approach

The potential interdependence of the parity conditions, discussed in the last section, requires a joint modelling approach of all the relevant variables, altogether seven in our final 'large' model. The statistical approach is based on the 'general-to-specific' principle discussed in Juselius (1992) and Hendry and Mizon (1993). The baseline is the unrestricted VAR model with a constant term, μ, seasonal dummies, S_t, and intervention dummies, D_t:

$$\begin{aligned} \Delta x_t &= \Gamma_1 \Delta x_{t-1} + \alpha\beta' x_{t-2} + \mu + \Phi_1 S_t + \Phi_2 D_t + \varepsilon_t, \\ \varepsilon_t &\sim N_p(0, \Sigma), \; t = 1, \ldots, T \end{aligned} \tag{12}$$

where $\{\Gamma_1, \alpha, \beta, \mu, \Phi_1, \Phi_2, \Sigma\}$ are unrestricted. In this form the model is heavily over-parameterized and represents a convenient way of describing the covariances of the data rather than a meaningful empirical model. The idea is to sequentially test and impose data consistent restrictions on the VAR (such as reduced rank restrictions, zero parameter restrictions, and other linear or nonlinear parameter restrictions) so that the end result is a more parsimonious model with economically interpretable coefficients.

The vector x_t is defined by Δp_t = the Japanese inflation rate; Δp_t^* = the US inflation rate; i_t^l = the Japanese 10 years bond yield; i_t^{l*} = the US 10 years bond yield; i_t^s = the Japanese libor rate; i_t^{s*} = the US libor rate; $ppp_t = p_t - p_t^* - s_t$, where p_t = the log of the Japanese price index (CPI), p_t^* = the log of the US price index (CPI), s_t = the log of the spot exchange rate, defined as yen/\$. All variables, apart from the interest rates (which appear as fractions) are in natural logarithms and the exchange rate is the end of period rate. All variables have been extracted from the International Monetary Funds CD-Rom disc.

The sample covers the post-Bretton Woods period of flexible dollar rates. It starts in 1975:7 after the first turbulent years following the first oil shock and ends in 1998:1, 1 year before the start of the EMU regime. To achieve comparability the empirical design follows JMa as closely as possible. Because the Japanese market for 3 months treasury bill rates was very thin and regulated up to the 1980s we use libor rates. Since the libor rates have only been available since 1978:9 the sample period is, therefore, slightly shorter in the large system containing all seven variables.

The analysis of a system containing seven variables is econometrically quite demanding and, as in JMa, a specific-to-general approach in the choice of variables will be adopted: real exchange rates, inflation rates, and long-term bond rates will first be analyzed in a five-dimensional system and then extended by the inclusion of the libor rates. The motivation for first including the long-term bond rates is that they are likely to be more closely related to the long-term movements in real exchange rates.

The advantage of this approach is two-fold. First, the identification of long-run relations is facilitated by building upon the cointegration results from the smaller model. Since the cointegration property is invariant to extensions of the information set, the finding of a particular cointegration relationship in a small set of variables, should also hold in an extended data set. Second, the gradual expansion of the information set facilitates an analysis of the *ceteris paribus* assumption and its importance for the empirical analysis of the smaller set of variables. By this procedure the impact of the short-term rates on the system is likely to be more transparent. The change in the cointegration rank and in weak exogeneity status are particularly informative in this respect.

4. The VAR model for inflation rates, bond rates and *ppp*[2]

From an econometric perspective the first step of the empirical analysis should be based on a VAR analysis of prices, p_t and p_t^*, the spot exchange rate, s_t, and long-term bond rates, i_t^l and i_t^{l*}. However, a visual inspection of the inflation rates, and a formal $I(2)$ analysis, suggested that prices are $I(2)$. Furthermore, the exchange rate was also found to be borderline $I(2)$. Therefore, following JMa, we base our subsequent VAR analyses exclusively on inflation rates and the real exchange rate, rather than on prices and the spot exchange rate. The VAR model (12) is first estimated for the smaller set of variables:

$$x_t' = [(\Delta p_t, \Delta p_t^*, ppp_t, i_t^l, i_t^{l*}]. \tag{13}$$

To achieve approximate normality we controlled for the largest intervention outliers[3] by including the following dummies in the model:

$$D_t' = [D78.11_t, DI80.02_t, D80.05_t, D80.07_t, D81.11_t, DI82.01_t], \tag{14}$$

where $Dxx.yy_t = 1$ in $19xx{:}yy$, 0 otherwise, $DIxx.yy_t = 1$ in $19xx{:}yy$, -1 in $19xx{:}yy + 1$, 0 otherwise.

A variety of multivariate and univariate misspecification tests found no evidence of residual autocorrelation, some evidence of ARCH effects but violation of multivariate normality as a result of excess kurtosis. Since cointegration estimates have been shown to be robust to moderate deviations from the latter (Gonzalo, 1994) we disregarded this problem. Detailed test results and discussions can be found in JMb.

The trace test, reported in Table 2 in the next section, supports the choice of $r = 2$ and, hence, $p - r = 3$ common trends. Based on LR tests (Johansen and Juselius, 1992) we found that none of the variables could be excluded from the long-run cointegration space

[2] All cointegration analyses have been performed with the program package CATS for RATS, Hansen and Juselius (1995), while the graphs and the short-run model with GiveWin and PcFiml, Doornik and Hendry (1998).

[3] If a residual larger than $|3.3\sigma_\varepsilon|$ corresponds to a known event, we included it in the information set as a dummy variable.

Table 1
Cointegration properties of the parity conditions in the small model

	The restricted relation $(H_1\varphi_1)'$						
	Δp_1	$\Delta p*$	i^l	i^{l*}	*ppp*	$\chi^2(v)$	*P*-value
$\mathcal{H}_1$	1	−1	0	0	0	10.0 (3)	0.02
$\mathcal{H}_2$	0	0	1	−1	0	34.1 (3)	0.00
$\mathcal{H}_3$	1	0	−1	0	0	21.6 (3)	0.00
$\mathcal{H}_4$	0	1	0	−1	0	18.1 (3)	0.00
$\mathcal{H}_5$	1	0.1	−1	−0.1	0	12.6 (2)	0.00
$\mathcal{H}_6$	1	−1	−0.2	0.2	0	3.6 (2)	**0.16**
$\mathcal{H}_7$	1	−1	0	0	0.148	8.9 (2)	0.01
$\mathcal{H}_8$	0	0	−1	1	−0.046	34.1 (2)	0.00
$\mathcal{H}_9$	1	0	−1	0	−0.095	21.1 (2)	0.00
$\mathcal{H}_{10}$	0	1	0	−1	−0.010	17.2 (2)	0.00
$\mathcal{H}_{11}$	1	0.16	−1	−0.16	−0.004	5.1 (1)	0.02
$\mathcal{H}_{12}$	1	−1	−0.4	0.4	0.008	6.0 (1)	0.01
$\mathcal{H}_{13}$	1	−0.21	−1	1	−0.401	0.01 (1)	**0.91**
$\mathcal{H}_{14}$	−0.25	1	−0.75	0	−0.214	0.3 (1)	**0.61**

Bold face indicates an insignificant test statistics.

and also none could be considered stationary over the sample period (see JMb for detailed results).

The hypotheses $\mathcal{H}_1 - \mathcal{H}_{14}$ reported in Table 1 are of the form $\beta = \{H_1\varphi_1, \psi\}$, and provide a test of whether a single restricted relation is in $sp(\beta)$, leaving the other relation unrestricted (Johansen and Juselius, 1992). Table 1 has been divided into four parts. The first part reports tests of the simple parities on their own, the second part provides tests of combinations of the parities, the third part adds the *ppp* term into the previous relations, and, finally, the fourth part reports two slightly modified versions of the previous tests. $\mathcal{H}_1 - \mathcal{H}_{12}$ were all tested for the German case with similar results, whereas $\mathcal{H}_{13} - \mathcal{H}_{14}$ are specific to the Japanese data.

As for the German–US case, all hypotheses that do not involve the *ppp* term were rejected,[4] most of them strongly so. With ppp_t included, the results improved to some extent, but not decisively so. This is contrary to the US–German case where the real interest rate parity condition when combined with ppp_t was accepted as stationary. For the Japanese case stationarity was recovered in the slightly modified real interest rate parity and *ppp* relation described by $\mathcal{H}_{13}$. It shows that Japanese inflation has been positively related to US inflation with a coefficient of approximately 0.2 and to deviations from PPP relative to the bond spread. The stationary relation under $\mathcal{H}_{14}$, a homogeneous relation between US inflation, Japanese inflation and the Japanese bond rate combined with ppp_t, is similar to the one found between the US and Germany. Combining the two hypotheses $\mathcal{H}_{13}$ and $\mathcal{H}_{14}$ in a joint test of two overidentifying restrictions gave a LR test statistic of 0.27, which is asymptotically distributed as $\chi^2(2)$.

[4] $\mathcal{H}_6$ which was borderline not rejected, but with a very small coefficient to the interest rate spread.

Finally, we subjected our chosen model to a set of Hansen and Johansen (1999) recursive stability tests, which indicated a remarkable degree of stability for the α and β coefficients in the cointegrating space defined by $\mathcal{H}_{13}$ and $\mathcal{H}_{14}$. These results are reported in JMb.

5. The VAR model with libor rates

We now apply our knowledge of the small model to an analysis of the full model structure as given by the following vector:

$$x_t' = [ppp_t, \Delta p_t, \Delta p_t^*, i_t^l, i_t^{l*}, i_t^s, i_t^{s*}], \tag{15}$$

where $t = 1978{:}9\text{–}1998{:}1$.[5] The final parity condition considered in Section 2, namely the term structure relationship, can now be analyzed.

As mentioned above, the short-term interest rates were subject to many major interventions in this period. In particular, the short period of monetary targeting in the beginning of the 1980s witnessed wild fluctuations in the short-term rates. The following 15 dummy variables[6] were needed for the residuals to approximately satisfy the normality condition $\hat{\varepsilon}_t \leq 3.3\hat{\sigma}_\varepsilon$:

$$D_t' = [D78.11, D79.03, D79.08, DI80.02, D80.03, D8005, D80.11, D81.01,$$
$$DI81.03, D81.11, DI82.01, DI84.12, DI87.09, D95.08, D97.04]$$

where $Dxx.yy_t = 1$ in 19*xx*:*yy*, except for *D*80.11 which is 1 in 1980:11 and 1980:12, 0 otherwise, $DIxx.yy_t = 1$ in 19*xx*:*yy*, -1 in 19*xx*:*yy* + 1, 0 otherwise. While the residuals passed the test for autocorrelation when controlling for these interventions, normality was rejected, primarily due to excess kurtosis. Both libor rates exhibited residual ARCH. As discussed for the smaller system, excess kurtosis and heteroscedastic errors might affect efficiency but should not produce biased inference.

Adding the two treasury bill rates implies three possible outcomes for the cointegration rank:

- $r = 2$, i.e. the rank is unchanged but the stochastic trends have increased to $p - r = 5$, implying that the two libor rates are not cointegrated, neither between themselves nor with any of the other variables. A priori this does not seem a plausible case outcome.
- $r = 3$ and $p - r = 4$, i.e. by including the short-term interest rates we introduce one additional stochastic trend into the system and the libor rates are cointegrated either between themselves or with the other variables.
- $r = 4$ and $p - r = 3$, i.e. the number of common stochastic trends are unchanged and the short-term interest rates are cointegrated, both with themselves and with the other variables. A priori this is consistent with the simple parity conditions being stationary.

Table 2 reports the trace statistics associated with both systems. The trace test supports three common trends in the small model and four in the large model. It seems plausible that

[5] Because the Japanese libor rate is only available from 1978.11 the sample period is shorter than for the bond rate model.

[6] In terms of parameters added to the model they correspond to the equivalent of two additional lags.

Table 2
The trace tests in the small and big model

$p-r$	7	6	5	4	3	2	1
Q_{95}	132	102	76	53	35	20	9
Small model ($Q(r)$)	–	–	232	64	**17**	6	0
Big model ($Q(r)$)	314	160	87	**42**	21	9	3

Bold face indicates the first insignificant test statistics.

the new common trend associated with the short-term interest rates describes the cumulative effect of relative monetary intervention shocks between the USA and Japan. Note, however, that this 'central bank' trend is not completely integrated with the other variables in the system. Thus, there are some permanent shocks to the short-term interest rates which do not transmit through the term structure to the rest of the economy (compare with the citation by Alan S. Blinder in Section 1).

6. Long-run weak exogeneity

Table 3 reports the LR test results of weak exogeneity (Johansen and Juselius, 1990) for both systems. In the small model the Japanese long-term bond rate and the *ppp* term prove to be weakly exogenous based on both the single and joint tests (the latter is $\chi^2(4) = 5.58$, with a P-value 0.23). That the US bond rate is not weakly exogenous is a surprising result considering that US financial shocks are generally believed to lead international capital markets.[7] A tentative explanation is that the large US trade deficits and the low levels of national savings relative to Japan have made the US economy more dependent on cheap capital imports from Japan than the other way around.

The rejection of weak exogeneity for the inflation rates (similarly rejected in JMa) suggests that prices are primarily adjusting to deviations from long-run steady-states, rather than the real exchange rate.[8] This is a surprising empirical result as the theoretical prediction of a floating yen/$ rate and price stickiness suggests the opposite. Thus, the large fluctuations in exchanges rates cannot be interpreted as movements towards a fundamental purchasing power parity equilibrium, but instead as movements generated by traders' behavior in the foreign exchange market. This conforms with the result in Frydman and Goldberg (2002) which shows that with imperfect information expectations, traders' behavior is likely to push exchange rates away from the PPP benchmark level, even if expectations are based on macroeconomic fundamentals.

Since weak exogeneity is not invariant to changes in the information set, adding the two libor rates into the system can change the previous findings of long-run weak exogeneity. Indeed, a change of weak exogeneity status is a sign of a reversal in the long-run feedback and is, therefore, of particular interest. The tests for the large model show that the weak exogeneity result is altered for the *ppp* term, but not for the Japanese bond rate. This result, together with the rejection of weak exogeneity of the short-term interest rates, suggests that

[7] In the analysis of the US–German data the US bond rate was, indeed, found to be weakly exogenous.

[8] Because the residual covariances are very small in this model as demonstrated later in Section 9, the conclusion is robust to linear transformations of the model.

Table 3
Tests of long-run weak exogeneity

	Δp_t	Δp_t^*	i_t^l	i_t^{l*}	ppp	i_t^s	i_t^{s*}	$\chi^2(v)$
Single test								
Small model	141.6	25.9	**2.7**	12.4	**3.7**	–	–	6.0 (2)
Big model	125.5	43.5	**2.5**	19.7	8.1	19.0	12.3	7.8 (3)

Bold face indicates an insignificant test statistics.

monetary policy shocks are influencing the real exchange rates. Similar results were found in JMa, where the weak exogeneity of ppp_t in the small system disappeared when the 3 months treasury bill rates were added. We interpret this as evidence of the importance of monetary shocks for short-term changes in exchange rates, whereas the bond rates do not seem much influenced.

7. Long-run relations and short-run adjustment

Because the cointegration property is invariant to changes in the information, set the two steady-state relations found in the small system should be equally valid in the large system. By restricting the first two relations in $\beta = \{H_1\varphi_1, H_2\varphi_2, \psi\}$ to H_{13} and H_{14}, the 'additional' impact of the libor rates on the system can be described by the third unrestricted cointegration vector, ψ. However, relation $H_1\varphi_1$ (defined by $\mathcal{H}_{13}$ in Table 1) was improved by replacing the Japanese long-term bond rate with the Japanese libor rate (see also Section 11 of JMa). Given this change in cointegration design, the unrestricted cointegration relation ψ normalized on the US treasury bill rate became:

$$\psi' = [-0.04, -0.03, -1.01, 1.00, 1.00, -0.85, 0.09].$$

Thus, the 'new' cointegration relation seems to contain information about an international term structure relationship in which the libor spread is proportional to the bond spread. Using this we were able to estimate the fully identified cointegration structure $\beta = \{H_1\varphi_1, H_2\varphi_2, H_3\varphi_3\}$ reported in Table 4. The eight overidentifying restrictions were strongly accepted based on the LR test in Johansen and Juselius (1994), with $\chi^2(8) = 1.03$ (P-value $= 1.00$). All of the estimated β_{ij} coefficients are strongly significant, and the estimated structure is both generically and empirically identified. The recursively calculated graphs of the estimated coefficients reported in Juselius and MacDonald (2000) show remarkable constancy over the last 10 years, a total of 120 observations!

Table 4
Three fully identified steady-state relations in the big system

	Δp_t	Δp_t^*	i_t^l	i_t^{l*}	i_t^s	i_t^{s*}	ppp_t[a]	P-value
β_1'	1.0	−0.37 (7.2)	0	0.37 (7.2)	−0.37 (7.2)	0	0.18 (2.5)	−0.000
β_2'	−0.50 (7.5)	1.0	−0.50 (7.5)	0	0	0	−0.24 (3.0)	−0.002
β_2'	0	0	−1.0	1.0	1.0	−1.0	0	0.000

[a] ppp has been divided by 100 to avoid reporting small coefficients.

Table 5
A multivariate equilibrium-correction model

Eq.	$\Delta^2 p_t$	$\Delta^2 p_t^*$	Δi_t^{l*}	Δi_t^s	Δi_t^{s*}	Δppp_t
Δi_t^l	1.88 (2.2)	2.67 (5.5)	0.31 (4.6)	0.21 (3.0)	–	0.44 (5.2)
Δi_{t-1}^l	–	–	–	0.44 (6.7)	–	0.14 (2.2)
Δi_{t-1}^{l*}	–	–	0.21 (4.1)	–	1.15 (14.0)	−0.14 (2.2)
Δi_{t-1}^s	–	0.54 (2.0)	−0.13 (3.3)	−0.14 (3.4)	–	
Δi_{t-1}^{s*}	–	0.63 (3.8)	–	–	0.17 (4.7)	–
$ecm1_{t-1}$	−1.20 (19.4)	−0.31 (6.7)	–	–	–	–
$ecm2_{t-1}$	–	−0.63 (9.7)	0.02 (3.7)	–	–	–
$ecm3_{t-1}$	–	−0.33 (4.5)	–	−0.03 (3.6)	0.04 (3.3)	0.04 (3.8)

The standardized residual covariance matrix (standard errors in diagonal)

$\Delta^2 p_t$	(0.00322)					
$\Delta^2 p_t^*$	0.08	(0.00178)				
Δi_t^{l*}	−0.06	0.19	(0.00023)			
Δi_t^s	−0.08	0.02	−0.11	(0.00024)		
Δi_t^{s*}	−0.12	0.18	−0.13	0.01	(0.00038)	
Δppp_t	0.04	−0.03	−0.05	0.02	0.01	(0.00031)

The short-run dynamic adjustment structure was first estimated for the full system by conditioning on the identified cointegration relations in Table 4. The weakly exogenous JP bond rate was not Granger caused by other variables and the system was reestimated conditional on this variable. The lagged inflation rates and the real exchange rate had no significant effects on the system and were left out altogether. By removing insignificant coefficients based on an LR test we arrived at the parsimonious model reported in Table 5. To save space the dummy variables are not included in Table 5, but they are reported in JMb. The LR test of overidentifying zero restrictions, distributed as $\chi^2(127)$, was 137.8 and the restrictions were accepted with a P-value of 0.24. Most of the 127 exclusion restrictions (103) are associated with the many interventions and seasonal dummies,[9] whereas only 24 are 'true' model restrictions associated with the system variables. The latter restrictions were tested separately and accepted with a P-value of 0.63. Finally, restricting the coefficients of Δi_{t-1}^l and Δi_{t-1}^{l*} in the *ppp* equation to be equal with opposite signs was accepted with a P-value of 0.83.

We note the following points regarding the large system:

1. The current change of the Japanese bond rate appears in all equations except in the Japanese libor rate equation. No additional significant contemporaneous effects were discovered, consistent with the small residual correlation coefficients of Table 5.
2. Japanese inflation and interest rates adjust primarily to changes in domestic determinants and much less to US variables, whereas the US inflation and US long-term bond rate exhibit considerable effects from the Japanese variables.
3. Both libor rates react only to the domestic determinants in the short-run.

[9] Monthly seasonal dummy variables were restricted to zero in all equations except in the US and Japanese inflation rate equations.

4. The real exchange rate and the short-term interest rates, but not the bond rates, are adjusting to *ecm*3, the international parity relation between the long-term and short-term spread. This seems to be against the simple expectation's hypothesis, which predicts that short-term interest rates drive long-term rates.
5. The real exchange rate has exclusively been affected by movements in the interest rates, both short and long, but not in inflation rates, indicating the crucial role of traders' behavior in the foreign exchange market.

The above results are quite similar to the US–German case. For example, JMa established a relation towards which German inflation was adjusting, a relation towards which US inflation was adjusting, and an international term structure relationship. Hence, both studies find evidence of price rather than exchange rate adjustment towards long-run steady-states. Both studies find evidence that interest rate spreads, long as well as short, have counterbalanced the long swings in the real exchange rate.

8. The long-run impact of shocks

The results of the previous section described how the system reacts in the short-run to a change in the system variables. This section focuses on the long-run impact of a shock to the system. Based on the MA representation of (12) it is straightforward to calculate the impulse response functions for a unitary change of $\hat{\varepsilon}_{it}$. Because we are primarily interested in the final impact of a permanent shock to the variable Δx_i, only the estimate of the final impact matrix C is reported in Table 6. Standard errors of estimates are calculated using results in Paruolo (1997). Significant coefficients with a P-value of 0.05 or less are indicated with bold face. The entries of a column in the C-matrix can be interpreted as the total (cumulated) impact of a shock, ε_{it}, on the other variables of the system, whereas a row can be interpreted as the weights with which permanent shocks to the variables of the system have influenced the long-run movements in the variable x_{it}. Hence, the significance of each entry, c_{ij}, gives an indication if the shock, ε_i, to the variable x_i has exhibited a permanent effect on the variable x_j.

We note that shocks to:

1. the two inflation rates have very small and generally insignificant effects on the other variables of the system;

Table 6
The estimates of the long-run impact matrix C

	$\Sigma\varepsilon_{\Delta p}$	$\Sigma\varepsilon_{\Delta p^*}$	$\Sigma\varepsilon_{i^l}$	$\Sigma\varepsilon_{i^{l*}}$	$\Sigma\varepsilon_{i^s}$	$\Sigma\varepsilon_{i^{s*}}$	$\Sigma\varepsilon_{ppp}$
Δp_t	0.0 (0.6)	−0.0 (1.1)	**0.5** (4.9)	**−0.7** (5.4)	**0.3** (3.5)	**0.3** (2.6)	**−0.2** (4.2)
Δp_t^*	−0.0 (1.1)	−0.0 (0.5)	**0.8** (8.1)	**−0.3** (2.6)	**0.2** (3.1)	0.1 (0.9)	**0.1** (2.8)
i_t^l	−0.01 (1.5)	0.0 (0.9)	**1.3** (7.5)	−0.1 (0.6)	−0.0 (0.4)	0.2 (1.2)	−0.1 (0.8)
i_t^{l*}	**−0.03** (3.0)	**0.1** (2.3)	**0.5** (2.3)	**1.0** (3.6)	−0.3 (1.8)	0.2 (1.0)	0.1 (1.0)
i_t^s	**−0.02** (2.0)	0.0 (0.5)	**1.0** (5.2)	**−0.5** (2.2)	**0.5** (3.7)	**0.6** (3.1)	−0.0 (0.3)
i_t^{s*}	**−0.03** (3.3)	**0.1** (2.0)	0.1 (0.6)	**0.7** (2.3)	0.2 (1.3)	**0.7** (2.6)	0.1 (1.1)
ppp_t	0.0 (0.2)	−0.0 (0.2)	−0.5 (0.2)	0.6 (0.7)	0.5 (0.1)	**−0.8** (2.6)	**1.1** (10.0)

Bold face indicates coefficients with t-values ≥ 1.8.

2. the two long-term bond yields have significant cumulative impacts on inflation rates and also on short-term interest rate yields;
3. the short-term interest rates have some positive long-run effects on the inflation rates, but primarily on each other and the real exchange rate;
4. the *ppp* term has significant long-run effects on itself and the two inflation rates.

A row-wise inspection of Table 6 shows that inflation rates are primarily influenced by shocks to the bond rates, the short-term interest rates and real exchange rates. The Japanese bond rate, being weakly exogenous, is not influenced by any of the other variables, whereas the US bond rate is to some extent influenced by permanent shocks to the Japanese variables. The libor rates are primarily influenced by permanent shocks to the bond rates and to each other, whereas the *ppp* term is significantly affected by shocks to the US libor rate.

These results reinforce the findings from the previous section that the long-term bond rates are the main driving force in this system, that inflation rates are strongly influenced by shocks to the other variables, and that inflationary shocks do not influence real exchange rates.

9. The value-added of libor rates

The results from our analysis of the common trends and the long-run relations conflict with the basic premise of the expectations hypothesis of the term structure and the Fisher conditions. Since the conduct of monetary policy is supposed to work from short-term interest rates to the rest of the economy it seems important to gain a further perspective on the role of short- relative to long-term interest rates. Therefore, Table 7 reports a

Table 7
The combined long-run effects in the extended Japanese model

Eq.	The combined effects $\hat{\Pi} = \hat{\alpha}\hat{\beta}'$						
	Δp_t	Δp_t^*	i_t^l	i_t^{l*}	ppp_t	i_t^s	i_t^{s*}
$\Delta^2 p_t$	**−1.30** (−14.2)	**0.54** (5.3)	**0.97** (7.6)	**−1.21** (−13.2)	**−0.57** (13.9)		
$\Delta^2 p_t^*$	0.02 (0.5)	**−0.27** (−5.2)	**0.26** (3.9)	−0.05 (1.1)	0.04 (1.8)		
Δi_t^l	−0.00 (0.2)	0.00 (1.7)	−0.01 (−1.2)	0.00 (0.3)	−0.00 (−0.6)		
Δi_t^{l*}	**−0.02** (-2.6)	**0.02** (3.4)	−0.01 (0.6)	−0.01 (−1.7)	**−0.01** (3.2)		
Δppp_t	−0.01 (1.3)	−0.01 (1.2)	**0.02** (2.2)	−0.01 (−1.7)	−0.00 (0.7)		
$\Delta^2 p_t$	**−1.34** (−13.7)	**0.57** (4.6)	0.02 (0.1)	**−0.54** (2.9)	**−0.24** (9.0)	**0.38** (2.7)	0.08 (0.5)
$\Delta^2 p_t^*$	−0.09 (1.7)	**−0.50** (−6.9)	**0.83** (6.6)	**−0.66** (6.1)	**0.07** (5.0)	**−0.32** (3.9)	**0.47** (5.4)
Δi_t^l	−0.01 (1.3)	0.01 (1.1)	−0.00 (0.2)	−0.00 (0.2)	0.00 (1.3)	0.00 (0.1)	0.00 (0.1)
Δi_t^{l*}	**−0.02** (3.2)	**0.03** (3.6)	−0.02 (1.0)	**−0.00** (0.9)	**0.01** (4.0)	0.00 (0.4)	−0.00 (−0.1)
Δppp_t	−0.01 (0.8)	0.00 (0.0)	**−0.04** (1.8)	**0.04** (2.0)	0.00 (0.6)	**0.04** (2.9)	**−0.04** (2.5)
Δi_t^s	−0.01 (1.4)	−0.01 (0.8)	**0.06** (3.5)	**−0.05** (−4.1)	0.00 (0.5)	−0.04 (−3.9)	**0.05** (4.1)
Δi_t^{s*}	**−0.03** (−2.5)	**0.04** (2.7)	**−0.07** (2.6)	**0.05** (2.1)	**0.01** (3.3)	**0.05** (3.0)	**−0.05** (2.6)

Bold face indicates coefficients with t-values ≥ 1.8.

comparative analysis of the combined long-run effects $\hat{\alpha}_r\hat{\beta}_r' = \hat{\Pi}_r$, where the subscript r stands for the restricted estimates in the small and the large system.

Comparing the Japanese inflation rate equations with and without the short-term interest rates demonstrated why the first cointegration relation, $H_1\varphi_1$, needed to be modified when moving from the small to large system: when including the libor rates into the analysis it replaces the Japanese bond rate as a significant determinant of Japanese inflation. Interestingly, the equation for US inflation with the short yields included changes quite dramatically: it is now significantly adjusting to the bond spread (negatively) and to the US–Japanese libor spread (positively) and much more significantly to the real exchange rate.

This may suggest that the yield gap plays a different role in this system from the one predicted by the pure expectations model of the term structure. According to the latter, the long bond yield should contain information on the current short rate and some average of expected future short rates. In this view, the addition of the short rates should not significantly affect the existing results. The fact that this was the case suggests that short rates contain important information over-and-above that contained in the long rates. If shocks to the short rates are related to the operation of monetary policy (as usually believed), the result confirms the previous findings that monetary shocks do not transmit to the bond rates.

It is noteworthy that the two inflation rates and the US bond and libor rates have reacted significantly to deviations from long-run PPP, whereas there is no significant steady-state adjustment towards the real yen/$ rate in the *ppp* equation. This was not the case for Germany–US where the *ppp* term was significant in the *ppp* equation as well as in US inflation rate equation.

The bond rate equations reported in Table 7 are essentially unchanged with the inclusion of the short rates: the Japanese bond rate is still weakly exogenous and the US bond rate is affected by the inflation rate differential relative to the *ppp* term both in the small and the extended system.

Both the US and Japanese short interest rates show significant reaction towards each other, but also effects from the bond yield spread. The US libor rate is also affected by the inflation rate spread and the real exchange rate, but this does not seem to be the case for the Japanese libor rate, (possibly) suggesting that it has been more influenced by monetary policy interventions than by market forces.

Finally, it is worth contrasting the lack of significant inflationary effects in the interest rate equations with the significant interest rate effects in the inflation rate equations. Similar results were found in JMa. It strongly suggests that the short-run adjustment effects are from bond rates to short rates, which then, in turn, influence inflation rates.

10. Summary and conclusions

In this paper we have investigated the existence of interest rate and inflation rate linkages between Japan and the USA for the post-Bretton Woods period of floating exchange rates. This was done by empirically examining the joint determination of a number of key parity conditions, such as uncovered interest rate parity, purchasing power parity, the Fisher condition and a term structure relationship. Our starting point was a similar study based on US–German data which strongly suggested that these parity conditions have not been valid as stationary relationships on their own (see Juselius and MacDonald, 2000). Only by allowing for interactions between the standard parities could stationarity be recovered. The analysis of the new Japanese–US data has further corroborated this result.

Since many of the hypotheses tested in this paper were motivated by our US–German study we will first give a brief summary of the similarities and dissimilarities between the two studies and then discuss how the new results have corroborated the hypothetical explanations of our previous study:

1. The finding in JMa that both the German and US bond rates were weakly exogenous was very strong in the German–US data. In the Japan–US system this was the case for the Japanese bond rate, but not for the US bond rate. In both cases, the results provide strong evidence of more than one stochastic trend driving the term structure of interest rates and suggests that the link is primarily from long-term to short-term interest rates, and this would seem to have important implications for the conduct of monetary policy.
2. In both cases the nonstationarity of the real dollar rates was primarily related to the nonstationary movements in interest rates and only to some minor extent to the inflation rates.
3. The finding that the main adjustment towards sustainable real exchange rates took place in the inflation rates was very strong in both cases. Since both dollar rates have been floating in this period, the substantial variability in spot exchange rates (compared to the much lower price variability) cannot be interpreted as movements toward sustainable real exchange rates, but rather as the outcome of traders' behavior in the exchange market. This conforms with the interpretation in Krugman (1993) and even more so with the imperfect knowledge expectations framework of Frydman and Goldberg (2002).
4. Another closely related finding was that inflation rates were found to have essentially no effects at all for our nominal interest rates, whereas the effects from nominal interest rates to inflation rates was positive (the so called price puzzle effect). This was a strong result in both studies suggesting that the Fisher parity condition works very poorly in open economies with an external float.
5. In both cases the deviations from fundamental purchasing power parity were compensated by corresponding movements in both the long-term and short-term interest rate spread, but interestingly with different signs: the yen/$ rate appreciated when the US-JP long-term bond spread increased, but depreciated with an increase in the short rate spread, whereas the DM/$ rate appreciated when the US–German treasury bill spread increased, but depreciated with an increasing US–German bond spread. For the Japan–US case this kind of behaviour might indicate central bank interventions in the yen/$ market to prevent the exchange rate appreciating. In the German–US case, traders might have bid up the dollar rate when buying US bonds, thereby counteracting an adjustment towards steady-state.

The above findings were shown to be remarkably robust (empirically as well as econometrically) over a period of many fundamental changes. The following conclusions in JMa were further strengthened in the Japanese–US system:

1. The desire to hold dollars seems to have facilitated the financing of the large US current account deficits during the post-Bretton Woods period. The large differences between national savings rates, and, in particular, the large US trade deficits, seems to be an important reason why the long-term bond rates were found to be so crucial in both systems. This points to the importance of capital markets, rather than goods markets, in explaining one of the 'market failure' puzzles: that is, why an adequate adjustment toward purchasing power parity between the USA and the other two major currency blocks has not taken place, or, if so, only very slowly.
2. Though the role of central bank policy for stabilizing the short-term capital market has evidently been crucial as the turbulent years of monetary targeting in the 1980s demonstrated, its role for controlling inflation seems much more modest than usually believed. This relates directly to the concern expressed by Blinder (1997), and cited in the introduction, about the empirical failure of the term structure and its monetary policy implications.
3. Finally, the estimated equation systems were able to explain the variation in the data with a remarkable degree of precision. In that sense it seems quite unlikely that one would be able to estimate competing models that could beat the present results in terms of precision and stability. In that sense the results could be used as a benchmark against which theoretically more sophisticated models are judged.

In sum, the Japanese–US linkages between interest rates, inflation rates and exchange rates reported in this paper do not conform to a standard textbook interpretation. We believe these results are challenging and merit further analysis.

Acknowledgements

Financial support from the Danish Social Sciences Research Council, Grant no. 9800363, is gratefully acknowledged.

References

Blinder, A., 1997. Is there a usable core in macroeconomics? The Bulletin of American Economic Association.

Campbell, J.Y., 1995. Some lessons from the yield curve. Journal of Economic Perspectives 9 (3), 129–152.

Doornik, J.A., Hendry, D.F., 1998. GiveWin. An Interface to Empirical Modelling. Timberlake Consultants.

Frydman, R., Goldberg, M., 2002. Imperfect knowledge expectations, uncertainty adjusted uncovered interest rate parity and exchange rate dynamics. In: Aghion, P., Frydman, R., Stiglitz, J., Woodford, M. (Eds.), Knowledge, Information and Expectations in Modern Macroeconomics (In Honor of Edmund S. Phelps). Princeton University Press, Princeton, NJ.

Hansen, H., Johansen, S., 1999. Recursive estimation in cointegrated VAR-models. The Econometric Journal 2, 306–333.

Hansen, H., Juselius, K., 1995. CATS in RATS. Manual to Cointegration Analysis of Time Series. Estima, Evanstone, IL.

Hendry, D.F., Mizon, G.E., 1993. Evaluating econometric models by encompassing the VAR. In: Phillips, P.C. (Ed.), Models, Methods and Applications of Econometrics, Blackwell Scientific Publications, Basil.

Johansen, S., Juselius, K., 1992. Testing structural hypotheses in a multivariate cointegration analysis of the PPP and the UIP for UK. Journal of Econometrics 53, 211–244.

Johansen, S., Juselius, K., 1994. Identification of the long-run and the short-run structure. An application to the ISLM model. Journal of Econometrics 63, 7–36.

Juselius, K., 1992. Domestic and foreign effects on prices in an open economy. The case of Denmark. Journal of Economic Policy Modeling 14, 401–428.

Juselius, K., MacDonald, R., 2000. International parities between Germany and the USA. European University Institute, unpublished report.

Juselius, K., MacDonald, R., 2002. Interest rate and price linkages between the USA and Japan: evidence from the post-Bretton Woods period. CESifo Working paper, in press.

Krugman, P., 1993. Exchange-Rate Instability. The MIT Press, Cambridge, MA.

Paruolo, P., 1997. Asymptotic inference on the moving average impact matrix in cointegrated $I(1)$ VAR systems. Econometic Theory 13, 79–118.

NORTH-HOLLAND

Available online at www.sciencedirect.com

SCIENCE @ DIRECT•

Global Finance Journal 15 (2004) 29–56

Global Finance Journal

Filtering the BEER: A permanent and transitory decomposition

Peter B. Clark[a], Ronald MacDonald[b,*]

[a] *International Monetary Fund, UK*

[b] *Department of Economics, University of Strathclyde, Curran Building, 100 Cathedrahl Street, Glasgow Scotland G14 0LN, UK*

Received 2 August 2002; received in revised form 11 June 2003; accepted 18 October 2003
Available online 28 April 2004

Abstract

In this paper, we extend the behavioral equilibrium exchange rate (BEER) approach which identifies an estimated equilibrium relationship between the real exchange rate and economic fundamentals. Here, the economic fundamentals (real interest rate differential, net foreign assets, and relative price of nontraded/traded goods) are decomposed using Johansen cointegration methods into transitory and permanent components, with the latter used to estimate the permanent equilibrium exchange rate (PEER) for the U.S. and Canadian dollars and the pound sterling. The BEER and the PEER move closely together for the U.S. and Canadian dollars and generally track the actual exchange rate. By contrast, for the pound sterling, the BEER and the PEER diverge sharply, with the latter following the actual exchange rate quite closely.
© 2004 Elsevier Inc. All rights reserved.

JEL classification: F31; F32; F41
Keywords: Equilibrium real exchange rates; Economic fundamentals; Permanent–transitory decomposition

1. Introduction

As the exchange rates of many industrial and developing countries have shown substantial fluctuations over the past 25 years, there has been considerable interest in exploring the factors that may be able to account for these movements. In particular, the substantial changes in the nominal and real exchange value of the U.S. dollar, the yen, and the pound sterling have raised questions as to whether exchange rates are driven in a systematic fashion by fundamental economic forces or are more a reflection of the perhaps

* Corresponding author.
E-mail addresses: Pclark1@imf.org (P.B. Clark), r.r.macdonald@strath.ac.uk (R. MacDonald).

1044-0283/$ - see front matter © 2004 Elsevier Inc. All rights reserved.
doi:10.1016/j.gfj.2003.10.005

irrational whims of market participants.[1] In attempting to answer this question, one strand of analysis has tried to identify a relatively small set of economic variables that can be used to explain these movements and to ascertain the extent to which exchange rates are misaligned (i.e., can be said to depart from economic fundamentals).

Some of the recent contributions to this literature have gone under the rubric of "equilibrium exchange rates," such as those contained in Baffes, Elbadawi, and O'Connell (1999), MacDonald and Stein (1999), and Williamson (1994). Two main approaches have been developed to assess the degree to which exchange rates are consistent with economic fundamentals. One is the macroeconomic balance approach which calculates the real exchange rate that is consistent with the economy operating at capacity output and a sustainable current account position. This method has been popularized by Williamson, who referred to the exchange rate computed in this manner as the fundamental equilibrium exchange rate (FEER). A recent extension and refinement of this methodology is contained in Isard and Faruqee (1998). An alternative approach involves the direct econometric analysis of a model of the behavior of the real exchange rate, which can be called the behavioral equilibrium exchange rate (BEER). The BEER approach produces a measure of misalignment that is different from the FEER, as it relates to the deviation between the actual exchange rate and the value given by the estimated equilibrium relationship between the real exchange rate and economic fundamentals.

In an earlier paper, Clark and MacDonald (1999) used the multivariate cointegration methods of Johansen (1995) to construct estimates of the BEER for the real effective exchange rates (REERs) of the U.S. dollar, the German mark, and the Japanese yen. The estimated BEERs were then compared to FEERs as tools for assessing misalignments in exchange rates. We noted that the direct application of the behavioral approach yielded a measure of *current misalignment*, namely, the difference between the actual value of the exchange rate and the estimated level of the exchange rate given by the current values of all the economic fundamentals. As the current values of these determinants may depart from sustainable or long-run levels, as emphasized in the FEER approach, it is also useful to calculate the *total misalignment*, which is the difference between the actual exchange rate and that given by the sustainable or long-run values of the economic fundamentals.[2] As an illustration of this type of calculation, we used the Hodrick–Prescott filter to obtain smoothed series for the economic fundamentals to generate long-run trend values for the REERs of the U.S. dollar, the German mark, and the pound sterling.

The BEER estimates presented in Clark and MacDonald (1999) and in this paper may also be contrasted with the popular PPP hypothesis. The latter ignores any fundamentals and empirical estimates indicate that there is a very long convergence to PPP. Our approach stresses two points: (i) There are real fundamentals which can be used to explain systematic exchange rate movements, and (ii) convergence in our estimated models is relatively rapid.

As it is generated from variables that are highly persistent and indeed often nonstationary, the measured BEER is itself likely to be a highly persistent series. Using

[1] This topic is the focus of a recent Controversy (1999) section of the *Economic Journal* on Exchange Rates and Fundamentals (see MacDonald, 1999).

[2] For a recent application of this approach, see Lim (2000).

the methods of Beveridge and Nelson (1981), a number of papers (see, e.g., Clarida & Gali, 1995; Huizinga, 1987) have in fact interpreted the persistent, or permanent, component of the real exchange rate as a measure of equilibrium. Recently, Granger and Gonzalo (1995) have shown how the Johansen cointegration method can be used to extract the permanent component from a vector of variables which exhibit cointegration, thereby producing a measure of equilibrium which is close in spirit to the BEER. In this paper, we use the method of Granger and Gonzalo to estimate the permanent components of the REERs of the U.S. dollar, the Canadian dollar, and the pound sterling. We refer to these measures as the permanent equilibrium exchange rate (PEER). As the approach used to extract the permanent component involves the cointegration methods used by Clark and MacDonald (1999) to estimate a BEER, a natural question to ask is "How similar are the BEER and PEER estimates?" To the extent that the BEER is a persistent series, as noted above, it would be expected that there are similarities between the two.

Aside from this comparison, we also argue that there may be advantages in supplementing a BEER analysis with a PEER-based approach to modeling equilibrium exchange rates. First, the latter approach produces estimates of the permanent and transitory components of all of the variables, and this may be useful in circumstances where the BEER and PEER are very different. Given the way the PEER is measured, any difference between it and the BEER must be due to the way the latter measure incorporates any transitory elements. Clearly, it is likely to be important for policy purposes to assess the extent to which a currency misalignment is due to significant transitory elements. Second, as a by-product of the permanent–transitory decomposition, it is possible to identify which variables are the main contributors of any system-wide nonstationarity (the common trends) and which variables, in turn, are affected by these common trends. For example, is it the net foreign asset position which is the key driving variable in a particular exchange rate system, or is it some combination of the underlying variables which drive the system? A third advantage of our approach, although one which is not pursued here, is that it is possible to analyze an exchange rate relationship in isolation, using a common factor analysis, and then go on in a second stage to analyze the joint interaction of this common factor with the common factor(s) from, say, other currency systems. Given that currencies and, indeed, other asset prices are interrelated, this may be a useful exercise. The common factor approach facilitates this type of analysis because instead of analyzing the complete currency systems simultaneously, all that is required is to estimate the interactions of the common factors. A final advantage of our approach is that because the common factors are derived from a vector error correction model (VECM), the problem with unit roots/nonstationarity does not arise, and hypothesis testing on linear combinations of the common factors can be conducted using standard chi-square tests.

The remainder of the paper is as follows. In the next section, we provide a brief overview of the BEER approach to defining an equilibrium exchange rate. Section 3 then describes the methodology used to decompose a vector which exhibits cointegration into permanent and transitory components. Section 4 then uses this decomposition to yield estimates of the total misalignment of three currencies: the U.S. and Canadian dollars, and the U.K. pound. Section 5 provides some concluding comments.

2. The BEER approach

2.1. The model

The model we apply is the same as that used in an earlier paper (Clark & MacDonald (1999)). The starting point is the familiar uncovered interest parity (UIP) condition;[3]

$$E_t(\Delta s_{t+k}) = -(i_t - i_t^*), \tag{1}$$

where s_t is the foreign currency price of a unit of home currency, i_t denotes a nominal interest rate, Δ is the first difference operator, E_t is the conditional expectations operator, $t+k$ defines the maturity horizon of the bonds, and the symbol * denotes a foreign variable. Eq. (1) can be converted into a relationship between real variables by adding the expected inflation differential, $E_t(\Delta p_{t+k} - \Delta p_{t+k}^*)$ to both sides of the equation. After rearrangement, this gives:

$$q_t = E_t(q_{t+k}) + (r_t - r_t^*) + e_t \tag{2}$$

where $r_t = i_t - E_t(\Delta p_{t+k})$ is the ex ante real interest rate, q_t is the real exchange rate, and e_t is a disturbance term. Eq. (2) describes the current equilibrium exchange rate as determined by two components, the expectation of the real exchange rate in period $t+k$ and the real interest differential with maturity $t+k$.

The use of the UIP relationship may appear suspect, as many researchers, e.g., Campbell and Clarida (1987), Edison and Pauls (1993), Froot (1990), and Meese and Rogoff (1988), have failed to uncover a systematic, robust relationship between exchange rates and interest rates. However, some recent research provides greater support for UIP. For example, Chinn and Meredith (1998) find that looking at longer time horizons, namely, from 3 up to 10 years, reveals a quite strong and consistent relationship between the change in the nominal exchange rate and the level of the interest differential across a range of currencies. Edison and Melick (1999), MacDonald (1997), and MacDonald and Nagayasu (1999) confirm that the finding of Meredith and Chinn also holds for the real uncovered interest differential. Thus, there is greater support than a few years ago for using UIP as our point of departure in modeling real exchange rates.

We assume that the unobservable expectation of the exchange rate, $E_t(q_{t+k})$, is the "long-run" equilibrium exchange rate, $\bar{q}_t$. The current equilibrium rate is defined as q_t' to distinguish it from the actual rate q_t:[4]

$$q_t' = \bar{q}_t + (r_t - r_t^*) \tag{3}$$

In summary, therefore, our approach posits that the current equilibrium exchange rate given by Eq. (3) comprises two components: the systematic component, $\bar{q}_t$, and the real interest differential.

---

[3] Our operationalisation of the short-run real exchange rate equation follows Baxter (1994), Edison and Pauls (1993), Isard (1983), MacDonald (1997), and Meese and Rogoff (1988).

[4] It is straightforward to modify Eq. (3) to include a risk premium (see Meese & Rogoff, 1988). However, in our empirical work, the risk premium always proved to be insignificant, and therefore, it is not included here.

The factors likely to introduce systematic variability into $\bar{q}_t$ have been discussed elsewhere in some detail (see Faruqee, 1995; MacDonald, 1997; Stein, 1999) and are not considered here in any depth. Suffice to say that for our purposes, the long-run equilibrium rate is assumed to be a function of two key variables:

$$\bar{q}_t = f(\overset{+}{\text{tnt}_t}, \overset{+}{\text{nfa}_t}) \tag{4}$$

where "tnt" is our proxy for the Balassa–Samuelson effect (i.e., the relative price of nontraded to traded goods[5]) and "nfa" is net foreign assets, and the signs above the right-hand side variables denote the partial derivatives.[6] As in the internal–external balance approach to modeling the real exchange rate, we see nfa being driven by the determinants of national savings and investment and, in particular, demographics and structural fiscal balances.[7] The definitions of the three variables entering Eq. (4) are described below.

As real interest rates appear in Eq. (3), which describes the current equilibrium exchange rate, we have not included them as a determinant of the long-run equilibrium rate, $\bar{q}_t$. However, some models of the equilibrium exchange rate (such as that of Stein, 1999) would ascribe to real interest rates an influence on the systematic component of the real exchange rate through productivity and thrift channels. The reason for separating real interest rates from $\bar{q}_t$ in Eq. (3) is that they are thought to reflect business cycle developments rather than the longer run systematic trends (see MacDonald & Swagel, 2000). However, in as much as the equation we estimate is a reduced form, it may be that real interest rates do have their effect through the systematic component of the real exchange rate. Indeed, our permanent and transitory decomposition of the data allows us to determine which effect dominates for our currency systems. As will be seen below, this is especially the case for the U.K. pound.

2.2. Data sources and definitions[8]

The REERs analyzed in this paper are the U.S. and Canadian dollars and the pound sterling. The sample period is from 1960–1997, and the data are annual. The definitions of the variables and sources of the data are given below.

[5] Using tnt as a proxy for the Balassa–Samuelson effect has been proposed by Kakkari and Ogaki (1993). However, a number of authors have issued a cautionary note about how good a measure tnt actually is of the Balassa–Samuelson effect (see, e.g., Clostermann & Friedmann, 1998; Duval, 2002). However, in as much as our concern in this paper is to illustrate the usefulness of the BEER/PEER methodology, we do not regard this as a particular issue in our work.

[6] The importance of nfa as a determinant of real exchange rates has recently been highlighted in Lane and Milesi-Ferretti (2000). In his NATREX model, Stein (2003) stresses the importance of the dynamic interactions between the real exchange rate and foreign debt (which is the negative of nfa).

[7] For a recent analysis that derives this relationship from internal and external balance considerations, see Alberola, Cervero, Lopez, and Ubide (1999).

[8] The authors are indebted to Jeff Gable for constructing the data set used in this paper.

2.2.1. REER: q

This is a multilateral consumer price index (CPI)-based REER of the currency of the domestic economy relative to its G-7 partner countries. It is defined in terms of foreign currency per unit of domestic currency, so that that an increase in q is a real effective appreciation. The methodology is described in Zanello and Desruelle (1997). This variable is expressed in logs: lq.

The basic data for the weights come from the IMF's information notice system (INS). In the INS system, for each "home" country, there are 146 partner countries that have some positive weight. To reduce the number of partner countries, the INS uses a threshold of 1%. Those partners with weights of less than 1% for a home country are eliminated, and the remaining partner country weights are renormalized to sum to unity. Typically, this leaves home countries with between one dozen and two dozen partners for the calculation of the weights. The REERs in this paper are constructed in a parallel fashion, with partner countries limited to the G-7 only. Typically, about 40% (36% for the United States and 43% for Germany) of a G-7 country's partner weights come from non-G-7 partners.

To assess the degree to which our narrower set of trading partners affects our REER calculations, correlations were calculated between our G-7-only REERs and those REERs calculated by the INS using the 1% cutoff for inclusion of partners. With exchange rates measured as annual percent changes, the correlation coefficient between the two exchange rate measures was at least .97 for the three currencies in our sample, indicating that our calculated exchange rates are very close to the CPI-based REERs published by the IMF.

2.2.2. Relative price of nontraded to traded goods: tnt

The relative price of nontraded to traded goods is defined as the ratio of the domestic CPI to the domestic wholesale or producer price index (PPI) relative to the corresponding weighted average of partner country ratios, using the same weights as described above. This variable is expressed in logs: ltnt (source: CPI, IMF *World Economic Outlook* database; PPI, IMF Unit Labor Cost database).

2.2.3. Net foreign assets: nfa

This variable is the stock of net foreign assets, defined as total foreign assets (less official gold holding) minus total liabilities to foreigners, expressed as a ratio to GNP. In the empirical analysis below, the stock of net foreign assets is scaled by dividing by the nominal value of GDP, which is denoted by "nfay" (source: Masson, Kremers, and Horne (1993) for data from 1960–1990; data from 1991–1997 obtained from the same publications cited in the source for this variable).

2.2.4. Real interest rates: r, r^*

The domestic real interest rate, r, is defined as the average annual nominal long-term (10-year) government bond yield minus the change in the CPI from the previous year. The foreign interest rate, r^*, is a weighted average of partner G-7 real interest rates computed in the same manner (source: IMF *World Economic Outlook* database).

Hence, our specification of the overall, or gross vector, x, is

$$x_t' = [\mathrm{l}q_t, (r_t - r_t^*), \mathrm{ltnt}_t, \mathrm{nfa}_t] \tag{5}$$

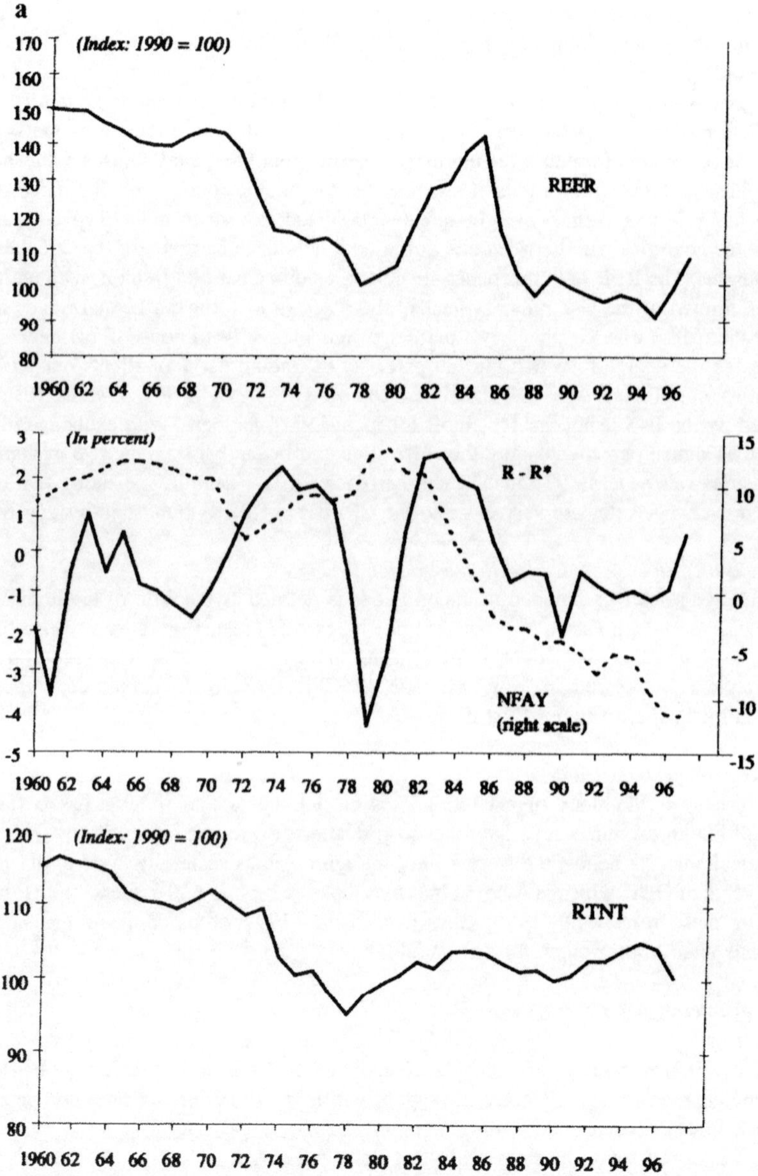

Fig. 1. The real exchange rate and fundamentals for (a) United States, (b) Canada, and (c) United Kingdom.

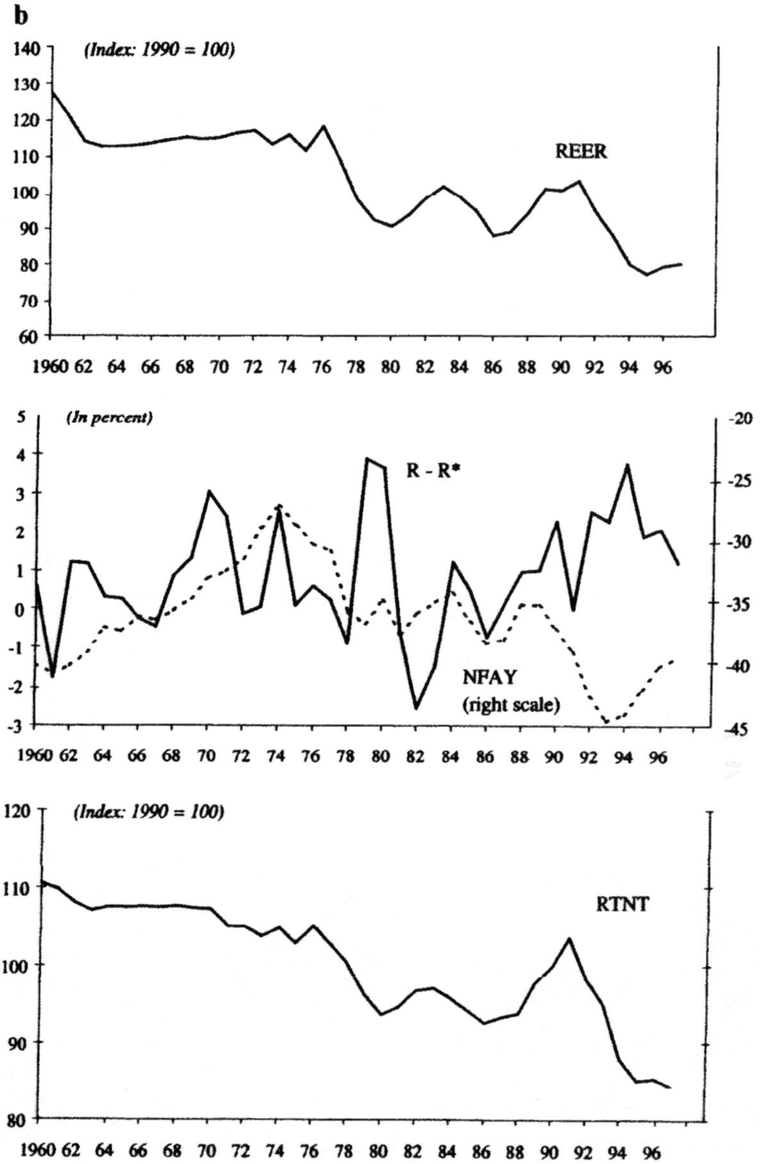

Fig. 1 (*continued*).

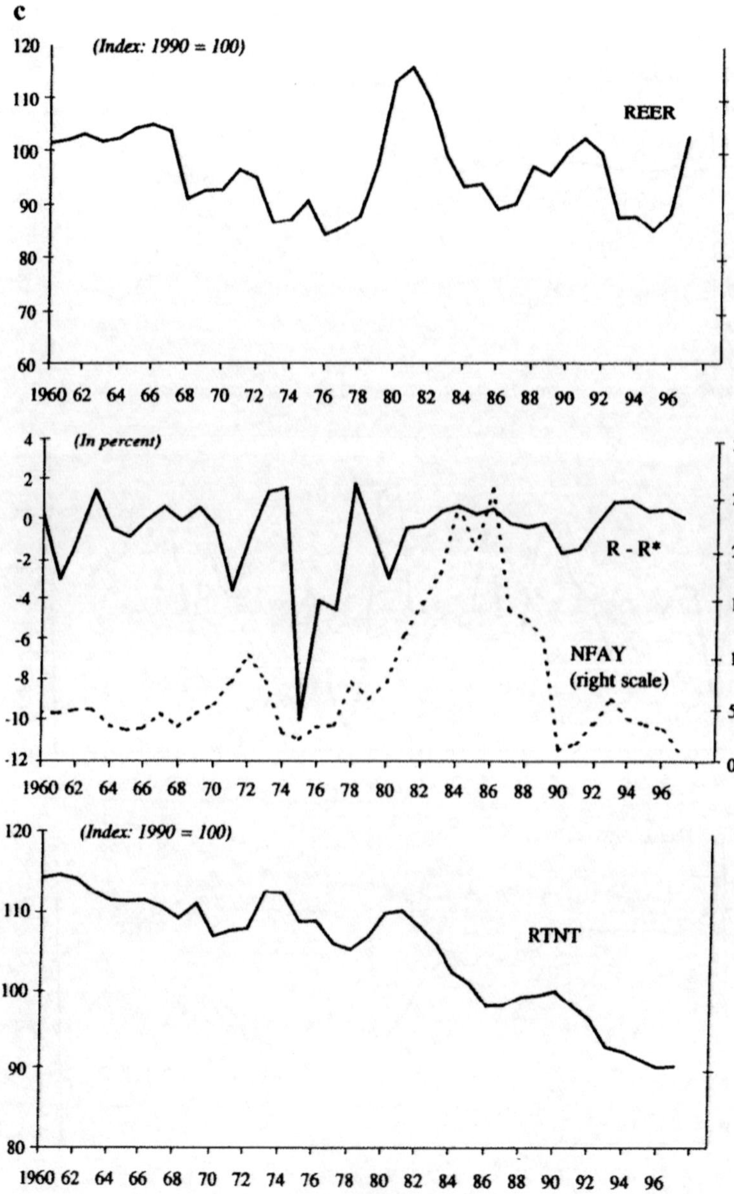

Fig. 1 (*continued*).

2.3. The behavior of the three exchange rates

Fig. 1 plots the REER for the United States, Canada, and the United Kingdom, as well as the three explanatory variables. Looking first at the U.S. dollar, there appear to be five distinct periods: a depreciation from 1960 to 1978, a fairly sharp appreciation from 1978 to 1985 followed by a sharp depreciation to 1988, a period of fairly limited movement from 1988 to 1995, and a real appreciation from 1995 to 1997. The first period of depreciation appears to be associated only with the gradual downward trend in the relative price of nontraded to traded goods, whereas the following sharp appreciation may reflect the substantial rise in the U.S. real interest rate relative to its G-7 partners'. The subsequent reversal in interest rates and declining net foreign assets can perhaps in part account for the depreciation from 1985 to 1988, and the appreciation at the end of the sample period appears to be associated with a rise in the interest differential in favor of the United States. This is of course a very impressionistic description of the relationships between the explanatory factors and the real exchange rate compared with the statistical analysis presented below, which shows the net effect of all three factors together.

Turning to the Canadian dollar, there is a general trend of depreciation over most of the sample period which may reflect the downward trend in the relative price of nontraded to traded goods. The behavior of the other two variables over this period does not reveal any obvious association with the real value of the Canadian dollar, but the statistical analysis below indicates that they are important explanatory variables. It is noteworthy that the real interest rate differential shows sharp year-to-year movements, which may reflect an attempt by the Bank of Canada to affect the value of the Canadian dollar through changes in monetary policy, in which case, one would not see a positive bivariate association between the interest rate differential and the exchange rate.

The real value of the pound shows no clear trend over the period, with beginning and ending values the same. Moreover, there is no obvious association between the three explanatory variables and the real value of the pound. Nonetheless, as shown below, the ability of the model to capture major movements in the pound is as impressive as for the other two currencies, the major difference being that it is the PEER, not the BEER, which provides the explanatory power in the case of the pound.

3. A permanent and transitory decomposition

3.1. Using the VECM representation

The recent literature on the decomposition of series into their permanent and transitory components has as its starting point the paper by Beveridge and Nelson (1995). In this literature, the permanent component of a series is normally interpreted as an I(1) process, while the transitory component is stationary, or I(0). The original work of Beveridge and Nelson involved both univariate and multivariate decompositions of the series. In as much as the sum of an I(1) and I(0) series is also I(1), one important issue that has to be addressed in this type of analysis is how the two components are

Table 1
Multivariate stationarity tests

Country	lq	$(r-r^*)$	ltnt	nfa	χ^2 (5)
United States	24.42	15.54	20.90	27.88	11.07
Canada	40.28	29.79	40.48	40.75	11.07
United Kingdom	27.86	21.59	34.41	34.26	11.07

identified. Often this involves assuming that the permanent component follows a random walk or that the two components are orthogonal at all leads and lags (see, e.g., Quah, 1989). Here, however, we follow Granger and Gonzalo (1995) and use the identification implicit in the cointegration of the series. In particular, Stock and Watson (1988) have demonstrated that if cointegration exists amongst a number of variables, then the vector will also have a common trend, or factor, decomposition. Granger and Gonzalo demonstrate that the common factor can be estimated if it is assumed to be a linear combination of the series in question and if it is further assumed that the residuals from this model do not have a permanent effect on the original series. The former assumption makes the common factor observable, while the second permits identification. As Granger and Gonzalo show, the linear combination may be estimated from a VECM, and as this approach takes care of any nonstationarity, it facilitates statistical inference on the common factor.

In this paper, we use the methods of Johansen (1995) to extract all the necessary information from the VECM. Briefly, this approach involves the following. Define a $(n \times 1)$ vector of variables, consisting of the variables specified in Eq. (5), and the associated definitional equations [these terms may be I(1) or I(0)], and assume that it has a vector autoregressive representation of the following form:

$$x_t = \eta + \sum_{i=1}^{p} \Pi_i x_t + \varepsilon_t, \tag{6}$$

where η is a $(n \times 1)$ vector of deterministic terms, and ε is a $(n \times 1)$ vector of white noise disturbances, with mean zero and covariance matrix Ξ. Eq. (6) may be reparameterised into the VECM as:

$$\Delta x_t = \eta + \sum_{i=1}^{p-1} \Phi_i \Delta x_{t-i} + \Pi x_{t-1} + \varepsilon_t \tag{7}$$

where Δ denotes the first difference operator, Φ_i is a $(n \times n)$ coefficient matrix (equal to $-\sum_{j=i+1}^{p} \Pi_j$), $\mathbf{\Pi}$ is a $(n \times n)$ matrix (equal to $\sum_{i=1}^{p} \Pi_i - I$) whose rank determines the

Table 2
Multivariate diagnostics—U.S. dollar

LB (9)	LM (1)	LM (4)	NM (10)
134.92	14.04	8.80	4.28
(.24)	(.60)	(.92)	(.83)

Table 3
Significance of cointegrating vectors

H_0:r	Trace	Trace 95
0	62.93	53.12
1	37.66	34.91
2	15.25	19.96
3	4.23	9.24

number of cointegrating vectors. If Π is either of full rank, n, or zero rank, $\Pi=0$, there will be no cointegration amongst the elements in the long-run relationship (in these instances, it will be appropriate to estimate the model in, respectively, levels or first differences). If, however, Π is of reduced rank, r (where $r<n$), then there will exist $(n \times r)$ matrices α and β such that $\Pi=\alpha\beta'$ where β is the matrix whose columns are the linearly independent cointegrating vectors and the α matrix is interpreted as the adjustment matrix, indicating the speed with which the system responds to last period's deviation from the equilibrium level of the exchange rate. Hence, the existence of the VECM, relative to, say, a VAR in first differences, depends upon the existence of cointegration.[9]

We test for the existence of cointegration amongst the variables contained in x_t using the Trace test as proposed by Johansen (1995). For the hypothesis that there are at most r distinct cointegrating vectors, this has the following form:

$$\mathrm{TR} = \mathrm{T}\sum_{i=r+1}^{N} \ln(1-\hat{\lambda}_i), \tag{8}$$

where $\hat{\lambda}_{r+1},\ldots,\hat{\lambda}_N$ are the $N-r$ smallest squared canonical correlations between x_{t-k} and Δx_t series [where all of the variables entering x_t are assumed I(1)], corrected for the effect of the lagged differences of the x_t process.[10]

For our purposes, it will prove useful to present the moving average representation of Eq. (7). Johansen (1995) has demonstrated that Eq. (7) has a vector moving average representation of the following form:

$$x_t = \mathbf{C}\sum_{i=1}^{t} \varepsilon_i + \mathbf{C}\eta + \mathbf{C}(L)(\varepsilon_t+\eta), \tag{9}$$

where

$$\mathbf{C} = \beta_\perp(\alpha'_\perp(\mathrm{I}-\sum_{1}^{k-1}\Phi_i)\beta_\perp)^{-1}\alpha'_\perp$$

where $\alpha_\perp$ and $\beta_\perp$ denote the orthogonal complements to α and β (that is, $\alpha'\alpha_\perp=0$ and $\beta'\beta_\perp=0$) and $\alpha_\perp$ determines the vectors defining the space of the common stochastic

[9] The so-called Granger representation theorem (see Frigle & Granger, 1987) implies that if there exists cointegration amongst a group of variables, there must also exist an error correction representation.

[10] For details of how to extract the λ's, see Johansen (1988), and Johansen and Juselius (1992).

trends, and therefore should be informative about the key 'driving' variable(s) in each of the systems. The $\beta_\perp$ vector gives the loadings associated with $\alpha_\perp$ (i.e., the series which are driven by the common trends). Thus, the **C** matrix measures the combined effects of these two orthogonal components.

If the vector x is of reduced rank, r, then Granger and Gonzalo (1995) have demonstrated that the elements of x can be explained in terms of a smaller number $(n-r)$ of I(1) variables called common factors, f_t, plus some I(0) components, the transitory elements, $\tilde{x}_t$:

$$x_t = A_1 f_t + \tilde{x}_t. \tag{10}$$

The identification of the common factors may be achieved in the following way. If it is assumed that the common factors, f_t, are linear combinations of the variables x_t:

$$f_t = B_1 x_t, \tag{11}$$

and if $A_1 f_t$ and $\tilde{x}_t$ form a permanent–transitory decomposition of x_t, then from the VECM representation (Eq. (7)), the only linear combination of x_t, such that $\tilde{x}_t$ has no long-run impact on x_t, is:

$$f_t = \alpha'_\perp x_t. \tag{12}$$

As Granger and Gonzalo point out, these are the linear combinations of Δx_t which have the 'common feature' of not containing the levels of the error correction term in them. This identification of the common factors enables Granger and Gonzalo to obtain the following permanent–transitory decomposition of x_t:

$$x_t = A_1 \alpha'_\perp x_t + A_2 \beta' x_t, \tag{13}$$

where, of terms not previously defined, $A_1 = \beta_\perp(\alpha'_\perp \beta_\perp)^{-1}$ and $A_2 = \alpha(\beta'\alpha)^{-1}$. It is straightforward to demonstrate that the common factor, f_t, corresponds to the common trend in the analysis of Stock and Watson (1988). This has the advantage that it is straightforward to estimate and also that hypotheses on the common trends can be tested. It also has the added advantage that it produces a permanent estimate of the equilibrium exchange rate which is consistent with the underlying VECM specifications; other extant measures of the permanent component of the equilibrium exchange rate often apply ad hoc moving average filters.

Table 4
Alpha adjustment matrix

Variable	alpha1	*t* alpha
lq	− 0.669	− 3.988
$(r-r^*)$	− 0.022	− 0.508
ltnt	0.119	1.881
nfa	− 0.094	1.864

4. Estimation results

The Johansen cointegration methodology used below presupposes that at least some (although not necessary all) of the variables entering the x_t vector are nonstationary. As a check on this, we used the multivariate stationarity test of Johansen (1995). This tests the

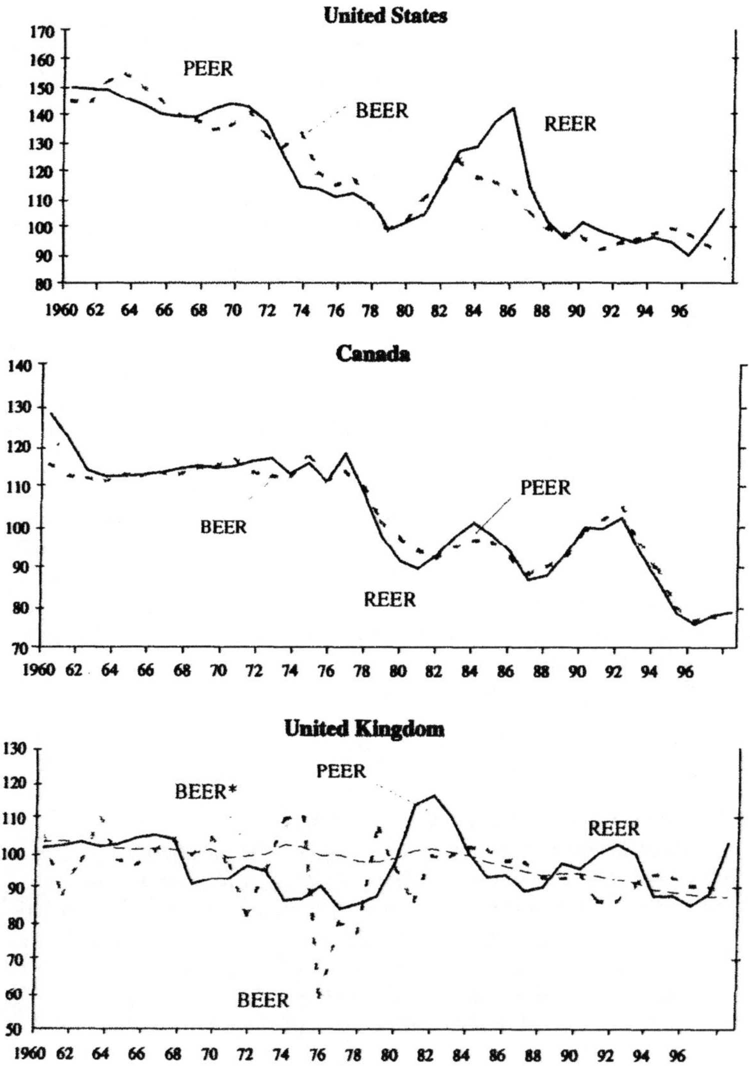

Fig. 2. BEER and PEER compared with REER.

Table 5
Alpha orthogonal components for the U.S. system

Variable	lq_t	$r_t - r_t^*$	$ltnt_t$	nfa_t
$\alpha_\perp^1$	0.003	−0.002	−0.608	−0.794
$\alpha_\perp^2$	−0.220	−0.045	−0.774	0.592
$\alpha_\perp^3$	0.041	−0.998	0.030	−0.020

null hypothesis of stationarity against the alternative of nonstationarity, subject to the chosen cointegrating rank, which, as we shall see below, is one in each system. The results, along with the X^2 Eq. (5) critical value, are reported in Table 1. These results clearly indicate that all of the variables in each of the systems are nonstationary.[11]

4.1. The U.S. dollar

We first consider the results for the United States. The lag length, p, in the underlying VAR system (Eq. (6)) was set equal to two, and the Pantula principle of jointly testing the rank and deterministic specification was used to specify the VECM. For the United States and indeed all of the other systems, this resulted in the constant term being constrained to lie in the long-run relationship. Table 2 reports a number of residual diagnostics from the estimated U.S. system, and this confirms that the estimated VAR is well specified.

The LB, LM, and NM statistics are multivariate residual diagnostic tests: LB (9) is the Hoskings multivariate Ljung–Box statistic, LM (1) and LM (4) are multivariate Godfrey (1988) LM-type statistics for first- and fourth-order autocorrelation, and NM (10) is a Doornik and Hansen (1994) multivariate normality test. Numbers in parentheses are P values and indicate an absence of serial correlation and normally distributed errors.

The estimated values of the Trace statistics for the U.S. system are reported in Table 3. On the basis of the Trace statistics, there is clear evidence of one significant cointegrating vector—perhaps two. However, a visual inspection of the second vector indicated some nonstationarity, and this was reinforced by an analysis of the roots of the companion matrix. We therefore focus solely on the first vector, which, normalized on the exchange rate, produces the following equation, with standard errors in parentheses:

$$lq_t = \underset{(0.62)}{1.592}(r - r^*) + \underset{(0.16)}{2.030}\,\text{ltnt} + \underset{(0.12)}{1.107}\,\text{nfa} + \underset{(0.012)}{4.618} \tag{14}$$

All of the coefficients have the correct sign and are of a plausible magnitude. On the basis of the Fisher standard errors, all of the variables are statistically significant. The alpha, or adjustment, matrix associated with this equation is reported in Table 4.

The significantly negative alpha coefficient in the exchange rate equation indicates that the exchange rate moves to close the gap of a disequilibrium by approximately 70% per annum. This means that most of the adjustment to a shock to the real exchange rate will be offset after 2 years. This result reinforces the usefulness of conditioning a real exchange rate on an appropriate set of fundamentals, as half-life estimates recovered from

[11] In the estimated equation below, q and tnt are expressed in logs and are represented in Table 1 as lq and ltnt, respectively.

Table 6
Beta orthogonal components for the U.S. system

Variable	$\beta_{\perp}^{1}$	$\beta_{\perp}^{2}$	$\beta_{\perp}^{3}$
lq_t	− 3.263	− 0.270	− 1.105
$r_t - r_t^*$	− 0.463	− 0.131	− 1.118
$ltnt_t$	− 0.570	− 0.822	0.309
nfa_t	− 1.237	1.451	0.042

regressions which condition the real exchange rate solely on lagged real exchange rates are about 20 years for the recent floating period (see MacDonald, 1995). It is noteworthy that significant adjustment to the exchange rate disequilibrium does not occur in the other equations.

The top panel in Fig. 2 shows the estimated BEER calculated from Eq. (14), together with the actual real exchange rate for the sample period from 1960 to 1997 as well as the PEER, which has been constructed from the common factor representation (Eq. (13)). The close relationship between the BEER and the PEER series for the U.S. dollar is quite striking, which indicates that the BEER has only a small transitory component. Given the similarity of the BEER and PEER, our discussion of the U.S. dollar below simply focuses on the PEER.

It is noteworthy that from the beginning of the sample to the end of the 1970s, the trend path of the U.S. dollar REER is mirrored quite closely in the PEER, although there are periods, such as 1963–1964 and 1972–1974, when transitory components are important. The period 1972–1974 corresponds to the breakdown of the Bretton Woods system when there was a general recognition that the dollar was overvalued. The largest discrepancy between the estimated PEER and the REER in this period is in 1973, when the latter depreciated sharply and the PEER rose somewhat. As can be seen in Fig. 1, the increase in the PEER appears to be accounted for by a rise in relative U.S. interest rates. Thus, for 1973, it would appear that the model is giving the wrong signal regarding the appropriate valuation of the U.S. dollar.

By contrast, the top panel in Fig. 2 shows that in the period 1983–1985, the REER substantially exceeds the estimated PEER by about 20% and thus corresponds to the widely held view that the U.S. dollar was overvalued during this period. Transitory factors drove the actual exchange rate far above the value suggested by the permanent components of economic fundamentals identified in the model.[12] Once these transitory factors had dissipated, the real value of the dollar returned to its equilibrium level given by the PEER. Similarly, at the end of the sample period, economic fundamentals in the model indicate that the dollar should have weakened, whereas it strengthened instead, probably on account of cyclical factors not captured by the model.

In constructing the PEER, we have made use of the moving average representation of the VECM. This representation is of particular interest in as much as it yields information on which variables drive the common stochastic trends, measured by $\alpha_{\perp}'\Sigma_{i=1}^{t}\varepsilon_i$, and which variables are most affected by the common trends, as measured

[12] This is a common finding in papers that provide empirical estimates of the behavior of the U.S. dollar. See, for example, Faruqee (1995), Kramer (1996), MacDonald (1997), and Stein and Allen (1995).

Table 7
The estimates of the long-run impact matrix for the U.S. system

Variable	$\Sigma\varepsilon_{lq}$	$\Sigma\varepsilon_{r-r^*}$	$\Sigma\varepsilon_{ltnt}$	$\Sigma\varepsilon_{nfa}$
lq_t	0.004 (0.01)	1.123 (1.47)	2.159 (2.42)	3.454 (2.50)
$r_t - r_t^*$	− 0.019 (0.22)	1.123 (5.40)	0.349 (2.02)	0.3131 (1.17)
$ltnt_t$	0.192 (1.38)	− 0.271 (0.81)	0.992 (3.56)	− 0.041 (0.09)
nfa_t	− 0.321 (1.71)	− 0.104 (0.23)	− 0.371 (0.98)	1.840 (3.14)

by the $\beta_\perp$ weights. In as much as the U.S. system contains four I(1) variables and one stationary relationship implied by the significant cointegrating vector, we can infer that there must be three common trends. For the U.S. system, the alpha and beta orthogonal components are reported in Tables 5 and 6, respectively. These tables should be read in the following way. In Table 5, the row headings indicate the three common trends, while the column headings indicate the contributions of the variables to the trends. Reading across a row, the cell with the largest absolute number indicates that the shock to the variable in the column heading makes the largest contribution to the trend in the row heading. In Table 6, the column headings indicate the weights attached to the common trends, and the rows indicate how the weights are distributed amongst the variables. Reading down a column we see how a particular common trend gets distributed amongst the variables in the row headings. Alternatively, reading across a row information is obtained on which trend has the largest effect on a particular variable. In as much as there are currently no significance levels available for these numbers, they should be regarded as informative rather than definitive.

The results in Table 5 indicate that the first and second common trends appear to correspond to unanticipated shocks to the net foreign asset and Balassa–Samuelson terms, while the third is driven by the long-run real interest differential.

Table 6 indicates that the real exchange rate appears to be driven by the first common trend, with the Balassa–Samuelson variable and net foreign assets driven by the second. Both the exchange rate and the real interest differential are driven by the third common trend.

Further insight into the driving variables in our systems may be obtained by calculating the **C** matrix from Eq. (9). This measures the combined effects of the alpha and beta orthogonal components and gives an indication if a shock to a particular variable has a permanent effect on the other variables in the system. The estimated **C** matrix for the United States is reported in Table 7. The *t* ratios in parentheses are based on the asymptotic standard errors suggested by Paruolo (1997). These results reinforce the message from Tables 5 and 6: shocks to net foreign assets and the Balassa–Samuelson effect have a significant cumulative impact on the real exchange rate and are correctly signed.

Table 8
Multivariate diagnostics

LB (9)	LM (1)	LM (4)	NM (10)
157.25	25.84	7.28	6.85
(0.02)	(0.06)	(0.97)	(0.55)

p-values in parenthesis.

Table 9
Significance of cointegrating vectors

H_0:r	Trace	Trace 95
0	56.96	53.12
1	26.65	34.91
2	8.50	19.96
3	1.48	9.24

4.2. The Canadian dollar

The VAR specification for the Canadian system is the same as that for the U.S. system, namely, two lags and the constant restricted to the cointegrating space. The residual diagnostics for the Canadian system are reported in Table 8 and indicate an absence of serial correlation and that the errors are normally distributed.

The estimated values of the Trace statistics for the Canadian system, which are reported in Table 9, also indicate that there is a single unique cointegrating vector for the Canadian dollar. Normalizing this vector on the real exchange rate produces the following equation:

$$lq_t = \underset{(0.31)}{0.532}(r - r^*) + \underset{(0.06)}{1.489}\,\mathrm{ltnt} + \underset{(0.09)}{0.633}\,\mathrm{nfa} + \underset{(0.04)}{4.849}. \quad (15)$$

The results are similar to those for the U.S. dollar, as all of the variables enter with the correct sign and all are statistically significant. The alpha matrix associated with Eq. (15) is reported in Table 10.

Similar to the findings above for the U.S. dollar, the real exchange rate adjusts significantly to the error correction term. The adjustment speed is also approximately the same as in the case of the U.S. exchange rate and suggests that adjustment is essentially complete within 2 years.

The BEER and PEER implied by Eq. (15) are plotted in the middle panel of Fig. 2. We note that again, as in the case of the U.S. dollar, there is a very close correspondence between these two measures of the equilibrium exchange rate. Further, there is also a very tight link between the estimated PEER and the actual exchange rate; in fact, it is much tighter than in the case of the U.S. dollar. The most significant difference is at the very beginning of the period when the Canadian dollar was significantly above the value indicated by the PEER. This may reflect the large capital inflows in the late 1950s that strengthened the Canadian dollar and contributed to a current account deficit. The economic fundamentals that explain the PEER can account for only a small fraction of the higher value of the Canadian dollar. In 1961 the Canadian Government took measures to counter what it viewed as an overvalued exchange rate, including exchange market intervention and expansionary monetary and fiscal policies. These measures had the desired effect of changing market sentiment, and the exchange rate weakened during the second half of 1961 and into 1962. On May 2, 1961 the currency was pegged at 92.5 U.S. cents, which compares with an average value of 102.7 U.S. cents from 1952–1960.[13]

[13] For a discussion of the factors affecting the value of the Canadian dollar during this period and the exchange rate policy of the government, see Yeager (1966).

Table 10
Alpha adjustment matrix

Variable	alpha1	*t*-alpha1
Δlq	− 0.605	− 2.307
$\Delta r - r^*$	0.158	1.429
Δltnt	− 0.035	− 0.232
Δnfa	0.132	1.137

Thus, the empirical results here suggest that the Canadian dollar moved toward its equilibrium value when it depreciated and was then pegged in the early 1960s.

The results from the moving average representation for the Canadian dollar are reported in Tables 11 and 12. The first common trend appears to correspond to unanticipated shocks to the net foreign asset term, the second to the Balassa–Samuelson effect, and the third to the long-run real interest differential. This pattern is similar to the U.S. dollar system, indicating a degree of commonality between the two systems.

As shown in Table 12, the variables which adjust most to the first two trends are the real exchange rate, the Balassa–Samuelson effect, and nfa; real interest rate appear to be affected most by the third trend.

The estimated **C** matrix for the Canadian dollar is reported in Table 13. As in the U.S.-based system, we note that the cumulative nfa term is significant for the real exchange rate and also for the Balassa–Samuelson effect. The latter result seems perverse, although it may simply reflect the way we have measured the Balassa–Samuelson effect.

4.3. The pound sterling

For the pound sterling system, three lags were required to produce well-behaved residual diagnostics, and these are reported in Table 14. The diagnostics indicate an absence of serial correlation, although the NM (10) statistic is marginally significant, suggesting that there is some evidence of nonnormality in the residuals, which seems to arise from heteroscedasticity in the real interest rate equation.

The estimated values of the Trace statistics for the U.K. system are reported in Table 15. These indicate that, as for the other two currencies, there is a single cointegrating vector for the pound sterling.

Normalizing the significant cointegrating vector on the real exchange rate, we obtain

$$lq_t = \underset{(0.55)}{5.038}(r - r^*) + \underset{(0.13)}{0.678}\,\text{ltnt} + \underset{(0.12)}{0.030}\,\text{nfa} + \underset{(0.02)}{4.549} \quad (16)$$

All variables enter Eq. (16) with the correct sign, and all are statistically significant apart from the nfa term. In the light of the discussion to follow, it is worth noting that the

Table 11
Alpha orthogonal components for the Canadian system

Variable	lq_t	$r_t - r_t^*$	ltnt$_t$	nfa$_t$
$\alpha_\perp^1$	− 0.209	0.014	− 0.011	− 0.978
$\alpha_\perp^2$	0.023	− 0.131	− 0.991	0.005
$\alpha_\perp^3$	− 0.250	− 0.960	0.121	0.038

Table 12
Beta orthogonal components for the Canadian system

Variable	$\beta_\perp^1$	$\beta_\perp^2$	$\beta_\perp^3$
lq_t	−1.929	−1.070	0.026
$r_t - r_t^*$	0.138	0.026	−0.739
$ltnt_t$	−0.822	−1.092	0.284
nfa_t	−1.230	0.856	−0.006

coefficient on the relative interest rate term is much larger for the U.K. system than in the other systems. The insignificance of the nfa term in the U.K. equation contrasts with the results for both Canada and the United States and perhaps reflects the dominance of relative interest rates for the United Kingdom. The alpha matrix associated with Eq. (16) is reported in Table 16.

As in the other two systems, the real exchange rate adjusts significantly to the exchange rate disequilibrium. However, in contrast to the other systems, all of the other variables are also significantly reacting to the error correction term, suggesting that adjustment to equilibrium is not so transparent in the U.K. system.

The BEER and PEER implied by Eq. (16) are plotted in the bottom panel of Fig. 2. The picture here is quite distinct from that given in the other panels of Fig. 2, as the BEER and PEER are quite different, with the former being much more volatile than the actual rate in the period up to the early 1980s. This volatility is driven by the volatility of real interest rates that was an important feature of this period. What explains this difference between the BEER and PEER? As we argued above, one advantage of estimating the PEER is that we have access to the permanent and transitory components of all of the variables in our systems. In contrast to the United States and Canada, for the United Kingdom, there is a much closer correlation between the actual and the transitory components of the real interest differential than between the actual and the permanent component. For example, the correlation between the actual and the transitory component for the U.K. real interest rate is .8, while for the United States it is only .06. This is underscored by an examination of Fig. 3, where we have graphed the permanent and transitory components of the real interest differentials against the actual values for all three countries.

We believe that one advantage of the PEER decomposition is that it clarifies the extent to which a misalignment implied by the BEER is permanent or transitory. Referring back to our discussion in Section 2, it would seem that as the real interest differential for Canada and the United States is driven in large measure by the permanent component, it should perhaps be thought of having its affect on the real exchange rate through $\bar{q}_t$. For the United

Table 13
The estimates of the long-run impact matrix for the Canadian system

Variable	$\Sigma\varepsilon_{lq}$	$\Sigma\varepsilon_{r-r^*}$	$\Sigma\varepsilon_{ltnt}$	$\Sigma\varepsilon_{nfa}$
lq_t	0.371 (0.64)	0.088 (0.19)	1.085 (0.91)	1.882 (2.98)
$r_t - r_t^*$	0.156 (1.25)	0.708 (7.26)	−0.117 (0.45)	−0.163 (1.18)
$ltnt_t$	0.075 (0.21)	−0.141 (0.52)	1.125 (1.58)	0.809 (2.11)
nfa_t	0.278 (1.02)	−0.124 (0.58)	−0.835 (1.49)	1.206 (4.01)

t-ratios in parenthesis.

Table 14
Multivariate diagnostics

LB (9)	LM (1)	LM (4)	NM (10)
129.412	24.63	16.47	17.38
(0.01)	(0.08)	(0.42)	(0.03)

p-values in parenthesis.

Kingdom, however, the prominence of the transitory component in the real interest differential suggests that it is more closely associated with business cycle developments, and therefore, its influence on the real exchange rate should be separate from $\bar{q}_t$. However, it turns out that the permanent component of the real interest differential follows closely the real exchange rate and would therefore be part of $\bar{q}_t$.

The pronounced volatility of real interest rates in the mid-1970s corresponds to the almost hyperinflationary environment of that period, combined with rising nominal interest rates, which did not quite catch up with the inflationary spiral until the late 1970s. We believe that the U.K. BEER is of interest in itself, in as much as, for one thing, it clearly illustrates how different the monetary environment has been for the United Kingdom compared to the United States and Canada. However, given the importance of interest rate volatility for the United Kingdom, it may be instructive to produce a BEER which is neutral with respect to interest rate effects [i.e., a BEER which is based only on the $\bar{q}_t$ component of $\bar{q}_t'$ in Eq. (3)]. This is shown as BEER* in the bottom panel of Fig. 2. We note that its profile is much smoother than the BEER and the REER for the United Kingdom.[14]

More generally, it is clear from Fig. 2 that the BEER provides a generally poor explanation of the behavior of the pound, as compared with the remarkably good fit for both the U.S. and Canadian dollars. One reason for this may be that the real effective value of the pound shows no clear trend, starting and ending the sample period at an index value of 100, whereas the estimated BEER does have a downward trend, reflecting the unit root characteristics of the three explanatory variables. By contrast, the PEER provides a remarkably good explanation for the real value of the pound, capturing well the devaluation in 1967, the substantial appreciation in the late 1970s, and the sharp appreciation in 1997. As noted above, this would appear to reflect the importance of the permanent component of the real interest differential in explaining the behavior of the pound, which is clearly evident in Fig. 4. By contrast, in the United States and Canada, the permanent component of the real interest differential is much less closely related to the PEER and the REER.

The set of results from the moving average representation for the United Kingdom are reported in Tables 17–19. The first common trend appears to correspond to the real interest differential, the second is driven by nfa and lq, while the third is driven by the Balassa–Samuelson effect.

The real exchange rate has the largest loading on all three common trends, although the second gets a large loading into nfa, and the third gets a relatively large loading into the

[14] BEER* in Fig. 2 is constructed on the basis that the real interest rate observed in the first year of the sample remains constant throughout the sample.

Table 15
Significance of cointegrating vectors

H_0:r	Trace	Trace 95
0	70.26	53.12
1	24.23	34.91
2	11.47	19.96
3	2.68	9.24

Balassa–Samuelson term. This is a rather different pattern from that contained in the U.S. and Canadian systems, where no single variable is strongly affected by all three common trends.

The estimates of the **C** matrix reported in Table 19 confirm the importance of real interest rates for the U.K. real exchange rate and that the real exchange rate, in turn, is important for the real interest differential, although the coefficient on the latter is much smaller.

In contrast to the other two systems, we note that shocks to net foreign assets do not have a cumulative effect on the pound. Consistent with what we said above, shocks to the real interest rate differential have a significantly positive cumulative effect on the real exchange rate and also on the ltnt term. We interpret this as a demand side influence on the relative price of traded to nontraded goods.

5. Concluding comments

The BEER estimates of equilibrium exchange rates presented in this paper are in sharp contrast to those that would be obtained from the popular PPP hypothesis. The latter hypothesis ignores any fundamentals, and empirical estimates indicate that there is a very long convergence to PPP. Our approach stresses two points: (i) There are real fundamentals that can be used to explain systematic exchange rate movements, and (ii) convergence in our estimated models is relatively rapid. For example, the half-life reported here for the U.S. dollar is only 1 year.

The main focus of this paper has been to provide an extension of the BEER approach to exchange rate analysis by providing a decomposition of the BEER into its permanent and transitory components. The BEER approach to identifying equilibrium exchange rates involves estimating an equilibrium relationship between the real exchange rate and

Table 16
Alpha adjustment matrix variable

	alpha1	t-alpha1
Δlq	−0.460	−3.653
$\Delta(r-r^*)$	0.238	5.541
Δltnt	−0.117	−3.008
Δnfa	0.237	3.118

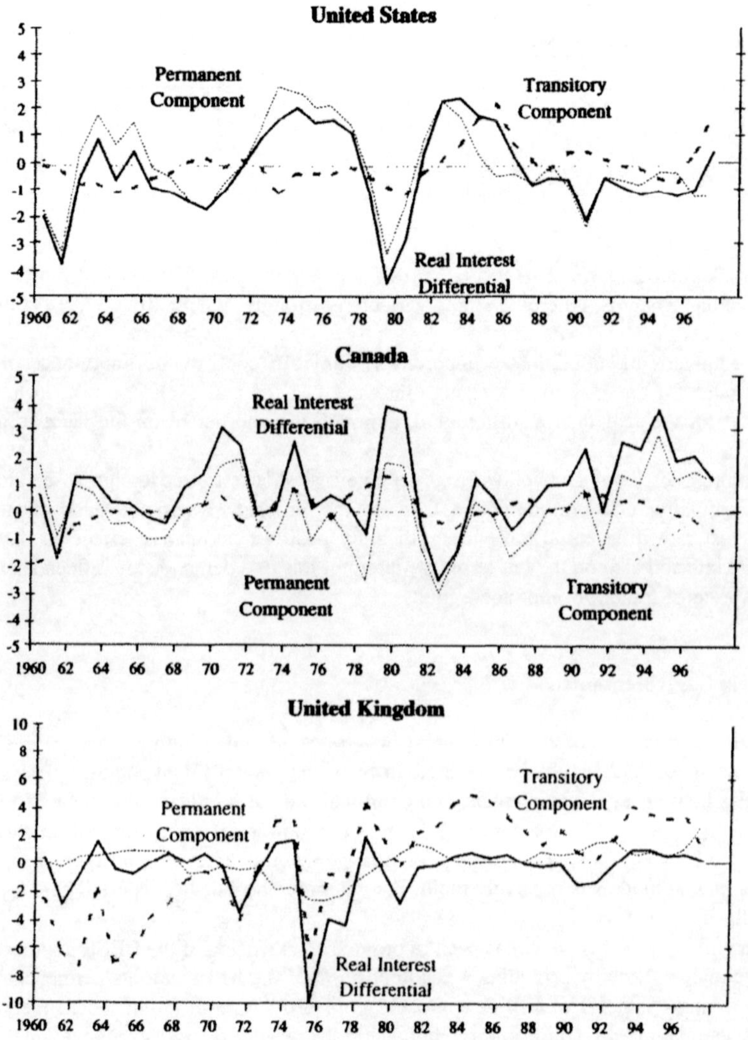

Fig. 3. Transitory and permanent components of the real interest differential.

economic fundamentals. In an earlier paper (Clark & MacDonald, 1999), we noted that in analyzing exchange rate behavior and making judgements about exchange rate sustainability, it is important to ascertain whether the economic fundamentals themselves are at their equilibrium values. In this paper, the explicit calculation of the permanent components of the REERs of the U.S. and Canadian dollars and the U.K. pound (and the related transitory components) provides one method of calibrating fundamentals at their 'equi-

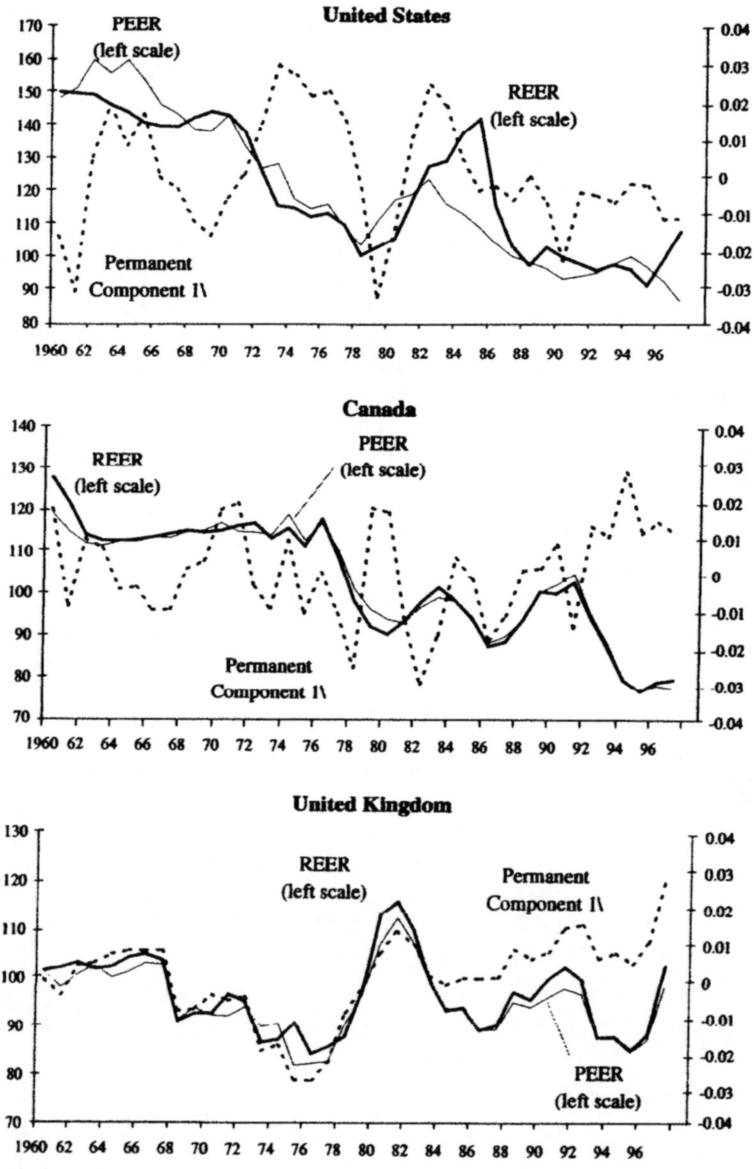

1\ Permanent component of real interest differential (right scale).

Fig. 4. REER, PEER, and permanent components of the real interest differential.

Table 17
Alpha orthogonal components for the U.K. system

Variable	lq_t	$r_t - r_t^*$	$ltnt_t$	nfa_t
$\alpha_\perp^1$	0.213	0.881	0.190	−0.377
$\alpha_\perp^2$	−0.574	−0.237	0.375	−0.688
$\alpha_\perp^3$	−0.017	−0.005	−0.884	−0.466

librium' values. Does such a calibration produce a measure of equilibrium, which is distinct from that provided by the BEER?

For the U.S. and Canadian dollars, we found that the BEER and the PEER move very closely together, implying that the current values of the economic variables driving the BEER have only a very small transitory component. Moreover, both the BEER and the PEER track the actual values of these two real exchange rates extremely well, with the exception of the 1983–1985 period for the U.S. dollar, which shows clearly that the highly appreciated value of the U.S. dollar during this period was a transitory phenomenon. By contrast, in the case of the U.K. pound, the BEER and the PEER diverge sharply, with the latter generally following the movements of the actual real value of the pound, thereby illustrating the value of the permanent–transitory decomposition. Moreover, much of the volatility of the pound appears to be driven by fluctuations in the permanent component of the real interest rate differential. There is a much higher correlation between the actual and the transitory component of U.K. interest rates compared to U.S. interest rates, for example, which would appear to account for the poor fit of the BEER with the real value of the pound.

The permanent–transitory decomposition adopted here has a number of additional advantages. One of these is that it is possible to identify which variables are the main contributors of system-wide nonstationarity (the common trends) and which variables in turn are affected by these common trends. Moreover, this approach yields information on the combined effects of the permanent and transitory components and gives an indication if a shock to a particular variable has a permanent effect on the other variables in the system. It is noteworthy that net foreign assets have a long-run impact on the real value of the U.S. and Canadian dollars; by contrast, the only variable that has a significant long-run effect on the U.K. pound is the real interest differential. Finally, it should be noted that this approach lends itself to extending the analysis to common

Table 18
Beta orthogonal components for the U.K. system

Variable	$\beta_\perp^1$	$\beta_\perp^2$	$\beta_\perp^3$
lq_t	1.777	−1.128	1.336
$r_t - r_t^*$	0.278	−0.224	0.385
$ltnt_t$	0.595.	0.046	−0.869
nfa_t	−0.843	−0.998	−0.398

Table 19
The estimates of the long-run impact matrix for the U.K. system

Variable	$\Sigma\varepsilon_{lq}$	$\Sigma\varepsilon_{r-r*}$	$\Sigma\varepsilon_{ltnt}$	$\Sigma\varepsilon_{nfa}$
lq_t	1.002 (2.98)	1.827 (3.11)	− 1.267 (1.27)	− 0.518 (0.77)
$r_t - r_t^*$	0.181 (3.01)	0.296 (2.81)	− 0.372 (2.07)	− 0.130 (1.08)
ltnt_t	0.115 (0.92)	0.518 (2.36)	0.899 (2.41)	0.150 (0.59)
lnfa_t	0.401 (1.68)	− 0.504 (1.21)	− 0.183 (0.26)	1.190 (2.50)

t-ratios in parenthesis.

factors across currency systems, as such systems and relevant interest rates are obviously interrelated. This extension is left for further work.

References

Alberola, E., Cervero, S. G., Lopez, H., & Ubide, A. (1999). *Global equilibrium exchange rates: Euro, Dollar, "ins," "outs," and other major currencies in a panel cointegration framework*, IMF Working Paper 99/175 (Washington: International Monetary Fund).

Baffes, J., Elbadawi, I. A., & O'Connell, S. A. (1999). Single-equation estimation of the equilibrium real exchange rate. In L. E. Hinkle, & P. J. Montiel (Eds.), *Chapter 10 in estimating equilibrium exchange rates in developing countries* (pp. 405–461). Washington: World Bank.

Baxter, M. (1994). Real exchange rates and real interest rate differentials: Have we missed the business-cycle relationship? *Journal of Monetary Economics, 33*, 5–37.

Beveridge, S., & Nelson, C. R. (1981). A new approach to decomposition of economic time series into permanent and transitory components with particular attention to measurement of the 'business cycle'. *Journal of Monetary Economics, 7*, 151–174.

Campbell, J. Y., & Clarida, R. H. (1987). The dollar and real interest rates. In A. Meltzer, & K. Brunner (Eds.), *Carnegie-Rochester conference series on public policy, vol. 24* (pp. 203–240). Amsterdam: North Holland.

Chinn, M. D. & Meredith, G. (1998). *Long-horizon uncovered interest rate parity*, NBER Working Paper No. 6797.

Clarida, R., & Gali, J. (1995). Sources of real exchange rate fluctuations: How important are nominal shocks? *Carnegie-Rochester series on public policy, vol. 41* (pp. 1–56). Amsterdam: North-Holland.

Clark, P. B., & MacDonald, R. (1999). Exchange rates and economic fundamentals: A methodological comparison of BEERs and FEERs. In R. MacDonald, & J. L. Stein (Eds.), *Chapter 10 in equilibrium exchange rates* (pp. 285–322). London, UK: Kluwer Academic Publishing.

Clostermann, J., & Friedmann, W. (1998). What drives the real effective D-mark exchange rate? *Konjunkturpolitik, 44*, 207–230.

Doornik, J., & Hansen, H. (1994). *Practical test of multivariate normality, unpublished paper*. Oxford: Nuffield College.

Duval, R. (2002). What do we know about long run equilibrium real exchange rates? *PPPs vs Macroeconomic Approaches Australian Economic Papers, 41*(4), 382–403.

Edison, H., & Pauls, D. (1993). Re-assessment of the relationship between real exchange rates and real interest rates: 1974–1990. *Journal of Monetary Economics, 31*, 165–188.

Edison, H. J., & Melick, W. R. (1999). Alternative approaches to real exchange rates: Three up and one down. *International Journal of Finance and Economics, 4*, 93–111.

Engle, R., & Granger, C. (1987). Cointegration and error correction: Representation, estimation and testing. *Econometrica, 55*, 251–276.

Faruqee, H. (1995). Long-run determinants of the real exchange rate: A stock-flow equilibrium approach, staff papers. *International Monetary Fund, 42*, 80–107.

Froot, K. A. (1990, January). *Short rates and expected asset returns*, NBER Working Paper No. 3247.

Godfrey, L. G. (1988). *Misspecification tests in econometrics*. Cambridge, MA: Cambridge University Press.

Granger, C., & Gonzalo, J. (1995). Estimation of common long-memory components in cointegrated systems. *Journal of Business and Economic Statistics*, *13*, 27–35.

Huizinga, J. (1987). An empirical investigation of the long-run behaviour of real exchange rates. *Carnegie-Rochester conference series on public policy, vol. 27* (pp. 149–214). Amsterdam: North-Holland.

Isard, P. (1983). An accounting framework and some issues for modeling how exchange rates respond to the news. In J. Frenkel (Ed.), *Exchange rates and international macroeconomics*. Chicago: Chicago University Press.

Isard, P. & Faruqee, H. (1998). *Exchange rate assessment: Extensions of the macroeconomic balance approach*, IMF Occasional Paper No 167 (Washington: International Monetary Fund).

Johansen, S. (1988). Statistical analysis of cointegrating vectors. *Journal of Economic Dynamics and Control*, *12*, 231–254.

Johansen, S. (1995). *Likelihood based inference in cointegrated vector autoregressive models*. Oxford: Oxford University Press.

Johansen, S., & Juselius, K. (1992). Maximum likelihood estimation and inference on cointegration—With applications to the demand for money. *Oxford Bulletin of Economics and Statistics*, *52*, 169–210.

Kakkari, V. & Ogaki, M. (1993). Real exchange rates and non-tradables, University of Rochester, mimeo.

Kramer, C. (1996). *The real effective value of the U.S. dollar, the fiscal deficit, and long-run balance of payments equilibrium: An empirical note*. Washington: International Monetary Fund (unpublished).

Lane, P. & Milesi-Ferretti, G. M. (2000). *The transfer problem revisited: Net foreign assets and real exchange rates*, unpublished paper, Trinity College Dublin and International Monetary Fund.

Lim, G. (2000). *Misalignment and managed exchange rates: An application to the Thai baht*, IMF Working Paper 00/63 (Washington: International Monetary Fund).

MacDonald, R. (1995). *Asset market and balance of payments characteristics: An eclectic exchange rate model for the dollar, mark and yen*, IMF Working Paper 95/55 (Washington: International Monetary Fund).

MacDonald, R. (1997). *What determines real exchange rates: The long and short of it*, IMF Working Paper 97/21 (Washington: International Monetary Fund).

MacDonald, R. (1999, November). Controversy: Exchange rate fundamentals. *Economic Journal*, *109*(459), F652–F691.

MacDonald, R. & Nagayasu, J. (1999). *The long-run relationship between real exchange rates and real interest differentials: A panel study*, IMF Working Paper 99/37.

MacDonald, R., & Stein, J. L. (Eds.). (1999). *Equilibrium exchange rates*. London, UK: Kluwer Academic Publishing.

MacDonald, R. & Swagel, P. (2000). *Real exchange rates and the business cycle*, IMF Working Paper forthcoming (Washington: International Monetary Fund).

Masson, P., Kremers, J., & Horne, J. (1993). "*Net foreign assets and international adjustments: The United States, Japan, and Germany*," IMF Working Paper 93/33 (Washington: International Monetary Fund).

Meese, R., & Rogoff, K. (1988). Was it real? The exchange rate–interest differential relation over the modern floating-rate period. *Journal of Finance*, *43*, 4.

Paruolo, P. (1997). Asymptotic inference on the moving average impact in cointegrated I(1) VAR systems. *Econometric Theory*, *13*, 79–118.

Quah, D. (1989). *The relative importance of permanent and transitory components: Identification and some theoretical bounds*, working paper, MIT.

Stein, J. L. (1999). The evolution of the real value of the U.S. dollar relative to the G7 currencies. In R. MacDonald, & J. L. Stein (Eds.), *Chapter 3 in equilibrium exchange rates*. London, UK: Kluwer Academic Publishing.

Stein, J. L. (2003). The equilibrium real exchange rate of the Euro: An evaluation of research. CESifo. *Economic Studies*, 1–33.

Stein, J. L. (1995). *Fundamental determinants of exchange rates*. Oxford, UK: Clarendon Press.

Stock, J. H., & Watson, M. W. (1988). Testing for common trends. *Journal of the American Statistical Association*, *83*, 1097–1107.

Williamson, J. (Ed.). (1994). *Estimating equilibrium exchange rates*. Washington: Institute for International Economics.

Yeager, L. B. (1966). *International monetary relations: Theory, history, and policy*, University of Virginia, Harper & Row, New York.

Zanello, A. & Dominique, D. (1997). *Primer on the IMF's information notice system*, IMF Working Paper 97/71 (Washington: International Monetary Fund).

[12]

THE REAL EXCHANGE RATE AND THE BALASSA–SAMUELSON EFFECT: THE ROLE OF THE DISTRIBUTION SECTOR

Ronald MacDonald* *University of Strathclyde*
Luca Antonio Ricci* *IMF, Washington, DC*

Abstract. This paper investigates the long-run impact of the distribution sector on the real exchange rate. The main result is that an increase in the productivity and product market competition of the distribution sector with respect to foreign countries leads to an appreciation of the real exchange rate, similar to what a relative increase in the domestic productivity of tradables does. This contrasts with the result that one would expect by considering the distribution sector as belonging to the non-tradable sector. One explanation may lie in the use of the services from the distribution sector in the tradable sector.

1. Introduction

Very few authors discuss the importance of the distribution sector in influencing the real exchange rate. When the sector is analysed, it is normally considered – either explicitly or implicitly – as non-tradable. This paper investigates, both theoretically and empirically, the long-run impact of the distribution sector on the real exchange rate (RER) and shows that the common intuition that such a sector behaves as a non-tradable is not consistent with the empirical evidence.

The issue is important, given the size of the distribution sector (wholesale and retail trade) in the economy, which in industrial countries often reaches 20% of industrial activity, in terms of both value added and employment (see Table 1), and might therefore account for a large component of prices. For example, using US input–output data, Burstein *et al.* (2000) show that consumption goods in the USA contain distribution services accounting for about 47% of the final price in the agricultural sector and 42% in manufacturing. Dornbusch (1989) mentions the importance of the distribution sector in influencing the RER via 'the service content of the consumer prices of goods'. Recent studies of the Balassa–Samuelson effect, which use sectoral data to derive measures of relative productivity of tradables and non-tradables, include the distribution sector in the non-tradable sector (De Gregorio *et al.*, 1994;

**Address for correspondence*: Ronald MacDonald, University of Strathclyde, Scotland, UK; Email: r.r.macdonald@strath.ac.uk. We would like to thank Tamim Bayoumi, Charles Engel, Peter Isard, Jacques Melitz, Sam Ouliaris and Eswar Prasad; seminar participants at the Copenhagen Business School, the CESifo Area Conference in Macroeconomics, Munich, the International Monetary Fund, Netherlands Central Bank and the University of Strathclyde for insightful discussions and comments; Peter Pedroni for helpful advice on panel econometrics; and Bennet Sutton for excellent research assistance. The project was started when Ronald MacDonald was visiting at the IMF Research Department during the summer of 1998.

© 2005 Blackwell Publishing Ltd

Table 1. Sectoral composition of economic activity: 1970–92 average of 10 European countries

	Sectoral share in industrial activity		*Sectoral share in national GDP*	
Sector	*Gross domestic value added (GDP)*	*Total employment (ET)*	*Gross domestic value added (GDP)*	*Total employment (ET)*
Community, social and personal services (*SOC*)	10.15	11.34	8.71	9.18
Finance, insurance, real estate, business services (*FNI*)	15.37	9.18	12.84	7.12
Transport, storage and communication (*TRS*)	8.51	8.10	7.15	6.36
Wholesale and retail trade (*RWH*)	15.21	18.68	12.87	14.91
Construction (*CST*)	8.21	9.73	6.92	7.73
Electricity, gas and water (*EGW*)	3.44	1.14	2.91	0.90
Manufacturing (*MAN*)	28.91	30.03	24.47	23.87
Mining and quarrying (*MID*)	1.85	0.67	1.57	0.54
Agriculture, hunting, forestry and fishing (*AGR*)	5.24	10.15	4.40	8.16
Other	3.11	0.97	18.17	21.23
Total industry (*TIN*)	100.00	100.00		
Total economic activity (*TET*)	100.00	100.00		

Source: OECD International Sectoral Database; OECD data code in parenthesis.

De Gregorio and Wolf, 1994; Chinn and Johnson, 1999).[1] Both Devereux (1999) and Burstein *et al.* (2000) explicitly discuss the role of the distribution sector in explaining the RER, but still treat the sector as a non-tradable. (In both papers it is assumed to influence the domestic consumption price of tradables, after international price equalization.) Obstfeld and Rogoff (2000) briefly mention, but do not pursue, the role of the distribution sector as an alternative explanation for the relatively slow mean reversion in RERs. Engel (1999) has suggested the distribution sector as one explanation for the variability of the relative price of non-traded goods in explaining US CPI-based RER movements.

The view that the distribution sector influences the RER through the non-tradable sector stems directly from the observation that arbitrage in the goods market occurs not at the consumer level but at the producer level.[2] Even abstracting from transportation costs and market pricing, and even if global market integration equalizes prices at the producer level, consumer prices for the same good may still differ across countries. For example, if one country

[1] The Balassa–Samuelson effect states that an increase in the relative productivity of tradables over non-tradables of one country *v.* those of foreign countries raises that country's relative wage, thus increasing its relative price of non-tradables and its relative average price, and inducing an appreciation of the real exchange rate (RER). For the original analysis, see Balassa (1964) and Samuelson (1964).

[2] It is interesting to note that when internet trade, or other forms of direct producer–consumer trade, will have developed internationally, goods arbitrage will tend to occur also at the consumer level, controlling for transportation costs.

© 2005 Blackwell Publishing Ltd

has a more efficient distribution sector (say, large retail outlets in the USA) than other countries (that have, say, small shops, e.g. some European countries), it will enjoy lower prices for the distribution services and a lower consumer price index than its foreign counterpart, as both prices of tradables and non-tradables would, *ceteris paribus*, be lower. This would, in turn, be reflected in a more depreciated RER. To the extent that differences in the efficiency of the distribution sector across countries remain constant over time, they would simply generate constant gaps in consumer price levels across countries. In other words, they would affect absolute PPP. Of course, this cannot be tested with the aggregate price series usually exploited in PPP-based studies, since these series are in index form. However, to the extent that these differences change over time (say, because of productivity growth or changes in the market structure of the retail sector), they would induce converging or diverging trends in relative prices and hence could explain systematic movements in RERs. In the previous example, an empirically testable implication would be the following: an increase (decrease) in the relative efficiency of the distribution sector with respect to the foreign country induces a depreciation (appreciation) of the RER. But is this, in fact, the case?

This paper addresses the issue by examining the importance of the distribution sector in explaining deviations of the RER from purchasing power parity (PPP) and by assessing how the sector influences the RER. The remainder of the paper is organized as follows. Section 2 provides a comparative description of our analysis versus the existing literature. Section 3 develops a simple theoretical model to explore the main intuition behind the influence of the distribution sector on the RER in the long run. Sections 4 and 5 empirically investigate the long-run relations between the RER and a measure of efficiency of the distribution sector, by applying a dynamic panel methodology to data for nine countries over a 20-year period. Section 6 draws conclusions.

2. OUR ANALYSIS AND THE RELATED LITERATURE

A natural framework for our investigation is the one that features the Balassa–Samuelson analysis. Most empirical studies of the Balassa–Samuelson effect on the RER compare aggregate measures of productivity across countries, such as GDP per capita, GDP per worker or labour productivity in the manufacturing sector. Ito *et al.* (1997) report a statistically significant relationship between the RER change and the change in per capita GDP, their proxy for the Balassa–Samuelson effect, for a group of Asian currencies. They do not find an association between the per capita differential and the relative price of non-traded to traded goods, and suggest that one explanation for this latter result is that per capita GDP is not a good proxy for productivity differences. However, there are a number of existing studies that test the Balassa–Samuelson hypothesis directly, via the effect of productivity in the tradable and non-tradable sectors on CPI-based RERs, rather than using proxies. For example, Hsieh (1982), Marston (1990) and De Gregorio and Wolf (1994) examine the relationship in growth terms and report evidence that is favourable to the

© 2005 Blackwell Publishing Ltd

Balassa–Samuelson hypothesis, in the sense that the coefficients on productivity in the two sectors are statistically significant and correctly signed. As Chinn and Johnson (1999) point out, however, the use of growth rates in these papers allows for permanent shocks to the relationship in levels, which may be undesirable. By applying cointegration analysis and employing OECD sectoral total factor productivity data, the authors find significant long-run relationships between the CPI-based RERs and the relative price of non-traded to traded goods, as well as between the RERs and productivity differentials, thus again supporting the Balassa–Samuelson proposition. Similar results are derived by Canzoneri *et al.* (1996), who, using panel cointegration methods, find a significant long-run relationship between the relative price of non-traded to traded goods and relative labour productivity in the traded to non-traded sectors.

Section 3 provides a very simple framework to illustrate the role of the distribution sector in the context of a standard Balassa–Samuelson setting with tradable and non-tradable sectors. (The model shares some features with Devereux, 1999, as discussed later.) Our motivation is to minimize the assumption changes in the basic Balassa–Samuelson framework in order to highlight the likely role the distribution sector will have on the RER.

One key assumption in the standard Balassa–Samuelson model is that the law of one price (LOOP) holds and therefore that systematic movements in RERs arise from movements in the relative price of non-traded to traded goods. However, using disaggregate CPI data, Engel (1993, 1999) has demonstrated that the vast majority of the variation in RERs is attributable to variations in the relative price of traded goods, rather than the relative price of non-traded to traded goods. This finding has been confirmed using more finely disaggregated prices by Rogers and Jenkins (1995) and Betts and Kehoe (2001).[3]

In our empirical testing of the effect of the distribution sector on the RER, we do not require the LOOP to hold; indeed, our empirical results are consistent with those researchers who have reported violations of the LOOP at the wholesale level. In particular, following MacDonald and Ricci (2002), we will introduce, in some specifications, the wage into our regressions as an extra conditioning variable in order to determine the channel of influence of the productivities in the various sectors and the importance of violations of the LOOP. If the LOOP holds, productivity shocks get transmitted into the RER via the wage, and the significance of productivity in the tradable sector should disappear once the wage is introduced into the regression.

In addition to the Balassa–Samuelson effect, other variables have been shown to be related to the RER in the long run, both in theoretical and empirical contributions (see e.g. Obstfeld and Rogoff, 1996; Devereux, 1999; Lane and Milesi-Ferretti, 2000; MacDonald, 1995). In order to ensure that our results with respect to productivity and distribution are not spurious, we include net foreign assets and the real interest differential in our empirical analysis.

[3] Terms-of-trade fluctuations have also been considered an important determinant of the real exchange rate, especially for developing countries.

© 2005 Blackwell Publishing Ltd

Our work also has a bearing on the recent PPP literature, which has produced the so-called PPP puzzle (Rogoff, 1996), indicating that the mean reversion in RERs is too slow to be consistent with a traditional form of PPP. In particular, studies that use long historical time spans on a single currency to estimate PPP (see Edison, 1987; Frankel, 1988; Diebold *et al.*, 1991), and those applying panel estimators to data for the recent floating period (see Frankel and Rose, 1995; MacDonald, 1995; Oh, 1996) have shown that the half-life in RERs is between three and five years. A variety of avenues have been explored to try to explain the 'PPP puzzle'. One of these simply involves explicitly recognizing the role of macroeconomic factors, such as the Balassa–Samuelson effect, net foreign assets and interest rate differentials, in driving RERs.[4] We will show that, taking into account these effects, as well as the one of the distribution sector, brings the estimated half-life of deviations close to one year.

3. A SIMPLE MOTIVATIONAL MODEL

The model assumes constant returns to labour in all primary activities, i.e. the production of intermediate inputs (I), distribution services (D), non-tradables goods (N) and the aggregation services (A) necessary to manufacture tradables from intermediate inputs.[5,6] The technology for secondary activities are Cobb–Douglas: in goods I, D and A for the production of tradables (T), and in goods T and D in order to make tradables available to consumers (TC). The model is then completed by assuming different technologies in the primary activities across countries, identical Cobb–Douglas preferences in tradables and non-tradables across countries, wage equalization within countries, international price equalization for tradables and non-tradability of intermediate inputs. In formulas, for country i ($I = 1, 2$),

[4] An alternative approach has capitalized on the evident failure of the LOOP and focuses on the relative price of traded goods, rather than the relative price of non-traded to traded goods. For example, one such explanation lies in exporters' pricing to market behaviour, which effectively prevents traditional arbitrage forcing PPP (see Feenstra and Kendall, 1997; Cheung *et al.*, 2001). A second explanation stresses the importance of transaction costs, relating to the distance between trading centres, in preventing arbitrage between trading centres. Such costs are usually captured in a nonlinear framework, such as a threshold autoregressive model, and the application of these models indicates adjustment speeds for real exchange rates that are consistent with a traditional form of PPP (see e.g. Obstfeld and Taylor, 1997). However, transaction costs are only a small proportion of traded goods prices and therefore seem insufficient on their own to explain the large observed deviations from PPP. For example, Hummels (1999) estimates the average trade-weighted freight cost in the USA in 1994 at 3.8%, which is clearly very small compared with the effects of distribution costs referred to above. A much more significant set of costs relates to the distribution of goods, which can affect the real exchange rate through both the relative price of traded goods and the relative price of non-traded to traded goods.

[5] In reality, the distribution sector delivers both intermediate inputs to the firms that use them in the final stage of production, and final goods to consumers. For the sake of simplicity, we assume that intermediate inputs are used only in the tradable sector and that distribution of final goods is necessary only in the tradable sector; relaxation of these assumptions would deliver qualitatively identical results. This choice of assumptions is also in line with the fact that most non-tradable activities (utilities, social services) have a vertically integrated distribution sector.

[6] Our model is similar to that of Devereux (1999), which we discuss below.

© 2005 Blackwell Publishing Ltd

$$Y_{ki} = \frac{L_{ki}}{\beta_{ki}}, \quad k = I, D, N, A,$$

$$Y_{Ti} = \frac{Y_{Ii}^{\gamma\eta} Y_{Di}^{1-\gamma} Y_{Ai}^{\gamma(1-\eta)}}{(\gamma\eta)^{\gamma\eta}(1-\gamma)^{1-\gamma}(\gamma(1-\eta))^{\gamma(1-\eta)}},$$

$$Y_{TCi} = \frac{Y_{Ti}^{1-\phi} Y_{Di}^{\phi}}{\phi^{\phi}(1-\phi)^{1-\phi}},$$

$$U_i = \frac{y_{Ni}^{\alpha} y_{TCi}^{1-\alpha}}{\alpha^{\alpha}(1-\alpha)^{1-\alpha}},$$

where L_{ki} and β_{ki} represent, respectively, employment and the unit labour input requirement prevailing in sector k and country i (for $k = I, D, N, A$), and Y_{ki} is the output in sector k of country i (for $k = I, D, N, A, T, TC$); U_i and y_{ki} stand for, respectively, the utility of one individual of country i and her/his demand for good k (for $k = N, TC$).

In equilibrium, given firms and consumer maximization problems and goods market-clearing, the following equations for the price of the various goods and services of the two countries must hold:

$$p_{ki} = \beta_{ki} w_i, \quad k = I, D, N, A,$$

$$p_{Ti} = p_{Ii}^{\gamma\eta} p_{Di}^{1-\gamma} p_{Ai}^{\gamma(1-\eta)} = w_i \beta_{Ii}^{\gamma\eta} \beta_{Di}^{1-\gamma} \beta_{Ai}^{\gamma(1-\eta)} \equiv w_i \beta_{Ti}^{\gamma} \beta_{Di}^{1-\gamma},$$

$$p_{TCi} = p_{Ti}^{1-\phi} p_{Di}^{\phi},$$

$$p_{T1} = e p_{T2},$$

$$p_i = p_{Ni}^{\alpha} p_{TCi}^{1-\alpha},$$

$$RER \equiv \frac{p_1}{ep_2} = \frac{p_{N1}^{\alpha} p_{TC1}^{1-\alpha}}{ep_{N2}^{\alpha} p_{TC2}^{1-\alpha}},$$

where w_i is the wage prevailing in country i, $\beta_{Ti} \equiv \beta_{Ii}^{\eta}\beta_{Ai}^{1-\eta}$ is the average productivity of the two stages of production of tradable goods in country i, and e is the nominal exchange rate (units of currency 1 for one unit of currency 2).

The price equalization of tradable goods (we discuss this assumption further below) determines relative wages and provides the familiar relation for the RER, which is now augmented for the distribution sector:

$$\frac{w_1}{ew_2} = \left(\frac{\beta_{T2}}{\beta_{T1}}\right)^{\gamma} \left(\frac{\beta_{D2}}{\beta_{D1}}\right)^{1-\gamma},$$

$$RER = \left(\frac{w_1}{ew_2}\right)^{\alpha+(1-\alpha)\phi} \left(\frac{\beta_{N1}}{\beta_{N2}}\right)^{\alpha} \left(\frac{\beta_{D1}}{\beta_{D2}}\right)^{(1-\alpha)\phi} = \left(\frac{\beta_{T2}}{\beta_{T1}}\right)^{\alpha\gamma+(1-\alpha)\phi\gamma} \left(\frac{\beta_{N2}}{\beta_{N1}}\right)^{-\alpha} \left(\frac{\beta_{D2}}{\beta_{D1}}\right)^{(1-\gamma)\alpha-(1-\alpha)\phi\gamma}$$

Hence the RER of country 1 versus that of country 2 will appreciate with the relative productivity of tradables (β_{T2}/β_{T1}) and will depreciate with the relative productivity of non-tradables (β_{N2}/β_{N1}). It will also appreciate with the relative productivity of the distribution sector (β_{D2}/β_{D1}), if this sector plays a bigger

© 2005 Blackwell Publishing Ltd

role in delivering goods in the tradable industry than to consumers. This is because the productivity of the distribution sector has two effects: on the one hand, it tends to lower the price of tradables (by lowering the cost of distributing intermediate inputs), thereby raising the relative wage and appreciating the RER (similar to the effect of the productivity of tradables); on the other hand, it lowers the consumer price of tradables, depreciating the RER (similar to the effect of the productivity of non-tradables).[7,8]

Our model is similar in spirit to that presented in Devereux (1999), who also analyses the effect of the distribution sector on the RER in the context of a Balassa–Samuelson framework. In particular, Devereux (1999) presents a general equilibrium model in which productivity in the traded sector, by raising consumption, leads to growth in the size of the distribution sector. This in turn generates an endogenous increase in productivity in the distribution sector, pushing the price of distribution services down. The latter effect, consequently, reduces the traded goods prices facing consumers, which in turn can generate a depreciation of the RER. As in our own model, Devereux (1999) assumes that the LOOP holds at the producer price level but not at the CPI level. A key difference is that an autonomous increase in the productivity of the distribution sector would depreciate the RER in Devereux's model, while in our model it could either depreciate or appreciate the RER (depending on parameter values).

In the presence of violations of the LOOP at the producer price level, the effect of both the Balassa–Samuelson and distribution effects on the RER would be less clear-cut. The productivity shocks would be transmitted to the RER also via the relative price of traded goods. Our empirical work will allow for failure of the LOOP, which has been chosen at the theoretical level simply for presentation of the main intuition behind the effect.

4. DATA SOURCES, VARIABLE DEFINITIONS AND ECONOMETRIC METHODS

This section presents a brief discussion of the construction of the data set, relegating a more complete description of the construction of the variables to the Data Appendix. Ten countries feature in our analysis: Belgium (BEL), Denmark (DNK), Finland (FIN), France (FRA), Italy (ITA), Japan (JPN), Norway (NOR), Sweden (SWE), West Germany (WGR) and the United States

[7] The net effect of the distribution sector would be positive if $\phi < (1-\gamma)\alpha/[(1-\alpha)\gamma]$. Note that, if $\phi = 0$ and $\gamma = 1$, the distribution sector would disappear from the model and we would obtain the usual Balassa–Samuelson framework, where the exponent of the relative productivity of both tradables and non-tradables is α and $-\alpha$. In our model the relative productivity of the tradable sector presents two differences with respect to a basic Balassa–Samuelson model: on the one hand it has a smaller effect, as its impact on wages is less than proportional; on the other hand it has an additional positive effect, as its impact on wages also raises the consumption price of tradables via the employment cost of the distribution sector. Note also that the sum of all the exponents in the RER expression is zero. Allowing for intermediate inputs in the non-tradable sector would lower the exponents (and hence the impact) of the productivities in both tradable and non-tradable sectors.

[8] Our model does not feature policy or preference shocks, which can have an independent effect on the relative price of traded to non-traded goods in the short run.

© 2005 Blackwell Publishing Ltd

(USA).[9] Variables for each of the first nine countries are defined relative to the USA, bringing the cross-sectional dimension of our panel to nine. Annual data are used for the period 1970–91. Both the cross-sectional and time series dimensions of the panel were determined by the availability of consistent data, especially for the distribution sector variables, and by the need to balance the panel for the panel unit root test employed. All variables, apart from the Balassa–Samuelson terms, are from IFS, OECD, World Bank, and WEO macroeconomic databases.

The key dependent variable in our study is the logarithm of the RER (*LRER*), which is CPI-based: an increase in *LRER* of country *j* corresponds to an appreciation of the real exchange rate of *j* against the USA. The relative productivity in tradables and non-tradables are calculated by drawing from the OECD International Sectoral Database. Like De Gregorio *et al.* (1994) and Cheung *et al.* (2001), we classify agriculture, manufacturing and transportation sectors as tradables, and utilities, construction and social services sectors as non-tradables.[10] Notably, we exclude the distribution sector from the non-tradables, in order to focus on this sector separately.[11]

We then sequentially introduce into the regressions variables capturing the relative efficiency in the distribution sector with respect to the USA (our proxies for β_{D2}/β_{D1}), calculated from the OECD International Sectoral Database. The most obvious measure of efficiency is the relative total factor productivity in this sector. The database however allows the calculation of another proxy for efficiency: the ratio of the number of employees to total employment (E) in the distribution sector. This employment variable is designed to capture product market competition in the sector. For example, imagine a family-owned retail store in the centre of Rome with three members of the family employing three employees: the E variable would equal ½. Imagine now a Wal-Mart in the USA, with 10 managers (maybe even just 1!) and 100 employees: the E variable would equal 10/11 (if not 100/101). This employment structure is likely to be reflected in the markup charged: in particular, a change in the E variable would imply a change in the price of the distribution services.[12] We therefore

[9] Data refer to West Germany only, even for the period after German reunification.

[10] De Gregorio *et al.* (1994) define as tradable those sectors for which the export share in total production is larger than 10%. A similar classification was used by Stockman and Tesar (1995). In the export content measurement exercise, the distribution sector is considered part of services activity, as specific data within this activity are not available. Note that in this classification the services the distribution sector sells to the tradable sector would still be classified as non-tradable, inducing an undervaluation of the importance of the distribution sector as a tradable sector.

[11] Mining was not included in the tradable sector for lack of data for Belgium and Italy. The financial sector was not included in the non-tradable sector for lack of data for Belgium, Italy and Netherlands.

[12] This variable is motivated by a simple model of monopolistic competition *à la* Dixit and Stiglitz, with a CES utility function and a production function characterized by a fixed cost and a constant marginal cost, both costs being in terms of labour. In the equilibrium of this model, if one assumes that the fixed employment cost is given by the managers (the difference between total employment and number of employees) and the marginal cost by the employees, our E variable would equal the inverse of the markup. Hence a lower markup could be interpreted as a more competitive sector. The framework presented above does not include imperfect competition or economies of scale for the sake of presentational simplicity.

© 2005 Blackwell Publishing Ltd

explore the empirical effect of each measure of efficiency in the distribution sector, both jointly and separately.

Finally, by introducing the aggregate wage in industrial activity (and in the tradable sector defined above), as well as measures of productivity and product market competition in the distribution sector (both series from the OECD International Sectoral Database), we are able to analyse how the distribution effect gets transmitted into the RER.

The relatively small available time series samples for each country necessitates using panel methods to improve the power of our tests. (Data on productivity, for example, are available only at an annual frequency.) In particular, we use a version of the panel DOLS (dynamic ordinary least squares) estimator which allows for limited heterogeneity in the form of fixed effects, i.e.

$$y_{it} = \theta_{1i} + \theta_{2t} + \theta_3 x_{it} + \sum_{j=-p}^{+n} \theta_{4j} \Delta x_{it+j} + \omega_{it}, \quad (1)$$

where y_{it} is a scalar, x_{it} is a vector with dimension k, θ_{1i} is an individual fixed effect, θ_{2t} is a time effect, θ_3 represents a cointegration vector, p is the maximum lag length, n is the maximum lead length and ω is a Gaussian vector error process. The leads and lags of the difference terms are included to ensure that the error term is orthogonalized. Our representation of the panel DOLS estimator assumes that the dynamics are the same across individuals. The estimator can address potential cross-sectional dependence by the inclusion of time dummies, and that is accomplished here by removing the cross-sectional mean of each variable.[13] As Pedroni (1997) notes, the residuals from an equation like (1) will have the same distribution as the raw data, and hence it is possible to use a standard unit root test to check for the existence of cointegration among the variables in the vector of interest. We therefore use the Levin–Lin (1993) panel unit root statistic to test for cointegration:

$$\Delta\omega_{it} = \delta\omega_{it-1} + \Sigma_{j=1}^{n} \theta_{4i} \Delta\omega_{it-j} + u_{it}, \quad (2)$$

where δ represents the adjustment speed[14] and the t-ratio on this term, denoted 'PUR test' in the empirical section of this paper, denotes the significance of the adjustment speed.[15] The null hypothesis that each time series of residuals has a unit root is rejected if δ is significantly negative; that is, in the current application there is panel cointegration. As Levin and Lin demonstrate, under the null hypothesis that $\delta = 0$ the PUR test diverges to minus infinity. However, they propose a simple adjustment to this statistic which produces a test statistic

[13] The inclusion of the time dummies neutralizes the role of the reference country (USA): measuring the real exchange rate with respect to different reference countries (say, Germany as opposed to USA) would yield different coefficients in the absence of time dummies. Our results on the adjustment speed do not depend on time dummies, as discussed in Section 5.5.

[14] Equation (1) represents the re-parameterization of a levels autoregression for ω, and therefore δ represents the difference between the sum of the levels autoregressive coefficients and one.

[15] Since fixed effects are included in our cointegrating regression, we use the adjustment proposed by Levin and Lin (1993) for the case of a constant term.

© 2005 Blackwell Publishing Ltd

that has a standard normal distribution, and it is the adjusted t-statistic that we use in this paper. We calculate the half-life mean reversion speed for our panel of RERs using the formula $\ln(0.5)/\ln(1 - \hat{\delta})$, where $\hat{\delta}$ is the estimated value of δ in expression (2).

5. RESULTS

This section discusses the empirical results. We first estimate a base-line model for equation (1), which consists of a regression of the CPI-based RER on net foreign assets, a real interest differential and a Balassa–Samuelson term. We next proceed to investigate the role of the distribution sector, via the inclusion on the basic model of variables measuring the efficiency of this sector. We then discuss our implications for the 'PPP puzzle'.

5.1. *A basic Balassa–Samuelson model of the real exchange rate*

Table 2 presents the basic model of the RER, which is dependent on two macroeconomic control variables (relative net foreign assets, *NFA*, and relative real interest rates, *INT*), and on the Balassa–Samuelson effect or on its two components (the relative productivity of tradable and of non-tradables). Robustness tests are performed here by dropping variables from the regression. In the first column of Table 2 we present the panel unit root (PUR) test for our RER series, taking into account fixed effects.[16] The RER appears to be non-stationary. However, given the limited power of the test with about 20 years of data, one may find it interesting that, if the RER were indeed stationary, the implied half-life of the deviations would be approximately three years, which is in the range reported by other researchers using panel data sets (see Section 2).

In the basic model specification, all of the variables enter with the correct sign and all are statistically significant. When the two productivity variables are entered separately, the control variables are no longer significant, suggesting that the macroeconomic variables are less important than the real variables capturing the Balassa–Samuelson effect. The PUR t-ratio is highly significant, and we get a marked rise in the adjustment speed with the implied half-life of the real exchange rate, with respect to its equilibrium, now very close to the one-year horizon. It is also worth noting that the two macroeconomic variables – net foreign assets and the real interest rate differential – on their own do not produce evidence of cointegration (see the final column of Table 2). It is only when the productivity and distribution effects are added in that we find evidence of cointegration, and this would seem to underscore the importance of these variables in explaining systematic movements in RERs.

[16] Implicitly, we also account for time dummies, as our variables have the cross-sectional mean removed.

© 2005 Blackwell Publishing Ltd

Table 2. Basic model of RER and its robustness (dynamic OLS)

	Basic model									
	*LRER**	*LRER*	*LRER*	*LRER*	*LRER*	*LRER*	*LRER*	*LRER*	*LRER*	*LRER*
Net foreign assets (*NFA*)	–	**0.004**	**0.001**	**0.004**	**0.001**	–	–	–	–	**0.005**
	2.02	0.41	1.92	0.61	–	–	–	–	2.94	
Real interest rates (*INT*)	–	**0.013**	**0.007**	–	–	**0.014**	**0.012**	–	–	**0.03**
	1.91	0.87	–	–	2.23	1.83	–	–	4.20	
Balassa–Samuelson (*LBAL2WT*)	–	**0.769**	–	**0.815**	–	**0.760**	–	**0.785**	–	–
	6.45	–	7.58	–	6.67	–	7.26	–	–	
Productivity in tradables (*LATRDWT*)	–	–	**0.418**	–	**0.425**	–	**0.271**	–	**0.315**	–
	–	1.93	–	2.04	–	1.37	–	1.66	–	
Productivity in non–tradables (*LANTRD*)	–	–	**–0.948**	–	**–0.934**	–	**–0.909**	–	**–0.910**	–
	–	–7.15	–	–7.95	–	–7.67	–	–8.07	–	
Testing restrictions on Balassa–Samuelson										
χ^2	4.92	4.76	9.63	8.64						
Probability	0.03	0.03	0.00	0.00						
Panel unit root analysis										
PUR test	–0.62	–3.81	–3.25	–4.28	–3.24	–3.47	–2.53	–2.95	–2.35	–0.87
Delta (from text)	–0.22	–0.44	–0.42	–0.44	–0.42	–0.38	–0.35	–0.32	–0.35	–0.28
Half–life time (years)	2.8	1.2	1.3	1.2	1.3	1.4	1.6	1.8	1.6	2.1
No. of observations	153	153	153	153	153	153	153	153	153	153

Notes: Absolute *t*–ratios below coefficients.
Wald Test on restrictions. H0: *LATRDWT* = –*LANTRD*. Do not reject if *P*–value above desired alpha (0.05).
Panel unit root (PUR) test: 'adjusted' Levin and Lin (1993) *t*–ratios discussed in the text.
Half–life time of deviations of the real exchange rate from estimated relation (years): log(0.5)/log(1 + delta).
*First column provides PUR test on residual of *LRER* on fixed effects.

© 2005 Blackwell Publishing Ltd

The magnitude of the coefficient on the Balassa–Samuelson term, as well as on the two components, are about in the middle of the range of coefficient estimates of previous work (Chinn and Johnston, 1996, report a range of 0.1–1.6 for the absolute value of these coefficients) and are particularly close to the estimates related to bilateral exchange rates (as opposed to multilateral). An estimate of approximately 0.8 (with a standard error of about 0.1) could appear to be somewhat high: in the neoclassical world of Balassa–Samuelson the theoretical prediction for this elasticity is that it should equal the expenditure share on non-tradables. However, our result is consistent with those of Chinn and Johnson (1999), who apply a similar methodology and discuss this empirical anomaly. Note also that the theoretical prediction for this elasticity would be higher than the one suggested by the Balassa–Samuelson framework if tradables, in order to be available for consumption, needed to be aggregated with non-tradables (see Burstein *et al.*, 2000).

Most empirical studies that include the Balassa–Samuelson effect focus either on aggregate measures of productivity (such as GDP per worker or labour productivity in manufacturing) or on productivity in the tradable sector or on the aggregate Balassa–Samuelson term. This is due partly to the lack of data for a large set of countries and/or extensive time series, but also to the presumption that all of the action should come from the tradable sector.[17] Our data set facilitates entering the two components of the Balassa–Samuelson term separately and testing the constraint that the coefficients on the two terms are equal and opposite, as the basic Balassa–Samuelson theory would suggest. On the basis of the reported χ^2 test, this hypothesis is rejected in the basic model. Perhaps more interestingly, the larger coefficient (in absolute value) is the one on productivity in the non-traded sector. We note that dropping the control variables, either one at a time or simultaneously, does not significantly affect the size or alter the significance of the Balassa–Samuelson terms or components, or of the stationarity of the residuals.

5.2. *The influence of the distribution sector on the real exchange rate*

Table 3 presents econometric evidence of the effects of the distribution sector on the RER. The two benchmark models (the one with the control variables and the Balassa–Samuelson term, and the one with the control variables and the productivity of tradables and of non-tradables separately) are expanded by adding, either one at a time or simultaneously, the two measures of relative efficiency in the distribution sector (relative productivity and product market competition).

The distribution sector does not alter the sign, size or significance of the coefficient on the Balassa–Samuelson variable. When the two Balassa–Samuelson components are entered separately, however, their coefficients tend to be closer (in absolute value) than when the distribution sector is not in the

[17] In many simple textbook representations of the Balassa–Samuelson effect, productivity in the non-traded sector is even assumed to be fixed across countries.

© 2005 Blackwell Publishing Ltd

Table 3. Influence of the distribution sector on RER (dynamic OLS)

	Benchmark model					
	LRER	*LRER*	*LRER*	*LRER*	*LRER*	*LRER*
Net foreign assets (*NFA*)	**−0.003**	**−0.003**	**−0.001**	**−0.002**	**−0.002**	**−0.002**
	1.44	1.32	0.44	0.85	1.55	1.29
Real interest rates (*INT*)	**0.012**	**0.011**	**0.018**	**0.018**	**0.016**	**0.017**
	2.02	1.59	3.34	2.65	2.82	2.6
Balassa–Samuelson (*LBAL2WT*)	**0.687**	–	**0.893**	–	**0.832**	–
	6.59	–	9.41	–	8.45	–
Productivity in tradables (*LATRDWT*)	–	**−0.664**	–	**0.733**	–	**0.857**
	–	3.36	–	3.98	–	4.58
Productivity in non–tradables (*LANTRD*)	–	**−0.706**	–	**−0.934**	–	**−0.82**
	–	−5.79	–	8.63	–	7.22
Productivity in distribution (*LARWH*)	**0.797**	**0.767**	–	–	**0.422**	**0.437**
	7.92	6.43	–	–	3.63	3.39
Product market competition in distribution (*LERWH*)	–	–	**2.043**	**1.979**	**1.482**	**1.518**
	–	–	8.85	7.49	5.35	5.14
Testing restrictions on coefficients						
χ^2		6.463				3.024
Probability		0.011				0.082
Testing restrictions on Balassa–Samuelson						
χ^2		0.03		0.98		0.03
Probability		0.011		0.32		0.86
Panel unit root analysis						
PUR test	−4.31	−3.79	−2.78	−2.69	−3.62	−3.74
Delta (from text)	−0.44	−0.44	−0.46	−0.45	−0.5	−0.51
Half–life time (years)	1.2	1.2	1.1	1.2	1.0	1.0
No. of observations	153	153	153	153	153	153

Notes: Absolute *t*–ratios below coefficients.
Wald test on restrictions. H0: $LATRDWT + LANTRD + LARWH = 0$. Do not reject if *p*–value above desired alpha (0.05).
Panel unit root (PUR) test: 'adjusted' Levin and Lin (1993) *t*–ratios discussed in the text. Half–life time of deviations of the real exchange rate from estimated relation (years): log(0.5)/log(1 + delta).

regression.[18] In terms of the control variables, the coefficient on the relative interest rate differential is correctly signed, of similar size and more significant than without the distribution sector. The coefficient of the net foreign asset variable, instead, becomes insignificant. The coefficients on both productivity and product market competition in the distribution sector are strongly significant and positive. (As one would expect, the size of these coefficients is reduced when they are both present in the regression, although they are both still largely significant.)

[18] Indeed, one can actually accept the hypothesis that they are identical. However, our model suggests that, once the distribution sector is taken into account, the relation among the coefficients should be different: more precisely, the coefficient of the productivity of non-tradables should equal (in absolute value) the sum of the coefficients of the productivity of tradables and of the distribution sector. This new restriction hypothesis cannot properly be tested with our empirical result, as we find two empirically useful measures of efficiency in the distribution sector. Readers may none the less be interested in knowing that, if one ignores this problem (i.e. focuses on the productivity in the distribution sector), the new restriction hypothesis can be rejected in column (2) and accepted in column (6) of Table 2 at the 5% level of significance.

© 2005 Blackwell Publishing Ltd

These results suggest that the distribution sector influences the RER as a traded sector rather than as a non-traded sector, contrary to what the few earlier contributions speculating on the role of this sector have assumed. In terms of our simple theoretical model, this would suggest that the role of the distribution sector via the traded sector is stronger than via the non-traded sector. This plausibly reflects the fact that some components of the non-traded sector – such as utilities and social services – have vertically integrated distribution sectors, while most of the services of the distribution sector get imputed into the traded components of manufacturing and agriculture.

Note that all of the PUR statistics are statistically significant (which is evidence of the stationarity of the estimated residuals) in Table 3. In the model with both measures of efficiency in the distribution sector, the implied half-life in this regression falls to unity, which is precisely the starting point for the PPP puzzle. Note also that our results hold even if we were to drop the control variables NFA and INT (see MacDonald and Ricci, 2001).

5.2.1. *Controlling for the wage: productivity effects and imperfect substitutability*
Following the approach adopted in MacDonald and Ricci (2002), this section attempts to further analyse the Balassa–Samuelson mechanism, in order to assess whether the distribution sector follows the same channel of influence on the RER. As noted in Section 3, the key variable in the Balassa–Samuelson effect is the wage rate. An increase in the productivity of tradables raises the domestic wage (as tradable prices are given), which in turn raises the price of non-tradables and induces an appreciation of the RER. Hence in a standard Balassa–Samuelson framework one would expect the coefficient on the productivity of tradables to become zero (i.e. insignificant) when the wage enters the regression, as the wage would capture all of the effect of the productivity of tradables.

The first four columns of Table 4 introduce the wage in the basic model and in the benchmark model with the distribution sector. We use two measures for the wage rate: the wage rate in the overall industrial activity is the measure suggested by the theory; then as a check we employ the average wage in the tradable sector (built similarly to the productivity index – see the Appendix). Not surprisingly, both measures yield similar results, given that wages are largely correlated across sectors within countries. The wage term is always positive and highly significant, with a plausible coefficient. (Theoretically, it should equal the share of expenditure on non-tradables.)

Note that the coefficient on the productivity of tradables becomes statistically negative after the introduction of the wage. MacDonald and Ricci (2002) document this result and discuss the theoretical underpinnings: while a standard Balassa–Samuelson approach cannot explain why the coefficient is significantly negative, imperfect substitutability across international goods produced in different countries may explain this finding. More specifically, in the presence of imperfect substitutability of tradables, productivity of tradables would not only directly and positively affect the aggregate wage, and hence indirectly and positively the overall price index and RER, but also would directly and negatively affect the price of tradables, and hence indirectly and negatively the

© 2005 Blackwell Publishing Ltd

Table 4. The influence of the distribution sector on RER: controlling for the wage effect (dynamic OLS)

	LRER	*LRER*	*LRER*	*LRER*	*LRER*	*LRER*
Net foreign assets (*NFA*)	**−0.002**	**−0.001**	**−0.003**	**−0.003**	**−0.003**	**−0.002**
	2.37	1.65	3.97	4.00	3.42	3.29
Real interest rates (*INT*)	**0.004**	**0.002**	**0.007**	**0.005**	**0.006**	**0.005**
	1.58	1.02	2.74	2.53	2.54	2.71
Productivity in tradables (*LATRDWT*)	**−0.587**	**−0.566**	**−0.253**	**−0.278**	**−0.120**	**−0.153**
	6.67	7.30	2.78	3.60	1.37	2.13
Productivity in non-tradables (*LANTRD*)	**−0.259**	**−0.221**	**−0.306**	**−0.283**	**−0.459**	**−0.393**
	4.83	4.54	6.08	6.46	8.38	8.50
Productivity in distribution (*LARWH*)	–	–	**0.230**	**0.182**	**−0.010**	**−0.021**
	–	–	4.47	4.04	0.16	0.39
Product market competition	–	–	**0.353**	**0.392**	**1.008**	**0.978**
in distribution (*LERWH*)	–	–	2.69	3.46	5.91	6.96
Wage in tradables (*LWTRDWT*)	**0.719**	–	**0.580**	–	**0.530**	–
	22.06	–	16.45	–	16.29	–
Wage in industry (*LWIND*)	–	**0.737**	–	**0.606**	–	**0.566**
	–	25.09	–	19.71	–	20.44
Profits in distribution (*ORWH*)	–	–	–	–	**0.104**	**0.095**
	–	–	–	–	3.47	3.77
Testing restrictions on coefficients, H0: *LATRDWT* = *LANTRD*						
χ^2	7.80	10.97	0.20	0.00	9.03	6.52
Probability	0.01	0.00	0.66	0.96	0.00	0.01
Panel unit root analysis						
PUR test	−1.88	−2.31	−3.81	−2.38	−4.13	−5.01
Delta (from text)	−0.26	−0.28	−0.41	−0.38	−0.50	−0.60
No. of observations	153	153	153	153	153	153

Notes: Absolute *t*–ratios below coefficients.
Panel unit root (PUR) test: 'adjusted' Levin and Lin (1993) *t*–ratios discussed in the text.

price index and the RER. The coefficient of the productivity of tradables would thus be positive in a normal regression without the wage, but would be negative once we control for the wage effect. This result is consistent with evidence presented by Engel (1993, 1999), Rogers and Jenkins (1995) and Betts and Kehoe (2001) that the majority of variation of RERs comes from the relative price of tradables across countries.

We now turn to the effect that the introduction of the wage has on the distribution sector. Unlike the coefficient on productivity in the tradables sector, the coefficients of the two measures of efficiency in the distribution sector maintain their sign as in the regression without the wage, although their size is smaller in absolute terms (third and fourth columns of Table 4). This suggests that, although productivity and product market competition in the distribution sector have a similar effect to the productivity of tradables on the RER, wages do not appear to be the only conduit that facilitates the effect of distribution sector efficiency.

Through which other channel could the distribution sector influence the RER? One potential channel is profits. In fact, as demonstrated in the last two columns of Table 4, the inclusion of operating profits in the regression

© 2005 Blackwell Publishing Ltd

for the distribution sector makes the coefficient on productivity in the distribution sector insignificant, leaving unaltered the significance and the signs of other variables. Note, however, that product market competition in the distribution sector remains positive and significant, perhaps suggesting that this variable also captures an externality in market structure, which should affect prices via game-theoretic incentives and would not show up in aggregate wages or sectoral operating profits.

One possible explanation for the role of profits is that international price equalization holds both for intermediate inputs and for final tradables. The equalization of prices of intermediate inputs determines wages and provides the channel for the productivity of intermediate goods (part of tradables) to positively influence the RER, consistent with the Balassa–Samuelson effect. Then intermediate inputs are conveyed though the distribution sector to the production of a second stage of tradables. The prices of this second stage of tradables, which includes the cost of distribution of such intermediate inputs, are also equalized internationally. If the distribution and the non-tradable sectors use a commonly specific factor such as land (or are similarly less competitive than tradables), and hence face similar operating profit margins, both sectors would see their profit margins being affected by the productivity of the distribution sector.[19] In this case operating profit margins would be the channel for the effect of productivity of the distribution sector on the RER. Productivity in tradables and productivity in the distribution sector would both similarly affect the RER, thanks to international price equalization, but one via wages and one via profits. A model consistent with such results is presented in MacDonald and Ricci (2001).[20]

In passing, it is worth noting how our results relate to the literature that seeks to decompose the sources of the variance of the real exchange into demand, supply and nominal shocks. Starting with Clarida and Gali (1997), a number of researchers have used trivariate structural VARs (SVARs), comprising relative output, relative inflation and the RER, to show that demand and nominal shocks dominate the variability of RERs. (This result has been confirmed in a number of other papers using such a trivariate structure.) However, when the supply side is made richer in such SVAR models (see Weber, 1997; Rogers, 1999), it is seen to play a significant role in explaining the variance of RERs. Since the supply side is, at least in part, attributable to a Balassa–Samuelson effect in such papers (see e.g. Weber, 1997), this would seem to be consistent with the results reported here for the level of the RER.[21]

[19] Note that in the OECD data set the operating profit margins include, for example, land rent.

[20] We checked the robustness of our results by using different panel estimators, different conditioning variables and different sample periods. These tests, reported in MacDonald and Ricci (2001), confirm the results reported in this section.

[21] We performed various robustness tests on the benchmark specification identified in Table 3: we excluded one country at a time; we changed the time span of the sample; we eliminated the two control variables, one at a time as well as simultaneously; and, finally, we ran plain static OLS. These additional experiments, which are reported in MacDonald and Ricci (2001), indicate that our original results are robust.

© 2005 Blackwell Publishing Ltd

5.2.2. *The PPP puzzle*

Although the main focus of our paper is on the role played by the distribution sector on the RER, our econometric results would seem to have an important bearing on the PPP puzzle. As noted in Section 2, this puzzle relates to the finding by a number of researchers that the mean reversion in RERs is too slow to be consistent with a traditional form of PPP. We now bring together the different mean reversion speeds mentioned at various places in this paper. First, we note that the half-life mean reversion speed for our RER series on its own is around three years (see Table 2), which is entirely consistent with the PPP puzzle. However, expanding the information set to include the usual determinants of the RER raises the speed significantly: including only the relative net foreign asset position and the real interest differential reduces the half-life of the deviation of the real exchange rate to its equilibrium, i.e. to 2.1, while including only the Balassa–Samuelson term produces a real exchange rate half-life of 1.6–1.8 years. In the basic model encompassing all these variables, the half-life drops to around 1.2–1.3 years. Perhaps our most striking finding is that adding our measures of efficiency in the distribution sector to the basic model produces a half-life of about one year (Table 3). It would seem therefore that at least one important explanation for the PPP puzzle (there may of course be others, as we noted in Section 2) is to be found in the fundamental determinants of RERs.

6. CONCLUSIONS

This paper finds that an increase in productivity, and in product market competition of the distribution sector with respect to foreign countries, leads in the long run to an appreciation of the real exchange rate, similar to the effect that a relative increase in the domestic productivity of tradables would have. This contrasts with the result that one would expect when considering the distribution sector as belonging to the non-tradable sector, as several authors have assumed. Notably, this effect is coexistent with the usual Balassa–Samuelson effect of productivity in the other tradable and non-tradable sectors (and holds also when controlling for other macro-determinants of the real exchange rate, such as net foreign assets and real interest rates). One possible explanation offered for this result is that the use of services from the distribution sector to deliver the intermediate goods used in the production of tradables has a larger impact on the real exchange rate than the use of distribution services to deliver final goods to consumers.

Accurate estimates of the long-run relations are obtained by employing dynamic panel estimation methods (dynamic OLS, or DOLS). Panel unit root tests support the hypothesis of panel cointegration among the series. Accounting for our explanatory variables (including the distribution sector) raises the speed of adjustment of temporary deviations of the real exchange rate from its long-run path by lowering the half-life of such deviations to approximately one year; and, as we have argued, this result would seem to contribute to solving the PPP puzzle. In other words, although the real exchange rate has

© 2005 Blackwell Publishing Ltd

a slow reversion to its average level (half-life of deviations of about three years), it has a reasonable speed of adjustment towards its equilibrium level (half-life of deviations of about one year), which depends on macroeconomic variables (such as net foreign assets position, real interest rate differential) but in particular on real variables measuring the Balassa–Samuelson effect and the efficiency in the distribution sector.

It is interesting to note that the channel of transmission of the distribution sector appears to be somewhat different from that predicted by the Balassa–Samuelson effect. The introduction of an aggregate wage variable does not crowd out the effect of productivity and product market competition in the distribution sector. However, the introduction of operating profits in the distribution sector makes the productivity of this sector insignificant. This would be consistent with a model that entails two stages of price equalization (of intermediate inputs and of final tradables, with the latter making use of these intermediate inputs once delivered by the distribution sector) and equalization of operating profits margins across the distribution sector and non-tradables.

REFERENCES

Balassa, B. (1964) 'The Purchasing Power Parity Doctrine: A Reappraisal', *Journal of Political Economy* 72, 584–96.

Betts, C. and P. Kehoe (2001) 'Tradability of Goods and Real Exchange Rates', Federal Reserve Bank of Minneapolis, Research Department Staff Paper.

Burstein, A. T., J. C. Neves and S. Rebelo (2000) *Distribution Costs and Real Exchange Rate Dynamics during Exchange-Rate-Based Stabilizations*, NBER Working Paper no. 7862.

Canzoneri, M. B., R. E. Cumby and B. Diba (1996) 'Relative Labor Productivity and the Real Exchange Rate in the Long Run: Evidence for a Panel of OECD Countries', *Journal of International Economics* 47, 245–66.

Cheung, Y.-W., M. Chinn and E. Fujii (2001) 'Market Structure and the Persistence of Sectoral Real Exchange Rates', *International Journal of Finance and Economics* 6, no. 2, pp. 95–114.

Chinn, M. and L. Johnson (1996) *Real Exchange Rate Levels, Productivity, and Demand Shocks: Evidence from a Panel of 14 Countries*, NBER Working Paper no. 5709.

—— and L. Johnson (1999) *The Impact of Productivity Differentials on Real Exchange Rates: Beyond the Balassa–Samuelson Framework*, University of California Santa Cruz Department of Economics, Working Paper no. 442.

Clarida, R. and J. Gali (1997) 'Sources of Real Exchange Rate Fluctuations: How Important are Nominal Shocks?' *Carnegie–Rochester Series on Public Policy* 41, 1–56.

De Gregorio, J. and H. C. Wolf (1994) 'Terms of Trade, Productivity, and the Real Exchange Rate', NBER Working Paper no. 4807.

—, X. X. Giovannini and H. C. Wolf (1994) 'International Evidence on Tradables and Nontradables Inflation', *European Economic Review* 38, 1225–44.

Devereux, M. (1999) 'Real Exchange Rate Trends and Growth: A Model of East Asia', *Review of International Economics* 7, 000–00.

Diebold, F. X., S. Husted and M. Rush (1991) 'Real Exchange Rates under the Gold Standard', *Journal of Political Economy* 99, 1252–71.

Dornbusch, R. (1989) 'Real Exchange Rates and Macroeconomics: A Selective Survey', *Scandinavian Journal of Economics* 91, 401–32.

Edison, H. J. (1987) 'Purchasing Power Parity in the Long Run: A Test of the Dollar/Pound Exchange Rate (1890–1978)', *Journal of Money, Credit and Banking* 19, 376–87.

Engel, C. (1993) 'Real Exchange Rates and Relative Prices: An Empirical Investigation', *Journal of Monetary Economics* 32, 35–50.

—— (1999) 'Accounting for US Real Exchange Rate Changes', *Journal of Political Economy* 107, 507–38.

—— (2000) 'Long-Run PPP May Not Hold After All', *Journal of International Economics* 57, 243–73.

© 2005 Blackwell Publishing Ltd

Feenstra, R. C. and J. D. Kendall (1997) 'Pass-Through of Exchange Rates and Purchasing Power Parity', *Journal of International Economics* 43, 237–61.

Frankel, J. (1988) *International Capital Mobility and Domestic Economic Policies*, NBER Conference Report, Chicago: University of Chicago.

—— and A. Rose (1995) 'A Panel Project on Purchasing Power Parity: Mean Reversion within and between Countries', *Journal of International Economics* 40, 209–24.

Hsieh, D. (1982) 'The Determination of the Real Exchange Rate: The Productivity Approach', *Journal of International Economics* 12, 355–62.

Hummels, D. (1999) 'Toward a Geography of Trade Costs', mimeo, University of Chicago.

Ito, T., P. Isard and S. Symansky (1997) *Economic Growth and Real Exchange Rate: An Overview of the Balassa–Samuelson Hypothesis in Asia*, NBER Working Paper no. 5979.

Lane, P. and G. Milesi-Ferretti (2000) *The Transfer Problem Revisited: Net Foreign Assets and Real Exchange Rates*, CEPR Discussion Paper Series no. 2511.

Levin, A. and C.-F. Lin (1993) 'Unit Root Tests in Panel Data: Asymptotic and Finite-Sample Properties', mimeo, University of California.

MacDonald, R. (1995) 'Long-Run Exchange Rate Modeling: A Survey of the Recent Evidence', *International Monetary Fund Staff Papers*, 42, 437–89.

—— and L. Ricci (2001) *PPP and the Balassa–Samuelson Effect: The Role of the Distribution Sector*, International Monetary Fund Working Paper no. 01/38.

—— and L. Ricci (2002) *Purchasing Power Parity and New Trade Theory*, International Monetary Fund Working Paper no. 02/32.

Marston, R. (1990) 'Real Exchange Rates and Productivity Growth in the United States and Japan', in S. W. Arndt and J. Davidson Richardson (eds.), *Real Financial Linkages among Open Economies*, town?: name of publisher?, pp. 71–96.

Obstfeld, M. and K. Rogoff (1996) *Foundations of International Macroeconomics*, Cambridge, Mass.: MIT Press.

—— and K. Rogoff (2000) 'New Directions for Stochastic Open Economy Models', *Journal of International Economics* 50, 117–53.

—— and A. M. Taylor (1997) 'Nonlinear Aspects of Goods-Market Arbitrage and Adjustment: Heckshers's Commodity Points Revisited', *Journal of Japanese and International Economies* 11, 441–79.

Oh, K.-Y. (1996) 'Purchasing Power Parity and Unit Root Tests Using Panel Data', *Journal of International Money and Finance* 15, 405–18.

Pedroni, P. (1997) 'Panel Cointegration: Asymptotic and Finite Sample Properties of Pooled Time Series Tests with an Application to the PPP Hypothesis (New Results)', mimeo, Indiana University.

Rogers, J. H. (1999) 'Monetary Shocks and Real Exchange Rates', *Journal of International Economics* 49, 269–88.

—— and M. Jenkins (1995) 'Haircuts or Hysteresis? Sources of Movements in Real Exchange Rates', *Journal of International Economics* 38, 339–60.

Rogoff, K. (1996) 'The Purchasing Power Parity Puzzle', *Journal of Economic Literature* 34, 647–68.

Samuelson, P. (1964) 'Theoretical Notes on Trade Problems', *Review of Economics and Statistics* 23, 1–60.

Stockman, A. and Tesar and L. (1995) 'Tastes and Technology in a Two-Country Model of the Business Cycle', *American Economic Review* 85, 168–85.

Weber, A. (1997) 'Sources of Purchasing Power Disparities between the G3 Economies', *Journal of Japanese and International Economies* 11, 548–83.

DATA APPENDIX : VARIABLE DEFINITIONS

For brevity, the OECD International Sectoral Database will be referred to as OCDE ISD. The corresponding three-letter sectoral code or variable name code is provided.

Real exchange rate: $LRER_j = \log(CPI_j/(e_j * CPI_{usa}))$, for CPI = consumer price index, e = exchange rate (currency units of j per US$). *Source*: IFS.

Relative real interest rate: $INT_j = (i_j - \pi_j) - (i_{usa} - \pi_{usa\,j})$; for i_j = nominal interest rate (long-term government bond yield) π_j = CPI inflation rate. *Source*: IFS.

© 2005 Blackwell Publishing Ltd

Relative net foreign assets: $NFA_j = (NFA_j * e_j/GDP_j) - (NFA_{usa}/GDP_{usa})$, for NFA = net foreign asset position, GDP = gross domestic product, e = exchange rate (currency units of j per US$). *Source*: IFS, OECD.

Relative public expenditure size: $GOVY_j$ = (government expenditure/GDP)$_j$ – (government expenditure/GDP)$_{usa}$. *Source*: World Bank, World Economic Outlook (IMF) database.

Relative productivity in tradables: $LATRDWT_j = \log(\Sigma_k(\omega_{kj}TFP_{kj})/\Sigma_k(\omega_{k,usa}TFP_{usa}))$, for k = agricultural sector (AGR), manufacturing sector (MAN) and transport, storage and communication sector (TRS), the weights being the country-specific relative size of the sectoral value added, averaged over the sample period. *Source*: OECD ISD.

Relative productivity in non-tradables: $LANTRD_j = \log(\Sigma_k(\omega_{kj}TFP_{kj})/\Sigma_k(\omega_{k,usa}TFP_{usa}))$, for k = community, social and personal services (SOC); electricity, gas and water (EGW); construction (CST); again the weights are the country-specific relative size of the sectoral value added, averaged over the sample period. *Source*: OECD ISD.

Balassa–Samuelson term: $LBAL2WT_j = LATRDWT_j - LANTRD_j$

Relative productivity in the distribution sector: $LARWH_j = \log(TFP_{kj}/TFP_{usa})$, for k = wholesale and retail trade sector (RWH). *Source*: OECD ISD.

Relative product market competition in the distribution sector: $LERWH_j = \log((EE_{kj}/ET_{kj})/(EE_{k,usa}/ET_{k,usa}))$, for k = wholesale and retail trade sector (RWH), EE = number of employees, ET = total employment. *Source*: OECD ISD.

Relative wage in tradables: $LWTRDWT_j = \log(\Sigma_k(\omega_{kj}(WSSS_{kj}/(e_j * EE_{kj})))/\Sigma_k(\omega_{k,usa}(WSSS_{k,usa}/EE_{k,usa}))$, for k = agricultural sector (AGR), manufacturing (MAN) and transport, storage and communication sectors (TRS); $WSSS$ = compensation of employees at current prices in national currency, EE = number of employees; e = exchange rate (currency units of j per US$), the weights being the country-specific relative size of the sectoral value added, averaged over the sample period. *Source*: OECD ISD.

Relative wage in industrial activity: $LWTIN_j = \log((WSSS_{kj}/(e_j * EE_{kj})))/(WSSS_{k,usa}/EE_{k,usa}))$, for k = total industry (TIN), $WSSS$ = compensation of employees at current prices in national currency, EE = number of employees, e = exchange rate (currency units of j per US$). *Source*: OECD ISD.

Relative profit margin in distribution sector: $LORWH_j = \log(OP_{kj}/OP_{usa})$, for k = wholesale and retail trade sector (RWH), and OP = ratio of gross operating surplus to value added less indirect taxes. *Source*: OECD ISD.

Relative wage in distribution sector: $LWRWH_j = \log((WSSS_{kj}/(e_j * EE_{kj}))/(WSSS_{k,usa}/EE_{k,usa}))$, for k = wholesale and retail trade sector (RWH), $WSSS$ = compensation of employees at current prices in national currency, EE = number of employees, e = exchange rate (currency units of j per US$). *Source*: OECD ISD.

Relative price in distribution sector: $LDRWH_j = \log((GDP_{kj}/(e_j * GDPV_{kj}))/(GDP_{k,usa}/GDPV_{k,usa}))$, for k = wholesale and retail trade sector (RWH), GDP = value added at market prices and current prices in national currency, $GDPV$ = value added at market prices and 1990 prices in national currency, e = exchange rate (currency units of j per US$). *Source*: OECD ISD.

© 2005 Blackwell Publishing Ltd

Available online at www.sciencedirect.com
ScienceDirect
ELSEVIER
Journal of Macroeconomics 29 (2007) 639–664
Journal of MACROECONOMICS
www.elsevier.com/locate/jmacro

Real exchange rates, imperfect substitutability, and imperfect competition

Ronald MacDonald [a,*], Luca Antonio Ricci [b]

[a] *Department of Economics, University of Glasgow, Glasgow G12 8RT, United Kingdom*
[b] *Research Department, International Monetary Fund, Washington, DC 20431, United States*

Received 9 August 2004; accepted 14 November 2005
Available online 3 April 2007

Abstract

This paper theoretically derives and empirically tests the implications of a trade theory framework with imperfect substitution of tradables for the systematic movements in the real exchange rate. Using a panel DOLS estimator, we derive long-run coefficients for relative productivity and product market competition (for which we construct an original proxy) in both the tradable and non-tradable sectors, controlling for standard macroeconomic variables. The implications of imperfect substitutability of tradables fit the data better than the standard neoclassical assumption of price equalization, and our new measure of product market competition is a statistically significant determinant of the real exchange rate.
© 2007 Elsevier Inc. All rights reserved.

JEL classification: F31

Keywords: PPP puzzle; Imperfect substitution

1. Introduction

This paper contributes to the understanding of how the relaxation of standard neoclassical trade theory assumptions helps explaining the long-run behavior of the real exchange rate and the deviations from purchasing power parity (PPP).

* Corresponding author. Tel.: +44 141 330 1988; fax: +44 141 330 4940.
E-mail addresses: r.macdonald@socsci.gla.ac.uk (R. MacDonald), lricci@imf.org (L.A. Ricci).

0164-0704/$ - see front matter © 2007 Elsevier Inc. All rights reserved.
doi:10.1016/j.jmacro.2005.11.007

The failure of PPP is neatly summarized by the so-called PPP puzzle (Rogoff, 1996), which indicates that the mean reversion evidenced in CPI-based real exchange rates is too slow to be consistent with PPP.[1] Empirical work has shown that macroeconomic variables, such as the relative real interest rate and relative net foreign assets positions, as well as relative productivity levels in the tradables and non-tradables sectors (the so-called Balassa–Samuelson effect; see Balassa, 1964 and Samuelson, 1964), are important in explaining deviations from PPP.[2] In particular, the Balassa–Samuelson effect suggests that in the presence of price equalization of tradables, productivity of tradables appreciates the real exchange rate via its positive impact on wages—and prices of non-tradables—while productivity of non-tradables depreciates the real exchange rate via its negative impact on prices of non-tradables. Several contributions have provided empirical support to the Balassa–Samuelson hypothesis, particularly recent ones based on a more accurate disaggregation of the tradable and non-tradable sector (such as De Gregorio et al., 1994; Canzoneri et al., 1999; Chinn and Johnson, 1999; and MacDonald and Ricci, 2005).[3]

In its traditional form, the Balassa–Samuelson hypothesis assumes that the law of one price holds at all points in time and therefore suggests that changes in the real exchange rate should be accounted for by changes in the internal price ratio (that is, the domestic price ratio of traded to non-traded goods, relative to the one in the foreign country). However, Engel (1999) has demonstrated that the source of systematic movements in real exchange rates seems to come from movements in the relative price of traded goods, rather than the internal price ratio (see also Engel and Rogers, 1996).[4]

There are a number of theoretical explanations for the persistence of the deviations of relative prices of traded goods across countries. One is in terms of the frictions introduced into international trade by transactions costs (see Obstfeld and Rogoff, 2000), such as transportation costs, tariffs and non-tariff barriers. Another theoretical explanation for this persistence is when multinational firms engage in pricing to market (see, for example, Betts and Devereux, 1996), or when countries face differences in productivities or market structure (Faruqee, 1996). Benigno and Theonissen (2003) generate a model encompassing three factors affecting the real exchange rate: a Balassa–Samuelson effect via the price of tradable and non-tradables, a demand bias towards home goods, and international price discrimination. One of the main results of their paper is that an increase in the relative productivity of the domestic tradable sector does not necessarily appreciates the real exchange rate (as in the standard Balassa–Samuelson framework) because of the additional direct negative effect on domestic prices of tradables (allowed by the imperfect substitutatibility of tradables).

From the empirical point of view, some evidence for the role of trade costs has been offered by Obstfeld and Taylor (1997). The empirical relevance of market structure in explaining real exchange rate persistence is highlighted by Cheung et al. (1999). These

[1] Recent research, however, suggests that mean reversion could be much higher if one takes into account a dynamic aggregation bias (Imbs et al., 2005).

[2] For recent contributions on the importance of net foreign assets or interest rate differentials, see, *inter alia*, Lane and Milesi-Ferretti (2004) and Obstfeld and Rogoff (1996).

[3] For studies based on comparisons of aggregate productivity across countries, see for example Hsieh (1982), Marston (1990) and Ito et al. (1999).

[4] In a related empirical work to ours, Zachariadis (2004) uses microeconomic price data for Europe, over the period 1975–1990, and finds a robust negative relationship between the productivity of manufactures (tradables) and international price differences.

authors apply a panel estimator to data for 14 OECD countries related to US dollar-based sectoral real exchange rates and two proxies for market structure: a price-cost margin and an intra industry trade index. The authors find that the two measures of market imperfection have a significantly positive impact on sectoral real exchange rate persistence and that this is robust across different model specifications.

This paper develops a theoretical and empirical contribution which encompasses in a coherent and compatible fashion three key ingredients of the analysis of long-run real exchange rate behavior: the main Balassa–Samuelson intuition, the failure of the law of one price, and the role of competition in the product market.[5] First, along the lines of Benigno and Theonissen (2003), we produce a simple model with: different productivity levels across countries and sectors (as in a standard Balassa–Samuelson approach), imperfect substitutability of internationally traded goods, different levels of product market competition—or of economies of scale—in different countries (which are two key ingredients of the several trade theory models, particularly since Helpman and Krugman, 1985 and Krugman, 1990), and home bias in demand.[6] Second, we test the implications of our model for the impact on the real exchange rate of the levels of productivity and product market competition in each sector, providing empirical evidence supporting each of the three ingredients discussed above. To that purpose, a proxy of product market competition is constructed on the basis of our model.[7]

Our empirical results are consistent with the assumption of imperfect substitutability of tradables. The Balassa–Samuelson-type effect of the productivity of tradables on the real exchange rate is not fully offset by the direct negative effect on prices: hence the real exchange rate still appreciates following an increase of such productivity at home. Also, product market competition in tradables has a positive effect on the real exchange rate, similar to the one of productivity.

The outline of the remainder of this paper is as follows. In the next section we develop the model. Section 3 contains a brief description of the data set and methodology employed and Section 4 summarizes our results. A final section provides some conclusions.

2. A trade theory model with imperfect substitution: The impact of productivity and product market competition on the real exchange rate

The model encompasses two countries (1 and 2), each with a tradable (T) and a non-tradable sector (N). Each of these sector is composed of many varieties which enters the utility function in a Dixit and Stiglitz (1977) form. Each variety is produced by a different firm under increasing return to scale with a fixed cost and a constant marginal cost, both in terms of labor. Trade is assumed to be free. Labor mobility within countries ensures

[5] While sharing several similarities, our model presents several key differences from Faruqee (1996), which focuses on transitional dynamics arising from monetary shocks. First, our model also incorporates a non-traded sector, which is crucial to a Balassa–Samuelson effect. Second, it does not require the law of one price to hold in the long-run. We also show how a measure of competitiveness can be proxied using readily available data.

[6] The effect of home bias on the relative price of tradables has been highlighted by Backus et al. (1992), and Warnock (2003). The symmetric effect of productivity and mark-up (i.e. product market competition) has been discussed by Obstfeld and Rogoff (2000).

[7] In Dixit–Stiglitz based trade theory models, the higher the demand elasticity of substitution, the lower the mark-up and the economies of scale, in equilibrium. We denote such an environment as more competitive.

domestic wage equalization across sectors. International labor immobility prevents agglomeration effects.[8] Preferences are similar across countries: Cobb-Douglas in tradables and non-tradables, CES between domestic and foreign tradables, and CES of the Dixit–Stiglitz type among varieties of each sector.

The choice of assumptions reflects the following objectives. In order to inspect the impact on the real exchange rate of different productivities and product market competition across sectors and countries, the elasticity of substitution and the marginal labor input requirement are chosen to be specific to each sector in each country. In order to allow for imperfect substitution of tradables and its impact on relative prices, the utility function is assumed to be CES between tradables and non-tradables. Within each sector of each country, firms have identical production functions, as is standard in several trade theory models.

2.1. Consumer maximization problem

A representative individual of country k ($k = 1,2$) maximizes the following preferences:

$$U_k = \left(\delta \left(\sum_{i=1}^{n_{\mathrm{T}k}} (c^k_{\mathrm{T}ki})^{\theta_{\mathrm{T}k}} \right)^{\frac{\theta}{\theta_{\mathrm{T}k}}} + (1-\delta) \left(\sum_{j=1}^{n_{\mathrm{T}k'}} (c^k_{\mathrm{T}k'j})^{\theta_{\mathrm{T}k'}} \right)^{\frac{\theta}{\theta_{\mathrm{T}k'}}} \right)^{\frac{1-\gamma}{\theta}} \left(\sum_{h=1}^{n_{\mathrm{N}k}} (c^k_{\mathrm{N}kh})^{\theta_{\mathrm{N}k}} \right)^{\frac{\gamma}{\theta_{\mathrm{N}k}}}$$

Subject to:

$$\sum_{i=1}^{n_{\mathrm{T}k}} p^k_{\mathrm{T}ki} c^k_{\mathrm{T}ki} + \sum_{j=1}^{n_{\mathrm{T}k'j}} p^k_{\mathrm{T}k'j} c^k_{\mathrm{T}k'j} + \sum_{h=1}^{n_{\mathrm{N}k}} p^k_{\mathrm{N}kh} c^k_{\mathrm{N}kh} = w_k L_k$$

where $\{c^k_{\mathrm{T}ki}, c^k_{\mathrm{T}k'j}, c^k_{\mathrm{N}kh}\}$ are, respectively, the consumption from the part of the representative consumer of country k of the $\{i$th, jth, hth$\}$ variety of the {tradables produced in country k, tradables produced abroad—i.e. in country k'—,and non-tradables produced in country k}. Similarly $\{p^k_{\mathrm{T}ki}, p^k_{\mathrm{T}k'j}, p^k_{\mathrm{N}kh}\}$ are the prices in location k of the varieties as respectively listed above. Prices of foreign varieties in the domestic market will equal foreign prices multiplied by the nominal exchange rate, e.[9,10] The labor supply and the wage rate of location k are denoted by L_k and w_k, respectively.

The relative weights of domestic and foreign tradables are assumed to be such that, *ceteris paribus* (i.e. if prices were identical), expenditure on domestic goods would be at least as large as expenditure on foreign goods ($0 < 1 - \delta \leqslant \delta < 1$). This introduces an expenditure bias on domestic tradables to the extent that $\delta > 1 - \delta$.[11] It is important to

[8] See Ricci (1999) for an economic geography model investigating the relation between agglomeration effects and comparative advantage (based on different productivities across countries and sectors).

[9] We introduced the notation of the nominal exchange rate for convenience in order to facilitate comparison with the macroeconomic literature on the real exchange rate. In this model, however, the nominal exchange rate is a redundant variable and can be set to one so that each variety has the same price in both locations.

[10] As Crucini et al. (2000) demonstrate, the law of one price is in fact violated for price comparisons of identical brands across relatively homogeneous European countries. In our work deviations from PPP depend essentially only on differences in the composition of the basket across countries (due to home bias) rather than on price differences in the elements of the basket.

[11] Note that in our framework the expenditure bias is assumed via the choice of δ. However, it may also be derived endogenously via the introduction of the trade costs, as in many economic geography models.

remark that the expenditure bias due to preferences (associated with δ) is identical across countries. Hence, such bias does not imply that the CPI weights for domestic and imported goods should be different across countries.[12]

The parameters θ_{T1}, θ_{T2}, θ_{N1}, θ_{N2} allow for the elasticity of substitution of demand to differ across sectors and countries.

The Consumers' maximization problem implies that consumers will spend a share γ and $1-\gamma$ of their income on non-tradable and tradable goods, respectively. Within tradable goods, the relative expenditure between domestic and foreign tradables will depend on the relative (domestic versus foreign) prices as well as on the expenditure bias towards domestic goods. Within each of the three sub-utility consumption baskets (domestic tradables, foreign tradables, and non-tradables), expenditure will be allocated equally among varieties, as the latter are all symmetric. Formally, the optimal expenditure functions of the representative consumer of country k on the typical varieties of domestic tradables (c^k_{Tk}), foreign tradables ($c^k_{Tk'}$), and domestic non-tradables (c^k_{Nk}) are given by

$$c^k_{Tk} = \frac{1}{n_{Tk}} \frac{(n_{Tk})^{\frac{\rho}{\rho-1}\frac{\theta_{Tk}-1}{\theta_{Tk}}} (p^k_{Tk})^{\frac{1}{\rho-1}} (\delta)^{\frac{1}{1-\rho}}}{(n_{Tk})^{\frac{\rho}{\rho-1}\frac{\theta_{Tk}-1}{\theta_{Tk}}} (p^k_{Tk})^{\frac{\rho}{\rho-1}} (\delta)^{\frac{1}{1-\rho}} + (n_{Tk'})^{\frac{\rho}{\rho-1}\frac{\theta_{Tk'}-1}{\theta_{Tk'}}} (p^k_{Tk'})^{\frac{\rho}{\rho-1}} (1-\delta)^{\frac{1}{1-\rho}}} (1-\gamma) E_k$$

$$c^k_{Tk'} = \frac{1}{n_{Tk'}} \frac{(n_{Tk'})^{\frac{\rho}{\rho-1}\frac{\theta_{Tk'}-1}{\theta_{Tk'}}} (p^k_{Tk'})^{\frac{1}{\rho-1}} (1-\delta)^{\frac{1}{1-\rho}}}{(n_{Tk})^{\frac{\rho}{\rho-1}\frac{\theta_{Tk}-1}{\theta_{Tk}}} (p^k_{Tk})^{\frac{\rho}{\rho-1}} (\delta)^{\frac{1}{1-\rho}} + (n_{Tk'})^{\frac{\rho}{\rho-1}\frac{\theta_{Tk'}-1}{\theta_{Tk'}}} (p^k_{Tk'})^{\frac{\rho}{\rho-1}} (1-\delta)^{\frac{1}{1-\rho}}} (1-\gamma) E_k$$

$$c^k_{Nk} = \frac{1}{n_{Nk} p^k_{Nk}} \gamma E_k$$

2.2. *Firms maximization problem*

The labor input (l_{sk}) required to produce x_{sk} units of a typical variety in sector s(T, N) in country $k(1, 2)$ is given by

$$l_{sk} = \alpha + \frac{x_{sk}}{\pi_{sk}}$$

where π_{sk} represent the marginal productivity of labor in the respective sector of each country. The firm's profit maximization implies the usual mark-up pricing. Within each sector, all firms face the same wage, the same productivity, and the same elasticity of demand. Hence, the optimal price in domestic currency of the representative firm of sector s of country k is given by

$$p^k_{sk} = \frac{w_k}{\pi_{sk} \theta_{sk}}$$

[12] The actual shares of expenditure on—and hence the CPI weights of—domestic and foreign goods are also influenced by relative prices and can therefore differ across countries if prices differ.

As is usual in the Dixit–Stiglitz framework, θ_{sk} (a parameter of the utility function) equals the inverse of the optimal mark-up, and we will refer to it as a measure of product market competition in the respective sector.[13] The zero-profit condition associated with monopolistic competition implies the following equilibrium output and employment for the typical firm:

$$x_{sk} = \alpha\pi_{sk}\frac{\theta_{sk}}{1-\theta_{sk}}, \quad l_{sk} = \alpha\frac{1}{1-\theta_{sk}}$$

Note that in each sector of each country, the ratio of variable employment to total employment equals the corresponding θ_{sk} parameter:

$$\frac{\text{variable employment}}{\text{total employment}} \equiv \frac{\frac{x_{sk}}{\pi_{sk}}}{\alpha + \frac{x_{sk}}{\pi_{sk}}} = \theta_{sk}$$

This relationship will turn out to be useful when we move to the empirical estimation.

2.3. Equilibrium

Equilibrium in the goods and labor market require the following conditions hold:

$$L_{Nk} - n_{Nk}l_{Nk} = \gamma L_k, \quad L_{Tk} = n_{Tk}l_{Tk} = (1-\gamma)L_k, \quad L_{Nk} + L_{Tk} = L_k$$
$$w_k L_{Tk} = n_{Tk}p^k_{Tk}x_{Tk} = n_{Tk}p^k_{Tk}(c^k_{Tk} + c^{k'}_{Tk})$$
$$w_k L_{Nk} = n_{Nk}p^k_{Nk}x_{Nk} = n_{Nk}p^k_{Nk}c^k_{Nk}$$

where L_{sk} is employment in sector s of country k and L_k is the labor supply of country k.

Equilibrium in the tradable sector implies the following trade balance equilibrium condition:

$$n_{Tk}p^k_{Tk}c^{k'}_{Tk} = n_{Tk'}p^k_{Tk'}c^k_{Tk'}$$

which provides a non-linear solution for the equilibrium relative wage:

$$w = \frac{N_{T1}L_2}{N_{T2}L_1}\frac{\left(N_{T1}\left(\frac{w}{\theta_T\pi_T}\right)^{\frac{\theta}{\theta-1}}(v)^{\frac{1}{1-\theta}} + N_{T2}\right)}{\left(N_{T1} + N_{T2}\left(\frac{\theta_T\pi_T}{w}\right)^{\frac{\theta}{\theta-1}}(v)^{\frac{1}{1-\theta}}\right)}$$

where

$$N_{Tk} \equiv (n_{Tk})^{\frac{\theta}{\theta-1}\frac{\theta_{Tk}-1}{\theta_{Tk}}}, \quad w = \frac{w_1}{ew_2}, \quad \theta_s = \frac{\theta_{s1}}{\theta_{s2}}, \quad \pi_s = \frac{\pi_{s1}}{\pi_{s2}}, \quad v = \frac{\delta}{1-\delta} \geqslant 1$$

By linearizing the model around this equilibrium we can determine, via a comparative static exercise, the percentage changes in the real exchange rate associated with changes in the parameters of interest: π_T, π_N, θ_T, θ_N; that is, respectively, the relative productivity in tradables and non-tradables, as well as the relative product market competition in tradables and non-tradables.

[13] The parameter θ_{sk} is directly related to the elasticity of substitution of demand for the respective variety (which equals $1/(1-\theta_{sk})$) and inversely related to the equilibrium economies of scale (as proxied by the ratio of average cost, equal to the optimal price, and marginal cost) in the respective sector.

2.4. Initial equilibrium

For simplicity, we characterize the initial equilibrium as symmetric. We are in fact interested in the impact on the real exchange rate of changes in the above parameters rather than characterizing the patterns of trade, production, and location. We leave for future work the investigation of the impact of the second order effects of such different cross country patterns of changes in productivities and product market competition would have on the real exchange rate.

We therefore initially assume that countries have the same overall labor supply, the same productivities and product market competition in the respective sector s (a subscript 0 denotes an initial value):

$$L_1 = L_2 = L, \quad \pi_{s1} = \pi_{s2} = \pi_{s0}, \quad \theta_{s1} = \theta_{s2} = \theta_{s0}$$

This is sufficient to generate an equilibrium, where in each sector, prices, output, employment, the mark-up, and the number of varieties is identical across countries; and the wage is identical across countries.

$$L_{T1} = L_{T2} = L_{T0} = (1-\gamma)L, \quad L_{N1} = L_{N2} = L_{N0} = \gamma L,$$
$$n_{s1} = n_{s2} = n_{s0} = L_{s0}(1-\theta)/\alpha \quad e = 1, \quad w_1 = w_2 = w_0, \quad p^1_{s1} = p^2_{s2} = p_{s0}$$

Note that even if prices of all varieties are initially identical across countries, this is not necessarily the case once shocks arise: if productivity and product market competition differ across countries, so do prices for the respective variety. For any specific variety, of course, the law of one price always holds, in the sense that the specific variety has the same price in the two countries.

The expenditure bias would be identical across countries, so that trade would be balanced. For future reference we identify the initial expenditure bias towards domestic goods as the difference in the initial shares of expenditures on domestic and foreign goods:

$$z = \frac{n_{Tk}p^k_{Tk}c^k_{Tk} - n_{Tk'}p^k_{Tk'}c^k_{Tk'}}{n_{Tk}p^k_{Tk}c^k_{Tk} + n_{Tk'}p^k_{Tk'}c^k_{Tk'}} = \frac{v^{\frac{1}{1-\theta}} - 1}{v^{\frac{1}{1-\theta}} + 1} \geqslant 0, \quad \text{if } \delta \geqslant 1-\delta$$

2.5. The real exchange rate

The real exchange rate, q,—the ratios of the true price indexes of the two countries—is given by:[14]

$$q = \left(\frac{(n_{N1})^{\frac{\theta_{N1}-1}{\theta_{N1}}}}{(n_{N2})^{\frac{\theta_{N2}-1}{\theta_{N2}}}}\frac{w}{\theta_N\pi_N}\right)^{\gamma}\left(\frac{\left(N_{T1}\left(\frac{w}{\theta_T\pi_T}\right)^{\frac{\theta}{\theta-1}}(v)^{\frac{1}{1-\theta}} + N_{T2}\right)}{\left(N_{T1}\left(\frac{w}{\theta_T\pi_T}\right)^{\frac{\theta}{\theta-1}} + N_{T2}(v)^{\frac{1}{1-\theta}}\right)}\right)^{\frac{(1-\gamma)(\theta-1)}{\theta}}.$$

[14] Using an empirically based real exchange rate, such as a geometric average of the prices of tradables and non-tradables (with weights given by the relative expenditures on the two components), would yield a simpler expression, and similar conclusions to those in Section 2.6 would be obtained.

As one can see, in the absence of an expenditure bias (i.e. if $v = 1$), the real exchange rate would depend only on the relative price of non-tradables. By differentiation, we can therefore derive the following expression in terms of percentage changes:

$$\hat{q} = (\gamma + (1-\gamma)z)w - (1-\gamma)z\hat{\pi_T} - \gamma\hat{\pi_N} - (1-\gamma)z(1-y_T)\hat{\theta_T} - \gamma(1-y_N)\hat{\theta_N} \tag{1}$$

where $y_S = 1 + \frac{\ln(n_{S0})}{\theta_{S0}}$, for $s = \mathrm{T},\ \mathrm{N}$.

The parameter y_s captures the impact on the real exchange rate due to the change in the number of varieties induced by the change in product market competition (or in the parameter of the utility function associated with it); for convenience we will separate this effect from the effect of product market competition directly on prices of individual varieties.

By differentiating the trade balance equilibrium we can derive the following expression for the percentage change in the relative wage:

$$\hat{w} = \frac{2v^{\frac{1}{1-\theta}}\frac{\theta}{1-\theta}}{1 + v^{\frac{1}{1-\theta}} + 2v^{\frac{1}{1-\theta}}\frac{\theta}{1-\theta}}((1-y_T)\hat{\theta_T} + \hat{\pi_T})$$

By substituting the expression for the wage in Eq. (1), the final expression for the percentage change in real exchange rate can be defined as

$$\hat{q} = \phi_{\pi T}\hat{\pi_T} + \phi_{\pi N}\hat{\pi_N} + \phi_{\theta T}\hat{\theta_T} + \phi_{\theta N}\hat{\theta_N} \tag{2}$$

where, recalling the definition of v,

$$\phi_{\pi T} = \frac{\gamma\left(\left(\frac{\delta}{1-\delta}\right)^{\frac{1}{1-\theta}}\left(\frac{1+\theta}{1-\theta}\right) - 1\right) + 1 - \left(\frac{\delta}{1-\delta}\right)^{\frac{1}{1-\theta}}}{\left(\left(\frac{\delta}{1-\delta}\right)^{\frac{1}{1-\theta}}\left(\frac{1+\theta}{1-\theta}\right) + 1\right)}$$

$$\phi_{\pi N} = -\gamma, \quad \phi_{\theta T} = (1-y_T)\phi_{\pi T}, \quad \phi_{\theta N} = -\gamma(1-y_N).$$

2.6. *Implications of the model for the real exchange rate*

Eq. (2) provides several implications for the behavior of the real exchange rate.

(1) The impact on the real exchange rate of the relative productivity in tradables is smaller than that of the relative productivity in non-tradables.
   - It can be easily shown that: $\phi_{\pi T} < \gamma$. This differs from the usual Balassa–Samuelson theoretical result, often calculated in a neoclassical framework with homogenous commodities and price equalization (where the coefficients are identical, and equal to the share of expenditure on non-tradables, γ). In fact, the imperfect substitutability of tradables implies that the productivity of tradables also has a direct negative impact on the prices of tradables in addition to the indirect positive impact—via wages—on the price of non-tradables. To the extent there is an expenditure bias towards domestic tradables, the direct negative impact would produce a depreciation of the real exchange rate (as domestic prices fall more than foreign ones). Such an effect would go against the usual positive impact on the real exchange rate of the indirect effect (via the wage) of the productivity of tradables.

(2) The overall impact of the productivity of tradables on q is positive, unless the share of expenditure on non-tradables is very small:
   - $\phi_{\pi T} > 0$, only if γ is not too small.[15] If the share of expenditure on non-tradables were to be too small, the direct negative impact of productivity of tradables on the real exchange rate can be larger than the indirect positive impact via wages. As we discuss later, we find empirically that $\phi_{\pi T} > 0$.

(3) The impact of relative product market competition in the tradable (non-tradable) sector on the real exchange rate is similar to the impact of relative productivity in the tradable (non-tradable) sector, if we neglect the price effect of changes in the number of varieties of tradables (non-tradables) captured by y_T (y_N).
   - If we neglect y_T and y_N, then $\phi_{\theta T} = \phi_{\pi T}$ and $\phi_{\theta N} = -\gamma$. Neglecting the price effect of changes in the number of varieties makes sense if the objective is to derive an expression that can be empirically estimated with Consumer Price Index (CPI) data, which do not properly—or at all—capture such an effect. Then, the model provides the intuitive result that product market competition affects prices—and hence the real exchange rate—in a similar way to productivity. For example, consider the case of an increase in θ_{T1} (and hence of θ_T) and assume $\phi_{\theta T} > 0$ (as is empirically the case). This induces, the mark-up in tradables of country 1 to drop (that is, higher product market competition), which both lowers the prices of varieties of tradables and increases the relative wage of country 1. The net effect on the real exchange rate is identical to that of an increase in productivity of tradables, which is discussed above.
   - Alternatively, if we consider the price effect of the change in the number of varieties captured by y_T and y_N, then $\phi_{\theta T} = -(\ln(n_{T0})/\theta_{T0})\phi_{\pi T}$, $\phi_{\theta N} = \gamma(\ln(n_{N0})/\theta_{N0})$, and the effect of product market competition on the real exchange rate is now the opposite of what we have when that effect is neglected. To illustrate the intuition for the influence of the price effect of the change in the number of varieties consider the same example as above; that is, an increase in θ_{T1} when $\phi_{\theta T} > 0$. In addition to the effect mentioned above (a reduction in the mark up for T1), the number of firms that can survive the stiffer competition within the T1 sector is reduced, so that every firm can produce a larger output and recover the same fixed cost despite the lower mark-up. However, due to the peculiar nature of the Dixit–Stiglitz utility functions (and its 'love for variety' property), a reduction in the number of firms increases the true price index of T1, thus inducing an opposite set of effects to a drop in the mark-up. It turns out that the price effect of the change in the number of varieties dominates the mark-up effect, so that an increase in θ_{T1} (hence an increase in product market competition of tradables of 1) would depreciate the real exchange rate of country 1. However, as we noted above, since it is unlikely that estimated CPIs capture the variety effect, we expect the effect of product market competition on the real exchange rate to be as in the case where the effect of y_T and y_N is neglected.

We conclude this section by stressing that the effect on the real exchange rate of the relative productivity in tradables, net of its indirect impact via the wage, is negative, as

[15] The exact condition being: $\gamma > \frac{\left(\frac{1}{1-\beta}\right)^{\frac{1}{1-\beta}}-1}{\left(\frac{1}{1-\beta}\right)^{\frac{1}{1-\beta}\frac{1+\beta}{1-\beta}}-1}$.

is visible from Eq. (1). The intuition has already been provided in the discussion to point 1 above: the direct effect is to reduce the relative price of domestic tradables. To the extent that there is an expenditure bias towards domestic tradables, such a reduction of the price of domestic tradables would reduce the overall domestic price level more than the foreign one and this generates a depreciation of the real exchange rate. It is useful to remember that in the standard neoclassical Balassa–Samuelson setup the effect of productivity of tradables on the real exchange rate operates exclusively via its positive impact on wages, and hence its coefficient would become zero once we net out wage adjustments. In both our framework, and that of Balassa–Samuelson, the productivity of non-tradables does not operate via wages, hence its coefficient is identical when we net out wage adjustments.[16]

3. Data sources, variable definitions, and econometric methods

This section presents a brief discussion of the construction of the data set, relegating a more complete description of the construction of the variables to the data appendix. Ten countries feature in our analysis: Belgium (BEL), Denmark (DNK), Finland (FIN), France (FRA), Italy (ITA), Japan (JPN), Norway (NOR), Sweden (SWE), West Germany (WGR), and the United States (USA).[17] Variables for each of the first nine countries are defined relative to the USA, bringing the cross-sectional dimension of our panel to nine. Annual data are used for the period 1970–1992 (this gives a total of 230 observations which reduces to 153 after allowing for leads and lags in the panel DOLS framework). Both the cross-sectional and time series dimensions of the panel were determined by the availability of consistent data for all the variables.[18] The correlation among variables, conditional on fixed effects (i.e. the correlation among the residuals of the regression of each variable on fixed effects) are presented in Table 1.

Our key objective in this section is to test a variant of Eq. (2). The dependent variable used in our empirical implementation of such an equation is the logarithm of the real exchange rate (LRER), which is CPI-based: an increase in LRER of country j corresponds to an appreciation of the real exchange of j versus the USA.[19] In addition to the key conditioning variables predicted by our theory—productivity and competitiveness in tradables and non-tradables—we condition the LRER term on two macroeconomic control variables: the relative size of net foreign assets to GDP ratios and a relative real interest rate term. The theoretical and empirical importance of these variables has been assessed in various contributions and we believe it is important to control for them in our study. Net foreign assets appears in many theoretical models as the key tie down condition for

[16] We focus on the relative productivity, as competitiveness was not present in the Balassa–Samuelson framework. However, also for competitiveness, the direct impact of on the real exchange rate of the relative competitiveness in tradables has the opposite sign than the overall effect.

[17] Data refer to West Germany only, even for the period after German reunification.

[18] We would have preferred to use a sample period defined purely for the post Bretton Woods period but this was not possible given data availability on the variables used for the construction of the competitiveness term.

[19] We use CPI-based real exchange rates in order to make our results comparable with the many studies on the PPP puzzle. We recognize, however, that there are a number of problems with such prices, such as the use of different weights in different countries and also that these weights can be time-varying over time. As Crucini et al. (2000), and others, have demonstrated such compositional biases can produce spurious findings of very long half-lives for real exchange rates.

R. MacDonald, L.A. Ricci / Journal of Macroeconomics 29 (2007) 639–664 649

Table 1
Correlation matrix among variables, accounting for fixed effects; i.e. correlation b/w residuals of regression of each variable on fixed effect

	LRER	NFA	INT	LBAL2WT	LATRDWT	LANTRD	LE2BALWT	LETRDWT	LENTRD	LWTRDWT	LWIND	LWMAN
LRER	1.0	0.1	0.2	0.4	−0.1	−0.5	0.0	−0.6	−0.4	0.9	0.9	0.9
NFA		1.0	−0.1	0.2	−0.3	−0.3	−0.2	−0.2	0.0	0.0	0.0	0.0
INT			1.0	0.1	0.1	−0.1	0.1	0.2	0.1	0.1	0.1	0.1
LBAL2WT				1.0	0.3	−0.8	−0.5	−0.1	0.3	0.5	0.5	0.5
LATRDWT					1.0	0.2	−0.4	0.2	0.4	0.3	0.2	0.2
LANTRD						1.0	0.2	0.2	0.0	−0.3	−0.3	−0.4
LE2BALWT							1.0	0.0	−0.7	−0.3	−0.3	−0.2
LE2TRDWT								1.0	0.7	−0.5	−0.5	−0.5
LE2NTRD									1.0	−0.1	−0.2	−0.2
LWTRDWT										1.0	1.0	1.0
LWIND											1.0	1.0
LWMAN												1.0

the long-run real exchange rate (see, for example, Lane and Milesi-Ferretti, 2004) and real interest differentials are often cited as determinants of the business cycle related component of the real exchange rate (see Obstfeld and Rogoff, 1996) and also the longer run real exchange rate (see Stein and Allen, 1995).

We then add productivity in tradables and non-tradables (we introduce them both separately and jointly, the latter being the usual way to analyze the Balassa–Samuelson effect). All of these variables, apart from the productivity terms, are from the IFS, OECD, World Bank, and WEO macroeconomic data bases. The relative productivity in tradables and non-tradables are calculated by drawing from the OECD International Sectoral data base. Similar to De Gregorio et al. (1994) and Cheung et al. (1999) we classify agriculture, manufacturing, and transportation sectors as tradables; and utilities, construction, and social services sectors as non-tradables.[20]

We then introduce into the regressions variables capturing the product market competition terms (θ_{sk}). In trade theory models such as ours, θ_{sk} equals the equilibrium ratio of variable employment to total employment, as shown before. We build a proxy for θ_{sk} by calculating for each sector the ratio of employees to total employment from the OECD ISD database. As with the Balassa–Samuelson effect, the product market competition terms for tradables and non-tradables are entered both separately and jointly. Finally, by introducing different measures of the aggregate wage in industrial activity (again from the OECD International Sectoral database), we are able to analyze how the Balassa–Samuelson and product market competition terms get transmitted into the real exchange rate.

The relatively small available time series samples for each country necessitates using panel methods to improve the power of our tests (data on productivity, for example, are only available at an annual frequency). Recent developments in the econometrics of panel data sets has sought to address the potential non-stationarity of the series entering the panel.[21] In particular, McCoskey and Kao (1999), Pedroni (2004) and Phillips and Moon (1999) have proposed panel equivalents to the single equation fully modified estimator, while McCoskey and Kao (1999) and Mark and Sul (1999) have proposed using a panel dynamic OLS (DOLS) estimator. Since Kao and Chiang (2000) have demonstrated that the panel DOLS procedure exhibits less bias than the panel OLS and panel fully modified estimators and Mark and Sul (1999) have emphasized the tractability of the estimator, we employ a panel DOLS estimator for all our regressions. This has the following form:

$$\text{LRER}_{it} = \theta_{1i} + \theta_{2t} + \theta_3 x_{it} + \sum_{j=-p}^{+n} \theta_{4j} \Delta x^{+}_{it+j} \omega_{it}, \tag{3}$$

where x_{it} is a vector with dimension v, θ_{1i} is an country fixed effect, θ_{2t} is a time effect, θ_3 represents a cointegration vector, p is the maximum lag length, n is the maximum lead

[20] De Gregorio et al. (1994) define as tradable those sectors for which the export share in total production is larger than 10%. A similar classification was used by Stockman and Tesar (1995). Following MacDonald and Ricci (2005) we exclude the distribution sector from the non-tradable sector. Mining was not included in the tradable sector for lack of data for Belgium and Italy. The financial sector was not included in the non-tradable sector for lack of data for Belgium, Italy, and Netherlands.

[21] On the basis of a Levin et al. (2002) panel unit root test with a constant, all variables are identified as having a unit root, apart from interest rates, wage in manufacturing, and product market competition when constructed as Balassa–Samuelson. No trend was introduced, as the objective of this study is to check whether the right hand side variables are able to explain any pattern of the real exchange rate. As the literature on testing for panel unit root is far from conclusive, we also run the regressions with OLS, obtaining similar results (see Section 4).

length and ω is a Gaussian vector error process. The leads and lags of the difference terms are included to ensure that the error term is orthogonalized. Our representation of the Panel DOLS estimator assumes that the dynamics are the same across individuals. The estimator can address potential cross-sectional dependence by the inclusion of time dummies, and that is accomplished here by removing the cross-sectional mean of each variable.[22]

The levels terms (x_{it}) entering Eq. (3) are the same levels terms as appear in Eq. (2), with the addition of net foreign assets and the real interest differential. Our interest is in the coefficients on the levels terms—and particularly productivity and competitiveness in tradables and non-tradables—since their sign and magnitude will shed light on our theoretical model. The dynamic terms included in Eq. (3) do not have a bearing on the model discussed in section and are therefore not reported in our empirical tests.

Pedroni (2004) has noted that the residuals from an equation like (3) will have the same distribution as the raw data and hence it is possible to use a standard unit root test to check for the existence of cointegration amongst the variables in the vector of interest. We therefore use the Levin et al. (2002) panel unit root statistic to test for cointegration:

$$\Delta\omega_{it} = \delta\omega_{it-1} + \sum_{j=1}^{n} \theta_{4i}\Delta\omega_{it-j} + u_{it}, \tag{4}$$

where—δ represents the adjustment speed[23] and the t-ratio on this term, denoted "PUR test" in the empirical section of this paper, denotes the significance of the adjustment speed.[24] The null hypothesis that each time series of residuals has a unit root is rejected if δ is significantly negative; that is, in the current application there is panel cointegration. As Levin et al. (2002) demonstrate, under the null hypothesis that $\delta = 0$ the PUR test diverges to minus infinity. However, they propose a simple adjustment to this statistic that produces a test statistic which has a standard normal distribution and it is this adjusted t-statistic which we use in this paper.

4. Empirical results

In Table 2 we present our base line set of results with the macro variables. The simplest model in which the real exchange rate is conditioned on NFA and the real interest differential indicates that both these variables are correctly signed and statistically significant. They contribute to reducing the half-life of a deviation from the long-run equilibrium level from 3.3 years to 2.1 years. In column 3, the introduction of a traditional Balassa–Samuelson term—i.e. the ratio of relative productivity in tradables and non-tradables—into such an equation, produces a significant coefficient and a sign which is consistent with the traditional Balassa–Samuelson effect. This is a common result in the literature on real exchange rates. However the results in column 4 indicate that the restriction that the

[22] The inclusion of the time dummies neutralizes the role of the reference country (USA): measuring the real exchange rate with respect to different reference countries (say Germany as opposed to USA) would yield different coefficients in the absence of time dummies. Our results on the adjustment speed do not depend on time dummies.

[23] Eq. (3) represents the reparameterization of a levels autoregression for ω, and therefore δ represents the difference between the sum of the levels autoregressive coefficients and one.

[24] We use the adjustment proposed by Levin et al. (2002) for the case of a constant terms as we employed fixed effects in the original regression that generated the residuals. We also implemented the Im et al. (2003) panel unit root test, with similar results.

Table 2
The base-line model of RER (dynamic OLS)

	LRER						
	(1)	(2)	(3)	(4)	(5)	(6)	(7)
Net foreign assets (NFA)		**0.005**	**0.003**	**0.001**	**−0.002**	**−0.001**	**−0.001**
		2.94	2.02	0.41	2.37	1.65	1.39
Real interest rates (INT)		**0.03**	**0.013**	**0.006**	**0.004**	**0.002**	**0.001**
		4.20	1.91	0.87	1.57	1.02	0.21
Balassa–Samuelson – BS		–	**0.77**	–	–	–	–
(LBAL2WT)		–	6.45	–	–	–	–
Productivity in tradables		–	–	**0.417**	**−0.587**	**−0.566**	**−0.412**
(LATRDWT)		–	–	1.92	6.66	7.30	4.41
Productivity in non-tradables		–	–	**−0.948**	**−0.259**	**−0.221**	**−0.259**
(LANTRD)		–		7.16	4.83	4.54	4.32
Wage in tradables		–	–	–	**0.719**	–	–
(LWTRDWT)		–	–	–	22.06	–	
Wage in industry (LWIND)		–	–	–	–	**0.736**	–
		–	–	–	–	25.08	–
Wage in manufacturing		–	–	–	–	–	**0.675**
(LWMAN)			–	–	–	–	19.27
Testing restrictions on coefficients							
Chi-square				4.92			
Probability				0.03			
Panel unit root analysis							
PUR test	−0.62	−0.87	−3.81	−3.25	−1.88	−2.31	−1.72
Delta (from text)	−0.22	−0.22	−0.44	−0.42	−0.26	−0.28	−0.27
Half lifetime (years)	2.8	2.1	1.2	1.3			
Number of observations	153	153	153	153	153	153	153

Absolute t-ratios below coefficients.
Wald Test on restrictions. H0: LATRDWT + LANTRD = 0. Do not reject if p-value above desired alpha (0.05).
Panel unit root (PUR) test: 'adjusted' Levin et al. (2002) t-ratios discussed in the text. Half lifetime of deviations of the real exchange rate from estimated relation (years): log(0.5)/(log(1 + delta)).

coefficient on productivity in tradables and non-tradables be equal and opposite is easily rejected using a 5% significance level. In fact, consistent with our model, the coefficient of the productivity of tradables is, in absolute terms, significantly lower than the coefficient of the productivity of non-tradables.

We now inspect the channel of influence of the difference in productivities on the real exchange rate. In the final three columns of the table we introduce three different measures of the relative wage: the wage in the tradable sector, the overall industry wage, and the wage in manufacturing. According to the standard Balassa–Samuelson framework, the wage is the only channel through which improvements in productivity in the tradable sector gets transmitted to the CPI based real exchange rate, and including the wage in our regression should make the coefficient on tradable productivity become zero (since the wage would capture all of the effect of the productivity of tradables). However, in all of the regressions which include the wage, the coefficient on the productivity of tradables becomes statistically negative, which is consistent with our model.

Both of the new results above (the significantly lower effect of the productivity of tradables versus the effect of non-tradables and the reverse in sign of the productivity of tradables when the wage enters the regression) can be ascribed to the imperfect substitutability of tradables in the presence of a home expenditure bias. As discussed in Section 2, in this case, productivity of tradables would not only directly and positively affect the aggregate wage (and hence indirectly and positively the overall price index and RER) but also directly and negatively the price of tradables (and hence indirectly and negatively the price index and the RER). The Balassa–Samuelson result would still hold if the first effect dominates, although once we control for the wage effect, only the second effect would be ascribed to the productivity of tradables. In other words, in the presence of imperfect substitutability of goods and expenditure bias towards domestic tradables, both productivity in tradables and non-tradables would have a direct negative impact on the real exchange rate once we control for the indirect effect via the wage channel.

Note also that the coefficient of productivity of non-tradables drops, in absolute terms, when the wage enters the regression. Our model (as well as the standard Balassa–Samuelson framework) cannot account for such an effect. However, one possible explanation for this result is that some components of non-tradables might indirectly be traded. It is in fact easy to conceive that services (such as the utilities) normally classified as non-tradable may constitute intermediate inputs for tradable goods. Productivity in these components would thus behave as productivity of tradables, so that the overall coefficient would be the average of two factors: pure non-tradables whose impact is unchanged when accounting for the wage, and spurious non-tradables, whose impact would become lower or negative when accounting for the wage. The net result would be a reduction of the coefficient when accounting for the wage effect.

Regarding the adjustment speeds, note that the introduction of the productivity terms dramatically reduces the half-lives of deviations of the real exchange rate from its long-run equilibrium level (the cointegrating relationship) to 1.2–1.3 years, which is the end point for the PPP puzzle (1 year).[25]

In Table 3 the two product market competition terms—in tradables and in non-tradables—are introduced instead of the productivity terms. Our discussion in Section 2 suggests that the coefficients on these terms should have opposite signs. Their signs should also mirror those of the productivities (positive for tradables and negative for non-tradables) to the extent the CPI-based real exchange rate cannot capture the effect of changes of the number of varieties on the true price index (i.e. the price of one unit of marginal utility); otherwise, these signs should be the reverse of those for productivities.

The first column shows that when both product market competition in the tradables and non-tradables enters the regression, their signs are, respectively, significantly positive and negative (similarly to the signs of productivities); NFA is now insignificant. However, when the product market competition term is entered separately (column 2 and 3), the sign of product market competition of tradables maintains its sign, while the coefficient on the product market competition of non-tradables is reversed (column 3). We attribute the last reversal of sign to multicollinearity, as the variables are strongly and negatively correlated (−0.7, as from Table 1).[26] In the last column, we constrain the coefficients of the two product market competition terms to be equal and opposite (thus building a term equivalent to

[25] The last 3 columns do not report an adjustment speed as the equation is deliberately overspecified.

[26] One explanation for the two competitiveness terms to be so closely correlated is that market structure might move more similarly across the traded and non-traded sectors than productivity does across sectors, a topic which is left for future investigation.

Table 3
Relative product market competition (dynamic OLS)

	LRER			
	(1)	(2)	(3)	(4)
Net foreign assets (NFA)	**0.001**	**0.003**	**0.003**	**0.003**
	0.20	2.06	1.84	1.51
Real interest rates (INT)	**0.034**	**0.040**	**0.032**	**0.019**
	5.38	6.67	4.25	2.55
P. m. competition like BS (LE2BALWT)	–	–	–	**0.101**
	–	–	–	0.23
P. m. competition in tradables (LE2TRDWT)	**3.554**	**2.526**	–	–
	7.32	9.01	–	–
P. m. competition in non-tradables (LE2NTRD)	**−0.994**	–	**1.119**	–
	2.83	–	4.74	–
Testing restrictions on coefficients				
Chi-square	89.09			
Probability	0.00			
Panel unit root analysis				
PUR test	−1.83	−0.88	−0.52	−0.94
Delta (from text)	−0.39	−0.28	−0.25	−0.33
Half lifetime (years)	1.4	2.1	2.4	1.7
Number of observations	153	153	153	153

Absolute-ratios below coefficients.
Wald Test on restrictions. H0: LE2TRDWT + LE2NTRD = 0. Do not reject if p-value above desired alpha (0.05).
Panel unit root (PUR) test: "adjusted" Levin et al. (2002) t-ratios discussed in the text.
Half lifetime of deviations of the real exch. rate from estimated relation (years): log (0.5)/(log(1 + delta)).

a Balassa–Samuelson term for product market competition): this term is not significant, as the difference of two collinear variable could have any sign (the last result is also not surprising given that in the first column we strongly reject the coefficient restriction). This last result is, however, of little importance to us, as our model does not support coefficients of identical size and opposite sign.

The results in Table 3 suggest that the best specification is the one with just the product market competition term in the tradable sector included: both terms cannot be simultaneously present or be constrained because of multicollinearity, and the coefficient on product market competition in the tradable sector is more stable than the other. Note that the residuals are non-stationary, suggesting that dropping productivity measures (present in Table 2) induces misspecification. However, a question arises as to whether our product market competition terms provide additional information to a setup where productivity terms are included. This issue is addressed in Table 4.

In Table 4 we add our various measures of product market competition into the model with constrained (first four columns) and unconstrained (last four columns) productivity terms. First, the introduction of the product market competition terms does not crowd out the significance of the coefficient on the productivity terms, although some of the specifications already rejected on the basis of Table 3 (i.e. columns 3, 4, 7, and 8 in Table 4) alter substantially the coefficients of the productivity terms. Also the coefficient on NFA is now consistently insignificant.

Table 4
Relative productivity and product market competition: in search of a model (dynamic OLS)

	LRER							
	(1)	(2)	(3)	(4)	(5)	(6)	(7)	(8)
Net foreign assets (NFA)	**0**	**0.001**	**0.002**	**0.002**	**−0.001**	**−0.000**	**0.002**	**−0.0004**
	0.04	0.99	1.09	1.15	0.87	0.19	1.34	0.18
Real interest rates (INT)	**0.018**	**0.024**	**0.014**	**0.033**	**0.021**	**0.028**	**0.017**	**−0.005**
	3.31	4.65	2.44	0.49	3.43	4.97	2.61	0.75
Balassa–Samuelson – BS	**0.769**	**0.736**	**0.997**	**0.944**	–	–	–	–
(LBAL2WT)	7.99	8.87	10.83	7.21	–	–	–	–
Productivity in tradables	–	–	–	–	**0.506**	**0.494**	**1.144**	**0.668**
(LATRDWT)	–	–	–	–	2.34	3.19	5.99	2.29
Productivity in non-tradables	–	–	–	–	**−0.766**	**−0.772**	**−0.955**	**−0.976**
(LANTRD)	–	–	–	–	7.64	8.10	9.38	7.40
P. m. competition like BS	–	–	–	**−1.590**	–	–	–	**−1.017**
(LE2BALWT)	–	–	–	3.57	–	–	–	1.82
P. m. comp. in tradables	**1.808**	**2.486**	–	–	**2.296**	**2.669**	–	–
(LE2TRDWT)	3.93	11.14	–	–	4.27	10.38	–	–
P. m. comp. in non-tradables	**0.479**	–	**1.704**	–	**0.131**	–	**1.844**	–
(LE2NTRD)	1.39	–	9.51	–	0.30	–	8.14	–
Testing restrictions on coefficients								
Chi-square	1.92							
Probability	0.16							
Panel unit root analysis								
PUR test	−4.67	−3.91	−2.36	−3.19	−5.04	−3.92	−2.42	−3.31
Delta (from text)	−0.59	−0.54	−0.42	−0.44	−0.63	−0.54	−0.42	−0.47
Half lifetime (years)	0.8	0.9	1.3	1.2	0.7	0.9	1.3	1.1
Number of observations	153	153	153	153	153	153	153	153

Absolute *t*-ratios below coefficients.
Wald Test on restrictions. H0: LE2TRDWT + LE2NTRD = 0. Do not reject if *p*-value above desired alpha (0.05).
Panel unit root (PUR) test: 'adjusted' Levin et al. (2002) *t*-ratios discussed in the text.
Half lifetime of deviations of the real exch. rate from estimated relation (years): log(0.5)/(log(1 + delta)).

The coefficient on the competitive terms reinforces our presumption that the specification with product market competition in tradables is the best one (column 2 and 6): not only are the coefficients of the productivity terms very similar to those in Table 2, but the multicollinearity of the two product market competition terms is again evident: product market competition in non-tradables is not significant in the specification with both terms unconstrained (columns 1 and 5); both product market competition terms are positive and significant when entered separately (columns 2, 3, 6, 7); and the constrained product market competition term (columns 4 and 8) changes sign with respect to the previous Table and now has the opposite sign than both product market competition terms entered separately.

One of the notable features of the regression presented in Table 4 is the fact that the half-life adjustment speed drops below unity in four instances, with the fastest adjustment speed occurring when both the product market competition and productivity terms are entered unconstrained.

In Table 5 we further inspect the mechanism through which the variable of interest affects the real exchange rate. To this end, as in Table 2, we introduce the three different measures of the wage discussed above into the best specification that our previous analysis delivered: a specification which comprises the basic macro variables, the productivity in tradables and non-tradables (separately), and the product market competition in trad-

Table 5
Relative productivity and product market competition: controlling for the wage effect (dynamic OLS)

	LRER			
	(1)	(2)	(3)	(4)
Net foreign assets (NFA)	**−0.000**	**−0.002**	**−0.001**	**−0.001**
	0.19	2.28	1.83	1.78
Real interest rates (INT)	**0.028**	**0.012**	**0.009**	**0.010**
	4.97	4.78	4.26	3.95
Productivity in tradables (LATRDWT)	**0.494**	**−0.328**	**−0.349**	**−0.169**
	3.19	3.85	4.67	2.11
Productivity in non-tradables (LANTRD)	**−0.772**	**−0.337**	**−0.297**	**−0.344**
	8.10	7.18	6.96	7.10
P. m. competition in tradables (LE2TRDWT)	**2.669**	**0.950**	**0.824**	**1.124**
	10.38	6.54	6.25	7.92
Wage in tradables (LWTRDWT)	–	**0.560**	–	–
	–	14.45	–	–
Wage in industry (LWIND)	–	–	**0.599**	–
	–	–	16.77	–
Wage in manufacturing (LWMAN)	–	–	–	**0.509**
	–	–	–	13.78
Panel unit root analysis				
PUR test	−3.92	−2.15	−2.05	−2.27
Delta (from text)	−0.54	−0.32	−0.37	−0.35
Half lifetime (years)	0.9			
Number of observations	153	153	153	153

Absolute *t*-ratios below coefficients.
Panel unit root (PUR) test: 'adjusted' Levin et al. (2002) *t*-ratios discussed in the text.
Half lifetime of deviations of the real exch. rate from estimated relation (years): log(0.5)/(log(1 + delta)).

Table 6
The base-line model of RER (OLS)

	LRER						
	(1)	(2)	(3)	(4)	(5)	(6)	(7)
Net foreign assets (NFA)		**0.004**	**0.003**	**0.001**	**−0.001**	**−0.0004**	**−0.001**
		2.97	2.50	1.23	2.11	0.88	1.22
Real interest rates (INT)		**0.007**	**0.003**	**0.004**	**0.001**	**0.0004**	**0.0003**
		1.99	1.05	1.25	1.37	0.42	0.23
Balassa–Samuelson – BS		–	**0.568**	–	–	–	–
(LBAL2WT)		–	5.84	–	–	–	–
Productivity in tradables		–	–	**0.252**	**−0.453**	**−0.387**	**−0.365**
(LATRDWT)		–	–	1.57	6.66	6.53	5.43
Productivity in non-		–	–	**−0.608**	**−0.180**	**−0.184**	**−0.163**
tradables (LANTRD)		–		6.39	3.84	4.45	3.44
Wage in tradables		–	–	–	**0.769**	–	–
(LWTRDWT)		–	–	–	27.53	–	
Wage in industry (LWIND)		–	–	–	–	**0.763**	–
		–	–	–	–	31.82	–
Wage in manufacturing		–	–	–	–	–	**0.740**
(LWMAN)			–	–	–	–	27.45
Testing restrictions on coefficients							
Chi-square				6.070			
Probability				0.01			
Panel unit root analysis							
PUR test	−0.66	−1.26	−2.85	−3.08	−0.97	−0.88	−1.61
Delta (from text)	−0.22	−0.29	−0.37	−0.39	−0.20	−0.22	−0.21
Half lifetime (years)	2.7	2.0	1.5	1.4			
Number of observations	153	153	153	153	153	153	153

Absolute t-ratios below coefficients.
Wald Test on restrictions. H0: LATRDWT + LANTRD = 0. Do not reject if p-value above desired alpha (0.05).
Panel unit root (PUR) test: 'adjusted' Levin et al. (2002) t-ratios discussed in the text. Half lifetime of deviations of the real exchange rate from estimated relation (years): log(0.5)/(log(1 + delta)).

ables. The addition of the product market competition terms does not alter the main results we found in Table 2 with respect to the productivity terms: regardless of the measure of the wage chosen, the coefficient on productivity in the tradable sector becomes significantly negative. However, the sign and significance of the product market competition term remains unchanged, although it falls to roughly one half the pre-wage equation. This last finding cannot be explained in terms of our model.

Tables 6–9 replicate the regressions in Tables 2–5, but with simple OLS rather than DOLS. Overall these results are remarkably similar to those outlined above, although the coefficients are generally lower.[27]

[27] We also conducted sensitivity tests in which the two macroeconomic control variables—the real interest differential and the net foreign asset term—were excluded from all of the key specifications. The results with respect to the key conditioning variables were unchanged. These results are available from the authors upon request.

Table 7
Relative product market competition (OLS)

	LRER			
	(1)	(2)	(3)	(4)
Net foreign assets (NFA)	**0.002**	**0.002**	**0.004**	**0.005**
	1.23	1.69	3.01	2.92
Real interest rates (INT)	**0.010**	**0.011**	**0.010**	**0.007**
	3.24	3.47	2.94	1.98
P. m. competition like BS (LE2BALWT)	–	–	–	**−0.050**
	–	–	–	0.12
P. m. competition in tradables (LE2TRDWT)	**2.716**	**2.082**	–	–
	5.31	6.98	–	–
P. m. competition in non-tradables (LE2NTRD)	**−0.526**	–	**0.966**	–
	1.52	–	4.41	–
Testing restrictions on coefficients				
Chi-square	51.48			
Probability	0.00			
Panel unit root analysis				
PUR test	−1.71	−2.00	−1.13	−1.22
Delta (from text)	−0.33	−0.33	−0.30	−0.29
Half lifetime (years)	1.8	1.7	2	2
Number of observations	153	153	153	153

Absolute t-ratios below coefficient.
Wald Test on restrictions. H0: LE2TRDWT + LE2NTRD = 0. Do not reject if p-value above desired alpha (0.05).
Panel unit root (PUR) test: 'adjusted' Levin et al. (2002) t-ratios discussed in the text.
Half lifetime of deviations of the real exch. rate from estimated relation (years): log(0.5)/(log(1 + delta)).

5. Concluding comments

This paper derives the theoretical implications for the real exchange rate of a trade theory model with imperfect substitution as well as different productivity and product market competition in the tradable and non-tradable sectors. It then tests such implications empirically, by estimating the long-run coefficients using a panel dynamic OLS estimator and testing for the cointegratedness of the variables entering the relationship. Results are compared with those of the standard Balassa–Samuelson approach. In the empirical section, a proxy for our product market competition term is developed by following a simple equilibrium relationship derived in the model (and common to the Dixit–Stiglitz-based trade theory literature): the inverse of the mark-up equals the equilibrium ratio of variable employment to total employment. Such a parameter is also directly related to the elasticity of substitution and inversely related to the equilibrium economies of scale.

Several results arise from our empirical analysis:

- First, the coefficient of the relative productivity of tradables is significantly lower than the coefficient of the relative productivity of non-tradables, in absolute terms.
- Second, the coefficient of the relative productivity of tradables changes sign if we introduce the wage into the estimation.

Table 8
Relative productivity and product market competition: in search of a model (OLS)

	LRER							
	(1)	(2)	(3)	(4)	(5)	(6)	(7)	(8)
Net foreign assets (NFA)	**0.001**	**0.001**	**0.002**	**0.004**	**0.001**	**0.000**	**0.002**	**0.003**
	1.38	0.99	2.40	3.09	0.41	0.04	1.86	1.99
Real interest rates (INT)	**0.007**	**0.007**	**0.006**	**0.004**	**0.007**	**0.007**	**0.006**	**0.004**
	2.63	2.57	2.38	1.29	2.73	2.72	2.40	1.37
Balassa–Samuelson – BS	**0.651**	**0.580**	**0.752**	**0.719**	–	–	–	–
(LBAL2WTM)	7.29	7.25	8.84	6.81	–	–	–	–
Productivity in tradables	–	–	–	–	**0.435**	**0.347**	**0.666**	**0.504**
(LATRDWT)	–	–	–	–	2.74	2.62	4.84	2.67
Productivity in non-tradables	–	–	–	–	**−0.701**	**−0.675**	**−0.781**	**−0.768**
(LANTRD)	–	–	–	–	7.47	7.48	8.29	6.91
P. m. competition like BS	–	–	–	**−1.212**	–	–	–	**−0.994**
(LE2BALWT)	–	–	–	3.18	–	–	–	2.41
P. m. comp. in tradables	**1.423**	**2.114**	–	–	**1.644**	**2.061**	–	–
(LE2TRDWT)	3.02	3.28	–	–	3.37	8.15	–	–
P. m. comp. in non-tradables	**0.577**	–	**1.419**	–	**0.356**	–	**1.381**	–
(LE2NTRD)	1.74	–	7.74	–	1.00	–	7.21	–
Testing restrictions on coefficients								
Chi-square	23.50							
Probability	0.00							
Panel unit root analysis								
PUR test	−4.99	−5.26	−4.12	−3.19	−4.29	−4.32	−4.25	−2.67
Delta (from text)	−0.52	−0.56	−0.48	−0.40	−0.49	−0.51	−0.48	−0.39
Half lifetime (years)	0.9	0.8	1	1.3	1	1	1	1.4
Number of observations	153	153	153	153	153	153	153	153

Absolute *t*-ratios below coefficients.
Wald Test on restrictions. H0: LE2TRDWT + LE2NTRD = 0. Do not reject if *p*-value above desired alpha (0.05).
Panel unit root (PUR) test: 'adjusted' Levin et al. (2002) *t*-ratios discussed in the text.
Half lifetime of deviations of the real exch. rate from estimated relation (years): log(0.5)/(log(1 + delta)).

Table 9
Relative productivity and product market competition: controlling for the wage effect (OLS)

	LRER			
	(1)	(2)	(3)	(4)
Net foreign assets (NFA)	**−0.000**	**−0.001**	**−0.001**	**−0.001**
	0.04	2.75	1.56	1.96
Real interest rates (INT)	**0.007**	**0.003**	**0.001**	**0.002**
	2.72	2.38	1.52	1.45
Productivity in tradables (LATRDWT)	**0.347**	**−0.362**	**−0.312**	**−0.276**
	2.62	5.49	5.46	4.36
Productivity in non-tradables (LANTRD)	**−0.675**	**−0.219**	**−0.218**	**−0.206**
	7.48	4.95	5.60	4.68
P. m. competition in tradables (LE2TRDWT)	**2.061**	**0.621**	**0.552**	**0.677**
	8.15	4.87	4.89	5.45
Wage in tradables (LWTRDWT)	–	**0.690**	–	–
	–	23.85	–	–
Wage in industry (LWIND)	–	–	**0.703**	–
	–	–	27.75	–
Wage in manufacturing (LWMAN)	–	–	–	**0.671**
	–	–	–	24.31
Panel unit root analysis				
PUR test	−4.32	−1.74	−1.43	−2.57
Delta (from text)	−0.51	−0.27	−0.28	−0.29
Half lifetime (years)	1			
Number of observations	153	153	153	153

Absolute *t*-ratios below coefficients.
Panel unit root (PUR) test: 'adjusted' Levin et al. (2002) *t*-ratios discussed in the text.
Half lifetime of deviations of the real exch. rate from estimated relation (years): log(0.5)/(log(1 + delta)).

These two results are consistent with the hypothesis of imperfect substitutability of tradables, coupled with an expenditure bias towards domestically produced tradables. An increase in productivity in tradables has two effects: first, a direct negative impact on the price of tradables, and therefore pressure towards a depreciation of the real exchange rate. Second, the lower price induces a larger demand and hence a higher wage (the standard Balassa–Samuelson effect), which instead tends to appreciate the real exchange rate via an increase in the price of non-tradables. The first effect ensures that the direct impact of the productivity of tradables on the real exchange rate—i.e. net of the wage channel—is negative. The ambiguity of the overall effect in a theoretical model is also highlighted by Benigno and Theonissen (2003), who, however, do not test empirically which effect tends to dominate.[28] We find that the impact of tradable productivity is lower than that for the productivity of non-tradables (the first result above), so that the standard Balassa–Samuelson result still apply: an increase in the productivity of tradables induces an appreciation of the real exchange rate.

[28] In a related empirical work to ours, Zachariadis (2004) uses microeconomic price data for Europe, over the period 1975–1990,and finds a robust negative relationship between the productivity of manufactures (tradables) and international price differences.

- Third, the coefficient of productivity on non-tradables drops when the wage enters the regression.

This result is likely to be due to the impossibility of deriving perfect measure of tradables and non-tradables: some components of non-tradables index (such as the utilities) might be used as intermediate inputs and therefore be indirectly traded. Productivity in these components would thus behave as productivity of tradables and would slightly offset other components.

- Fourth, a measure of product market competition in the tradable sector is significant and positive.
- Fifth, the coefficient of product market competition in the tradable sector remains significant and positive, although it drops in size, when we introduce the wage.[29]

The fourth result suggests that an increase in product market competition of tradables acts exactly like an increase in productivity, which is consistent with the model if we neglect the effect of the change in the number of varieties (i.e. if we believe that the CPI-based real exchange rate cannot capture the effect of the change in the number of varieties on the true price index—the price of one unit of marginal utility). The fifth result cannot be explained in terms of our model and requires further investigation of the mechanism through which product market competition affects the real exchange rate, as it suggests that the product market competition in tradables does not have the same transmission mechanism as the productivity of tradables.

Some caveats are in order. Given the novelty of our measure of product market competition, it is important to acknowledge that our proxy for product market competition is probably imperfect, as it is based on a too literal interpretation of our model. The existence of other factors of production in addition to labor, the unrealism of equilibrium relationship, and the fact that "number of employees" in the OECD ISD classification might not correspond to what the model requires to be variable employment, point to the imperfection of such a measure. However, our results clearly show that such a measure, which has not to our knowledge been used before, is powerful in explaining systematic changes of the real exchange rate. Further research is necessary to obtain a better understanding of the role of market structure, competition, and economies of scale in influencing the real exchange rate.

We would like to conclude with a suggestion for further research. We maintained a simple framework by assuming an initial symmetric equilibrium. In the absence of such restrictions, the model would have implied that the impact of relative productivity and product market competition in the two sectors depends also on factors such as the relative size and the initial relative prices. We leave for future research to investigate these interesting aspects, perhaps using a panel regression framework with heterogeneous slopes.

[29] The competitiveness measure in the non-tradable is found to be collinear with the one in tradables, and its effect dominated by the first one. Hence, specific implications for such measure cannot be derived.

Acknowledgements

The authors would like to thank Tamim Bayoumi, Tito Cordella, Charles Engel, Sam Ouliaris, Eswar Prasad, Kenneth Rogoff and two anonymous referees for useful comments and discussions.

Appendix. Variable definitions

For brevity, OECD International sectoral Database will be referred to as OCDE ISD. The corresponding three letter sectoral code or variable name code is provided.

Real exchange rate: $LRER_j = Log(CPI_j/(e_j * CPI_{usa}))$, for CPI = consumer price index, e = exchange rate (currency units of j per US$); Source: IFS.

Relative real interest rate: $INT_j = (i_j - \pi_j) - (i_{usa} - \pi_{usa\,j})$; for i_j = nominal interest rate (long term government bond yield) π_j = CPI inflation rate; source: IFS.

Relative net foreign assets: $NFA_j = (NFA_j * e_j/GDP_j) - (NFA_{usa}/GDP_{usa})$, for NFA = Net foreign asset position, GDP = gross domestic product, e = exchange rate (currency units of j per US$). Source: IFS, OECD.

Relative productivity in tradables: $LATRDWT_j = Log(\sum_k(\omega_{kj}TFP_{kj})/\sum_k(\omega_{k,usa}TFP_{usa}))$, for k = agricultural sector (AGR), manufacturing sector (MAN) and transport, storage and communication sector (TRS); the weights being the country-specific relative size of the sectoral value added, averaged over the sample period. Source: OECD ISD.

Relative productivity in non-tradables: $LANTRD_j = Log(\sum_k(\omega_{kj}TFP_{kj})/\sum_k(\omega_{k,usa}TFP_{usa}))$, for k = community, social and personal services (SOC); electricity, gas and water (EGW); construction (CST); again the weights being the country-specific relative size of the sectoral value added, averaged over the sample period. Source: OECD ISD.

Balassa–Samuelson term: $LBAL2WT_j = LATRDWT_j - LANTRD_j$.

Relative product market competition in tradables: $LE2TRDWT_j = Log(\sum_k(\omega_{kj}(EE_{kj}/ET_{kj}))/\sum_k(\omega_{k,usa}(EE_{k,usa}/ET_{k,usa})))$, for k = agricultural sector (AGR), manufacturing sector (MAN) and transport, storage and communication sector (TRS); the weights being the country-specific relative size of the sectoral value added, averaged over the sample period. EE = number of employees, ET = total employment. Source: OECD ISD.

Relative product market competition in non-tradables: $LE2NTRD_j = Log(\sum_k(\omega_{kj}(EE_{kj}/ET_{kj}))/\sum_k(\omega_{k,usa}(EE_{k,usa}/ET_{k,usa})))$, for k = community, social and personal services (SOC); electricity, gas and water (EGW); construction (CST); again the weights being the country-specific relative size of the sectoral value added, averaged over the sample period. EE = number of employees, ET = total employment. Source: OECD ISD.

Product market competition like Balassa–Samuelson: $LE2BALWT = LE2TRDWT_j - LE2NTRD_j$.

Relative wage in tradables: $LWTRDWT_j = Log(\sum_k(\omega_{kj}(WSSS_{kj}/(e_j * EE_{kj})))/\sum_k(\omega_{k,usa}(WSSS_{k,usa}/EE_{k,usa})))$, for k = agricultural sector (AGR), manufacturing sector (MAN) and transport, storage and communication sector (TRS); WSSS = compensation of employees at current prices in national currency, EE = number of employees; e = exchange rate (currency units of j per US$); the weights being the country-specific relative size of the sectoral value added, averaged over the sample period. Source: OECD ISD.

Relative wage in industrial activity: $LWTIN_j = Log((WSSS_{kj}/(e_j * EE_{kj}))/(WSSS_{k,usa}/EE_{k,usa}))$, for k = total industry (TIN), WSSS = compensation of employees at current prices in national currency, EE = number of employees, e = exchange rate (currency units of j per US$). Source: OECD ISD.

References

Backus, D., Kehoe, P., Kydland, F., 1992. International real business cycles. Journal of Political Economy 100, 745–775.

Balassa, B., 1964. The purchasing power parity doctrine: A reappraisal. Journal of Political Economy 72, 584–596.

Benigno, G., Theonissen, C., 2003. Equilibrium exchange rates and supply-side performance. The Economic Journal 113, C103–C124.

Betts, C., Devereux, M., 1996. The exchange rate in a model of pricing to market. European Economic Review 40, 1007–1021.

Canzoneri, M., Cumby, R., Diba, B., 1999. Relative labor productivity and the real exchange rate in the long run: Evidence for a panel of OECD countries. Journal of International Economics 47, 245–266.

Cheung, Y.W., Chinn, M., Fujii, E., 1999. Market structure and the persistence of sectoral real exchange rates. International Journal of Finance and Economics 6 (2), 95–114.

Chinn, M., Johnson, L., 1999. The impact of productivity differentials on real exchange rates: Beyond the Balassa Samuelson framework. University of California Santa Cruz, Department of Economics, Working Paper, No. 442.

Crucini, M., Telmer, C.I., Zachariadis, M., 2000. Dispersion in real exchange rates. University of Vanderbilt, Working Paper No. 00-W13.

De Gregorio, J., Giovannini, A., Wolf, H., 1994. International evidence on tradables and nontradables inflation. European Economic Review 38, 1225–1244.

Dixit, A., Stiglitz, J., 1977. Monopolistic competition and optimal product diversity. American Economic Review, 67.

Engel, C., 1999. Accounting for US real exchange rate changes. Journal of Political Economy 107, 507–538.

Engel, C., Rogers, J., 1996. How wide is the border? American Economic Review 86, 1112–1125.

Faruqee, H., 1996. Real exchange rates and the pattern of trade: Comparative dynamics for north and south. Journal of International Money and Finance 15 (2), 313–336.

Helpman, E., Krugman, P., 1985. Market Structure and Foreign Trade. MIT Press.

Hsieh, D., 1982. The determination of the real exchange rate: The productivity approach. Journal of International Economics 12, 355–362.

Im, K.S., Hasnem Pesaran, M., Shin, Y., 2003. Testing for unit roots in heterogenous panels. Journal of Econometrics 115, 53–74.

Imbs, J., Mumtaz, H., Ravn, M.O., Rey, H., 2005. PPP strikes back: Aggregation and the real exchange rate. Quarterly Journal of Economics 120 (1), 1–44.

Ito, T., Isard, P., Symansky, S., 1999. Economic growth and real exchange rate: An overview of the Balassa–Samuelson hypothesis in Asia. In: Ito, T., Krueger, A. (Eds.), Changes in Exchange Rates in Rapidly Developing Countries: Theory, Practice, and Policy Issues. The University of Chicago Press, Chicago, pp. 109–130.

Kao, C., Chiang, M.-H., 2000. Nonstationary panels, panel cointegration, and dynamic panels. Advances in Econometrics 15, 179–222.

Krugman, P., 1990. Rethinking International Trade. MIT Press, Cambridge.

Lane, P., Milesi-Ferretti, G., 2004. The transfer problem revisited: Net foreign assets and real exchange rates. Review of Economics and Statistics 86 (4), 841–857.

Levin, A., Lin, C.-F., Chu, C.-S.J., 2002. Unit root tests in panel data: Asymptotic and finite-sample properties. Journal of Econometrics 108 (1), 1–24.

MacDonald, R., Ricci, L.A., 2005. The real exchange rate and the Balassa–Samuelson effect: The role of the distribution sector. Pacific Economic Review 10 (1), 29–48.

McCoskey, S., Kao, C., 1999. Comparing panel data cointegration tests with an application of the twin deficits problem. Mimeo.

Mark, N., Sul, D., 1999. Nominal exchange rates and monetary fundamentals: Evidence from a small Post-Bretton woods panel. Journal of International Economics 53 (1), 29–52.

Marston, R., 1990. Real exchange rates and productivity growth in the United States and Japan. In: Arndt, S.W., Davidson Richardson, J. (Eds.), Real Financial Linkages Among Open Economies. MIT Press, Cambridge, pp. 71–96.

Obstfeld, M., Rogoff, K., 1996. Foundations of International Macroeconomics. MIT Press, Cambridge.

Obstfeld, M., Rogoff, K., 2000. New directions for stochastic open economy models. Journal of International Economics 50, 117–153.

Obstfeld, M., Taylor, A., 1997. Nonlinear aspects of goods-market arbitrage and adjustment: Hecksher's commodity points revisited. Journal of Japanese and International Economies 11, 441–479.

Pedroni, P., 2004. Panel cointegration: Asymptotic and finite sample properties of pooled time series tests with an application to the purchasing power parity hypothesis (New Results). Econometric Theory 20, 597–625.

Phillips, P., Moon, H., 1999. Linear regression limit theory for nonstationary panel. Econometrica 67 (5), 1057–1111.

Ricci, L.A., 1999. Economic geography and comparative advantage: Agglomeration versus specialization. European Economic Review 43, 357–377.

Rogoff, K., 1996. The purchasing power parity puzzle. Journal of Economic Literature XXXIV, 647–668.

Samuelson, P., 1964. Theoretical notes on trade problems. Review of Economics and Statistics 23, 1–60.

Stein, J., Allen, P.R., 1995. Fundamental Determinants of Exchange Rates. Oxford University Press, Oxford.

Stockman, A., Tesar, L., 1995. Tastes and technology in a two-country model of the business cycle: Explaining international comovements. American Economic Review 85, 168–185.

Warnock, F., 2003. Exchange rate dynamics and the welfare effects of monetary policy in a two-country model. Journal of International Money and Finance 22, 343–363.

Zachariadis, M., 2004. Productivity and prices in Europe: Micro-evidence for the period 1975–1990. Mimeo, Louisiana State University.

PART III

EXPECTATIONS FORMATION, NEWS AND RISK

[14]

£M3 Surprises and Asset Prices

By R. MacDonald and T. S. Torrance

University of Aberdeen

Final version received 22 October 1986. Accepted 11 November 1986.

In this paper the relationship between unanticipated sterling M3 (£M3) and a variety of asset prices is investigated for part of the UK's experience with monetary targeting. The unanticipated component of monetary growth is generated using Money Market Services (UK) survey data and an ARIMA model. It is demonstrated that the UK survey data are rational, in that they are an unbiased and efficient forecast, and that the market efficiently incorporates unanticipated money growth into asset prices. The sign of the unanticipated monetary component in our asset price equations tends to indicate that the Fisher (the inflation expectations) hypothesis is better supported during the sample period.

In the United States there has appeared recently a large number of papers exploring the effect on a range of interest rates and asset prices of the unanticipated component in the announced change in M1.[1] Such money supply announcements take place there weekly, and the effect on a wide range of financial and monetary indicators has been well documented using market expectations data supplied by Money Market Services Inc. of San Francisco.

Similar empirical work for the UK experience with monetary targeting is still in its infancy, and until recently has in fact received little serious attention from economic theorists.[2] Although Money Market Services (UK) have produced a monthly survey of market expectations for the monetary aggregate £M3 since 1981, the data series has not been used in a comparable UK study.

In the UK the move to set annual targets for £M3 in late 1976 was based on the belief that such targets could have a profound effect on inflationary expectations. Announcements of the provisional growth of £M3 are made monthly by the Bank of England. They usually take place on the first Tuesday of each month and relate to the change in £M3 over the previous month. For many financial analysts this announcement is one of the main economic events of the month, and the revelation of whether the growth of the central British monetary aggregate is within its target band is a piece of eagerly awaited economic news in the financial community.

It should now be noted that on 17 October 1985 Nigel Lawson, the Chancellor of the Exchequer, decided that the chief UK monetary indicator would cease to be £M3, and that in the future M0, the measure of the much narrower monetary base, would be the object of the government's policy on money supply targets. Notwithstanding this major change in the attitude of the British government to £M3 as a policy indicator (which many commentators have characterized as the 'end of monetarism'), it is undoubtedly still true that in the City of London itself £M3 remains the most closely watched monetary aggregate.

The enquiry starts from the fact that observations in both the United States and the United Kingdom show that, when the announced money supply figures show a rate of growth greater than what had been expected, short-term (nominal) interest rates tend to rise. Researchers have typically advanced two competing hypotheses to explain this phenomenon:[3] the Policy Anticipation hypothesis, or real interest rate effect, and the Fisher (inflation expectation) hypothesis. Under the former, what is conjectured is that market operators expect a tightening of monetary policy by the Bank of England to bring the growth in the future of £M3 back within the target range: hence short-term rates rise in anticipation of such a policy move. According to the second theory, however, what is suggested is that the monetary overrun is a harbinger of future inflation: hence short-term rates rise in expectation of such an eventuality.

Establishing a decisive preference between these two offered theories has produced a great deal of discussion and debate. Much of this involves the examination of the performance of other variables that, in theory, ought to move in contrariwise directions according to the hypothesis held. Cornell (1983a) argues that the two hypotheses yield different predictions on the behaviour of long-term (nominal) interest rates. For example, if the Policy Anticipation hypothesis is correct, and to the extent that the expected future monetary tightness is expected to last for an extended time period, long-term interest rates will fall since agents' inflationary expectations will be reduced. Cornell (1983b) further argues that examining share prices should give a further clue as to which of the two hypotheses is relevant: if the Policy Anticipation effect is correct, the higher short-term interest rates would induce agents to switch from stocks to bills, resulting in a fall in share prices. Engel and Frankel (1984) argue that, if the Policy Anticipation effect is correct, an unanticipated increase should result in an exchange rate appreciation. In further attempts to distinguish between the two hypotheses Hardouvelis (1984) concentrates on long forward interest rates, while Frankel and Hardouvelis (1985) consider commodity prices.

In this paper we examine some of the issues in this debate within a British context. We examine the effect of the announcement of a survey supply figure that differs from market expectations on two indexes of long-term interest rates, on an index of UK ordinary shares, on two short-term interest rates, and on the behaviour of the dollar-pound foreign exchange rate.

The outline of the remainder of this paper is as follows. In Section I the data used in our study are discussed, the rationality of the Money Market Services (UK) expectational series is investigated, and a monetary expectational series, using the Box-Jenkins methodology, is derived. Our empirical results from regressing the unanticipated and anticipated growth of £M3 on a variety of asset prices are considered in Section II. Finally, some concluding comments are drawn.

I. The Data and the Expected Monetary Growth Variables

In this section the data used in our study are outlined and the properties of the expected money supply series considered.

Our data on money supply consist of the announcements by the Bank of England of the provisional change in £M3 over the previous month. These announcements are normally made on the first Tuesday of each month, and are to be found published in the *Financial Times* of the following day.

Our data on asset prices are as follows. Our short rates are the closing three-month interbank rate for wholesale deposits and the three-month UK

Treasury bill rate, both as reported in the *Financial Times*. We decided to make use of both of these short rates as a safeguard against distortions arising from possible market stickiness in either of them. Two yields were chosen to represent the longer end of the market: the 5-year and the 25-year FT-Actuaries Index of the redemption yields of UK government medium coupon stocks. (These two indices of redemption yields were chosen in preference to two representative stocks because of the distortions that would occur in readings of the gross redemption yields as the stocks moved towards maturity.) The chosen index of quoted equity prices is the FT-Actuaries All-Share Index in daily percentage changes. The exchange rate used is the dollar-pound exchange rate at the close of trading in London as given by the *Financial Times*. The calculation of asset price changes is discussed below.

Two measures of the expected change in £M3 are utilized. First, the median value of the Money Market Services (UK) monthly survey is used. Each month since September 1981, Money Market Services (MMS) surveyed by telephone approximately 20 money market dealers and economists on the Monday in the week prior to the Tuesday announcements by the Bank of England of the provisional £M3 figures. These expectational figures are gathered eight days before the actual announcement, and, obviously, this gap is sufficiently large for other developments to occur (such as interest rate changes) to enable possibly a further part of the Tuesday announcement to be anticipated. Our investigation, however, utilizes not the original MMS figures (collected eight days before the announcement), but rather the figures obtained by the MMS as a check on the Monday immediately preceding the Bank of England announcement. We believe that the use of this checked expectational data provides the most accurate possible indication of market expectations of the monthly announcements of the provisional £M3 figures. Our second measure of expected monetary growth utilizes the Box-Jenkins ARIMA methodology. Each of these expectational schemes is now considered in further detail.

Before using the market expectation series in our tests of the impact of unanticipated money on asset prices, it must be determined whether market operators have utilized available information rationally. In order to determine this, unbiasedness and error orthogonality tests were conducted. The unbiasedness test involves estimating equation (1) by OLS:

$$(1) \qquad \dot{M} = a_0 + a_1 \dot{M}^e + u_t$$

where $\dot{M}$ is the actual money supply growth, $\dot{M}^e$ is the expected money supply growth, and it is expected that a_0 and a_1 are equal to zero and unity, respectively, and the error term is a white noise process. Furthermore, if expectations are rational they should incorporate all available information efficiently. This proposition is tested by determining whether the error term in equation (1) is orthogonal to an information set on which agents form their expectations of the money supply (i.e. $E(u_t|I_{t-1})$ where I represents the information set). The error orthogonality property is tested by running the following regression:

$$(2) \qquad \dot{M} - \dot{M}^e = b_0 + b_j \sum_{j=1}^{4} I_{t-j} + v_t$$

where, for efficiency, it is expected that b_0 and b_j differ insignificantly from zero and v_t is a white noise process.

Our estimated version of equation (1) using the MMS (UK) data for the period September 1981–April 1985 is

$$\text{(3)} \qquad \underset{(0\cdot24)}{\dot{M} = 0\cdot053} + \underset{(4\cdot06)}{1\cdot075\dot{M}^e}$$

$$\bar{R}^2 = 0\cdot27, \qquad DW = 2\cdot13, \qquad Q_{20} = 31\cdot10,$$

$$t = 0\cdot28, \qquad F_{(2,41)} = 0\cdot024$$

where t-ratios are in parentheses, $\bar{R}^2$ is the adjusted coefficient of determination, DW is the Durbin–Watson statistic, Q_{20} is the Box–Pierce statistic with 20 degrees of freedom, t is a t-test for the hypothesis that $a_1 = 1$, and the F-statistic tests the joint hypothesis that $a_0 = 0$ and $a_1 = 1$. The market clearly passes this test of unbiasedness.

The hypothesis that the slope coefficient in (3) equals unity cannot be rejected at the 95 per cent level (i.e. critical value for t_{95} is 2·02). The joint hypothesis that $a_0 = 0$ and $a_1 = 1$ also cannot be rejected at the 95 per cent level (critical $F_{(2,41)} = 3\cdot23$). Furthermore, the Durbin–Watson statistic is consistent with the hypothesis of the absence of first-order autocorrelation, and the Box–Pierce statistic indicates the absence of higher-order autocorrelation.

Our tests of the error orthogonality equation, (2), were implemented in stages. First, we regressed the forecast error, $\dot{M} - \dot{M}^e$, on four lagged values of the forecast error, and this result is reported as equation (4). Although the fourth lag in (4) has a significant t-ratio, the F-statistic, which tests the joint hypothesis that all the coefficients are equal to zero, is insignificant at the 95 per cent level (critical value of $F_{(4,34)} = 2\cdot66$).

$$\text{(4)} \qquad \dot{M} - \dot{M}^e = \underset{(0\cdot46)}{-0\cdot045} - \underset{(0\cdot63)}{0\cdot102}(\dot{M} - \dot{M}^e)_{t-1} - \underset{(0\cdot51)}{0\cdot082}(\dot{M} - \dot{M}^e)_{t-2}$$

$$+ \underset{(0.76)}{0\cdot119}(\dot{M} - \dot{M}^e)_{t-3} - \underset{(2.22)}{0\cdot334}(\dot{M} - \dot{M}^e)_{t-4}$$

$$\bar{R}^2 = 0\cdot18, \qquad DW = 1\cdot87, \qquad F_{(4,34)} = 1\cdot87.$$

Next, other lagged variables on which agents may base their expectations were separately introduced into equation (2). In particular, we used lagged values of the variables considered in the next section, namely, interest rates and the exchange rate. The relevant F-statistics are reported in Table 1 and all are insignificantly different from zero at the 95 per cent level. Thus, on the basis of the information set chosen, the MMS (UK) data would appear efficiently to utilize such information. This is supportive of similar tests conducted on the US data by Grossman (1981), Cornell (1983b), Engel and Frankel (1984) and Urich and Wachtel (1981). In sum, therefore, the MMS (UK) expectations series is rational.

Our alternative expectational series was generated from the actual money growth series using the Box–Jenkins methodology. The final model fitted, using maximum likelihood, is of the form ARIMA (004):

$$\text{(5)} \qquad \dot{M} = \underset{(38\cdot55)}{0\cdot771} - \underset{(1\cdot98)}{0\cdot316}\varepsilon_{t-1} - \underset{(1\cdot01)}{0\cdot162}\varepsilon_{t-2} - \underset{(1\cdot03)}{0\cdot169}\varepsilon_{t-3} - \underset{(1\cdot75)}{0\cdot262}\varepsilon_{t-4}$$

$$\bar{R}^2 = 0\cdot54, \qquad Q_{20} = 11\cdot96.$$

TABLE 1

F-STATISTICS TESTING THE ERROR ORTHOGONALITY PROPERTY

Information*	$\sum_{j=1}^{4} I_{t-j}$ $F_{(4,34)}$
DIB	1·15
DTB	0·94
DB5	1·12
DB25	0·23
DFT	0·95
DS	0·69

* The critical value of $F_{(4,34)}$ at the 5% level is 2·65. *D* denotes a change in a variable, *IB* is the inter-bank rate, *TB* is the Treasury bill rate, *B5* is the 5-year bond rate, *B25* is the 25-year bond rate, *FT* is the *FT*-Actuaries All Share index, *S* is the dollar-pound exchange rate.

The residuals from equation (5) represent our alternative measure of the unexpected change in the money supply.

II. UNANTICIPATED £M3 AND ASSET PRICES

In Tables 2-5 we present our results from regressing the two measures of unanticipated money on the chosen changes in asset prices. Two periods are examined: period 1 and period 2. For period 1, asset price changes are measured as the difference between the close of trading price on the day preceding the money supply announcement and the closing rate on the day of the money supply announcement. (Interest rates are measured as level changes while the FT-Actuaries All-Share Index and the exchange rate are measured as percentage changes.) For period 2 the asset price changes are measured as the difference between the close of trading price on the day of the money supply announcement and the closing rate on the day after the money supply announcement. If the market is efficient, we would expect the impact of unanticipated £M3 on asset prices to be insignificant.

In Table 2 the results from regressing the anticipated and unanticipated growth of £M3 (as measured by the difference between actual growth and expected growth given by MMS (UK)) on various asset prices are presented. Thus we are estimating equations of the form

$$(6) \qquad DX1 = a_0 + a_1(\dot{M} - \dot{M}^e)$$

and

$$(7) \qquad DX1 = a_0 + a_1(\dot{M} - \dot{M}^e) + a_2\dot{M}^e$$

where *DX1* is the change in the asset price for period 1, a_0 and a_2 are expected

TABLE 2

ANTICIPATED AND UNANTICIPATED MONEY SUPPLY ANNOUNCEMENTS AND CHANGES IN ASSET PRICES, PERIOD 1 (MARKET EXPECTATIONS)*

	a_0	a_1	a_2	R^2	DW
DIB1	−0·008	0·023	—	0·002	1·92
	(0·21)	(0·36)			
DIB1	−0·132	0·019	0·163	0·054	1·93
	(1·41)	(0·29)	(1·46)		
DTB1	0·062	0·095	—	0·024	1·89
	(1·49)	(1·44)			
DTB1	−0·048	0·091	0·145	0·042	1·78
	(0·52)	(1·39)	(1·31)		
DB51	0·022	0·044	—	0·061	1·86
	(1·28)	(1·63)			
DB51	0·003	0·044	0·025	0·067	1·91
	(0·78)	(1·60)	(0·53)		
DB251	−0·013	0·084	—	0·084	1·76
	(0·48)	(1·94)			
DB251	−0·092	0·082	0·105	0·085	1·65
	(1·49)	(1·89)	(1·42)		
DFT1	−0·169	−0·187	—	0·018	1·59
	(1·27)	(0·88)			
DFT1	−0·018	−0·182	−0·199	0·026	1·62
	(0·06)	(0·85)	(0·55)		
DS1	−0·245	0·005	—	0·00003	1·43
	(2·54)	(0·03)			
DS1	−0·287	0·004	0·056	0·001	1·43
	(1·29)	(0·03)	(0·21)		

* See Table 1 for variable definitions. A '1' denotes period 1. t-ratios in parenthesis.

to differ insignificantly from zero, and a_1 should be either significantly positive or negative. The results have a number of interesting features.

First, the coefficient a_1 in the 25-year bond equation is marginally significant at the 95 per cent level, and significant at the 80 per cent level in the Treasury bill and 5-year bond equations; estimates of a_1 in the other equations are all statistically insignificant. Second, the coefficient a_2 is statistically significant at the 80 per cent level in three cases, but this may reflect the use of the survey median forecast rather than any market inefficiency. (See Hafer, 1984, for a discussion of the use of median forecast values.) Third, the sign pattern on the short-term interest rates is consistent with both the Fisher hypothesis and the Policy Anticipation effect. However, the sign on the long-term bond rates is also positive, which, following Cornell (1983a), is supportive of the Fisher hypothesis, though we admit that this result is not accepted by all commentators. Perhaps this conflict can be reconciled, as Engel and Frankel (1984) have suggested, with reference to the foreign exchange market. In fact, the positive sign on a_1 in the exchange rate equation is supportive of the Policy Anticipation effect. (We should recall that the exchange rate is the foreign currency price of a unit of home currency, and therefore a rise indicates an appreciation.) But unfortunately, little value can be placed on the sign of a_1 in the exchange rate equation since it is completely insignificant. We shall return to the exchange rate equations below. Interestingly, the sign on the change in the share price index is also supportive of the Policy Anticipation effect but again is insignificant.

In Table 3 equations (6) and (7) are re-estimated for period 2 to determine if the market absorbs any unexpected money supply change on the day of publication. Although the sign pattern is similar to that for period 1, the coefficients on unanticipated and anticipated money growth are all insignificant. This finding suggests that the market is efficient in incorporating the new information about money growth into asset prices.

The period 1 results from regressing the news about money growth, generated from our ARIMA model, on asset price changes are given in Table 4. Interestingly, the sign pattern is, with the exception of the interbank rate, identical to that derived from the market expectations data. Furthermore, using the ARIMA 'news' pulls up the significance level of the a_1 coefficient in the interest rate equations: all are significant at the 95 per cent level or better. The a_1 coefficients in the exchange rate and share index equations are again completely insignificant.

The period 2 results using the ARIMA 'news' (Table 5) are again supportive of the proposition that the market discounts the new information about money supply growth on the day of receipt.

One interesting feature of the above results is the completely insignificant impact of unanticipated monetary 'news' on the percentage change in the

TABLE 3

ANTICIPATED AND UNANTICIPATED MONEY SUPPLY ANNOUNCEMENTS AND CHANGES IN ASSET PRICES, PERIOD 2 (MARKET EXPECTATIONS)*

	a_0	a_1	a_2	R^2	DW
DIB2	0·018	−0·031	—	0·006	1·96
	(0·48)	(0·48)			
DIB2	0·098	−0·028	−0·104	0·028	1·96
	(1·08)	(0·44)	(0·96)		
DTB2	0·002	−0·004	—	0·00008	1·44
	(0·05)	(0·05)			
DTB2	−0·002	−0·004	0·006	0·0001	1·44
	(0·03)	(0·05)	(0·05)		
DB52	−0·024	0·017	—	0·006	1·74
	(1·16)	(0·52)			
DB52	0·015	0·019	−0·053	0·027	1·82
	(0·32)	(0·56)	(0·93)		
DB252	−0·021	0·014	—	0·008	1·72
	(1·29)	(0·57)			
DB252	0·020	0·015	−0·054	0·046	1·81
	(0·57)	(0·63)	(1·27)		
DFT2	0·256	−0·102	—	0·007	2·64
	(2·18)	(0·55)			
DFT2	0·059	−0·108	0·259	0·023	2·67
	(0·22)	(0·51)	(0·82)		
DS2	0·121	0·032	—	0·0009	1·28
	(1·23)	(0·20)			
DS2	−0·044	0·076	0·219	0·017	1·29
	(0·19)	(0·16)	(0·81)		

* See Table 1 for variable definitions. A '2' denotes period 2. *t*-ratios in parenthesis.

TABLE 4

ANTICIPATED AND UNANTICIPATED MONEY SUPPLY ANNOUNCEMENTS AND CHANGES IN ASSET PRICES, PERIOD 1 (ARIMA EXPECTATIONS)*

	a_0	a_1	a_2	R^2	DW
DIB1	0·026	−0·039	—	0·003	2·03
	(0·22)	(0·32)			
DIB1	0·028	−0·033	0·079	0·045	1·85
	(0·25)	(0·27)	(1·29)		
DTB1	0·072	0·111	—	0·075	1·82
	(1·78)	(1·85)			
DTB1	0·011	0·111	0·069	0·08	1·81
	(0·10)	(1·85)	(0·58)		
DB51	0·028	0·051	—	0·091	2·05
	(1·64)	(2·05)			
DB51	0·036	0·050	−0·010	0·092	2·06
	(0·78)	(2·01)	(0·20)		
DB251	−0·004	0·087	—	0·103	1·65
	(0·15)	(2·19)			
DB251	−0·076	0·088	0·083	0·126	1·67
	(1·04)	(2·23)	(1·06)		
DFT1	−0·185	−0·186	—	0·021	1·66
	(1·41)	(0·96)			
DFT1	−0·052	−0·188	−0·153	0·025	1·64
	(0·14)	(0·96)	(0·39)		
DS1	−0·771	0·024	—	0·0006	1·41
	(2·70)	(0·16)			
DS1	−0·340	−0·022	0·080	0·002	1·39
	(1·25)	(0·15)	(0·28)		

* See Table 1 for variable definitions. A '1' denotes period 1. *t*-ratios in parenthesis.

exchange rate and the share index. For the former variable, this result contrasts with the findings of Engel and Frankel (1984) and Cornell (1982) for the United States and Smith and Goodhart (1985) for the United Kingdom. Perhaps the key to understanding the poor performance of the exchange rate equations lies in the low *DW* statistics. Thus, if the exchange rate change is non-white—that is to say, if the exchange rate does not follow a random walk—this will introduce autocorrelation into our estimated relationships and produce inefficient estimates. As a check on the autocorrelation properties of the asset price changes, we computed correlograms and Box–Pierce statistics. The random walk hypothesis is relatively well supported for the interest rates and share price changes,[4] and this is supportive of the evidence of Pesando (1978) and Sargent (1979), who report results that corroborate the random walk version of the term structure. The correlograms and Box–Pierce statistic for the exchange rate change[5] indicated substantial non-whiteness, which is supportive of the theoretical work on exchange rates, which indicates that the efficient markets hypothesis implies only that the exchange rate follows a random walk under special circumstances. (See Levich, 1979, for a useful discussion.)

In an attempt to account for first-order autocorrelation, the exchange rate equation was re-estimated with a first-order autoregressive scheme specified for the error term (using maximum likelihood), and the result is reported here

TABLE 5

ANTICIPATED AND UNANTICIPATED MONEY SUPPLY ANNOUNCEMENTS AND CHANGES IN ASSET PRICES, PERIOD 2 (ARIMA EXPECTATIONS)*

	a_0	a_1	a_2	R^2	DW
DIB2	0·013	0·007	—	0·00009	1·94
	(0·12)	(0·06)			
DIB2	0·011	0·019	−0·060	0·025	1·98
	(0·09)	(0·02)	(1·02)		
DTB2	0.001	−0·017	—	0·002	1·65
	(0·24)	(0·26)			
DTB2	−0·052	−0·015	0·061	0·007	1·63
	(0·43)	(0·23)	(0·47)		
DB52	−0·026	−0·022	—	0·012	1·92
	(1·24)	(0·72)			
DB52	−0·101	−0·020	0·087	0·061	1·89
	(1·82)	(0·67)	(1.45)		
DB252	−0·021	−0·014	—	0·009	1·84
	(1·33)	(0·60)			
DB252	−0·059	−0·013	0·044	0·031	1·85
	(1·38)	(0·56)	(0.90)		
DFT2	0·238	0·036	—	0·001	2·75
	(2·01)	(0·21)			
DFT2	0·482	0·031	−0·282	0·016	2·78
	(1·48)	(0·18)	(0·81)		
DS2	0.106	0.058	—	0.004	1.41
	(1·06)	(0·39)			
DS2	0·059	0·059	0·054	0·005	1·42
	(0·21)	(0·39)	(0·18)		

* See Table 1 for variable definitions. A '2' denotes period 2. *t*-ratios in parenthesis.

as equation (8):

$$(8)\qquad DS1 = \underset{(1\cdot 27)}{-0\cdot 288} + \underset{(0\cdot 28)}{0\cdot 039}(\dot{M} - \dot{M}^e) + \underset{(0\cdot 27)}{0\cdot 067}\dot{M}^e$$

$$R^2 = 0\cdot 005, \qquad DW = 1\cdot 98, \qquad \rho = \underset{(1\cdot 74)}{0\cdot 27}.$$

Unfortunately, although the DW statistic is now acceptable, the coefficient on the unanticipated money supply change remains statistically insignificant.

III. SUMMARY AND CONCLUSIONS

In this paper we have examined the effects of unanticipated money supply announcements on a range of asset prices for the UK, using Money Market Services (UK) survey data. A number of interesting findings emerged. First, the MMS (UK) monthly forecast of £M3 was shown to be rational in the sense of being an unbiased forecast of the growth of £M3 and efficiently incorporating a relevant information set. Furthermore, it was demonstrated that the market considers the information content contained in the monetary announcements as important and discounts this information rapidly into current asset prices. Interestingly, this contrasts with Smith and Goodhart

(1985), who found that two-thirds of the impact of a UK monetary surprise occurred on the day after the announcement.

Do the data allow us to come to any firm conclusions on whether the Policy Anticipation or the Fisher hypothesis better describes the beliefs of market operators about the Bank of England's short-term monetary policy? The behaviour of UK short-term interest rates is supportive of the findings of researchers into the US experience with monetary targeting: short-term interest rates rise in response to a monetary surprise. This observed behaviour is obviously supportive of both hypotheses. However, the observed behaviour of UK long-term rates, especially since they appear to react even more strongly in the same direction, is supportive of the Fisher hypothesis. Interestingly, this finding seems to corroborate Cornell's (1983a) evidence for the United States. We had hoped to find further confirmation of support for the Fisher hypothesis by examining the reaction of the exchange rate and the FT index to the unanticipated component of money supply announcements. Although the sign of the coefficient of unanticipated money in our exchange rate and share index equations is supportive of the Policy Anticipation effect, the coefficients turned out to be quite insignificant. This finding contrasts with that of Smith and Goodhart (1985), and also with the findings of authors using US data. An explanation for this difference could lie in the fact that the importance and significance attached to £M3 was beginning to decline during the sample period utilized in this paper.[6]

There are, however, other ways in which a researcher may discriminate between the Policy Anticipation and the Fisher hypotheses. Thus, useful topics for future research would be for researchers to investigate the effects of unanticipated £M3 on long-run forward interest rates, as suggested by Hardouvelis (1984), on commodity prices, as suggested by Frankel and Hardouvelis (1985), and on forward exchange rate premiums, as suggested by Husted and Kitchen (1985). Such research should help to shed further light on whether the Policy Anticipation or the Fisher hypothesis is the more appropriate for the UK's experience with monetary targeting.

ACKNOWLEDGMENTS

We would like to thank Laurence Copeland, David Peel and two anonymous referees for helpful comments, and Money Market Services (UK) for kindly providing the market expectation data used in this study.

NOTES

1. See, *inter alia*, Grossman (1981), Urich and Wachtel (1981), Cornell (1982, 1983a, b), Engel and Frankel (1984), Hardouvelis (1984), Frankel and Hardouvelis (1985), Husted and Kitchen (1985) and Loeys (1985).
2. See Smith and Goodhart (1985) and Goodhart and Smith (1985). These authors use the expectational series of a City of London broker, Messel and Co. This series is not derived from a market survey.
3. We are aware that a number of other hypotheses have also been advanced, most notably the Real Activity hypothesis and the Tobin Risk hypothesis. For a discussion of these theories, and for a further elaboration of the Policy Anticipation and Fisher hypotheses, see Cornell (1983b). An additional hypothesis of note is presented by Siegel (1985), who develops a version of the Real Activity hypothesis in which there is neutrality of money but where money supply information, via a connection between money demand and money supply, can relay signals to the market on the future level of real activity and this can be said to have an effect on such activity.

4. The Box-Pierce statistics, with 20 degrees of freedom, for the changes in interest rates are as follows:

   DTBI, 27·4; *DB5I*, 18·7; *DB25I*, 15·7; *DFTI*, 19·3.

5. The Box-Pierce statistic, with 20 degrees of freedom for the percentage change in the exchange rate, is 38·1.
6. In a further paper (MacDonald and Torrance, 1986), we examine the effects of unanticipated £M3 on a selection of five currencies. It is documented, *inter alia*, that monetary surprises are more important for the earlier part of the UK's experience with monetary targeting.

REFERENCES

CORNELL, B. (1982). Money supply announcements, interest rates and foreign exchange. *Journal of International Money and Finance*, **1**, 201-8.

—— (1983a). Money supply announcements and interest rates: another view. *Journal of Business*, **56**, 1-24.

—— (1983b). The money supply announcements puzzle: review and interpretation. *American Economic Review*, **83**, 644-57.

ENGEL, C. and FRANKEL, J. (1984). Why money announcements move interest rates: an answer from the foreign exchange market. *Journal of Monetary Economics*, **13**, 31-9.

FRANKEL, J. and HARDOUVELIS, G. (1985). Commodity prices, money surprises and FED credibility. *Journal of Money Credit and Banking*, **17**, 425-38.

GOODHART, C. and SMITH, R. (1985). The impact of news on financial markets in the United Kingdom. *Journal of Money Credit and Banking*, **17**, 507-11.

GROSSMAN, J. (1981). The rationality of money supply expectations and the short-run response of interest rates to monetary surprises. *Journal of Money Credit and Banking*, **13**, 409-24.

HAFER, R. W. (1984). Comparing time series and survey forecasts of weekly changes in money: a methodological note. *Journal of Finance*, **39**, 1207-13.

HARDOUVELIS, G. A. (1984). Market perception of Federal Reserve policy and the weekly monetary announcements. *Journal of Monetary Economics*, **14**, 225-40.

HUSTED, S. and KITCHEN, J. (1985). Some evidence on the international transmission of US money supply announcement effects. *Journal of Money Credit and Banking*, **17**, 456-66.

LEVICH, R. (1979). On the efficiency of markets for foreign exchange. In R. Dornbusch and J. Frenkel (eds), *International Economic Policy Theory and Evidence*, pp. 246-67. Baltimore: John Hopkins Press.

LOEYS, J. C. (1985). Changing interest rate responses to money announcements: 1977-1983. *Journal of Monetary Economics*, **15**, 323-32.

MACDONALD, R. and TORRANCE, T. S. (1986). Exchange rates and the 'news': some evidence using UK survey data. Forthcoming, *The Manchester School.*

MUSSA, M. (1979). Empirical regularities in the behaviour of exchange rates and theories of the foreign exchange market. In K. Brunner and A. H. Meltzer (eds), *Policies for Employment, Prices and Exchange Rates*. Amsterdam: North-Holland.

PESANDO, J. E. (1978). On the efficiency of the bond market: some Canadian evidence. *Journal of Political Economy*, **86**, 1057-76.

SARGENT, T. J. (1979). Rational expectations and the term structure of interest rates. *Journal of Money Credit and Banking*, **4**, 74-97.

SIEGEL, J. (1985). Money supply announcements and interest rates: does monetary policy matter? *Journal of Monetary Economics*, **15**, 164-76.

SMITH, R. and GOODHART, C. (1985). The relationship between exchange rate movements and monetary surprises: results for the United Kingdom and the United States compared and contrasted. *The Manchester School*, **L111**, 2-22.

URICH, T. J. and WACHTEL, P. (1981). Market response to weekly money supply announcements in the 1970s. *Journal of Finance*, **36**, 1063-72.

Oxford Economic Papers 42 (1990), 544–561

EXPECTATIONS FORMATION AND RISK IN FOUR FOREIGN EXCHANGE MARKETS*

By RONALD MACDONALD *and* THOMAS S. TORRANCE

[Scientific enquiry] is a matter of comparing the corollaries of a whole group of hypotheses to a whole group of facts.

Pierre Duhem, *The Aim and Structure of Physical Theory*, Paris, 1906.

ONE of the most controversial issues in the International Finance literature concerns the interpretation of the finding that the forward premium on foreign exchange is a biased predictor of the exchange rate change.[1] Researchers like Bilson (1981), Cumby and Obstfeld (1984) and Longworth (1981) take the view that the rejection of the unbiasedness hypothesis is due to the irrationality of market participants: speculation is in some sense excessive (i.e. destabilising) with respect to the information set. In contrast, Fama (1984), Hodrick and Srivastava (1984) and Bilson (1985) argue that it is the risk averse behaviour of economic transactors which explains the rejection. Until recently it has proved impossible to discern which of these interpretations was correct. However, the recent availability of survey data on agents' expectations allows a researcher to determine whether the failure is due to irrationality or risk aversion or to some combination of both factors.

Survey data has been used to discern whether irrationality or risk aversion explain rejection of the joint unbiasedness hypothesis by Dominguez (1986), Frankel and Froot (1986), MacDonald and Torrance (1988) and Taylor (1988). In this paper we present some further tests of these issues. Our study has a number of novel features. First, we use a survey data base which has only been partially utilised hitherto. In particular, we use a survey data base constructed by Money Market Services Ltd. (UK) for four currencies, namely the US dollar–British pound, the deutschemark–US dollar, the Swiss franc–US dollar and the Japanese yen–US dollar.[2] A second novel feature of our work is that the data base is sufficiently large to allow tests of various expectational mechanisms for individual currencies: other researchers, such Frankel and Froot (1986 and 1987), have had to pool their data in order to achieve sufficient degrees of freedom. But we believe it is of interest to see if speculators treat

* We are grateful to two anonymous referees for their helpful comments on an earlier draft of this paper. Helpful comments were also received from seminar participants at the University of Connecticut, the University of Dundee, the fifth International Forecasting Symposium (Amsterdam), the Scottish Economic Society Conference (1988) and Queen's University (Canada). The usual disclaimer applies.

[1] Useful surveys of this topic are provided by Levich (1985), Hodrick (1987), Booth and Longworth (1986), MacDonald (1988) and MacDonald and Taylor (1989).

[2] MacDonald and Torrance (1988) utilize part of this data base (04.02.85 to 28.04.86) for a study of the deutschemark–US dollar exchange rate.

© Oxford University Press 1990

currencies homogeneously. The third novel feature of our study is that the size of the data base allows examination of the behaviour of exchange rate expectations for parts of our full sample. In particular, our data sample encompasses a period in which the other major currencies were generally depreciating against the US dollar and a period in which they were appreciating; and the question that thus naturally arises is whether the estimates of a standard unbiasedness equation have the same interpretation when the currency is appreciating as when it is depreciating.

The outline of the remainder of this paper is as follows. In Section 1 we discuss the data set used in our study and present some simple descriptive statistics. In Section 2 we use the survey data to discern whether the common empirical finding of rejection of the unbiasedness hypothesis is due to risk or irrationality. Finally, a concluding section is presented.

1. The data and some descriptive statistics

Our basic survey data, supplied by Money Market Services Ltd of London—MMS(UK), is of expected exchange rates against the US dollar of the deutschemark, the Japanese yen, the Swiss franc and the British pound. As is customary, the initial data was in the form of units per dollar in the case of the first three of these currencies, while in the case of the British pound the original data specified the number of dollars per pound.

For the four exchange rates against the dollar, we have drawn on two series of MMS(UK) data. The first, which is of weekly data and runs from 02.07.84 to 13.04.87 inclusive, consists of the expected spot rate a week ahead. The second series, which is of two-weekly data and which is from 12.07.82 to 13.04.87, comprises the expected spot rate four weeks later.[3] Since the sample for the latter data, as mentioned earlier, covers a period in which all our currencies were appreciating against the dollar and one in which they were depreciating, we thought it important to investigate the properties of our models for these sub-periods, with the aim of ascertaining whether speculators behave differently when currencies are depreciating against the dollar compared to periods when they are appreciating. Our sub-samples run from 12.07.82 to 18.02.85 for all four currencies, from 04.03.85 to 13.04.87 for the British pound, deutschemark and Japanese yen, and 04.03.85 to 28.04.86 for the Swiss franc.

In gathering these two series of data, MMS(UK) sought the views of approximately thirty major financial institutions, many of them large banks, situated both in London and in the financial centres of continental Europe. The first series is a set of the median values of weekly surveys conducted each Monday with the aim of ascertaining dealers' forecasts of the relevant closing London rate of the Monday of the following week. The second series consists of a set of the median values of two-weekly surveys conducted also on a Monday

[3] In the case of both series, the data on expected Swiss franc rates terminates on 28.04.86.

and requesting dealers' views on the closing London rate on the Monday of four weeks hence.[4]

Our data on spot and forward rates are taken from the *Financial Times*. For each currency, the spot rate is the mid-market London closing rate on the Monday of each week that falls into the survey period. The one-week forward rates we use are theoretical rates calculated from the relevant one-week currency and the one-week US dollar euro-interest rates published as prevailing at the close of the London financial markets each Monday. The four-week forward rates are those given by the use of the appropriate forward extensions published as a part of the table of dollar exchange rates in the *Financial Times*.

Before turning to regression based tests, we present some descriptive statistics of the raw data. These statistics spring from understanding the efficient market hypothesis (EMH) as a joint-hypothesis of a view of equilibrium returns and the contention that agents are endowed with rational expectations. For our purposes, the latter proposition can be stated as:

$$\Delta s_{t+k} = \Delta s^e_{t+k} + \eta_{t+k}, \quad \Delta s^e_{t+k} = E[\Delta s_{t+k}|I_t], \tag{1}$$

where $\Delta s_{t+k} = s_{t+k} - s_t$, $\Delta s^e_{t+k} = s^e_{t+k} - s_t$, s denotes the log of the spot rate (home currency price of the dollar, with the exception of the British pound where it is the dollar price of the pound), s^e denotes the log of the expected spot rate, E is the mathematical expectations operator, I_t is the information set on which agents base their expectations and η_{t+k} is a random forecast error, orthogonal to the information set.

The first half of the EMH as a joint-hypothesis can be expressed either on the assumption that agents are risk neutral or that they are risk averse. On the first assumption we have the proposition that agents will act to ensure that the forward premium (discount) equals the expected currency appreciation (depreciation), namely:

$$f_t^{t+k} - s_t = fp_t = s^e_{t+k} - s_t = \Delta s^e_{t+k}, \tag{2}$$

where f_t^{t+k} denotes the log of the relevant forward rate and fp_t denotes the log of the forward premium. On the alternative assumption of risk aversion, however, we have:

$$fp_t = \Delta s^e_{t+k} + \pi_t, \tag{3}$$

where π_t represents a risk premium (required to compensate agents from exposure to open positions in the currency in question at time t).

In using (1) and (3) we obtain a statement of the joint-hypothesis under risk aversion as follows:

$$fp_t = \Delta s_{t+k} + \varepsilon_{t+k} + \pi_t. \tag{4}$$

[4] Each expectational series contains a small number of missing observations, corresponding to public holidays. To obtain expectations points for these missing values we regressed the survey data expectations against the actual series and a constant up to the break point; the point estimates were then used to obtain expected values. We do not believe that this procedure affects our results in any sufficient way. If anything, this process should bias our tests in favour of rationality.

where $\varepsilon_{t+k} = -\eta_{t+k}$ of equation (1). As we shall see in the next section, researchers, in trying to interpret the often quoted finding that the forward premium is a biased predictor of the exchange rate change, either assume that π_t is zero (and therefore rejection is attributed to "irrationality") or assume agents are rational and therefore rejection is due to a significant value of π. However, the availability of survey data on agents' expectations permits us to deploy a single hypothesis test of the EMH as in (4) by regressing the empirically obtained change in the expected exchange rate against the forward premium. The use of survey expectational data thus allows us directly to generate the risk premium as in (4) and to compare its properties with those of the forward premium and of the expected change in the exchange rate. We are aware, nevertheless, that the use of survey expectational data involves its own special problems.

More specifically in this connection, we do appreciate that there is, in some parts of the economics literature, an inherent mistrust of survey data. It is commonly argued, for instance, that the use of actual price data (in the context of, say, a rational expectations test) is better than using survey expectational data since the former reflects actual trading behaviour and thus what economic agents actually believe; while the latter, since agents do not have to make any monetary commitment on the basis of their survey views, may not reflect their true beliefs. Such criticism is perhaps justifiable in certain studies, such as those using inflationary expectations, where the survey respondents may not have much, if any, effect on the overall price level. However, it is probably less justifiable in the present context, since the respondents to the MMS survey are direct participants in the spot-forward exchange markets, being traders themselves or economists in foreign exchange dealing rooms. As Frankel and Froot (1986) forcefully argue: "at the very least exchange rate survey data contain some useful information that warrants study".

As we argued above, a major advantage in using survey data is that it allows us to test the efficiency of the forward exchange premium without imposing the usual auxiliary hypothesis that there are no systematic prediction errors in the sample; and this auxiliary hypothesis is something one would like to test rather than simply to impose.

A central supposition, therefore, concerning the survey data we use is that it is equal to the "true" expectational series, $\Delta\bar{s}^e$, plus a random error term which reflects our use of the median and the existence of, perhaps, heterogeneous beliefs. That is:

$$\Delta s^e_{t+k} = \Delta\bar{s}^e_{t+k} + \zeta_t \tag{5}$$

where ζ_t is the random measurement error. It turns out that all but one of our regression based tests are robust to such measurement error since the expectational variable enters as a regressand. Furthermore, and as we shall attempt to show, there is evidence to suggest that the survey data represents a less noisy expectational series than that derived by imposing rational expectations.

Before we come to our main analysis, let us briefly consider certain descriptive statistics, relating to mean and variance, which help to shed light on the issues raised in our discussion surrounding equations (1) and (4). In Table 1 such statistics are reported for the one-week horizon and in Table 2 for the four-week horizon.

In the Tables it can be seen that in general the mean of the change in the expected exchange is in the same direction as the mean of the actual change (the exceptions being the British pound in Table 1 and Table 2 sub-sample 2, and all of the currencies in Table 1 sub-sample 1). Essentially, the same is true for the mean of the forward premium, though with this measure the mean of the forward premium on the British pound is correctly signed in Table 1. The wide difference between the mean of the expected change in the spot rate and the mean of the forward premium gives rise in the final column to a risk premium that is large relative to the forward premium. This finding is particularly interesting since it indicates that it is hazardous to draw conclusions, as other researchers have done (e.g. Fama 1984), about the sign or magnitude of the risk premium from an analysis of forward forecast errors (for example, in Table 1 for the SF and BP rates the sign of the risk premium is opposite to the forecast error in two cases and for the remaining two cases the magnitude is very different). Notice also, that as predicted by Mussa (1979), the variance of the spot rate change is considerably greater than that of the expected rate change and, most noticeably, than that of the variance of the forward premium.

Also in Tables 1 and 2, it is interesting to compare the relative size of the variance of the risk premium and the variance of the expected change in the

TABLE 1

Comparisons of Means and Variances of Weekly Exchange Rate Series, in Per Cent per Annum

		$(s_{t+1} - s_t)$	$(s^e_{t+1} - s_t)$	$(f_t^{t+1} - s_t)$	$(s^e_{t+1} - s_{t+1})$	$f_t^{t+1} - s_{t+1}$	π_t
BP	M	3.852	−6.708	3.468	−10.560	−0.384	10.176
	V	1.898	0.153	0.0006	2.465	1.882	0.154
DM	M	−16.276	−8.112	−3.406	8.164	12.870	4.706
	V	1.737	0.231	0.008	2.309	1.763	0.217
JY	M	−19.188	−7.176	−2.064	12.012	17.124	5.112
	V	1.331	0.136	0.0003	1.576	1.232	0.138
SF	M	−15.496	−4.602	−6.136	10.894	9.360	−1.534
	V	2.402	0.262	0.0008	3.058	2.413	0.266

Where BP denotes the US dollar–British pound, DM denotes the deutschemark–US dollar, JY denotes the Japanese yen–US dollar, SF denotes the Swiss franc–US dollar, M denotes the mean expressed in per cent per annum, V denotes the variance expressed in per cent per annum and other symbols have the same interpretation as in the text.

The sample for BP, DM and JY runs from 02.07.84 to 13.04.87, whilst that for SF runs from 02.07.84 to 28.04.86.

TABLE 2

Comparisons of Means and Variances of Two-Weekly Exchange Rate Series, in Per Cent per Annum

		$(s_{t+2}-s_t)$	$(s^e_{t+2}-s_t)$	$(f_t^{t+2}-s_t)$	$(s^e_{t+2}-s_{t+2})$	$f_t^{t+2}-s_{t+2}$	π_t
Full Sample							
BP	M	− 3.302	− 0.215	− 4.082	3.087	− 0.780	− 3.867
	V	3.042	0.189	0.011	3.588	3.198	0.181
DM	M	− 12.688	− 16.952	− 15.262	− 4.264	− 2.574	1.690
	V	3.302	0.278	2.704	3.900	4.628	0.031
JY	M	− 23.582	− 19.552	− 6.188	4.030	17.394	13.364
	V	3.328	0.237	0.004	3.822	3.406	0.241
SF	M	− 5.330	− 15.912	− 6.656	− 10.582	− 1.326	9.256
	V	4.550	5.356	4.654	0.952	0.006	0.949
Sub Sample 1							
BP	M	− 35.620	3.432	0.202	39.052	35.418	− 3.230
	V	1.682	0.083	0.004	1.914	1.695	0.087
DM	M	22.308	− 19.942	− 9.438	− 42.250	− 31.746	10.504
	V	2.233	0.157	0.002	2.527	2.272	0.158
JY	M	2.192	− 23.556	− 8.164	− 25.748	− 10.356	15.392
	V	2.514	0.180	0.003	2.808	2.558	0.188
SF	M	22.750	− 23.764	− 13.884	− 46.514	− 36.634	9.880
	V	3.328	0.328	0.003	2.990	3.328	0.341
Sub Sample 2							
BP	M	35.620	− 4.576	− 9.230	− 40.196	− 44.850	− 4.654
	V	3.640	0.307	0.0009	4.368	3.692	0.296
DM	M	− 54.340	− 13.416	− 22.256	41.924	32.084	− 8.840
	V	3.380	0.419	5.928	4.134	6.656	6.630
JY	M	− 54.340	− 14.716	− 3.848	39.624	50.492	10.868
	V	3.692	0.291	0.001	4.212	3.692	0.302
SF	M	− 66.040	− 15.808	− 7.878	50.232	58.162	7.930
	V	5.252	2.350	0.959	7.722	5.278	2.322

For definitions of terms, *see* Table 1. The full sample period for BP, DM and JY runs from 12.07.82 to 13.04.87. Sub-sample 1 runs from 12.07.82 to 18.02.85 for all four currencies whilst sub-sample 2 runs from 04.03.85 to 13.04.87 for the BP, DM and JY rates and from 04.03.85 to 28.04.86 for the Swiss franc.

exchange rate. A number of researchers (*see* Fama 1984, Hodrick and Srivastava 1986 and Bilson 1985) have argued that exchange rate expectations are essentially static and that thus changes in the forward premium primarily reflect changes in the risk premium. If this view is correct, then it follows that the variance of the risk premium should be of much greater magnitude than the variance of the change in the expected exchange rate. However, as can be observed, the relative *similarity* of these two sets of variance results tends to cast doubt on this particular thesis. It therefore follows that the relatively small and stable forward premium variances reported in Tables 1 and 2 contain within it greater volatility of its components.[5] Another noteworthy feature of the variance measures reported in Tables 1 and 2 is that the variance of the exchange rate change is greater than that of the variance of our survey expected change. Assuming that both the survey and actual exchange rate contain only the market expectation plus white noise, then this information implies that the actual exchange rate data is noisier than the survey data, and therefore more precise point estimates may be obtained from use of the survey data in a standard unbiasedness test (i.e. the estimated slope coefficient from regressing the actual change in the exchange rate on the forward premium would be less precise than that obtained from a regression of the expected change in the exchange rate on the forward premium).

Also reported in Table 1 are the mean prediction errors (and associated variances) using both the survey expectational data and the forward rate (as a proxy for the expected rate). Both types of prediction error are extremely large: we find that the survey forecast errors are lower in two instances (that for the deutschemark and Japanese yen), very similar in one case (the Swiss franc), and much greater, in absolute terms, for the British pound. The variability, however, of all four currencies is greater for the survey prediction errors.

The main difference in the results contained in Table 2 to those in Table 1 relates to the homogeneity of the sample. For although both the expected change in the exchange rate and the change in the forward premium in the full sample both correctly reflect, in all cases, the actual change in the exchange rate, both measures are wholly inaccurate with regard to all the currencies in the earlier of the two sub-samples. This, not surprisingly, leads to substantial mean forecast errors in this sub-sample. When we compare overall mean forecast errors, we find that the relative performance of the two measures differs according to the sample period.

2. Forward premia, expectations and risk premia

As we mentioned previously, researchers, in attempting to gain information about exchange rate expectations, have frequently used the forward rate as a proxy for the expected exchange rate. In this section we propose to investigate the legitimacy of this practice and also to shed further light on the effects of speculation in the foreign exchange market.

One way to test the unbiasedness of market exchange rate expectations is to run the following regression:

$$\Delta s_{t+k} = \alpha_0 + \beta_0 \Delta s^e_{t+k} + \varphi_{t+k}. \tag{6}$$

If agents' expectations are unbiased then in an estimated version of (6), α_0 would be expected to differ insignificantly from zero, β_0 insignificantly from unity, and the error term would be expected to be white noise, orthogonal to the information set on which speculators base their expectations

[5] This gives clear support to Fama's (1984) proposition that the risk premium and the expected change in the spot rate are negatively correlated.

(i.e. $E[\varphi_{t+k}|I_t] = 0$, where I_t represents the information set upon which the speculators base their expectations). With access to direct information of agents' expectations, (6) may be tested directly. However, in the absence of survey data, most researchers have tested (6) by employing the forward premium as a proxy for the expected change in the exchange rate. An equation like the following is thus tested instead of one like (6):

$$\Delta s_{t+k} = \alpha_1 + \beta_1 fp_t^{t+k} + \varepsilon_{t+k}, \tag{7}$$

where again α_1 is expected to be zero, β_1 unity and the error term a white noise process orthogonal to the information set. However, if in an estimated version of (7), $\hat{\beta}_1$ differs significantly from unity, the interpretation placed on this must be clouded by the jointness of the hypothesis under scrutiny. Thus, in testing (7) one is testing not only that agents are rational but also whether they are risk neutral (i.e. we are imposing $\Delta s_{t+k}^e = fp_t^{t+k}$ which, we pointed out earlier, is true only if the risk premium π_t is equal to zero). The jointness of the hypothesis hence makes any inference about agents' expectations highly questionable.

As a matter of fact, the broad conclusion to emerge from numerous estimates of (7) is that the joint EMH is resoundingly rejected. In particular, a number of investigators report estimates of $\hat{\beta}_1$ which are significantly different from unity. Fama (1984), Hodrick and Srivastava (1984) and Bilson (1985) argue that such a result is evidence of a significant time-varying risk premium. But this conclusion must be based on the (implicit) supposition that agents are rational. By way of contrast, Bilson (1981), Longworth (1981) and Cumby and Obstfeld (1984) take the opposing view that the rejection is due to the irrationality of the market participants. But this conclusion is founded on the assumption of risk neutrality. It is clear, therefore, that in interpreting the results of an estimation of (7), the light that can be shed on the behaviour of speculators' expectations is somewhat limited if a researcher is constrained by the need simply to *assume* that one leg of the joint hypothesis continually holds.

The use of survey data, which does not require the imposition of the assumption of rationality, can, however, be used to determine which of the two competing interpretations of estimations of (7) is to be preferred. To this end, we proceed as follows. Given the decomposition of the risk premium π_t as in Section 1, we decompose the probability limit of β_1 in (7) into:

$$\beta_1 = \frac{\text{Cov}(\varepsilon_{t+k}, fp_t) + \text{Cov}(\Delta s_{t+k}^e, fp_t)}{\text{Var}(fp_t)}. \tag{8}$$

Following Frankel and Froot (1986), β_1 may be written as:

$$\beta_1 = 1 - \beta_{re} - \beta_\pi. \tag{9}$$

That is, β_1 is equal to one (the null) minus a term due to the failure of rational expectations to hold, β_{re}, minus a term due to the existence of a risk premium (reference here to a failure of rational expectations need not literally mean that agents are irrational processors of information—this is discussed more fully in the concluding section). In (9) we understand:

$$\beta_{re} = \frac{\text{Cov}(\varepsilon_{t+k}, fp_t)}{\text{Var}(fp_t)} \tag{10a}$$

$$\beta_{\pi} = \frac{\text{Var}(\pi_t) + \text{Cov}(\Delta s^e_{t+k}, \pi_t)}{\text{Var}(fp_t)} \tag{10b}$$

The availability of independent information on expectations, other than from the use of the forward premium as a proxy, should permit us to determine whether deviations of β_1 from unity are due to "irrationality" or risk aversion (or some combination of both).

Before presenting our estimates of the βs we must say a few words about the estimation technique employed. First, the observational frequency of our one month forecast data is greater than the forecast horizon, thereby imparting a moving average error equal to $k - 1$. In order to deal with this we follow Hansen and Hodrick (1980) in estimating our coefficients by O.L.S. (since they are unbiased even in the presence of autocorrelation) and correcting the coefficient covariance matrix using Hansen's (1981) generalised method of moments (MOM). In constrast to Hansen and Hodrick, however, we do not assume homoscedastic errors. Thus a large number of researchers (*see*, for example, Gregory and McCurdy 1983 and Cumby and Obstfeld 1982) have demonstrated that the variance of foreign exchange forecast errors are heteroscedastic (as we demonstrate this indeed is a feature of both our data sets) and we allow for this using a heteroscedastic consistent covariance matrix which does not require knowledge of the form of the heteroscedasticity.

More specifically, our estimation strategy consists of estimating the basic model, written here in general form, by O.L.S.

$$y^k_t = X^k_t \beta + v^k_t \tag{11}$$

where k is the number of periods in the forecast horizon, y is the dependent variable, X is the matrix of explanatory variables and the variance-covariance matrix of the coefficient estimates, $\hat{\beta}$, is

$$\hat{\Lambda} = (X'X)^{-1}X'\hat{\Omega}X(X'X)^{-1} \tag{12}$$

where $\hat{\Omega}$ is the variance-covariance matrix of the residuals, and the ijth element of $\hat{\Omega}$ is given by:

$$\begin{aligned} \hat{\lambda}(i, j) &= \hat{v}_i \hat{v}_j \quad \text{for } |i - j| \leq (k - 1) \\ &= 0 \qquad \text{otherwise.} \end{aligned}$$

where $\hat{\lambda}$ is the estimated autocovariance.[6] We now turn to estimates of β_1, β_{re} and β_{π} for our currencies and chosen samples.

[6] As Newey and West (1985) have emphasized there is no guarantee that the variance-covariance matrix will be positive definite in finite samples, particularly when the MA process is of a high order. In our study, with an MA1 error, we did not encounter problems of positive-definiteness. However, in order to check the accuracy of our standard errors we estimated them with a variety of different damping factors, and in all cases we found that the standard errors were not sensitive to the damp factor.

We first consider some estimates of equation (7), reported in Table 3. The column headed WH contains White's (1980) heteroscedasticity statistic (approximate chi-squared distribution, with 2 degrees of freedom) along with the corresponding P values. Notice that in all cases the statistic is strongly significant, which is supportive of the findings of other researchers (i.e. Cumby and Obstfeld 1982 and Gregory and McCurdy 1982) and therefore underscores our use of a heteroscedastic consistent estimator.[7] The column denoted LB contains Liung-Box statistics and their associated P values. As expected, the one-month horizon data exhibit fairly strong autocorrelation across currencies/samples whilst the one-week horizon data portray little evidence of autocorrelation (the LB statistic is significant at the 4% level for the Japanese yen).[8,9] For both forecast horizons and for all three samples the point estimates of β_1 are often negative and widely different from unity. Six of the $\hat{\beta}_1$ estimates are statistically different from zero using the method of moments covariance matrix. A number of constant terms are also statistically significant which, combined with estimates of $\hat{\beta}_1$, results in a number of rejections of the joint null $\alpha_1 = 0/\beta_1 = 1$. The results reported in Table 3 are very similar to the findings of a large number of other researchers (*see* Hodrick 1987 and MacDonald 1988 for a further discussion of the extant evidence on equation (7)). But, however, in contrast to other investigators, our use of survey data allows us to apportion responsibility for the estimated deviations of $\hat{\beta}_1$ from 1 between the factors of "irrationality" and risk aversion.

In Table 4 estimates of β_{re} are presented for the same data as in Table 3. Thus estimates of β_{re} can be obtained by regressing the forecast error, $s^e_{t+k} - s_{t+k}$, onto the forward premium, that is:

$$s^e_{t+k} - s_{t+k} = \alpha_{re} + \beta_{re} fp_t + \varepsilon_{t+k}. \tag{14}$$

A test of rationality can be accomplished by testing whether $\alpha_{re} = \beta_{re} = 0$. Interestingly, half the estimates of β_{re} in Table 4 are significantly different from zero at the 95% level (on the basis of the MOM standard errors), and a number of the estimates of α_{re} are also significant. Moreover, the sub-sample patterns that emerge from the forward premium regressions seem to carry over into these rational expectations estimates, in that, for instance, the full sample and sub-sample 2 results for the deutschemark–dollar rate are similar (in respect of sign, magnitude and significance), while the sub-sample 1 results are dramatically different. Not surprisingly, the above results give a number of rejections of the null hypothesis $\alpha_{re} = 0/\beta_{re} = 0$.

Our estimates of the β_π term are obtained in the following way. As we have noted, the derivation of (7) relies crucially on the supposition that

[7] We also estimated ARCH statistics for all the currencies and these also indicated substantial heteroscedasticity.

[8] Ljung-Box and White statistics were also estimated for our other equations, but since the pattern of results was very similar to those recorded in Table 3 they are not reported.

[9] Correction for serial correlation for the one-week JY equations, using a MOM estimator, made very little difference to the standard errors and therefore we do not report them.

TABLE 3

The Forward Premium as a Predictor of the Exchange Rate Change

$$\Delta s_{t+k} = \alpha_1 + \beta_1(f_t^{t+k} - s_t)$$

		$\hat{\alpha}_1$	$\hat{\beta}_1$	R^2	LB	WH	$W^{\alpha=0}_{\beta=1}$	DF
BP	Full	− 0.012	− 6.825	0.17	57.05	28.71	21.35	121
		(3.38)(3.39)	(4.98) (3.56)		(0.00)	(0.00)	(0.00)	
1mo	1	− 0.013	− 1.195	0.00	27.74	16.06	12.98	65
		(4.36)(3.27)	(0.46) (0.40)		(0.27)	(0.00)	(0.00)	
	2	− 0.061	− 21.027	0.11	24.08	24.01	8.89	54
		(2.08)(1.42)	(2.59) (1.67)		(0.28)	(0.00)	(0.01)	
1wk		− 0.008	13.618	0.05	23.34	32.83	8.48	142
		(2.15)(2.55)	(2.82) (3.14)		(0.15)	(0.00)	(0.01)	
DM	Full	− 0.003	0.253	0.05	86.27	50.35	2921.89	121
		(1.06)(0.76)	(2.58)(14.57)		(0.00)	(0.00)	(0.00)	
1mo	1	− 0.018	− 7.472	0.06	44.34	23.68	11.73	65
		(1.34)(0.99)	(2.02) (1.57)		(0.00)	(0.00)	(0.00)	
	2	− 0.019	0.223	0.08	34.62	23.57	292551.8	54
		(4.04)(3.24)	(2.26)(13.55)		(0.03)	(0.00)	(0.00)	
1wk		− 0.004	− 1.141	0.01	32.17	47.36	19.04	142
		(2.25)(2.44)	(0.94) (2.25)		(0.65)	(0.00)	(0.00)	

TABLE 3

$$\Delta s_{t+k} = \alpha_1 + \beta_1(f_t^{t+k} - s_t)$$

		$\hat{\alpha}_1$	$\hat{\beta}_1$	R^2	LB	WH	$W^{\alpha=0}_{\beta=1}$	DF
JY	Full	−0.028	−7.879	0.07	54.15	34.39	0.02	121
		(4.07)(0.14)	(3.08)(0.11)		(0.01)	(0.00)	(0.00)	
1mo	1	−0.019	−6.526	0.05	35.13	14.97	0.00	65
		(1.71)(0.05)	(1.88)(0.06)		(0.06)	(0.00)	(0.99)	
	2	−0.010	7.072	0.01	31.82	16.84	0.02	54
		(0.81)(0.03)	(0.88)(0.03)		(0.06)	(0.00)	(0.98)	
1wk		−0.006	−5.088	0.01	52.06	30.47	0.002	142
		(2.27)(0.04)	(0.95)(0.02)		(0.04)	(0.00)	(0.99)	
SF	Full	−0.44	−9.148	0.10	49.78	28.96	10.17	96
		(3.32)(2.35)	(3.32)(2.57)		(0.00)	(0.00)	(0.01)	
1mo	1	0.003	−1.154	0.00	30.30	13.33	6.29	65
		(0.12)(0.13)	(0.29)(0.34)		(0.18)	(0.00)	(0.04)	
	2	−0.063	−12.378	0.02	37.06	15.16	5.59	29
		(1.51)(1.47)	(0.92)(0.94)		(0.00)	(0.00)	(0.06)	
1wk		−0.009	−5.802	0.01	17.23	31.75	3.91	92
		(1.46)(1.96)	(1.08)(1.58)		(0.93)	(0.00)	(0.14)	

Where, of variables not previously defined, R^2 is the coefficient of determination, DF denotes degrees of freedom, LB is the Ljung-Box statistic, W is a linear Wald test of the null hypothesis, WH is White's (1980) test for heteroscedasticity. LB, W and WH all have an asymptotic chi squared distribution, and the numbers in parenthesis below the estimated statistics are P values. The numbers in parenthesis immediately below the point estimates are OLS t ratios, while the numbers to their right are t ratios calculated using Hansen's (1981) generalised method of moments (*see* main text for further details).

TABLE 4

Regression Based Tests of Rational Expectations

$$s^e_{t+k} - s_{t+k} = \alpha_{re} + \beta_{re}(f_t^{t+k} - s_t)$$

		α_{re}	β_{re}	R^2	$W^{\alpha=0}_{\beta=0}$		DF
BP	Full	0.013	7.698	0.18	18.95	(0.00)	121
		(3.46)(3.51)	(5.19) (3.58)				
1 month	1	0.015	1.222	0.00	12.37	(0.00)	65
		(4.48)(3.34)	(0.45) (0.38)				
	2	0.079	26.759	0.14	6.65	(0.04)	54
		(2.55)(1.70)	(3.08) (1.93)				
1 week		0.006	− 13.855	0.04	8.68	(0.01)	142
		(1.60)(1.90)	(2.55) (2.79)				
DM	Full	− 0.003	− 0.279	0.05	388.14	(0.00)	121
		(0.95)(0.69)	(2.62)(16.15)				
1 month	1	0.012	7.714	0.05	16.31	(0.00)	65
		(0.79)(0.64)	(1.96) (1.66)				
	2	0.013	− 0.247	0.08	31388.38	(0.00)	54
		(2.62)(2.18)	(2.26)(13.95)				
1 week		0.003	2.474	0.02	37.41	(0.00)	142
		(1.62)(1.77)	(1.78) (6.11)				
JY	Full	0.020	7.846	0.06	7.17	(0.03)	121
		(2.75)(2.08)	(2.85)(2.60)				
1 month	1	0.008	5.714	0.04	9.05	(0.01)	65
		(0.65)(0.50)	(1.55)(1.37)				
	2	− 0.003	− 12.211	0.04	9.17	(0.01)	54
		(0.20)(0.21)	(1.45)(1.72)				
1 week		0.003	1.996	0.00	2.65	(0.27)	142
		(1.13)(1.31)	(0.34)(0.45)				
SF	Full	0.039	9.911	0.11	13.05	(0.01)	96
		(2.28)(1.92)	(3.36)(2.61)				
1 month	1	− 0.018	− 0.072	0.00	10.11	(0.01)	65
		(0.89)(0.76)	(0.02)(0.02)				
	2	0.088	22.529	0.06	5.84	(0.05)	29
		(1.76)(1.89)	(1.39)(1.52)				
1 week		0.007	4.378	0.01	1.84	(0.39)	92
		(0.95)(1.34)	(0.72)(1.12)				

For definitions, *see* Table 3.

$\Delta s^e_{t+k} = fp_t^{t+k}$, i.e. on the supposition that there is no risk premium. This contention can be tested by use of the survey data in an estimation of the following by O.L.S:

$$\Delta s^e_{t+k} = \rho_0 + \rho_1 fp_t + \phi_{t+k}. \qquad (15)$$

If agents are risk neutral, then it would be expected that $\rho_1 = 1$. But in fact a test of $\rho_1 = 1$ is equivalent to a test of $\beta_\pi = 0$ since:

$$\rho_1 = 1 - \frac{\mathrm{Var}(\pi_t) + \mathrm{Cov}(\Delta s^e_{t+k}, \pi_t)}{\mathrm{Var}(fp_t)} \tag{16}$$

$$\rho_1 = 1 - \beta_\pi, \text{ or: } \beta_\pi = 1 - \rho_1.$$

The results reported in Table 5 indicate that the hypothesis that $\beta_\pi = 0$ may be rejected in a number of cases, in that the hypothesis that $\rho_1 = 1$ is rejected at

TABLE 5

Regressions of the Expected Changes in the Exchange Rate on the Forward Premium: A Test of Perfect Substitutability

$$\Delta s^e_{t+k} = \rho_0 + \rho_1(f^{t+k} - s)_t$$

		ρ_0	ρ_1	R^2	$t_{\rho_1=1}$	$W^{\rho^*=0}_{\rho_1=1}$	DF
BP	Full	0.001	0.873	0.04		4.82 (0.09)	121
		(1.35)(2.17)	(2.37)(1.95)		−0.28		
1 month	1	0.001	0.028	0.00		5.05 (0.08)	65
		(1.89)(1.87)	(0.05)(0.05)		—		
	2	0.018	5.732	0.09		7.43 (0.02)	54
		(2.18)(2.49)	(2.42)(2.65)		2.19*		
1 week		−0.001	−0.237	0.00		19.43 (0.00)	142
		(1.10)(1.37)	(0.17)(0.18)		—		
DM	Full	−0.007	−0.026	0.01		905902 (0.00)	121
		(7.04)(5.55)	(0.91)(6.73)		342*		
1 month	1	−0.007	0.242	0.00		1486 (0.00)	65
		(1.79)(1.66)	(0.24)(0.24)		—		
	2	−0.005	−0.024	0.01		2879622 (0.00)	54
		(3.09)(2.32)	(0.66)(3.57)		146*		
1 week		−0.007	1.333	0.06		8.97 (0.01)	142
		(1.12)(1.20)	(3.10)(8.05)		2.02*		
JY	Full	−0.008	−0.033	0.00		25.73 (0.00)	121
		(4.02)(3.28)	(0.05)(0.04)		—		
1 month	1	−0.012	−0.812	0.01		28.07 (0.00)	65
		(3.68)(2.56)	(0.86)(0.58)		—		
	2	−0.013	−5.139	0.10		35.01 (0.00)	54
		(3.85)(5.44)	(2.39)(2.86)		−3.42*		
1 week		−0.003	−3.092	0.02		13.54 (0.00)	142
		(3.29)(3.66)	(1.84)(2.40)		−3.18*		
SF	Full	−0.005	0.764	0.00		4.96 (0.08)	96
		(0.72)(0.57)	(0.57)(0.52)		—		
1 month	1	−0.015	−1.226	0.02		13.74 (0.00)	65
		(2.34)(2.13)	(1.00)(0.87)		—		
	2	0.025	10.151	0.04		3.20 (0.20)	29
		(0.89)(1.72)	(1.13)(1.98)		1.78		
1 week		−0.003	−1.424	0.01		7.53 (0.02)	92
		(1.15)(1.74)	(0.80)(1.49)		2.54*		

For definitions, *see* Table 3. A * denotes significance at the 5% level.

the 95% level in seven cases (on the basis of a t-test). Again, there is evidence of differences across the sample periods.

The results from Tables 4 and 5 indicate that the reason for the rejection of $\alpha_1 = 0/\beta_1 = 1$ in Table 3 is attributable in some cases to a failure of the RE leg of the joint-hypothesis (i.e. the SF 4-week (full-sample); the BP 1-week), but that in the majority of cases it is due to a failure of both legs of the joint-hypothesis. The conclusions, therefore, to be drawn from estimates of (7) are not as clear-cut as a number of researchers have asserted.

TABLE 6
Regression Based Tests of Excessive Speculation

$$s^e_{t+k} - s_{t+k} = a + b(s^e_{t+k} - s_t)$$

		a	b	R^2	$W^{\alpha=0}_{\beta=0}$	DF
BP	Full	0.001	1.988	0.21	14.14 (0.00)	121
		(0.45)(0.32)	(5.63)(3.52)			
1 month	1	0.013	1.889	0.15	36.21 (0.00)	65
		(3.98)(2.73)	(3.44)(2.23)			
	2	− 0.012	1.667	0.19	9.61 (0.00)	54
		(2.48)(1.97)	(3.62)(2.64)			
1 week		0.0002	2.348	0.34	56.65 (0.00)	142
		(0.16)(0.16)	(8.61)(7.26)			
DM	Full	0.008	1.591	0.18	24.30 (0.00)	121
		(2.32)(1.74)	(5.16)(4.90)			
1 month	1	− 0.005	1.427	0.13	31.33 (0.00)	65
		(1.05)(0.82)	(3.07)(3.57)			
	2	0.023	1.423	0.20	18.08 (0.00)	54
		(4.45)(3.59)	(3.72)(3.33)			
1 week		0.004	1.734	0.30	55.55 (0.00)	142
		(2.82)(2.71)	(7.82)(7.44)			
JY	Full	0.013	1.534	0.14	25.41 (0.00)	121
		(3.19)(2.48)	(4.54)(5.04)			
1 month	1	0.002	1.291	0.11	12.64 (0.00)	65
		(0.32)(0.26)	(2.79)(2.89)			
	2	0.023	1.379	0.13	19.32 (0.00)	54
		(4.01)(3.21)	(2.85)(3.87)			
1 week		0.004	1.385	0.16	17.59 (0.00)	142
		(3.06)(3.09)	(5.29)(3.58)			
SF	Full	0.008	0.849	0.13	7.82 (0.02)	96
		(0.18)(0.13)	(3.81)(2.66)			
1 month	1	− 0.018	− 0.005	0.00	16.26 (0.00)	65
		(3.31)(3.60)	(0.01)(0.01)			
	2	0.026	1.029	0.32	14.91 (0.00)	29
		(3.05)(2.50)	(3.71)(3.41)			
1 week		0.003	1.753	0.26	40.78 (0.00)	92
		(1.67)(1.67)	(5.74)(6.38)			

For definitions, *see* Table 3.

As a final exercise we present a test of whether speculators have had excessive expectations throughout the period of our samples. That is, in forming their expectations, have speculators placed too much or too little weight on the current spot rate as compared to all other variables in their information set. Such a test may be obtained by re-expressing equation (6). Thus, (6) may be derived from (17) by noting that the left hand side of (17) is $\Delta s^e_{t+k} - \Delta s_{t+k}$

$$s^e_{t+k} - s_{t+k} = a + b(s^e_{t+k} - s_t) + \phi_{t+k}, \tag{17}$$

where $\alpha_0 = -a$, $\beta_0 = 1 - b$. Thus if agents are rational, regression of the expectational error on the change in the expected exchange rate should result in point estimates of a and b differing insignificantly from zero: the null hypothesis is $a = b = 0$.

With one exception, all the estimates of $\hat{b}$ in Table 6 are statistically different from zero. Furthermore, a number of the $\hat{a}$ terms are also statistically significant and the combined effect of this and the deviation of $\hat{b}$ from zero results in a convincing rejection of the null for all the estimated equations.[10] Thus, we can say that the results of Table 6 indicate evidence of excessive speculation for our sample periods: in other words, in forming their expectations, agents would have done better by giving more weight to the spot exchange rate.

Concluding comments

In this paper we employed exchange rate survey data to shed fresh light on the formation of expectations in four foreign exchange markets in the context of the experience of the 1980s with floating exchange rates. A number of interesting results emerged. First, for all currencies, regardless of the sample period, our descriptive statistics pointed to both the risk premium and the expected change in the spot rate as being important ingredients of the forward premium. Secondly, and as a corollary of this, we found that expectations are not static, a fact which has important implications for theoretical models which include such an assumption. Thirdly, we discovered evidence to suggest that the common finding that the forward premium is a biased predictor of an exchange rate change is due to *both* risk aversion and the characteristics of expectations formation on the part of agents. And, finally, we found that exchange rate expectations seem to be fairly homogeneous across exchange markets and sub-samples in that our findings appear robust with respect to such differences.

In conclusion, it is perhaps worth remarking on our finding that, on the basis of our survey data, agents do not seem to be exploiting all available information as suggested by the rational expectations hypothesis. Perhaps the simplest rationalisation for this finding is that agents are irrational information processors, and this is a conclusion that would find favour in some quarters

[10] It is straightforward to demonstrate that measurement error will bias b to unity. However, the fact that our reported b coefficients are all (with two exceptions) greater than unity suggests that it is not measurement error which results in rejection of rational expectations.

(*see* e.g. Tobin 1982). We, however, are inclined to be more cautious in our interpretation of the results. There are in fact two main explanations, that do not rely on irrational information processing, for our finding that forecast errors are correlated with available information. First, it is possible that agents were still learning the data generation process for the exchange rate series during our sample and this could have resulted in violation of the error orthogonality condition. Second, the "peso problem", first suggested by Krasker (1980), could explain the biasedness of the forecasts, to the extent that there was a small probability of a large exchange rate change which did not occur in sample (thus biasing our test statistics towards rejection). Whichever view is correct, we believe that our use of survey data indicates that researchers should be more cautious in their interpretations of rejection of the unbiasedness proposition.

Department of Economics, University of Dundee
Department of Economics, University of Aberdeen

REFERENCES

BILSON, J. F. O. (1981). "The 'Speculative Efficiency' Hypothesis", *Journal of Business*, 54, 435–51.

BILSON, J. F. O. (1985). "Macroeconomic Stability and Flexible Exchange Rates", *American Economic Review*, Papers and Proceedings, 75, 62–7.

BOOTH, P. and LONGWORTH, D. (1986). "Foreign Exchange Market Efficiency Tests: Implications of Recent Empirical Findings", *Journal of International Money Finance*, 5, 135–52.

CUMBY, R. E. and OBSTFELD, M. (1984). "International Interest Rate and Price Level Linkages under Flexible Exchange Rates: A Review of Recent Evidence". In *Exchange Rate Theory and Practice*, Chicago, Chicago University Press.

DOMINGUEZ, K. (1986). "Are Foreign Exchange Forecasts Rational? New Evidence from Survey Data", *Economics Letters*, 21, 277–81.

DORNBUSCH, R. (1976). "Exchange Rates Expectations and Monetary Policy", *Journal of International Economics*, 231–44.

FAMA, E. (1984). "Forward and Spot Exchange Rates", *Journal of Monetary Economics*, 14, 319–38.

FRANKEL, J. A. and FROOT, K. (1986). "Interpreting Tests of Forward Discount Bias Using Survey Data on Exchange Rate Expectations", *NBER Working Paper*, 1963.

FRANKEL, J. A. and FROOT, K. (1987). "Using Survey Data to Test Some Standard Propositions Regarding Exchange Rate Expectations", *American Economic Review*, 77, 133–53.

GREGORY, A. W. and MCCURDY, T. H. (1984). "Testing Unbiasedness in the Forward Foreign Exchange Market: A Specification Analysis", *Journal of International Money and Finance*, 3, 357–68.

HANSEN, L. P. (1982). "Large Sample Properties of Generalized Method of Moments Estimators", *Econometrica*, 50, 1029–54.

HANSEN, L. P. and HODRICK, R. J. (1980). "Forward Exchange Rates as Optimal Predictors of Future Spot Rates: An Econometric Analysis", *Journal of Political Economy*, 88, 829–53.

HODRICK, R. (1987). *The Empirical Evidence on the Efficiency of the Forward and Futures Foreign Exchange Markets*. Harwood Academic Press, New York.

HODRICK, R. and SRIVASTAVA, S. (1984). "An Investigation of Risk and Return in Forward Foreign Exchange", *Journal of International Money and Finance*, 3, 5–30.

HODRICK, R. and SRIVASTAVA, S. (1986). "The Covariation of Risk Premiums and Expected Future Spot Rates", *Journal of International Money and Finance*, 5 (Supplement), S5–S22.

KRASKER, W. S. (1980). "The 'Peso Problem' in testing the efficiency of Forward Exchange Markets", *Journal of Monetary Economics*, 6, 269–76.

LEVICH, R. (1985). "Empirical Studies of Exchange Rates: Price behavior, Rate Determination and Market Efficiency". In R. Jones and P. Kenen (eds.), *Handbook of International Economics*, vol. 2, North-Holland, Amsterdam.

LONGWORTH, D. (1981). "Testing the Efficiency of the Canadian–US Exchange Market under the Assumption of no Risk Premium", *Journal of Finance*, 36, 43–9.

MACDONALD, R. (1988). *Floating Exchange Rates: Theories and Evidence*. London, Unwin-Hyman.

MACDONALD, R. and TORRANCE, T. S. (1988). "On Risk, Rationality and Excessive Speculation in the Deutschemark–US Dollar Exchange Market: Some Evidence Using Survey Data", *Oxford Bulletin of Economics and Statistics*, 50, 107–23.

MACDONALD, R. and TAYLOR, M. P. (1989). "Economic Analysis of Foreign Exchange Markets: An Expository Survey". In R. MacDonald and M. P Taylor (eds.), *Exchange Rates and Open Economy Macroeconomics*, Oxford, Blackwell.

MUSSA, M. (1979). "Our Recent Experience with Fixed and Flexible Exchange Rates", *Carnegie-Rochester Supplement*, 3, 1–50.

NEWEY, W. and WEST, K. (1985). "A Simple Positive Definite Heteroscedasticity and Autocorrelation Consistent Covariance Matrix", *Discussion Paper no. 92*, Woodrow Wilson School, University of Princeton, New Jersey.

TAYLOR, M. P. (1989). "Expectations, Risk and Uncertainty in the Foreign Exchange Market: Some Results based on Survey Data", forthcoming, *The Manchester School*.

TOBIN, J. (1982). "The State of Exchange Rate Theory: Some Sceptical Observations". In R. Cooper, P. B. Kenen, J. De Macedo and J. U. Ypersele (eds.), *The International Monetary System*, Cambridge, Mass., Ballinger.

WHITE, H. (1980). "A Heteroscedasticity-Consistent Covariance Matrix Estimator and a Direct Test for Heteroscedasticity", *Econometrica*, 48, 817–38.

Journal of Forecasting, Vol. 13, 313–332 (1994)

Combining Exchange Rate Forecasts: What is the Optimal Consensus Measure?

RONALD MACDONALD and IAN W. MARSH
University of Strathclyde, U.K.

ABSTRACT

In this paper a high-quality disaggregate database is utilized to examine whether individual forecasters produce efficient exchange rate predictions and also if the properties of the forecasts change when they are combined. The paper links a number of themes in the exchange rate literature and examines various methods of forecast combination. It is demonstrated, *inter alia*, that some forecasters are better than others, but that most are not as good as a naive no-change prediction. Combining forecasts adds to the accuracy of the predictions, but the gains mainly reflect the removal of systematic and unstable bias.

KEY WORDS Combining forecasts Exchange rates Information sets

Recently it has become popular to use survey-based measures of expectations to test a range of hypotheses about the behaviour of foreign exchange rates.[1] One particular advantage of such data is that, in principle, they enable a researcher to conduct tests of the efficiency of foreign exchange markets without imposing auxiliary assumptions about agents' risk preferences. However, the majority of research in this area uses some measure of the 'consensus' forecast, such as the mean or median. Often the use of such measures simply reflects the fact that the institution conducting the survey is unwilling to provide information on the individual responses. However, many interesting issues can only be addressed with the availability of the disaggregate data. For example, one common finding in the extant literature is that the consensus forecast measure is a biased predictor of the future exchange rate. But do all agents produce biased estimates or are some better than others? Also, is it possible to combine forecasts in such a way that an unbiased consensus forecast can be produced? These kinds of questions can only be addressed with a disaggregate survey database.

In this paper we use a novel database of disaggregate exchange rate forecasts, gathered from over 100 institutions in the leading financial centres of the world, to examine the issues referred to above. In particular, we examine whether individual forecasters produce expectations which are unbiased and orthogonal to a publicly available information set.[2] Although such tests are of interest in themselves, their presentation in this paper is more for motivational purposes;

[1] See, *inter alia*, Dominguez (1986), Frankel and Froot (1987, 1989), MacDonald (1990), and MacDonald and Torrance, (1988, 1990).

[2] This part of the paper may be viewed as an update of the estimates presented in MacDonald (1992).

CCC 0277–6693/94/030313–20
© 1994 by John Wiley & Sons, Ltd.
Received August 1992
Revised October 1993

our main objective is to examine whether such individual forecasts may be combined in ways which outperform other consensus measures. Our forecast combination strategy draws on a variety of techniques suggested by the optimal forecast combination literature.

The outline of the remainder of this paper is as follows. In the next section we present a brief survey of the literature on how best to combine forecasts and we relate this to the recent exchange rate modelling literature. The third section contains a description of the database used and also a discussion of the testing methodology employed. The issue of how well different forecast combinations perform is addressed in the fourth section. The paper closes with a summary and conclusions.

FORECAST COMBINATIONS AND EXCHANGE RATE FORECASTING

The optimal way of combining forecasts

Bates and Granger (1969) noted that the complexity of the economic system means that different forecasters will, in general, employ different information. While it would be best to combine this information and produce a forecast based upon this wider pool of knowledge, in practice only the forecasts themselves are available. Bates and Granger considered methods of using this one-step-removed data to provide better predictions. Earlier researchers had noted the strong performance of averages of forecasts, and Bates and Granger extended this idea by weighting the forecasts in various ways dependent on the quality of predictions in recent periods. The weights were restricted to sum to one, under the assumption that the forecasts were unbiased.

Newbold and Granger (1974) took up this theme empirically, and demonstrated that the in-sample performance of a weighted average forecast can indeed be superior to both individual forecasts and the simple average. In contrast, however, later studies found little advantage from sophisticated combination methods over simple averaging of forecasts.[3]

Granger and Ramanathan (1984) demonstrated how to analyse forecast combinations in a regression format.[4] Bates and Granger's earlier work, with presupposed unbiased forecasts, was seen to be equivalent to a linear regression of the actual variable on a set of forecasts with no constant and the constraint that coefficients sum to unity. However, this is an inefficient combination, because, as Granger and Ramanathan demonstrate, when forecast errors are stationary and the covariance matrix is constant optimal weights can be retrieved from an unrestricted regression with a constant included, even if forecasts are biased. By construction, this optimal combination will perform at least as well as the simple average within-sample. Empirical work has, however, cast doubt on the practical use of this method out-of-sample, when it cannot necessarily be assumed that the structure of forecast errors and the covariance matrix are invariant (see, for example, Figlewski and Urich, 1983; Winkler, 1984). The most often cited reasons for this breakdown are the actions of forecasters themselves. The performance of individual forecasters often determines their continued employment,[5] theoretical developments lead to major changes in the equations underlying the macroeconometric models of the economy,[6] and when a substantial amount of judgement is

[3] See, for example, Makridakis and Hibon (1979).

[4] This was not a totally innovative idea as it had been suggested as early as 1967 in the work of Crane and Crotty (1967), and revived by Reinmuth and Geurts (1979).

[5] Cyriax (1978) pointed out that over 70 organizations make macroeconomic forecasts in the UK alone, and while it needs few qualifications to provide such predictions, competition from the 'big' organizations whose forecasts are widely reported should force the correction of biases through time (see Webb, 1984).

[6] See, for example, Ball *et al.* (1979) for a history of the changes made to the London Business School model.

incorporated into a forecast there is no reason to suppose that optimal weights will remain constant through time. As a result, Clemen (1986) advocated the imposition of restrictions and used GNP forecasts to provide an example of how a regression with constrained coefficients can outperform an unrestricted 'optimal' forecast. Diebold and Pauly (1987) investigated the use of the most recent T^* observations in calculating optimal weights. They noted, however, that the choice of T^* is arbitrary and that the choice can have a large impact on the optimal weights.

Exchange rate forecasts

The problems of producing fundamentally determined exchange rate forecasts have been well documented since Meese and Rogoff (1983) compared the out-of-sample performance of several asset-based models of the exchange rate to a random walk for a range of currencies. The conclusion that emerged from their study was that none of the models could outperform the simple random walk over any forecast horizon considered, with the sole exception of one-month forecasts of the deutschmark. Furthermore, constrained combinations of all the forecasts (weights forced to sum to unity) failed to improve performance.[7] Meese and Rogoff (1984) produced forecasts from their models with coefficients constrained to values taken from the empirical literature on money demand functions which could outperform the no-change prediction, but only over horizons above one year. These results[8] may be interpreted as supporting the view that the exchange rate is an asset price determined in an efficient market. If this is the true representation of the way the foreign exchange market works, then trading on the basis of forecasts made by models or 'experts' cannot be profitable.

Evidence on this point is mixed. Boothe and Glassman (1987) found profitable trading rules based on a real interest differential model for the Canadian dollar and the deutschmark, though profits for the latter currency were highest from the random walk model. Boothe and Glassman noted, however, that the unexploited profit opportunities could be the result of risk bearing and did not necessarily indicate market failure. Bilson and Hsieh (1987) did account for risk and still found evidence of profitable speculation. However, their results were heavily influenced by a few highly profitable opportunities which could be associated with the 'peso' problem.[9] Guerard (1989) combined a time-series forecast, the forward rate and a forecast from a single US bank using a ridge regression technique but found the forward rate itself very hard to beat, indicating market efficiency.

Though the out-of-sample evidence may be unclear, the in-sample performance of most models is also unsatisfactory in terms of having wrongly signed coefficients, low R^2 values and insignificant magnitudes.[10] This has led some researchers to conclude that the operation of the foreign exchange market is influenced by technical analysts, or chartists, who base their predictions of currency movements on patterns in the history of exchange rate movements.

---

[7] Pairwise constrained combinations did beat a random walk over a one-month horizon, but never for more than one of the four exchange rates considered.

[8] Other researchers have managed to produce models capable of matching or beating a prediction of no change, but rarely for a wide range of currencies. Finn (1986) added partial adjustment dynamics to a flexible price model which subsequently performed as well as a random walk. Wolff (1987) repeated Meese and Rogoff's work using a Kalman filter which allowed coefficients to change with time. His results indicate an ability to predict the dollar/deutschmark rate, but a random walk model still outperformed the dollar–yen and dollar–sterling models at all forecast horizons. See MacDonald and Taylor (1992) for a more detailed discussion of the out-of-sample performance of economic models.

[9] That is, a small probability of an adverse event which did not occur within sample. In-sample occurrence of this event could then offset the profits made elsewhere. See Krasker (1980) for a more detailed discussion.

[10] See Dornbusch and Frankel (1987), MacDonald (1988), and MacDonald and Taylor (1992).

That these analysts play a role in the market is beyond doubt. Taylor and Allen (1992) found from survey results that over a short-term (intra-day to one week) forecasting horizon over 90% of chief foreign exchange dealers in London, the largest currency market in the world, use some type of chart analysis in formulating their expectations, and that over half of their respondents felt that these charts to be at least as important as fundamental determinants of the exchange rate. This is less surprising when one notes that Allen and Taylor (1990) found that some of the chart analysts could consistently outperform a random walk over a one-week and four-week forecast horizon. Theoretical models are now being devised which incorporate non-fundamentalist traders.[11]

Work carried out to date on the accuracy of exchange rate forecasts has used the forecasts of either econometric- or time-series-based models (economics-based), or technical analysts' predictions. Goodman (1979) used various measures of predictive power to evaluate the output of ten forecasting services; six used economics-based techniques and four used chartist-based methods. His broad conclusions were that the economics-oriented services did rather poorly and were not notably profitable, while the technical services did much better, producing high returns on speculated capital. Blake *et al.* (1986) investigated the performance of three British, economics-based forecasters and were able to reject the hypothesis of unbiasedness in both the individual forecast series and in an optimally combined series.

DISAGGREGATE INTERNATIONAL FORECASTS

To date, researchers have not systematically examined the performance of individuals who speculate in the foreign exchange market. We cannot, unfortunately, correct for this deficiency here, as market participants are, not surprisingly, reluctant to reveal their trading record.[12] What we can offer is an analysis of predictions made by traders and economists in banks, financial houses, and corporations from around the world, gathered by Consensus Economics of London. These predictions differ from the forecasts previously examined since our data consist of the survey respondents' subjective and potentially time-varying combinations of fundamentals-based forecasts, chartist predictions and other considerations.[13] Furthermore, most previous studies have concentrated on forecasters from one country, typically the United Kingdom or the U.S.A. A primary reason for combining forecasts is to capture a wider set of information. Focusing on a single country (or even worse, a single financial centre), where traders have largely common information sources, will limit potential gains.

Consensus Economics have surveyed leading financial institutions, forecasting units, and multinationals in the G7 countries on the first Monday of each month since October 1989, concerning their expectations of the dollar–sterling, mark–dollar, and yen–dollar spot exchange rates 3 and 12 months ahead. In this study we only use the 3-month forecasts for the period October 1989 to December 1991—a total of 27 overlapping observations. The number of forecasters surveyed differs from country to country; the response rate is not always perfect and varies across currencies. For this study we have only included those companies

[11] See Frankel and Froot (1986, 1990) for a model which helps to explain the behaviour of the US dollar in the mid-1980s, and Kirman (1991) for a model in which traders switch between chartist advice and fundamentalist predictions.

[12] Hartzmark (1991) analysed daily futures positions of large-volume traders in a variety of US exchanges using non-parametric techniques. He finds that returns to futures trading are randomly generated. However, he did not have any data on currency futures trades.

[13] In fact Goodman (1979) neglected to analyse the performance of 13 of his total sample of 23 forecasting agencies on the grounds that they combined both econometric and technical methods in making their predictions.

which responded to all surveys for a currency. We have also excluded specialist forecasting companies whose responses are likely to be model determined and not a mix of a variety of inputs. This has left us with 24 forecasters for the mark–dollar, 19 for the dollar–sterling, and 20 for the yen–dollar exchange rates. Thirteen of these are common to all three currencies. To preserve the anonymity of the survey respondents, we identify each by a country abbreviation and a number (thus F12 denotes company 12 for France).[14] Consensus, as their name suggests, also produce a variety of consensus forecasts. We follow their practice, but again only use our restricted data set, and produce mean forecasts from each country, a mean forecast for the entire sample, and the mean value from our core subset of thirteen forecasters.

In addition to the survey data, we collected data on spot exchange rates from the *Financial Times*. We took the closing spot rate (average of bid–ask spread) on the Monday the survey was made as the current spot rate, S_t. The corresponding 3-month forward rate was also collected. We also noted the spot rate which prevailed at the close of the day falling 3 calendar months from the survey date—the 'forecast day'. If this fell on a Saturday, the Friday rate was used, while if it fell on a Sunday we used the Monday rate. From this entire database we then calculated the actual and expected changes (in terms of our forecasts and the forward rate) for each currency.

Before turning to our forecast combinations, we first, as a preliminary exercise, test the individual forecasts for unbiasedness and error orthogonality. These tests were performed by running the following regressions:

$$\Delta S_{t+k} = \rho + \delta\, \Delta S^{e}_{t+k} + \varphi_{t+k} \quad (1)$$

$$S^{e}_{t+k} - S_{t+k} = \Phi_0 + \Phi_1 X_t + \zeta_{t+k} \quad (2)$$

where S denotes the (logarithm) of the spot exchange rate, superscript e denotes an expectation, Δ is the first difference operator, and X_t is the period-t information set available to agents at the time their k-period forecasts were formed. Unbiasedness in the forecasts implies that ρ should equal zero and δ should equal unity in equation (1), while error orthogonality implies that the Φ coefficients in equation (2) should jointly equal zero.[15] Since the forecast horizon of the forecasts is greater than the sampling frequency we have overlapping data, rendering estimated variance–covariance matrices inefficient. We therefore use Hansen's (1982) generalized method of moments (GMM), in its heteroscedasticity-consistent form, to correct the coefficient covariance matrix.[16]

The results of the OLS/GMM estimation of equations (1) and (2) are presented in Tables I and II. Unbiasedness is resoundingly rejected. Individual, country average, and sample average forecasts typically have point estimates of δ which are much closer to minus one than plus one. In only five of the 63 individual forecasts can we accept the hypothesis of no bias in the forecasts at the 5% level. The information set used in computing the orthogonality tests was the change in the spot exchange rate over the previous week. In the efficient markets sense this is a weak test, but still it appears that many of these forecasts do not fully incorporate such elementary information into their forecasts. More stringent tests, in terms of a wider

[14] The mnemonics are those attached to the entire database and so are not necessarily sequential. In future papers using the same database we plan to use the same identifying codes to facilitate comparison. C denotes Canada, F France, I Italy, J Japan, B Britain, U the USA and G Germany.

[15] Note that equation (1) is formulated in terms of rates of change rather than levels. This transformation is necessary as the stochastic process generating the spot exchange rate may be non-stationary, which would invalidate hypothesis testing in a levels equation. Further details can be found in Hodrick (1987, pp. 27–31).

[16] See MacDonald (1992) for details of the use of this correction.

information set, resulted in almost uniform rejection of error orthogonality. It is worth noting the difference between these results and those reported in MacDonald (1992). Although the general tenor of MacDonald's disaggregate results are similar to those noted here, he did report some results which indicated that German forecasters produced unbiased forecasts. We attribute the difference in the two sets of results to the different sample periods and the

Table I. Unbiasedness test of individual and average forecasts

	Deutschmark		Sterling		Yen	
	δ	T_2	δ	T_2	δ	T_2
C1	−1.612	0.00	−0.903	0.00	−0.565	0.00
C5	−0.063	0.00	−0.084	0.00	−0.802	0.00
F2	−0.890	0.00				
F10	−0.876	0.00	−0.711	0.00	−0.641	0.00
F12	−0.318	0.00	−0.706	0.00	0.196	0.15
I6	−0.352	0.00			−0.249	0.00
I10	−0.094	0.00	−0.752	0.00	−0.625	0.00
J1					−0.358	0.00
J3					−0.697	0.00
J7					−0.210	0.00
J14	−0.025	0.00			−0.302	0.00
J20	−0.311	0.00	−0.498	0.00	−0.595	0.00
B16	−0.403	0.00	−0.183	0.00	−0.747	0.00
B25			−0.824	0.00		
B29	0.181	0.06	0.135	0.12		
B32			−0.560	0.03		
B35	−0.599	0.00	−0.552	0.00	−0.038	0.00
U1	−0.773	0.01				
U5			−0.211	0.00	−0.206	0.01
U20	0.290	0.30				
U24	0.210	0.38				
G5	−0.938	0.00	−1.218	0.00	−0.042	0.00
G8	−0.573	0.00	−0.523	0.00	−0.533	0.00
G10	−1.435	0.00			−0.721	0.00
G12	−0.312	0.00	−0.127	0.00		
G13	−0.623	0.00	−0.678	0.00	−0.281	0.00
G14	−0.119	0.00	−0.528	0.00	−0.427	0.00
G15	−0.268	0.00	−0.145	0.00	−0.376	0.00
G22	−0.648	0.00	−0.882	0.00		
G23	−0.411	0.00				
Averages						
Canadian	−0.887	0.00	−0.818	0.00	−0.787	0.00
French	−1.150	0.00	−1.015	0.00	−0.600	0.00
Italian	−0.341	0.00	−0.752	0.00	−0.430	0.00
Japanese	−0.177	0.00	−0.498	0.00	−0.746	0.00
British	−0.662	0.00	−0.900	0.00	−0.210	0.00
American	−0.032	0.18	−0.211	0.00	−0.206	0.01
German	−0.981	0.00	−0.997	0.00	−0.654	0.00
All	−1.091	0.00	−1.332	0.00	−0.753	0.00
Forward	3.947	0.10	−1.505	0.22	−3.664	0.09

T_2 denotes the marginal significance of a chi-square test of $\rho = 0/\delta = 1$.

selection of different forecasters (because of the criterion required for combining forecasts).

Biased forecasts are, however, not necessarily bad forecasts and in order to evaluate the accuracy of our forecasters we have used two measures. First, the root mean squared error (RMSE) was calculated over the full sample period for each individual forecaster, each country consensus, the mean of the full sample, and for our core group of thirteen. We also computed

Table II. Orthogonality test of individual and average forecasts (information set X is change in spot rate over previous week)

	Deutschmark		Sterling		Yen	
	T_1	T_2	T_1	T_2	T_1	T_2
C1	0.007	0.019	0.035	0.044	0.002	0.005
C5	0.003	0.002	0.036	0.015	0.024	0.049
F2	0.001	0.001				
F10	0.019	0.045	0.056	0.050	0.057	0.163
F12	0.001	0.005	0.036	0.103	0.044	0.030
I6	0.001	0.003			0.035	0.093
I10	0.011	0.036	0.091	0.071	0.103	0.255
J1					0.098	0.214
J3					0.405	0.531
J7					0.086	0.051
J14	0.035	0.043			0.016	0.020
J20	0.004	0.013	0.065	0.159	0.054	0.031
B16	0.006	0.010	0.031	0.048	0.013	0.028
B25			0.011	0.025		
B29	0.000	0.000	0.008	0.016		
B32			0.260	0.227		
B35	0.001	0.003	0.023	0.054	0.000	0.000
US	0.043	0.072				
U5			0.126	0.197	0.037	0.110
U20	0.003	0.011				
U24	0.013	0.046				
G5	0.016	0.035	0.049	0.029	0.016	0.033
G8	0.003	0.003	0.025	0.009	0.017	0.049
G10	0.029	0.056			0.027	0.082
G12	0.092	0.238	0.676	0.304		
G13	0.000	0.001	0.009	0.027	0.001	0.001
G14	0.016	0.026	0.016	0.017	0.007	0.025
G15	0.000	0.000	0.000	0.000	0.014	0.037
G22	0.036	0.087	0.069	0.090		
G23	0.000	0.001				
Averages						
Canadian	0.005	0.007	0.033	0.027	0.007	0.025
French	0.002	0.004	0.039	0.072	0.029	0.059
Italian	0.002	0.009	0.091	0.071	0.060	0.170
Japanese	0.011	0.023	0.065	0.160	0.057	0.152
British	0.001	0.001	0.024	0.045	0.001	0.001
American	0.011	0.035	0.126	0.197	0.037	0.110
German	0.003	0.009	0.024	0.024	0.005	0.014
All	0.002	0.006	0.030	0.040	0.011	0.033
Forward	0.111	0.112	0.296	0.081	0.244	0.386

T_1 denotes the marginal significance of a chi-square test of $\Phi_1 = 0$, T_2 the marginal significance of a chi-square test of $\Phi_0 = 0/\Phi_1 = 0$.

the RMSEs using the forward and current spot rates as forecasts.[17,18] The distributions of these errors for each currency are presented graphically in Figures 1–3, and numerically in Table III. Only two individual forecasters managed to beat a forecast of 'no change', using this measure of accuracy.[19] These results are very supportive of the Meese and Rogoff (1983) findings, and indicate that the spot rate is efficient. The forward rate is always outperformed by the current rate, which, in turn, supports the findings of Goodhart *et al.* (1992), who conclude that the forward premium/discount contains no information about subsequent changes in the exchange rate. Note that (only) two forecasters manage to beat the forward rate and a random walk.

As a second measure, we calculated the profits accruing from speculation in the forward market. If the forecast was for a depreciation of the dollar in excess of that priced into the forward rate, a 3-month forward contract is deemed to have been sold, and vice versa. This is clearly only an approximate measure of trading profits as the possibility of an early closing of the contract (cutting of losses) is ignored, but it has the advantage of showing the importance of the qualitative predictions embedded in our forecasts.[20] That is, the accuracy of a forecast in terms of RMSE is possibly less important to a trader than correctly predicting

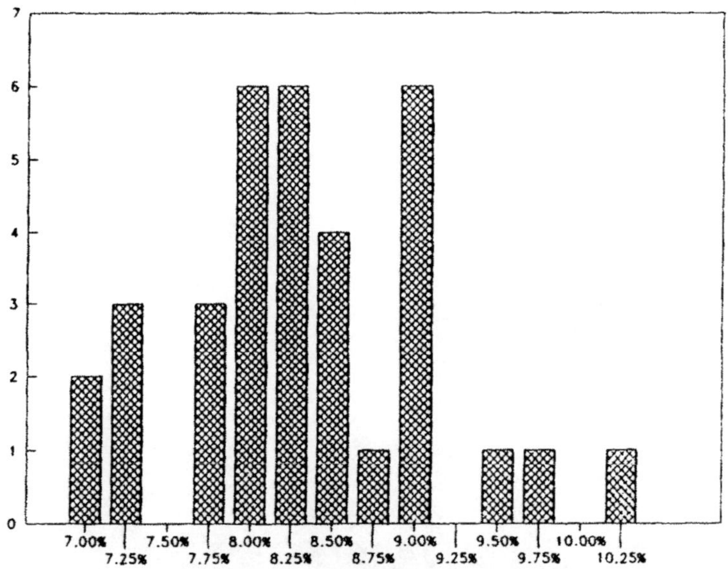

Figure 1. Distribution of RMSE – DEM

[17] The latter being the naive random walk forecast of no change.

[18] We initially transformed the data into logs which implies that the RMSE figures are approximately percentage measures.

[19] Unfortunately, these two forecasters, U20 and U24, only replied to the questionnaire regarding their forecasts of the deutschmark and so we cannot see whether they are equally good for the full range of currencies.

[20] An alternative measure would be the profits from a buy-and-hold strategy.

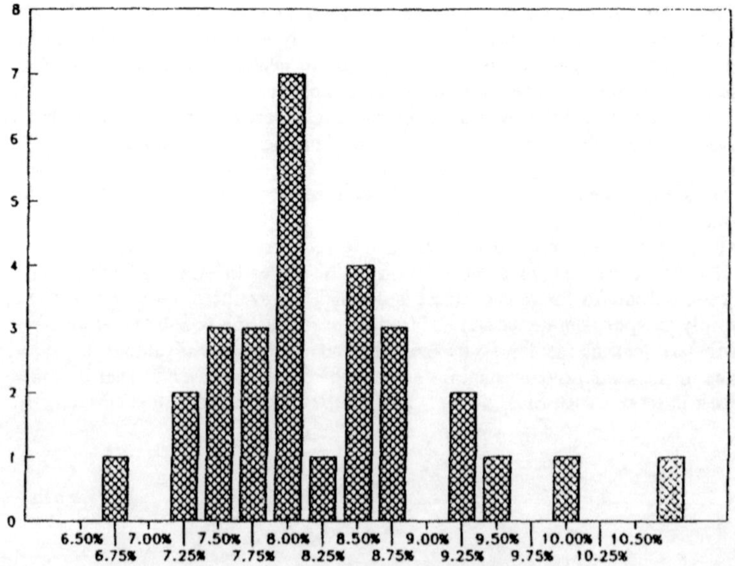

Figure 2. Distribution of RMSE – STG

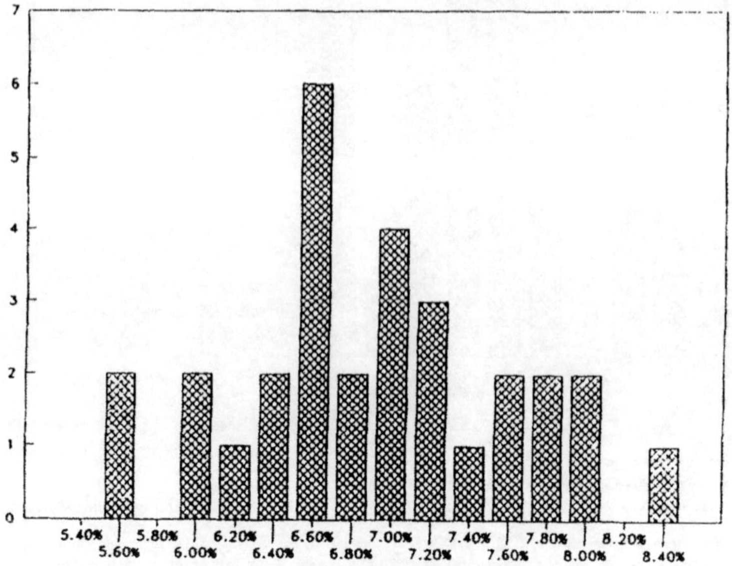

Figure 3. Distribution of RMSE – JPY

Table III. Errors and profits from forward speculation (uncorrected)

	Deutschmark		Sterling		Japanese yen	
	RMSE	Profit/ (loss)	RMSE	Profit/ (loss)	RMSE	Profit/ (loss)
Individuals						
C1	8.09	(44.40)[a]	7.77	(16.59)	6.82	8.16
C5	7.96	(70.46)	7.59	(11.81)	6.67	(79.02)
F2	8.80	(130.00)				
F10	8.84	(121.68)	8.31	(70.39)	7.17	(46.04)
F12	8.18	19.40[a]	7.76	69.91	6.00	18.78
I6	8.19	(7.82)[a]			7.42	(14.63)
I10	7.70	(33.28)[a]	7.98	(54.99)	6.79	(42.48)
J1					7.53	(12.46)
J3					6.58	(60.32)
J7					6.58	44.66[a]
J14	8.87	(12.18)[a]			7.99	(68.60)
J20	8.18	26.98[a]	8.28	62.51	7.05	30.98[a]
B16	7.70	(2.24)[a]	7.48	135.77	6.42	26.06[a]
B25			8.13	(12.51)		
B29	7.53	(74.14)	7.07	54.97		
B32			7.80	(19.23)		
B35	8.18	(35.34)[a]	8.52	11.57	8.35	17.94
U1	7.87	(145.86)				
U5			7.31	(16.03)	5.89	(4.74)
U20	6.93[b]	31.40[a]				
U24	6.94[b]	35.90[a]				
G5	8.17	(32.24)[a]	8.33	(156.77)	6.38	(25.12)
G8	9.69	(186.28)	9.43	(156.65)	7.87	(125.72)
G10	8.80	(42.80)[a]			7.39	(86.06)
G12	8.34	(48.82)[a]	10.59	(15.83)		
G13	10.01	(79.28)	9.97	(73.89)	7.68	(24.36)
G14	8.36	22.60[a]	9.20	(136.29)	7.19	(38.16)
G15	9.38	(27.78)[a]	9.09	20.51	7.70	(45.90)
G22	8.94	(116.14)	8.73	(132.49)		
G23	8.55	(31.90)[a]				
Averages						
Canadian	7.88	(59.84)	7.54	(15.43)	6.54	2.04
French	8.28	(98.26)	7.77	(33.73)	6.23	35.56[a]
Italian	7.78	(14.40)[a]	7.98	(54.99)	6.96	(70.18)
Japanese	8.19	(12.08)[a]	8.28	62.51	6.52	(9.66)
British	7.78	(15.70)[a]	7.52	(5.31)	6.95	18.68
American	7.07	3.72[a]	7.31	(16.03)	5.89	(4.74)
German	8.49	(87.96)	8.67	(128.85)	6.94	(35.60)
All	7.94	(35.72)[a]	7.87	(43.35)	6.50	6.36
Random walk	7.03[a]	(56.38)	6.62[a]	142.03	5.46[a]	21.44
Forward	7.04		7.12		5.55	

In RMSE columns, [a]smaller value than forward rate, [b]smaller value than forward rate and random walk.
In Profit columns, [a]higher profit than random walk.

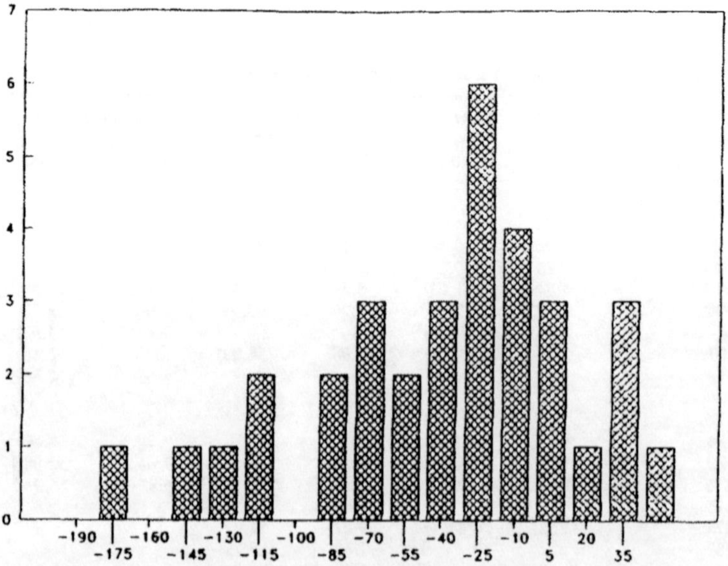

Figure 4. Distribution of profits – DEM

the direction of currency movements.[21] The results are given in Figures 4–6, and Table III. Comparison with the RMSE results is instructive. A random walk forecast no longer clearly dominates. Trading on the basis of a forecast of no change results in losses for the deutschmark, but is still the best strategy for the pound. It should also be noted that poor forecasts in terms of RMSE can be profitable. Forecaster B35, for example, has the highest RMSE for the yen and yet forward trading on the basis of his forecasts results in a profit. We leave for further research the question of whether these profits are a return for risk bearing, but we note that speculation based on individual forecasts resulted, on average, in losses, and that out of 63 forecast series only 17 forecasters (less than 27%) returned a profit. Of these 17, only eight outperformed their respective random walks.

If our forecasters are unable to clearly dominate a random walk forecast, can we detect any systematic difference between their performances? In analysing the performance of US forecasters, Stekler (1987) suggested the use of a non-parametric test which, when the analysis was corrected by Bachelor (1988), turned out to be Friedman's (1937) test for two-way analysis of variance by ranks. The procedure is as follows.

The absolute forecast errors are mapped into ranks for each forecast date. These ranks are then summed across time for each forecaster to produce a rank sum, r_j. Under the null hypothesis of no significant differences in rank, the expected value of r_j is $T(n+1)/2$, where T is the number of observations and n the number of forecasters. Similarly, the sampling variance of an individual rank statistic is $n(n+1)/12$ and so for T independent ranks is

[21] The authors are exploring the accuracy of forecast direction in current research.

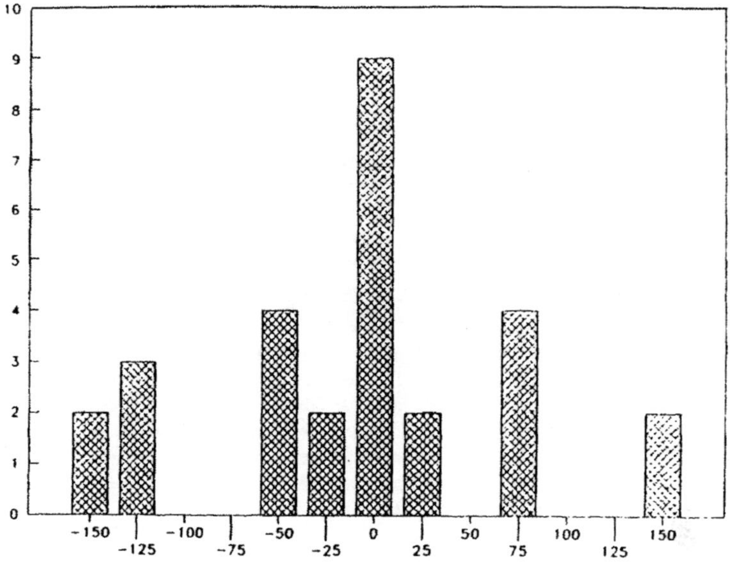

Figure 5. Distribution of profits – STG

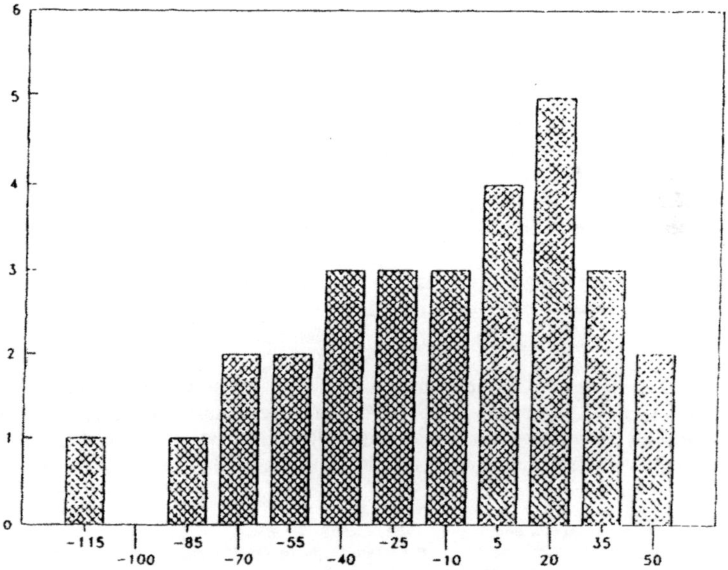

Figure 6. Distribution of profits – JPY

Table IV. Friedman's test of independence of rank

	T	n	Φ	$\chi^2_{(n-1)}$	Marg. sig.
Deutschmark	27	24	41.43	35.2	0.011
Sterling	27	19	43.05	28.9	0.001
Yen	27	20	29.08	30.1	0.065
Pooled 13	81	13	39.23	21.0	0.000

$Tn(n+1)/12$. The test statistic is:

$$\phi = \sum_{l=1}^{n} \frac{(r_l - T(n+1)/2)^2}{Tn(n+1)/12} \tag{3}$$

which under the null hypothesis of no systematic assignment of ranks will be asymptotically distributed as chi-square with $n-1$ degrees of freedom.[22] The values of ϕ for each of the three currencies are given in Table IV, together with that for a pooling of the three currencies for the core group of 13 forecasters. Given the low power of non-parametric tests, these results are strongly indicative of systematic differences in forecasting power. Nevertheless, although the forecasts are different, they are still not very good. We now turn to the question of whether by combining the forecasts we can improve their accuracy.

THE PERFORMANCE OF FORECAST COMBINATIONS

We have demonstrated that individual forecasts are not very accurate, are biased, and do not take full account of available information. There are exceptions (most notably U20 and U24) and for some currencies even the least accurate are still profitable to follow. We have also demonstrated that the performance of our forecasters is not randomly generated. It would seem that at least some of our forecasts contain information. We have noted that ideally we would like to pool the information sets on which the forecasts are conditioned. As these data are clearly not available, the next best method is to combine the forecasts themselves. In order to evaluate these composite forecasts we must note that within-sample, unconstrained combinations of forecasts must match or outperform the components in terms of accuracy (though not necessarily profitability). The only true test of performance is an out-of-sample comparison.

We shall use the simple Granger–Ramanathan method to optimally combine the forecasts, whereby the following regression is run:

$$\Delta S_{t+k} = \alpha + \sum \beta_i \, \Delta S^e_{it+k}, \qquad i = 1, \ldots, n \tag{4}$$

That is, the actual change in the spot exchange rate is regressed on a constant and a set of n forecast changes. Due to the substantial location and scale biases[23] in the forecasts noted above, no constraints are imposed on equation (4). Running this regression to combine a number of forecasts will result in negative weights on some of the components. This is not

[22] Iman and Davenport (1980) suggest a small-sample version of the Friedman statistic which has an approximate F-distribution. Computing this alternative form had little effect on the marginal significance levels found.

[23] Location bias indicates a constant non-zero mean error ($\alpha \neq 0$), while a scale bias occurs when a forecaster systematically under- or over-predicts ($\beta \neq 1$).

necessarily a comment on the forecaster's ability but, rather, indicates the way the predictions should be combined given the correlations between forecasts. However, running equation (4) with just one forecast is equivalent to unbiasing the forecast. We do this for each of our individual forecasters and test the out-of-sample accuracy of these 'corrected' forecasts.

We have a total of 27 observations available, eight of which are saved for the out-of-sample tests. Our in-sample period, then, is October 1989 to April 1991, while our test period is May 1991 through December 1991. However, a researcher looking to combine forecasts in May 1991, the first of our test months, would only have outcome errors for the months up to February 1991.[24] This leaves just 17 in-sample observations in which to construct the weights. For each currency we have at least 19 forecasters—a severe shortage of degrees of freedom. We chose to split our forecasters into subgroups to overcome this problem. For example, for forecasts of the mark exchange rate we formed three groups consisting of nine German, eight other European and seven Other (Canadian, Japanese, and US) forecasters. Noting that we are seeking to pool information and that grouping homogeneous forecasters will not yield maximum benefits, we also combined the forecasts of our core group of 13 (which contains representatives from all seven countries) and the best five forecasters (in terms of in sample RMSE) for each currency. (Details of the groups are given in the Appendix.)

From equation (4) we retrieve the optimal weights attached to each forecast and use them to construct a set of out-of-sample 'optimal' forecasts. Three 'optimal' forecasts for each grouping of forecasters were constructed. In the first instance, the initial in-sample weights are taken as fixed throughout the out-of-sample period. We also compute weights which are updated as new information about the performance of our forecasters is received, using the full set of historical information. Finally, following Diebold and Pauly (1987), we update the weights using only the last T^* observations in an attempt to lessen the effect of any shifts in the structure of the forecast errors or covariance matrix. The size of our largest group constrains our choice of T^* and we use the most recent twelve observations. This, of course, precludes this type of weighting for G13.

The accuracy of these various combinations in terms of root mean squared errors and mean absolute errors (MAE) are detailed in Tables V to VII.[25] A few general results emerge. Exchange rates in our test period are more stable than in the rest of our sample period, since the random walk RMSEs are up to 2.1% lower than those computed over the full data period and shown in Table IV. Second, the Average forecast (an unweighed mean of all forecasts of each currency), while a worse predictor than the current spot or forward rate, is frequently as accurate as the 'optimal' combinations. The Average forecasts also perform better in the test period than in the full sample. Third, combining large numbers of forecasts tends to give poor results. For the G13 grouping the weights are unstable as correlations change, and the resultant errors are very large. This also holds true for the combined German forecasts of the pound and mark. Finally, updating weights as new information becomes available generally reduces errors whereas using only the most recent (twelve) observations in calculations appears to be detrimental. This last point, even more than the others, may be due to the small sample size available.

Turning to more specific results, no grouping is able to beat the RMSE and MAE scores of

[24] In fact, it is possible that January's forecast error is the latest available as the February forecast day may be later than the day on which the May predictions are made (see MacDonald, 1992, for more detail). We ignore this point as the overlap is only of the order of a couple of days.

[25] With a large enough sample we would have liked to calculate speculative profits from these combinations. This is something we hope to do as our data sample extends.

the random walk model for the deutschmark and pound sterling, no matter how the weights are chosen. Combinations of the Best 5 deutschmark forecasters come closest, and using full sample updating can marginally beat the RMSE of a random walk (but not the mean absolute error). Given that this grouping includes two individual forecasts which clearly outperform a no-change prediction over the full sample, U20 and U24, this is an indictment of the other three forecasts.[26,27] No combination comes close to challenging the pre-eminence of the random walk for sterling.

The yen tells a slightly different story. Both the groupings of the German and Best 5

Table V. Root mean squared and mean absolute errors no updating of weights

	Deutschmark		Sterling		Yen	
	RMSE	MAE	RMSE	MAE	RMSE	MAE
Random walk	5.90	4.63	4.52	3.43	3.45	3.03
Forward rate	6.55	5.25	5.41	4.21	3.76	3.38
Average[c]	7.20	5.82	5.92	4.95	4.99	4.26
G13	33.22	31.04	13.06	11.58	12.48	10.92
Best 5[c]	6.18[a]	5.49	8.40	7.28	2.12[b]	1.80[b]
German[c]	31.77	27.82	29.18	17.24	2.80[b]	2.52[b]
British			7.33	5.81		
Japanese					5.48	3.99
European	12.69	10.37				
Others[c]	6.23[a]	5.26	11.76	9.71	9.00	7.74

[a] Smaller value than forward rate.
[b] Smaller than forward rate and random walk.
[c] Note that the composition of these groups changes for different currencies. See Appendix for group compositions.

Table VI. Root mean squared and mean absolute errors updating of weights over full sample

	Deutschmark		*Sterling*		*Yen*	
	RMSE	MAE	RMSE	MAE	RMSE	MAE
Random walk	5.90	4.63	4.52	3.43	3.45	3.03
Forward rate	6.55	5.25	5.41	4.21	3.76	3.38
Average[c]	7.20	5.82	5.92	4.95	4.99	4.26
G13	22.64	18.92	10.80	8.95	10.52	7.60
Best 5[c]	5.84[b]	5.21[a]	6.80	5.04	2.36[b]	2.13[b]
German[c]	22.88	17.75	30.72	20.07	2.70[b]	2.21[b]
British			6.53	4.96		
Japanese					3.84	3.00[b]
European	13.07	9.65				
Others[c]	7.56	6.13	8.12	5.77	8.55	7.34

[a–c] As Table V.

[26] In fact, in the out-of-sample period, both of these forecasters are beaten by J14, which is also included in the Best 5.
[27] U20, U24, and J14 are also in the 'Other' group which explains the reasonably good performance of this combination.

Table VII. Root mean squared and mean absolute errors updating of weights using previous twelve observations

	Deutschmark		Sterling		Yen	
	RMSE	MAE	RMSE	MAE	RMSE	MAE
Random walk	5.90	4.63	4.52	3.43	3.45	3.03
Forward rate	6.55	5.25	5.41	4.21	3.76	3.38
Average[c]	7.20	5.82	5.92	4.95	4.99	4.26
G13	NA	NA	NA	NA	NA	NA
Best 5[c]	6.55	5.84	6.40	5.19	4.24	4.15
German[c]	33.95	23.88	32.00	17.62	5.97	4.67
British			8.64	6.37		
Japanese					4.86	3.50
European	26.52	21.32				
Others[c]	8.06	4.86[a]	15.48	13.37	9.81	7.30

[a,c] As Table V.

Table VIII. Out-of-sample errors ('corrected' individual forecasts)

	Deutschmark		Sterling		Japanese yen	
	RMSE	MAE	RMSE	MAE	RMSE	MAE
Random walk	5.90	4.63	4.52	3.43	3.45	3.03
Forward rate	6.55	5.25	5.41	4.21	3.76	3.38
C1	4.88[b]	4.01[b]	3.71[b]	3.23[b]	1.90[b]	1.25[b]
C5	4.62[b]	6.59	3.48[b]	4.02[a]	1.91[b]	1.45[b]
F2	4.67[b]	5.75				
F10	5.69[b]	5.75	3.89[b]	3.27[b]	1.60[b]	1.38[b]
F12	6.40[a]	7.85	4.29[b]	3.67[a]	3.74[a]	1.61[b]
I6	5.48[b]	6.75			1.86[b]	2.45[b]
I10	4.67[b]	5.14[a]	4.47[b]	2.97[b]	2.87[b]	1.58[b]
J1					2.70[b]	1.53[b]
J3					1.64[b]	1.34[b]
J7					2.91[b]	1.89[b]
J14	7.26	8.95			1.70[b]	2.78[b]
J20	5.66[b]	7.15	7.59	3.71[a]	3.93	1.89[b]
B16	4.71[b]	5.53	3.52[b]	3.52[a]	2.68[b]	1.87[b]
B25			3.83[b]	3.23[b]		
B29	4.61[b]	5.50	3.42[b]	3.67[a]		
B32			4.23[b]	3.36[b]		
B35	5.10[b]	5.06[a]	3.94[b]	3.32[b]	3.55[a]	2.30[b]
U1	5.72[b]	4.41[b]				
U5			3.76[b]	3.26[b]	2.79[b]	1.15[b]
U20	4.53[b]	5.04[a]				
U24	4.77[b]	4.53[b]				
G5	4.44[b]	4.64[a]	5.12[a]	3.76[a]	3.78	1.22[b]
G8	5.00[b]	7.21	6.39	3.53[a]	2.65[b]	1.90[b]
G10	4.55[b]	4.15[b]			2.41[b]	1.10[b]
G12	5.46[b]	6.28	14.96	6.43		
G13	8.73	8.04	8.73	3.58[a]	2.36[b]	2.66[b]
G14	4.61[b]	5.54	3.92[b]	3.71[a]	1.63[b]	1.56[b]
G15	5.00[b]	8.50	3.44[b]	3.90[a]	1.65[b]	1.83[b]
G22	6.67	6.60	7.27	3.88[a]		
G23	4.96[b]	6.15				

[a–c] As Table V.

forecasters convincingly outperform the current spot rate as a predictor of future rates when the full in-sample information is used to construct the weights. Interestingly, the Best 5 forecasters come from five different countries, and the only forecaster common to both groups, G5, does not have a dominant influence in either combination. It appears that combining information contained in some forecasts can lead to significant gains in forecast accuracy for the Japanese yen, though not for the two European currencies.

As we noted above, however, an unconstrained combination of forecasts also corrects for the bias in the forecasts. Have the gains in accuracy found from combining yen forecasts been because of information pooling or because we have removed bias? The errors of the corrected or unbiased individual forecasts are given in Table VIII. They indicate that by combining corrected forecasts we have actually lost accuracy. For all three currencies, merely correcting the in-sample bias of individual forecasters usually results in a better performance than the spot rate in an out-of-sample context.[28]

The fact that supposedly optimal combinations do so badly is due to changing correlations between forecasters. These changing correlations represent, we feel, the substantial amount of judgement that go into making these forecasts. For this reason, we do not feel that the good performance of our corrected individual forecasts is robust to extensions in the data sample. Furthermore, forecasters learn from, and work to correct, their mistakes, and the parameters used to unbias these forecasts will change.

SUMMARY AND CONCLUSIONS

In this paper we have used a high-quality disaggregate database to examine whether individual forecasters produce efficient forecasts and also whether the properties of the forecasts change when they are combined. In terms of the former testing strategy, we found that some are better than others, but that most are not as good as a naive no-change prediction. Further, available information is not efficiently incorporated into forecasts and this is interpreted as reflecting irrationality. In terms of the second part of our testing strategy, we found that pooling forecasters information sets by combining their forecasts possibly adds to the accuracy of the predictions, but the gains mainly reflect the removal of systematic bias. This bias does not appear to be stable over time, and this may explain the poor performance of combined forecasts. The fact that adjusted forecasts can be more accurate than the spot and forward rates as predictors indicates that there is information available to traders that is not incorporated into the market rates. However, with just two possible exceptions, the fact that individual forecasters are unable to beat these rates over an extended period implies that this information is widely scattered. Our non-parametric tests, which indicated differing abilities, could reflect one of two possibilities. There may just be some very bad forecasters which make the merely poor look good by comparison. On the other hand, scarce but unincorporated information may not be randomly scattered, but rather lies in the hands of a select few. We hope that this will show up as our data set extends over time.

---

[28] Holden and Peel (1989) address aspects of forecast bias and combination. They show that the unrestricted regression method of combination which we have used not only corrects for in-sample bias but also includes the unconditional mean of in-sample exchange rate changes as an additional forecast. They argue that including the mean of the dependent variable as an extra forecast may not be appropriate as it is typically a very poor predictor. In our situation, however, the mean change in exchange rates is very close to zero and so is in fact a good forecast.

APPENDIX: DETAILS OF GROUPINGS

All currencies

G13	C1 C5 F10 F12 I10 J20 B16 B35 G5 G8 G13 G14 G15

Deutschmark

Best 5	J14 U20 U24 G23 G5
German	G5 G8 G10 G12 G13 G14 G15 G22 G23
European	F2 F10 F12 I6 I10 B16 B29 B35
Other	C1 C5 J14 J20 U1 U20 U24

Sterling

Best 5	B29 U5 B25 B16 F12
German	G5 G8 G12 G13 G14 G15 G22
British	B16 B25 B29 B32 B35
Other	F10 F12 I10 J20 C1 C5 U5

Japanese yen

Best 5	U5 G5 J7 F12 I10
German	G5 G8 G10 G13 G14 G15
Japanese	J1 J3 J7 J14 J20
Other	C1 C5 F10 F12 I6 I10 B16 B35 U5

ACKNOWLEDGEMENTS

We are grateful to Michael Sykes of Consensus Economics for providing the survey data together with the Nuffield Foundation and ESRC (Grant No: R000232945) for financial support. We would also like to thank two anonymous referees for their helpful comments.

REFERENCES

Allen, H. L. and Taylor, M. P., 'Charts, noise and fundamentals in the foreign exchange market', *Economic Journal*, **100** (Supplement) (1990), 49–59.

Ball, R. J., Burns, T. and Warburton, P. S., 'The London Business School model of the UK economy: an exercise in international monetarism', in P. Ormerod (ed.), *Economic Modelling*, (London: Heinemann, 1979.

Batchelor, R. A., 'All forecasters are equal', *Journal of Business and Economic Statistics*, **8** (1988), 143–4.

Bates, J. M. and Granger, C. W. J., 'The combination of forecasts', *Operational Research Quarterly*, **20** (1969), 451–68.

Bilson, J. F. O. and Hsieh, D. A., 'The profitability of currency speculation', *International Journal of Forecasting*, 3 (1987), 115–130.

Blake, D., Beenstock, M. and Brasse V., 'The performance of UK exchange rate forecasters', *Economic Journal*, **96** (1986), 986–99.

Boothe, P. and Glassman, D., 'Comparing exchange rate forecasting models: accuracy versus profitability', *International Journal of Forecasting*, **3** (1987), 65–79.

Clemen, R. T., 'Linear constraints and the efficiency of combined forecasts', *Journal of Forecasting*, **5** (1986), 31–8.

Crane, D. B. and Crotty, J. R., 'A two-stage forecasting model: exponential smoothing and multiple regression', *Management Science*, **13** (1967), B501–7.

Cyriax, G. (ed.), *World Index of Economic Forecasts*, Farnborough: Gower Press, 1978.

Diebold, F. X. and Pauly, P., 'Structural change and the combination of forecasts', *Journal of Forecasting*, **6** (1987), 21–40.

Dominguez, K. N., 'Are foreign exchange forecasts rational? New evidence from survey data', *Economics Letters*, **21** (1986), 277–82.

Dornbusch, R. and Frankel, J., 'The flexible exchange rate system: experience and alternatives', in S. Borner (ed.), *International Trade and Finance in a Polycentric World*, London: Macmillan, 1987.

Figlewski, S. and Urich, T., 'Optimal aggregation of money supply forecasts: accuracy, profitability and market efficiency', *Journal of Finance*, **28** (1983), 695–710.

Finn, M. G., 'Forecasting the exchange rate: a monetary or random walk phenomenon?' *Journal of International Money and Finance*, **5** (1986), 181–93.

Frankel, J. and Froot, K., 'Understanding the dollar in the eighties: the expectations of chartists and fundamentalists', *Economic Record*, (1986), 24–38.

Frankel, J. and Froot, K., 'Using survey data to test standard propositions regarding exchange rate expectations', *American Economic Review*, **77** (1987), 133–53.

Frankel, J. and Froot, K., 'Interpreting tests of forward discount bias using survey data on exchange rate expectations', *Quarterly Journal of Economics*, **104** (1989), 139–61.

Frankel, J. and Froot, K., 'Chartists, fundamentalists, and the demand for dollars', in A. S. Courakis and M. P. Taylor (eds), *Private Behaviour and Government Policy in Interdependent Economies*, Oxford: Clarendon Press, 1990.

Friedman, M., 'The use of ranks to void the assumption of normality implicit in the analysis of variance', *Journal of the American Statistical Association*, **32** (1937), 675–701.

Goodhart, C. A. E., McMahon P. C. and Ngama, Y. L., 'Does the forward premium/discount help to predict the future change in the exchange rate?' *Scottish Journal of Political Economy*, **39** (1992), 129–40.

Goodman, S. H., 'Foreign exchange forecasting techniques: implications for business and policy', *Journal of Finance*, **34** (1979), 415–27.

Granger, C. W. J. and Ramanathan, R., 'Improved methods of forecasting', *Journal of Forecasting*, **3** (1984), 197–204.

Guerard, J. B., 'Composite model building for foreign exchange rates, *Journal of Forecasting*, **8** (1989), 315–29.

Hansen, L. P., 'Large sample properties of generalised method of moments estimators', *Econometrica*, **50**, 1029–54.

Hartzmark, M. L., 'Luck versus forecast ability: determinants of trader performance in futures markets', *Journal of Business*, **64** (1991), 49–74.

Hodrick, R. J., *The Empirical Evidence on the Efficiency of Forward and Futures Foreign Exchange Markets*, Chur: Harwood, 1987.

Holden, K. and Peel, D. A., 'Unbiasedness, efficiency and the combination of economic forecasts', *Journal of Forecasting*, **8** (1989), 175–88.

Iman, R. L. and Davenport, J. M., 'Approximations of the critical region of the Friedman statistic', *Communications in Statistics*, **A9** (1980), 571–95.

Kirman, A., 'Epidemics of opinion and speculative bubbles in financial markets', in M. P. Taylor (ed.), *Money and Financial Markets*, Cambridge, MA: Basil Blackwell, 1991.

Krasker, W. S., '"The peso problem" in testing the efficiency of forward exchange markets', *Journal of Monetary Economics*, **6** (1980), 269–76.

MacDonald, R., *Floating Exchange Rates: Theories and Evidence*, London: Unwin Hyman, 1988.

MacDonald, R., 'Are foreign exchange market forecasters "rational"? Some survey-based tests', *Manchester School of Economic and Social Studies*, **58** (1990), 229–41.

MacDonald, R., 'Exchange rate survey data: a disaggregated G—7 perspective', *Manchester School of Economic and Social Studies*, **LX** (Supplement) (1992), 47–62.

MacDonald, R. and Torrance, T. S., 'On risk, rationality and excessive speculation in the deutschmark–US dollar exchange market: some evidence using survey data', *Oxford Bulletin of Economics and Statistics*, **51** (1988), 107–23.

MacDonald, R. and Torrance, T. S., 'Expectations formation and risk in four foreign exchange markets', *Oxford Economic Papers*, **42** (1990), 544–61.

MacDonald, R. and Taylor, M. P., 'Exchange rate economics: a survey', *International Monetary Fund Staff Papers*, **39** (1992), 1–57.
Makridakis, S. and Hibon, M., 'Accuracy of forecasting: an empirical investigation', *Journal of the Royal Statistical Society. Series A*, **142** (1979), 97–145.
Meese, R. A. and Rogoff, K., 'Empirical exchange rate models of the seventies: do they fit out of sample?' *Journal of International Economics*, **14** (1983), 3–24.
Meese, R. A. and Rogoff, K., 'The out-of-sample failure of empirical exchange rate models: sampling error or misspecification?' in J. A. Frenkel (ed.), *Exchange Rates and International Macroeconomics*, Chicago, IL: University of Chicago Press, 1984.
Newbold, P. and Granger, C. W. J., 'Experience with forecasting univariate time series and the combination of forecasts', *Journal of the Royal Statistical Society, Series A*, **137** (1974), 131–49.
Reinmuth, J. E. and Guerts, M. D., 'A multideterministic approach to forecasting', in S. Makridakis and S. C. Wheelwright (eds), *Forecasting*, Vol. 12, TIMS Studies in the Management Sciences, New York, North-Holland, 1979.
Stekler, H. O., 'Who forecasts better?', *Journal of Business and Economic Statistics*, **5** (1987), 155–8.
Taylor, M. P. and Allen, H. L., 'The use of technical analysis in the foreign exchange market', *Journal of International Money and Finance*, **11** (1992), 304–14.
Webb, R. H., 'Inadequate tests of the rationality of forecasts', Paper presented at 1984 meetings of Western Economic Association, Las Vegas.
Winkler, R. L., 'Combining forecasts', in S. Makridakis *et al.* (eds), *The Forecasting Accuracy of Major Time Series Methods*, New York: Wiley, 1984.
Wolff, C. P., 'Forward foreign exchange rates, expected spot rates and premia: a signal-extraction approach', *Journal of Finance*, **42** (1987), 395–406.

Authors' biographies:
Ronald MacDonald is Professor of International Finance in the Department of Economics and the Centre for International Macroeconomic Modelling at the University of Strathclyde. He is the author of numerous books and journal articles on international economics.
Ian Marsh is a research assistant in the Economics Department at the University of Strathclyde. He is currently reading for his PhD on exchange rate forecasting and modelling.

Authors' address:
Ronald MacDonald and **Ian Marsh**, Department of Economics, University of Strathclyde, Curran Building, 100 Cathedral Street, Glasgow G4 0LN, Scotland.

[17]

Pergamon

Journal of International Money and Finance, Vol. 15, No. 5, pp. 665–685, 1996
Copyright © 1996 Elsevier Science Ltd
Printed in Great Britain. All rights reserved
S0261-5606(96)00030-7 0261-5606/96 $15.00 + 0.00

Currency forecasters are heterogeneous: confirmation and consequences

RONALD MACDONALD

Department of Economics, University of Strathclyde, Glasgow G4 OLN, UK

AND

IAN W MARSH*

Department of Economics, University of Strathclyde, Glasgow G4 OLN, UK

Using a disaggregated international survey database we demonstrate that foreign exchange forecasters hold heterogeneous expectations. We find that a major cause of these differences of opinion is the idiosyncratic interpretation of widely available information, and that this heterogeneity translates into economically meaningful differences in forecast accuracy. Finally, we show that such disagreements are key variables in determining market trading volume. (JEL F31). Copyright © 1996 Elsevier Science Ltd

Recently it has become fashionable to use survey-based data to examine the behavior of financial asset prices.[1] One of the main advantages of such data is that it facilitates an examination of the behavior of asset prices without recourse to auxiliary assumptions concerning the formation of expectations. Much of the existing survey literature utilizes a 'consensus' measure of expectations, such as the mean or median response. Without doubt papers that have used this measure have shed considerable light on the operation of a variety of asset markets. For example, in terms of the foreign exchange market, the focus of this study, Frankel and Froot (1987, 1989) find considerable evidence to

*The authors are grateful to Agnes Benassy, the co-editor, Michael Melvin, an anonymous referee and participants at the colloquium La Formation des Anticipations Economiques, held at the Sorbonne, Paris 1995 for their very helpful comments on earlier versions of this paper, Michael Sykes of Consensus Economics for providing some of the data used in this study, and the Nuffield Foundation and the ESRC (Grant Number: R000232945) for financial support. The usual disclaimer applies.

support the view that exchange rate expectations are stabilizing and that time-varying foreign exchange risk premia are not important. But do studies that rely on a consensus measure of expectations actually conceal more than they reveal? There are in fact a number of reasons why one might want to utilize survey data which have a greater level of disaggregation than the mean or median response.[2]

For example, information is lost when just the mean or median forecast is used if forecasts differ. In terms of the foreign exchange market, speculative foreign exchange trades are most likely to occur if different valuation expectations are held,[3] and the immense turnover in this market suggests *a priori* that we should expect a degree of heterogeneity among market practitioners. Furthermore, aggregated forecasts have at best a very weak link with the marginal individuals who trade in the market and in many instances determine the price of foreign exchange (see Tagaki, 1991). However, the future spot price of currency is clearly related to individual forecasts weighted by the volume of trades that are made as a result of each forecast. The existence of heterogeneity in foreign exchange markets is the motivation for the recently developed market micro-structure literature (see Frankel and Rose, 1994), and a finding in support of such heterogeneity offers a base on which to build models such as those developed by Lyons (1991, 1993).

Although several researchers have begun to use survey data, most studies have relied on data sourced from a single country. However, due to the global nature of the foreign exchange market there are problems with using such forecasts, or even worse, forecasts from a single financial center. It is our contention that for there to be a reliable relationship between the individual forecasts and the (marginal) price, the survey must cover as large a section of market participants as possible—it should be disaggregated both within and across countries.

In this paper we utilize a survey database which is both wide ranging, in terms of the financial centers surveyed, and highly disaggregate in nature. By including corporate forecasters, professional forecasting agencies (whose predictions are used by other market participants) and financial institutions from the G-7 countries, as wide a coverage as possible is achieved. As the panel provides predictions on three exchange rates over two forecast horizons it is possible to examine any differences in an individual's forecasts across currencies and prediction periods.

We believe that an understanding of how asset prices are determined is crucial to both theoretical work and for making policy prescriptions. Thus the extent to which participants in asset markets are driven by fads (or other extraneous forms of asset pricing) may have an important bearing on the type of foreign exchange market policy that should be adopted. In this paper we hope to shed some further light on the operation of what is perhaps the key asset market and this, in turn, may aid both policy makers and theoretical modelers. Our investigation specifically concentrates on the degree of heterogeneity among foreign exchange market forecasters.

The outline of the remainder of this paper is as follows. In the next section we describe the disaggregate survey data set used for our empirical tests and the definitions of the market data utilized. In Section II we consider the causes of heterogeneity among our panel of exchange rate forecasters using a test due to Ito and a simple extension of his procedure. We then, in Section III, perform non-parametric tests designed to see whether the heterogeneity highlighted in Section I translates into systematically different forecast performances. The extent of such heterogeneous forecasting performance is the topic of Section IV. The final element in our investigation of heterogeneity is to determine if it is indeed (as suggested above) related to market turnover, and this is considered in Section V. The paper closes with a summary and some concluding comments.

I. Description of data and data sources

Since October 1989 Consensus Forecasts of London have surveyed and published the forecasts of economists, foreign exchange dealers and executives in over 150 companies and institutions in the G-7 nations. The companies surveyed are mainly commercial and investment banks, but industrial corporations and forecasting agencies (whose predictions form an input to the decisions of other forecasters) are also polled.[4] Respondents return a fax on the first Monday of each month containing their point forecasts of the dollar–sterling, Deutsche mark–dollar and yen–dollar exchange rates three and twelve calender months ahead. They are only requested to provide predictions for those exchange rates they are best able to estimate, which ensures that the forecasters analyzed are 'close to the market'. Response rates and currency/horizon coverage are not surprisingly less than perfect, and in the work that follows we constrain our analysis to subsets of the total panel (details are given in the relevant section).

We use both the three- and twelve-month forecasts for the three exchange rates over the period October 1989 to September 1992. The advantage of having two forecast horizons is that we can discern whether there is any differential forecasting performance among forecasters over the two periods. This may be of interest given the increasing popularity of the story that chartist techniques dominate forecasting behavior in the short-term while fundamentals dominate in long-term forecasts (see Frankel and Froot, 1990b).

We matched this survey database with actual market rates taken from the Barclays Bank International pages on Datastream. These are the middle market (mean of bid and ask) rates prevailing in the foreign exchange market at a time between 15:30 and 16:00 in London. Besides the spot rates in effect on the day the predictions were made, we also gathered rates for the days that fell three and twelve calendar months from the survey date—'the forecast days'. If any of these fell on a weekend or holiday the nearest business day was used. Since we cannot tell exactly when each forecast is received on the survey date our use of the afternoon London rates is admittedly arbitrary. The importance of timing is assessed by recomputing all results using the previous Friday's rates, which would have been known when the forecasts were made. The differences between the two sets of results are so small that we only report results pertaining to the Monday rates.

II. Are forecasters different?

Ito (1990) provides a simple and robust test for detecting differences among forecasts which he applies to a database of Japanese forecasters' predictions of the yen–dollar rate. Ito finds considerable heterogeneity in the form of what he terms 'individual effects'. The individual effects he detects emanate from a constant bias and not because of different modeling techniques. As an initial test of heterogeneity we utilize Ito's approach.

Suppose an individual j makes a forecast of the (log) exchange rate at time t that consists of two parts, part X_t based on public information, I_t, common to all forecasters, plus an individual, or idiosyncratic effect, g_j. This individual's forecast is then the sum of these two parts plus an individual random disturbance term, u_{jt}, which could occur through rounding or measurement errors

$$\langle 1 \rangle \qquad s^e_{jt} = X_t + g_j + u_{jt}.$$

The average forecast at time t is then

$$\langle 2 \rangle \qquad s^e_{At} = X_t + g_A + u_{At}.$$

Normalizing such that g_A equals zero and subtracting ⟨2⟩ from ⟨1⟩ we obtain

$$\langle 3 \rangle \qquad s^e_{jt} - s^e_{At} = g_j + [u_{jt} - u_{At}].$$

The individual effects g_j may then be retrieved from a regression of the difference between an individual and the average forecast on a constant term; a non-zero g_j indicates that an individual's forecasts are biased compared to those of the representative, or average, forecaster. Note that this test tells us nothing about the forecasting *ability* of the individual.

One attractive feature of the above tests is that there is no need to specify the common forecast element, X_t, or the information set, I_t, on which it is based, if it can be assumed common to all individuals. However, it is possible to test for idiosyncratic coefficient terms on information in I_t. Suppose that besides individual biases (the g_js) each forecaster places different weights on some element of the publicly available information set; for concreteness assume this element to be the forward premium that holds at time t, fp_t. Then

$$\langle 4 \rangle \qquad s^e_{jt} = X'_t + g'_j + \beta_j fp_t + u_{jt},$$

where X'_t is the common forecast term based on I_t less the forward premium, and g'_j is the new individual bias. Specifying the equivalent equation for the average forecast and subtracting as above implies that

$$\langle 5 \rangle \qquad s^e_{jt} - s^e_{At} = g'_t + [\beta_j - \beta_A] fp_t + [u_{jt} - u_{At}].$$

This richer formulation allows us to test for both individual biases ($g'_j \neq 0$) and idiosyncratic effects ($\beta_j - \beta_A \neq 0$).

Due to the international nature of our database we can push the above tests a little further. Our data set allows calculation of these effects with respect to the overall average and with respect to the relevant country average. This, in turn, allows us to examine, among other aspects, whether our individuals are more inclined towards, say, a dollar depreciation than the overall average or their compatriots. This distinction may be important if we cannot be sure that the information set is common to all forecasters, due to time zone or language-induced informational differences. Averaging within a country is less likely to result in problems arising from such informational asymmetries.

To cover as much of our panel as possible, and due to the simplicity of the regressions, we include all forecasters who replied in at least 20 months of the total survey for a currency. In examining idiosyncratic effects two information terms are included, the forward premium relevant for the forecast horizon and the lagged 1 month change in the spot rate.

The results of estimating equations ⟨3⟩ and ⟨5⟩ by OLS are summarized in Tables 1 and 2, and are available in greater detail from the authors on request. The main import of these results is that we find considerable evidence of heterogeneous expectations for both the three- and twelve-month forecast horizons. This is apparent when either the overall average or the country average is used as a benchmark. In contrast to Ito (1990), we find evidence of both idiosyncratic coefficients and individual effects. Since the standard variables used (lagged spot rate changes and the forward premium) are available at very little cost to all market participants, regardless of location, we would argue that these differing coefficients are not due to asymmetric information, but rather to the use of different forecasting models. The exclusion of these variables from equation ⟨3⟩ could bias the estimation of g_j, and this appears to be significant when we examine the interpretation of the forward premium. In almost all cases, including the relevant forward premium in equation ⟨5⟩ results in a fall in the number of significant individual effects, and more findings of idiosyncratic behavior (or occurrences of both effects). There is little evidence of an idiosyncratic interpretation of lagged spot rate changes in line with the findings of Ito.[5]

The striking similarity between the results in Tables 1 (overall consensus) and 2 (country-specific consensus) suggests that informational asymmetries between nations are small and that it is appropriate to think of a 'global foreign exchange market' with a common information set. This finding is consistent with the 'meteor shower' interpretation of the operation of foreign exchange markets (see, for example, Ito *et al.*, 1992 and Hogan and Melvin, 1994).

As noted in our discussion of ⟨1⟩, the error term in equations ⟨3⟩ and ⟨5⟩ reflects measurement error (that is, the gap between the reported survey response and the true forecast) and is assumed to be random. However, one feature of survey data is that an individual in producing a forecast may, for strategic reasons, not give their true forecast but an adjusted one (the fact that the individual participants to our surveys are not publicly quoted may or may not exacerbate this phenomenon).[6] Although this need not necessarily conflict with the assumption of the randomness it may, nevertheless, mean that measurement errors are large period-by-period. One way of gauging the magnitude of measurement errors for individual forecasters is to compare the standard errors of the equations and the coefficients of determination. As an illustration of this, let us examine the three-month forecasts for the mark using the global consensus as the average forecast and the forward premium as the

TABLE 1. Expectations heterogeneity with respect to overall consensus

	Indiv.	Idiosyn.	Both	Neither	Other	Total
Deutsche mark 3 month						
Eqn ⟨3⟩	53	—	—	54	—	107
Fwd prem.	16	29	12	40	10	107
Lag change	50	7	3	47	0	107
Sterling 3 month						
Eqn ⟨3⟩	47	—	—	46	—	93
Fwd prem.	5	1	11	44	32	93
Lag change	43	3	5	42	0	93
Japanese yen 3 month						
Eqn ⟨3⟩	43	—	—	64	—	107
Fwd prem.	27	14	20	46	0	107
Lag change	33	5	10	58	1	107
Deutsche mark 12 month						
Eqn ⟨3⟩	60	—	—	29	—	89
Fwd prem.	24	21	26	15	3	89
Lag change	52	1	8	27	1	89
Sterling 12 month						
Eqn ⟨3⟩	51	—	—	30	—	81
Fwd prem.	6	6	23	19	27	81
Lag change	45	0	7	29	0	81
Japanese yen 12 month						
Eqn ⟨3⟩	50	—	—	41	—	91
Fwd prem.	28	22	24	16	1	91
Lag change	48	3	4	35	1	91

Notes: The figures in each column give the number of forecasters in each category. Indiv indicates significant individual biases, Idiosyn denotes idiosyncratic coefficients on the specified information term, Both denotes that both individual and idiosyncratic effects were present, Neither that an F-test of no individual or idiosyncratic effects cannot be rejected, and Other denotes that while the t-tests each rejected individual and idiosyncratic effects, the F-test rejected joint zero terms. Where equation ⟨3⟩ is being estimated, the figures in the Neither column denote no findings of individual effects.

information variable in equation ⟨5⟩. The average standard error is 0.0276 with a range of 0.0146 to 0.0518,, indicating a wide degree of deviations from the consensus. The average R^2 is 0.126 with a range of 0.00 to 0.58. In those cases when our R^2 is very low, a variety of alternatives suggest themselves. The simplest case is that there is merely random measurement error. Alternatively, strategic behavior may mean that forecasts differ from the average because of

TABLE 2. Expectations heterogeneity with respect to country consensus

	Indiv.	Idiosyn.	Both	Neither	Other	Total
Deutsche mark 3 month						
Eqn ⟨3⟩	49	—	—	58	—	107
Fwd prem.	17	27	14	33	16	107
Lag change	50	6	5	46	0	107
Sterling 3 month						
Eqn ⟨3⟩	47	—	—	44	—	93
Fwd prem.	3	1	14	38	37	93
Lag change	45	5	5	38	0	93
Japanese yen 3 month						
Eqn ⟨3⟩	43	—	—	64	—	107
Fwd prem.	20	11	24	51	1	107
Lag change	34	4	10	58	1	107
Deutsche mark 12 month						
Eqn ⟨3⟩	63	—	—	26	—	89
Fwd prem.	19	17	26	13	14	89
Lag change	55	1	6	25	2	89
Sterling 12 month						
Eqn ⟨3⟩	54	—	—	27	—	81
Fwd prem.	8	4	19	18	32	81
Lag change	46	1	10	23	1	81
Japanese yen 12 month						
Eqn ⟨3⟩	52	—	—	39	—	91
Fwd prem.	33	20	22	15	1	91
Lag change	48	2	5	35	1	91

Notes: See notes in Table 1.

factors unrelated to any fundamental variable, or we have not used the variable about which interpretations differ. Thus we cannot rule out that some heterogeneity of reported predictions is due to strategic behavior. However, we can still explain, on average, 12.6 percent of the deviation from the consensus simply on the basis of differential interpretation of the forward premium. A significant proportion of the demonstrated heterogeneity appears to be because of the use of different forecasting models.

In this section we have presented strong evidence of heterogeneity among a panel of international foreign exchange market participants and advisers that confirm and extend the Japanese-specific results of Ito. Forecasters appear to maintain individual biases relative to their peers, and to interpret the importance of key variables in different ways.

III. Are some forecasters better than others?

The tests in this section are complementary to those contained in the previous section on individual and idiosyncratic effects. More specifically, we now investigate whether our previous findings—that our forecasters hold biases compared with each other and that they appear to use different forecasting methods—result in *statistically* different forecast performance, or whether the different methods are equally (in)accurate.

The analysis of performance accuracy is complicated by the differing response rates of the panellists in this study. It is not immediately apparent how to compare the performance of a forecaster who gives returns for, say, the first two years of the sample with another who only forecasts over the final two years. Assuming that rates are equally easy to forecast each month is, we feel, too heroic. MacDonald and Marsh (1994) avoid the problem by restricting their sample to only those with a perfect response record over 27 months, but for our longer data set this proves to be a severe selection criterion. Instead we use a non-parametric test due to Prentice (1979) that controls for imperfect response rates and hence allows us to include a larger proportion of our total database.

To introduce notation, suppose that we have m months of forecasts ($1 \leq i \leq m$) from p forecasters ($1 \leq j \leq p$). Each forecaster may have some months for which he did not provide predictions. For each forecast made the absolute forecast error, E_{ij}, is calculated. These errors are then ranked within each month, whereby $E_{11}, E_{12}, \ldots, E_{ip}$ are compared and rank 1 assigned to the largest absolute error, rank 2 to the next largest, etc. Suppose that r_{ij} is the rank of forecast error E_{ij}. Tied values are given their average rank. The null hypothesis that we are interested in is that the rankings of the errors within months are equally likely, against an alternative that at least one forecaster yields higher ranks than at least one other forecaster. In other words, are some forecasters systematically more accurate than others.

This can be tested by using the Prentice 'C' test which is summarized as

$$C = y'W^{-1}y,$$

where y is a $(p-1)$ vector whose jth element is

$$y_j = \sum_{i \in S_j} \left[r_{ij}(k_i + 1)^{-1} - \tfrac{1}{2} \right], \qquad \langle 6 \rangle$$

S_j is the set of months for which forecaster j supplied a forecast, k_i is the number of forecasts ranked in month i and one of the p possible sums is omitted from y to avoid singularity. W is the $(p-1) \times (p-1)$ covariance matrix of the $(p-1)$ remaining y_js, where the elements of W are given by

$$w_{jj} = \sum_{i \in S_j} \frac{\left((k_i - 1)(k_i + 1)^{-1}\right)}{12}, \qquad w_{jj'} = -\sum_{i \in S_j \cap S_{j'}} \frac{\left((k_i + 1)^{-1}\right)}{12} \; (j \neq j').$$

The asymptotic distribution of C under the null of no difference in performance is chi-squared with $(p-1)$ degrees of freedom.

We compute values for Prentice's C for all of the groupings listed above and these are reported in Table 3.[7] Over the three-month horizon, 10 out of 21 country groupings show significantly different forecast performance. This rises to 16 for the long-horizon forecasts. In all six combinations of currency and horizon, heterogeneous forecast ability is found when the forecasters are treated as one group. Overall, differential performance is indicated for all three currencies at both horizons, but is strongest for the twelve-month forecasts and, in particular, the Japanese yen. Such differences in results between both horizon and currency are recurring themes in the paper.

We have established that our forecasters are different. They place different weights on variables when forecasting and hold individual biases. Furthermore, these differences translate into a distribution of forecast performance—some forecasters are significantly more accurate than others. We have said nothing so far about the forecast ability of our panellists, only their relative performance, and we remedy this in the next section.

TABLE 3. Prentice's non-parametric test of forecaster homogeneity

		Three-month forecast horizon					
		Deutsche mark		Pound sterling		Japanese yen	
All	(64)	126.99	(0.00)	115.19	(0.00)	145.32	(0.00)
Canadian	(8)	10.12	(0.26)	2.89	(0.94)	1.44	(0.99)
French	(4)	5.86	(0.21)	8.01	(0.09)	5.61	(0.23)
Italian	(4)	2.54	(0.64)	9.82	(0.04)	11.38	(0.02)
Japanese	(4)	3.98	(0.41)	1.74	(0.78)	5.55	(0.24)
British	(17)	36.67	(0.00)	31.50	(0.02)	44.69	(0.00)
American	(7)	25.58	(0.00)	11.30	(0.13)	21.09	(0.00)
German	(14)	31.29	(0.01)	34.87	(0.00)	35.36	(0.00)

		Twelve month forecast horizon					
		Deutsche mark		Pound sterling		Japanese yen	
All	(65)	162.26	(0.00)	179.69	(0.00)	376.58	(0.00)
Canadian	(9)	26.21	(0.00)	10.99	(0.28)	52.06	(0.00)
French	(4)	16.94	(0.00)	17.09	(0.00)	22.21	(0.00)
Italian	(5)	6.41	(0.27)	13.01	(0.02)	17.58	(0.00)
Japanese	(3)	5.70	(0.13)	6.84	(0.08)	23.96	(0.00)
British	(17)	50.16	(0.00)	55.25	(0.00)	98.72	(0.00)
American	(7)	17.45	(0.01)	27.88	(0.00)	85.04	(0.00)
German	(14)	22.21	(0.07)	32.94	(0.00)	37.39	(0.00)

Notes: The figures in each column give the value of the test statistic. The figures in parentheses after the grouping give the degrees of freedom associated with each test, and the figures in parentheses after the test statistics are the marginal significance levels.

IV. How good are the forecasters?: Statistical evaluation vs. market value

One key feature of the results reported in the last section is the finding of differences in the forecast performance in terms of absolute errors. This finding is confirmed when we conduct a standard Meese and Rogoff (1983a) type exercise of comparing the forecasting performance of a simple random walk model to that of our forecasters using the RMSE and the MAE criteria. In particular, we calculate for each forecaster considered in Section II the ratio of the RMSE (and MAE) to that of a naive 'no-change' prediction (constructed only over those months in which the panel member provided a forecast). A summary of our results is reported in Table 4 where we record the number of forecasters who generate a ratio of less than unity. Very few forecasters produce smaller errors than a random walk over the shorter horizon, but a substantial proportion of panel members (a majority in the case of the yen) do so over a twelve-month horizon. Furthermore, many of the good long-term forecasters are substantially better than a random walk alternative. For example, four yen forecasters have RMSE ratios of less than one-half. These results are very much in accordance with Meese and Rogoff (1983a, b) who find that simple asset price models only perform well in comparison to naive alternatives over longer forecast horizons.

However, it could be argued that accuracy in terms of error statistics is more relevant to an evaluator of forecasts than an end-user. In the case of asset price forecasts, a consumer is likely to use a prediction as a guide to speculative opportunities. The user is likely to be more concerned with some form of profit measure than the RMSE. Therefore as an alternative to the error statistics we calculate a simple measure of profit based on forward market speculation. We use the method of Booth (1983) and Boothe and Glassman (1987), in which a foreign currency purchase or sale is made in the forward market dependent on the forecast. If the currency is forecast to be stronger than that indicated by the forward rate US$100 equivalent of the currency is bought, and if weaker US$100 equivalent is sold.[8] The profits and losses of these trades are then cumulated to give a final total profit figure. Again, adjustments have to be made for the imperfect response rates. The first stage is to express these profits in a 'per trade' format (i.e. divide total profits by the number of forecasts made). Second, to allow comparison with the performance of a naive forecast of no-change, the difference, or spread, between forecaster profit per trade and random walk profit per trade is computed. For correct comparison the random walk alternative is only calculated for those months in which the forecaster responds. The profit spread calculations are summarized in Table 4.

Between one-quarter and one-half of the three-month forecasters prove profitable to follow, according to our speculative strategy. The proportions rise to between one-half and three-quarters over the longer forecast horizon. However, when we compare our forecasters' performances to a random walk alternative, the picture changes somewhat. Typically, over our sample period, a no-change prediction proves costly to follow for the Deutsche mark over three

TABLE 4. Forecasters vs. the random walk—error measures and forward profits

	Number	RMSE	MAE	Profits	Excess profits
Deutsche mark 3 month	107	4	5	27	34
Sterling 3 month	93	5	2	44	6
Japanese yen 3 month	107	2	2	35	25
Deutsche mark 12 month	89	26	23	55	27
Sterling 12 month	81	14	35	62	9
Japanese yen 12 month	91	56	62	68	67

Notes: The first column gives the number of forecasters to supply the required number of predictions for each currency/horizon combination. The second and third columns give the number of forecasters whose RMSE and MAE ratios are less than unity, the fourth column gives the number of forecasters whose profit per trade proves positive, and the final column gives the number of forecasters whose profit per trade exceeds the profit per trade of a random walk.

months and hence while 27 forecasters give positive returns, 34 give returns in excess of a random walk. This is reversed over the twelve-month horizon, where roughly half of the profitable forecasters beat the no-change alternative. For the yen over both horizons a random walk approximately breaks even as the same number of profitable forecasters earn what we term excess profits. A prediction of no-change proves very profitable for the pound over both three and twelve months. Thus, the number of forecasters earning excess profits is substantially lower than the relatively high count of profitable forecasters.

An interesting, and perhaps natural, result to emphasize is that there is a correspondence between accurate and profitable forecasters. For the three-month Duetsche mark, for example, all four forecasters with RMSE ratios less than unity have positive profit spreads. However, the relationship does not always hold in reverse, since several forecasters are particularly profitable yet have RMSE ratios greater than unity. Table 5 presents the correlations between profit spread and our two error ratios for each currency/horizon combination.

Although all of these correlations have the expected sign and are significant, the relatively weak relationship between profit and forecast error, at least over the shorter horizon, is evident. An example is given in Figure 1, where the RMSE ratios and profit spreads of each three-month yen forecaster are plotted. The body of forecasters in the upper right quadrant (i.e. profitable but inaccurate forecasters) is of particular relevance. Why do these panel members make large errors yet still return profits in excess of the random walk alternative?

This anomaly is also noted by Leitch and Tanner (1991) who calculate a range of error measures together with profit from speculation, using methods akin to ours, to evaluate a range of forecasts of US Treasury bill rates. Based on correlation analysis, they show that profits derived from forecasts bear little relationship to measures of forecast error, but that they are closely related to

TABLE 5. Error measures and profit correlations

	Simple correlations		
	RMSE–MAE	RMSE–profit	MAE–profit
Deutsche mark 3 month	0.936	−0.608	−0.597
Sterling 3 month	0.929	−0.529	−0.556
Japanese yen 3 month	0.963	−0.399	−0.371
Deutsche mark 12 month	0.967	−0.837	−0.804
Sterling 12 month	0.957	−0.895	−0.832
Japanese yen 12 month	0.981	−0.865	−0.885
	Spearman's rank correlations		
	RMSE–MAE	RMSE–profit	MAE–profit
Deutsche mark 3 month	0.862	−0.369	−0.363
Sterling 3 month	0.768	−0.306	−0.308
Japanese yen 3 month	0.884	−0.183	−0.168
Deutsche mark 12 month	0.898	−0.742	−0.660
Sterling 12 month	0.848	−0.766	−0.600
Japanese yen 12 month	0.962	−0.794	−0.789

directional accuracy.[9] Leitch and Tanner conclude from their results that speculative profits are a better method of financial forecast evaluation. However, our speculative strategy, in common with that of Leitch and Tanner, takes no account of risk. Since risk is generally related to some measure of error, the fact that we find only a weak negative correlation between forecast accuracy and profit suggests that both types of evaluation criteria are important in assessing predictive performance: profit alone is not a good measure of forecast ability if it is not always accompanied by small errors.

One final point worth addressing in this section concerns the forecasting performance across currencies and horizons.[10] In particular, are good forecasters of one currency also good forecasters of another currency, or are good short horizon forecasters of a currency also good long horizon forecasters?[11] With few exceptions the answer to the first question is no. Of the ten most accurate three-month mark forecasters only two are also in the top ten three-month sterling forecasters and just one makes the top ten three-month yen list. However, good short horizon forecasters do seem more likely to be good long horizon forecasters. Of the ten most accurate forecasters of the mark (pound sterling) [yen] over three months, three (three) [four] enter the top ten over twelve months.[12] Similar patterns emerge when profitability is used as the benchmark.

V. Differences of opinion and trading volume

We turn now to a more direct investigation of the apparent heterogeneity in forecasting performance that the above tests reveal, regardless of the forecast

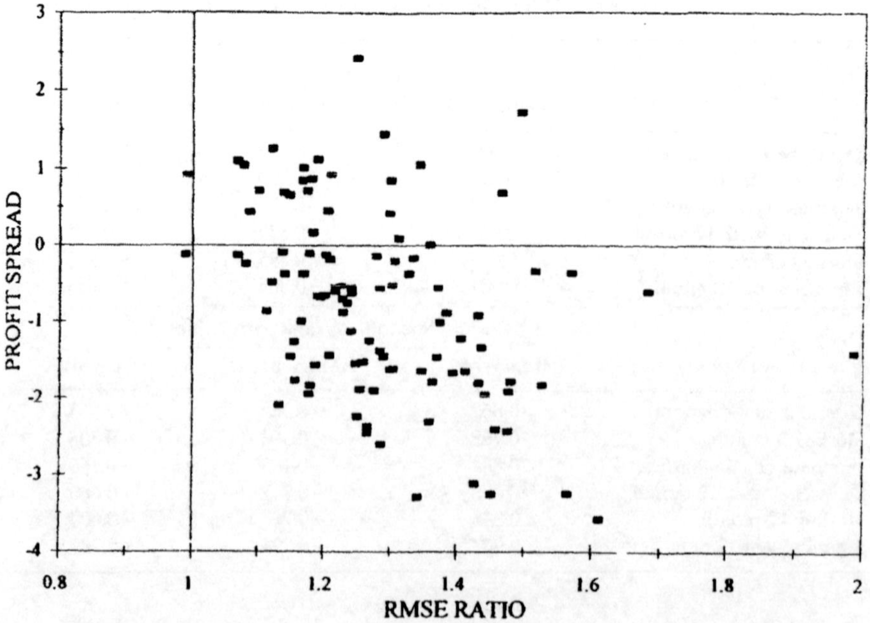

FIGURE 1. Relationship between accuracy and profitability of 3-month Japanese yen forecasts.

horizon. Such an investigation should shed light on whether disaggregate survey data are any more insightful than analysis based on a consensus measure. More specifically, we examine the implications for turnover resulting from differences of opinion noted in the previous sections. Although the theoretical implications of heterogeneity for trading volumes have been theoretically derived by Varian (1989), very little empirical work has been conducted. The bulk of the extant empirical work relates to the stock market and this has established a positive association between the dispersion of stock analysts' forecasts of company earnings and share trading in the USA.[13] With respect to the foreign exchange market, Frankel and Froot (1990a) show that the standard deviation of exchange rate predictions, price volatility and futures trading volume exhibit complex Granger causality relationships over very short forecast horizons (one week). In this section, we show that the degree of heterogeneity of our panellists' forecasts is positively related to turnover in the Chicago currency futures pits, even after controlling for other potential determinants of trading volume.

An annex contains a brief outline of the mean-variance model of trading volume due to Grossman (1976, 1978) and Varian (1989) which results in the following estimated equation:

$$\langle 7 \rangle \qquad T_t = a + b \text{ std.dev}\,(s^e_{it}) + c \text{ std.dev}\,(s_t) + d\, T_{t-1} + \text{seasonals},$$

where T is turnover, calculated as the daily average dollar value of trade in the relevant IMM futures pit on the Chicago Mercantile Exchange (measured over a period that covers the two weeks prior to the day on which expectations are surveyed together with the two subsequent weeks). Volumes for all contract maturities are combined, though the total is always dominated by the nearest dated.

The term std.dev denotes a standard deviation such that std.dev(s_{it}^e) is our survey-based measure of the dispersion of expectations and std.dev(s_t) is the standard deviation of the current period price change. The latter variable is included since it is well known that price changes generate turnover. Several explanations have been put forward for this relationship. Varian's (1989) model, for example, contains a mechanism in which trading volume depends on the idiosyncratic interpretation of news (as demonstrated in Section II). The news itself, even if from private sources, will reveal itself to all participants through price changes.

We include lagged turnover for two reasons. First, previous studies have shown that volume is Granger causal to both forecast dispersion and price volatility and we wish to control for these effects. Second, the mean-variance model implies that differences in initial currency holdings will also induce trading volume. In a world of costly adjustment to equilibrium holdings, lagged turnover can act as a proxy for asymmetric initial currency holdings.

Seasonal and trend terms are included where necessary due to the nature of trading on the futures markets. Figure 2 shows the pattern of turnover in the three currency futures pits over our period of estimation. A strong downward trend in yen turnover is evident, while, to a lesser extent, there may be changes in the behavior of trading volume for both the pound and the Deutsche mark around the end of 1990. The break for sterling appears around September 1990 which suggests an ERM effect, given that Britain joined the Mechanism on October 8 of that year. This is discussed further below. For the mark, weak evidence exists of a jump in the mean of daily turnover in the early months of 1991. We can find no strong rationale for this, although it could be related to reunification and German elections or to a transfer of sterling business to the more liquid Deutsche mark market once the pound joined the ERM. This latter explanation would account for both of the above changes in behavior, but initially we make no modeling provisions.

The results of estimating equation ⟨7⟩ using the three-month forecasts[14] are given in Table 6. For the pound and yen two estimated equations are presented; for both currencies version I is closest to the theoretical model, but II is empirically more valid. Further lags of independent variables for all three currencies are found to be statistically insignificant and are not reported. For the yen and mark, the dispersion of expectations [std.dev(s_{it}^e)] is positive and significant at the 5 percent level. The current period price change [std.dev(s_t)] is also significant, though at differing levels. For the yen, lagged turnover is not significant and its inclusion has little impact on the coefficients of interest.

Sterling is somewhat different. Lagged turnover is very important in explaining current volumes, and while the current period price change is not significant, lagged values are strongly so. Incorporating this lagged term drives up the

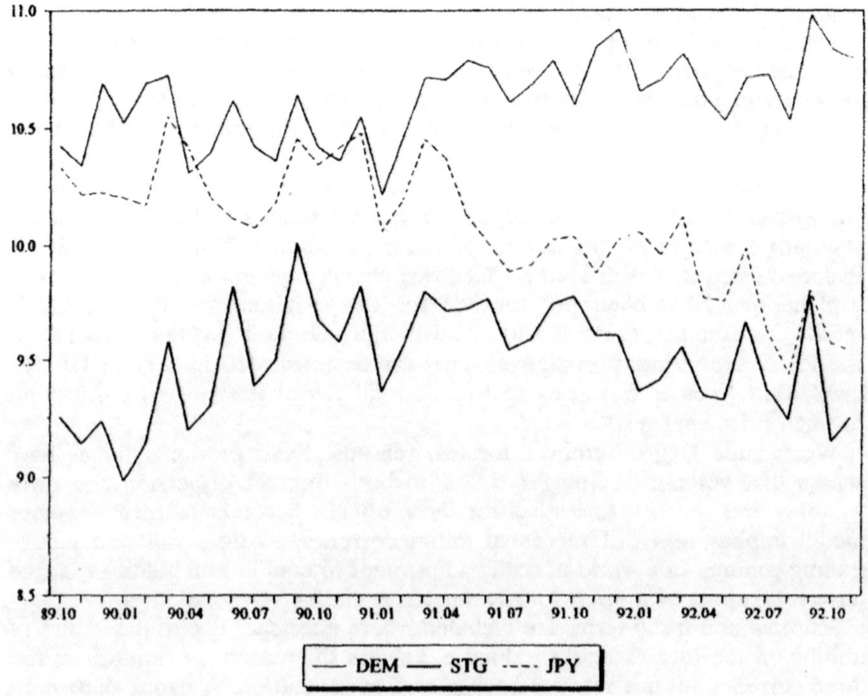

FIGURE 2. Log of turnover in Chicago turnover futures pits.

coefficient on expectations dispersion such that it becomes significant at the 11.5 percent level. Nevertheless, the fit of the models for sterling is poor in comparison with the others, a fact we ascribe to distortions caused by the pound's entry to and exit from the ERM. In particular, there is a marked change in the seasonality of turnover after sterling's entry accompanied by a reversal of trend. This may have been caused by future traders switching into the more liquid Deutsche mark contract once the sterling/mark cross rate was quasi-fixed. Incorporating three dummies to remove the excess seasonal turnover peaks in 1990 and one to account for the jump in turnover in September 1992 results in a rise of coefficient on forecast dispersion with little change to the value of other significant terms in Model II.[15]

$$
\begin{aligned}
T_t = {} & \underset{(2.37)}{13.305}\,\text{std.dev}(s^e_{it}) - \underset{(1.08)}{4.282}\,\text{std.dev}(s_t) - \underset{(2.94)}{9.724}\,\text{std.dev}(s_{t-1}) \\
& + \underset{(4.91)}{0.687}T_{t-1} + \text{constant, seasonal and deterministic dummies.}
\end{aligned}
$$

Our results provide strong support for the mean-variance model of Varian. For the yen and Deutsche mark the variables are correctly signed and typically

Forecast heterogeneity: R MacDonald and I W Marsh

TABLE 6. Trading volume, forecast dispersion and volatility

	Deutsche mark	Pound sterling		Japanese yen	
	I	I	II	I	II
Standard deviation (s_{it}^e)	11.098	2.978	10.238	13.871	17.976
	(3.34)	(0.51)	(1.64)	(2.09)	(3.32)
Standard deviation (s_t)	4.949	0.179	−1.527	0.948	1.051
	(1.82)	(0.05)	(2.28)	(2.21)	(2.56)
Standard deviation (s_{t-1})			−8.459		
			(2.28)		
T_{t-1}	0.376	0.659	0.582	0.211	
	(2.74)	(4.03)	(3.78)	(1.09)	
Time				−0.011	−0.014
				(3.35)	(7.31)
R^2	0.83	0.73	0.78	0.90	0.89
SEE	0.095	0.164	0.150	0.115	0.113

Notes: *t*-statistics given in parentheses.

significant. For all three currencies the trading volume of the currency future pits in Chicago is positively related to the dispersion of our panellists' forecasts, even when other determinants of turnover are accounted for.[16]

VI. Summary and conclusions

In this paper we have been concerned to establish the importance of heterogeneity in the foreign exchange market using a high quality disaggregated survey database. The respondents to the survey, based in the financial centers of the G-7 countries, are polled simultaneously on a monthly basis regarding their forecasts of three exchange rates three and twelve months ahead. A number of findings emerge from our study.

The hypothesis of heterogeneity is confirmed when we use tests designed to gauge heterogeneous expectations formation.[17] Forecasters appear to use common information differently in making their forecasts. While this in itself may not be surprising, we also show that the differences in forecasts result in systematically different forecast ability.

An interesting finding that emerged from our evaluation of the potential profitability of following the advice given by the forecasters is that even when the performance of forecasters is poor, as measured by standard statistical criteria (such as the RMSE or MAE), they may still produce forecast advice that would have been profitable to follow. In a finite sample, however, the mere existence of positive returns is not sufficient evidence of forecast ability since the profit also needs to compensate for the risk associated with the trading positions.

The final component of our study involves relating the evident heterogeneity that exists among our panel members to turnover in the foreign exchange market. We use a simple mean-variance model that highlights the key relationship between turnover and market sentiment. The model is shown to have empirical validity for at least two of the three currencies studied in this paper.

What are the policy implications of our work? One key element in our results concerns the differential forecasting performance in predicting the exchange rate three and twelve months ahead; forecasters seem consistently better at forecasting currencies at relatively long horizons. This finding may be attributed to the widespread use of chartist and other non-fundamental techniques in short-term trading strategies, while fundamentals are seen as more important determinants of longer term exchange rate movements (see De Long *et al.*, 1990; Frankel and Froot, 1990b). The use of non-fundamental techniques introduces considerable noise into exchange rate behavior which makes forecasting currencies at the short end an especially hazardous occupation.

This, together with our finding of heterogeneity among forecasters at both short and long horizons may have implications for the choice of an appropriate exchange rate regime and for how a particular regime is managed. For example, with flexible exchange rates the existence of heterogeneity suggests that macroeconomic policy, and in particular interest rate policy, should be framed in a clear and unambiguous fashion so that there can be little doubt about its interpretation by market participants. Unclear and ambiguous policy may well produce important exchange rate misalignments.

A proponent of greater fixity of exchange rates may find some comfort in the existence of heterogeneity. To the extent that some forecasters are dominant actors in the foreign exchange market and additionally are, say, driven by non-fundamental/irrational factors, the clearest signal that the authorities can give about their dislike of misalignments is simply to fix the exchange rate.

Of course, the heterogeneity, need not necessarily be a reflection of irrationality and for trade to take place in a financial market there must, by definition, be a degree of heterogeneity. It may therefore be more appropriate to ensure that the market structure within which traders take their positions is the most conducive for attenuating any potentially unpleasant consequences of heterogeneity. We interpret the recently developed market micro-structure literature as a move in this direction and, indeed, our findings are supportive of this work since the existence of heterogeneity (and its relatedness to trading volume) is a key element in this explanation of the behavior of foreign exchange rates.

Appendix

In this Appendix we detail the model of turnover suggested by Varian (1989) and estimated in Section V.

Assume there are two assets, one with a certain payoff (domestic currency) and one risky (foreign currency). The price in the next period of this risky asset is P_1. For simplicity the return on the domestic currency is assumed to be zero. There are n individual investors, and each investor i has a subjective prior distribution for the price of foreign exchange that is assumed to be Normal with mean P_{1i} and variance $1/\alpha$. Varian terms α the 'precision' of the prior belief. Assuming that investors all have constant absolute risk-tolerance utility functions, with Arrow–Pratt measures of absolute risk aversion equal to $1/\tau$, it is straightforward to demonstrate that each agent's demand function for foreign currency will be of the form

$$D_i = \frac{\tau[E_i(P_1) - P_0]}{\mathrm{var}_i\,(P_1)}(P_1) = \tau\alpha(P_{1i} - P_0), \tag{A.1}$$

where P_t is the period t price. Supposing that each investor has a supply X_i of currency and that the price adjusts to equate aggregate supply and demand, the current period equilibrium price will be

$$P_0^* = \bar{P}_1 - \frac{\bar{X}}{\tau\alpha}, \tag{A.2}$$

where P^* denotes the equilibrium price and a bar denotes a mean value of the variable across investors.

Solving for the demand of each investor yields

$$D_i = \tau\alpha(P_{1i} - \bar{P}_1) + \bar{X}. \tag{A.3}$$

That is, each investor's demand is a function of the difference between his individual and the average opinion of the future price of currency. Given each investor's initial endowment of the asset, the net trade of individual i is

$$T_i = \tau\alpha(P_{1i} - \bar{P}_1) - (X_i - \bar{X}), \tag{A.4}$$

and aggregating over the n investors in the market then gives the total volume of trade. At this stage, market turnover results from differences in prior beliefs and/or from differences in initial holdings of currency.

An additional effect due to price changes may be introduced by considering the effect of 'news'. In Grossman's (1976) work, the price system acts as an aggregator of information whereby the current spot rate reveals all information available in the economy, whether private or otherwise. Varian extends this by considering the effect of idiosyncratic interpretation of news. He shows that price changes will still reveal all information flows but that the demand of each individual will now also depend upon that individual's interpretation of the news. A representative trader's demand now becomes

$$T_i = \tau[\alpha(P_{1i} - \bar{P}_1) + \beta(\delta_i - \bar{\delta})\bar{Y}] + (X_i - \bar{X}), \tag{A.5}$$

where $\bar{Y}$ is the 'magnitude' of the information as revealed by price changes and $(\delta_i - \bar{\delta})$ measures the degree of idiosyncrasy with which the information is interpreted.

The implication of the above model is that in assessing the effect on turnover of differences in forecaster opinion we have to control for the impact of heterogeneous interpretation of new information. In an empirical test of this model a proxy for the flow of information is needed. The most obvious proxy to use is the change in the price level, since this is used by individuals to infer the aggregate information flow. Hence the operational equation that we estimate is equation ⟨7⟩ in the text.

Notes

1. For example, Dominguez (1986), Frankel and Froot (1987, 1990a), MacDonald (1991), MacDonald and Torrance (1988, 1990), Cavaglia *et al.* (1993) and Prat and Uctum (1995) use a variety of survey databases of exchange rate forecasts in order to gain insight into the efficiency of the foreign exchange market.
2. Very little work has been done with fully disaggregated exchange rate forecasts. Exceptions include Ito (1990), who uses Japanese exchange rate forecasts, MacDonald (1992), MacDonald and Marsh (1994) and Benassy and Raymond (1994) who examine

aspects of the Consensus Economics exchange rate database (specifically, the rationality and the pooling potential of the forecasts).

3. The most likely reason for trading when investors agree on valuation is for diversification purposes. However, Lyons (1991) points out the proportion of total trading that can be explained by shifts in wealth, taxes and return higher moments is very small in typical portfolio choice models. He concludes that '[t]he burden of explanation, then, appears almost certainly to fall on differences in beliefs regarding valuation' (p. 2).
4. Respondents retain confidentiality by the use of mnemonics that identify only their country of origin. We are thus unable to break down forecasters by type of institution.
5. Another notable feature of the results concerning the forward premium is the high count of 'Other' cases, particularly for the pound. This occurs when t-tests of significant intercept and slope are rejected but a joint F-test is not. This could be because the relative stability of sterling's forward premium for most of the sample period leads to near collinearity with the constant term, and hence large standard errors.
6. We are grateful to an anonymous referee for suggesting this point. See Batchelor and Dua (1990) for a discussion.
7. To ensure sufficient observations for the mean rank of a forecaster to be accurately determined, we restrict the panel to those forecasters who replied to at least 29 (23) questionnaires for each currency at the three (twelve) month horizon. Although this is a more strict selection criterion than the one employed in Section II to analyze expectations heterogeneity, restricting the analysis to the smaller panel results in no major differences in distributons from those presented in Tables 1 and 2.
8. This is clearly only an approximate measure of trading profits as the possibility of an early closing of the contract (cutting of losses) is ignored, but it has the advantage of showing the importance of the qualitative predictions embedded in our forecasts. An alternative measure would be the profits from a buy-and-hold strategy.
9. One problem with the paper is that to increase their degrees of freedom Leitch and Tanner (1991) were forced to pool a wide range of forecast horizons in calculating their figures. Our results show marked differences in correlation between horizons which questions the appropriateness of such a strategy.
10. Given the confidentiality restriction placed on the data set, we cannot indicate whether forecasters, say, operating within commercial banks forecast better than, say, those in industrial corporations, although this type of comparison would also be interesting.
11. These comparisons are complicated by the imperfect response records of individual forecasters, and the fact that they are not required to forecast all three currencies. Indeed, just 22 panellists respond frequently enough to be analyzed for all three currencies over the 3-month horizon. Marsh and Power (1995) provide an examination of the performance of these 22 across currencies.
12. There is a much stronger relationship between poor short-term mark and pound sterling forecasters; of the ten worst mark forecasters five also fall into the bottom ten when predicting the pound. This does not seem to hold for the yen, however.
13. See, for example, Ajinkya *et al.* (1991).
14. The dispersion of the twelve-month forecasts produces weaker results, probably because the futures market is not ideal for opening such long-term positions.
15. Dummies are included for the three months of March, June and September 1990, and September, 1992.
16. An anonymous referee has noted, correctly, that the correlation we find in this section between heterogeneity and trading volume does not necessarily indicate causality. Gallant *et al.* (1992), for example, have argued that trading volume, and its interpretation by market participants, may cause price volatility. We have run the reverse regression to ⟨7⟩ and trading volume proved to be a significant determinant of heterogeneity. Therefore, all we can say is that these two variables are related and not that heterogeneity is causal to turnover.
17. Our tests are based on an assumption of constant bias, or individual effect, for individual forecasters. As more data for this panel of forecasters become available it

will be interesting to incorporate a learning process into the tests in order to examine how any bias evolves over time.

References

AJINKYA, BIPIN B., K. ROWLAND, K. ATIASE AND MICHAEL J. GIFT, 'Volume of trading and the dispersion of financial analysts' earnings forecasts,' *Accounting Review*, April 1991, **66**: 389–401.

BATCHELOR, ROY AND PAMI DUA, 'Product differentiation in the economic forecasting industry,' *International Journal of Forecasting*, September 1990, **6**: 311–316.

BENASSY, AGNES AND HELENE RAYMOND, 'The heterogeneity of exchange rate expectations according to survey data,' Document de travail du THEMA 9418, November 1994.

BOOTHE, PAUL, 'Speculative profit opportunities in the Canadian foreign exchange market, 1974–1978,' *Canadian Journal of Economics*, November 1983, **16**: 603–611.

BOOTHE, PAUL AND DEBRA GLASSMAN, 'Comparing exchange rate forecasting models: Accuracy vs. profitability,' *International Journal of Forecasting*, June 1987, **3**: 65–79.

CAVAGLIA, STEFANO, WILLEM F.C. VERSCHOOR AND CHRISTIAN C.P. WOLFF, 'Further evidence on exchange rate expectations,' *Journal of International Money and Finance*, April 1993, **12**: 78–98.

DE LONG, J. BRADFORD, A. SHLEIFER, L.H. SUMMERS AND R.J. WALDMANN, 'Noise trader risk in financial markets,' *Journal of Political Economy*, 1990, **98**: 703–738.

DOMINGUEZ, KATHRYN, 'Are foreign exchange forecasts rational? New evidence from survey data,' *Economics Letters*, 1986, **21**: 277–282.

FRANKEL, JEFFREY A. AND KENNETH A. FROOT, 'Using survey data to test standard propositions regarding exchange rate expectations,' *American Economic Review*, March 1987, **77**: 133–153.

FRANKEL, JEFFREY A. AND KENNETH A. FROOT, 'Interpreting tests of forward discount bias using survey data on exchange rate expectations,' *Quarterly Journal of Economics*, February 1989, **104**: 139–161.

FRANKEL, JEFFREY A. AND KENNETH A. FROOT, 'Exchange rate forecasting techniques, survey data, and implications for the foreign exchange market,' NBER Working Paper No. 3470, 1990 (1990a).

FRANKEL, JEFFREY A. AND KENNETH A. FROOT, 'Chartists, fundamentalists, and the demand for dollars,' in Courakis, Anthony S. and Mark P. Taylor, eds, *Private Behavior and Government Policy and Interdependent Economies*, Oxford: Clarendon Press, 1990 (1990b).

FRANKEL, JEFFREY A. AND ANDREW ROSE, 'A survey of empirical research on nominal exchange rates,' NBER Working Paper, No. 4865, 1994.

GALLANT, A. RONALD, P.E. ROSSI AND GEORGE TAUCHEN, 'Stock prices and volume,' *Review of Financial Studies*, 1992, **5**: 199–242.

GROSSMAN, SANFORD, 'On the efficiency of competitive stock markets where traders have diverse information,' *Journal of Finance*, May 1976, **31**: 573–585.

GROSSMAN, SANFORD, 'Further results on the informational efficiency of competitive stock markets,' *Journal of Economic Theory*, 1978, **18**: 81–101.

HOGAN, KEDRETH C. AND MICHAEL T. MELVIN, 'Sources of meteor showers and heat waves in the foreign exchange market,' *Journal of International Economics*, 1994, **37**: 239–247.

ITO, TAKATOSHI, 'Foreign exchange rate expectations: Micro survey data,' *American Economic Review*, June 1990, **80**: 434–439.

ITO, TAKATOSHI, ROBERT F. ENGLE AND W. LIN, 'Where does the meteor shower come from? The role of stochastic policy coordination,' *Journal of International Economics*, 1992, **32**: 221–240.

LEITCH, GORDON AND J. ERNEST TANNER, 'Economic forecast evaluation: Profits vs. the conventional error measures,' *American Economic Review*, June 1991, **81**: 589–590.

LYONS, RICHARD D., 'Private beliefs and informational externalities in the foreign exchange market,' mimeo, 1991.

LYONS, RICHARD D., 'Tests of microstructural hypothesis in the foreign exchange market.' NBER Working Paper No. 4471, 1993.

MACDONALD, RONALD, 'Are foreign exchange market forecasters rational?: Some survey based tests', *The Manchester School of Economic and Social Studies*, June 1991, **58**: 229–241.

MACDONALD, RONALD, 'Exchange rate survey data: A disaggregated G-7 perspective.' *Manchester School of Economic and Social Studies*, June 1992, **60**: 47–62.

MACDONALD, RONALD AND IAN W. MARSH, 'Combining exchange rate forecasts: What is the optimal consensus measure?,' *Journal of Forecasting*, May 1994, **13**: 313–332.

MACDONALD, RONALD AND THOMAS C. TORRANCE, 'On risk, rationality and excessive speculation in the Deutsche mark–US dollar exchange market: Some evidence using survey data,' *Oxford Bulletin of Economics and Statistics*, May 1988, **50**: 544–561.

MARSH, IAN W. AND DAVID POWER, 'A note on the performance of foreign exchange forecasters in a portfolio framework,' *Journal of Money and Banking*, 1995, forthcoming.

MEESE, RICHARD A. AND KENNETH ROGOFF, 'Empirical exchange rate models of the seventies: Do they fit out of sample?,' *Journal of International Economics*, February 1983, **14**: 345–373, (1983a).

MEESE, RICHARD A. AND KENNETH ROGOFF, 'The out-of-sample failure of empirical exchange rate models: Sampling error or misspecification?,' in Jacob A. Frenkel ed, *Exchange Rates and International Macroeconomics*, Chicago: University of Chicago Press, 1983 (1983b).

PRAT, GEORGE AND REMZI UCTUM, 'Analyse de l'hypothesis de changements endogenes dans le process anticipatif: L'example des anticipations de change,' University of Paris, mimeo, 1995.

PRENTICE, M.J., 'On the problem of *m* incomplete rankings,' *Biometrika*, 1979, **66**: 167–170.

TAGAKI, SHINJI, 'Exchange rate expectations: A survey of survey studies,' *International Monetary Fund Staff Papers*, March 1991, **38**: 156–183.

VARIAN, HAL R., 'Differences of opinion in financial markets,' in Stone, Courtnay C., ed, *Financial Risk: Theory, Evidence and Implications*, Boston: Kluwer Academic Publishers, 1989.

Available online at www.sciencedirect.com
SCIENCE @ DIRECT•

ELSEVIER

Int. Fin. Markets, Inst. and Money 13 (2003) 113–136

Journal of INTERNATIONAL FINANCIAL MARKETS, INSTITUTIONS & MONEY

www.elsevier.com/locate/econbase

Models of exchange rate expectations: how much heterogeneity?

Agnès Bénassy-Quéré [a], Sophie Larribeau [b], Ronald MacDonald [c,*]

[a] *University of Paris X (THEMA) and CEPII, Paris, France*
[b] *University of Rennes and THEMA, Rennes, France*
[c] *Economics Department, University of Strathclyde, 100 Cathedral Street, Glasgow G4 0LN, UK*

Received 27 March 2001; accepted 24 June 2002

Abstract

In this paper we use a unique disaggregate expectations data base to model the expectations formation of around 40 leading foreign exchange forecasters/dealers. Panel estimators are used to increase the power of the tests and to study various types of heterogeneities across forecasters. We find that both model heterogeneities and coefficient heterogeneities are important across individual forecasters, although the latter seem to be reduced at the 12-month compared with the 3-month horizon.
© 2002 Elsevier Science B.V. All rights reserved.

Keywords: Foreign exchange rates; Expectations formation; Heterogeneity

JEL classifications: C33; D84; F31

1. Introduction

The dynamic properties of exchange rates (particularly their excessive volatility) has proved a challenge to theorists, who emphasise the importance of economic fundamentals in explaining exchange rate movements. This is perhaps most clearly seen in the apparent failure of fundamentals-based exchange rate models to

* Corresponding author. Tel.: +44-141-548-3861; fax: +44-141-552-5589.
E-mail address: r.r.macdonald@strath.ac.uk (R. MacDonald).

1042-4431/02/$ - see front matter © 2002 Elsevier Science B.V. All rights reserved.
PII: S1042-4431(02)00040-9

outperform a simple random walk, a finding which 'continues to exert a pessimistic effect on the field of empirical exchange rate modelling in particular and international finance in general' (Frankel and Rose, 1995)[1]. One way in which theorists have tried to address this issue is by relaxing the assumption of rational expectations which is central to many traditional theoretical models, such as the monetary approach to the exchange rate. Indeed, several approaches have been developed where the market 'consensus' is the result of heterogenous beliefs based on differing models (chartists vs. fundamentalists, Frankel and Froot, 1986), and differing information sets (informed vs. uninformed, Lyons, 1991), differing capabilities (sophisticated vs. naive agents, De Long et al., 1990). Although some efforts have been made to show that specific forecasting methods like imitation can be reconciled with rational expectations (see for example, Orléan, 1986), little empirical work has been conducted to support the often ad hoc assumptions made in the theoretical literature[2].

In order to understand the behaviour of foreign exchange market participants, researchers have turned to examining the properties of survey based expectations, and this has recently become a very popular research avenue. Much of this work focuses on explaining the biasedness of the forward premium in terms of either a time-varying risk premium or expectational errors, or both (see Frankel and Froot, 1986, or Liu and Maddala, 1992). A relatively smaller portion of this work focuses on the actual formation of expectations. For example Frankel and Froot (1987a,b, 1990). Cavaglia et al. (1993a,b). MacDonald and Torrance (1988). Prat and Uctum (1994) find that bandwagon effects tend to be prevalent at short horizons (3 months and less) while expectations appear to be stabilising at longer horizons (greater than 3 months). In a further paper, Prat and Uctum (2000), using consensus expectations, show that the best model to describe aggregated (average) predictions is a model mixing extrapolative, adaptive and regressive forecasts. However, the interpretation of such a result is difficult since it is unclear if it stems from individuals using different models, or from heterogeneous interpretation of the same information structure.

A preliminary answer to this question comes from the work of Ito (1990). MacDonald and Marsh (1996); Elliott and Ito (1999). All of these studies are based on the following type of regression equation:

$$s_{jt}^{e} - s_{At}^{e} = g_j + \varepsilon_{jt}$$

where s_{jt}^{e} is the individuals expectation, s_{At}^{e} is the (cross section) average forecast and ε_{jt} is an error term. In an estimated version of this equation, a finding that g_j is significantly different from zero indicates that individuals j's forecast differs significantly from the cross section average and this may be interpreted as evidence

---

[1] Although this view is not universally accepted—see MacDonald (1995).

[2] Such models have typically been simulated to reproduce some stylised features of exchange-rate dynamics, especially chaos-like dynamics (De Grauwe et al., 1993) and fat tail distributions (Lux, 1998). Such tests are, however, reduced-form in nature.

of individual heterogeneity. Using a disaggregate survey data base constructed from the forecasts of Japanese-based exchange rate forecasters, Ito finds that there is extensive evidence of such heterogeneity and that this varies across various groups of exchange rate forecasters. MacDonald and Marsh demonstrate, using a panel survey data base of foreign exchange expectations from seven financial centres, that forecasters exhibit considerable heterogeneity, both in terms of a statistically significant value for g and also in terms of their interpretation of common information. Elliott and Ito update the work of Ito for Japan and they also find substantial evidence of individual heterogeneity in terms of statistically significant values of g.

In this study, we attempt to analyse the origins of the evident heterogeneity of foreign exchange market expectations by explicitly examining the expectations formation processes of individual foreign exchange market participants. To our knowledge such a study has not been undertaken before and should, therefore, provide useful information about a key aspect of expectations behaviour. In particular, we use individual data from the forecasts of Consensus Economics of London panel survey. These forecasts are for 3- and 12-month horizons and relate to the US dollar bilateral rates of the DM, yen and pound sterling for the period 1990–1994. Three basic models are estimated on each panel data base: an extrapolative, a regressive and an adaptive model. The coefficients are allowed to vary across individuals, and we test for the homogeneity of all individual coefficients using a Swamy test on the whole sample and on the sub-sample of those individuals displaying significant estimates. This facilitates making inferences on coefficient heterogeneities within each expectational framework, which is substantially different to the kind of test employed by others and discussed above. Finally, we estimate a mixed model, which nests the three basic ones, in order to test for model heterogeneities. This last exercise allows us to assess whether the 'consensus' forecast is made by heterogenous forecasters, or whether each forecaster himself uses a mixed model.

The outline of the remainder of this paper is as follows. In the next section, we present the methodology and data used in this paper. Section 3 contains our results concerning coefficient heterogeneities based on the estimation of the three basic models. Section 4 deals with model heterogeneities on the basis of mixed model estimations. Section 5 concludes.

2. Methodology and data

2.1. General strategy

Three basic expectational models are generally considered in the literature. According to the *extrapolative* model, forecasters are essentially chartists: their expectations are based on the past evolution of the variable, its present value summing up available information. In the *regressive* framework, the exchange rate is assumed to return gradually to the equilibrium value, which can itself move over

116 *A. Bénassy-Quéré et al. / Int. Fin. Markets, Inst. and Money 13 (2003) 113–136*

time. If the equilibrium is a moving average of the actual exchange rate, the regressive model could also be classified as a chartist model. Alternatively, the equilibrium can be related to fundamentals, such as relative prices. Finally, the *adaptive* model is a form of learning process where forecasters try to learn the 'true' level of the variable rather than its underlying process.

Heterogeneities across forecasters can show up either in the use of different basic models (extrapolative/regressive/adaptive), or in the use of different coefficients within the same basic model (e.g. different mean-reverting coefficients in the regressive model). We study the latter by estimating each basic model on a panel sample of forecasts and allowing individual coefficients to differ across forecasters. However, this method does not account for heterogeneities in the models selected by the various forecasters. This more fundamental form of heterogeneity is studied here through the estimation of a mixed model which nests within it the three basic models, and through the tests performed on the coefficients of this mixed model for each forecaster.

Given the generality of the mixed model, it may seem more appropriate to estimate only this model rather than estimating the basic models sequentially. However, we believe there is value added to be obtained from looking at each model separately. This is because the particular empirical specification of, say, the extrapolative model may depend on the underlying data dynamics, which would be difficult to discern if the general model was first tested with no pre-testing on the underlying components. In addition, it is difficult to study the heterogeneity of individual coefficients within the mixed model where the individual coefficients on the various explanatory variables are never significant at the same time. Finally, 12 observations per individual are dropped in the adaptive as well as in the mixed model for the 12-month horizon. This loss of information is especially severe for the mixed model where many coefficients must be estimated.

Previous survey-based work on expectational processes generally utilises the consensus measure of the survey, such as the mean or median[3]. Exceptions are Ito (1990), MacDonald (1992), who both analyse individual survey data. For example, Ito (1990) estimates an extrapolative model with idiosyncratic coefficients effects, using a panel data set of biweekly surveys on yen/dollar, 1-, 3- and 6-month expectations of 44 Japanese institutions, over the period May 1985 to June 1987. He finds that 'the heterogeneity is more like a constant bias rather than the differences in reacting to the recent changes in the exchange rate' (p. 440). However, the scope of this study is limited both geographically (only Japanese forecasts of the yen/dollar exchange rate are available) and temporally (the period covered was dominated by the dramatic fall of the dollar against the yen).

MacDonald (1992) tested the null of static expectations against the alternative of extrapolative, adaptive and regressive expectations, using the disaggregate data set produced by Consensus Economics of London, for the period October 1989 to March 1991. Implementing single equation estimations on each individual, he was

[3] See Takagi (1991), Bénassy-Quéré and Raymond (1997), MacDonald (2000) for reviews.

unable to reject the null hypothesis of static expectations for the vast majority of forecasters. However, this failure to reject the null may simply reflect the econometric method used and/or the relatively short data span available.

In this paper, we also attempt to model the expectations formation process of individual forecasters, and, in particular, the extent of individual heterogeneity in expectations formation. Our approach has certain advantages over earlier studies, noted above: we have access to forecasts produced in all of the G7 financial centres; our sample period is longer than that used in the above studies; most notably, we use panel data sets which potentially have more power to discriminate amongst the various hypotheses and facilitates a specific test for heterogeneity across individuals.

2.2. Econometric methodology

Two different classes of panel estimators are used here: a base-line model, which we take to be a fixed effects model, and a model with random coefficients. The general form of the constant coefficients model with fixed effects is:

$$S^{a}_{i,t,h} - S_t = \alpha_{i,h} + \beta_{i,h} x_{i,t,h} + u_{i,t,h}, \tag{1}$$

where $S^{a}_{i,t,h}$ is the logarithm of the exchange rate that is expected by individual i, at time t, for time $t+h$ (in this paper, $h=3$ or 12 months), S_t is the logarithm of the nominal exchange rate observed at time t, α_{ih} is a constant that varies across individuals, β_h is constant and identical for all individuals, and $x_{i,t,h}$ is the vector of explanatory variables in the adaptive, regressive, extrapolative or mixed model[4]. The general form of the random coefficients model is:

$$S^{a}_{i,t,h} - S_t = \alpha_{i,h} + \beta_{i,h} x_{i,t,h} + u_{i,t,h}, \tag{2}$$

where α_{ih} and β_{ih} are each the sum of a constant, common mean, λ_h, and of a random term, $\lambda_{i,h}$, with zero mean and a constant variance (the idiosyncratic term). Hence, the vector of coefficients $\Lambda_{i,h} = \begin{pmatrix} \alpha_{i,h} \\ \beta_{i,h} \end{pmatrix}$ can be written[5]:

$$\Lambda_{i,h} = \lambda_h + \lambda_{i,h} \text{ with } E\lambda_{i,h} = 0 \quad \text{for each } i$$

and

$$E\lambda_{i,h}\lambda'_{j,h} = \begin{cases} \Delta & \text{if } i=j \\ 0 & \text{if } i \neq j \end{cases}.$$

In the first model, individual effects are reduced to differing constants across individuals, whereas in the second model all coefficients are random and vary across individuals, meaning that individuals can differ in their interpretation of the

---

4 $x_{i,t,h} = x_{t,h}$ in the extrapolative and regressive models.

5 See Hsiao (1986) (chapter 6) and Hsiao (1992).

information driven by the explanatory variables[6]. The residuals are assumed to have the following properties:

$$u_{i,t,h} = e_{i,t,h} - \theta_1 e_{i,t-1,h} - \theta_2 e_{i,t-2,h},$$

$$e_{i,t,h} \rightarrow N(0, \sigma^2_{i,h}) \quad \text{for each } t,$$

$$Ee_{i,t,h}e_{i,t',h} = 0 \quad \text{if } t \neq t',$$

$$Ee_{i,t,h}e_{j,t',h} = 0 \quad \text{if } i \neq j \text{ for each } (t, t'),$$

$$Eu_{i,h}u'_{j,h} = \begin{cases} \sigma^2_{i,h}\Theta_h & \text{if } i = j \\ 0 & \text{if } i \neq j' \end{cases}$$

where $u_{i,h}$ is the vector of the individual residuals and Θ_h is derived from the MA2 structure of the residuals. The latter assumption arises because of the overlapping nature of the data which imparts a second order moving average error process (see for example, Hansen and Hodrick, 1980)[7] and, indeed, this kind of process was borne out by our initial diagnostic testing. Besides, the use of such a process has the added advantage that it does not affect the interpretation of the extrapolative coefficient (which it would were we to use an autoregressive structure for the error process).

In the fixed effects model, individual heterogeneity is evaluated through a Fisher test where the null hypothesis is H_0: $\alpha_{i,h} = \alpha_h$. In the random coefficients model, individual heterogeneity is tested using a Swamy test where the null hypothesis is:

$$H_0{:}\Lambda_{1h} = \Lambda_{2h} = \ldots = \Lambda_{Nh},$$

where N denotes the number of individuals. The statistic of the test is:

$$F^* = \sum_{i=1}^{N} \frac{1}{\hat{\sigma}^2_{ih}} (\hat{\Lambda}_{ih} - \hat{\Lambda}^*_h)' x'_{ih} \Theta_h^{-1} x_{ih} (\hat{\Lambda}_{ih} - \hat{\Lambda}^*_h),$$

where x_{ih} is the vector of explanatory variables for each individual, $\hat{\Lambda}_{ih}$ is the least-squares estimator for each cross-sectional unit and $\hat{\Lambda}^*_h$ is a matrix-weighed average of $\hat{\Lambda}_{ih}$, the weights being inversely proportional to $\hat{\sigma}^2_{ih}\Theta_h$. Under H_0, F^* has an asymptotic χ^2 distribution with $K(N-1)$ degrees of freedom as T, the number of

[6] Although there is little doubt that there will be large heterogeneities in individual fixed effects, we want to check their significance (through a Fisher test) before looking at a somewhat more meaningful type of heterogeneity. In addition, estimating the fixed-effect model first allows us to select the functional form which will be the same for the random-coefficient estimation.

[7] Hansen and Hodrick show that when data overlap, as is the case here, the residuals by construction follow an MA(h-1) process, where h is the forecast horizon. However, this result applies only when the endogeneous variable is the forecast error, as in unbiaseness tests for instance. Here, the endogeneous variable contains the expectation error, although it is not equal to it.

periods, tends to infinity and N is fixed, K being the number of parameters[8]. This test can also be performed on a sub-vector of coefficients.

The Swamy test is, however, not very powerful since only one different coefficient can be enough to reject global homogeneity. We, therefore, subsequently estimate each model on each individual separately and construct sub-panels for individuals, who display significant estimates. We then re-run our panel estimates, and perform the Swamy test on the sub-panels. We also test for any individual discrepancy from the sub-panel behaviour with the following Student test:

$$\begin{vmatrix} H_0{:}\Lambda_h^k(i) = \Lambda_h^k \\ H_1{:}\Lambda_h^k(i) \neq \Lambda_h^k, \end{vmatrix}$$

where $\Lambda_h^k(i)$ is the kth component of the vector of estimated parameters in the individual regression for individual i, and Λ_h^k is the kth component of the estimated parameter for the sub-panel. The actual statistic for this test is:

$$\mathrm{ST} = \frac{\Lambda_h^k(i) - \hat{\Lambda}_h^k}{\hat{\sigma}_{\Lambda_h^k(i)}}$$

where $\hat{\sigma}_{\hat{\Lambda}_h^k(i)}$ is the estimated standard error of $\hat{\Lambda}_h^k(i)$ in i-individual regression. Under the null hypothesis, ST follows a Student distribution with (TT$-K$) degrees of freedom, TT being the number of observations per individual and K, the number of explanatory variables (both TT and K vary across the models). It should be noted that the common coefficient used in the latter test ($\hat{\Lambda}_h^k$) is the estimated common coefficient of the sub-panel, while the common coefficients used in the Swamy test ($\hat{\Lambda}_h^*$) are weighted averages of individual coefficients. These two measures of common behaviour can differ when there are few individuals in the sub-panel. This is because an individual coefficient estimated with a large uncertainty, $\hat{\sigma}_{ih}^2$, is far away from the weighed average by construction (its weight in the average is low). Thus, the null hypothesis is easily rejected in the Swamy test, which is not the case in the individual Student test.

2.3. The data set

Our survey data are from Consensus Economics of London, who collect foreign exchange forecasts from various individuals and financial institutions in the capital cities of the G7. The salient features of the survey data base are summarised in Table 1. The reliability of survey data has been questioned in a number of ways. For example, respondents to a particular survey may have no idea of the future exchange rate because their working horizon does not fit that of the survey. Additionally, surveyed forecasters may not reveal their true expectations because of their desire to manipulate the overall outcome. A response to the former kind of criticism has been given by Goodhart (1988): 'there is little incentive for those paid to forecast the

---

[8] This statistics is derived from Hsiao (1986) with an MA2 residual process represented by the matrix.

Table 1
The salient features of the survey data

Surveying institution	Consensus Forecasts, London
Exchange rates	DM/$, yen/$, £/$
Horizons of the forecasts	3 and 12 months
Frequency	Monthly
Period of the survey	1990:01–1994:12
Participants of the survey	133 individuals from various cities, of which 3/4 are financial institutions
Collecting method	by fax, on the first Monday of each month

future to confess that it cannot be done, so they are unlikely to put much weight on the random walk view' (p. 451). In addition, Ammer and Brunner (1997) show that at least some of the US commercial banks run dealing positions 'with a view as to how markets will move over a period of several weeks or more' (p. 9). This result is based on first-order autocorrelations showing that the reported positions (in the monthly FFIEC regulatory form number 035) are persistent, although mean-reverting. A response to the second kind of criticism would be to argue that only consensus forecasts (i.e. average or median forecasts) are published, and that the publication intervenes with a lag which prevents such information being used for immediate speculation.

Fig. 1 depicts the average expectation of the panel, together with the extreme forecasts and the realisations for the three currencies and the two horizons. Two features of the survey data emerge from this figure:

i) The uncertainty band is larger for the 12-month horizon than for the 3-month horizon, which is consistent with larger expected variations for longer horizons.
ii) The average 3-month expectation follows the realisations with a 3-month lag, showing that the market average behaviour is close to that of a random walk: the expected rate is close to the observed rate by the time of the forecast. This feature does not apply to the 12-month expectation which appears more independent of the realisations[9]. The former result is consistent with existing econometric results showing that the null hypothesis of a random walk is generally not rejected for short horizons (Bénassy-Quéré and Raymond, 1997). One motivation for the present study is to determine if this result applies to individual expectations formation processes.

During 5 years, 133 forecasters were asked for six predictions each month (three exchange rates over two horizons)[10]. Only seven individuals never failed to give their six expectations, i.e. only seven provided a total of $60 \times 3 \times 2 = 360$ predictions each.

[9] An exception is the pound crisis of September 1991: this crisis was not expected, but it lead to a strong revision of expectations.

[10] Although more forecasters than those studied in this paper responded to the survey poll, only 133 remained the same throughout the 5-year time period.

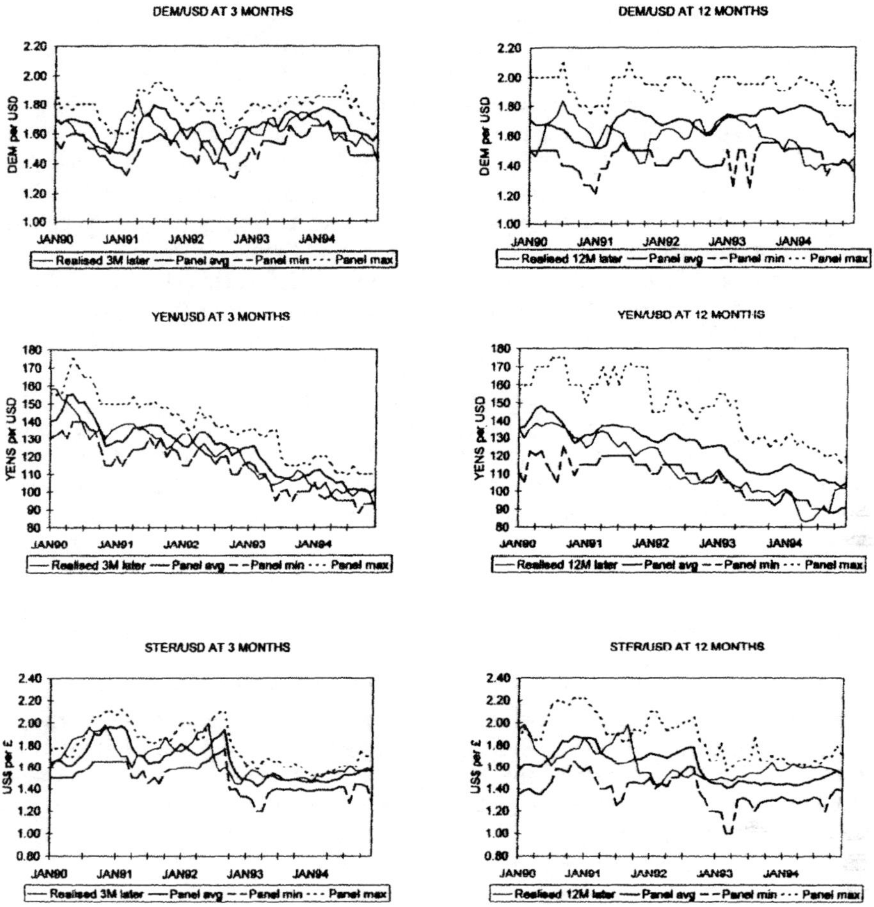

Fig. 1. Panel expectations.

All other individuals failed at least once. Some of them participated in the panel only during one sub-period. Others sometimes did not answer, for reasons that are unknown but can easily be understood (holiday, staff restructuring, no time, etc). However, standard econometric methods are not well disposed towards missing values (especially in a model with random coefficients), and it is, therefore, necessary to address this issue. Limiting the panel to those individuals who never failed to respond would have been too costly since it would have meant dropping 123–125 individuals (out of 133), depending on the forecast horizon/currency including those who failed only once or twice. Against this, working with the whole data set with incomplete panel data techniques (mixing various forecasting periods) could have lead us to confuse individual heterogeneities and time heterogeneities (given the limitation of our time span, we have to assume constant coefficients over time). On balance, we decided to follow MacDonald and Marsh (1996) in retaining those individuals, who did not fail more than four times (i.e. less than once a year on average) for each exchange rate at each horizon. The blanks were then filled in with the mean expectation of the panel. This solution produces a balanced panel of individuals (depending on the currency and on the horizon)[11]. For the DM this procedure produced 38 individuals at the 3 months horizon and 36 at the 12 months horizon, for the yen, it produced 38 individuals at both horizons, while for the pound sterling it produced 33 at the 3-month and 34 at the 12-month horizon.

In extracting reliable statistical inferences from our estimated relationships, it is important that the variables used are stationary. The variables employed in this study are either first differences or quasi-differences. In particular, the stationarity properties of the expected change in the exchange rate should be similar to the stationarity properties of the actual change in the exchange rate. In order to check this, we ran standard augmented Dickey–Fuller unit root tests for each of the series used in the study. These tests gave a very clear rejection of the null of non-stationarity (when a constant and constant plus time trend were used as deterministic series), thereby confirming the above assertion regarding the use of quasi-difference series. Furthermore, we also used the panel unit root tests of Levin and Lin (1993) to test if each variable considered in a panel context was stationary. Not surprisingly, given the stationarity on an individual unit basis, the panel tests gave a very clear rejection of the null of non-stationarity (having, on average, adjusted t-ratios of -16.0, compared with the 5% critical values of -2.0)[12].

Section 3 presents the results of the estimations performed for each of the three basic models (extrapolative/regressive/adaptive), and the conclusions they embody in terms of coefficient heterogeneities across individuals within each model. Section 4 turns to the results obtained for the mixed model, which allows conclusions on the heterogeneities across individuals in the choice of a particular basic model to be made. Section 5 concludes.

3. Coefficient heterogeneities

3.1. The extrapolative model

As already noted, in the extrapolative model the expected variation of the exchange rate depends on its past variations. The basic extrapolative model is usually defined as:

$$S^{a}_{i,t,h} - S_t = b(S_t - S_{t-1}), \quad b > 0, \tag{3}$$

---

[11] A preliminary statistical analysis indicated no relationship between the number of missing values and the S.D. of the forecasts over time and also the mean absolute error. In any case, our chosen method of replacing missing values will bias the results against finding heterogeneity.

[12] These results are available from the authors on request.

where $S^a_{i,t,h}$ is the logarithm of the exchange rate that is expected by individual i, at time t, for time $t+h$ (in this paper, $h=3$ or 12 months). S_t is the logarithm of the nominal exchange rate observed at time t. In implementing this model, we started with a richer lag structure than that given in Eq. (3). In particular, we experimented with up to three lagged changes in the exchange rate. Since the last lag was never significant in any specification, we do not report estimates with it included. However, to be consistent, we report the estimated two lags even when they are not significant. Additionally, a time trend was included in each of the estimated equations to capture the potential systematic movements in currencies which are not explicitly modeled, and a dummy was added to the pound equation to take account of the September 1992 currency crisis.

For our 'base-line' fixed effects model, the specification used is:

$$S^a_{i,t,h} - S_t = a_{i,h} + b^1_h(S_t - S_{t-1}) + b^2_h(S_{t-1} - S_{t-2}) + c^1_h t + c^2_h \text{Crisis}_t + u_{i,t,h}, \qquad (4)$$

where Crisis_t is a dummy, which takes the value of 1 only for the £/USD exchange rate in October 1992; i.e. for the first forecast made on this exchange rate after the pound left the European exchange rate mechanism (otherwise, $\text{Crisis}_t = 0$). The random-coefficient estimation follows the same specification.

The estimates with fixed effects are reported in the top half of Table 2 and indicate that all but one of the slope coefficients are significantly negative. This implies that, on average, a currency appreciation generates the expectation of a depreciation. This is a surprising result and conflicts with the basic premise of the model. However, it is, in fact, consistent with the results usually obtained when average data are used. Such studies indicate that for horizons of 3 months or more the coefficient of extrapolation is negative, while for shorter horizons, the coefficients are positive or zero[13].

The moving average coefficients are statistically significant thereby confirming our use of an MA2 model for the residuals. The time trend is positive for the mark and yen at both horizons, and negative for the pound[14]. Given that the pound is certain-priced while the two other currencies are uncertain-priced, this result can be interpreted as indicating that the dollar was expected to appreciate against the three currencies to an increasing extent over the period. Since the dollar tended to depreciate against the yen over the period (Fig. 1), this result can be interpreted as evidence of mean-reverting expectations. If this interpretation is correct, then a regressive model should be more appropriate for this currency. Finally, the coefficient on the crisis dummy is significant and negative, indicating that the expected value of the pound was revised downwards by 6–7% following the crisis.

We tested for homoscedastic errors using an ARCH test (since it is widely accepted that ARCH effects constitute the most likely source of heteroscedasticity

[13] See Takagi (1991), Bénassy-Quéré and Raymond (1997).

[14] It is worth noting that the inclusion of the time trend does not effect the signs or the significance of the estimates of the extrapolative coefficients; its main effect is to increase the explanatory power of the equation.

Table 2
Extrapolative model

	DM/$		Yen/$		£/$	
	3 months	12 months	3 months	12 months	3 months	12 months
The fixed effects model						
Number of individuals	38	36	38	38	33	34
b^1	−0.306**	−0.483**	−0.317**	−0.396**	−0.371**	−0.453**
b^2	−0.041*	−0.185**	−0.034*	−0.150**	0.005	−0.074**
c^1	6×10^{-4}**	0.001**	8×10^{-4}**	0.002**	-2×10^{-4}**	-9×10^{-5}
c^2	–	–	–	–	−0.061**	−0.067**
θ_1	−0.372**	−0.525**	−0.351**	−0.494**	−0.328**	−0.514**
θ_2	−0.207**	−0.362**	−0.187**	−0.293**	−0.197**	−0.289**
Adjusted R^2	0.255	0.287	0.285	0.401	0.217	0.233
DW	1.880	1.761	1.790	1.721	1.821	1.828
Arch test[a]						
χ^2 statistic[a]	0.041	9.626	2.644	0.315	0.108	5.176
P-value	0.838	0.002	0.104	0.574	0.742	0.023
Fixed effects: $H_0: a_i = a$						
Fisher statistic	6.083	11.832	5.284	11.666	7.682	14.089
P-value	0.000	0.000	0.000	0.000	0.000	0.000
Measuring individual heterogeneities						
Random coefficients model						
Adjusted R^2	0.370	0.376	0.426	0.551	0.353	0.362
Swamy tests on panel estimates						
On all coefficients	536.9*	498.7*	626.8*	879.3*	622.9*	711.5*
On (b^1, b^2)	250.8*	70.9	227.4*	89.1	380.6*	101.6*
Individuals with significant bi^1 *(at 10%) in individual regressions*						
% of the panel	81.6	83.3	84.2	81.6	88.2	90.9
S.D. of b_i^1 (%)	47.4	22.3	50.7	29.6	47.7	27.9
Swamy test on sub-panel estimates (individuals with significant b_i^1*)*						
On all coefficients	336.5*	433.0*	539.9*	751.2*	589.5*	621.8*
On (b^1, b^2)	163.8*	48.2	165.6*	58.7	316.6*	61.2*
Percent of significantly different individual coefficients in the sub-panel						
b_i^1	29.0	13.3	28.1	12.9	33.3	13.3
bi^2	29.0	23.3	31.3	16.1	43.3	36.7
c_i	25.8	40.0	40.6	61.3	20.0	30.0

** Significant at 1%; *, significant at 5%; ##, significant at 10%; #, significant at 15%. Swamy tests, *, means that the null hypothesis of homogeneity of all coefficients or of a sub-vector of coefficients across individuals is rejected at 10%. Individual tests, individual coefficients are those estimated in individual regressions.

[a] $H_0: \rho = 0$ in $(\frac{1}{N}\Sigma_{i=1}^{N} e_{i,t,h}^2) = \rho(\frac{1}{N}\Sigma_{i=1}^{N} e_{i,t-1,h}^2) + \varepsilon_{t,h}$.

for exchange rates). The null hypothesis of no ARCH effects cannot be rejected, except for the £/$ at 12 months where it is rejected at the 5% level (but accepted at the 1% level), and for the DM/$ at 12 months, where it is rejected at any level.

The null hypothesis of no fixed effects is strongly rejected for this panel, with the estimated Fisher statistics all having P-values of 0.000. Given this, we now explore whether there is a richer form of heterogeneity embedded in our panel estimates by examining the random coefficients model.

The estimation results for the extrapolative model using a random coefficients estimator are detailed in Bénassy-Quéré et al. (1999). As in the fixed effects case, we find that the common b coefficients are negative and the coefficient on the last observed exchange rate variation, b^1, is always significant. However, in the random effects estimates b^2 (the coefficient on the lagged exchange rate variation) is significant at only the 12-month horizon for two currencies: at longer horizons, forecasters use more information on the dynamic exchange rate process than they do at short horizons. Table 2 reports the adjusted R^2s from the random regressions, which range from 40 to 70% above their values in the fixed effects models, and we attribute this to the greater flexibility this model has in capturing individual heterogeneities. The null hypothesis of homoscedastic residuals cannot be rejected except, again, in the case of the pound at the 12-month horizon.

An important advantage of the random coefficient model is that it provides a test for global heterogeneity (Swamy test in Table 2). For the extrapolative model, we always reject the null hypothesis of homogeneity at the 3-month horizon for the whole vector of coefficients and also for the sub-vector containing b_{ih}^1 and $b_{ih}^2()$. At the 12-month horizon, the homogeneity of all the coefficients is also rejected, but the homogeneity of the individual b_{ih}^1 and b_{ih}^2 coefficients is not rejected at the 10% level for the DM and yen forecasts. This result may stem from the fact that individual forecasters rely more heavily on public forecasts for long horizons.

In order to get a more precise representation of the heterogeneities, noted above, we estimated extrapolative models for individuals, who produced a significant b^1 coefficient. The percentage of individuals who use a version of the extrapolative model is summarised in the bottom half of Table 2. These indicate that about 20% of the forecasters do not extrapolate, and this figure is independent of the horizon. Among the remaining individuals, the dispersion of the b_{ih}^1 coefficient is high. For instance, the standard deviation (S.D.) of b^1 across individuals at 3 months is around 50%. However, the dispersion of b^1 is much smaller for the 12-month horizon, which is consistent with the Swamy tests.

Finally, we re-ran the panel estimates, limiting the sample to those individuals displaying a significant b_i^1 in the individual regressions. The results are contained in the rows with the label 'sub-panel' in Table 2. The Swamy tests give the same results as for the whole panel. The extent of individual heterogeneities is obtained by testing the equality of each individual coefficient relative to the sub-panel average. Depending on the coefficient and on the exchange rate concerned, between 13 and 61% of individual coefficients differ significantly from the panel average. It should be noted that the number of individual heterogeneities is systematically smaller for the 12-month horizon: for b^1 (our filter), the percentage of heterogeneities falls from 28 to 33% at 3 months to 13% at 12 months.

The heterogeneities found in our extrapolative tests can be summarised as follows. Around 20% of forecasters do not extrapolate. Among the 80%, who use a version of the extrapolative model, there are still many heterogeneities in the coefficients. However, the Swamy test fails to reject the null hypothesis of homogeneity for the most important coefficients (b^1 and b^2) at the 12-month horizon, although detailed analysis confirms a smaller heterogeneity grouping at 12 months. We believe that this latter result can be interpreted as indicative of a higher reliance on public forecasts at longer horizons.

3.2. The regressive model

In the regressive model, the exchange rate is expected to move towards a reference level, $\bar{S}_t$, which can be a constant, a moving average, or a fundamental rate based, for instance, on purchasing power parity (PPP). The basic regressive model is defined as:

$$S^a_{i,t,h} - S_t = d(\bar{S}_t - S_t), \quad 0 < d < 1, \tag{5}$$

where $\bar{S}_t$ denotes a measure of the equilibrium exchange rate. Here, we use a PPP reference rate: $\bar{S}_t$ is the nominal exchange rate that would have maintained the real exchange rate at a level equal to its mean over the estimation period (1990:01–1994:12)[15].

Following Prat and Uctum (2000), we introduce a second order term into the regressive equation: that is, when the target exchange rate depreciates more quickly than the observed exchange rate, the expected speed of depreciation rises. Finally, a dummy is introduced for the £/USD exchange rate in order to take the regime shift of September 1992 into account: because the pound moved from a fixed to a floating exchange rate regime, forecasters may have switched to another long run reference rate after September 1992. Thus, we define Float_t as a dummy which is equal to 1 only for the pound after September 1992, zero otherwise. For the fixed effects model the specification is:

$$S^a_{i,t,h} - S_t = a_{i,h} + d^1_h(\bar{S}_t - S_t) + d^2_h((\bar{S}_t - \bar{S}_{t-1}) - (S_t - S_{t-1})) + c^3_h\text{Float}_t + u_{i,t,h} \tag{6}$$

Eq. (6) can be re-expressed to explain exchange rate expectations with two regressive terms:

$$S^a_{i,t,h} - S_t = a_{i,h} + (d^1_h + d^2_h)(\bar{S}_t - S_t) + d^2_h(S_{t-1} - \bar{S}_{t-1}) + c^3_h\text{Float}_t + u_{i,t,h} \tag{6'}$$

In Table 3, we present the fixed effects results. Although the adjusted R^2s have the same orders of magnitude as in the extrapolative model, this specification may be deemed more satisfactory since the equations do not feature a trend[16]. The residual

[15] The real exchange rate is calculated with monthly consumer prices (OECD). We alternatively used a Hodrick–Prescott filter over a longer period (1974:01–1994:12), calibrated in order to generate an overvaluation of the dollar between 1983 and 1986. The results (not reported here) were, however, less significant than with the PPP rate.

[16] The interpretation of the positive trend coefficient in the extrapolative model as a mean reversion behaviour is thus confirmed for the yen.

Table 3
The regressive model

	DM/$		Yen/$		£/$	
	3 months	12 months	3 months	12 months	3 months	12 months
The fixed effects model						
Number of individuals	38	36	38	38	33	34
d^1	0.0388*	0.395**	0.111**	0.320**	0.029#	0.287**
d^2	0.282**	0.221**	0.251**	0.175**	0.252**	0.230**
c^3	–	–	–	−0.010**	−0.042**	
θ_1	−0.420**	−0.515**	−0.386**	−0.483**	−0.303**	−0.455**
θ_2	−0.252**	−0.356**	−0.214**	−0.281**	−0.190**	−0.235**
Adjusted R^2	0.154	0.283	0.255	0.402	0.166	0.245
DW	1.886	1.741	1.830	1.704	1.796	1.727
Arch test(1)						
$\chi^2(1)$ statistic	0.006	9.161	2.675	1.332	0.008	10.214
P-value	0.937	0.002	0.102	0.248	0.930	0.001
Fixed effects: $H_0{:}a_I = a$						
Fisher statistic	5.4638*	11.902*	4.992*	11.424*	7.317*	14.474*
Measuring individual heterogeneities						
Random coefficients model						
Adjusted R^2	0.238	0.331	0.369	0.539	0.289	0.408
Swamy tests on panel estimates						
On all coefficients	411.3*	420.3*	480.1*	793.6*	462.9*	768.2**
On (d^1, d^2)	243.2*	53.2	279.0*	197.6*	43301.9*	17097.0*
Individuals *with significant* d_i^1 *(at 10%) in individual regressions*						
% of the panel	18.4	69.4	63.2	84.2	27.3	70.6
S.D. of d_i^1 (%)	–	23.3	54.3	49.6	–	61.6
Swamy test on sub-panel 1 estimates (individuals with significant d_i^1*)*						
On all coefficients	336.5*	433.0*	539.9*	751.2*	589.5*	621.8*
On (d^1, d^2)	163.8*	48.2	165.6*	58.7	316.6*	61.2*
Percent of significantly different individual coefficients in sub-panel 1						
d_i^1	n.a.	12.0	25.0	53.1	n.a.	16.7
d_i^2	n.a.	24.0	45.8	28.1	n.a.	20.8
Individuals with significant d_i^2 *(at 10%) in individual regressions*						
% of the panel	73.7	44.4	86.8	50.0	84.8	58.8
S.D. of d_i^2 (%)	31.4	30.5	70.4	68.7	52.3	36.1
Swamy test on sub-panel 2 estimates (individuals with significant d_i^2*)*						
On all coefficients	259.6*	218.1*	418.8*	482.9*	389.8*	476.1*
On (d^1, d^2)	165.9*	154.6*	246.0*	414.7*	22289.7*	94880.9*
Percent of significantly different individual coefficients in sub-panel 2						
d_i^1	14.3	25.0	36.4	63.2	28.6	55.0
d_i^2	25.0	12.5	30.3	21.1	25.0	35.0

See **Table 2,** n.a., Not available (sub-panel too small to perform the regression).

autocorrelation seems to have been well captured by the MA2 process; however, the null hypothesis of homoscedasticity is still rejected for the 12-month DM and pound expectations. Both d^1 and d^2 are positive and almost always highly significant. A positive d^1 implies that the nominal exchange rate is expected to return to its PPP level: forecasters believe in absolute PPP. It should be noted that d^1 is higher at the 12-month horizon than at the 3-month horizon. But consistency between 3- and 12-month expectations would imply d^1_{12} to be roughly four times d^1_3 (in the case of a linear expected adjustment), which is not the case here[17].

Some interpretation may be put on the d^2 coefficient in the following way. Since the assumption of PPP implies a constant real exchange rate, the variation in the PPP exchange rate must equal the inflation differential:

$$\bar{S}_t - \bar{S}_{t-1} = (P_t - P_{t-1}) - (P^*_t - P^*_{t-1}),$$

where P_t denotes the logarithm of the domestic consumer price index and P^*_t the foreign consumer price index. Under the maintained hypothesis, therefore, the acceleration term is equal and opposite to the observed variation of the real exchange rate:

$$(\bar{S}_t - \bar{S}_{t-1}) - (S_t - S_{t-1}) = (P_t - P_{t-1}) - (P^*_t - P^*_{t-1}) - (S_t - S_{t-1}).$$

Hence, a positive d^2 means that the last real exchange rate variation is expected to be reversed, without any level anchor: forecasters believe in relative PPP. Note that d^2 is larger for 3-month than for 12-month expectations, which means that variations in the real exchange rate are expected to revert quickly. This is consistent with the negative coefficients obtained in the extrapolative model (the PPP exchange rate moves only slowly, so the acceleration term resembles an extrapolative term over short horizons).

As in the extrapolative model, fixed effects are highly significant, which encourages us to explore the individual heterogeneities in more detail. Using a random coefficients estimator, the common coefficients, d^1 and d^2, are still positive, but d^1 is no longer significant in 2 of the 3-month cases (see Bénassy-Quéré et al., op. cit.). Hence, forecasters seem to believe in relative PPP at this horizon, while they believe in absolute PPP at the 12 months horizon. This would seem to accord with our economic intuition, in the sense that absolute PPP is more likely to hold at long horizons. Other results using the random coefficient model are in line with the extrapolative model: (i) except for the 12-month expectations of the DM, the adjusted R^2s are between 40 and 70% above those obtained with fixed effects; (ii) the two cases of heteroscedasticity obtained with fixed effects remain in the random coefficients model.

The Swamy test statistic reported in Table 3 produces a rejection of the homogeneity of the coefficients across individuals, except for (d^1, d^2) in the 12-

[17] Time-consistency tests suggested by **Pesaran (1989)** cannot be performed here because we do not have a forecasting model for the 1-month exchange-rate variation, which appears significant in the 12-month expectation.

month DM/$ regression. The Swamy statistic is very high for (d^1, d^2) in the £/$, due to significantly negative values for two individuals. Those individuals seem to extrapolate past deviations from PPP. In sum, we note that individual heterogeneity seems more important here than in the extrapolative case. For example, in two cases, less than 1/3rd of the forecasters produce a significant value of d^1_{ih}. The heterogeneities on d^1_i are more frequent in the case of the 3-month horizon. This result may be due to the fact that many individuals only believe in relative PPP for the 3-month horizon (displaying significant $d^2_{i,h}$).

Interpreting individuals who produce a significant d^1 coefficient as those using absolute PPP, we see that significant heterogeneities remain: the Swamy tests reject homogeneity of the individual coefficients (except, again, for the 12-month DM/$ expectations), and $d^1_{i,h}$ differs from the panel average for 12–53% of the individuals[18].

In order to test for heterogeneity among relative PPP forecasters, we subsequently used the significance of the d^2_{ih} coefficient as a filter, and in Table 3, we report sub-panel results which only include individuals who had a significant d^2_{ih} in individual regressions. More individuals are kept in the sub-panel than in the previous case for the 3-month horizon, but less individuals are kept for two currencies at the 12-month horizon. This result confirms that 3-month individual expectations generally follow relative PPP, while 12-month individual expectations follow absolute PPP. Among regressive forecasters, the dispersion of d^2_i is specially high for the yen. Sub-panel results confirm this high heterogeneity for the yen[19].

3.3. *The adaptive model*

The adaptive expectations model is defined as:

$$S^a_{i,t,h} - S^a_{i,t\ h,h} = (1+f)(S_t - S^a_{i,t-h,h}), \quad 0 < (1+f) < 1. \tag{7}$$

which here is estimated as:[20]

$$S^a_{i,t,h} - S_t = a_{i,h} + f_h(S_t - S^a_{i,t-h,h}) + c^1_h t + u_{i,t,h}, \tag{8}$$

Since the error on the £/USD exchange rate happened to be very large in September 1992, there is no need for a crisis dummy in the adaptive model (the correction made in the forecasts is automatically large in October 1992). Because $(1+f_h)$ should be bounded by 0 and 1, f_h should be negative in Eq. (8). This is what we obtain: f is always significantly negative (Table 4). Generally, the value of f is

---

[18] Sub-panel estimates were not calculated for the DM and the yen at 3 months because the sub-sample were too small.

[19] This heterogeneity is confirmed by plotting of the coefficient distributions (see Bénassy-Quéré et al., op. cit.).

[20] Although this formulation entails an important loss of information at the 12-month horizon, it is preferred to an 'early revision' formulation proposed by **Prat and Uctum (2000)** where the explanatory variable is not an expectation error.

Table 4
The Adaptive model

	DM/$		Yen/$		£/$	
	3 months	12 months	3 months	12 months	3 months	12 months
The fixed effects model						
Number of individuals	38	36	38	38	33	34
f	−0.124**	−0.170**	−0.129**	−0.093**	−0.087**	−0.078**
c^1	5×10^{-4}**	3×10^{-4}**	6×10^{-4}**	10^{-3}**	-2×10^{-4}**	2×10^{-4}#
θ_1	−0.304**	−0.406**	−0.308**	−0.422**	−0.292**	−0.425**
θ_2	−0.179**	−0.293**	−0.193**	−0.248**	−0.126**	−0.198**
Adjusted R^2	0.233	0.282	0.253	0.353	0.148	0.235
DW	1.872	1.725	1.799	1.697	1.823	1.761
Arch test(1)						
$\chi^2(1)$ statistic	0.277	1.393	0.053	0.122	0.003	0.286
P-value	0.598	0.237	0.818	0.726	0.952	0.593
Fixed effects: $H_0: a_i = a$						
Fisher statistic	4.578*	10.717*	4.057*	14.138*	5.902*	12.175*
Measuring individual heterogeneities						
Random coefficients model						
Adjusted R^2	0.344	0.396	0.353	0.498	0.240	0.377
Swamy tests on panel estimates						
On all coefficients	393.2*	410.9*	369.1*	760.9*	312.6*	454.1*
On f	236.8*	169.9*	149.4*	443.5*	151.6*	124.2*
Individuals with significant f_i (at 10%) in individual regressions						
Percent of the panel	57.9	63.9	50.0	26.3	48.5	29.4
S.D. of f_i (%)	63.8	32.0	28.7	20.4	61.7	68.2
Swamy test on sub-panel estimates (individuals with significant b_i^1)						
On all coefficients	131.2*	212.8*	163.1*	195.7*	142.4*	118.2*
On (b^1, b^2)	116.5*	73.1*	53.9*	187.9*	64.8*	51.2*
Percent of significantly different individual coefficients in the sub-panel						
f_i	22.7	8.7	10.5	0.0	12.5	40.0
c_i^1	13.6	17.4	21.1	20.0	25.0	20.0

See Table 3.

around −0.1, so $(1+f)$ is around 0.9: a 10% undervaluation of the dollar in the last forecast period produces an increase in the expected dollar value of 9%.

It is worth noting that for the first time, the null hypothesis of homoscedasticity is accepted for every currency/horizon, which could be explained by the fact that the adaptive model is the only one of our basic models in which the explanatory variable varies across individuals. As in the other models, the null hypothesis of no fixed effects is again strongly rejected for this panel.

The random effects estimates are detailed in Bénassy-Quéré et al. (op. cit.). The adjusted R^2's, reported in Table 4, are raised by 40–80%, compared with the fixed effects model, and the residuals do not display ARCH effects. The common coefficient on the expectation error, f_h, is always significantly negative, varying from

−0.1 to −0.2. As in the extrapolative model, the trend is not significant as a common variable, but it is important for some individuals. Those individuals expect that the exchange rate will move more and more rapidly in one direction, but less rapidly if they have overvalued the last rise. The Swamy tests (reported in Table 3) always reject the null hypothesis of homogeneity for all the coefficients or for $f_{i,h}$, for the whole panel and also in the sub-panel containing those individuals displaying a significant $f_{i,h}$ in individual regressions. Individual regressions never show more than 64% of individuals as adaptive, which is a lower percentage than for other models.

Among adaptive individuals, however, there is less heterogeneity than for other models: the rejection of the null hypothesis of homogeneity seems to be due to a small number of individuals, and the values of f are concentrated around −0.2 for the 3-month horizon and −0.3 for the 12-month horizon. This relative homogeneity can be due to the fact that explanatory variables differ across individuals, which is not the case for other models[21]. Finally, there is no systematic difference in heterogeneity across the horizons, which contrasts with other models.

In sum, the analysis of simple expectational models highlights the existence of two types of individual heterogeneities:

i) Coefficient heterogeneities: among individuals that use a specific model, there is evidence of important heterogeneity in the coefficients, especially when a model is used by a large number of forecasters. Within the extrapolative specification, there is less heterogeneity for the 12-month horizon than for the 3-month horizon, meaning that forecasters rely more heavily on public forecasts in the latter case.
ii) Model heterogeneities: a large number of individuals do not use each type of model. This is especially the case for the adaptive model at both horizons, as well as for the absolute PPP model at the 3-month and the relative PPP model at the 12-month horizon. Even the most widely used models (the extrapolative model at both horizons and the relative PPP model at 3 months) are not used by 20% of the individuals. However, the basic models do not allow us to make a definitive conclusion on model heterogeneities, for two reasons. First, each basic model is implicitly tested against a naive model rather than against other basic models. Second, it is possible that the same individuals use the three basic models, while the others use none of them. The objective of estimating a model, which is a mix of the three basic models is to identify the existence of model heterogeneities across individuals.

[21] For 12-month expectations of the yen/$, no individual $f_{i,12}$ significantly differs from the panel f_{12}, although the Swamy test rejects the homogeneity of all $f_{i,12}$. This contradictory result may be explained by the fact that individual estimates are not compared to the same coefficient in both tests.

4. Model heterogeneities

There are two basic reasons for merging the three simple processes, estimated separately above, into a single model. The first is econometric and arises from our estimation results. Specifically, the extrapolative model seems to be the most widely used specification, while the regressive model provides a nice interpretation of the trend included in the two other models. However, it is only in the adaptive model that we see the explanatory variables differing across individuals, and it is only in this model that we observe no evidence of heteroscedasticity. So combining the models should give a more satisfactory overall specification.

The second justification for estimating the mixed model is economic. We have shown that an important number of forecasters do not use the extrapolative, regressive or adaptive models. This raises the question of whether the various models are used by different forecasters, or whether the same forecasters use various models at the same time, other forecasters, perhaps, using none of them. This would seem to be an important question for models which attempt to explain exchange rate fluctuations by interactions between market agents with different expectations, such as that of De Long et al. (1990).

The model estimated in this section mixes the three basic specifications. Since the trend term will be captured by the regressive terms, it is dropped from the relationship. However, the dummies used in the extrapolative and regressive models are also introduced here:

$$\begin{aligned} S^{a}_{i,t,h} - S_t = {} & a_{i,h} + b^1_h(S_t - S_{t-1}) + b^2_h(S_{t-1} - S_{t-2}) + d^1_h(\bar{S}_t - S_t) \\ & + d^2_h((\bar{S}_t - \bar{S}_{t-1}) - (S_t - S_{t-1})) + f_h(S_t - S^{a}_{i,t-h,h}) + c^2_h\text{Crisis}_t \\ & + c^2_h\text{Float}_t + u_{i,t,h} \end{aligned} \tag{11}$$

The results for the mixed model are presented in Table 5. Most coefficients are significant with high confidence levels. When significant, their values generally resemble those obtained for the three basic models. However, the second order term of the regressive model (d^2) becomes negative (generally not significant), and the adaptive term is significantly positive in one case.

The adjusted R^2 statistics do not always exceed those obtained with the simple models. This may be due to a variety of factors: (i) there is likely to be multicolinearity amongst the right-hand-side variables (however, our experiments with sequentially removing variables had little effect on the remaining coefficients); (ii) it may be due to a lack of degrees of freedom resulting from the incorporation of the adaptive term (which means that three and 12 observations per individual are dropped for the 3- and 12-month horizon models, respectively, while a total of eight coefficients are estimated (ten for the pound)); (iii) the fact that the trend term has been dropped. However, the null hypothesis of homoscedasticity is not rejected with a high confidence level. Furthermore, fixed effects are highly significant, which constitutes some first evidence that the mixed model estimated with some success on

Table 5
The mixed model

	DM/$		Yen/$		£/$	
	3 months	12 months	3 months	12 months	3 months	12 months
No of individuals	38	36	38	38	33	34
b^1	−0.402#	−0.924**	−0.422**	−0.963**	−0.466**	−0.565**
b^2	0.010	−0.107**	0.035#	−0.125**	0.002	−0.045##
d^1	−0.029	0.323**	0.089**	0.231**	−0.066**	0.303**
d^2	−0.162	−0.633#	−0.213	−0.657**	−0.092	−0.228
F	−0.092**	0.016	−0.065**	−0.002	−0.026*	0.046**
c^2	–	–	–	–	0.006#	−0.032**
c^3	–	–	–	–	−0.065**	−0.043**
θ_1	−0.400**	−0.442**	−0.383**	−0.462**	−0.291**	−0.415**
θ_2	−0.253**	−0.325**	−0.224**	−0.272**	−0.175**	−0.206**
Adjusted R^2	0.181	0.391	0.256	0.375	0.216	0.342
DW	1.883	1.755	1.826	1.685	1.744	1.702
Arch test (1)						
$\chi^2(1)$ statistics	0.182	1.686	1.829	0.342	0.280	1.249
P-value	0.669	0.194	0.176	0.558	0.597	0.264
Fixed effects: $H_0: a_i = a$						
Fisher statistics	4.600	17.083	4.636	16.478	7.305	17.905
P-value	0.000	0.000	0.000	0.000	0.000	0.000
Swamy test	602.3*	640.4*	603.6*	1145.2*	804.3*	1234.7*

See Table 2.

average expectations by Prat and Uctum (2000), is not that of a representative agent, but rather the result of aggregating heterogeneous individuals.

The fixed effects results for the mixed model were confirmed in the random coefficients model: the common coefficients are almost never significant, suggesting that the mixed model is not an accurate representation of common behaviour.

The Swamy tests, reported in the final row of Table 4, all produce a rejection of the null hypothesis of individual homogeneity in the random effects model. We estimated the mixed model for each individual separately, and plotted the Student or Fisher statistics of the relevant coefficients for each individual (see Bénassy-Quéré et al., op. cit Appendix 2). The six individual coefficients are never significant at the same time, which again rules out a schizophrenic interpretation of the mixed model. More specifically, the models used differ across individuals, currencies and horizons. At the 12-month horizon, the most frequent model used for all currencies is a regressive model; at the 3-month horizon, the most frequent model is also a regressive one for the yen, while an adaptive process is best for the pound[22]. In all cases, some individuals use several methods simultaneously, but they are not in the majority.

[22] However, these differences across currencies can be due to the specific time span.

5. Conclusion

A key theme in recent theorising on the operation of financial markets concerns the importance of heterogeneous expectations amongst agents. The purpose of this paper was to determine the nature of the expectations processes governing agents' expectations formation and the degree of heterogeneity of such processes. We are unaware of any other study which has focussed on the expectational processes of individual foreign exchange rate forecasters. In contrast to other studies in this area, we used panel estimators, and focused both on coefficient heterogeneities (within a single basic model, either extrapolative, regressive or adaptive) and on model heterogeneities (i.e. on differences across individuals in the basic models used). The expectational series used were extracted from the survey data base of Consensus Economics of London, and consisted of 3- and 12-month expectations of the US dollar bilateral rates of the German mark, Japanese yen and pound sterling, for the period January 1990 to December 1994. Our testing methods centred around two panel estimators, namely a fixed effects model and a random coefficients model. The former is seen as a base-line model in which we capture heterogeneities solely in terms of differing intercepts across individuals, whereas in the latter heterogeneity also exhibits itself in terms of differing coefficients and is summarised with a Swamy test.

Our main finding is that both model and coefficient heterogeneities are large. Specifically, a large number of individuals do not use each basic (i.e. extrapolative, regressive or adaptive) model, while few individuals use the three models at the same time (the mixed model performs poorly when coefficients are allowed to vary across individuals). This finding shows that the mixed behaviour of the panel average found in previous studies results from the aggregation of heterogeneous individuals. Among individuals who use a specific model, there are important heterogeneities in the coefficients used. For example, some individuals produce very small (and sometimes negative) coefficients of reversion in the regressive model. We believe our finding of heterogeneous expectation processes across individuals justifies the building of models of exchange rate determination which are based on the coexistence of various types of agents. This finding may also be important for policy makers who should not expect all speculators to behave in the same way in the foreign exchange market.

Notwithstanding individual heterogeneities, some regularities show up across horizons. Namely, the regressive model, with absolute PPP reversion, performs better for the 12-month horizon, while relative PPP performs better for the 3-month horizon. Within the extrapolative specification, there is less heterogeneity for the 12-month horizon than for the 3-month horizon, implying that forecasters probably rely more heavily on public forecasts in the latter case. Hence, our results support the building of models of exchange rate determination based on the interaction between heterogeneous forecasters at relatively short horizons (3 months or less) as well as models contrasting forecasting behaviour at various horizons.

Acknowledgements

The authors are grateful to an anonymous referee for helpful comments on an earlier draft of this paper.

References

Ammer, J., Brunner, A.D., 1997. Are banks market timers or market makers? Explaining foreign exchange trading profits. Journal of International Financial Markets Institutions and Money 7 (1), 43–60.

Bénassy-Quéré, A., Raymond, H., 1997. Les anticipations de change d'après les données d'enquêtes: un bilan de la littérature. Revue d'Économie Politique 107 (4), 421–456.

Bénassy-Quéré, A., Larribeau S., MacDonald R., 1999. Models of Exchange Rate Expectations: How Much Heterogeneity", CEPII Discussion paper nb 1999-03 **http://www.cepii.fr/anglaisgraph/workpap/summaries/1999/wp99-14.htm.**

Cavaglia, S., Verschoor, W.F.C., Wolff, C.P., 1993a. Further evidence on exchange rate expectations. Journal of International Money and Finance 12, 78–98.

Cavaglia, S., Verschoor, W.F.C., Wolff, C.P., 1993b. On the biasedness of forward foreign exchange rates: irrationality or risk premium. Journal of Business 67, 321–343.

De Grauwe, P., Dewachter, P.H., Embrechts, M., 1993. Exchange Rate Theory: Chaotic Models of Foreign Exchange Markets. Blackwell Scientific Publication, Cambridge.

De Long, J.B., Shleifer, A., Summers, L.H., Waldmann, R.J., 1990. Positive feedbacks, investment strategies and destabilizing rational speculation. Journal of Finance XLV (2), 250–271.

Frankel, J.A., Froot, K., 1986. The Dollar as a Speculative Bubble: a Tale of Fundamentalists and Chartists, NBER Working Paper No 1854.

Frankel, J.A., Froot, K., 1987a. Using survey data to test standard propositions regarding exchange rate expectations. American Economic Review 77, 133–153.

Frankel, J.A., Froot, K., 1987. Exchange Rate Forecasting Techniques, Survey Data and Implications for the Foreign Exchange Market, NBER Working Paper No 3470.

Frankel, J. and Froot, K., 1990. Exchange Rate Forecasting Techniques, Survey Data and Implications for the Foreign Exchange Market, NBER Working Paper No 3470, Cambridge, MA.

Frankel, J.A., Rose, A., 1995. A survey of empirical research on nominal exchange rates. In: Grossman, S., Rogoff, K. (Eds.), The Handbook of International Economics. North Holland, Amsterdam.

Goodhart, C., 1988. The foreign exchange market: a random walk with a dragging anchor. Economica 55, 437–460.

Hansen, L.P., Hodrick, R.J., 1980. Foreign exchange rates as optimal predictors of future spot rates: an econometric analysis. Journal of Political Economy 88, 829.

Hsiao, C., 1986. Analysis of Panel Data. Cambridge University Press.

Hsiao, C., 1992. Random coefficients models. In: Matyas, L., Sevestre, P. (Eds.), The Econometrics of Panel Data (Chapter 5). Kluwer Academic Publishers.

Ito, T., 1990. Foreign exchange expectations: micro survey data. American Economic Review 80, 3.

Levin, A., Lin, C.F., 1993. Unit Root Tests in Panel data: Asymptotic and Finite—Sample properties, mimeo, Federal Reserve Board of Governors.

Lyons, R., 1991. Private beliefs and information externalities in the foreign exchange market, NBER working paper 3889.

Liu, P.C., Maddala, G.S., 1992. Rationality of survey data and tests for market efficiency in the foreign exchang market. Journal of International Money and Finance 11, 366–381.

Lux, T., 1998. The socio-economic dynamics of speculative markets: interacting agents, chaos, and the fat tails of return distributions. Journal of Economic Behavior and Organization 33, 143–165.

MacDonald, R., 1992. Exchange Rate Survey Data: a Disaggregated G7 Perspective, The Manchester School LX, 47–62.

MacDonald, R., 1995. Long-run exchange rate modeling: a survey of the recent evidence. International Monetary Fund Staff Papers 42 (3), 437–489.

MacDonald, R., 2000. Expectations formation and risk in three financial markets: surveying what surveys say. In: Gardes, F., Prat, G. (Eds.), Price Expectations in Goods and Financial Markets. Edward Elgar.

MacDonald, R., Torrance, T., 1988. On risk rationality and excessive speculation in the Deutschemark–US dollar exchange market: some evidence using survey data. Oxford Bulletin of Economics and Statistics 50, 544–561.

MacDonald, R., Marsh, I.W., 1996. Foreign exchange forecasters are heterogeneous: confirmation and consequences. Journal of International Money and Finance 15 (5), 665–685.

Orléan, A., 1986. Mimétisme et anticipations rationnelles: une perspective keynésienne. Recherches Économiques de Louvain 52, 1–22.

Pesaran, H., 1989. Consistency of short-term and long-term expectations. Journal of International Money and Finance 8, 511.

Prat, G., Uctum, R., 1994. Formation des anticipations de change: les enseignements des enquêtes du Consensus Forecasts, AFFI 16th Annual Meeting, Paris, December.

Prat, G., Uctum, R., 2000. The evidence of a mixed expectation generating process in the foreign exchange market. In: Gardes, F., Prat, G. (Eds.), Price Expectations in Goods and Financial Markets. Edward Elgar.

Takagi, S., 1991. Exchange rate expectations: a survey of survey studies. IMF Staff Papers 38 (1), 156–183.

PART IV

THE ECONOMICS OF FIXED EXCHANGE RATES AND CREDIBILITY ISSUES

ELSEVIER European Economic Review 42 (1998) 1493–1523

EUROPEAN ECONOMIC REVIEW

On the mean-reverting properties of target zone exchange rates: Some evidence from the ERM

Myrvin Anthony, Ronald MacDonald*

Department of Economics, University of Strathclyde, Glasgow, G4 0LN, UK

Received 1 November 1994; accepted 7 July 1997

Abstract

One key prediction of the target zone model is that the exchange rate should be mean-reverting within the band. Although this property is widely referred to in the target zone literature, little work has been done to test it. In this paper we seek to remedy this important lacuna in the literature by examining the time-series properties of the seven currencies participating in the Exchange Rate Mechanism (ERM) of the European Monetary System, for the period 13 March 1979 to 9 April 1992. Using standard univariate unit root tests we find little evidence of mean reversion. However, using variance ratio test statistics, which control for heterogeneity in the distribution of exchange rate behaviour, we find much more evidence of mean reversion. Another part of our work includes implementing a panel unit-root test. © 1998 Elsevier Science B.V. All rights reserved.

JEL classification: F31; G12; G15

Keywords: Exchange rates; Target zones; Mean-reversion

1. Introduction

For the formulators of the Delors Committee Report, one of the key elements in the process towards European monetary integration was the Exchange Rate

* Corresponding author. Tel.: (+44)141-548-3861; fax: (+44)141-552-5589; e-mail: r.r.macdonald@strath.ac.uk.

0014-2921/98/$ – see front matter © 1998 Elsevier Science B.V. All rights reserved.
PII S0014-2921(97)00087-1

Mechanism (ERM) of the European Monetary System (EMS). Although the ERM is now effectively in abeyance, the period of its existence in its original form has generated a very useful data base on which to test the process of exchange rate determination within predetermined bands. It is now widely accepted that to understand this process a theoretical framework which views the exchange rate as determined in a target zone should be adopted. One key prediction of the target zone literature is that if an exchange rate band is credible the exchange rate within the band should exhibit strongly mean-reverting behaviour, thus imparting a degree of stability to an exchange rate which is absent under freely floating rates, and which may also be absent even in a conventional managed float. Although this mean-reverting attribute has been widely referred to in the literature (see for example, Krugman, 1991; Svensson, 1992, 1993; Rose and Svensson, 1994), and perhaps even taken for granted as a natural property of a target zone system, little effort has been devoted to testing its validity. Of the work that has been done to test this hypothesis, it is our belief that it has not been correctly implemented. In this paper we seek to rectify this important lacuna in the target zone literature.

In particular, we offer in this paper a careful dissection of the mean-reverting properties of all seven of the participating member currencies of the ERM, for the period 13 March 1979 to 9 April 1992. Usually, discussion of ERM exchange rates concentrates on only the German mark bilateral rates. However, we believe it to be of interest to examine all of the ERM rates (i.e. all of the cross bilateral rates in addition to the mark bilateral) to see if the other rates have the same properties as the key central ERM rate; if the system was operating correctly they should have. The comprehensitivity of our tests necessarily implies that the paper is rather lengthy and results-orientated; however, this comprehensitivity should be a useful reference source for others on the behaviour of target zone exchange rates. For each currency we conduct our tests using data for each of the realignment periods, where the periods are modified to exclude potentially turbulent observations generated by the realignments. Our testing method consists of two sets of tests. The first set are univariate in nature and consist of standard unit root and variance ratio tests. The latter test has useful advantages over the standard unit root test since a significance test can be computed which controls for heterosecdastic processes and non-normal errors and also gives a clear picture of any mean reversion that actually exists.

One potential disadvantage of univariate unit-root tests, such as the Dickey–Fuller class of statistics, is that they can have poor power properties in small samples. One way of increasing the power of such tests is to increase the span of the data on an historical or cross sectional basis. In terms of the former method, it has now become fashionable in international finance research to utilise very long runs of annual data (for at least one hundred years) or to construct panel data sets consisting of pooled cross section/time-series data.[1] Clearly, the former option is not available to a researcher analysing an historical episode with a fixed start point, but in the context of the ERM experiment, where time-series data is available on a group of currencies, it is possible to construct panel data sets and implement panel unit root tests. This is a test which we implement in this paper.

The outline of the remainder of this paper is as follows. In the next section we give a brief discussion of why exchange rates should be mean-reverting in a target zone and also outline the univariate methods we propose using to test for such mean-reversion. In Section 3 our univariate unit-root and variance ratio test results are presented, along with a full listing of realignment dates. In Section 4 we discuss our panel unit-root testing methods and results. The paper closes with a concluding section.

2. Mean reversion: Target zone behaviour and univariate testing methods

The assumptions, and predictions, of the target zone model are now well known and are not surveyed hear in any detail (see Svensson (1992) for an excellent survey). However, for motivational purposes, it is worth briefly discussing why exchange rates should be mean-reverting within a target zone.[2] In the basic target zone model of Krugman, it is assumed that the target zone is credible and no realignments are expected. Credibility requires that the authorities purposely or automatically adapt monetary policy to defend the zone. As a simplification, it is further assumed that the target zone is 'defended' only when the exchange rate reaches the upper or lower edges of the zone (the so-called intra-marginal intervention is ruled out). The exchange rate is determined as

$$s_t = m_t + v_t + \alpha \mathrm{E}_t[\mathrm{d}s_t]/\mathrm{d}t, \qquad (1)$$

where, in natural logarithms, s_t is the domestic currency price of foreign exchange, m_t is the money supply (which is an exogenous policy variable), α is the semi-elasticity of the demand for money, v_t is a 'general purpose' term (that includes anything else impacting on the demand or supply for money (e.g. changes in real income) and E_t is the conditional expectations operator. Most simply v_t is taken to be the 'cumulative value of velocity' (Miller and Weller, 1991). Shocks to velocity are random with mean-zero, and normally distributed such that the cumulative value of v follows a continuous-time random walk. The sum of m_t and v_t is usually referred to as the 'composite fundamental term', f_t.

---

[1] See MacDonald (1995) and Froot and Rogoff (1995) for surveys of this research.

[2] The discussion here draws on Hallwood and MacDonald (1994).

1496 M. Anthony, R. MacDonald / European Economic Review 42 (1998) 1493–1523

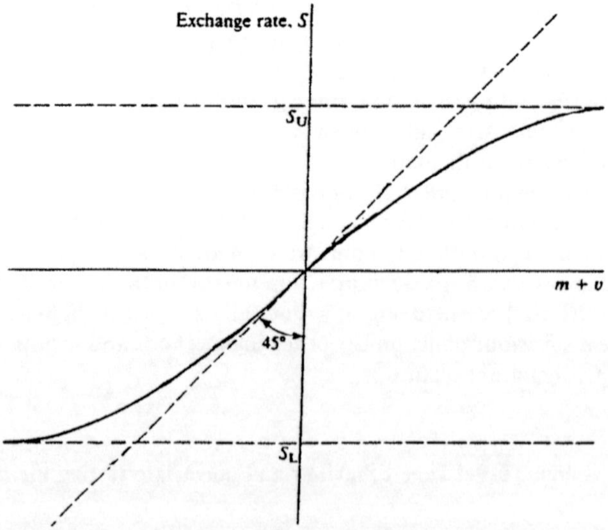

Fig. 1. The behaviour of the exchange rate in a target zone.

The final term, $E_t[ds_t]/dt$, is the instantaneous rationally expected rate of change of the exchange rate. Absolute purchasing power parity – $s_t = p_t - p_t^*$ – and uncovered interest rate parity (UIP) – $i_t = i_t^* + E_t[ds_t]/dt$ – are assumed to hold continuously. Moreover, as the country is assumed small, p_t^* and i_t^* are parametrically given.

Fig. 1 shows how the exchange rate is expected to behave in response to shocks to v_t. If the exchange rate was permitted to float freely, then from Eq. (1), we see that it would be expected to move along the dashed 45° ray line (because the exchange rate is homogeneous of degree one with respect to both the fundamentals entering f_t). However, there is a target zone with s^u as the maximum depreciation and s^l as the maximum appreciation permitted. According to the theory of target zones the 'S'-shaped curve defines the relationship between the exchange rate and its' fundamental determinants.[3]

To see how the exchange rate behaves inside the band suppose that there is a positive random shock to v_t. In this case f_t increases and, to balance the domestic money market, i_t falls. However, given (UIP) a fall in i_t is only possible if $E_t[ds_t]/dt$ is negative – the exchange rate is expected to appreciate. From Eq. (1) we see that a negative value of $E_t[ds_t]/dt$ will attenuate the movement of

[3] This predicted non-linear behaviour of the exchange rate within target zone bands has been tested by Flood et al. (1991).

s_t; i.e., s_t moves by less than it would have done had $E_t[ds_t]/dt$ does not become negative. This is called the honeymoon effect and represents a free benefit from the announcement of a credible target zone. The generation of the expected appreciation of s_t may be illustrated by considering the situation whereby s has already reached the upper edge of the band. A further random increase in v_t will be offset by a reserve outflow induced reduction in m_t. Therefore, s_t cannot rise because f_t has an upper limit; but it might fall because the next random shock to v_t could be negative in which case f_t and s_t fall. Thus on balance, s_t must be expected to fall. It is this expected appreciation, or negative expected depreciation, given that UIP holds at all times, that allows i_t to fall below i_t^*. Moreover, the argument holds for any value of s between its upper and central limit.

This negative association between the exchange rate within the band and the expected rate of currency depreciation within the band implies that the exchange rate within the band displays mean-reversion. To quote Svensson (1992):

> "... that is the expected future exchange rate within the band is closer to the long run mean of the exchange rate within the band the further away in time it is. This mean reversion is *an important general property* of target zone exchange rates that is independent of the validity of the specific Krugman model ..." (emphasis added).[4]

In periods of less than perfect credibility, and, in particular, in periods when agents expected rate of realignment is non-zero, there would be no necessary requirement for the exchange rate to display a negative association with respect to the *total* expected rate of currency depreciation within the band, rather it should be negatively related to the expected rate of currency depreciation within the band, a measure derived by subtracting the expected rate of realignment from the total expected rate of currency depreciation. Hence, the importance of examining the mean-reverting properties of exchange rates within periods in which the exchange rate was not actually realigned should be obvious and is one we are careful to adopt in this study (this is discussed again in Section 3). We believe that testing for mean-reversion within the band is simpler than Svensson's 'simplest test' and it may be appropriate to christen our approach the 'simplest simple test'!

We propose using two univariate methods for testing the mean-reverting properties of our ERM exchange rates (we consider a multivariate or panel test in Section 5): a standard Augmented Dickey–Fuller t-ratio and a variance ratio test. Both tests may be illustrated in the following way. Our null hypothesis is that an exchange rate, s_t, is generated by a random walk process with drift

$$s_t = \phi + s_{t-1} + \gamma_t, \tag{2}$$

[4] Svensson (1992, p. 127).

where $\gamma_t - \text{NID}(0, \sigma^2)$. If this is the case, the exchange rate will not exhibit any mean-reverting properties: a current shock to the exchange rate is permanent. The alternative hypotheses is that the time-series properties of s_t are described by

$$s_t = \phi + \beta s_{t-1} + \gamma_t, \quad |\beta| < 1. \tag{3}$$

The alternative hypothesis in Eq. (2) places the restriction on β that it should lie between -1 and 1. In this case, the exchange rate series is stationary and, in particular, mean-reverting. The standard way of testing the null is to estimate the following regression equation:

$$\Delta s_t = \gamma_0 + \gamma_1 t + (\beta_0 - 1)s_{t-1} + \sum_{j=1}^{n-1} \beta_{j+1}\Delta s_{t-j} + \upsilon_t, \tag{4}$$

where t denotes a time trend. Since $\phi(B)$ will contain a unit root if $\sum_1^n \phi = 1$ the presence of a unit root is formally equivalent to a test of whether $\beta_0 = 1$ or $(\beta_0 - 1) = 0$. This hypothesis may be tested using a standard t-test although, as Dickey and Fuller (1979) and many others note, this will have a non-standard distribution and, therefore, one has to use the percentiles tabulated by Fuller (1976) or MacKinnon (1991). The inclusion of the correct specification of deterministic variables in (4) is crucial to the power of the test (see Banerjee et al., 1993). In view of this, we compute both the τ_τ (based on Eq. (4)) and the τ_μ test, where τ_μ is obtained from a regression equation *without* the time trend t. However, since in the context of target zones the exchange rates are expected to be stationary around the central parity, it seems more appropriate to use a regression model without t. We therefore only report the results for the τ_μ test in the paper (although the results from the τ_τ test are principally similar for all the bilateral rates).[5]

An additional practical issue which must be resolved when conducting Dickey–Fuller unit root tests is the choice of the lag parameter, n, in Eq. (4). Since n will usually be unknown, some procedure must be employed to ensure that the appropriate lag structure in Eq. (4) is being applied. Failure to do this can adversely affect the validity of the test because too few lags may not eliminate serial correlation in υ_t; whilst, on the contrary, too many lags can reduce the efficiency of the test since more parameters have to be estimated than is required (see Banerjee et al., 1993). In order to address this problem, we follow the simple model selection procedure suggested in Hall (1990) and Campbell

[5] Unit-root tests for the first-difference of these bilateral exchange rates were also computed using both the t_μ and t_τ tests. These results, as well those for the t_τ test on the level of the exchange rates, can be obtained from the authors by request.

and Perron (1991). In particular, we estimate an autoregression as in Eq. (5), where the lag parameter $n = 20$ initially. If the coefficient on the last included lag is statistically significant from zero we set $n = 20$ in Eq. (5); if not we successively reduce the order of the autoregression until the coefficient on the last included lag in the reduced model is statistically significant. If none of the lags is statistically significant we set $n = 0$.

$$s_t = \gamma_0 + \sum_{j=1}^{n} \beta_j s_{t-j} + \mu_t . \tag{5}$$

It is now widely accepted that standard unit-root tests based on Eq. (4) are not very powerful in detecting whether a series is stationary or not, particularly when the series contains a root which lies close to the unit circle (see, for example, Campbell and Perron, 1991). Lo and MacKinlay (1988) have demonstrated that the variance ratio test has greater power to reject the null hypothesis of a unit root, when it is in fact false, than the standard Dickey–Fuller test, essentially because it is better able to capture the underlying time-series properties of the data. The variance ratio test was introduced into the recent economics literature by Cochrane (1988) and has the further advantage that it offers a very straightforward interpretation of how rapidly a series reverts back to, or diverges from, its mean value.

First,[6] an unbiased estimator of the variance of an exchange rate series, σ^2, is given by

$$\hat{\sigma}_1^2 = \frac{1}{(T-1)} \sum_{t=1}^{T} \left[s_t - s_{t-1} - \frac{1}{T}(s_T - s_0) \right]^2 , \tag{6}$$

where T denotes the number of observations. If s_t does indeed follow a random walk, then the variance of the kth difference of s_t will also give an unbiased estimator of σ^2:

$$\hat{\sigma}_k^2 = \frac{T}{k(T-k)(T-k+1)} \sum_{t=k}^{T} \left[s_t - s_{t-k} - \frac{k}{T}(s_T - s_0) \right]^2 . \tag{7}$$

Hence under the null hypothesis that s_t follows a random walk the ratio of the variance of $\hat{\sigma}_k^2$ to $\hat{\sigma}_1^2$ should equal unity:

$$\hat{V}_k = \frac{\hat{\sigma}_1^2}{\hat{\sigma}_k^2} = 1, \tag{8}$$

[6] The notation in Eqs. (6)–(10) follows Mills (1993).

where $\hat{V}_k$ denotes the estimated variance ratio. If, however, $\hat{V}_k$ is either above or below unity the random walk null is rejected. However, it is only in the latter case that the series exhibits mean reversion, and we therefore take values for $\hat{V}_k$ of one or above as evidence against the target zone model. How do we determine if $\hat{V}_k$ is indeed significantly different from one or not? Lo and MacKinlay (1988) define the test statistic:

$$M(k) = \hat{V}_k - 1,$$

and show that

$$z_1(k) = M(k)\left(\frac{2(2k-1)(k-1)}{3nk^2}\right)^{-1/2}, \tag{9}$$

where $n = T/k$, is asymptotically N(0, 1). Usefully Lo and MacKinlay, also derive a version of the variance ratio test which is robust to a wide range of heteroscedastic processes and non-normal errors. Given that financial market data often exhibit substantial heterogeneity we believe that this is especially useful in the current application. The test statistic which allows for heterogeneous errors in the underlying exchange rate process (2) is

$$z_2(k) = M(k)\Omega^{-1/2}(k), \tag{10}$$

where

$$\Omega(k) = \sum\left[\frac{2(k-j)}{k}\right]^2 \delta(j)$$

and

$$\delta = \frac{\sum_{t=j+1}^{T} \alpha_{0t}\alpha_{jt}}{\left(\sum_{t=1}^{T} \alpha_{0t}\right)}, \qquad \alpha = \left(s_{t-j} - s_{t-j-1} - \frac{1}{T}(s_T - s_0)\right)^2.$$

If the estimated value of V_k is insignificantly different from unity the null hypothesis of a random walk cannot be rejected. If $\hat{V}_k$ is significantly less than unity, the null hypothesis may be rejected in favour of mean-reversion. If, however, $\hat{V}_k$ is significantly above unity the series is non-stationary. Since Lo and MacKinlay have demonstrated that the variance ratio constructed using k lags is equal to one plus the sum of the k autocorrelations of the series, a value of $\hat{V}_k$ above 1 implies that an exchange rate exhibits positive serial correlation whereas a value below 1 implies negative serial correlation and therefore mean reversion.

To our knowledge the only tests of the mean-reverting properties of the ERM currencies are those contained in Svensson (1993), Rose and Svensson (1994), and Nieuwland et al. (1994). Svensson (1993)[7] is, in fact, concerned to estimate the expected rate of exchange rate depreciation using the following regression equation:

$$\Delta x_{t+k} = \sum_j \beta_{0j} d_j + \beta_1 x_t + \beta_2 i_t^k + \beta_3 i_t^{*k} + \varepsilon_{t+k}, \tag{11}$$

where, of terms not previously defined, x_t is the exchange rate *within the band* (that is, the exchange rate less the central parity), d_j is a dummy for 'regime j', that is, each period between realignments, i_t^k denotes an interest rate with maturity k and an asterisk denotes a foreign magnitude. Svensson estimates this relationship for the six German mark exchange rates used in this paper (with the same data set used in this paper) and interprets the t-ratio on β_1 as the Dickey–Fuller statistic discussed above. Based on this interpretation he finds strong evidence of mean-reversion in the x_t process. It is not, however, clear that this interpretation is correct.

First, the critical values calculated by Dickey and Fuller are for a regression consisting of simply the first difference of the variable on the lagged level of the variable and a constant (it does not include the other deterministic elements or the interest rate variables used by Svensson).

Second, the regressand (Δx_{t+k}) in Eq. (11) is not the first-difference of the exchange rate within the band (as would be the case in the standard Dickey–Fuller equation) but the *sixty-fifth difference* (when Eq. (11) is estimated for the 3-month horizon). Third, although x_t is properly adjusted to exclude observations which may reflect realignment expectations (when Eq. (11) is estimated for the 3-month horizon), and a set of dummy variables (d_j) which account for 'shifts' in regimes is included in Eq. (11), we do not think that this equation is a legitimate variant of the class of unit-root tests which consider deterministic breaks (or regime or structural shifts) in the time-series process (see, for example, Perron, 1989; Banerjee et al., 1992).[8] Thus, in this context, this t-ratio is difficult to interpret as a normal Dickey–Fuller statistic used to

---

[7] The equation estimated in Rose and Svensson (1994) is

$$\Delta x_{t+k} = \sum_j \beta_{0j} + \beta_1 x_t + \beta_2 (i_t^k - i_t^{*k}) + \varepsilon_{t+k}. \tag{11a}$$

Since the same criticisms of Eq. (11) are applicable to Eq. (11a) we do not discuss the equations separately.

[8] Svensson correctly points out (Svensson (1993, p. 779) that the critical values of this class of unit-root tests tend to be larger than those for the standard tests, and therefore his use of the critical values of standard Dickey–Fuller test would not invalidate his conclusions; but this is not an adequate justification for using Eq. (11) to evaluate the unit-root hypothesis, given the other limitations of this equation which we have adumbrated above.

evaluate the null hypothesis of a unit root in a time series. Indeed, in the context of constructing panel unit-root tests, Levin and Lin (1992) have demonstrated that the introduction of extra deterministic elements (that is, over and above a constant and time trend) requires very large t-ratios, in absolute terms (around 10 in value), to reject the null of a unit root.

Moreover, no lagged changes in the exchange rate (within the band) appear in the estimated version of Eq. (4), which is desirable in the presence of serially correlated disturbances. Svensson does, however, calculate standard errors for the coefficient based on a Newey–West correction and his t-ratio on β_1 may therefore be (broadly) interpreted as a Phillips–Perron adjusted Dickey–Fuller statistic; but even this interpretation is questionable. Further, there is now growing evidence to suggest that Phillips–Perron type unit-root tests have "... serious size distortions in finite samples when the data-generating process has a predominance of negative autocorrelations in first differences. This suggests that the Phillips–Perron tests may be less reliable than the Dickey–Fuller methodology where a parametric correction is applied".[9] As we indicated above, a further problem with unit root tests based on the Dickey–Fuller approach is that even if they are implemented correctly they are not, in circumstances when the null hypothesis is rejected, informative about the profile of mean-reversion.

In their study, Nieuwland et al. (1994) use weekly German mark bilateral exchange rate data (for the currencies examined by Svensson (1993) and also the British pound and the Spanish peseta) for the period 15 March 1979 to 27 February 1992. They utilise predominantly a variety of Phillips–Perron unit-root tests (as well as the Dickey–Fuller test) to check for mean-reversion in these exchange rates, and found little evidence of it, with the exception of the Dutch guilder/German mark exchange rate. However, as these tests are conducted over the *entire sample* which contains several realignments (changing parities or means) they may be unable to detect mean-reversion in these exchange rates because, as is well-known (see Perron, 1989), these standard unit-root tests perform poorly in the context of time-series with 'trend- or other deterministic-breaks' – a point which the authors themselves acknowledge. In order to deal with this difficulty, the authors re-compute these unit-root tests on data (for the *whole sample period*) which exclude *only* the realignments and arrive at the same conclusion. It is our opinion however, that the deletion of *only* the realignments is not a sufficiently satisfactory way of adjusting these exchange rates to check for mean-reversion because observations which are close to (but preceding) realignment dates may reflect realignment expectations, as we explained above.

---

[9] Campbell and Perron (1991).

3. Univariate tests of mean-reversion

3.1. The data and realignment dates

The data for this study were originally extracted from the BIS database and run from 13 March 1979 to 9 April 1992 (observational frequency is daily).[10] All of the exchange rates are spot ecu-rates and are recorded at a daily central bank telephone conference at 2.30 p.m. Swiss time and they are: the Belgian/Luxembourg franc (BF), the Danish krone (DK), the Deutsche mark (DM), the French franc (FF), the Italian lira (IL), the Irish punt (IP) and the Netherlands guilder (NG). The bilateral exchange rates have been calculated from these ecu-rates. All have been transformed using the natural logarithm operator and missing values, all of which appear to correspond to holidays, have been deleted.[11]

As we noted in Section 2, it is clearly important that our tests for mean-reversion be conducted in periods in which there was no realignment, and no expectation of such. We have therefore taken our full sample period and sub-divided it into sub-periods corresponding to periods between realignment dates.[12] Our mean-reversion statistics are then calculated for these sub-sample periods. However, even during periods of no realignment there may still be a non-zero expected rate of realignment which could potentially bias our results. For example, in a period immediately before a realignment there would in all likelihood be a non-zero expected rate of realignment. In order to exclude any exchange rate turbulence associated with a realignment date we have truncated each of these periods 10 observations before the end (we experimented with other truncation periods and obtained qualitatively similar results).[13]

3.2. The Dickey–Fuller (DF) results

3.2.1. German mark bilateral rates

Table 1 contains the results of the DF (τ_μ) tests for the DM bilateral rates.

---

[10] The data set was kindly provided by Lars Svensson.

[11] Due to space limitations we only present here a subset of the tables containing our Dickey–Fuller and variance ratio tests' results. Interested readers can refer to our discussion paper (see Anthony and MacDonald, 1997) to obtain the full compliment of these tables for the 21 exchange rates we discuss. The discussion paper also contains a list of all the cross exchange rates considered in this paper, and a complete set of realignment dates for all of the cross rates is also provided.

[12] Using data for the full sample would not in any case be a feasible option since, and as we noted in Section 2, it would have to include a large number of non-standard deterministic elements for each currency (to capture realignment dates).

[13] We are grateful to an anonymous referee for suggesting this point.

Table 1
Dickey–Fuller (τ_μ) test for unit roots

Period	DM-based exchange rates					
	BFDM	DKDM	FFDM	ILDM	IPDM	NGDM
1	– 3.42 (16)[a]	– 1.39 (3)	– 0.61 (11)	– 2.56 (16)	– 3.86 (18)[c]	– 1.25 (0)
2	– 1.71 (12)	– 1.19 (8)	– 0.70 (17)	0.05 (13)	– 1.32 (1)	– 3.13 (16)[a]
3	0.32 (12)	– 2.79 (19)[b]	1.21 (17)	0.84 (1)	0.13 (1)	– 2.78 (16)[b]
4	0.13 (19)	– 2.21 (19)	0.73 (17)	0.97 (18)	0.84 (1)	
5	0.89 (19)	– 2.09 (19)	– 0.91 (17)	1.03 (12)	– 0.36 (2)	
6	– 0.55 (19)	– 0.82 (19)	– 0.36 (17)	– 0.22 (19)	0.07 (2)	
7	– 0.38 (19)	– 1.78 (19)	– 1.75 (17)	0.08 (12)	– 0.07 (15)	
8	– 1.79 (19)	– 1.53 (12)		0.68 (19)	– 1.57 (5)	
9		– 2.83 (19)[b]		– 1.38 (19)		
10				– 1.88 (19)		

Notes: [a] Denotes significance at 5% level.
[b] Denotes significance at 10% level.
[c] Denotes significance at 1% level.
No. of lags used for ADF tests are given in parentheses.

Consider first the BF/DM exchange rate. With the exception of regime 1 (79:03:13–79:09:23), we find evidence in favour of the unit-root hypothesis, and thus the absence of mean-reversion in the other regimes. Similarly, the first regime (79:03:13–79:09:23) of the IP/DM exchange rate also demonstrates evidence of a mean-reverting tendency; but in all theother seven regimes we find support for the non-stationarity of the exchange rate. There is also evidence of stationarity for the DK/DM exchange rate in regimes 3 (79:11:30–81:10:04) and 9 (87:01:12–92:04:09), respectively – though in both cases the unit-root hypothesis is only rejected at the 10% level of significance.

The Netherlands guilder suffered the least number of devaluations (relative to the German mark) in the ERM, and in this respect, the NG/DM exchange rate was the most 'stable' rate within the system. We find no evidence in favour of mean-reversion during the first regime (79:03:13–79:09:23); but cannot reject the mean-reversion hypothesis for the final two regimes (79:09:24–83:03:20, and 83:03:21–92:04:09).

Probably, the more interesting cases of mean-reversion cited above relate to the final regimes of both the DK/DM and NG/DM exchange rates. Both regimes coincide with the period of relative stability in the ERM, and the evidence for mean-reverting behaviour in these instances, would seem to give some credence to the theoretical postulation of the target zone literature. In particular, the result for the NG/DM exchange rate suggests that the most 'stable' exchange rate in the ERM was also probably the only one to have behaved most consistently like a typical target zone exchange rate. The initial instability in the Dutch guilder (relative to the German mark) in the formative years of the ERM, eventually gave way to stability in the later years. This result is, however, probably not surprising since during the 1980s Netherlands had effectively ceded monetary sovereignty to Germany by pegging the guilder to the German mark. The behaviour of the NG/DM exchange rate is, therefore, merely a reflection of the de facto monetary union between these two countries.

In stark contrast to the results for the BF/DM, DK/DM, IP/DM, and NG/DM exchange rates, the results for the FF/DM, and IL/DM exchange rates are much stronger in their rejection of mean-reversion in the sense that we cannot reject the unit-root hypothesis for these exchange rates in any of the regimes. Thus, the weight of evidence, taken over all the regimes for all the DM exchange rates, is mainly supportive of their non-stationarity, and thus the absence of a mean-reverting tendency.

In general terms, the foregoing findings are not in concordance with the results for the DM rates presented in Svensson (1993) and Rose and Svensson (1994). Unlike these papers, we find that the behaviour of the DM exchange rates within most regimes is typically non-stationary: in 39 instances out of a total of 45, we fail to reject the unit root hypothesis for these DM exchange rates. However, this is above the number that would be expected to occur by chance at the 5% level and, to the extent to which these tests have power to reject the null, this may imply a lack of credibility within the nonstationary periods.

3.2.2. Non-German mark exchange rates

3.2.2.1. 'Inner core' exchange rates. The ERM is a cooperative arrangement in which the participating currencies are restricted to fluctuate within bands which are defined around bilateral central par values relative to each other. Although the DM bilateral exchange rates, in practice, have been the most important exchange rates in the ERM, it is, nonetheless, worthwhile to examine the time-series properties of the other cross exchange rates in the system since they also would be expected to demonstrate mean-reverting behaviour. But before we discuss the findings for the other bilateral exchange rates we wish to highlight that the results for a set of bilateral rates have certain implications for the other cross exchange rates.

Given any set of bilateral exchange rates, we can compute the relevant cross exchange rates that exist among the various currencies. Thus, if we have $s_{i/j}$ and $s_{k/j}$, where $s_{i/j}$ is the (log) exchange rate between currency *i* and *j* (expressed as the number of units of currency *i* per unit of currency *j*), and $s_{k/j}$ is the (log) exchange rate between currency *k* and *j* (expressed as the number of units of currency *k* per unit of currency *j*), the cross exchange rate $s_{i/k}$ is derived from the linear

Table 2
Dickey–Fuller (τ_μ) test for unit roots

Period	FF-based exchange rates				
	BFFF	DKFF	ILFF	IPFF	NGFF
1	− 2.02 (17)	− 1.91 (14)	− 1.12 (18)	− 2.56 (16)	− 0.62 (17)
2	− 1.50 (11)	− 1.16 (14)	− 1.22 (15)	− 0.55 (16)	1.76 (17)
3	− 0.23 (18)	− 2.36 (12)	− 1.37 (19)	− 1.07 (16)	0.57 (8)
4	− 0.63 (19)	− 2.39 (12)	− 1.08 (19)	− 1.04 (16)	− 0.26 (16)
5	− 0.27 (19)	− 2.48 (12)	− 1.60 (19)	− 1.70 (2)	0.17 (8)
6	0.34 (19)	− 2.17 (12)	− 1.65 (19)	− 2.44 (16)	− 0.87 (5)
7	0.71 (19)	− 0.98 (12)			
8		− 0.62 (15)			
9		− 0.19 (15)			

Notes: See Table 1.

expression in Eq. (12)

$$s_{i/k} = s_{i/j} - s_{k/j}. \tag{12}$$

From Eq. (12) the following relationships would hold: (a) if $s_{i/j}$ and $s_{k/j}$ are both stationary, then $s_{i/k}$ will also be stationary; (b) if $s_{i/j}$ and $s_{k/j}$ both have a unit root, then it will generally be the case that $s_{i/k}$ will also have a unit root, *unless* $s_{i/j}$ and $s_{k/j}$ are cointegrated in which case $s_{i/k}$ will be stationary; and (c) if either $s_{i/j}$ or $s_{k/j}$ has a unit root and the other is stationary, then $s_{i/k}$ will have a unit root because the exchange rate with the unit root will dominate. The relationships (a)–(c) can be expected to hold for the entire sample and for regimes which are identical, but not necessarily for regimes which may overlap and clearly not for regimes which differ. We should therefore anticipate a certain degree of consistency in the unit-root tests for the other cross exchange rates.

In Table 2 (and Tables 4–6 in Anthony and MacDonald (1997)) our findings for the French franc, Belgium–Luxembourg franc and Netherlands guilder are presented (excluding of course, DM/FF, DM/BF and DM/NG since these are merely the reciprocals of the DM rates discussed in the previous section).

Looking first at the cross exchange rates among the 'inner core' currencies (that is, BF/FF, NG/FF and NG/BF exchange rates) we once more find no evidence of mean-reversion: we cannot refute the unit-root hypothesis for any of the regimes of these bilateral rates.

The picture is quite similar across the bilateral rates between these 'inner core' currencies and the remaining ('peripheral') currencies in the ERM. The results from these unit root tests are unanimous in their rejection of mean-reversion. Apart from two exceptions – regime 1 (79:03:13–79:09:23) for BF/IP and

Table 3
Dickey–Fuller (τ_μ) test for unit roots

Period	Peripheral exchange rates					
	DKNG	ILNG	IPNG	DKIL	IPIL	IPDK
1	− 1.71 (19)	− 0.79 (18)	− 1.48 (4)	− 1.78 (18)	− 0.87 (8)	− 1.21 (19)
2	− 0.78 (16)	0.40 (1)	0.17 (10)	− 2.61 (9)	− 0.22 (8)	− 0.95 (19)
3	− 2.10 (17)	0.39 (18)	1.42 (7)	− 2.86 (12)	− 0.09 (8)	− 1.85 (17)
4	− 0.82 (17)	0.36 (18)	0.08 (10)	− 1.67 (5)	− 0.65 (1)	− 1.92 (19)
5	− 1.40 (19)	− 0.18 (18)	0.58 (10)	− 1.76 (9)	− 0.31 (1)	− 1.81 (19)
6	0.18 (15)	− 0.48 (18)	1.24 (7)	− 1.35 (9)	− 1.18 (1)	− 1.72 (19)
7	− 0.84 (15)	− 0.78 (18)	− 1.70 (10)	− 1.35 (12)	− 1.45 (1)	− 0.49 (8)
8	− 0.65 (15)	− 1.03 (12)		0.20 (12)	− 1.55 (1)	
9	− 2.02 (17)	− 1.76 (18)		− 0.17 (12)		
10				− 0.19 (12)		
11				− 0.28 (12)		

Notes: See Table 1.

regime 3 (79:11:30–82:02:21) for DK/BF – we cannot reject the unit-root hypothesis for these bilateral exchange rates.

3.2.2.2. 'Peripheral' exchange rates. The time-series properties of the 'peripheral' exchange rates (i.e. IP/IL, DK/IL, and IP/DK exchange rates), reported in Table 3, bear a familiar resemblance to the other bilateral rates discussed previously. In common with the other bilateral rates, these exchange rates also depict clear evidence of being generally non-stationary. In all regimes for these three cross exchange rates we fail to reject the unit-root hypothesis.

The main conclusion to be drawn from these unit-root results is that, in general terms, the ERM bilateral rates do not behave like typical target zone rates in that they do not demonstrate a consistent tendency towards mean-reversion. The strike record is that in only 8 instances out of a potential 159 is there any evidence of mean reversion. A total of 8 is only marginally greater than the number that would be expected by chance at the 5% level. However, this may, in fact, be a reflection of the nature of the test used rather than an inherent lack of mean reversion in the data.

3.3. Variance ratio results

We have constructed our variance ratio tests for lags 2 to 24, since we believe that with daily data any evidence of mean reversion should have revealed itself after approximately one month's trading. Before presenting a blow-by-blow account of our variance ratio statistics it is worth giving an overall impression of the results since they portray a quite different picture from the ADF statistics considered in the previous section. In particular, out of a potential of 1272 instances (159 exchange rate regimes *times* the eight different lags reported in each table) there are 707 rejections of the random-walk hypothesis (based on the $z_2(k)$ statistic at 10% level of significance).[14] These rejections can be split into two groups. The first group (191 instances) consists of variance ratios significantly above unity and the second (516 instances) comprises variance ratios significantly below one. Since it is the latter set of results which are of interest in the current context we comment only on these variance ratios which are below unity; the variance ratios above one are regarded as non-stationary. We present an elaboration of the non-stationary result in the concluding section.

For comparative purposes, we scrutinise more closely our results at a relatively short lag – in this case lag 12 – and at a longer lag – the 24th lag. There are 106 instances out of a potential 159 in which the variance ratio is below one after 12 lags and 88 (again out of 159) when it is below one at 24 lags. Using the z_2 statistic as the metric of significance, there are 62 variance ratios significantly below one (using a 10% significance level) at lag 12 and 58 at lag 24. This picture contrasts quite sharply with the overall impression gleaned from the univariate ADF results.

To conserve space we do not list all of the variance ratio tables although we do refer to results contained in the discussion paper version (see Anthony and MacDonald, 1997). We turn now to a more specific examination of these results.

3.3.1. German mark bilateral rates

In Tables 4–7 (see Tables 7–12 in Anthony and MacDonald (1997)) we present our variance ratio results for the German mark bilateral rates. Although for a number of currency/time periods, the pattern is similar to that unearthed by the Dickey–Fuller tests there is now much more evidence of mean reversion. There are 205 instances (out of a total of 360) in which the estimated variance ratio is below unity. Of these 205 cases, 89 were statistically significant.

Consider, the variance ratios for the key German mark–Belgium franc rate, BF/DM, reported in Table 4. Four of the periods display estimated variance ratios which are numerically below unity (38 instances). A number of these (16 instances) are statistically less than one but the most noticeable depiction of mean-reversion is perhaps in period 8, a period categorised by a large number of observations and one which is generally seen as one of the most tranquil of the ERM experience. A U-shaped pattern exists for period 1: the value for $\hat{V}_k$ falls below one to lag 4 and then rises until it becomes significantly greater than one

[14] Throughout our discussion of these variance ratio results we emphasise the $z_2(k)$ statistic rather than $z_1(k)$ because the former is the more appropriate of the two test statistics in the present context, as was explained in Section 2.

Table 4
Variance ratio statistics and significance levels. Exchange rate: BF/DM

		2	4	6	8	12	16	20	24
1	V	0.91	0.62	0.71	0.74	0.96	1.23	1.52	1.77
	Z1	(0.30)	(0.02)	(0.19)	(0.33)	(0.90)	(0.57)	(0.29)	(0.12)
	Z2	(0.48)	(0.02)	(0.10)	(0.16)	(0.82)	(0.26)	(0.01)	(0.00)
2	V	0.89	0.86	0.89	0.92	0.93	0.91	0.90	0.91
	Z1	(0.02)	(0.10)	(0.32)	(0.53)	(0.68)	(0.64)	(0.67)	(0.71)
	Z2	(0.06)	(0.54)	(0.16)	(0.32)	(0.44)	(0.32)	(0.32)	(0.35)
3	V	0.92	0.65	0.64	0.60	0.45	0.32	0.27	0.33
	Z1	(0.47)	(0.09)	(0.17)	(0.22)	(0.18)	(0.18)	(0.21)	(0.35)
	Z2	(0.80)	(0.33)	(0.34)	(0.31)	(0.18)	(0.10)	(0.08)	(0.12)
4	V	1.00	1.37	1.80	2.19	2.94	3.93	4.59	4.78
	Z1	(0.97)	(0.12)	(0.01)	(0.00)	(0.00)	(0.00)	(0.00)	(0.00)
	Z2	(0.98)	(0.11)	(0.00)	(0.00)	(0.00)	(0.00)	(0.00)	(0.00)
5	V	1.01	1.04	1.00	0.96	0.98	1.06	1.05	1.06
	Z1	(0.90)	(0.77)	(0.99)	(0.85)	(0.95)	(0.85)	(0.90)	(0.89)
	Z2	(0.88)	(0.62)	(0.98)	(0.66)	(0.88)	(0.59)	(0.68)	(0.64)
6	V	0.82	0.77	0.81	0.81	0.86	0.87	0.89	0.90
	Z1	(0.00)	(0.00)	(0.03)	(0.08)	(0.30)	(0.43)	(0.55)	(0.60)
	Z2	(0.01)	(0.01)	(0.03)	(0.04)	(0.14)	(0.20)	(0.27)	(0.31)
7	V	1.33	1.55	1.60	1.57	1.73	2.08	2.45	2.83
	Z1	(0.00)	(0.00)	(0.00)	(0.01)	(0.01)	(0.00)	(0.00)	(0.00)
	Z2	(0.01)	(0.00)	(0.00)	(0.00)	(0.00)	(0.00)	(0.00)	(0.00)
8	V	1.02	0.88	0.85	0.84	0.85	0.83	0.83	0.86
	Z1	(0.40)	(0.02)	(0.03)	(0.05)	(0.13)	(0.17)	(0.22)	(0.34)
	Z2	(0.67)	(0.07)	(0.04)	(0.04)	(0.05)	(0.04)	(0.05)	(0.10)

Notes: The numbers in column one denote the sub-sample period (regime) used to construct the variance ratio statistic (V), and its associated significance levels – Z1 and Z2 – (see Eqs. (9) and (10) in the text for definitions). The numbers at the head of each column denote the lag length (*K*) used to construct the variance ratio statistic. The numbers not in parenthesis in each column are the estimated variance ratios; whilst the numbers in parenthesis are the marginal significance levels of the Z1 and Z2 statistic.

at lag 24. The unusual pattern for period 1 may simply reflect the time taken for investors to gain experience and confidence in the operation of the ERM system. It is unlikely, though, that one can appeal to the newness of the system to explain the rather puzzling results for period 7. Are there, therefore, any other explanations to explain these results? We consider some in the concluding section.

Three other DM bilateral exchange rates – DK/DM, FF/DM, and IL/DM – exhibit a similar kind of behaviour as the BF/DM rate, in the sense that there

Table 5
Variance ratio statistics and significance levels. Exchange rate: FF/DM

		2	4	6	8	12	16	20	24
1	V	0.78	0.76	0.83	0.83	0.85	0.92	0.96	1.00
	Z1	(0.02)	(0.16)	(0.44)	(0.52)	(0.68)	(0.84)	(0.93)	(0.97)
	Z2	(0.03)	(0.04)	(0.18)	(0.21)	(0.33)	(0.60)	(0.80)	(0.99)
2	V	0.95	0.82	0.82	0.86	0.85	0.82	0.73	0.69
	Z1	(0.27)	(0.04)	(0.11)	(0.28)	(0.39)	(0.36)	(0.23)	(0.21)
	Z2	(0.56)	(0.08)	(0.11)	(0.21)	(0.23)	(0.16)	(0.04)	(0.02)
3	V	1.14	1.11	1.22	1.21	1.21	1.35	1.48	1.65
	Z1	(0.07)	(0.45)	(0.27)	(0.39)	(0.48)	(0.32)	(0.24)	(0.15)
	Z2	(0.23)	(0.46)	(0.18)	(0.23)	(0.25)	(0.08)	(0.02)	(0.00)
4	V	0.93	0.64	0.74	0.74	0.82	0.98	1.07	1.19
	Z1	(0.31)	(0.01)	(0.16)	(0.24)	(0.52)	(0.94)	(0.85)	(0.64)
	Z2	(0.54)	(0.02)	(0.12)	(0.15)	(0.36)	(0.91)	(0.73)	(0.37)
5	V	0.94	0.90	0.89	0.90	0.98	0.97	0.97	0.95
	Z1	(0.08)	(0.16)	(0.22)	(0.36)	(0.86)	(0.87)	(0.87)	(0.81)
	Z2	(0.41)	(0.29)	(0.25)	(0.32)	(0.81)	(0.81)	(0.78)	(0.67)
6	V	1.09	1.29	1.47	1.62	2.01	2.36	2.86	3.36
	Z1	(0.21)	(0.03)	(0.01)	(0.01)	(0.00)	(0.00)	(0.00)	(0.00)
	Z2	(0.29)	(0.00)	(0.00)	(0.00)	(0.00)	(0.00)	(0.00)	(0.00)
7	V	0.94	0.90	0.90	0.90	0.93	0.94	0.96	1.00
	Z1	(0.02)	(0.05)	(0.14)	(0.22)	(0.49)	(0.62)	(0.79)	(0.98)
	Z2	(0.33)	(0.21)	(0.25)	(0.27)	(0.46)	(0.55)	(0.72)	(0.97)

Notes: See Table 4.

are several instances in which the variance ratio is less than unity and some significantly so. For example, the Italian lira–German mark rate (Table 6) displays an almost identical mix of mean-reverting and non-stationary behaviour, as does the BF/DM. There are 51 instances in which the variance ratio lies below unity, half of which are statistically significant. Regimes 2 and 8, respectively, display clear evidence of mean reversion.

The DK/DM and the FF/DM rates (see Table 8 in Anthony and MacDonald (1997) for the former and Table 5) have 38 and 36 instances, respectively, in which the estimated variance ratio is less than one. However, they both have relatively fewer significant variance ratios below unity than we find for both the BF/DM and IL/DM exchange rate. More importantly, these significant variance ratios are much more dispersed across several regimes and juxtaposed with either other insignificant variance ratios and/or variance ratios which are bigger than one. Thus, the evidence for mean-reversion for these two rates is much less obvious than we find for the BF/DM and IL/DM rates.

Table 6
Variance ratio statistics and significance levels. Exchange rate: IL/DM

		2	4	6	8	12	16	20	24
1	V	0.90	0.99	1.09	1.15	1.19	1.19	1.19	1.02
	Z1	(0.26)	(0.95)	(0.69)	(0.56)	(0.60)	(0.64)	(0.71)	(0.96)
	Z2	(0.38)	(0.94)	(0.56)	(0.33)	(0.27)	(0.29)	(0.31)	(0.90)
2	V	0.76	0.75	0.81	0.85	0.86	0.78	0.73	0.68
	Z1	(0.00)	(0.01)	(0.13)	(0.32)	(0.48)	(0.35)	(0.31)	(0.27)
	Z2	(0.01)	(0.02)	(0.10)	(0.21)	(0.28)	(0.10)	(0.04)	(0.02)
3	V	0.81	0.64	0.55	0.56	0.48	0.46	0.47	0.46
	Z1	(0.03)	(0.05)	(0.05)	(0.10)	(0.14)	(0.19)	(0.24)	(0.28)
	Z2	(0.04)	(0.00)	(0.00)	(0.00)	(0.00)	(0.00)	(0.00)	(0.00)
4	V	0.90	0.90	1.00	0.99	1.09	1.16	1.30	1.51
	Z1	(0.21)	(0.52)	(0.99)	(0.98)	(0.76)	(0.64)	(0.46)	(0.26)
	Z2	(0.43)	(0.51)	(0.99)	(0.97)	(0.59)	(0.35)	(0.09)	(0.01)
5	V	0.93	0.93	0.91	0.95	1.01	1.04	1.10	1.18
	Z1	(0.36)	(0.63)	(0.64)	(0.81)	(0.97)	(0.90)	(0.78)	(0.65)
	Z2	(0.45)	(0.55)	(0.48)	(0.68)	(0.94)	(0.76)	(0.48)	(0.22)
6	V	0.85	0.88	0.92	0.97	1.06	1.11	1.17	1.27
	Z1	(0.00)	(0.14)	(0.41)	(0.79)	(0.71)	(0.54)	(0.42)	(0.25)
	Z2	(0.01)	(0.10)	(0.27)	(0.68)	(0.49)	(0.20)	(0.07)	(0.00)
7	V	0.96	0.99	0.96	0.95	0.94	0.89	0.80	0.76
	Z1	(0.63)	(0.93)	(0.84)	(0.82)	(0.84)	(0.76)	(0.63)	(0.60)
	Z2	(0.59)	(0.88)	(0.70)	(0.62)	(0.61)	(0.39)	(0.14)	(0.09)
8	V	0.66	0.51	0.47	0.46	0.41	0.44	0.46	0.45
	Z1	(0.00)	(0.00)	(0.00)	(0.02)	(0.04)	(0.09)	(0.15)	(0.17)
	Z2	(0.00)	(0.00)	(0.00)	(0.00)	(0.00)	(0.00)	(0.00)	(0.00)
9	V	0.94	1.00	1.02	1.03	1.02	1.03	1.05	1.09
	Z1	(0.09)	(0.94)	(0.83)	(0.82)	(0.90)	(0.84)	(0.77)	(0.64)
	Z2	(0.32)	(0.95)	(0.80)	(0.76)	(0.84)	(0.72)	(0.57)	(0.31)
10	V	1.07	1.03	0.96	0.92	0.94	0.97	0.99	1.04
	Z1	(0.08)	(0.69)	(0.67)	(0.49)	(0.71)	(0.89)	(0.97)	(0.87)
	Z2	(0.22)	(0.68)	(0.61)	(0.35)	(0.54)	(0.80)	(0.93)	(0.72)

Notes: See Table 4.

Interestingly, the Irish punt–German mark rate (see Table 11 in Anthony and MacDonald (1997)) exhibits rather different time-series properties relative to the other currencies. Thus, in the initial two sub-sample periods and in the last there is considerable evidence of mean-reversion (both numerically and statistically); in all other sub-periods there is clear evidence of non-stationary behaviour. The strong mean-reversion evidenced at the start of the overall sample perhaps

Table 7
Variance ratio statistics and significance levels. Exchange rate: NG/DM

		2	4	6	8	12	16	20	24
1	V	1.06	1.08	1.15	1.21	1.32	1.60	2.03	2.38
	Z1	(0.54)	(0.66)	(0.51)	(0.44)	(0.36)	(0.14)	(0.04)	(0.01)
	Z2	(0.60)	(0.55)	(0.28)	(0.14)	(0.03)	(0.00)	(0.00)	(0.00)
2	V	0.91	0.87	0.94	1.01	1.05	1.05	1.05	1.05
	Z1	(0.01)	(0.05)	(0.51)	(0.94)	(0.67)	(0.74)	(0.76)	(0.79)
	Z2	(0.08)	(0.03)	(0.40)	(0.91)	(0.47)	(0.52)	(0.52)	(0.55)
3	V	0.90	0.85	0.78	0.73	0.68	0.64	0.61	0.59
	Z1	(0.00)	(0.00)	(0.00)	(0.00)	(0.00)	(0.00)	(0.00)	(0.00)
	Z2	(0.00)	(0.00)	(0.00)	(0.00)	(0.00)	(0.00)	(0.00)	(0.00)

Notes: See Table 4.

reflects the significant initial gains in credibility the punt obtained by participating in the ERM, whilst the mean-reversion in the last period reflects the relative tranquility of this period. The pattern for the NG/DM rate is in concordance with the Dickey–Fuller results: strong evidence of mean reversion is indicated for the long and tranquil period 3, a period in which the system was at perhaps its most credible.

3.3.2. Non-German mark exchange rates

3.3.2.1. 'Inner core' exchange rates. The variance ratio results for the cross rates of the French franc, Belgian franc and Dutch guilder are reported in Tables 13–24 in Anthony and MacDonald (1997). Since the sub-sample periods may differ for these cross currencies, relative to those with respect to the DM rates, the sub-samples in this sub-section are not strictly comparable with those in the previous section and therefore caution should be exercised in any exact comparison. Although the general tenor of these results is similar to the DM rates there are, nevertheless, some important differences.

Consider first the French franc cross rates. One general impression to be gleaned from these results is that there is slightly more evidence in favour of mean-reversion for the French franc-based cross rates than those based on the mark. About one-quarter (89 instances out of 360) of the reported mark-based variance ratios are significantly less than unity; whilst slightly more than one-half (141 instances out of 272) of the reported French-franc based variance ratios are significantly smaller than one.

For example, for the BF/FF rate (presented in Table 8) all of the periods apart from period 6 produce evidence of mean reversion and this is strongly significant

Table 8
Variance ratio statistics and significance levels. Exchange rate: BF/FF

		2	4	6	8	12	16	20	24
1	V	0.92	0.78	0.71	0.68	0.64	0.62	0.54	0.54
	Z1	(0.05)	(0.00)	(0.00)	(0.01)	(0.02)	(0.03)	(0.02)	(0.04)
	Z2	(0.27)	(0.01)	(0.00)	(0.00)	(0.00)	(0.00)	(0.00)	(0.00)
2	V	0.87	0.67	0.65	0.62	0.46	0.31	0.23	0.24
	Z1	(0.22)	(0.11)	(0.19)	(0.25)	(0.18)	(0.17)	(0.18)	(0.28)
	Z2	(0.68)	(0.36)	(0.36)	(0.33)	(0.18)	(0.10)	(0.07)	(0.07)
3	V	0.80	0.51	0.53	0.51	0.45	0.43	0.44	0.49
	Z1	(0.11)	(0.04)	(0.14)	(0.19)	(0.27)	(0.33)	(0.43)	(0.47)
	Z2	(0.22)	(0.02)	(0.04)	(0.04)	(0.03)	(0.04)	(0.04)	(0.07)
4	V	0.98	0.89	0.86	0.83	0.78	0.76	0.66	0.60
	Z1	(0.80)	(0.42)	(0.45)	(0.43)	(0.42)	(0.47)	(0.37)	(0.32)
	Z2	(0.78)	(0.17)	(0.12)	(0.07)	(0.04)	(0.03)	(0.00)	(0.00)
5	V	0.76	0.62	0.61	0.61	0.58	0.54	0.47	0.43
	Z1	(0.00)	(0.00)	(0.00)	(0.00)	(0.00)	(0.00)	(0.00)	(0.00)
	Z2	(0.00)	(0.00)	(0.00)	(0.00)	(0.00)	(0.00)	(0.00)	(0.00)
6	V	1.08	1.03	0.96	0.90	1.00	1.06	1.17	1.27
	Z1	(0.29)	(0.84)	(0.82)	(0.64)	(0.97)	(0.86)	(0.66)	(0.50)
	Z2	(0.40)	(0.80)	(0.72)	(0.42)	(0.99)	(0.68)	(0.25)	(0.07)
7	V	0.90	0.79	0.74	0.73	0.75	0.76	0.78	0.81
	Z1	(0.00)	(0.00)	(0.00)	(0.00)	(0.01)	(0.04)	(0.10)	(0.21)
	Z2	(0.07)	(0.00)	(0.00)	(0.00)	(0.00)	(0.00)	(0.01)	(0.04)

Notes: See Table 4.

in many instances. This pattern contrasts quite markedly with the experience for the BF/DM rate, discussed above. For other French franc cross rates a similar story can be told, even when the peripheral currencies are considered. For example, for the IL/DM around a third (27 out of 88) of the variance ratios are above unity whereas only one-fifth (10 out of 48) of the IL/FF entries (contained in Table 9) are above unity (and of those that are below unity, many are significantly so).

In the majority of instances, the patterns for the Belgian franc are similar to the French franc cross rates – there is more evidence of mean reversion (slightly more than one-half (122 out of 232) of the estimated variance ratios are significantly smaller than unity) for these rates than the comparable German mark rates. However, the pattern of mean reversion is less marked for the Dutch guilder cross rates and these are much more similar to the German mark rates, a finding reflecting the previously noted close links between the guilder and mark throughout the ERM period.

Table 9
Variance ratio statistics and significance levels. Exchange rate: IL/FF

		2	4	6	8	12	16	20	24
1	V	0.77	0.73	0.75	0.80	0.88	0.94	1.01	1.03
	Z1	(0.00)	(0.00)	(0.02)	(0.13)	(0.46)	(0.76)	(0.97)	(0.92)
	Z2	(0.01)	(0.01)	(0.02)	(0.07)	(0.29)	(0.62)	(0.95)	(0.83)
2	V	0.92	0.77	0.71	0.65	0.60	0.55	0.46	0.46
	Z1	(0.17)	(0.03)	(0.04)	(0.05)	(0.07)	(0.08)	(0.06)	(0.11)
	Z2	(0.31)	(0.01)	(0.01)	(0.00)	(0.00)	(0.00)	(0.00)	(0.00)
3	V	0.98	0.95	0.95	0.96	0.93	0.86	0.83	0.84
	Z1	(0.64)	(0.41)	(0.54)	(0.73)	(0.59)	(0.39)	(0.35)	(0.43)
	Z2	(0.83)	(0.56)	(0.61)	(0.75)	(0.56)	(0.30)	(0.23)	(0.26)
4	V	0.90	0.90	0.91	0.93	0.90	0.81	0.72	0.70
	Z1	(0.20)	(0.48)	(0.62)	(0.77)	(0.73)	(0.49)	(0.49)	(0.50)
	Z2	(0.20)	(0.29)	(0.37)	(0.55)	(0.41)	(0.16)	(0.05)	(0.04)
5	V	0.86	0.84	0.83	0.82	0.81	0.84	0.88	0.91
	Z1	(0.00)	(0.01)	(0.04)	(0.06)	(0.12)	(0.26)	(0.44)	(0.62)
	Z2	(0.00)	(0.01)	(0.01)	(0.01)	(0.01)	(0.03)	(0.11)	(0.26)
6	V	1.12	1.08	1.06	1.06	1.20	1.35	1.46	1.54
	Z1	(0.01)	(0.31)	(0.56)	(0.63)	(0.20)	(0.06)	(0.03)	(0.02)
	Z2	(0.14)	(0.42)	(0.57)	(0.59)	(0.09)	(0.01)	(0.00)	(0.00)

Notes: See Table 4.

3.3.2.2. 'Peripheral' exchange rates. Most of the peripheral rates have already been addressed in the previous two sub-sections. Those that have not, are contained in Tables 10 and 11 (Tables 25–27 in Anthony and MacDonald (1997)). The pattern here is in general agreement with the German mark rates, although it is worth highlighting the Irish punt–Danish krone which produces variance ratios which are below unity in every instance bar one.

4. Panel unit-root tests

One potential problem with the unit-root tests conducted in the previous section is that they may have low power to reject the null hypothesis of a unit root when it is, in fact, false (i.e. a type II error – see Campbell and Perron for a discussion). This is an issue which has been addressed in other related areas by expanding the span of the data (see, for example, the recent literature on PPP, surveyed in Froot and Rogoff (1995); MacDonald (1995)). In principle, there are two ways to expand the span of the data. One involves extending the historical span by increasing the number of years covered by the data set. In the literature

Table 10
Variance ratio statistics and significance levels. Exchange rate: DK/IL

		2	4	6	8	12	16	20	24
1	V	1.09	1.37	1.66	1.99	2.40	2.65	2.91	3.11
	Z1	(0.31)	(0.03)	(0.00)	(0.00)	(0.00)	(0.00)	(0.00)	(0.00)
	Z2	(0.28)	(0.00)	(0.00)	(0.00)	(0.00)	(0.00)	(0.00)	(0.00)
2	V	0.87	0.62	0.79	0.98	1.19	1.23	1.07	0.81
	Z1	(0.43)	(0.23)	(0.60)	(0.97)	(0.79)	(0.82)	(0.94)	(0.85)
	Z2	(0.40)	(0.03)	(0.27)	(0.92)	(0.39)	(0.32)	(0.77)	(0.43)
3	V	0.78	0.69	0.66	0.64	0.63	0.66	0.70	0.72
	Z1	(0.00)	(0.00)	(0.02)	(0.03)	(0.08)	(0.18)	(0.30)	(0.37)
	Z2	(0.10)	(0.04)	(0.04)	(0.03)	(0.03)	(0.06)	(0.10)	(0.13)
4	V	0.82	0.67	0.68	0.79	0.83	0.85	0.85	0.78
	Z1	(0.04)	(0.05)	(0.15)	(0.43)	(0.64)	(0.71)	(0.74)	(0.66)
	Z2	(0.02)	(0.00)	(0.00)	(0.09)	(0.23)	(0.31)	(0.33)	(0.17)
5	V	0.76	0.51	0.60	0.56	0.61	0.60	0.68	0.76
	Z1	(0.02)	(0.02)	(0.14)	(0.19)	(0.34)	(0.43)	(0.58)	(0.73)
	Z2	(0.06)	(0.00)	(0.02)	(0.02)	(0.05)	(0.06)	(0.14)	(0.28)
6	V	0.87	0.81	0.96	1.01	1.15	1.25	1.43	1.69
	Z1	(0.28)	(0.43)	(0.90)	(0.97)	(0.76)	(0.66)	(0.55)	(0.33)
	Z2	(0.32)	(0.25)	(0.83)	(0.95)	(0.44)	(0.23)	(0.05)	(0.00)
7	V	0.96	0.82	0.81	0.79	0.81	0.79	0.74	0.80
	Z1	(0.55)	(0.18)	(0.29)	(0.33)	(0.51)	(0.52)	(0.49)	(0.62)
	Z2	(0.71)	(0.18)	(0.19)	(0.17)	(0.26)	(0.22)	(0.14)	(0.26)
8	V	0.86	0.84	0.82	0.84	0.90	0.93	0.98	1.04
	Z1	(0.00)	(0.04)	(0.08)	(0.20)	(0.51)	(0.70)	(0.91)	(0.87)
	Z2	(0.00)	(0.01)	(0.01)	(0.04)	(0.20)	(0.40)	(0.79)	(0.66)
9	V	0.91	0.89	0.87	0.89	0.95	1.06	1.21	1.28
	Z1	(0.23)	(0.43)	(0.48)	(0.63)	(0.86)	(0.86)	(0.61)	(0.53)
	Z2	(0.35)	(0.33)	(0.29)	(0.40)	(0.71)	(0.66)	(0.17)	(0.07)
10	V	0.93	0.94	0.99	1.06	1.11	1.17	1.25	1.31
	Z1	(0.04)	(0.30)	(0.93)	(0.55)	(0.38)	(0.23)	(0.13)	(0.09)
	Z2	(0.22)	(0.32)	(0.91)	(0.41)	(0.15)	(0.02)	(0.00)	(0.00)
11	V	1.05	0.96	0.90	0.89	0.93	0.96	0.98	1.01
	Z1	(0.25)	(0.61)	(0.33)	(0.36)	(0.68)	(0.84)	(0.91)	(0.96)
	Z2	(0.39)	(0.55)	(0.17)	(0.14)	(0.43)	(0.66)	(0.79)	(0.89)

Notes: See Table 4.

on testing whether real exchange rates contain stochastic unit roots, such an extension has been demonstrated to have a dramatic effect on the ability of a researcher to reject the null of non-stationarity (see Froot and Rogoff, 1995; MacDonald, 1995). In the current application such an extension is, unfortunately,

Table 11
Variance ratio statistics and significance levels. Exchange rate: IP/DK

		2	4	6	8	12	16	20	24
1	V	0.75	0.72	0.68	0.74	0.76	0.75	0.81	0.85
	Z1	(0.01)	(0.10)	(0.15)	(0.33)	(0.51)	(0.54)	(0.70)	(0.77)
	Z2	(0.01)	(0.02)	(0.02)	(0.07)	(0.12)	(0.12)	(0.24)	(0.38)
2	V	0.74	0.58	0.47	0.46	0.49	0.43	0.45	0.46
	Z1	(0.11)	(0.19)	(0.19)	(0.28)	(0.47)	(0.57)	(0.58)	(0.59)
	Z2	(0.16)	(0.06)	(0.02)	(0.03)	(0.06)	(0.04)	(0.05)	(0.06)
3	V	0.76	0.60	0.57	0.50	0.46	0.45	0.43	0.40
	Z1	(0.00)	(0.00)	(0.00)	(0.00)	(0.00)	(0.00)	(0.01)	(0.01)
	Z2	(0.00)	(0.00)	(0.00)	(0.00)	(0.00)	(0.00)	(0.00)	(0.00)
4	V	0.89	0.73	0.76	0.72	0.70	0.72	0.71	0.74
	Z1	(0.08)	(0.02)	(0.11)	(0.13)	(0.20)	(0.31)	(0.36)	(0.46)
	Z2	(0.12)	(0.00)	(0.01)	(0.01)	(0.01)	(0.02)	(0.03)	(0.05)
5	V	0.94	0.84	0.76	0.73	0.67	0.61	0.57	0.56
	Z1	(0.08)	(0.02)	(0.01)	(0.01)	(0.02)	(0.02)	(0.02)	(0.03)
	Z2	(0.23)	(0.01)	(0.00)	(0.00)	(0.00)	(0.00)	(0.00)	(0.00)
6	V	1.04	0.99	0.86	0.70	0.65	0.69	0.66	0.55
	Z1	(0.72)	(0.95)	(0.63)	(0.40)	(0.44)	(0.59)	(0.63)	(0.53)
	Z2	(0.71)	(0.91)	(0.34)	(0.06)	(0.05)	(0.09)	(0.07)	(0.02)
7	V	0.99	0.88	0.87	0.89	0.89	0.90	0.89	0.90
	Z1	(0.57)	(0.02)	(0.05)	(0.14)	(0.25)	(0.37)	(0.40)	(0.48)
	Z2	(0.80)	(0.08)	(0.07)	(0.13)	(0.15)	(0.20)	(0.18)	(0.23)

Notes: See Table 4.

not an option. However, the recent literature on PPP demonstrates that precisely the same result as is obtained from a long-run of annual data may also be obtained by expanding the panel dimensions of the data set.[15] In this section, therefore, we propose expanding the span of the data by pooling across the currencies participating in the ERM and testing for a unit root across the panel. Panel unit-root tests may be motivated using the following equation:

$$\Delta s_{it} = \alpha + \delta s_{t-1} + \left\{\sum_i \gamma_i D_i\right\} + \left\{\sum_t \gamma_t D_t\right\} + \left\{\sum_i \beta_i t_i\right\} + v_{it}, \tag{13}$$

[15] In particular, Frankel and Rose (1995) and MacDonald (1995) have demonstrated that with long runs of historical data the proposition that real exchange rates contain a unit root may be rejected in favour of the alternative hypothesis that they are mean reverting with a half-life of around 4 years. Exactly the same result may be obtained by expanding the cross-sectional dimensions of a given time-series data set.

where i denotes a currency, D_i and D_t denote, respectively, country-specific and time-specific fixed effects dummy variables, a t_i denotes a country-specific time trend. Eq. (13) is essentially the panel analogue to Eq. (4) and of interest is the magnitude of δ, which will indicate the speed of mean reversion, and its significance as judged by the estimated t-ratio. As Levin and Lin (1992, 1993) have demonstrated the critical values for the latter statistic are affected by the particular deterministic specification used.

In circumstances where all of the deterministic elements in Eq. (13) are excluded apart from the single constant term, α, Levin and Lin (1992) demonstrate that the t-statistic on converges to a standard normal distribution. Including individual specific effects (either $\{\sum_i \gamma_i D_i\}$ or $\{\sum_i \beta_i t_i\}$) or both), but excluding time specific intercepts, Levin and Lin (1992) demonstrate that the t-ratio converges to a non-central normal distribution, with substantial impact on the size of the unit-root test (and they tabulate critical values). However, Levin and Lin (1993) argue that unless there are very strong grounds for exclusion, time specific intercepts should always be included in these kind of panel tests. The reason for this is that the inclusion of such dummies is equivalent to subtracting the cross-section average in each period. This subtraction may be dispensed with in cases where the units in the panel are independent of each other; however, in cases where this is not the case such a subtraction is vital to ensure independence across units.

In addition to facilitating the removal of time means, the panel methods of Levin and Lin (1993) have a number of other advantages such as allowing the residual term to be heterogeneously distributed across individuals (in terms of both non-constant variance and autocorrelation), rather than a white noise process. Since, as we have argued previously, such heterogeneity is a feature of daily exchange rate data the Levin–Lin method has clear advantages in the current context.

The testing method has the null hypothesis that each individual time series in the panel has a unit root, against the alternative that all individual units taken as a panel are stationary. The procedure consists of four steps which we now briefly note (these steps do not correspond exactly to the steps in Levin and Lin).

The first step involves subtracting the cross section mean from the observed exchange rate series. Thus, we now have s_{it} where i runs from 1 to N, where N denotes the total number of currencies in the ERM, and we construct $\bar{s}_t = (1/N)\sum_{i=1}^{N} s_{it}$. In the following steps the term s_{it} is interpreted as having been adjusted by $\bar{s}_t$.

Step two involves performing the following two regressions:

$$\Delta s_{it} = \sum_{L=1}^{p_i} \hat{\pi}_{iL} \Delta s_{it-L} + \hat{\alpha}_{mi} d_{mt} + \hat{e}_{it}, \tag{14a}$$

$$s_{it-1} = \sum_{L=1}^{p_i} \hat{\phi}_{iL} \Delta s_{it-L} + \hat{\alpha}_{mi} d_{mt} + \hat{v}_{it-1}, \tag{14b}$$

where a $\hat{}$ denotes a fitted value, $\hat{e}_{it}$ and $\hat{v}_{it-1}$ denote estimated residuals and d_{mt} denotes appropriate deterministic variables defined for three different models $m = 1, 2, 3$. Model 1 contains no exchange rate specific deterministic elements, Model 2 contains a (country-specific) constant term and Model 3 contains a (country-specific) constant and a deterministic trend. Having estimated Eq. (14b), the following regression is run:

$$\hat{e}_{it} = \delta_i \hat{v}_{it-1} + \varepsilon_{it}. \tag{15}$$

The t-ratio calculated on the basis of $\hat{\delta}_i$ is the panel equivalent to an ADF calculated on the basis of (4). In order to control for heterogeneity across individuals both $\hat{e}_{it}$ and $\hat{v}_{it-1}$ are deflated by the regression standard error from Eq. (15); these adjusted errors are labelled, $\tilde{e}_{it}$ and $\tilde{v}_{it-1}$. Under the null hypothesis these normalised innovations should be independent of each other and this may be tested by running the following regression:

$$\tilde{e}_{it} = \delta \tilde{v}_{it-1} + \tilde{\varepsilon}_{it}. \tag{16}$$

Under the null hypothesis that $\delta_i = 0$ for all $i = 1, \ldots N$, the asymptotic theory in Section 4 of Levin and Lin indicates that the regression t-statistic t_δ has a standard normal distribution for model 1, but diverges to negative infinity for models 2 and 3. However, Levin and Lin demonstrate that the following adjusted t-ratio has an N(0,1) distribution and the critical values of the standard normal distribution can be used to test the null hypothesis that $\delta_i = 0$ for all $i = 1, \ldots, N$:

$$t_\delta^* = \frac{t_\delta - N\tilde{T}\hat{S}_{NT}\hat{\sigma}_\varepsilon^{-2}\,\mathrm{RSE}(\hat{\delta})\,\mu_{m\tilde{T}}^*}{\sigma_{m\tilde{T}}^*}. \tag{17}$$

The terms in Eq. (17), other than t_δ, are calculated under step 4. In particular, $\hat{S} = (1/N)\sum_{i=1}^{n} \hat{s}_i$, $\hat{s}_i = \hat{\sigma}_{si}/\hat{\sigma}_{ei}$, $\hat{\sigma}_{ei}$ is the residual standard error from Eq. (15) and $\hat{\sigma}_{si}$ is an estimate of the long-run standard deviation, RSE(δ) is an estimate of the reported standard error of $\hat{\delta}$ (the latter being a least-squares estimate) $\hat{\sigma}_\varepsilon$ is the estimated standard error of regression (16), $\tilde{T} \equiv (T - \bar{p} - 1)$ is the average number of observations per individual in the panel and $\bar{p} \equiv (1/N)\sum_{i=1}^{N} p_i$ is the average lag order for the individual ADF statistics. $\sigma_{m\tilde{T}}^*$ and $\mu_{m\tilde{T}}^*$ represent the mean and standard deviation adjustments, respectively, and are tabulated in Table 1 of Levin and Lin for different deterministic specifications ($m = 1, 2, 3$).

In implementing the Levin and Lin (1993) test we combined our data to form panels in the following way. We examined each realignment period and for those which contained five or six overlapping currencies a panel was then formed. From the full-sample period this generated five separate panel data sets: 79:03:13–79:09:23, 86:04:07–86:08:03, 86:08:04–87:01:11, 87:01:12–90:01:08 and 90:01:08–92:04:09. Since country-specific fixed effects dummy variables were significantly different across currencies, we did not compute a panel ADF test

Table 12
Panel unit-root tests

	Panel 1	Panel 2	Panel 3	Panel 4	Panel 5
t_δ	− 3.96	− 5.56	− 6.04	− 2.34	− 3.81
t_δ^*	− 0.58	0.11	− 1.43	2.77	0.65

Notes. t_δ and t_δ^* are, respectively, the unadjusted and adjusted panel unit root t-ratios, defined in the text. The t_δ^* statistic has a standard normal distribution and none are significant at conventional significance levels. The five panel data sets used to construct these statistics are defined in the text.

across the panel. Rather, we constructed the Levin and Lin (1993) t-ratios which allow for differing fixed effect dummies across countries; that is, for each of the data periods we constructed an unadjusted panel unit-root t-test, δ_t, and the adjusted t-ratio given by (17).

Our panel results are reported in Table 12. We note that the unadjusted t-ratio, t_δ, is negative and, in all cases apart from panel 4, is less than the standard Dickey–Fuller 5% critical value of − 2.97. However, these statistics are not valid for reasons we have just noted. The adjusted t-ratios, the t_δ^*'s, portray a rather different story in that only two of the statistics are negative and none of these are significant at the 5% level. However, there is some evidence of rejection of the joint null in the case of panel three, where the t_δ^* is significant on the basis of a one tail test at the 8% level.

We attribute the failure to reject the null of non-stationarity in the panel setting to two factors. First, our variance ratio tests demonstrate that within a particular realignment period some currencies do exhibit mean reversion while others do not. If the failure to reject the null for some currencies is due to a lack of credibility then this may simply confound the rejection signal from other currencies when all of the currencies are stacked into a panel format. Second, it is well known that panel testing methods work best when the dimensions of the panel are approximately square (i.e. the time-series dimension is approximately equal to the cross-sectional dimension). Unfortunately, the nature of our data base makes it impossible to construct square panel data sets and so our failure to reject the null in a panel context could simply be a reflection of the relatively low power of the test (relative to a square panel).

5. Concluding comments

In this paper we have implemented a battery of tests concerning the mean-reverting properties of currencies participating in the ERM up to 1992. Although the mean-reverting properties of such currencies is a central prediction

1520 *M. Anthony, R. MacDonald / European Economic Review 42 (1998) 1493–1523*

of the target zone literature, little research effort has been devoted to verifying it (and indeed as we demonstrated the tests that have been undertaken have been flawed). The main conclusion to stem from our work is that in the majority of instances ERM exchange rates appear to be non-stationary. Although we have emphasised the relatively low power that our univariate tests have to reject the null of a random walk, we nevertheless find that there are important and significant exceptions to our failure to reject the null hypothesis of a unit root.

The exceptions we find to the unit-root null are perhaps explicable in terms of the kinds of policies that have to be pursued by national governments if they are to be truly committed to an ERM-style arrangement. For example, Netherlands guilder–German mark exchange rate exhibited strong mean-reversion. Since a de facto monetary union existed between these two currencies for our sample periods, this perhaps indicates the kind of monetary policy a country needs to adopt to effectively participate in an exchange rate mechanism like the ERM. An interesting sub-plot in our story, which we do not wish to emphasise too much, is the finding that of the instances where mean-reversion does occur (based on the evidence from our variance ratio results) it seems to be more prevalent for French franc and Belgian franc bilateral rates than for German mark bilaterals. The fact that these rates exhibit more of the characteristics of a target zone perhaps indicates that the rejections we observe for the DM-based rates cannot be wholly attributable to a power problem; they are, perhaps, evidence of a lack of credibility.

To a large extent, the lack of support for a mean-reverting tendency among the ERM bilateral rates for the period prior to January 1987 is not totally unexpected. First, there was the period from February 1985 to December 1987 in which the dramatic depreciation of the US dollar resulted in speculation against the dollar towards other currencies, including participants in the ERM. This period was therefore seen as exceptional and led to the dramatic realignment in January 1987 and the Basle–Nyborg agreement of 1987.[16] Thus, even considering within-realignment data may not ensure mean-reverting exchange rate behaviour.

Secondly, from its commencement in March 1979 to January 1987 there were 11 realignments in the ERM – a clear indication of the relative instability of this early phase in the operation of the system. The frequency of realignments in this period depicted the persistence of inflation differentials across the EMS currencies. As was pointed out by De Grauwe (1989), the volatility of inflation rates across the EMS countries rose between 1979 and 1983, and remained substantial until 1986. Similar (but weaker) conclusions were made by Robertson and Symons (1990). Looking for mean-reversion using within-realignment data may

[16] This was an agreement designed to strengthen foreign intervention against speculative attacks and encourage policy coordination (see Eichengreen and Wyplosz, 1993).

have been expected to overcome this problem. However, the fact that prices were trended for the whole period means that such trending behaviour will also manifest itself in the behaviour of ERM exchange rates in the sub-sample constituents of the full sample and this, in turn, could generate non-mean-reverting behaviour, which is indeed what we find.

Although there was undeniably some improvement in convergence in prices (and policy objectives) after January 1987, there was still lingering divergences which meant that "*neither the necessary (convergence of costs and prices) nor the necessary and sufficient conditions (convergence of costs, prices, and policies) for irrevocably fixed exchange rates among all ERM participants have been fulfilled*" (Ungerer et al., 1990) (emphasis is ours). Despite this, policy makers pursued a no-realignment strategy, in the process, creating a de facto pegged exchange rate system.[17]

This post-1987 period also witnessed two important developments which (as the September 1992 events would subsequently confirm) had deleterious implications for the EMS. First, commencing in 1990, the German economic and monetary unification (GEMU) imposed a massive asymmetric shock on the EMS, which implied a (long-run) depreciation of the German mark. Second, 1990 also saw the removal of existing capital controls in some EMS countries, as part of the 1992 Single Market Programme. But the removal of controls on capital flows substantially reduced the monetary authorities' ability to withstand speculative attacks – a necessary precondition for the viability of any fixed exchange rate system.

Although an analysis of the September 1992 crisis in the ERM is beyond the purview of this paper,[18] with hindsight, it is apparent that the absence of realignments in the post-1987 period temporarily masked the intrinsic pressures which were already built-up in the ERM. Our findings of a general absence of a mean-reverting tendency after 1987 would therefore be consistent with such a view. The nominal exchange rates in the ERM were not as stable as the absence of realignments superficially suggested. But the instances in which we do observe mean reversion are suggestive of the kinds of policies that have to be pursued if an ERM arrangement is to be successful.

Acknowledgements

We are grateful to Francesco Giavazzi and to two anonymous referees for their helpful comments on an earlier draft of this paper. We would also like to

---

[17] The Italian lira was devalued on 8 January 1990 by placing it in the narrow 2.25% band.

[18] See Eichengreen and Wyplosz (1993) for an excellent analysis of the causes of the September 1992 crisis in the ERM.

thank John McConnell, Alison Wright and Andrew Deykin for their efficient research assistance. MacDonald acknowledges financial support from the ESRC (L120251023) and the Leverhulme foundation.

References

Anthony, M., MacDonald, R., 1997. On the mean-reverting properties of target zone exchange rates: Some evidence from the ERM. Discussion paper 3. Centre for Financial Research, Glasgow.

Banerjee, A., Dolado, J., Galbraith, J.W., Hendry, D.F., 1993. Cointegration, Error-Correction, and the Econometric Analysis of Non-Stationary Data. Oxford University Press, Oxford.

Banerjee, A., Lumsdaine, R.L., Stock, J.H., 1992. Recursive and sequential tests of the unit root and trend-breaking hypothesis: Theory and international evidence. Journal of Business and Economic Statistics 10, 271–287.

Campbell, J.Y., Perron, P., 1991. Pitfalls and opportunities: What macroeconomists should know about unit roots. In: Blanchard, O.J., Fischer, S. (Eds.), NBER Economic Annual. MIT Press, Cambridge.

Cochrane, J.H., 1988. How big is the random walk in GNP? Journal of Political Economy 96, 893–920.

De Grauwe, P., 1989. The cost of disinflation and the European monetary system . Discussion paper 326. Centre for Economic Policy Research, London.

Dickey, D., Fuller, W.A., 1979. Distribution of the estimators for autoregressive time series with a unit root. Journal of the American Statistical Association 74, 427–431.

Eichengreen, B., Wyplosz, C., 1993. The unstable EMS. Discussion paper 817. Centre for Economic Policy Research, London.

Flood, R., Rose, D., Matheson, D., 1991. An empirical exploration of exchange rate target zones. Carnegie Rochester Series on Public Policy 35, 7–65.

Froot, K., Rogoff, K., 1995. Perspectives on PPP and long-run real exchange rates. In: Grossman, E., Rogoff, K. (Eds.), The Handbook of International Economics. North-Holland, Amsterdam.

Fuller, W.A., 1976. Introduction to Statistical Time Series. Wiley, New York.

Hall, A., 1990. Testing for a unit root in time series with preset data based model selection. Mimeo. North Carolina State University, Durham, NC.

Hallwood, P., MacDonald, R., 1994. International money and finance. Blackwell, Oxford.

Krugman, P., 1991. Target zones and exchange rate dynamics. Quarterly Journal of Economics 106, 669–682.

Levin, A., Lin, C.F., 1992. Unit roots in panel data: Asymptotic and finite sample properties. Mimeo. University of California, San Diego, CA.

Levin, A., Lin, C.F., 1993. Unit roots in panel data: asymptotic anf finite sample properties. Revised Mimeo. University of California, San Diego, CA.

Lo, A., MacKinlay, C., 1988. Stock prices do not follow random walks: Evidence from a simple specification test. The Review of Financial Studies 1, 41–66.

MacDonald, R., 1995. Long-run exchange rate modeling: A survey of the recent evidence. International Monetary Fund Staff Papers 42 (3), 437–489.

MacKinnon, J., 1991. Critical values for cointegration tests. In: Engle, R.F., Granger, C.W.J. (Eds.), Long-Run Economic Relationships: Readings in Cointegration. Oxford University Press, Oxford, pp. 267–276.

Miller, M., Weller, P., 1991. Currency bands, target zones and price flexibility. International Monetary Fund Staff Papers 38, 184–215.

Mills, T., 1993. The Econometric Modelling of Financial Time Series. Cambridge University Press, Cambridge.

Nieuwland, F.G.M.C., Verschoor, W.F.C., Wolff, C.C.P., 1994. Stochastic jumps in EMS exchange rates. Journal of International Money and Finance 13, 699–727.

Perron, P., 1989. The great crash, the oil price shock, and the unit root hypothesis. Econometrica 57 (6), 1361–1401.

Robertson, D., Symons, J., 1990. Output, inflation, and the ERM. Discussion paper 43. Centre for Economic Policy Research, London.

Rose, A.K., Svensson, L.E.O., 1994. European exchange rate credibility before the fall. European Economic Review 38, 1185–1216.

Svensson, L.E.O., 1992. An interpretation of recent research on exchange rate target zones. Journal of Economic Perspectives 6 (4), 119–144.

Svensson, L.E.O., 1993. Assessing target zone credibility. European Economic Review 37, 763–802.

Ungerer, H., Hauvonen, J.J., Lopez-Claros, A., Mayer, T., 1990. The EMS: Developments and perspectives. International Monetary Fund Occasional Paper 73. International Monetary Fund, Washington, DC.

[20]

EXPLORATIONS IN ECONOMIC HISTORY **34,** 174–194 (1997)
ARTICLE NO. EH970668

Crash! Expectational Aspects of the Departures of the United Kingdom and the United States from the Inter-War Gold Standard*

C. Paul Hallwood†

Department of Economics, University of Connecticut, Storrs, Connecticut 06371

and

Ronald MacDonald‡ and Ian W. Marsh‡

Department of Economics, University of Strathclyde, Glasgow, G4 0LN, United Kingdom

This paper contains an investigation of the pressures on the UK and the USA to devalue their currencies against gold in 1931 and 1933, respectively. We derive time-series of realignment expectations for the pound and the dollar. Among our findings is that expectations are quite well explained by fundamental economic variables. The implication is drawn that macroeconomic events, some of them directly or indirectly under the influence of the authorities, were in part responsible eventually for jolting the UK and the USA off the gold standard. Furthermore, quantitative evidence is presented supporting the view that Federal Reserve monetary policy was constrained by international considerations. © 1997 Academic Press

Within the space of 19 months, beginning in September 1931 and ending in March 1933, both the United Kingdom and the United States departed from the gold-exchange standard system which had been reconstructed as an international regime following World War I. In this paper the commonalities of the experiences of these two central players in the "game" of the inter-war gold standard are examined, and, in particular, the extent to which macroeconomic events were responsible for encouraging the speculative runs against the pound and the dollar that encouraged both of them to abandon the gold standard. The paper also

* MacDonald and Marsh gratefully acknowledge funding from the ESRC's Global Economic Institutions program (Grant L120-25-1014). The authors thank Peter Temin, two anonymous referees and the Editor, Larry Neal, for their comments on an earlier draft of this paper.

† E-mail: hallwood@uconnvm.uconn.edu.

‡ E-mail: economics@strath.ac.uk.

0014-4983/97 $25.00
Copyright © 1997 by Academic Press
All rights of reproduction in any form reserved.

addresses the controversial matter of whether Federal Reserve policy was constrained by international considerations.[1]

Some of our conclusions that are of general relevance to the economic history of the inter-war gold standard period are as follows. First, we are not in agreement with the view that the Federal Reserve was a free agent with respect to the choice of monetary policy; rather, we believe that its action were constrained by the American commitment to the gold standard. This is contrary to the view of Friedman and Schwartz (1963) but is in agreement with those of some more recent writers cited below. Second, our tests suggest that domestic and international factors were intertwined as causes of the United States suspending its adherence to the gold standard. Third, because we find systematic relationships between bank failures in the United States, dollar realignment expectations, and international gold flows going back for over 6 years, we think it is a misperception to treat President Roosevelt's role in the Bank Panic of March 1933 as a single event, separate from what had gone before. While we do not deny that his election may have influenced expectations that the dollar was about to be devalued, we also note that, according to our calculations, these expectations were not that much different from those in some earlier episodes of dollar weakness such as 1931(10)–1932(6). Fourth, our calculations indicate that financial markets did not seriously question the adherence of the pound to gold at a fixed price until the summer of 1931. We believe that this finding sheds light on the debate over whether the United Kingdom was playing by the "rules of the game" from 1925 until that summer. While various economic historians have defined the rules and their violation in different ways, it is our assertion that the financial markets of the day were in fact the best judge. Thus, while the Bank of England may not have been following the rules exactly, it was not deviating from them sufficiently to seriously worry the financial markets.

The approach adopted in this paper involves using target zone methods to extract time series of unobserved realignment probabilities for the British pound from the observed interest rate differentials between the United Kingdom and the United States. As already noted, these realignment series show that the markets did not expect devaluations of the pound until mid-1931, consistent with the hypothesis of a speculative attack. However, it also seems that the expected devaluation of the pound is related to several key economic fundamentals, including the differential between money supplies and industrial production levels. The main lesson is that macroeconomic fundamentals between pairs of countries must move in tandem if exchange rate target zones are to remain credible in financial markets. While this lesson is not new, we do offer a demonstration of it as drawn from an important part of 20th century experimentation with pegged exchange rates.

Using interest differentials between France and the United States, a series for

[1] An excellent collection of papers on the classical gold standard can be found in Bordo and Schwartz (1984).

dollar devaluation expectations is also generated. Again these show little sign of tension until the pound left the gold standard, after which there are three clear episodes: a 9-month period during which the dollar was consistently expected to depreciate, followed by 7 months of tranquillity when no parity changes were expected, and finally 2 months of renewed dollar devaluation expectations.

A variety of techniques are used to relate devaluation expectations to two key economic determinants, the widespread United States bank failures and gold flows into and out of the United States. The results confirm the hypothesis of Brown (1940), who argued that increases in the money supply of the United States induced fears in Europe of American inflation at a time when American short-term liabilities to foreigners were still well in excess of the country's free gold. The inflation expectations gave rise to devaluation expectations and the external gold drain as residents feared suspension of the gold standard, which was also a factor in the accelerating banking crisis of early 1932.

Our findings would seem to support the position that the Federal Reserve in this period was being hemmed in by commitment to the gold standard. And, therefore we come down on the side of Kindleberger (1986), Eichengreen (1992a), and Temin (1989) that US monetary policy was constrained by international considerations—a position that Friedman and Schwartz (1963) have strongly denied. The Federal Reserve found itself in a dilemma: if it increased the money base to "save the banks" it was not playing by the rules of the game given the preponderance of gold outflows at this time. However, if it did nothing, which turned out to be the chosen policy, this risked the bank failures that also put pressure on the dollar. Adherence to the gold standard quickly became untenable.

In short, we conclude that in both the United Kingdom and the United States domestic and international macroeconomic events, some of them directly or indirectly under the influence of the authorities, were responsible for both the countries leaving the gold standard during the inter-war period. Furthermore, as our results indicate that economic factors can to quite a large extent explain the 1933 American episode, we do not agree that the election of President Roosevelt was an important causal factor in it.

We proceed as follows: Section I sets out the theory of target zones and how it can be manipulated to reveal rationally held realignment expectations in financial markets. In Section II we empirically implement the target zone model to reveal realignment expectations for the pound and the dollar. In Section III attention is turned to modelling the determinants of realignment expectations, and finally, Section IV presents our conclusions.

I. REALIGNMENT EXPECTATIONS: THEORY

Krugman (1988, 1991) models an exchange rate that is restricted to a narrow band, such as between the gold points, as a "target zone."[2] A target zone is

[2] Empirical investigation of gold standard as a target zone is undertaken by Hallwood *et al.* (1996), Giovannini (1993) and Flood *et al.* (1991).

credible, in the sense that the market believes that the exchange rate will be contained within it, if it is believed that the monetary authorities are committed to managing fundamentals, such as its discount rate and the monetary base, to that end. Thus, at the edges of the target zone monetary policy must be geared exclusively to the exchange rate and not towards influencing, say, domestic business conditions.

To investigate the credibility of the inter-war gold standard we need a measure of *realignment expectations,* and in this we follow the methodology of Svensson (1991, 1993) and Bertola and Svensson (1993).[3] In natural logarithms, define the current exchange rate, s_t, as

$$s_t = x_t + c_t, \tag{1}$$

where c_t is the central parity and x_t is the proportionate deviation from parity. Taking time derivatives,

$$E_t[ds_t]/dt = E_t[dx_t]/dt + E_t[dc_t]/dt, \tag{2}$$

so the rationally expected rate of change of the exchange rate is divided into the expected movement "within the band," $(E_t[dx_t]/dt)$, plus the expected rate of depreciation of the central parity, $(E_t[dc_t]/dt)$.

Furthermore, for any given x_t, the movement within the band is bounded by the gold import and gold export points,

$$(x_t^l - x_t)/dt \leq E_t[dx_t]/dt \leq (x_t^u - x_t)/dt, \tag{3}$$

where x^l is the lower bound of s_t, the gold import point, and x^u, is the upper bound or gold export point.

On using Eqs. (2) and (3) we discover the so called "100%" confidence interval for realignment expectations,

$$(i_t - i_t^*) - (x_t^u - x_t\}/dt \leq E_t[dc]/dt \leq (i_t - i_t^*) - (x_t^l - x_t)/dt, \tag{4}$$

where i_t is the home country's interest rate and i_t^* is a comparable interest rate in the foreign country. The term $(i_t - i_t^*)$— the interest differential—has been substituted for $E_t[ds_t]/dt$ because we are assuming uncovered interest parity. As Svensson (1993, p. 766) points out, if agents arbitraging between national money markets demand a risk premium, the interest differential measures the expected change in the exchange rate plus the risk premium. Svensson also shows, however, that the risk premium must be small in any credible target zone.

Equation (4) defines the minimum and maximum bounds of the market's rationally expected central parity realignment. Svensson called this the "simplest test" for realignment expectations.[4] It is only when both the left and right sides of

[3] Calomiris (1993), using a different methodology, has calculated realignment expectations for the short period 1893–1896. Giovannini (1993) uses a methodology similar to ours, applying it to the years 1889–1909.

[4] A numerical illustration may be helpful. Suppose that the expected change in the exchange rate as

the inequality signs are of the same sign that we reject the null hypothesis of no realignment expectation.[5]

One problem with the simplest test is that it supposes that the edges of the zone are known for certain, but this was probably not the case as the gold points varied (see Officer, 1993). Another problem is that it ignores the mean reverting tendency of the exchange rate within the band, which is strongly implied by the target zone theory. Svensson complements the former technique with that of the "drift adjustment method," which uses an econometric estimate of expected reversion of the exchange rate to parity (Svensson, 1993, p. 768). This may be demonstrated in the following way.

Rearranging Eq. (2) we obtain a statement of the rationally expected realignment expectation as

$$E_t[dc]/dt = E_t[ds]/dt - E_t[dx]/dt. \tag{5}$$

This realignment expectation can be calculated if we know both the expected change in the exchange rate, $E_t[ds]/dt$, which is easily calculated from the interest differential, and the expected movement of the exchange rate within the band, $E_t[dx]/dt$.

As far as the calculation of the latter is concerned, it is only necessary to mention that it is based on the theoretical proposition due to Krugman (1988, 1991) and to Miller and Weller (1991) that within a target zone the exchange rate should be a mean reverting—or stationary—time-series. Based upon this, Svensson (1993) calculates the expected movement of the exchange rate within the band as a linear function of the current deviation, x_t, of the exchange rate from the central parity. Imposing rational expectations, the expected movement of the exchange rate within the band over the subsequent m months is the fitted value

---

measured by the interest differential is 5% and that the exchange rate is currently at the centre of the zone (i.e., $x_t = 0$ and, therefore, $x_t^u - x_t = 0.5\%$ or approximately half the width of the historical gold points). It follows that $4.5\% \le E_t[dc]/dt \le 5.5\%$ and we are confident that depreciation of the central parity is expected. The idea that we are "100%" confident derives from the fact that we are assuming the edges of the target zone, x^l and x^u, are known for certain. But supposing that the exchange rate is again in the center of its zone but that the expected depreciation is only 0.25%, we now calculate $-0.25\% \le E_t[dc]/dt \le 0.75\%$. In this case the range of expectations spans both a possible appreciation of the central parity and a depreciation. As this range spans zero, we do not reject the null hypothesis that no realignment is expected.

[5] The expected rate of realignment can be interpreted as the expected devaluation size multiplied by the frequency of realignment. Suppose that, conditional on there being a devaluation, the devaluation will be 5%. An expected rate of realignment of 2.5% (roughly the average for the sterling-dollar rate through the less credible early part of the classical gold standard, for the USA, 1879–1896—see Hallwood *et al.* 1996) implies that the expected frequency of realignment is 0.5 per annum. That is, the market expects a 5% devaluation within the year to happen with a 50% probability. Equivalently, the expected time to a 5% devaluation of the dollar is two years. Thus, though the average expected rate of realignment may appear to be small it can be consistent with quite substantial devaluation expectations. Of course, when the confidence interval spans zero we cannot reject the hypothesis that the expected probability of a devaluation of any magnitude is zero.

from the regression,

$$x_{t+m} - x_t = \alpha_0 + \alpha_1 x_t + u_t, \tag{6}$$

where if α_1 is significantly less than zero, mean reversion is occurring.

The final step in implementing Eq. (5) is to take the 95% confidence interval for mean reversion (calculated using Eq. (6)) and combine it with the interest rate differential (the proxy for $E_t[ds]/dt$) to calculate the 95% confidence intervals for realignment expectations. This is Svensson's drift adjustment method.

The main questions we address in this paper are: to what extent does the expected rate of realignment predict the currency crises in the United Kingdom and in the United States? and, more fundamentally, can the expected rate of realignment be explained using fundamental variables? In general terms this latter proposition may be considered in terms of the expression

$$E_t[dc]/dt = f(z^1_{t-1}, z^2_{t-1}, \ldots, z^n_{t-1}), \tag{7}$$

where f denotes a general functional form and $z^1_{t-1}, z^2_{t-1}, \ldots, z^n_{t-1}$ represent the fundamental determinants of the expected rate of realignment. In this paper we are guided by previous studies as to the relevant fundamental variables for each of our currencies. In Sections III and IV we propose methods for empirically testing (7).

II. REALIGNMENT EXPECTATIONS: EMPIRICAL EVIDENCE

We constrain our analysis of the pound–dollar rate to the interval May 1925 to August 1931, the latter being the last full month during which the pound/gold link was maintained. To examine dollar devaluation expectations we had to choose a currency to measure it against. The obvious choice was the French franc as France remained on the gold standard until 1936, and became the most important country remaining on gold following the American suspension. We use the franc/dollar rate from December 1926 (shortly after France had *de facto* settled on the gold standard) until February 1933, the last full month before the US interfered with the gold convertibility of the dollar.[6] The exchange rate series were extracted from Einzig (1937); and short term interest rates were taken from the Board of Governors of the Federal Reserve (1943). Specifically, we use the 3 month UK Treasury bill–US commercial paper differential to provide the total expected change in the sterling–dollar exchange rate.[7] For expectations of the franc–dollar rate we use the three month forward premium (computed by triangular arbitrage

[6] For further discussion of the French franc exchange rate during some of this period see Eichengreen (1986, 1992b) and Sicsic (1992).

[7] Ideally we would have used a differential between identical instruments. However, the US treasury bill market was undeveloped during this period, and the average spread between UK treasury bills and UK bankers' acceptances was less than one basis point. We therefore chose to use the differential between the most liquid short-term instruments in each country.

TABLE 1
Expected Change in Exchange Rate within the Band

	Pound/Dollar	Franc/Dollar
	1925(5)–1931(8)	1927(3)–1933(2)
Constant	0.0009	−0.0009
	(1.85)	(1.79)
x_t	−0.619	−0.758
	(3.38)	(5.14)
R^2	0.309	0.345

Notes. Figures in parentheses are t-statistics computed with Generalized Method of Moments standard errors.

based on sterling exchange rates taken from Einzig (1937)[8]) due to a lack of sufficiently comparable French interest rate data.[9]

Table 1 shows mean reversion in the pound/dollar and franc/dollar rates, i.e., Eq. (6). Using the 95% confidence intervals derived from these equations we calculate the 95% confidence intervals for realignment expectations, i.e., Eq. (4). These are shown in Figs. 1 and 2. As explained earlier, in Fig. 1 it is only when both the upper and lower confidence intervals are in the *positive* section that we are 95% confident that markets expect devaluation of the pound (against the dollar). Similarly with Fig. 2, except that in this case markets expect dollar devaluation (i.e. fewer francs per dollar) when both the upper and lower bounds are in the *negative* section. We discuss these figures in greater detail below.

III. EXPLAINING DEVALUATION EXPECTATIONS

The Experience of the United Kingdom

It is known that the United Kingdom was financing a basic (on current and long-term capital accounts) balance of payments deficit by a short term capital inflow throughout the 1925–1931 period. Furthermore, as the MacMillan Committee (1931) acknowledged, this practice was "precarious." It was precarious because its continuation depended on international investors sustaining their

[8] The Einzig data are sampled weekly. We extract data relating to the final week of each month to provide a monthly database. To avoid complications arising from instability in the foreign exchange markets after sterling's departure from the system, the end-September 1931 observation of the franc-dollar forward rate is in fact that holding on September 19, rather than the September 26.

[9] We note that a forward premium rather than an interest rate differential is also used in Eichengreen (1982). Both approaches are equivalent if covered interest parity holds—an assumption made here and in Eichengreen In our other work on the pound–dollar rate in the period up to 1931 we have found that it makes little difference whether we use interest rates or the forward premium (see Hallwood *et al.* 1996). However, the interest differential will contain liquidity, risk, and maturity premia unless very similar instruments are used. The forward premium will only contain a risk premium, and as we note in the text this should be small in a target zone. Furthermore, forward premium data are more sensitive to exchange rate expectations than are some interest rate series when the latter are changed only at fairly long intervals.

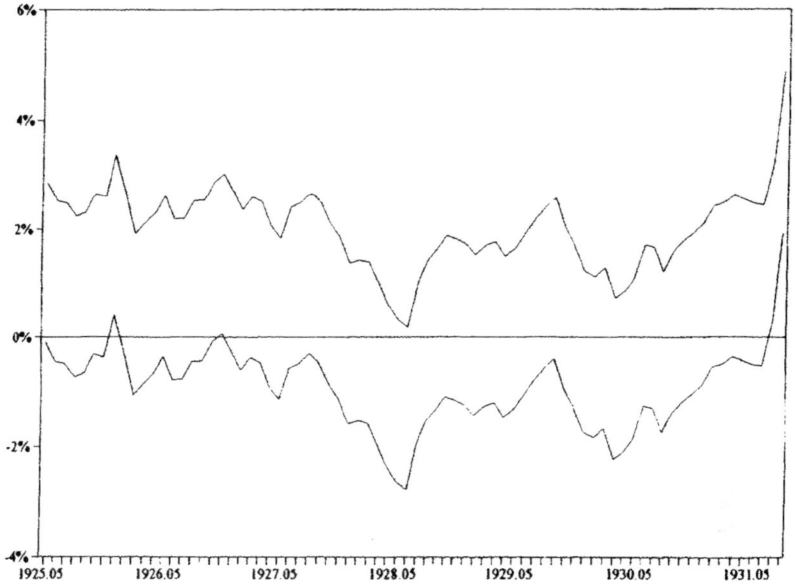

FIG. 1. Expected rate of realignment 95% confidence interval, sterling–dollar.

confidence in the value of the pound. According to our evidence in Fig. 1, they did so until the summer of 1931.

Just when did strong speculation against the pound first start? Cairncross and Eichengreen (1983) dissect the speculative runs of 1927, 1929, and 1931, commenting that they were of increasing severity, and we find some evidence for this in Fig. 1. In both 1927 and 1929 realignment expectations turned to favor devaluation of the pound, but not particularly significantly.[10] In fact, the pound was generally weak against the dollar throughout the period 1925–1931, lying nearer to the gold export point than to the gold import point (for statistical evidence on this see Officer, 1993), and the mean realignment expectation over the period as an entirety was positive (i.e., more pounds per dollar).

But it is the final run on the pound, the one that led to Britain leaving the gold standard, that is of greater interest. It can be seen from Fig. 1 that it was *not* a long drawn out affair. The market's confidence in the pound was sustained even up to the summer of 1931. Contemporary evidence (Einzig, 1937, the *Federal Reserve Bulletin*, and *The Economist*) points to a short sharp speculative attack which cost the Bank of England about $1 billion (at £1 = $4.86) over the period July–September 1931. Cairncross and Eichengreen (1983) support this view, although they do point out that on some bourses, as early as January, the forward pound had, for a while, moved outside of the gold export point. But they also point out

[10] The marginal significance levels of devaluation expectations in the peak months of August 1928 and September 1929 were 11.5% and 14.9%.

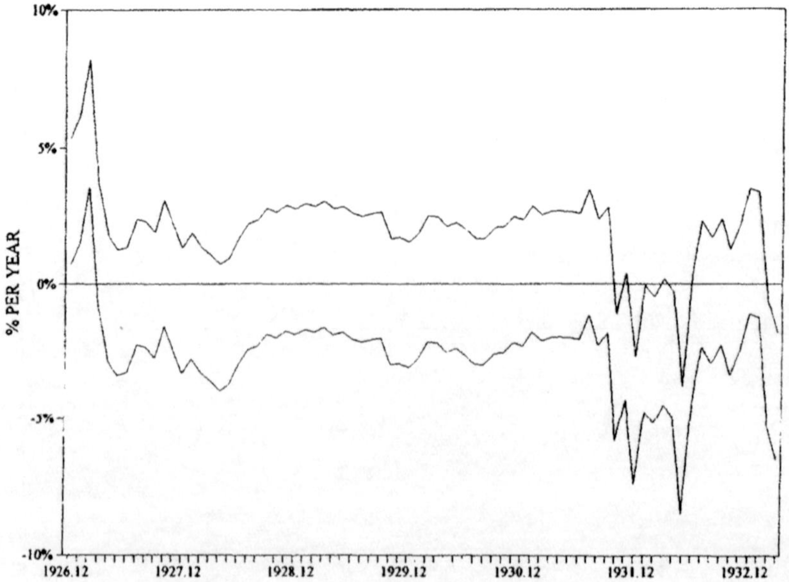

FIG. 2. Expected rate of realignment 95% confidence interval, franc–dollar.

that well into the summer of 1931 the financial press remained sanguine about the value of the pound. Cairncross and Eichengreen (1983) produce econometric evidence that strong speculation against the pound began only in midsummer 1931—being provoked by the collapse of Austria's largest bank, Creditanstalt, and bank failures in Germany. These bank failures both reduced the Bank of England's accessible foreign assets held in Austria and Germany, and alerted the markets to the possibility of inconvertibility crises in other countries, including the United Kingdom.

The Cairncross and Eichengreen (1983) econometric evidence is as follows: they estimate a monetary model of the balance of payments for the period 1926 to the beginning of 1931 for the determinants of the Bank of England's gold and foreign exchange reserves. They then simulate it out-of-sample for the rest of 1931. Their main finding is that although the model predicts the behavior of reserves well during the in-sample period, in the third quarter of 1931 it over-predicts them (a case of missing reserves). Thus, in this quarter, on the basis of the actual monetary determinants of the UK's balance of payments, the Bank of England's gold and foreign exchange reserves should have risen when in fact they fell. As Cairncross and Eichengreen (1983) explain: "the conventional view, that the 1931 crisis is properly understood as a consequence of a scramble for liquidity only indirectly related to the fundamental determinants of Britain's balance of payments position, remains the logical candidate" (p. 76–77). This view would appear to be consistent with our own finding that realignment expectations only turned significantly (in a statistical sense) against the pound in July and August 1931—they account for the run on the gold reserves of the United Kingdom as foreign investors withdrew funds from London.

Nevertheless we may still want to investigate whether there were any motivating factors for the attack. Referring back to Eq. (7), we specifically ask whether realignment expectations can be explained by the kind of fundamental variables which enter into standard models of balance of payments and exchange rate determination as proposed by Cairncross and Eichengreen (1983): that is, we assume the z variables consist of the relative money supplies, inflation, output, the current account and the real exchange rate.[11] The evidence in this section suggests that macroeconomic events ultimately did play a significant role in pushing the United Kingdom off the gold standard. But it remains true that for the 6 years until mid-1931 macroeconomic variables behaved well enough for financial markets to believe that the United Kingdom would remain on the gold standard.

In econometrically implementing Equation (7) for the United Kingdom/United States relationship we use the projection equation[12]

$$E_t[dc_t]/dt = \beta_0 + \beta_1(\pi - \pi^*)_{t-1} + \beta_2(m - m^*)_{t-1} + \beta_3(ca - ca^*)_{t-1} + \beta_4(y - y^*)_{t-1} + \beta_5(d\text{real})_{t-1} + \epsilon_t, \tag{8}$$

where π denotes the inflation rate, m the money supply, y income (proxied by industrial production), ca the current account ratio (exports/imports), and *d*real the change in the real exchange rate. All variables are in logarithms, and an asterisk denotes a foreign variable.[13] Seasonal dummies are also included in the estimated version but not reported.

The regression results for Eq. (8), shown in Table 2, have good explanatory power with a highly significant chi-squared test statistic for the explanatory variables taken together, and a reasonable R^2. Encouragingly, the significant explanatory variables bear signs that would seem to accord with economic intuition. For example, the money supply term is strongly significant and has a positive sign, suggesting that excessive domestic monetary expansion creates expectations of a devaluation (the inflation differential is perhaps insignificant because it captures the same information as the money supply magnitudes). The strong negative effect of relative industrial production indicates that an increase in output in the United Kingdom relative to that in the United States reduces the expected rate of devaluation, possibly because it increases the demand for money relative to supply. Both of the other variables (ca and *d*real) are insignificant.

We can now answer two key questions. First, how well does the model fit

[11] The latter two variables enter such models via the wealth and risk premium channels, respectively (see MacDonald, 1988, for a fuller discussion).

[12] A similar approach to determining the fundamental determinants of expected realignments for ERM currencies has been advocated by Chen and Giovannini (1994).

[13] Tests of the order of integration of dependent and independent variables are not reported but are available from the authors. They indicate that all variables are indeed stationary.

TABLE 2
Fundamental Determinants of Realignment Expectations

	Pound/Dollar
	1925(7)–1931(8)
$(\pi - \pi^*)_{t-1}$	0.1312
	(0.19)
$(m - m^*)_{t-1}$	0.1540
	(3.55)
$(y - y^*)_{t-1}$	−0.0127
	(2.79)
$(\text{ca} - \text{ca}^*)_{t-1}$	0.0102
	(1.82)
$d\text{real}_{t-1}$	−0.1373
	(0.24)
Observations	74
R^2	0.407
Standard error of equation	0.0065
χ^2 test	17.165 [0.00]

Notes. Figures in parentheses under the coefficient estimates are t-statistics computed with Generalized Method of Moments standard errors. π denotes inflation, m denotes money supply (M1), ca denotes the current account ratio (exports/imports), y denotes income, and *d*real denotes the change in the real exchange rate. All independent variables are lagged by one period and a * denotes a foreign (US) variable. The χ^2 test is a test that the fundamental determinants are jointly insignificant. The figure in brackets after the test statistics is the marginal significance level.

experience in the crucial final few months? This is easiest shown in Fig. 3, where we report the actual rate of realignment expectations together with the fitted value from the equation reported in Table 2. From this figure it is clear that the upturn in devaluation expectations in the summer of 1931 is at least partially captured by the model based on fundamental factors. Second, which variables are driving this increased expectation of devaluation? Sequentially dropping variables from the model leads to the conclusion that differences in relative money supplies is the key cause. Plots of the money supply series (not reported) for the United Kingdom and United States show clearly that the authorities in the United Kingdom were sterilizing the effects of the gold outflow, and that the authorities in the United States, as has already been well documented elsewhere, were reducing the money supply against all the rules of the game. Thus it does seem that the refusal of the United Kingdom to allow the gold outflows to reduce the money supply, coupled with the contrarian strategy in the United States of tightening the monetary stance

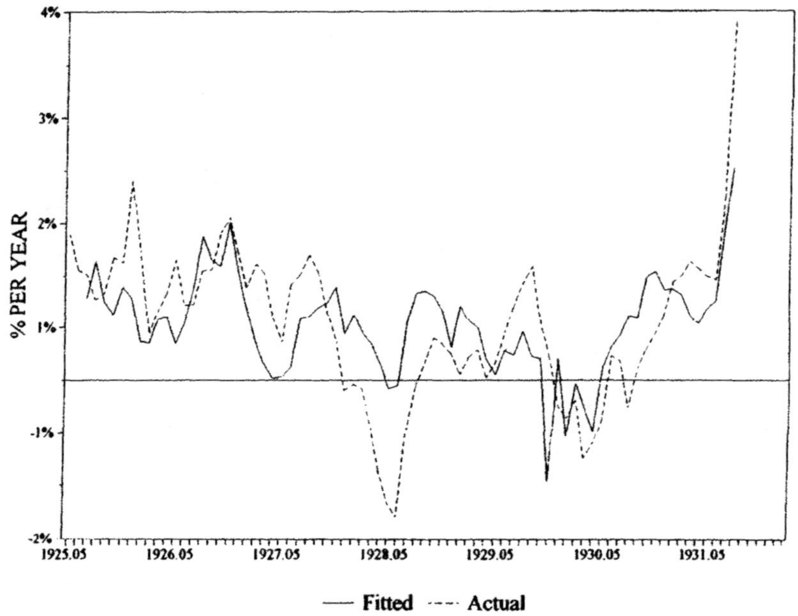

FIG. 3. Fitted devaluation expectations, sterling–dollar.

at a time of gold inflows, contributed to initiating the speculative attack which ended the United Kingdom's gold link.

The Experience of the United States

Like the United Kingdom, the United States had a crucial weakness as an international financial center during the period of the inter-war gold exchange standard: its short-term liabilities to foreigners were much greater than its available gold reserve. Only free gold reserves could be counted as "available," as the Federal Reserve note issue required a minimum 40% gold backing, with the other 60% coming from eligible securities held by the Fed or from gold. As the Fed was short of eligible securities, free gold was even less than it otherwise might have been, as gold was needed to make up the difference. By January 1930 free gold was down to $600m (Friedman and Schwartz, 1963, p. 401, quoting an estimate made by Benjamin Anderson), while the New York banks' short-term liabilities to foreigners were more than four times this amount (Board of Governors, 1943, p. 574). In fact, at almost $900m, short-term liabilities to France alone exceeded the amount of free gold. About $2,000m was owed to European countries, and it was France, the Netherlands, Switzerland, and Belgium (four of the countries that were later to form the gold block, along with Poland and Italy) that were to exchange their deposits for monetary gold held by the United States,

TABLE 3
Three Phases of the Dollar after the UK Leaving and the US Suspension of the Gold Standard

	Mean realignment expectations (+: Dollar appreciation)	Change in US official gold stock, $M (+: inflow)	Banking crises[a]
[1] 1931(10)–1932(6)	−3.2%[b]	−91	Oct. peak month of losses is second crisis.
[2] 1932(7)–1933(1)	+0.2%[c]	+91	Begins calm, ends with third crisis.
[3] 1933(2)–1933(3)	−3.6%[d]	−135	Bank holidays.[e]

[a] As measured by deposits at suspended commercial banks.
[b] All months significant or very close to 95% significance.
[c] No months with significant realignment expectations.
[d] All months having significant realignment expectations.
[e] The bank holiday was proclaimed March 6, 1933 as a means of stemming further bank runs and failures. (Also suspended were gold convertibility of the dollar and gold exports from the US.)

Sources. Column 2: Fig. 2; Column 3: Board of Governors (1943, p. 537); Column 4: Friedman and Schwartz (1963) and Board of Governors (1943, p. 283).

$431 in 1931, $739 in 1932, and $219 in 1933 (Board of Governors, 1943, p. 540). By February 1932 free gold was down to $461 million (Brown, 1940, p. 1227), and short-term liabilities to foreigners were still about 2.5 times higher.

Counting from October 1931—the first full month after the United Kingdom abandoned the gold standard—until the suspension of the gold standard in the United States in April 1933 there are 18 complete months. We can divide this period into three successive phases (see Fig. 2); the 9 month period to June 1932 of statistically significant (or almost so) dollar devaluation expectations, the following 7 months to January 1933 of relative tranquility when no significant realignment expectations were recorded, and finally, the 2 month prelude-to-suspension of strong realignment expectations in February and March 1933. See Table 3.

The interesting aspects of these phases are:

[1] The 9 month period 1931(10)–1932(6): Over these months, the mean monthly realignment expectation was −3.2% (meaning dollar devaluation was expected—fewer francs per dollar), reaching highs of −5.1% in December 1931 and −6.1% in May 1932. These latter dollar devaluation expectations were the first to be statistically significant since the US banking crisis of 1907, and the worst since 1896, when Presidential candidate William Jennings Bryan campaigned to withdraw the United States from the gold standard and was only narrowly defeated.[14] Gold outflows accompanied these negative dollar realignment expectations. The gold outflow of October 1931 was a record in United

[14] We make the observations in this sentence on the basis of our findings published in Hallwood *et al.* (1996). Our monthly data for the pre-WWI period in fact ended in 1908, but our annual data are continuous from 1879 to 1913.

States history to that point in time. Of these 9 months, 6 saw net outflows of gold from the monetary gold stock, and they were especially great in May–June 1932 as well as in the previous October. Brown (1940, p. 1222) saw this as *two* separate episodes of speculative attack, but our calculations of realignment expectations suggests that the entire period was one of continuous dollar weakness: mean realignment expectations in all 9 months were negative, 6 of them being statistically significant at the 95% level and the other 3 almost so.

The Bank of France was the major destination of the monetary gold outflow. But, by the spring of 1932, it had almost entirely withdrawn its balances from the United States. Accordingly, the French withdrawals coincide with the strong dollar devaluation expectations, and the weathering of these coincides with the cessation of French pressure against the dollar.

[2] Next came the 7 months to January 1933. This represented a tranquil period in the foreign exchange market—no significant monthly realignment expectations were recorded, and the mean value was very close to zero. Gold on a net basis returned to the United States in every one of these months for a monthly average of $91 m.

[3] The final 2 full months before suspension of the gold standard by the United States saw the reemergence of strongly significant negative realignment expectations, with mean values of −2.9% in February, and −3.6% in March 1933. Suspension coincides with the third banking crisis.

There can be little doubt that gold outflows from the United States were provoked by the question of continued adherence to the gold standard. First, as described above, there is the correlation between our calculations of realignment expectations and gold flows. More formally, in a linear regression, we find a significant, at the 1% level, and correctly signed (i.e., positive) relationship between contemporaneous changes in the gold stock of the United States and realignment expectations, although the R^2 is only 0.16. The low R^2 is only to be expected as official gold holdings would be affected by developments in the "above the line" balance of payments as well as changes in the preferences of foreign central banks for holding gold rather than dollars. Second, at least three experts on the financial history of this period suggest it. Thus, Friedman and Schwartz (1963) comment that: "France was strongly committed to staying on gold, and the French financial community, the Bank of France included, expressed the greatest concern about the United States' ability and intention to stay on the gold standard" (p. 397). And Brown (1940) wrote that: "The uninterrupted large scale purchases of government securities [during spring 1932 after the passage of the Glass–Steagall Act] by Federal Reserve Banks [in an effort to stimulate the economy] seemed in the eyes of foreigners to be evidence of approaching inflation [*sic*] in the US. The gold outflow to the continental creditor countries was consequently sharply accelerated as this policy was vigorously pressed forward" (p. 1233).

Concurrent with dollar weakness and fluctuating official gold stock was the succession of American banking crises. Over the period from 1926(12) to 1933(2) there is a statistically significant, at the 1% level, negative relationship between bank failures (measured either as number of banks or value of assets) and changes in official United States gold stocks.[15]

This negative relationship indicates that losses of official gold and bank failures moved together and is consistent with the argument of Brown (1940). He suggested the following line of causation (pp. 1222–1240). The Federal Reserve, attempting to raise the money supply, induced fears in Europe of American inflation at a time when American short-term liabilities to foreigners were still well in excess of the country's free gold. The inflation expectations gave rise to devaluation expectations and the external drain of gold. The external drain then stirred an internal gold drain as residents feared suspension of the gold standard. Finally, the internal gold drain was a factor in the accelerating banking crisis of Spring 1932.[16]

In contrast with the United Kingdom where the lack of a clear theory to explain sterling's departure from gold forced us to rely on a reduced form monetary approach in specifying the fundamental determinants of the expected rate of realignment, for the United States we focus on Brown's hypothesis regarding the links between realignment expectations, changes in the gold reserve of the United States, and banking crises.[17] Our first step involves estimating a vector autoregression (VAR) for the period 1926(12) to 1933(2).[18] Our choice of the more powerful VAR method for this exchange rate, over the simple projection Eq. (8) used for the United Kingdom, is facilitated by the relatively small number of fundamental variables and the longer data sample (relative to the United Kingdom/United States relationship). The precise VAR used is

$$E_t[dc_t]/dt = \sum_{i=1}^{4} \alpha_i E_{t-i}[dc_{t-i}]/dt + \sum_{j=1}^{4} \beta_j \text{gold}_{t-j} + \sum_{k=1}^{4} \gamma_k \text{bankfail}_{t-k} + \epsilon_t$$

$$\text{gold}_t = \sum_{i=1}^{4} \delta_i \text{gold}_{t-i} + \sum_{j=1}^{4} \eta_j E_{t-j}[dc_{t-j}]/dt + \sum_{k=1}^{4} \theta_k \text{bankfail}_{t-k} + \mu_t \tag{9}$$

$$\text{bankfail}_t = \sum_{i=1}^{4} \psi_i \text{bankfail}_{t-i} + \sum_{j=1}^{4} \lambda_j E_{t-j}[dc_{t-j}]/dt + \sum_{k=1}^{4} \varphi_k \text{gold}_{t-k} + \zeta_t,$$

[15] There is no significant correlation between bank failures and dollar realignment expectations. It is true that the first banking crisis, beginning in late-1930, had no discernable effect on dollar realignment expectations. There seems to have been no real rush by foreigners to get out of dollar deposits at this time. Then, again, both the second and third banking crises were concurrent with dollar weakness, the latter in fact with American suspension of the gold standard.

[16] Contrary to the view that declining gold reserves were an important factor forcing the United States off gold, Coleman (1992) argues that the United States was not forced off gold in 1933 by this factor. Rather, the new president, Roosevelt, wanted to move the United States out of depression and saw raising the price of gold as a vital step. The fact is, however, that expectations of dollar devaluation and gold outflows were correlated.

[17] Furthermore, while it seems reasonable to expect that developments in the United States would have an important influence on the decision of the United Kingdom to leave gold, the size of the economy of the United States compared to that of France (the only reasonable choice as partner country), and the relatively closed nature of the United States mean that the reduced form approach of Eq. (8) is less applicable here.

[18] The sample is terminated in 1933(2) because of the declaration of bank holidays in March 1933.

TABLE 4
Granger Causality between Devaluation Expectations, Gold Flows, and Banking Crises

Direction of causality	Test statistic	Marginal significance
Gold → Devaluation	3.9412	0.0067
Bankfail → Devaluation	7.4624	0.0001
Devaluation → Gold	0.6155	0.6560
Bankfail → Gold	1.1327	0.3501
Devaluation → Bankfail	1.2050	0.3185
Gold → Bankfail	2.6849	0.0401

Notes. The test statistics reported in column 2 are distributed as $F(4,58)$. The marginal significance of these statistics is reported in column 3.

where devaluation expectations are taken from our calculations above, gold flows are measured by the change in official United States gold stocks, and banking crises (bankfail) are proxied by the deposits of suspended commercial banks.[19] The lag length of 4 was determined by LM-tests from a more general model, although alternative lag lengths produce very similar results. One particularly useful feature of a system such as (9) is that it facilitates Granger causality tests. For example, gold flows would be deemed Granger causal to devaluation expectations (denoted gold → devaluation) if the restrictions $\beta_j = 0$ ($j = 1$ to 4) could be rejected using a standard F-test. The results of the six combinations of Granger causality tests are given in Table 4.

The results of estimating (8) suggest three significant causal relationships. The most significant is between bank failures and devaluation. However, gold flows are also a significant determinant of devaluation expectations and of bank failures. This causality pattern does not fit particularly well the story put forward by Brown, but it is important to recognize that Granger causality tests are not designed to highlight contemporaneous causality. If foreign investors moved sufficiently quickly to ship gold out of the United States because of their devaluation fears, lagged expected realignment expectations might not explain gold flows in a monthly database.

To investigate this point further we calculate the impulse responses of the VAR expressed in (8). These are graphed in Fig. 4, together with ± 2 standard error bars (computed using bootstrap methods). Ignoring the autoregressive tendencies given by the graphs on the leading diagonal, we interpret the results as follows. A shock to realignment expectations causes a purely contemporaneous gold flow in the expected direction but has no impact on bank failures (row one). Similarly, gold flows have a contemporaneous impact on bank failures, together with a lagged effect on realignment expectations (row two). Finally, in row three, bank failures have a lagged effect on realignment expectations but no independent impact on gold flows. These results are fully compatible with Brown's hypoth-

[19] Unreported unit root tests indicate that each of these variables is stationary.

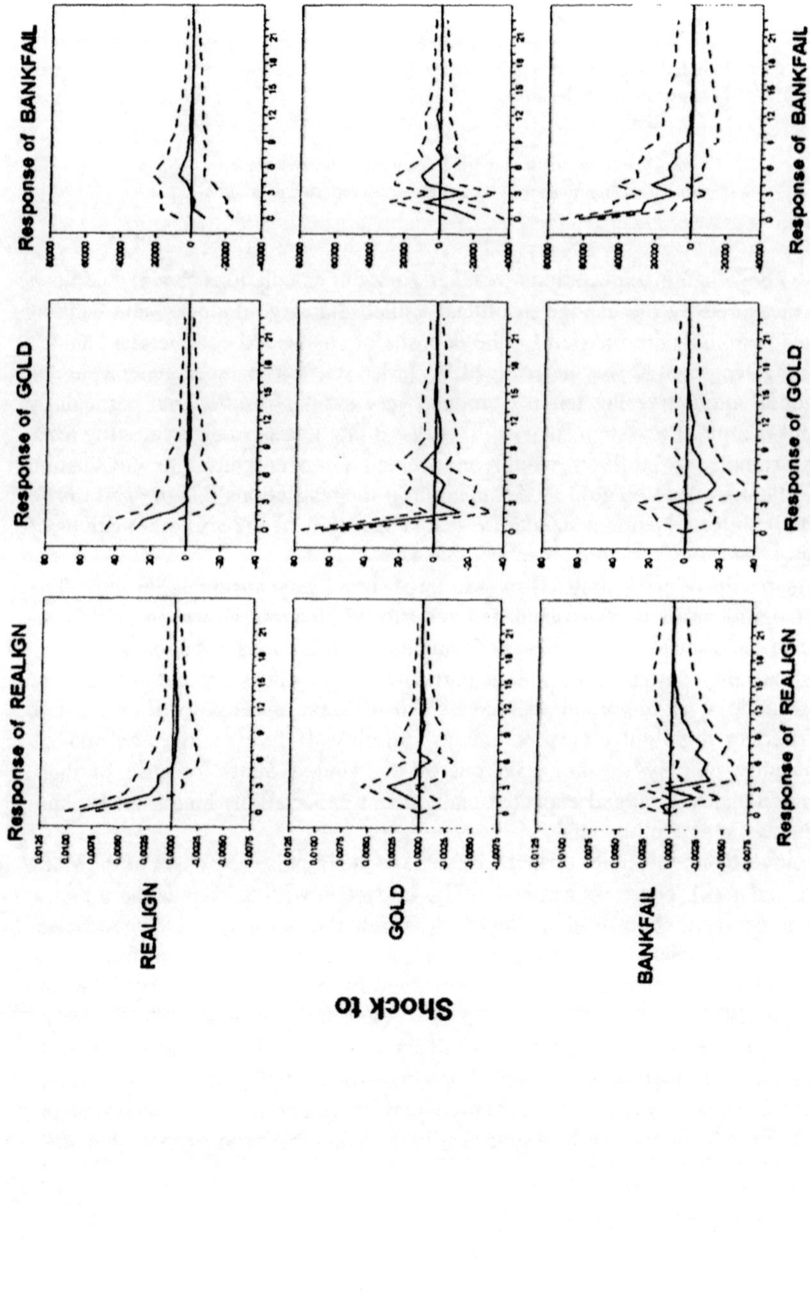

FIG. 4. Impulse responses.

esis.[20] An increase in devaluation expectations causes gold to flow out of the US which in turn causes bank failures to rise. Both gold flows and bank failures serve to strengthen devaluation expectations with a lag.[21]

Our findings throw light on what has been a disputed international aspect of the Great Depression: was the United States, in particular the Federal Reserve, hampered by its international commitments? Put differently, did the commitment of the United States to the gold standard constrain expansionary monetary policy during the Depression up until March 1933, when the United States suspended the gold standard? Kindleberger (1986) takes the view that the key constraints were international ones, but he does not analyze statistically the matter of international monetary constraints on Federal Reserve policy. Eichengreen (1990) has demonstrated international interactions between *global* money supply, key currency backing of non-key currencies, and the maldistribution of gold toward the United States and France. But this is not the same thing as demonstrating that the leading key currency country itself, the United States, was constrained by international monetary events. Eichengreen (1992a), *inter alia,* does show a keen awareness of the notion that United States monetary policy was most probably constrained by the fear of "endangering the gold parity" (p. 295). But it has never been demonstrated statistically that this was the case. In contrast, Friedman and Schwartz (1963) take the contrary position, arguing that the Federal Reserve could have undertaken substantial open market purchases if it had really wanted to.[22] Epstein and Ferguson (1984) have challenged the latter's position using data on the Fed's open market operations.[23]

Our evidence on United States monetary policy and international interactions supports the argument that the Federal Reserve's monetary policy was constrained by international considerations. The evidence is as follows: first, the fact that bank failures cause devaluation expectations with a lag (on both the Granger causality and VAR tests) suggests a domestic cause of the weakening of adherence to the gold standard. In other words, even more stringent monetary

[20] We appreciate that a common criticism of a standard VAR system is its nonstructural nature. However, since Brown's hypothesis suggests no particular structure other than a certain ordering of the variables we were unable to impose further restrictions. It is well known that the ordering of variables in a VAR may change the properties of the impulse responses, and this is true in our case. Since we specifically chose the ordering to be in line with Brown's hypothesis the strongest statement we can make is that the impulse responses provide evidence consistent with his story.

[21] These results are robust to changes in the sample period. In particular, our conclusions are unchanged if we terminate the sample in November 1932, excluding the final banking crisis.

[22] Friedman and Schwartz (1963) wrote "that a shortage of free gold did not in fact seriously limit the alternatives open to the [Federal Reserve] System. The amount was at all times ample to support large open market purchases. . . . The problem of free gold was largely an *ex post* justification for policies followed, not an *ex ante* reason for them" (p. 406).

[23] However, one may want to treat the Epstein and Ferguson (1984) results with caution for two reasons: (a) many of the significance levels are low even for one-tailed tests; (b) such tests are not appropriate when the hypothesized sign could be reversed (e.g., their hypothesis is for a negative relationship between currency inflow and open market purchases, but if the Fed were to take inflows as a sign of confidence in the dollar the sign would be reversed).

contraction and resulting bank failures would have caused even greater fragility of the dollar on the foreign exchanges. Even more significantly for our argument, we also find a positive feedback from gold outflows to bank failures (a lagged effect on the Granger causality tests and a contemporaneous effect from the VAR). That is, an international interaction was adversely affecting the banking system. Furthermore, gold outflows were having a lagged effect on dollar devaluation expectations (this time from both of our tests), which must also have been a worry for the Fed. These findings would seem to support the position of Kindleberger and Eichengreen rather than that of Friedman and Schwartz. The Federal Reserve was indeed being hemmed in by the commitment of the United States to the gold standard. The Federal Reserve found itself in a dilemma: if it increased the money base to "save the banks," which it did try to do with open market purchases in the spring and early summer of 1932, it was not playing by the rules of the game given the preponderance of gold outflows between September 1931—when sterling left gold—and June 1932. However, if it did nothing, which turned out to be the preferred policy, this risked the bank failures that, as we have shown, also put pressure on the dollar. Under these circumstances adherence to the gold standard was becoming untenable.

Furthermore, this evidence suggests that both domestic causes (banks → devaluation expectations) and international causes (gold → banks, and gold → devaluation expectations) were operative in the Bank Panic of 1933. Also, as these causal relationships are systematic across the period from 1926(12) to 1933(2), we do not think that the election of President Roosevelt represents a discontinuity in American inter-war financial history. But we do not deny that Wigmore (1987) (and references cited therein) may well be correct in arguing that the exact timing of the suspension of the gold standard by the United States was due to him.

IV. CONCLUSIONS

The pound was subjected to a short sharp speculative attack which, owing to the precariousness of its gold reserves and balance of payments, it was able to weather for less than 3 months. After the fall of the pound the attention of speculators turned to the dollar. But, largely owing to the greater strength of the United States balance of payments and gold reserve, it took 19 months for the dollar to fall. A 9 month phase to June 1932 of speculative attack was overcome and gold began to return to the United States for the 7 months to and including January 1933. Finally, however, another speculative attack combined with the third banking crisis lead to the United States suspending adherence to the gold standard.

What was driving exchange rate realignment expectations seem to be explained well by the relationships we have examined. We find support in our United Kingdom regression for the hypothesis that perverse monetary policies in the United Kingdom relative to the United States increased devaluation expectations. For the United States we focus on the huge gold flows and bank failures which characterized the run up to gold suspension. We provide results from a VAR analysis which were fully consistent with the hypothesis of Brown (1940) that devaluation expectations caused a withdrawal of gold which in turn precipitated waves of bank failures. In short, macroeconomic events, some of them directly or indirectly under the influence of the authorities, were ultimately responsible for both the United Kingdom and the United States leaving the gold standard during the inter-war period. But this is not necessarily to say that the authorities approximately played by the rules of the game for most of the inter-war experience with the gold standard. Only towards the end did they deviate sufficiently to bring the system down.

REFERENCES

Bertola, G., and Svensson, L. E. O. (1993), "Stochastic Devaluation Risk and the Empirical Fit of Target-Zone Models." *Review of Economic Studies* **60,** 689–712.

Board of Governors of the Federal Reserve Board (1943), *Banking and Monetary Statistics, 1914–1941.* Washington, D.C.

Bordo, M. D., and Schwartz, A. J. (1984), *A Retrospective on the Classical Gold Standard, 1821–1931.* NBER, Chicago.

Brown, W. A. (1940), *The International Gold Standard Reinterpreted 1914–1934.* NBER, New York.

Cairncross, A., and Eichengreen, B. (1983), *Sterling in Decline: The Devaluations of 1931, 1949 and 1967.* Blackwell, Oxford.

Calomiris, C. W. (1993), "Greenback Resumption and Silver Risk: The Economics and Politics of Monetary Regime Change in the United States, 1862–1900" In M. D. Bordo and F. Cappie (Eds.), *Monetary Regimes in Transition.* Cambridge Univ. Press, Cambridge, UK. Pp. 86–134.

Chen, Z., and Giovannini, A. (1994), "The Determinants of Realignments Expectations under the EMS: Some Empirical Regularities." London School of Economics Financial Markets Group Discussion Paper No. 184.

Coleman, W. (1992), "The New Deal's New Gold Policy: A Case Study in the Power of (Old) Ideas." Discussion Paper 1992–04, Dept. of Economics, Univ. of Tasmania.

Eichengreen, B. (1982), "Did Speculation Destabilize the French Franc in the 1920s?" *Explorations in Economic History* **19,** 71–100.

Eichengreen, B. (1986), "The Bank of France and the Sterilization of Gold, 1926–1932." *Explorations in Economics History* **23,** 56–84.

Eichengreen, B. (1990), *Elusive Stability: Essays in the History of International Finance.* Cambridge Univ. Press, Cambridge.

Eichengreen, B. (1991a), *Golden Fetters: The Gold Standard and the Great Depression, 1919–1939.* Oxford Univ. Press, Oxford/New York.

Eichengreen, B. (1992b), "Comment." *Explorations in Economic History* **29,** 93–98.

Einzig, P. (1937), *The Theory of Forward Exchange.* Macmillan & Co., London.

Epstein, G., and Ferguson, T. (1984), "Monetary Policy, Loan Liquidation and Industrial Conflict: The Federal Reserve and the Open Market Operations of 1932." *Journal of Economic History* **44,** 957–983.

Flood, R. P., Rose, A. K., and Mathieson, D. J. (1991), "An Empirical Exploration of Exchange Rate Target-Zones." *Carnegie–Rochester Series on Public Policy* **35,** 7–66.

Friedman, M., and Schwartz, A. J. (1963). *A Monetary History of the United States, 1867–1960.* Princeton Univ. Press, Princeton, NJ.

Giovannini, A. (1993), "Bretton Woods and Its Precursors: Rules versus Discretion in the History of the International Monetary System." In M. Bordo and B. Eichengreen (Eds.), *A Retrospective on the Bretton Woods System.* Chicago Univ. Press, Chicago. Pp. 109–53.

Hallwood, C. P., MacDonald, R., and Marsh, I. W. (1996), "Credibility and Fundamentals: Were The Classical and Inter-war Gold Standards Well-Behaved Target Zones?" In T. Bayoumi, B. Eichengreen, and M. Taylor (Eds.), *Modern Perspectives on the Gold Standard.* Cambridge Univ. Press, Cambridge.

Kindleberger, C. P. (1986), *The World in Depression 1929–1939.* Univ. of California Press, Berkeley.

Krugman, P. R. (1988), "Target Zones and Exchange Rate Dynamics." NBER Working Paper 2481, Cambridge, MA.

Krugman, P. R. (1991), "Target Zones and Exchange Rate Dynamics." *Quarterly Journal of Economics* **106,** 669–682.

MacDonald, R. (1988), *Floating Exchange Rates: Theories and Evidence.* Unwin Hyman, London.

MacMillan Committee on Finance and Industry (1931), Cmd 3897, HMSO.

Miller, M. and Weller, P. (1991), "Currency Bands, Target Zones and Price Flexibility." *International Monetary Fund Staff Papers* **38,** 184–215.

Officer, L. H. (1993), "Gold Point Arbitrage and Uncovered Interest Arbitrage Under the 1925–31 Dollar–Sterling Gold Standard." *Explorations in Economic History* **30,** 98–127.

Svensson, L. E. O. (1991), "The Simplest Test of Target Zone Credibility." *International Monetary Fund Staff Papers* **38,** 655–665.

Svensson, L. E. O. (1993), "Assessing Target Zone Credibility: Mean Reversion and Devaluation Expectations in the ERM: 1979–1992." *European Economic Review* **37,** 763–802.

Sicsic, P. (1992), "Was the Franc Poincaré Deliberately Undervalued." *Explorations in Economic History* **29,** 69–92.

Temin, P. (1989), *The Lessons from the Great Depression.* MIT Press, Cambridge, MA.

Wigmore, B. A. (1987), "Was the Bank Holiday of 1933 Caused by the Run on the Dollar?" *Journal of Economic History* **47,** 139–155.

[21]

ELSEVIER Journal of Monetary Economics 46 (2000) 605–620

Journal of MONETARY ECONOMICS

www.elsevier.nl/locate/econbase

Realignment expectations and the US dollar, 1890–1897: Was there a 'Peso problem'?☆

C. Paul Hallwood[a,*], Ronald MacDonald[b], Ian W. Marsh[c,d]

[a]*Department of Economics, University of Connecticut, Storrs, CT 06289, USA*
[b]*Department of Economics, University of Strathclyde, Glasgow G41 2BH, Scotland, UK*
[c]*Department of Banking and Finance, City University Business School, London EC2Y, UK*
[d]*CEPR, Goswell Road, London EC1V 7RR, UK*

Received 1 September 1994; received in revised form 17 January 2000; accepted 4 February 2000

Abstract

We investigate dollar–sterling exchange rate expectations during the period 1890–1908. We show that the dollar faced a 'Peso problem' in that for much of the period financial markets expected it to depreciate against sterling, but this never in fact happened – i.e. expectations were persistently biased. Drawing on the economic history of the period we identify 11 'events' which probably gave rise to realignment expectations. Once the dollar's adherence to the gold standard was settled as a political matter in the 1896 Presidential Election expectations of dollar realignment abruptly subsided and United States interest rates fell relative to British rates. © 2000 Elsevier Science B.V. All rights reserved.

JEL classification: C53; E58; F31; F33

Keywords: Gold standard; Fixed exchange rates; Peso problem; Credibility; Interest parity

☆MacDonald is grateful to the ESRC's Global Economic Institutions Programme for financial support (Grant No. L120251023). The authors would like to thank Lawrence Officer for supplying data, and Michael Bordo, Keith Cuthbertson, David Miles, an anonymous referee, and the Editor, Robert King, for useful comments.

* Corresponding author. Tel.: 860-434-1064.
E-mail address: hallwood@uconnvm.uconn.edu (C. Paul Hallwood).

0304-3932/00/$ - see front matter © 2000 Elsevier Science B.V. All rights reserved.
PII: S0304-3932(00)00040-4

1. Introduction

A number of papers have demonstrated that an important feature of the Classical gold standard period (circa 1875–1914) was the credibility it seemed to confer on the currencies of participating countries, especially the UK, France and Germany (Bordo and MacDonald, 1997; Hallwood et al., 1997; Officer, 1996; Giovannini, 1993). The United States dollar, however, was persistently weak against sterling during much of the 1890s and credibility appears to have been violated. It was not until after 1896 that the dollar's gold peg was fully trusted in the financial markets. In this paper we use data spanning 1890–1908 to illuminate the causes of dollar weakness and its subsequent strengthening. Using newly available theoretical advances in the modeling of pegged exchange rates, we unravel the different possible explanations, namely: economic fundamentals, political effects, expectational failures, time-varying risk premia.

Friedman and Schwartz (1963) state that the reason for persistent dollar weakness during 1879–1896 was not founded on economic fundamentals but on political factors. At this time, strong political forces were pushing for change from the gold standard to a bimetallic gold–silver standard. Such a change was expected to raise the US rate of inflation (Calomiris, 1992; Friedman, 1990a, b; Mitchell, 1913). Schwartz (1987) estimates that on average until 1897, because of higher expected inflation in the United States than in the UK, US nominal interest rates were about 2% higher than they would have been had America's adherence to the gold standard not been in question. As soon as it was settled in the Presidential Election of November 1896 that the US would continue to adhere to the gold standard, American nominal interest rates abruptly fell to a 1% markup over equivalent UK rates – a differential that reflected the actual higher American inflation rate. The juxtaposition during the 1890–1896 period of frequent expected dollar devaluation and no actual devaluation suggests a 'Peso' problem (Krasker, 1980); even though investors may have formed their expectations rationally, they still made persistently biased forecasting errors.

In this paper we demonstrate for the dollar–sterling exchange rate that the Peso effect is an important explanation for the biased forecast errors that did in fact persistently occur. However, we also find that a time-varying risk premium has a role to play. Our approach allows us to quantify the relative importance of these factors. Other contributions of this paper to United States monetary history relate to the effectiveness of the Morgan–Belmont syndicate in supporting the dollar in 1895; a finding that the size of an expected dollar devaluation had it occurred was large, supporting some contemporary opinion; and that after 1896 there was a shift in sentiment in favor of the dollar that helps to explain why the Fisher equation failed to hold – a point of contention ever since Fisher (1907).

2. Exchange rates and interest rates – a first pass through the data

Interpreting exchange rates in the Classical gold standard period in the context of the target zone literature is now widespread and follows Svensson's (1992) suggestion that all of the important regimes of the international monetary system in which exchange rate fixity was the *modus operandi* may be analyzed using a target zone framework. Since this framework is now well known we do not give a blow-by-blow account here. Rather, we note a few key relationships.

First, in a target zone in natural logs, the total expected change in the exchange rate is given as:

$$\mathrm{E}_t[\mathrm{d}s_t]/\mathrm{d}t = \mathrm{E}_t[\mathrm{d}x_t]/\mathrm{d}t + \mathrm{E}_t[\mathrm{d}c_t]/\mathrm{d}t. \tag{1}$$

If the target zone is perfectly credible, x, the deviation of the exchange rate from central parity (denoted c), should be mean-reverting and the expected rate of realignment, $\mathrm{E}_t[\mathrm{d}c_t]/\mathrm{d}t$, should be zero. Uncovered interest parity is assumed to hold and so the interest differential (with a maturity corresponding to the expectation horizon in (1)) will be equivalent to the total expected change in the exchange rate. A '100% confidence band' for the expected change in x can be determined if the edges of the band are known. In the gold standard these are the gold import and export points and below we use Officer's (1996) estimates. This confidence band is then used to calculate realignment expectations using

$$(i_t - i_t^*) - (x_t^u - x_t)/\mathrm{d}t \leq \mathrm{E}_t[\mathrm{d}c_t] \leq (i_t - i_t^*) - (x_t^l - x_t)/\mathrm{d}t \tag{2}$$

where $i_t - i_t^*$ is the domestic minus the foreign interest rate at time t and x_t^u and x_t^l are, respectively, the upper and lower edges of the target zone, measured as absolute deviations from central parity. If both sides of the inequality are above (or below) zero then we may infer that there was a non-zero expected rate of realignment.

A way of gaining further insight into the issue of credibility during the period, and one which is examined in some detail in the next section, is to focus on the uncovered interest parity condition, $\mathrm{E}_t[\mathrm{d}s_t] = i_t - i_t^*$. By assuming that expectations are formed rationally this can be rewritten as the standard unbiasedness regression equation:

$$\Delta s_{t+k} = \alpha + \beta(i_t - i_t^*) + \varepsilon_{t+k}. \tag{3}$$

For the sample period 1890–1908 our estimate of this equation is:

$$\Delta s_{t+k} = 0.0002355 - 0.04513(i_t - i_t^*) \tag{4}$$

and hence, in common with many studies for the inter-war and post-war periods, the slope coefficient is closer to minus one than plus one. Much of the rest of this paper may be interpreted as an attempt to explain this finding.

In summing up political-economic developments in the 1890s, Friedman and Schwartz (1963) write that 'agitation over silver reached its peak, and the political forces in favor of free silver came closest to victory. The effect was to create a lack of confidence both at home and abroad in the maintenance of the gold standard and to lead to something of a flight from the dollar – or rather a series of flights and returns as views altered' (p. 104). The target zone theory outlined above can add quantification to this insight. Using Officer's (1996) data, a plot of the 100% confidence band of realignment expectations, given in Fig. 1, clearly indicates that there are credibility problems for the period 1890 through to 1897, but that thereafter the violations of credibility are few and far between.

Between 1890 and 1897 the rate of inflation was lower in the United States than in the United Kingdom and yet US interest rates were higher. Friedman and Schwartz (1963, Chapter 3) explain this in terms of a perceived lack of confidence in the value of the dollar against gold and, hence, sterling. In particular, they point out that 'political agitation for an expansion of the money stock ... continued from 1879 to the end of the century' (p. 91). The loci of this agitation were the labor movement and agricultural interests suffering from the depression of trade brought about by a falling US price level. Both groups supported the re-monetization of silver (which had been demonetized after the Civil War in 1873) and were supported in this by the silver producing states. As bimetallism was also strongly supported by a faction in the Democratic Party it was a live political issue throughout the period to 1896 when, in the Presidential Election, the Democratic Candidate and strong silver supporter, William Jennings Bryan, was defeated by the pro-gold standard Republican candidate McKinley. Friedman (1990a) has calculated that if the United States had re-monetized silver the US price level would indeed have been higher. A higher US price level suggests that, ultimately, the dollar would have had to be devalued. Thus, given the political agitation, the devaluation expectations revealed in Fig. 1 are understandable.

Table 1 lists eleven major monetary or other events that probably impacted exchange rate expectations during the 1878–1897 period.[1] We will not enter into a full historical discussion as this is very adequately covered by Friedman and Schwartz (1963), instead a few points will suffice.

Events 1 and 2 taken together ambiguously committed the US Treasury to buy large amounts of silver and to a adhere to the gold standard, respectively. Event 3 is a straightforward financial panic which caused some flight from the dollar. Event 4, the Sherman Silver Purchase Act, introduced silver in large amounts into the US money supply, and could have been interpreted as heralding a regime change should the United States abandon the monometallic gold standard. Passed in July 1890, the Act was immediately followed by

[1] We follow Calomiris (1992) in not including Treasury deficits in Table 1 as Bohn (1991) suggests that these would not have been expected to impact the US money supply.

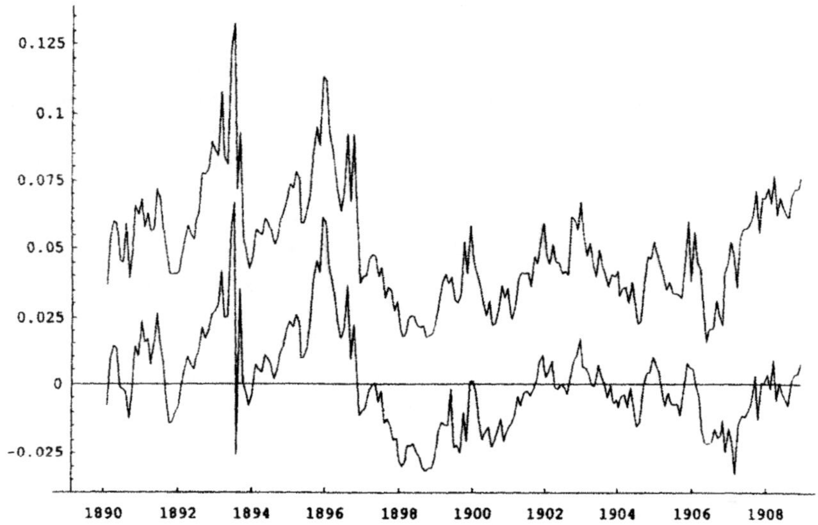

Fig. 1. '100%' confidence band of realignment expectations.

Table 1
US monetary and other 'events' impacting exchange rate expectations, 1878–1897[a]

	Year	Event
1	1878	Bland–Allison Act
2	1879	United States de facto onto gold standard
3	1884	Financial panic in United States
4	1890 July	Sherman Silver Purchase Act
5	1890 November	Financial strain in United States
6	1891 spring	Abnormally large gold outflows from New York
7	1891 fall to summer 1892	Record United States crop exports
8	1893 November	End of silver purchases under the Sherman Act
9	1895 January	US Treasury's gold reserve falls to record low
10	1895 February to September	Morgan–Belmont syndicate
11	1896 November	Defeat of free silver forces in Presidential Election

[a]Friedman and Schwartz (1963) is the source of the data.

significant realignment expectations (Fig. 1). These subsided temporarily after August for the next three months. But from December 1890 (after several financial firms failed in New York – event 5) until the repeal of the silver purchase clause on 1 November, 1893 the only major fall in devaluation expectations during this period coincided with the record crop exports of fall 1891 to summer 1892 (event 7). In the spring of 1891, large gold outflows were recorded (event 6), apparently confirming the pressure on the dollar.

Upon repeal of the Sherman Act (event 8) realignment expectations again fell dramatically, but this was not long lasting as the approaching Presidential Election held the possibility of the return of a 'President William Jennings Bryan' committed to the abandonment of monometallicism. The January 1895 record low for Treasury gold reserves (event 9) falls within the long run of dollar weakness. Event 10, the Belmont–Morgan syndicate providing gold reserves to the US Treasury, temporarily brought relief, but it was not until Bryan's defeat in the election that beliefs were more-or-less stilled that the United States would abandon the gold standard.

From then on to the end of our data in 1908 there are relatively few, scattered months of significant realignment expectations, and these were more weakly held than they had been before November 1896. The fact that these realignment expectations are rather scattered is important because it means that the long runs of biased forecasting errors had come to an end. There is no consistent explanation for the bouts of perceived dollar weakness that did occur after 1897, rather there is a series of *ad hoc* explanations. The behavior of US capital exports during this period would seem to be relevant to an explanation of changes in exchange rate expectations. However examination of them does not take us very far as for the period 1897–1906. Friedman and Schwartz comment that their 'course of events is most puzzling' (1963, p. 142). The significant realignment expectations towards the end of 1901 may well have been caused by May's stock market collapse; and those of summer 1902 may have been a reflection of tight money in New York as the US business cycle was moving to its peak in September. We have no explanation for the significant realignment expectations of spring 1903, but those of summer 1907 foreshadowed the severe financial panic of October.

In the rest of this paper we analyze expectations of exchange rate realignments in more detail. Specifically, we examine whether the biasedness findings in Eq. (3) are explained by a time-varying risk premium, or whether the silver forces caused investors seriously to doubt the dollar's link with gold and hence led to consistent expectational errors and a classic manifestation of the Peso problem.

3. Econometric methods and results

3.1. Expectational model

In attempting to unravel the sources of expectational bias during the period we give the data as many 'degrees of freedom' as possible. We rely on a model which highlights expectational factors but which also has a role for time-varying risk premia which have often been suggested as an explanation of apparently biased exchange rate expectations. We therefore focus on the following equation in our econometric analysis:

$$i_t - i_t^* = [(1 - p_t^k)\mathrm{E}_t[\Delta s_{t+k}|no\ deval.] + p_t^k\mathrm{E}_t[\Delta s_{t+k}|deval.] + RP_t]/k \quad (5)$$

where the dependent variable is the interest rate differential (US minus UK) on instruments of maturity k years, p_t^k denotes the time t probability of a realignment (US dollar devaluation) during the subsequent k years, s_t denotes the spot exchange rate, and RP_t is a time-varying risk premium. Eq. (5) states that the interest differential equals the risk premium plus the probability weighted change in the spot exchange rate under the alternative scenarios of a devaluation and no devaluation.

The various components in Eq. (5) may be 'identified' in the following ways. Consider first the magnitude of the expected change in the spot exchange rate. If there is no devaluation, the expected change in the spot rate is equivalent to the expected change in the deviation from the 'center' of the band. This center of the band could be the mint parity level but the mean spot rate over this period was above the \$4.866 parity level, and the gold import and export points were asymmetric about parity. Further, unlike today, the spot exchange rate shows substantial seasonality during this period, possibly due to the greater proportion of seasonal goods (e.g. agriculture) in US exports and the greater influence of international trade on foreign exchange trading. Following Bordo and MacDonald (1997) we first deseasonalize the spot exchange rate[2] and subsequently model the time-varying levels to which it regresses as the fitted values from the regression:

$$s_t = \alpha_0 + \alpha_1 + \alpha_2 s_{t-12} + \varepsilon_t \quad (6)$$

where the lagged dependent variable is introduced to capture stochastic seasonality effects, and the fitted values are denoted $\bar{s}_t$. Finally, if x_t denotes the deviation of the spot rate from fitted levels, $x_t = s_t - \bar{s}_t$, following Rose and Svensson (1995) we model Δx_t as

$$\mathrm{E}_t[\Delta s_{t+k}|no\ deval.] = \mathrm{E}_t[\Delta x_{t+k}|no\ deval.] = \beta_1 x_t. \quad (7)$$

Deriving the expected change in the spot rate at a devaluation is more problematic. Mizrach (1995) models the expected size of a devaluation of key ERM exchange rates as a linear function of the previous devaluation, but this is not an option in the Classical gold standard since the dollar never actually devalued. For simplicity, we model the size of devaluation as a constant (denoted β_2).

[2] The interest differential is also deseasonalized to avoid imposing spurious dynamics.

The probability of a devaluation, p_t^k, is modeled as a function of several (seasonally adjusted) economic fundamentals, two dummies designed to take account of expectations of a return to silver, a trend, and a constant. The fundamentals are the relative (US minus UK) month-on-month money supply and income growth rates, the deviation of the real exchange rate from trend, the change in US cotton exports (also detrended), the change in the Standard and Poor's stock market index and the change in the US Treasury's gold and silver holdings. These variables were chosen to highlight the importance of the events listed in Table 1. Thus, financial strains and panics are proxied by the S&P index, gold flows are captured by changes in Treasury reserves, and the performance of US exports are proxied by cotton exports. All fundamentals are included in the model with a one period lag to avoid endogeneity problems. Sources are detailed in Appendix A.

The two dummies proxy the effect of political pressures to move to silver. The first takes a value of one if the Sherman Silver Purchase Act is on the US statutes (1890/7–1893/10) and a zero otherwise. The second dummy takes a value of one if the bimetallism debate is still active in the United States, defined as the period from the start of our sample until the defeat of Bryan in 1896 (1890/1–1896/10). Writing the variables in vector form (z) and denoting the coefficient vector by γ, we make a probit transformation so that $p_t^k = \Phi(\gamma z_t)$ which is bounded [0, 1].

The risk premium is modeled with an asymmetric GARCH(1,1)-in mean specification such that it varies with both the magnitude and sign of past surprises (Glosten et al., 1993). Because of the potential number of constant terms in the model, the risk premium has the following slightly unusual specification:

$$\begin{aligned} RP_t &= \delta h_t, \\ h_t &= v_1 + v_2 \varepsilon_{t-1}^2 + v_3(\varepsilon_{t-1}^2 | \varepsilon_{t-1} < 0) + v_4 h_{t-1}. \end{aligned} \tag{8}$$

There is no constant risk premium. Instead, the constant element of the risk premium is subsumed into the constant Peso effect.

Substitution leads to the final econometric specification:

$$\begin{aligned} i_t - i_t^* &= [\beta_1 x_1(1 - \Phi(\gamma z_t)) + \beta_2 \Phi(\gamma z_t) + \delta h_t + \varepsilon_t]/k, \\ h_t &= v_1 + v_2 \varepsilon_{t-1}^2 + v_3(\varepsilon_{t-1}^2 | \varepsilon_{t-1} < 0) + v_4 h_{t-1}. \end{aligned} \tag{9}$$

This system is estimated using maximum likelihood methods (BFGS algorithm), with standard errors robust to heteroscedasticity and the serial correlation induced by the overlapping dependent variables.

3.2. Econometric results

The results from estimating Eq. (9) are presented in Table 2. We believe the estimated equation has a number of attractive properties which reveal the

Table 2
FIML estimation results, 1890/02–1908/12[a]

Variable	Coefficient	Std error	T-statistic
1. Mean reversion, β_1	− 0.260	0.122	− 2.132
Size of devaluation			
2. Devaluation size, β_2	0.581	0.020	29.741
Probability of devaluation, γ			
3. Constant	− 4.380	0.439	− 9.972
4. Money	1.609	1.660	0.969
5. Income	0.060	0.459	0.131
6. Real exchange rate	3.356	0.529	6.345
7. Cotton exports	− 0.038	0.024	− 1.586
8. S&P index	− 1.557	0.341	− 4.571
9. Gold reserves	0.009	0.057	0.166
10. Sherman dummy	0.163	0.039	4.234
11. Silver debate dummy	0.686	0.147	4.652
12. Trend	0.004	0.001	4.389
Risk premium			
13. Variance in mean, δ	1.218	0.312	3.907
14. Variance constant, v_1	0.048	0.016	2.915
15. ARCH, v_2	1.196	0.507	2.362
16. Asymmetric ARCH, v_3	− 0.907	0.406	− 2.232
17. GARCH, v_4	0.331	0.151	2.188

[a]The general form of the model is

$$i_t - i_t^* = [(prob.\ of\ deval.)(size\ of\ deval.) + (1 - prob.\ of\ deval.)(mean\ reversion) + risk\ premium]/k,$$

$$mean\ reversion = \beta_1 x_t,$$

$$size\ of\ deval. = \beta_2,$$

$$prob\ of\ deval. = \Phi(\gamma z_t),$$

$$\text{risk premium} = \delta h_t$$

$$h_t = v_1 + v_2 \varepsilon_{t-1}^2 + v_3(\varepsilon_{t-1}^2 | \varepsilon_{t-1} < 0) + v_4 h_{t-1}.$$

sources of the biasedness reported in (4). First, note that the estimated coefficient of mean reversion is negative, as predicted. This suggests that the dollar was expected to close around one-fourth of the distance from its time-varying mean level each quarter.

The size of the expected devaluation is 58% and is strongly significant. Although this seems a relatively large value, the crucial thing in terms of our modeling is the weight placed on this number by the probability of devaluation. We provide a more detailed discussion of the magnitude of the devaluation in the next section.

The probability of a devaluation is determined by coefficients 3 through 12. Six of these ten coefficients are statistically significant. From the perspective of a monetary framework, the effect of relative money supplies is correctly signed but insignificant, and while both relative income changes and gold reserves are incorrectly signed they are also insignificant. The deviation of the real exchange rate from trend and changes in the S&P index are significant at reasonable levels, and cotton exports are marginally so.

Importantly, the two dummy variables are significantly positive indicating that the political pressures to monetize silver raised the probability that the dollar would devalue. In terms of both magnitude and significance level, the continued debate over silver exerted a greater influence over expectations than the presence of pro-silver clauses in the statute book. This is consistent with Calomiris (1992) who has also argued that it was unlikely that the extant silver legislation would have been responsible for pushing the United States off the gold standard. The probability of a devaluation, which captures the joint effect of the above-noted elements, is given in Fig. 2. Typically less than half of one percent in the tranquil post silver period, it was over 1.5% during the two peak crisis points. Crucially, removing the effect of the silver debate results in very small devaluation probabilities. In fact, devaluation expectations based on fundamentals alone are higher in the relatively tranquil twentieth century portion of the period under question than in the volatile 1890s. The fact that the silver debate was active had a statistically and economically significant negative effect on the credibility of the dollar's link with gold.

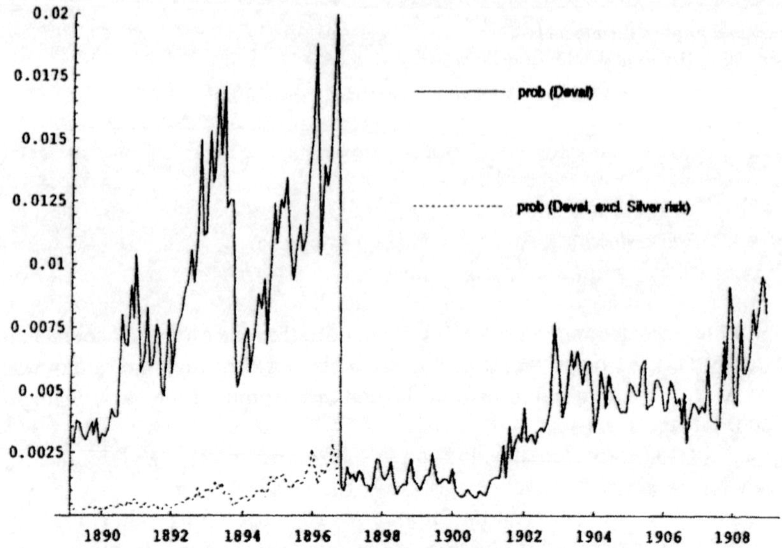

Fig. 2. Probability of devaluation.

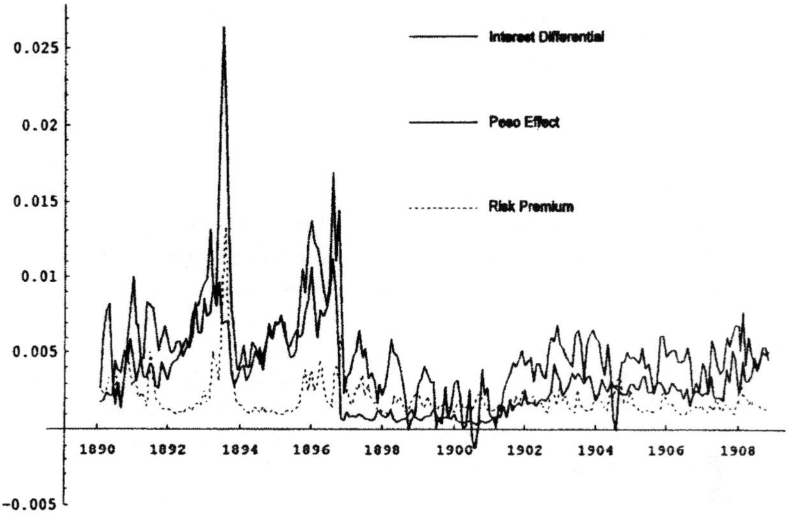

Fig. 3. Components of interest differential.

The variance-in-mean term, δ, is positive and statistically significant implying that, in contrast to the assumption of the basic target zone model, the interest differential does appear to contain a time-varying risk premium. Furthermore, this is well captured by the asymmetric GARCH(1,1) model employed. The asymmetry in particular is important – a positive error leads to very persistent risk effects, but a negative error much less so.

The relative importance of the risk premium and the Peso effect in the interest differential may be gauged from Fig. 3, where all three series are plotted. Note that the Peso effect (the expected probability of devaluation times the expected size of the devaluation) explains the majority of the interest differential in the early years and then dies effectively to zero in 1900, before rising slightly in the run-up to the end of our data sample (which coincides with the financial panic of 1907). The risk premium is positive and significant in the estimated equation. Fig. 3 reveals that it is quite small on average (0.25%) but with occasional large peaks in volatile periods. Nevertheless we would argue that the Peso problem explains noticeably more of the interest differential during the silver-crisis period, and that the likelihood of devaluation was dominated by political and not economic performance.

4. More commentary

Our findings do not support Grilli's (1990) claim that the probability of dollar devaluation built up only gradually following the passage of the Sherman Silver

Purchase Act in July 1890. We show in Fig. 2 an immediate jump in the probability of devaluation. This is consistent with warnings appearing in the financial press at the time: The Economist 12/20/1890, 5/16/1891, 11/21/1891 and 12/26/1891; and Mitchell (1913, p. 52). Nor do we support Grilli's calculation that the probability of speculative attack declined step-by-step in the two years leading up to the 1896 election. Rather, our findings support the opposite proposition that failure to deal with the overhang of paper money (note in Fig. 2 that the probability of devaluation excluding the effects of the silver dummies tends to *increase* after 1893), and the gathering momentum of the free silver movement was a threat to the United States' adherence to the gold standard.[3]

Our results allow us to comment on the Morgan–Belmont contract of February 1895 with the US government to support the dollar. We show the devaluation probability fell as soon as the syndicate began supporting the dollar, but in the second quarter of the year the probability increased somewhat. This ordering squares with the discussion of Simon (1968). He claims that the Morgan–Belmont syndicate met with initial success in reducing external pressure on the dollar (i.e. February–April 1895). However, increased capital exports (which Simon associates with renewed silver agitation in the United States, net sales by European investors of American railroad securities, and advice in the British financial press to avoid American shares) then undermined the dollar from May through August 1895.

We also find that once the Morgan–Belmont syndicate ceased its supportive operations, in September 1895, dollar devaluation prospects dramatically increased and, though fluctuating, were to remain high until November 1896. We ascribe this course of events over the 14 months to this date to both a slight worsening of economic fundamentals affecting exchange rates, and, more especially, to the agitation for free silver.

On the basis of our evidence, the prediction by the Morgan–Belmont syndicate – as recounted by Simon (1968, p. 406) – that their support would be needed only until September 1895 (when US agricultural exports, especially cotton and wheat should pick up) is not supported, possibly because the harvests of both major export crops were disappointing. We find a sharp increase in the probability of dollar devaluation in the later months of 1895. From this it is impossible to say whether the Morgan–Belmont syndicate 'saved the gold standard' both because we do not know how realignment expectations would

[3] There were frequent detailed reports in The Economist on the overhang (from November 1895 through June 1896) and on the deleterious effects of potential new silver legislation (May through October 1896). Other foreign publications such the Spectator also addressed the problems of the American currency in 1895 and 1896. These and received academic wisdom leave no doubt that the weakness of the US dollar troubled investors so much so that it influenced both the propensity to invest in US securities and international gold flows between the United States and the United Kingdom.

have developed in its absence in early 1895 and also what would have happened had the harvests turned out to be good. However, a dummy variable for the operational existence of the syndicate in that part of Eq. (9) which determines devaluation probabilities, while bearing the theoretically correct negative sign, is far from significant (t-statistic equals -0.946).

An issue of interest to contemporary investors was the combination of the probability of a dollar devaluation and its likely size should it have occurred. Our estimates of these variables support the judgment of the Economist (7/11/1896, p. 891) that (a) the danger of devaluation was remote (presumably because even if Bryan had won he would still have had Congress against him), and (b) if the devaluation had come it would have been large because the price of silver had fallen so low relative to gold. On the size of the devaluation, should it occur, The Economist (7/11/1896, p. 890) wrote: 'One of the two great parties in the States has deliberately adopted a policy of repudiation. The Democratic Party stands pledged to the most predatory set of proposals for dealing with the public currency ever set forth by a body of public men. They in effect demand that the debtor shall be allowed to pay his creditor ten shillings in the pound and demand a discharge in full' – equivalent to a fifty percent devaluation.

Confidence in our findings of a potentially large devaluation is supported by other recent work using different methodologies. Garber (1986) treats a bimetallic standard as an implicit option contract to deliver silver or gold in settlement of debts. He shows that, with the sharp fall in the price of silver relative to gold, in the years 1890–1896 an option to deliver silver 'was very much in the money' (page 1027). Further, some calculations by Friedman (1992) suggest that if the United States had adopted bimetallism rather than the gold standard the US price level would have increased very sharply compared with that in the UK.

Our findings are relevant to a debate on the apparent failure of the intertemporal purchasing power parity, the so-called Fisher equation, to hold after about 1896. As an empirical fact, for many years after this date, while the rate of inflation in the United States increased relative to that in the United Kingdom, US interest rates – also relative to those in the UK – failed to do so. This apparently confounded Irving Fisher's theory that, via uncovered interest parity, changes in relative price levels and interest rates should be positively related. As prior unsatisfactory attempts to explain the failure of the Fisher equation to hold including Fisher (1907, p. 278) are summarized in Barsky and De Long (1989) we will not rehearse them here. However, it is worth mentioning that our findings do not support Barsky and De Long's own explanation: namely, that while investors could have used publicly available information to predict inflation (hence moving interest rates in the appropriate direction), they failed to do so because they did not know how to process the relevant information into an inflation prediction. Rather, our econometric results give strong support to an explanation rejected in Barsky and De Long (1989, page 819, footnote 5) that after 1896 and the decline in influence of the free silver movement there was, unsurprisingly, a strong shift in sentiment in favor of the dollar. That is, the interest differential could narrow as either the risk premium and/or the probability weighted expected change in the exchange rate declined. This change in sentiment, we show, is due to a sharp reduction in the Peso effect as the probability of expected devaluation fell.

5. Summary and conclusions

In this paper we have examined an early example of a 'Peso problem' – the US dollar 1890–1897 – defined as investors holding apparently persistently biased forecasts of exchange rate changes. For many months prior to November 1896 financial markets were forecasting a dollar devaluation against gold (and sterling) that never came. In fact the dollar was not devalued against gold until March 1933.

Our explanation of this phenomenon is that financial markets were predicting a regime change – specifically the monetization of silver alongside gold – that would have increased both the US money supply and rate of inflation relative to the gold standard's 'core' country, Britain. The specific events which gave rise to the belief in a regime change were the Bland–Allison Act of 1878, the prolonged agitation for the free coinage of silver which lasted at least from 1879 until its weakening in late 1896, the Sherman Silver Purchase Act of 1890, the draining of US gold reserves during the 1890s, and the support given to the free silver movement by influential elements in the Democratic Party. Our finding of a significant dollar Peso problem quantifies the keen insights of Friedman and Schwartz (1963) and adds to the quantitative findings of some other investigators.

Appendix A. Data

Spot exchange rates for the last Saturday of each month were taken from Table 13 of National Monetary Commission (1910). For the years 1890–1895 the rates are the posted rates of sight exchange at New York on London for bankers' bills. After 1895 we use actual rates of exchange.

The US interest rates are those available on choice 60–90 day double name commercial paper, taken from Table 29 of National Monetary Commission (1910). The rates pertain to the last Saturday of each month.

The UK interest rates are prime bank bill rates for the last working day of each month from Table III (10) of Capie and Webber, 1985.

The US price level is proxied by the index of the general price level (NBER series 04051).

The UK price level is proxied by the wholesale price index of all commodities (NBER series 04053).

The US money supply data are from NBER series 14135 of total circulation outside the US Treasury.

The UK money supply data are from NBER series 14081 of total circulation in Great Britain.

US income is proxied by the index of the physical volume of business activity (NBER series 01001).

UK income data is proxied by an interpolated monthly series of annual railway receipt data (NBER series 04053).

As a proxy for the export performance of US agricultural interests we use physical US exports of raw cotton (NBER series 07043).

As a proxy for the health of the US financial system we use Standard & Poor's index of all common stock prices (NBER series 11025).

Treasury gold and silver stocks are computed as the sum of gold and silver held in the Treasury and Federal Reserve Banks, at the end of each month (NBER series 14137 and 14133 respectively).

References

Barsky, R.B., De Long, J.B., 1989. Forecasting pre-World War I inflation: the Fisher effect and the gold standard. Quarterly Journal of Economics 106, 815–836.

Bohn, H., 1991. Budget balance through revenue or spending adjustments? Some historical evidence for the United States. Journal of Monetary Economics 27, 333–359.

Bordo, M.D., MacDonald, R., 1997. Violations of the 'rules of the game' and the credibility of the classical gold standard, 1880–1914. NBER working paper no. 6115.

Capie, F., Webber, A., 1985. A Monetary History of the United Kingdom, 1870–1982, Vol. 1. Allen and Unwin, London.

Calomiris, C.W., 1992. Greenback resumption and silver risk: the economics and politics of monetary regime change in the United States, 1862–1900. NBER working paper no. 4166 (Reprinted in Bordo, M., Capie, F. (Eds.), 1994. Monetary Regimes in Transition, Cambridge University Press, Cambridge).

Fisher, I., 1907. The Rate of Interest. MacMillan, New York.

Friedman, M., 1990a. The crime of 1873. Journal of Political Economy 98, 1159–1194.

Friedman, M., 1990b. Bimetallism revisited. Journal of Economic Perspectives 4, 85–104.

Friedman, M., 1992. A counterfactual exercise: estimating the effect of continuing bimetallism after 1873. In: Money Mischief: Episodes of Monetary History. Harcourt Brace and Co., New York.

Friedman, M., Schwartz, A.J., 1963. A Monetary History of the United States, 1867–1960. NBER and Princeton University Press, New York.

Garber, P.M., 1986. Nominal contracts in a bimetallic standard. American Economic Review 76, 1012–1030.

Giovannini, A., 1993. Bretton Woods and its precursors: rules versus discretion in the history of the international monetary system. In: Bordo, M., Eichengreen, B. (Eds.), A Retrospective on the Bretton Woods System. University of Chicago Press, Chicago.

Glosten, L., Jagannathan, R., Runkle, D., 1993. On the relation between the expected value and the volatility of the nominal excess return on stocks. Journal of Finance 48, 1779–1801.

Grilli, V., 1990. Managing exchange risk: evidence from the 1980s. Journal of International Money and Finance 9, 258–275.

Hallwood, C.P., MacDonald, R., Marsh, I.W., 1997. Credibility and fundamentals: was the gold standard a well-behaved target zone? In: Bayoumi, T., Eichengreen, B., Taylor, M. (Eds.), Modern Perspectives on the Gold Standard. Cambridge University Press, Cambridge.
Krasker, W.S., 1980. The 'peso problem' in testing the efficiency of forward exchange markets. Journal of Monetary Economics 6, 269–276.
Mitchell, W.C., 1913. Business Cycles. Burt Franklin, New York.
National Monetary Commission, 1910. Statistics for the United States, 1867–1909. Government Printing Office, Washington DC, Document No. 570. 61st Congress, Second Session.
Mizrach, B., 1995. Target zone models with stochastic realignments: an econometric evaluation. Journal of International Money and Finance 14, 641–657.
Officer, L.H., 1996. Between the Dollar-Sterling Gold Points. Cambridge University Press, Cambridge.
Rose, A.K., Svensson, L.E.O., 1995. Expected and predicted realignments: the FF/DM exchange rate during the EMS. Scandinavian Journal of Economics 97, 173–200.
Schwartz, A.J., 1987. A century of British market interest rates, 1874–1975. In: Money in Historical Perspective. University of Chicago Press, Chicago.
Simon, M., 1968. The Morgan-Belmont syndicate of 1895 and intervention in the foreign-exchange market. Business History Review 42, 385–417.
Svensson, L.E.O., 1992. An interpretation of recent research on exchange rate target zones. Journal of Economic Perspectives 6, 119–144.

Available online at www.sciencedirect.com
SCIENCE DIRECT•

Journal of Monetary Economics 52 (2005) 307–327

Journal of MONETARY ECONOMICS
www.elsevier.com/locate/econbase

Interest rate interactions in the classical gold standard, 1880–1914: was there any monetary independence?☆

Michael D. Bordo[a,b,*], Ronald MacDonald[c,d]

[a]*Department of Economics, Rutgers University, New Brunswick, NJ 08901, USA*
[b]*NBER, Cambridge, MA 02138, USA*
[c]*University of Glasgow, Glasgow Scotland G128RT, UK*
[d]*CESifo, 81679 Munich, Germany*

Received 11 June 1998; received in revised form 17 March 2003; accepted 4 May 2004

Abstract

This paper examines an hypothesis of Svensson (1994) (Journal of Monetary Economics 33, 157–199) that a credible target zone can confer on a country a degree of independence in the operation of its monetary policy, even when exchange rates are fixed. We test this hypothesis for the Classical gold standard using a newly created monthly data base for the period 1880–1913. Building on the recently noted finding that the Classical gold standard represented a credible, well-behaved, target zone system we propose a number of ways of testing the Svensson' model. Our main finding is that the Classical gold standard did indeed confer some independence in the operation of monetary policy for participating countries. This would seem

☆We are grateful to Jose Campa, Marc Flandreau, Peter Garber, Bruce Mizrach, Lawrence Officer, Pierre Sicsic, Lars Svensson and Alan Taylor, participants at the 1996 AFSE (Paris) Conference, the 1997 NBER IFM Conference and the Quantitative Economic History Seminar, Rutgers University, an anonymous referee and Robert King for their valuable comments on an earlier draft of this paper. We are also grateful to Andrew Davies and Gillian Maciver for their excellent research assistance. We are also grateful to the ESRC (grant L120251023) for financial support.

*Corresponding author. Department of Economics, Rutgers University, New Brunswick, NJ 08901, USA. Tel.: +1 732 932 7069; fax: +1 732 932 7416.

E-mail address: bordo@econ.rutgers.edu (M.D. Bordo).

0304-3932/$ - see front matter © 2005 Elsevier B.V. All rights reserved.
doi:10.1016/j.jmoneco.2004.05.008

to have an important bearing on the kind of institutional framework required for a modern day target zone to function effectively and, in particular, to weather speculative attacks.
© 2005 Elsevier B.V. All rights reserved.

JEL classification: F31; F33; N23

Keywords: Target zone; Monetary independence

1. Introduction

This paper examines the operation of monetary policy within the context of the recent literature on target zones (Krugman, 1991). We argue that under the classical gold standard, gold parity was bounded by a two-sided target zone set by the gold points. Within the zone, stabilizing expectations allowed monetary authorities to use their policy tools to set short-term interest rates independently of those in the rest of the world. Our approach builds upon a recent paper by Svensson (1994). He argues that the conventional view on fixed exchange rate systems in a world of perfect capital mobility, that central banks have no power to conduct an independent monetary policy, does not hold in a system with exchange rate bands, such as the Bretton Woods regime or the Classical gold standard. In a fixed exchange rate system with bands, monetary authorities have the latitude for independent action because of stabilizing rational expectations.

For example, in the case where a central bank lowers short-term rates, instead of an immediate capital outflow as in the textbook case, the exchange rate (domestic currency price of foreign currency) rises above the central parity rate until the expected rate of depreciation relative to central parity has become so negative as to match the initial decline in the short-term rate. When the short-term interest rate is raised, the exchange rate declines (appreciates) relative to central parity such that the expected rate of depreciation relative to central parity matches the initial rise in the exchange rate. Thus, when central banks gear monetary policy to domestic goals they are simply exploiting mean reversion of the exchange rate relative to central parity towards the long-run mean (Svensson, 1994, p. 162).

The classical gold standard is an example of a fixed exchange rate system with bands and with a high degree of capital mobility (see, for example, Bordo et al., 1998; Obstfeld and Taylor, 1998; Officer, 1986), where the bands are determined by the gold points. It was also a system which monetary authorities in the core countries of Western Europe, on occasion, used their policy tools to influence domestic objectives. Although the monetary authorities were supposed to follow the 'rules of the game' in their use of monetary policy to speed adjustment to a balance of payments shock, the evidence in many cases is that the rules were violated (Bloomfield (1959) and the literature cited in Bordo and MacDonald (1997)).

That violations of the rules of the game occurred, in the sense that central banks often sterilized gold flows (Bloomfield, 1959) and had variables other than gold convertibility in their short-run reaction functions (Dutton, 1984; Giovannini, 1986;

Jeanne, 1995; Davatyan and Parke, 1995), while at the same time adhering to gold convertibility as a long-run objective is consistent with the view that the gold standard operated as a well-behaved target zone. Indeed, evidence that the Classical gold standard system represented a credible target zone within the gold bands is contained in a number of recent studies (Officer, 1996; Hallwood et al., 1996). According to the Svensson (1994) view, the monetary authorities potentially had the scope to conduct independent monetary policies within the gold points. However, the scope for violation was limited by the size of the bands and could only be temporary because the exchange rate must eventually revert towards central parity (Svensson, 1994, ibid).

This paper attempts to test Svennson's hypothesis for the monetary policy conducted by the central banks of the three core countries of the Classical gold standard: England, France and Germany, over the period 1880–1913. The outline of the remainder of the paper is as follows. Section 2 provides a motivation for our empirical results. In Section 3 we describe the data set. The econometric results are contained in Section 4. Section 5 gives our conclusions and discusses suggestions for future research.

2. Motivation and methodology

Under rigidly fixed exchange rates the condition of interest rate parity may be expressed as

$$i_t = i_t^*, \tag{1}$$

where i_t and i_t^* denote, respectively, the domestic and foreign currency interest rates with maturity k. Expression (1) indicates that the domestic interest rate cannot deviate from the foreign rate even momentarily. This is the standard assumption in many 'textbook' versions of the Mundell–Fleming model and it implies, of course, that domestic monetary policy can only have an effect on domestic variables, such as output and inflation, to the extent that the home country is 'large' (i.e. the US). For a small open economy (1) implies that its monetary policy is determined in the foreign country or, more realistically, the rest of the world. Condition (1) is often taken as a representation of perfect capital mobility (see, for example, Frankel, 1994).

However, as Svensson (1994) indicates there are few, if any, regimes of the international monetary system in which it can be said that exchange rates were rigidly fixed. The Classical gold standard, which is often cited as an example *par excellence* of a rigidly fixed exchange rate regime, in fact had (time-varying) exchange rate bands in the form of the gold export and import points (this is discussed in greater detail below). The existence of such bands introduces a wedge between the domestic and foreign interest rate in the form of a non-zero expected exchange rate change and this, in turn, means that domestic monetary policy will have some independence vis-a-vis foreign interest rate policy, even for a small open economy. This may be illustrated in the following way.

The ability of the domestic rate to deviate from the foreign rate is clearest when exchange rates are freely flexible. In this case the interest parity condition given in (1) has to be modified to

$$i_t = i_t^* + \Delta s_{t+k}^e, \tag{2}$$

where Δs_{t+k}^e represents the expected exchange rate change over the same maturity period defined for the interest rates. Two assumptions are necessary to interpret Eq. (2) as a representation of perfect capital mobility (see, for example, Frankel, 1994). First, an absence of impediments to capital movements and, second, the assumption that agents are risk neutral. If Δs_{t+k}^e is negative in Eq. (2), the domestic currency is expected to appreciate and the domestic interest rate can fall below the foreign interest rate by the extent of the expected appreciation. One way this can happen is if expectations are determined by a simple regressive expectations mechanism, such as that exploited in the classic Dornbusch (1976) model. The existence of exchange rate bands can have similar implications for interest rates under certain assumptions (discussed below). In the presence of an exchange rate band, s_t may be split into two components

$$s_t \equiv c_t + x_t, \tag{3}$$

where c_t denotes the central parity rate and x_t denotes the exchange rate's deviation from central parity. It follows from (3) that the expected currency depreciation in a fixed rate regime may be defined as

$$\Delta s_{t+k}^e = \Delta c_{t+k}^e + \Delta x_{t+k}^e. \tag{4}$$

Substituting (4) into (2) we obtain

$$i_t = i_t^* + \Delta c_{t+k}^e + \Delta x_{t+k}^e. \tag{5}$$

Now if the central rate is credible, in the sense that agents believe there will not be a devaluation or revaluation of the currency over the maturity horizon k, the Δc_{t+k}^e term will be zero and the domestic interest rate can rise above or below the foreign rate to the extent that Δx_{t+k}^e is non-zero. For example, if the domestic authorities increase the money supply the domestic interest rate will fall below the foreign rate and, as investors switch funds from the domestic interest bearing asset to the foreign asset, the exchange rate depreciates relative to the central parity. Under the assumption that the central parity is credible the depreciation will produce the expectation of an appreciation relative to c; i.e. $\Delta x_{t+k}^e < 0$.

As Svensson (1994) emphasizes, even a relatively small bandwidth can offer the monetary authorities substantial leverage over interest rates. For example, a 1% deviation of the exchange rate from the central parity which is expected to be removed in three months, implies an annualized expected appreciation of 4% per year—a non-trivial number from a monetary policy perspective. It is worth emphasizing that all of the above discussion presupposes capital is perfectly mobile, in the sense that the UIP condition holds. Therefore, one of the key empirical tests in this paper is a test of UIP for each of the country pairings considered.

There are, however, important limitations to the extent of any independence conferred by a country participating in a credible target zone. First, if the assumption that Δc^e_{t+k} is zero is violated and, in particular, if it is endogenously related to Δx^e_{t+k} and increasing in the exchange rate's deviation from central parity, then this will reduce the degree of monetary independence; in instances where Δc^e_{t+k}, moves in an equal and opposite direction to Δx^e_{t+k} there will be no monetary independence. For certain currencies and at certain times in the existence of the Bretton Woods system this may have been a reasonable working assumption. However, for the Classical gold standard system there is considerable evidence to suggest that the exchange rates studied in this paper were highly credible (see Hallwood et al., 1996; Officer, 1996). Second, the monetary independence can only be temporary since unless expectations are systematically violated (which would ultimately mean the expected rate of realignment was non-zero) the exchange rate must eventually revert back to its central parity. This, in turn, implies that the monetary independence will be limited to interest rates with short-term maturities.

Svensson argues that the monetary independence remaining after taking account of the above limitations offers a central bank scope to attempt to stabilize output and inflation and engage in interest smoothing objectives. Our main objective in this paper is to test the implications of this view of a banded exchange rate system (which we refer to as a target zone in the following) for three gold standard exchange rates. The main focus of our work concentrates on three interest rate systems (defined below) which are used to assess different aspects of monetary independence in a credible target zone. Since it has been demonstrated elsewhere (see Officer, 1996; Hallwood et al., 1996) that the gold standard system was indeed credible, we take that as a given here. In particular, studies show that for the country pairings considered in this paper, the Classical gold standard was credible period-by-period. Given that such tests are constructed using a strong form of UIP, we interpret this as indirect evidence on the absence of a time-varying risk premium for our sample period.

The three systems that we consider are designed to gauge the existence of short-run monetary independence and its relationship to the policy variables targeted by the monetary authorities. The systems are: system one, which consists of a home short interest rate, i^s_t, and a comparable short foreign rate, i^{s*}_t; system two, which consists of the variables in system one plus a home long interest rate, i^l_t; system three consists of the variables in system two plus the policy variables (discussed below) targeted by the monetary authorities. We now discuss these systems in a little more detail.

The Svensson (1994) story is that in the short-run there should be some scope for the home short interest rate to deviate from the comparable foreign rate, but in the longer term such scope vanishes. By examining system 1 we hope to capture this essential feature of the Svensson model. In particular, if home and foreign short term interest rates are individually non-stationary, or $I(1)$, then for them not to persistently deviate from each other in the longer term they should form a cointegrating relationship of the form first proposed by Engle and Granger (1982).[1] That is, in the context of an estimated version of Eq. (6)

$$i_t^s = \alpha + \beta i_t^{s*} + v_t, \tag{6}$$

it would be expected that the error process, v_t, is stationary, or $I(0)$, α would differ insignificantly from zero and β would be insignificantly different from unity (we discuss below how we propose estimating (6)).

The expected change in the exchange rate within the band does not appear in the cointegrating relationship since it is expected to be $I(0)$ and will not affect the long-run result (in a cointegration sense); it may be thought of as being subsumed in the error term. However, the non-zero Δx_{t+k}^e term will be captured in the short-run dynamic equations implied by (6). In particular, if the two interest rates defined in (6) are cointegrated then the Granger Representation theorem implies that a dynamic error correction representation of the following form must exist:

$$\Delta i_t^s = -\varphi(i_{t-1}^s - i_{t-1}^{s,*}) + \sum_{i=1}^{p} \kappa_i \Delta i_{t-i}^s + \sum_{i=1}^{p} \gamma_i \Delta i_{t-i}^{s,*}, \tag{7}$$

$$\Delta i_t^{s,*} = +\varphi(i_{t-1}^s - i_{t-1}^{s,*}) + \sum_{i=1}^{p} \kappa_i^* \Delta i_{t-i}^s + \sum_{i=1}^{p} \gamma_i^* \Delta i_{t-i}^{s,*}, \tag{7'}$$

where the first term on the right-hand side of each equation represents the error correction mechanism (ECM) recovered from the cointegration tests on (6) (in this example we have imposed the condition $\alpha = 0$ and $\beta = 1$ on the ECM relationship). The significance of this coefficient will be informative with respect to which of the interest rates adjusts in response to a disturbance of the levels terms. It should be significantly negative in the first equation, to the extent that the home interest rate is adjusting, and significantly positive in the second, to the extent that the foreign rate does the adjusting.

Additionally, the coefficients on the dynamic terms will give a feel for the amount of short-run policy independence available to the participating countries. Essentially, the existence of significant explanatory variables in (6) is prima facie evidence that the expected change within the band is non-zero. Of course this assumption relies crucially on the absence of a foreign exchange risk premium.

There are two ways of assessing the importance of a risk premium for our sample period. One is to take the extant tests of credibility of the gold standard period (see Officer, 1996; Hallwood et al., 1996). Such tests suggest that the currency pairings we consider were highly credible and therefore there was no uncertainty regarding the gold parity values of the currencies. A second way of assessing credibility involves a direct test of UIP and this is something we consider in the next section.

In addition to its implication for short rates, the Svensson model, as we have noted, also has implications for the behavior of long-term interest rates. Therefore, the second system we consider introduces a long rate into system one. We assume

[1] As we note in Section 4, all of the interest rates considered in this paper are $I(1)$ processes.

long rates are determined by a standard expectations model of the term structure formulation (see Campbell and Shiller, 1987):

$$i_t^l = (1-\delta)\sum_{j=0}^{\infty} \delta^j E_t i_{t+j}^s, \tag{8}$$

where δ is the discount factor and we have assumed, for simplicity, an infinite discounting horizon. From (8) we see that a current change in short interest rates which is expected to be reversed will have little impact on long bond yields. It follows, therefore, that long rates are not expected to move systematically with short rates and the yield gap, or spread (i.e. $i_t^l - i_t^s$), should open up after a shock to the short rate, but that this would be expected to be extinguished relatively quickly.

To examine the short–long interest rate interrelationships we again intend exploiting cointegration methods. In particular, Campbell and Shiller (1987) have demonstrated that if (8) is a valid representation of the long–short interest rate relationship, long and short interest rates should be cointegrated with a cointegrating coefficient equal to unity; an equivalent interpretation is that the spread should be stationary. That is, on subtracting i_t^s from both sides of (8) we may obtain

$$i_t^l - i_t^s = \sum_{j=1}^{\infty} \delta^j E_t \Delta i_{t+j}^s. \tag{8′}$$

Therefore, in a trivariate system consisting of a home and foreign short rate and a home long rate we should observe two long-run relationships: one governing short rates, from the interest parity condition, and the other governing the relationship between the home short and long rates given by the term structure relationship. On the basis of the Granger Representation theorem this kind of system will produce the following equation for the change in the domestic short-term interest rate

$$\Delta i_t^s = -\varphi(i_{t-1}^s - i_{t-1}^{s*}) - \delta(i_{t-1}^l - i_{t-1}^s) + \sum_{i=1}^{p} \kappa_i \Delta i_{t-i}^s + \sum_{i=1}^{p} \gamma_i \Delta i_{t-i}^{s*} + \sum_{i=1}^{p} \mu_i \Delta i_{t-i}^l, \tag{9}$$

where the 'l' superscript denotes a long rate, the first term on the right-hand side denotes the error correction term associated with the short-run interest parity relationship, the second term denotes the term structure effect, or 'spread', and the remaining terms are the dynamic terms.

In addition to (9) there would, of course, be a further two dynamic equations for the change in the foreign short rate and the change in the domestic long rate. Since with such a relatively complex system it can be difficult to interpret the coefficients on any one variable, we propose examining the interrelationships represented in (9), and the associated equations, using an impulse response analysis. This system will not only help to address the issue of the long–short relationship referred to above, it will also give further insight into the degree of monetary autonomy which a credible target zone confers and the degree of mean-reversion which exists for short rates.

Our third system involves examining the interrelationships between short-term interest rates and the variables to which they are targeted. In particular, if we can establish that there is some independence for short term interest rates we may ask: how could this independence have been used? The Svensson story is that it should facilitate standard counter-cyclical objectives such as stabilizing the output-inflation trade-off and allowing the authorities to engage in interest rate smoothing. More specifically, we investigate the effect on short term interest rates of changes in output (y), prices (p), and unemployment (u), variables designed to capture counter cyclical operations, the money supply (m), reflecting both external gold flows and internal demands for liquidity, and the volatility of interest rates $Vol(i)$), which the authorities are assumed to want to minimize if they had an interest rate smoothing objective. These variables, apart from the interest rate terms are log transformed and the volatility of interest rates is measured using the standard deviation from the sample mean.[2]

Defining the vector $\mathbf{z_t} = [\Delta y_t, \Delta p_t, \Delta u_t, \Delta m_t, \ Vol(i)]'$, we may gauge what effect the fundamentals have on the domestic interest rate change, over-and-above the influence of other interest rates, by introducing $\mathbf{z_t}$ into (9)

$$\Delta i_t^s = -\varphi(i_{t-1}^s - i_{t-1}^{s,*}) - \delta(i_{t-1}^l - i_{t-1}^s) + \sum_{i=1}^{p} \kappa_i \Delta i_{t-i}^s + \sum_{i=1}^{p} \gamma_i \Delta i_{t-i}^{s,*} + \sum_{i=1}^{p} \mu_i \Delta i_{t-i}^{l,*} + \sum_{i=0}^{p} \mathbf{f} \mathbf{z}_{t-1}. \tag{10}$$

More specifically, the Svensson model implies that the fundamentals can have an impact on the short-run behavior of the interest rate, but they do not impact on the long-run equilibrium relationships. This feature of the Svensson approach is captured in (10).

To summarize this section. Central to the Svensson hypothesis of limited monetary independence under flexible exchange rates is the UIP condition. This condition, in turn, requires the absence of impediments to capital movements and risk neutral investors. Clearly if UIP does not hold then the kind of interest rate dynamic equations that we have discussed in this section could equally be consistent with deviations from UIP and a time-varying risk premium. The existence of UIP is therefore central to the interpretation of our results.

3. Data sources

The data sample runs from January 1880 to December 1913. The data are collected for France, Germany and the UK. For each of these countries we have collected data on bank rate and a single long rate (which is country-specific). Since

[2] In the pre-1914 era, seasonal movements in interest rates in economies still largely dependent on agriculture—where crop movements were financed by short-term commercial loans—were often associated with financial stress and sometimes financial crises. Hence, smoothing short-term interest rates was an important objective of central bank policy and indeed was a rationale for the establishment of the Federal Reserve in 1913. See Miron (1996).

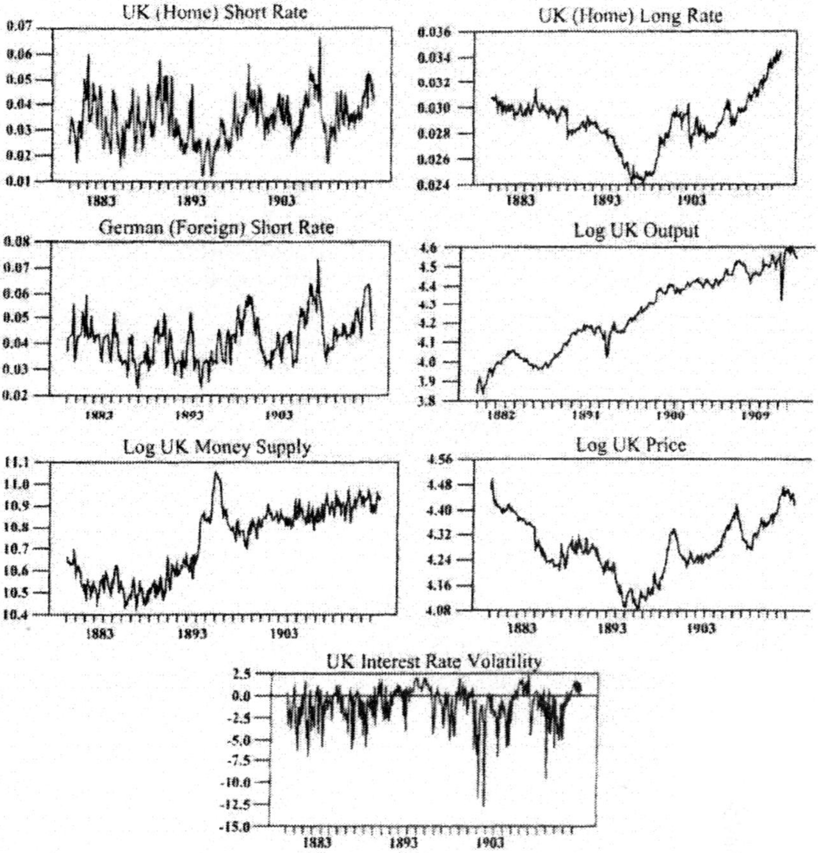

Fig. 1. Data for the UK–German system.

the former interest rate is directly targeted by the central bank we believe it is the most appropriate short rate to use in our analysis. Additionally, we have collected data on the spot exchange rates and, using shipping costs, insurance and an opportunity cost variable, have calculated the gold points for each country (the mean value of the gold points is taken to be our central parity rate). The fundamental variables which complete our data set are the money supply, industrial production, a consumer price index, and unemployment. All data were originally seasonally unadjusted and have been seasonally adjusted using the X11 filter.[3] In Fig. 1, we

[3]As Robert King has pointed out, use of the X11 filter could affect our econometric results. As a check we therefore re-estimated all of the relationships reported in this paper using seasonally unadjusted data and centered seasonal dummies. The results turned out to be extremely close to those reported here and are available from the authors on request as an appendix (containing both figures and tables).

present the data series used to test the interest rate interactions between the UK and Germany. A complete listing of all variables, their sources and construction are presented in Appendix of Bordo and MacDonald (1997). The calculation of the gold points follows the procedure used by Clark (1984), Officer (1986) and Giovannini (1993).

Three country pairings are examined, namely the UK–France, the UK–Germany and Germany–France. Given that the UK, and particularly London, was central to the operation of the Classical Gold Standard we regard the two pairings involving the UK as central to our analysis. However, we also implement our set of tests for the German–French pairing for comparative purposes; since neither of these countries can be regarded as credible as the UK, there is an expectation that this pairing will exhibit different properties to the UK-based pairings (evidence contained in Bordo and MacDonald (1997) supports this interpretation).

The calculations are based on the following formulae, for the gold import point, G_t^{I}, and gold export point, G_t^{X}, respectively

$$G_t^{\mathrm{I}} = \frac{X}{Y}\left[\frac{1}{(1+i)^{k/365}+c}\right],$$

where X is the official home currency price of an ounce of "fine" gold, Y is the official 'foreign' price of an ounce of fine gold, and X/Y is therefore the official exchange rate or "mint parity", i is the home interest rate, k is the shipping time and c denotes direct shipping costs which includes items such as freight and insurance costs, packing, loading and unloading, abrasion, charges for assay and minting and, finally, incidental expenses.

The gold export point is defined as

$$G_t^{\mathrm{X}} = \frac{X}{Y}\left[(1+i)^{k/365}+c\right]\left(\frac{1+i^{*}}{1+i}\right)^{k/365},$$

where, of terms not previously defined, i^* is the 'foreign' or overseas interest rate. For the home and foreign interest rates we have used the market rate of discount. In computing the gold points between London and Berlin (LB) and London and Paris (LP) we follow Einzig's (1931) calculations for shipping time and costs and set $k = 3$ in LB and $k = 1$ in LP. We estimate the cost of shipping for LB to be $c = 0.1152\%$ and for LP $c = 0.263\%$.[4]

4. Econometric results

We conducted a set of univariate root tests (both ADF and KPSS tests) on all of the variables used in this study and the general tenor of these results was that all of the series are approximately $I(1)$ processes (these results are available from the authors on request).

[4]These results essentially confirm the findings of Giovannini (1993).

Table 1
FIML estimates of interest rate parity

Interest rate combination	$i_t = \alpha + \beta i_t^* + v_t$					
	α	β	$t_\beta = 1$	l Max	Trace	LM(4)
Short rates						
UK–France, bank rate	−0.535	1.320	1.45	24.02*	31.45*	6.67
	(0.68)	(0.22)		7.43	7.43	(0.15)
UK–German, bank rate	0.056	0.805	0.42	18.71*	28.88*	2.17
	(0.59)	(0.14)		10.17	10.17	(0.70)
German–France, bank rate	0.552	1.195	0.57	17.20*	25.26*	11.02
	(1.03)	(0.34)		8.06	8.06	(0.03)
Long rates						
UK–France, long rates	0.004	1.167	0.64	19.56**	25.41*	7.16
	(0.01)	(0.26)		5.85	5.85	(0.13)
UK–German, long rates	0.003	1.031	0.11	13.94**	22.80*	6.69
	(0.02)	(0.29)		8.23	8.23	(0.15)
German–France, long rates	0.004	0.868	0.13	18.02**	24.02*	2.21
	(0.003)	(0.37)		6.02	6.02	(0.70)

Notes: The first column describes the interest rate/country combination. The numbers in the columns labeled α and β are the estimated constant and slope coefficient from the interest parity regression Eq. (6). The numbers not in parenthesis in the column headed $t_\beta = 1$ are tests of the hypothesis that the slope coefficient is unity. The numbers in the columns labeled l Max and Trace are the estimated values of Eqs. (17) and (16) in the text and LM(4) is a Lagrange Multiplier test for fourth-order serial correlation. Numbers in brackets below point estimates are Fisher standard errors, while numbers in brackets below the LM tests are marginal significance levels. A single *denotes significance at the 5% level, while **denotes significance at the 10% level.

4.1. System 1 results

In Table 1, we present our estimates of Eq. (6) using the methods of Johansen (1995). Since these methods are now well known we do not detail them here. In deciding on the deterministic specification, we have used the so-called 'Pantula (1989) principle' of testing the joint hypothesis of rank order and deterministic components. The deterministic elements reported in all Tables containing Johansen estimates are based on this principle.

In the short rate system the constant was constrained to lie in the cointegration space and evidence in favor of a single cointegration vector is fairly clear-cut across the short-rate systems. The coefficients on the 'foreign' interest rates are all positive and numerically close to unity.[5] More specifically, these values range from 0.81, for the UK–German bank rate relationship, to 1.32 for the UK–French bank rate relationship. Although the point estimates of β are numerically different from unity, on the basis of the standard errors, reported in parenthesis, none of the β coefficients are statistically different from plus one (the numbers in the columns labeled $t_\beta = 1$

[5]All of the systems are based on an 8 lag VAR model.

are t-ratios for the null hypothesis that $\beta = 1$). Furthermore, all of the constant terms are insignificantly different from zero.[6]

We regard these results as indicating very strong support for uncovered interest rate parity and are in marked contrast to results obtained for the recent floating period (see, for example, Frankel, 1994; Obstfeld, 1993). Hence, a key element of the Svensson model is confirmed for our data set. The reported Lagrange Multiplier tests statistics (LM4) for up to fourth-order autocorrelation indicate that the systems all have tolerably random residuals.

In terms of the long-rate systems, reported in the bottom half of the table, the evidence for cointegration is also clear but only when a time trend is included in the cointegrating space (the Pantula principle indicated that both a constant and a time trend were required in the cointegrating space). The existence of a time trend could be capturing the long-run change in capital mobility occurring in our period (for example, an increase in financial market integration). However, we again note that none of the β coefficients are statistically different from unity.[7]

Having established evidence of cointegration for all of the interest rate combinations, the next strand in our analysis involves estimating the dynamic relationships between interest rates. We do this by exploiting the Granger Representation theorem which states that if two (or more) series are cointegrated then there must exist an error correction representation of the form (7) for the two variables. The resulting error correction models are reported in Tables 2–4 for the combinations of short interest rates (the restriction $\beta = 1$ has been imposed in all of these systems).[8]

The results in Tables 2–4 may be summarized in the following way. First, in all of the systems the ECM term enters with a negative sign in the equation for the change in the domestic interest rate and positively in the equation for the foreign rate. Given the way the ECM term is defined, this means that adjustment occurs in both markets and since each system has at least one significant ECM, this confirms the cointegration tests discussed above.

Notice that the adjustment coefficient is always larger, in absolute terms, in the equation featuring the change in the 'domestic' interest rate (i.e. in the equations for the UK—in the UK–French and UK–German systems—and for Germany in the German–French system). In the UK–French system, the coefficient on the ECM term in the UK equation is approximately ten times larger, in absolute terms, than the corresponding number in the French equation, while in the UK–German system the adjustment coefficient in the UK equation is twice as large as the corresponding coefficient in the German equation.

[6] We also implemented a similar set of tests for market determined short interest rates. These results, reported in Bordo and MacDonald (1997) were qualitatively very similar; the main difference being that the constant terms in all cases were statistically significant, perhaps indicating the heterogeneity of the underlying assets.

[7] To model violations of the gold points, we experimented with including event dummies in the VECM, but this made little difference to the results.

[8] In constructing these dynamic ECM's we deleted insignificant lags and this resulted in more parsimonious models for the bank rate systems.

Table 2
Error correction system for UK–France

$$\Delta i_t = \alpha + \sum_{j=1}^{n} \Delta i_{t-j} + \sum_{j=1}^{n} \Delta i^*_{t-j} + \text{error correction}$$

Dependent variable	Δ UK rate ($t-1$)	Δ UK rate ($t-2$)	Δ UK rate ($t-3$)	Δ UK rate ($t-4$)	Δ UK rate ($t-5$)	Δ UK rate ($t-6$)	Δ UK rate ($t-7$)	R^2
Δ UK rate (t)	0.031	−0.126	−0.066	−0.070	0.0146	−0.044	−0.075	0.146
	[0.486]	[2.028]	[1.081]	[1.183]	[0.279]	[0.821]	[1.436]	
	Δ French rate ($t-1$)	Δ French rate ($t-2$)	Δ French rate ($t-3$)	Δ French rate ($t-4$)	Δ French rate ($t-5$)	Δ French rate ($t-6$)	Δ French rate ($t-7$)	ECM ($t-1$)
	−0.139	−0.144	0.107	−0.083	−0.079	−0.174	−0.008	−0.212
	[0.870]	[0.916]	[0.691]	[0.555]	[0.572]	[1.249]	[0.057]	[4.082]

$$\Delta i^*_t = \alpha + \sum_{j=1}^{n} \Delta i_{t-j} + \sum_{j=1}^{n} \Delta i^*_{t-j} + \text{error correction}$$

Dependent variable	Δ UK rate ($t-1$)	Δ UK rate ($t-2$)	Δ UK rate ($t-3$)	Δ UK rate ($t-4$)	Δ UK rate ($t-5$)	Δ UK rate ($t-6$)	Δ UK rate ($t-7$)	R^2
Δ French rate (t)	0.005	−0.022	0.007	−0.008	0.038	−0.012	0.011	0.087
	[0.217]	[1.062]	[0.322]	[0.415]	[2.025]	[0.698]	[0.652]	
	Δ French rate ($t-1$)	Δ French rate ($t-2$)	Δ French rate ($t-3$)	Δ French rate ($t-4$)	Δ French rate ($t-5$)	Δ French rate ($t-6$)	Δ French rate ($t-7$)	ECM ($t-1$)
	0.067	−0.056	−0.003	−0.136	−0.051	−0.164	−0.019	0.020
	[1.260]	[1.073]	[0.049]	[2.736]	[1.115]	[3.551]	[0.414]	[1.141]

Table 3
Error correction system for UK–Germany

$$\Delta i_t = \alpha + \sum_{j=1}^{n} \Delta i_{t-j} + \sum_{j=1}^{n} \Delta i^*_{t-j} + \text{error correction}$$

Dependent variable	Δ UK rate (t − 1)	Δ UK rate (t−2)	Δ UK rate (t−3)	Δ UK rate (t−4)	Δ UK rate (t−5)	Δ UK rate (t−6)	Δ UK rate (t−7)	R^2
Δ UK rate (t)	−0.051	−0.155	−0.114	−0.094	−0.015	−0.110	−0.076	0.124
	[0.471]	[2.267]	[1.689]	[1.432]	[0.239]	[1.847]	[1.293]	
	Δ German rate (t−1)	Δ German rate (t−2)	Δ German rate (t−3)	Δ German rate (t−4)	Δ German rate (t−5)	Δ German rate (t−6)	Δ German rate (t−7)	ECM (t−1)
	−0.059	−0.200	−0.043	−0.063	−0.056	−0.057	−0.095	−0.096
	[0.662]	[2.280]	[0.494]	[0.733]	[0.676]	[0.694]	[1.159]	[1.839]

$$\Delta i^*_t = \alpha + \sum_{j=1}^{n} \Delta i_{t-j} + \sum_{j=1}^{n} \Delta i^*_{t-j} + \text{error correction}$$

Dependent variable	Δ UK rate (t − 1)	Δ UK rate (t−2)	Δ UK rate (t−3)	Δ UK rate (t−4)	Δ UK rate (t−5)	Δ UK rate (t−6)	Δ UK rate (t−7)	R^2
Δ German rate (t)	−0.023	−0.006	0.047	0.029	0.055	−0.034	0.082	0.078
	[0.471]	[0.130]	[0.990]	[0.620]	[1.239]	[0.828]	[2.011]	
	Δ German rate (t−1)	Δ German rate (t−2)	Δ German rate (t−3)	Δ German rate (t−4)	Δ German rate (t−5)	Δ German rate (t−6)	Δ German rate (t−7)	ECM (t−1)
	−0.021	−0.096	−0.066	−0.129	−0.073	−0.040	−0.110	0.035
	[0.347]	[1.569]	[1.085]	[2.169]	[1.261]	[0.695]	[1.931]	[2.238]

Table 4
Error correction system for UK–France

$$\Delta i_t = \alpha + \sum_{j=1}^{n} \Delta i_{t-j} + \sum_{j=1}^{n} \Delta i^*_{t-j} + \text{error correction}$$

Dependent variable	Δ German rate $(t-1)$	Δ German rate $(t-2)$	Δ German rate $(t-3)$	Δ German rate $(t-4)$	Δ German rate $(t-5)$	Δ German rate $(t-6)$	Δ German rate $(t-7)$	R^2
Δ German rate (t)	0.020	−0.040	−0.004	−0.091	−0.021	−0.043	−0.065	0.066
	[0.364]	[0.726]	[0.069]	[1.704]	[0.393]	[0.809]	[1.236]	
	Δ French rate $(t-1)$	Δ French rate $(t-2)$	Δ French rate $(t-3)$	Δ French rate $(t-4)$	Δ French rate $(t-5)$	Δ French rate $(t-6)$	Δ French rate $(t-7)$	ECM $(t-1)$
	−0.051	−0.022	−0.083	0.076	0.000	−0.110	0.128	−0.086
	[0.452]	[0.200]	[0.761]	[0.719]	[0.001]	[1.119]	[1.279]	[2.938]

$$\Delta i^*_t = \alpha + \sum_{j=1}^{n} \Delta i_{t-j} + \sum_{j=1}^{n} \Delta i^*_{t-j} + \text{error correction}$$

Dependent variable	Δ German rate $(t-1)$	Δ German rate $(t-2)$	Δ German rate $(t-3)$	Δ German rate $(t-4)$	Δ German rate $(t-5)$	Δ German rate $(t-6)$	Δ German rate $(t-7)$	R^2
Δ French rate (t)	−0.070	−0.012	−0.004	0.015	0.008	0.007	0.006	0.092
	[2.775]	[0.485]	[0.069]	[0.593]	[0.340]	[0.287]	[0.253]	
	Δ French rate $(t-1)$	Δ French rate $(t-2)$	Δ French rate $(t-3)$	Δ French rate $(t-4)$	Δ French rate $(t-5)$	Δ French rate $(t-6)$	Δ French rate $(t-7)$	ECM $(t-1)$
	0.098	−0.064	0.083	−0.127	−0.029	−0.174	−0.029	0.026
	[1.888]	[1.258]	[0.761]	[2.576]	[0.636]	[3.797]	[0.615]	[1.912]

That much of the adjustment occurred in the UK is consistent with the width and depth of capital markets in the UK during this period vis-a-vis the markets in the other two countries (and also the fact that extensive bank balances were held in London by French and German nationals).[9] Using the coefficients on the error correction terms we calculated the implied half-lives as: 3 months, for UK–France, 6 months for UK–Germany and 7.5 months for the German–French system.

In sum: the results in Tables 2–4 clearly indicate that there were important and significant deviations of interest rates between countries, so that there is evidence of monetary independence for all three countries; as indicated by the relatively short half-lives, the interest rate deviations were not purely transitory, as predicted by the Svensson model; and the large, in absolute terms, error correction terms in equations for UK rates, suggest that London, as the primary financial center, played a fundamental role in attracting capital to restore interest rate parity.

4.2. System 2 results

Having established the simplest of the three systems discussed in Section 3, we now turn to an examination of the VECM system consisting of a home and foreign short rate and a home long rate (the equation for the home short interest rate from this system is reported as Eq. (9)). This system gives further insight into the independence conferred on monetary policy by facilitating an examination of the interaction between three interest rates, namely the domestic short and long rates and the foreign short rate.

These three rates give two potential equilibrium relationships: one an interest parity relationship, described by (1) or (2), and the other a term structure relationship linking the domestic short rate to the long rate.

As in the case of the two variable interest rate systems, we used the Johansen method to test for cointegration amongst these three rates.[10] The results are presented in Table 5. In all instances there is evidence of two cointegrating vectors. We attempt to interpret vector one as the interest parity relationship for short-term interest rates and vector two as the term structure relationship (i.e. the yield gap). This restriction cannot be rejected at the 5% level for any of the systems involving UK rates although it is marginally rejected in the two systems containing Germany and France (the reported χ^2 statistic is the relevant statistic, p-value in parenthesis).

Using these restricted vectors as our ECM terms we then constructed VECM models where each equation in the system has the explanatory variables given in (9). Rather than report the actual equations, which are difficult to interpret given the size of the system, we construct impulse response functions (with the two cointegrating vectors imposed on the system) for each of the country pairs.

[9]For a further discussion on the significance of the UK financial sector during this period see: Eichengreen (1987), Giovannini (1989) and Lindert (1969).

[10]The Hannan–Quinn lag length selection criterion was used to test the optimal lag length, which was 2 for each system.

Table 5
Tri-variate systems

$i^s_t = \alpha + \beta i^{s,*}_t + \phi i^l_t + v_t$
$i^s_t = \delta + \gamma i^{s,*}_t + \eta i^l_t + w_t$

Interest rate combination				χ^2	L-max	Trace	LM(4) $\chi^2_{(9)}$
	α	β	ϕ				
UK short bank (i^s_t)	−1.434	0.652	0.729	1.72	73.36*	104.5*	4.155
German short bank ($i^{s,*}_t$)	δ	γ	η	(0.42)	30.56*	31.22*	(0.90)
UK long (i^l_t)	86.461	−34.07	20.007		0.66	0.66	
	α	β	ϕ				
UK short bank (i^s_t)	2.141	1.391	−0.997	3.94	68.91*	94.57*	11.335
French short bank ($i^{s,*}_t$)	δ	γ	η	(0.14)	25.18*	25.66*	(0.25)
UK long (i^l_t)	−13.470	−8.762	14.815		0.49	0.49	
	α	β	ϕ				
German short bank (i^s_t)	−3.956	−0.496	2.603	8.15	86.00*	120.4*	13.081
French short bank ($i^{s,*}_t$)	δ	γ	η	(0.02)	31.92*	34.40*	(0.16)
German long (i^l_t)	12.202	3.758	−5.195		2.49	2.49	

Note: See Table 1 for definitions. χ^2 refers to a joint test that $\beta = 1$, $\phi = 0$, $\gamma = 0$, and $\eta = 1$ and has 2 degrees of freedom.

The impulse response functions, along with the 95% confidence intervals, are reported in Fig. 2 and the country combination is indicated at the top of each column. The first two impulse pictures in each column represent the effects of a one per cent increase in the 'domestic' rate on the 'foreign' short rate and the 'domestic' long rate, respectively. The third and fourth impulses in each column display a similar set of reactions (for the domestic short and long) to a 1% increase in the 'foreign' short rate. The variables are entered into the moving average representation in the following order: long rate, foreign short rate and domestic short rate. This ordering indicates that the long rate is regarded as the most exogenous followed by the foreign short, with the domestic short being the most endogenous.

The impulse plots all have the same general pattern and may be illustrated by focussing on the results for the UK–French system. This figure clearly demonstrates that in the short-run there is not a one-to-one lock between UK and French short interest rates: a 1% increase in the UK short rate produces a very small—2 basis point—increase in the French rate which is then rapidly offset (by about month 6). The UK long rate actually falls, which, through the term structure relationship, indicates that investors expect the current rise in short rates to be offset in the near future; however, notice that the long rate change is very small (less than one basis point) and the dynamics die out very rapidly. Interestingly, the corresponding French shock has a much bigger impact on the short UK bank rate (75 basis points) and the effect on UK rates is very rapidly offset.

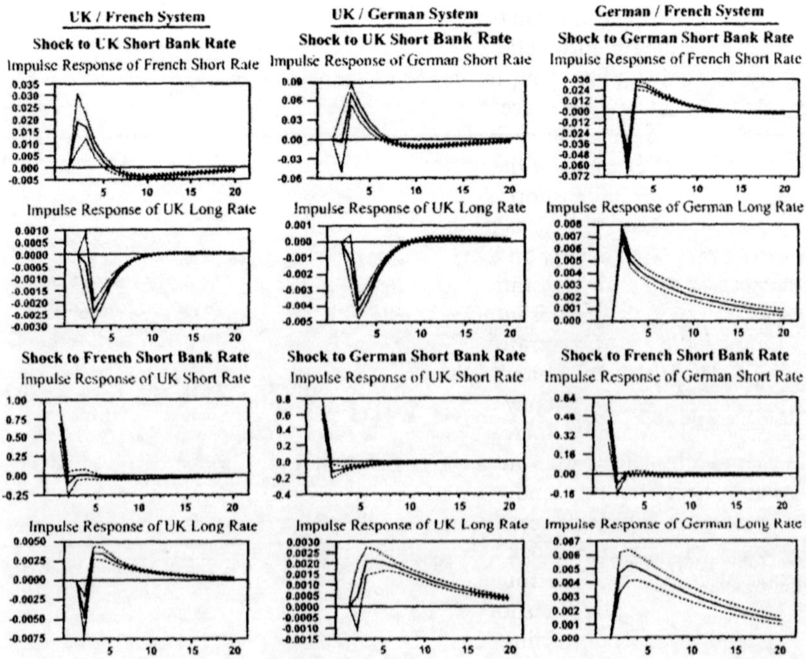

Fig. 2. Impulse response functions for system 2.

We attribute this contrasting adjustment of the UK and French rates to the importance of London as a financial center during the period.[11] The kind of patterns that we observe in Fig. 2 are, in general terms, repeated for the other interest rate combinations, although we note that the German–French system (final column in Fig. 2) is not as well-behaved as the two UK systems; this is consistent with the view expressed earlier that the UK played an important role in tying down interest relationships for the period. In general, then, interest rates seem to behave in the way predicted by the Svensson model.

In sum, the existence of a credible target zone means that in the short-run domestic interest rates can deviate from foreign rates and the yield gap opens up as short rates change. However, such changes are purely transitory and are offset relatively rapidly.

4.3. System 3 results

Finally we ran system 3, in which the fundamentals that the monetary authorities are presumed to be using their monetary independence to target enter the VAR. The

[11] This result is consistent with Eichengreen's (1992, p53) conclusion that London had considerably greater discretion than Paris to absorb interest rate shocks.

fundamentals are: the change in the logarithm of the money supply, the change in the logarithm of industrial production, the change in the logarithm of the price level and an interest rate volatility term, measured by the standard deviation of short term interest rates. To save on space, the results, which comprise an impulse response analysis for the three country pairings, are available in Bordo and MacDonald (1997). We briefly summarize them here.

We find that for both short and long rates there is a significant response to fundamentals, but that this is, as predicted by the Svennson model, much smaller for long rates (indeed the impact on long rates is miniscule). Through the term structure relationship, short and long rates move in the same direction in response to the shocks, and the sign pattern is intuitively plausible. For example, a positive shock to both output and prices generates an initial increase in the domestic interest rate, presumably through the demand for money channel, and this is rapidly offset. An increase in the domestic money supply produces a fall in interest rates, which is reversed by month 4. A 1% increase in interest rate volatility initially produces a fall in the domestic interest rate, but by a miniscule amount. There is no evidence of interest rate overshooting and, indeed, the required interest rate adjustment is relatively small in each instance. The magnitude of the response of the domestic rate to a foreign interest rate shock is essentially unchanged relative to system 2. In common with system 2, we found that the independence conferred on domestic monetary policy is purely transitory and evaporates after approximately 12 months.

It is perhaps worth contrasting some of the interest rate adjustments contained in our system 3 results with those sometimes required at crisis points during the ERM experience. Thus, the majority of interest rate adjustments generated in our system 3 estimation amounted to only a few basis points and this was sufficient to give independence for a number of months. In contrast, the Swedish example of a 75% increase in interest rates in September 1992 only gave the authorities several days of independence, at most.

5. Summary and concluding comments

In this paper, we have used a target zone framework to analyze the behavior of interest rates and exchange rates for France, Germany and the UK during the classical gold standard period. Our particular focus was to test a hypothesis proposed by Svensson (1994) that the existence of a credible target zone should confer on a country some independence in the operation of its monetary policy. This hypothesis is of particular interest for the Classical gold standard period since it is well known that countries did not play by the rules of the game, in the sense that they did not direct monetary policy to external objectives, yet the system seemed to operate effectively (in contrast to other regimes of the international monetary systems in which governments directed monetary policy to domestic objectives). We devised a number of tests to assess the Svensson hypothesis.

Central to our testing methods is the existence of UIP for our sample period. We confirmed that the strong-form version of this hypothesis held for all of the short and long rate systems considered in this paper. Using these long-run relationships we moved to three sets of dynamic (i.e. short-run) systems to explore if there was in fact any leeway for independent monetary policies during the Classical period. In the absence of a strong-form of UIP, these dynamic systems could be consistent with other interpretations, such as indicating a time-varying risk premium. However, we believe that our finding of strong-form UIP means they can be used to quantify the degree of monetary independence conferred on the currencies due to their participation in a credible target zone. The dynamic systems showed significant evidence of independence, although this proved, as expected, to be transitory and it was significantly related to certain key fundamentals. This finding is in agreement with the historical literature (e.g. Sayers, 1957) that the Bank of England (as well as other central banks) were on occasion concerned with the behavior of domestic macroeconomic variables.

Another aspect of our work was the finding that the particular combination of countries had a bearing on the results. Thus, the two bilateral systems which featured the UK worked well in the sense that adjustment was relatively rapid and fundamental variables bore a predictable relationship with interest rates; this was not, however, the case for the system which did not feature the UK (i.e. the German–French system). We believe this finding reinforces the view already prevalent in the literature that the UK, and particularly London, played a key role in the operation of the Classical gold standard system.

We conclude by noting that our findings have a bearing on the kind of institutional framework required for a modern day target zone to function effectively and, in particular, to weather speculative attacks. For example, there is currently much discussion about reforming the international monetary system (IMS) and, in particular, the institutional arrangements governing the tripolar three exchange rates—the dollar euro and yen. A number of politicians and economists have argued that the tripolar three should be governed by a target zone structure. The results presented in this paper suggest that for such a structure to be effective requires that credibility ultimately anchors both short-term interest rate policy and the term structure of interest rates and it has at its center an anchor country.

References

Bloomfield, A.I., 1959. Monetary policy under the International Gold Standard. Federal Reserve Bank of New York, New York.

Bordo, M.D., Eichengreen, B., Kim, J., 1998. Was there really an earlier period of international financial integration comparable to today? In: The Implications of Globalization of World Capital Markets, Bank of Korea, Seoul, pp. 27–82.

Bordo, M.D., MacDonald, R., 1997. Violations of the 'Rules of the Game' and the credibility of the Classical Gold Standard, 1880–1914. NBER Working Paper No. 6115.

Campbell, J., Shiller, R., 1987. Cointegration and tests of present value models. Journal of Political Economy 95, 1062–1088.

Clark, T.A., 1984. Violations of the Gold Points, 1890–1908. Journal of Political Economy 92, 791–823.

Davatyan, N., Parke, W.R., 1995. The operations of the Bank of England 1890–1908: a dynamic probit approach. Journal of Money Credit and Banking 27 (4 Part I), 1099–1112.

Dornbusch, R., 1976. Expectations and exchange rate dynamics. Journal of Political Economy 84, 1161–1176.

Dutton, J., 1984. The Bank of England and the rules of the game under the International Gold Standard: new evidence. In: Bordo, M.D., Schwartz, A.I. (Eds.), A Retrospective on the Classical Gold Standard 1821–1931. University of Chicago Press for the NBER, Chicago, 1984.

Eichengreen, B., 1987. Conducting the International Orchestra: Bank of England leadership under the Classical Gold Standard. Journal of International Money and Finance 6, 5–29.

Eichengreen, B., 1992. Golden Fetters: The Gold Standard and the Great Depression, 1919–1939. Oxford University Press, New York.

Einzig, P., 1931. International Gold Movements. Macmillan, London.

Engle, R., Granger, C., 1982. Cointegration and error correction: representation estimation and testing. Econometrica 55, 251–276.

Frankel, J., 1994. Quantifying International Capital Mobility in the 1980s. In: Frankel, J. (Ed.), On Exchange Rates. MIT Press, Cambridge, MA.

Giovannini, A., 1986. Rules of the game during the International Gold Standard: England and Germany. Journal of International Money and Finance 5, 467–483.

Giovannini, A., 1989. How fixed exchange rate regimes work: evidence from the Gold Standard, Bretton Woods and the European Monetary System. In: Miller, M., Eichegreen, B., Portes, R. (Eds.), Blueprints for International Monetary Reform. Cambridge University Press, Cambridge.

Giovannini, A., 1993. Bretton woods and its precursors: rules versus discretion in the history of International Monetary Regimes. In: Bordo, M.D., Eichengreen, B. (Eds.), A Retrospective on the Bretton Woods System: Lessons for International Monetary Reform. Chicago University Press, Chicago.

Hallwood, P., MacDonald, R., Marsh, I.W., 1996. Credibility and fundamentals: were the classical and inter-war gold standards well-behaved target zones? In: Bayoumi, T., Eichengreen, B., Taylor, M. (Eds.), Economic Perspectives on the Classical Gold Standard. Cambridge University Press, Cambridge.

Jeanne, O., 1995. Monetary Policy in England 1893–1914: a structural VAR analysis. Explorations in Economic History 32, 302–326.

Johansen, S., 1995. Likelihood-Based Inference in Cointegrated Vector Auto-Regressive Models. Oxford University Press, Oxford.

Krugman, P.R., 1991. Target zone and exchange rate dynamics. Quarterly Journal of Economics CVI (3), 669–682.

Lindert, P., 1969. Key Currencies and Gold, 1900–1913. Princeton Studies in International Finance, vol. 24, Princeton, New Jersey.

Miron, J., 1996. The Economics of Seasonal Cycles. MIT Press, Cambridge, MA.

Obstfeld, M., 1993. International capital mobility in the 1990s. NBER Working Paper No. 4534.

Obstfeld, M., Taylor, A., 1998. The great depression as a watershed: International Capital Mobility over the long-run. In: Bordo, M.D., Goldin, C., White, E. (Eds.), The Defining Moment: The Great Depression and the American Economy in the Twentieth Century. University of Chicago Press, Chicago.

Officer, L.H., 1986. The efficiency of the Dollar–Sterling Gold Standard, 1890–1908. Journal of Political Economy 94, 1038–1073.

Officer, L.H., 1996. Between the Dollar-Sterling Gold Points: Exchange Rates, Parity and Market Behavior. Cambridge University Press, Cambridge.

Pantula, S.G., 1989. Testing for unit roots in time series analysis. Econometric Theory 5, 256–271.

Sayers, R., 1957. Central Banking After Bagehot. Clarendon Press, Oxford.

Svensson, L.E.O., 1994. Why exchange rate bands? Journal of Monetary Economics 33, 157–199.